ALBION!

A Complete Record of West Bromwich Albion 1879-1987

ALBION!

A Complete Record of West Bromwich Albion 1879-1987

TONY MATTHEWS
WITH
COLIN MACKENZIE

Breedon Books Sport

First published in Great Britain by
The Breedon Books Publishing Company Limited
45 Friar Gate, Derby DE1 1DA
1987

ISBN 0 907969 23 2

Printed by Butler and Tanner Limited, Frome
Jacket designed by Graham Hales

Photographs supplied by *Birmingham Post and Mail* and Steve Hale.

ACKNOWLEDGEMENTS

Foremost, I have to acknowledge the splendid co-operation of my friend Colin Mackenzie, a civil servant based at Birmingham International Airport, who once again has provided so much valuable assistance over the past 12 months, and whose help in checking and re-checking the statistical information has been tremendous.

Colin, an Albion supporter for 35 years, has painstakingly, fingered through the many old newspapers and periodicals available at libraries in Birmingham and London, clarifying hundreds of facts and figures in an effort to make this book what it is - A *Complete Record* of *West Bromwich Albion* Football Club. Thankyou sincerely Colin.

Grateful acknowledgement is also made to my lady love, Margaret, for her unstinted effort in proof-reading the manuscript and for putting up with the continuous tapping of the typewriter as well as having heaps of pages scattered round the living room, bedroom, ante-room and bathroom.

Also I have to say thankyou to Anton Rippon and the staff at Breedon Books, Derby; to professional photographers Bill Goulden (Peerless Photography), Geoff Wright (*Express & Star*), and Dale Martin; to amateur photographers Barry Marsh and Lawrie Rampling; Dave Shaw, Barry Swash and Donald Seely for use of old pictures and newspaper cuttings; to former players Harold Pearson, Johnny Nicholls, Jimmy Sanders and the late Bill Richardson; to the *Birmingham Post and Mail*; the Provincial Press Agency (Southport); the *Express and Star* (Wolverhampton), and the Universal Pictorial Press & Agency (London), whose pictures of past and present Albion players and match-action have again proved so very useful in this publication.

There must be some people, somewhere, who have given their assistance in a small way, whom I have failed to mention here. But take it from me your work has been appreciated - thankyou all.

TONY MATTHEWS August 1987

Contents

Introduction

THIS book is probably the most comprehensive work ever compiled on one specific football club as far as facts and figures are concerned.

There are literally thousands upon thousands of statistics throughout the 320 pages of this 'Complete Record' of West Bromwich Albion Football club — a club which is now 108 years old, having been formed by an enthusiastic group of young cricketers, all of whom worked at the George Salter Spring Factory in the town.

It has taken Colin Mackenzie and myself three full years to get everything 'right' for publication, and believe me, it has been hard work, but extremely interesting and fascinating for all that.

Football statistics can be a nightmare for anyone who cares to dabble in them and, during the compilation of this book, all the vital statistics have been diligently researched, using every possible source available. It is known that over the years, a number of major errors have occurred and been passed down, errors, I might add, which have been a constant thorn in my side since I became Albion's statistician some 20 years ago. These, I sincerely hope, have now been rectified thanks to my colleague, Colin, and the help of material at hand from various archives. Indeed, frequent reference has been made to the club's official organ, the *Albion News and Record* which began in 1905 and which today is one of the top programmes in the country; and to the 'History of West Bromwich Albion Football Club' which was serialised in the club's programme from 1911 to 1930 inclusive and gave, on the whole, an excellent account of Albion's earlier years.

A variety of local and national newspapers have also been methodically scrutinised and exhaustively read, particularly copies of the *Sport Argus*, the *Free Press*, the *Weekly News*, the *Birmingham Daily Gazette*, *Saturday Night* and the *Midland Athlete* to name but a few.

Here I would like to point out that, in a number of these older publications, the details of certain Albion scorers vary considerably, especially during the Victorian era, but every conceivable effort has been made to produce accurate statistics from what is an extremely complicated subject bearing in mind that some goals were reported as being scored by the result of a 'scrimmage', and that in the days before the last war, players did not wear numbered jerseys, hence another worrying jigsaw to solve whereby in some team line-ups players were inserted 'out of position'

(i.e. defenders in a forward role, and vice-versa). But we've conquered these infuriating points, and each and every League and senior Cup game played by the Albion club since 1883 (when they first entered the FA Cup) has been detailed in full, with team line-ups in the League competition given in easy-to-read, 1-11 formation with the substitute (number 12) included only when he was used.

Attendances are from official Albion records, and not from newspapers or magazines. The information set out in other sections speaks for itself (ie club directors, managers, secretaries, chairmen, international honours, sendings-off, etc.) and with regard to transfer fees, these have been given in 'round' figures in most cases, and may differ with what the reader may have seen previously printed in other football annuals. The category featuring 'star' players has had to be restricted to a certain number and these have been chosen by myself, with no guidance from other people. And under Players' Records I have given the actual year of signing for Albion, when the man *first* put pen to paper, either as an amateur, an apprentice or as a full-time professional.

Colin and I have covered the complete history of West Bromwich Albion Football Club in this book. Very little, if anything, has been overlooked. Many photographs have been used, some of which have never been published before. Much of the information in this unique book has been up-dated from my previous Albion publications, and all the statistical records included are up to the end of season 1986-7. Entries in this book, however small or insignificant, supersede all previous statistical records appertaining to West Bromwich Albion FC. Colin and I sincerely believe that the contents in this latest Albion book will act as a permanent encyclopædia of The Hawthorns' club for many years to come. It is a COMPLETE RECORD.

As a final note, I would like to stress that all the views expressed in this publication are those of myself and Colin, and not necessarily those of West Bromwich Albion Football Club.

TONY MATTHEWS

May 1987

Foreword
by Bobby Robson

I WAS delighted when Tony Matthews asked me to pen a foreword to this 'Complete Record' of West Bromwich Albion Football Club, having spent six excellent years with Albion from 1956 to 1962.

While I was at The Hawthorns I made many friends both on and off the field, and I can recall the splendid times I had playing alongside, and socialising with, the likes of big Derek Kevan, Frank Griffin, Ronnie Allen, Maurice Setters, Ray Barlow, Len Millard, the late, great Joe Kennedy, 'Chippy' Clark, Alec Jackson, Don Howe and David Burnside. Indeed, Don and David are now key members of my coaching staff at international level and we frequently talk about the good old days at Albion.

In the world of football, Albion are, and always have been, regarded as a fine club. They've got a great tradition, especially as Cup fighters, and all their magnificent achievements down the years have been captured in this splendid publication.

When I first arrived at The Hawthorns in March 1956, on a transfer from Fulham, manager Vic Buckingham was in the process of rebuilding his Albion team following FA Cup glory in 1954 — and I was part of his plans. We had a fine side in those days and were perhaps a shade unlucky not to have reached Wembley again in 1957 and 1958.

In fact, Albion — the Baggies — never played at the Empire Stadium during the time I was with them, but I did, gaining international recognition for England as an inside-forward and wing-half. I played 20 times for my country, and in several games I teamed up with Don Howe and Derek 'The Tank' Kevan. And I am positive that it was Albion who made me into an international footballer.

The club's supporters were great to me, but they have been deprived of success in recent years. Nevertheless, you can't keep a good club down for long, and I am certain that Albion will be back in the First Division where they belong in the not-too-distant future.

Albion have been in existence for over 100 years. They have had their ups and downs, but generally speaking they have been one of England's top teams, having travelled the world playing good football in places as far afield as China and Hong Kong, the USSR, the USA and Canada, East Africa, Brazil and throughout Europe.

They have had many wonderful players: Jesse Pennington, Billy Bassett, 'W.G.' Richardson, who was trainer-coach at the club when I first signed for Albion, Billy Elliott and Jack Vernon from yesteryear; and Laurie Cunningham, Cyrille Regis, Willie Johnston, John Wile, Tony Brown, and Bryan Robson more recently. They will always be a club in the news, they will always produce great players.

This book is a work of art — an encyclopædia — and I am proud to be part of it. It will always be treasured by me, as it gives a quite fascinating insight into everything there is to know about West Bromwich Albion Football club, from League competition to Cup action, from attendances to transfers, from star players to chairmen, directors and secretaries, statistics and stories, facts and figures covering 108 years from those pioneer days of 1879 when the club — known then as The Strollers —began setting the Black Country alight on the road to becoming a major force in British football.

I congratulate Tony (and Colin) on this marvellous publication, and I wish them, and the club, every success in the future.

Foreword
by Vic Buckingham

I ACCEPTED the position of West Bromwich Albion manager in January 1953, and left for AFC Ajax of Holland in May 1959.

They were happy times for Albion, with such players as Ray Barlow, Ronnie Allen, Jim Dudley, Joe Kennedy and Frank Griffin greeting my arrival — and still around to wave me their goodbyes six years later.

The Board of Directors, chaired by Major Wilson Keys, were wholly supportive, and all echoed the Chairman's philosophy of "If you believe in it..then get on with it". Yes, indeed, happy days.

Those years had a 'zing' about them, with crowds of 30,000-plus the norm, and the 40,000 crowd not uncommon.

Together with the players and training staff, I liked to think that Albion played the game with skill and determination and, indeed for me, they always did. Yes, as any supporter did, I gasped at the thunderous volleys of Ronnie Allen; the long and accurate crossfield passes of the elegant Ray Barlow; the 'jinking' Frank Griffin; and the cat-like leaps of Joe Kennedy in the centre of defence .... exciting stuff indeed.

The Albion name was being recognised in faraway places and in 1957 an invitation to make a three-match tour of Russia was accepted. Our visit was reciprocated by the Russians sending a side to England the following season.

Young and experienced players of the calibre of Derek Kevan, Bobby Robson, Maurice Setters, Don Howe, Brian Whitehouse, Alec Jackson and Roy Horobin; a great trainer in Dick Graham; and Gordon Clark, a chief scout of the highest quality, were ready and able to take the club into the sixties.

West Bromwich Albion Football Club owes its existence to a group of working-class youths who, not relishing the prospect of another long winter with little to occupy themselves, looked to football as a way of passing the months until the cricket season came around again.

The lads were all from George Salter Spring Works in West Bromwich, where they played for the works cricket team. And on the Saturday afternoon of 20 September 1879, they took the decision to form a football team. What they could not have known, especially in those formative years of the game itself, was that their fledgling would grow into one of the most famous names in soccer.

They had heard good reports of the game from their pals in Wednesbury which, at that time, boasted no fewer than four football teams, the Old Athletic Club, Wednesbury Town, the Strollers, and Elwell's Works side. The lads from Salter's works believed they could raise a team capable of playing matches against anyone who cared to take them on.

Initially, 12 youngsters formed the new club. A seven-man committee comprised James Stanton, George Bell, his brother Harry Bell, John Stokes, Arthur Eld, George Timmins and Billy Bisseker.

A ball was needed — and as football had not been introduced to the folk of West Bromwich, none of the local shops stocked such an item. Committee members had to walk to Wednesbury where the necessary equipment was purchased after each individual member had donated sixpence to the club's funds.

Another meeting established that the team should be called West Bromwich Strollers — no doubt after that pilgrimage to Wednesbury to get their first ball. The committee decided unanimously on a weekly subscription of twopence, which met all requirements as there was no rent to pay.

> The most common name in Albion's first team over the years is Smith. Since 1879 a total of 17 players with that surname have represented Albion in various competitions and friendlies, the latest being John Smith, a defender, in 1983-4.
> Jack Smith, a wartime guest in Albion's colours (1939-45) was the club's first manager (1948) and Ephraim Smith was club secretary, as well as assistant-secretary, between 1906 and 1960.
> The next most common name in Albion's ranks is Williams (nine); there have been eight Joneses and six Daviesies.

Anybody who wanted to join the Strollers had to pay an introductory fee of sixpence. At the outset, wearing all types of coloured clothing, and various designs of footwear, the newly-formed Strollers kicked around on a piece of enclosed ground known as Cooper's Hill, adjacent to Dartmouth Park.

Practising as often as they could, the players began to show immense promise and arrangements were soon being made for their first competitive match. On 13 December 1879 they celebrated their first game with a 1-0 victory over Black Lake Victoria, watched by 500 people.

BLACK LAKE VICTORIA

The name of an obscure West Bromwich football club called Black Lake Victoria is forever enshrined in the long and colourful history of the Albion. When West Bromwich Strollers played their first recorded match on 13 December 1879 at Dartmouth Park, Black Lake Victoria were their opponents. Albion's line-up that day consisted of 12 players, of whom six were forwards, and they mastered the opposition by 1-0, the goal being scored, it is believed, by Harry Aston. The Albion pioneers (then bearing the name of Strollers) were: S.Biddlestone; H.Twist, H.Bell, T.Smith, J.Johnstone, J.Stanton, W.Bisseker (captain), J.T.Stokes, E.T.Smith, G.Timmins, H.Aston, G.Bell.

A week later Strollers played a second match, this time against the Bullock's Club. The venue was an excellent stretch of turf in Dartmouth Park, near the Beeches Road entrance, and again the Strollers excelled, winning convincingly by four clear goals.

Harry Aston hit two more, and Harry Evans notched the others. The attendance this time was around 1,000 and in the Strollers side at left-back was big Bob Roberts, later to become Albion's first international.

Roberts was nothing if not keen, and although he failed consistently wherever he played, he still managed to find his way into the side in some other position. Eventually he was tried in goal. It was a brilliant move, for Roberts became known as the 'Prince of Goalkeepers' and played three times for England.

Everything appeared to be running smoothly for the Strollers, and there is no record of them having lost a game in their initial season.

The annual general meeting of the club was held in July 1880 — and the following season the players chalked up a record 14-0 win over Oakfield. Bob Roberts played his first game in goal, against Hockley Belmont; in the same season Albion suffered their first defeat, having changed their name from Strollers.

Yet 1880-81 was a good season, and it seemed to justify a little enterprise. At the annual meeting of 1881 two decisions were made. George Bell was appointed club captain, in succession to Jimmy Stanton, who had hitherto held the post with Billy Bisseker. Bisseker was made 'sub-captain'; and a new ground, Bunn's Field, Walsall Street, was acquired on a 12-month lease.

The players and officials levelled and rolled the ground and put the fences in reasonably good order so that they might charge an entrance fee. They eventually called their new headquarters The Birches, and this ground was officially opened on 10 September 1881. Oldbury FC were Albion's guests and a crowd numbering about 300 paid 15s.2d to see Albion triumph 5-1 with Billy Bisseker grabbing two of the goals.

And that money taken at the turnstile — yes only one — was wealth indeed to the youthful enthusiasts of the Albion club.

Within three years of playing their first match, West Bromwich Albion, as they had now become, had beaten Aston Villa and were being talked about as a club with a great future.

That win over Villa, who were to become Albion's keenest rivals down the years, was achieved in 1882 and the forecast about great times ahead came from the secretary of the Birmingham County FA.

Albion had entered the Birmingham Cup for the first time in 1881 and it was their 3-2 win over Calthorpe that moved Mr J.H.Cofield, secretary of the County FA, to write a three-page letter congratulating the club on their performance. The game itself was played on Calthorpe's Bristol Road ground and in a cleanly fought tie, Albion won 3-2.

From that time forward Albion's yellow and white quartered jerseys, with the Staffordshire knot embroidered neatly on the front, became familiar on local grounds.

Albion went on to oust Elwell's in the second round (2-1), Fallings Heath (3-1) in the third, and Notts Rangers (5-2) in the quarter-final, but were then narrowly pipped for a Final place by the favourites, Wednesbury Old Athletic 3-2. Old Athletic went on to win the trophy that year, but Albion were becoming a power in Midland football circles.

The 1882-3 season found Albion competing for the Birmingham, Wednesbury and Staffordshire Cups, and Mr George Salter was made an enthusiastic president of the club.

Unfortunately Albion could not hold on to their Bunn's Field arena, yet luckily they were handed the Four Acres Cricket Ground by the local Dartmouth club, whose football section had been very much eclipsed by the rising performances of the Albion.

The tenancy agreement was dated 20 September 1882 and in view of the improved conditions, the club entrance fee was raised to five shillings with an annual subscription of 2s.6d. Season tickets were issued at three shillings but these were not valid for cup-ties.

Stoke 2   Albion 3

VICTORY over Stoke in the 1883 Staffordshire Cup Final at the Victoria Ground did much to put West Bromwich Albion on the football map and make the likes of Aston Villa and Wolverhampton Wanderers sit up and take notice. It was Albion's first appearance in any kind of Cup Final and their performance that day did them proud.

On the way to their meeting with Stoke, Albion ousted Bloxwich after a replay, and then removed Aston Villa, also at the second attempt. The win over Villa was indeed a feather in the Throstles' cap and it gave them a quarter-final match with another useful team, Mitchell St George's, who were eliminated with a similarly impressive display. In the semi-final, Leek White Star were whipped 8-1.

There was a great deal of excitement in the Black Country as Albion prepared to meet a well-balanced, efficient Stoke team which had scored 42 goals on their way to the Final. A cheap-day railway excursion was run from West Bromwich and more than 1,500 fans took advantage of it, decking themselves out in Albion favours for the big occasion.

Albion, who had trained at Malvern in the week before the big game, were able to select their strongest team, but they were still the underdogs when the game got underway — and when Johnson put Stoke ahead after only 15

minutes, it appeared that West Brom's second-best status was justified.

The Throstles, however, fought back hard and in a four-minute spell they scored twice through George 'Darkie' Timmins and Fred Bunn. Before the interval, Stoke drew level when Johnson notched his second of the match, making Stanton and While pay for their hesitancy.

Both sides went close in the opening period of the second half, but with 15 minutes remaining, it looked as though the issue would not be resolved that afternoon. Then Albion got a cross deep into the Stoke penalty area, up went winger George Bell to steer a powerful header past goalkeeper Wildin, and Albion were back in front.

When the final whistle sounded, West Brom's players and spectators alike were ecstatic. The fans chaired their heroes off the pitch and the celebrations in West Bromwich went on for three days after the team's triumphant homecoming. The *Athletic* reported: 'The atmosphere throughout the game was terrific and Albion thoroughly deserved their success.'

Stoke: Wildin; Stanford, Mellor, Brown, Bettany, Johnson, Brown, Shutt, Fennall, Myatt, Bennett.
Albion: Roberts; H.Bell, Stanton, E.Horton, Bunn, While, Aston, Whitehouse, Timmins, Bisseker, G.Bell.

Attendance: 6,150   Referee: Mr L.King (Leicester)

Albion's team which won the 1883 Staffordshire Cup Final, pictured with the trophy. Back row (l to r): A.Eld (secretary), H.Bell, R.Roberts, J.Stanton, J.Noons (umpire). Middle: R.Biddulph (reserve), J.While, Mr G.Salter (President), F.Bunn, E.Horton, H.Green (reserve). Front: G.Bell, G.Timmins, W.Bisseker, H.Aston, J.Whitehouse. Timmins, Bunn and Bell scored the goals which gave Albion victory in their first-ever Cup Final appearance.

Early action involving Albion in 1882, perhaps a practice match.

Albion's first season at the Four Acres saw them now running a useful second team and the fight for first-team places was beginning to hot up.

At the end of the campaign the annual report stated, in bold print, that the first team had played 39 matches, won 27, drawn seven and lost only five, scoring 177 goals and conceding 60. Harry Aston and George Bell were chief marksmen, each scoring over 40 goals.

The report added: 'Every club of importance in Birmingham has during the past season, succumbed to the prowess of the Albion, who even beat the famous Aston Villa by a goal to nil.'

It finished with the prophetic words: 'We hope the time is not far distant when even the English Cup (the FA Cup) will find a home in West Bromwich.'

In the 1882-3 Birmingham Cup, Albion ran up a mammoth score of 26-0 against Coseley in a first round tie on 11 November. Every player, except goalkeeper Bob Roberts, scored and the victory is still Albion's highest.

Violence and hooliganism at football matches is nothing new and was very much in evidence the first time Albion met Villa, at Perry Barr in November 1882 in the Staffordshire Cup.

The Albion party had to run a gauntlet of stones and clods of earth as they travelled to the ground. Villa, who had been established for eight years to Albion's mere three, reckoned they were on to an easy win and fielded an understrength team. They got a nasty shock when Albion, brimming with confidence and backed by some 3,000 fans, held on for a 3-3 draw.

Villa were still confident and sent an unchanged side to Albion for the replay. They paid the penalty as Albion overturned the form book with a 1-0 win, thanks to George 'Darkie' Timmins' solitary goal in the second half. A record crowd of 10,447 packed the Four Acres for that Christmastide replay, producing gate receipts of over £400.

Albion went on to lift the Staffordshire Cup with victory over Stoke in the Final. Thus, in less than five years, the boys who collected their sixpences to play were the proud holders of this sparkling silver prize. If anyone had any doubts about the position of Albion in the hearts of the locals, this was the occasion to dispell them.

In 1883, Albion entered the FA Cup for the first time. But any dreams they might have had of a spectacular triumph were rudely shattered when they were beaten 2-0 at home by Wednesbury Town.

Albion progressed in each of the other three cup competitions in which they participated in 1883-4 but carried off only one prize — the Birmingham Cup, beating Wolverhampton Wanderers in the Final, 2-1 after a replay.

In a friendly that season, Albion played Preston North End at home on Boxing Day and beat the country's top team 2-1 in front of a 3,600 crowd. It was only the second meeting between the clubs, Preston having won the previous encounter 3-1 in Lancashire earlier in the season.

Goalkeeper Joe Reader is the only player to appear for Albion on three different home grounds — Four Acres, Stoney Lane and The Hawthorns — in a competitive match.

In the 1884-5 FA Cup, Albion came into their own, and reached the sixth round before losing to high-riding Blackburn Rovers 2-0 before a record 16,393 crowd at the Four Acres. In a Birmingham Cup second round tie that season, Albion hammered Bloxwich 15-0.

With Tom Smith now club secretary and Joey Law the first-team trainer, Albion began season 1885-6 at another new ground — Stoney Lane — part of which is still there today. A 15-year lease was taken at £25 per annum. A total of £150 was spent on improving parts of the popular enclosure and helping towards the cost of a stand.

The Albion team for the opening of The Stoney Lane Ground, 5 September 1885, against Third Lanark Rifle Volunteers. Albion won 4-1. Back row (left to right): H.Green, H.Bell. Centre row: T.Green, T.Lavender, R.Roberts, E.Horton, G.Bell, G.Timmins, A.Loach. Front row: G.Woodhall, J.M.Bayliss, F.Bunn.

The year 1886 provided Albion with another landmark when they reached the FA Cup Final for the first time. Luck smiled on the club all the way. Every round brought a home draw until the semi-final where they beat Small Heath 4-1 at Aston to become the first Midlands team to reach the Final.

Blackburn Rovers were Albion's opponents in the Final at the Kennington Oval, which was jammed full with 15,156 people paying receipts of £650.

PROFESSIONALISM

Professionalism in football was very much frowned upon by the Football Association in the 1880s but eventually the officials of the FA came to realise that the paying of players could not be prevented. The Birmingham FA followed the official line for a while and suspended several local players, among them Tom Green who was Albion's FA Cup Final inside-right in 1886, for alleged professionalism. The authorities relented in 1885, however, and on 17 March 1885, the Albion committee appointed Henry Jackson and Tom Smith to represent the club at the FA meeting in London on 23 March to consider the question of the payment of players.

At Anderton's Hotel, London on 20 July 1885, the Football Association legalised the remuneration of players, and Albion wasted no time in adopting professionalism, a committee meeting resolving on 11 August 1885, that the club should be registered as professional. Albion's pioneer professionals received ten shillings (50p) a week but were not given training expenses nor was loss of time allowed. This sum of money was not that generous when one considers the discomforts players of the Victorian era had to put up with such as poor dressing-room facilities (invariably dimly lit and often without a bath), long hours spent in draughty railway carriages travelling to away matches, having to work Saturday mornings before home games and often having to take the field on a cold day without having had a square meal.

They saw a goalless draw, with Albion giving a good account of themselves despite being the underdogs. But in the Derby replay, which was witnessed by a crowd bigger than the initial game, 16,144, Rovers, who had won the trophy in the past two seasons, came out winners 2-0.

> *Bob Roberts was Albion's goalkeeper in successive FA Cup Finals of 1886, 1887 and 1888 and he was also the club's first full international, capped by England in 1887.*

Albion had the consolations of winning both the Birmingham and Staffordshire Cups in 1886, beating Walsall Swifts and Stoke in the respective Finals.

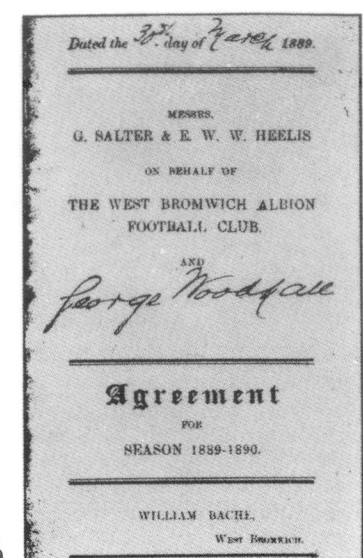

George Woodhall's contract, 1889.

Albion, 1888. Back row (left to right): Albert Aldridge, Ezra Horton, Harry Green, George Timmins, Bob Roberts (goal), Charlie Perry, Joe Wilson. Front row: George Woodhall, Billy Bassett, 'Jem' Bayliss, Tom Pearson.

The Woodman pub as it was in 1890, ten years before Albion moved to The Hawthorns.

Within 12 months they were back in the FA Cup Final again, this time facing local rivals, Aston Villa. And again Albion crashed — this time 2-0.

After defeats in successive FA Cup Finals, Albion were determined to make amends and in 1888 they won the Cup, beating the famous Preston 'Invincibles' in the Final.

The Black Country was aflame with enthusiasm for weeks, for never before had there been such football heroes — not even back in 1883 when Albion captured their first prize.

In 1888, Albion were invited to be one of the original 12 members of the Football League but there were no spectacular achievements for the Throstles in those early days, although they did have the honour of being the first club to top the League table. After just one match, a 2-0 away victory over Stoke, they headed the other 11 teams.

The FA Cup was still their 'lucky' competition. Twice they reached the semi-finals, only to lose out to old rivals Preston in 1888-9 and Blackburn Rovers in 1890-91.

World Championship

IN 1887-8 WEST BROMWICH ALBION played a grand total of 58 first-team matches. They won 43 of them, drew seven and lost only eight, scoring 195 goals and conceding 62 in the process.

They reached four Cup Finals, winning two and losing two, and one of those triumphs came in the FA Cup against 'Proud' Preston, whom they defeated 2-1 at The Oval.

Following this victory Albion were asked to play for the 'Championship of the United Kingdom'. The game, which was also dubbed the 'Championship of the World' took place at Hampden Park on 19 May 1888, and Albion's opponents were the Scottish Cup-holders, Renton, then one of the top teams North of the Border. The outcome was a 4-1 win for the Scots.

The football correspondent of the *Lennox Herald*, who rejoiced in the name of 'Saint Crispin', noted: 'Champions of the World is no doubt a very big title, nevertheless there is a club now holding that honour, and that club is Renton, as whoever are the Champions of the United Kingdom, can quite easily single themselves conquerors of the World.'

The match itself was an exciting affair. The rainy, windy weather was not conducive to footballing skill and it kept the crowd down to little over 6,000.

Renton defended stoutly at first, withstanding heavy pressure from Albion, whose right-wing pairing of Woodhall and Bassett went close on three occasions. 'Jock' Lindsay, the Renton goalkeeper, also saved a tremendous shot from 'Jem' Bayliss and then, seconds later, dived at the feet of the same player.

But in the 25th minute, in a breakaway, McNee put Renton ahead totally against the run of play, when he cashed in on a slip by Timmins to score from close range. Albion struck back fiercely, and held the upper hand right up until the break, yet their efforts failed to produce a goal.

Tom Pearson did equalise soon after the restart in a goalmouth melee, but within five minutes Renton had touched peak form and rattled in three goals in the space of a quarter of an hour to knock the stuffing out of the Baggies.

McNee rifled in his second goal from 20 yards, McCall sneaked in a third and after Charlie Perry had failed to clear a free-kick, J.Campbell slotted in a fourth, the ball hitting both uprights before crossing the line.

Albion tried to make the scoreline a little more respectable but as the rain poured down, so the saturated surface made ground football virtually impossible, and that was no use to Albion who were renowned for their quick man-to-man soccer.

Indeed, the weather became so bad that Mr Sinclair, the Irish referee, almost abandoned the game with ten minutes remaining. He was perhaps persuaded to carry on by the expressions displayed on the Rentonians' faces.

The final whistle sounded and Renton were deserved winners and thus 'World Champions'. Two weeks later they confirmed their status by beating another top English club, Preston North End.

The teams for the first-ever World Championship game were:
Renton: Lindsay; Hannah, McCall, Kelso, Kelly, McKechnie, H.Campbell, McColl, J.Campbell, McCallan, McNee.
Albion: Roberts; C.Mason, H.Green, E.Horton, C.Perry, Timmins, Woodhall, Bassett, Bayliss, Pearson, Wilson.

Albion team group showing ten of the players who contested the 'Championship of the World'. Back row (left to right): Mr Birch, Mr Jas Raybould, Mr George Salter, Mr Tom Smith, Mr H.Jackson, Mr Louis Ford. Middle: A.Aldridge, C.Perry, E.Horton, R.Roberts, G.Timmins, H.Green. Front: G.Woodhall, W.I.Bassett, J.M.Bayliss (captain), T.Pearson, J.J.Wilson. Tom Pearson managed to score for Albion but Renton were soon on top.

Albion on the attack before a packed Kennington Oval crowd in the 1888 FA Cup Final.

Match to Remember 2   24 March 1888

Albion 2   Preston North End 1

FOR two successive seasons Albion had fallen at the last hurdle in their attempt to win the FA Cup. In 1886, Blackburn Rovers had beaten them in the Final, and the following year it was the turn of arch-rivals Aston Villa to lift the Cup at Albion's expense.

When Albion reached the Final again in 1888, they opposed Preston North End, and once more it looked as though the Throstles were going to end up as runners-up, for Proud Preston were the favourites.

Indeed, Preston were so confident that they asked to be photographed with the trophy before the start. 'Had you not better win it first?' was the brisk reponse from referee Major Marindin.

The game certainly caught the imagination of the football public and the gates at The Oval were closed by kick-off time —the first time this had happened for a soccer match. It is a matter of history that almost 19,000 spectators saw Albion win the Cup 2-1, and there have been few more gallant, or popular, victories than the Throstles' success that afternoon.

Albion's team was comprised entirely of Englishmen and the club's weekly wage bill was no more than £10, yet they outfought mighty Preston with all their stars. And remember that 12 months later North End would become the first club to lift the double of League and Cup.

Albion played the long-passing game, backed up by a tremendous enthusiasm which swept aside the artistry of the Lancashire team. The man who proved Albion's greatest inspiration was 19-year-old Billy Bassett, who later that evening was selected for England and who was on the threshold of a great career.

Albion went ahead after only eight minutes when Bassett collected a poor clearance from Preston goalkeeper, Mills-Roberts. Bassett sprinted away down the right before laying on an inch-perfect cross for 'Jem' Bayliss to score from close range.

Preston clawed back and after 40 minutes of cut and thrust they equalised through Dewhurst, although West Brom complained that the ball had not crossed the line.

Undeterred, the Midlanders bounced back and in the 77th minute, George 'Spry' Woodhall grabbed the winner amidst wild cheering from the Black Country fans who had made the trip south.

Albion: Roberts; Aldridge, H.Green, E.Horton, C.Perry, Timmins, Woodhall, Bassett, Bayliss, Pearson, Wilson.
Preston North End: Mills-Roberts; Howarth, Holmes, N.Ross, Russell, Gordon, J.Ross, Goodall, Dewhurst, Drummond, Graham.

Attendance: 18,904 (Receipts £827.13s.0d)   Referee: Major Marindin (London)

Stoke 0   Albion 2

WHEN the Football League was formed in 1888, West Bromwich Albion were one of the founder members. The Throstles' first match in the new competition was against Stoke at the Victoria Ground and Albion went into the match brimming with confidence after friendly match victories over Sheffield Wednesday and Wolves.

Some 4,000 spectators — a good crowd for the first day of the brand-new competition — included a fair number of Albion supporters and their hopes of an early success were soon fulfilled as West Brom ran the match from the first whistle.

They pushed Stoke back into their own half from the onset and dominated the early exchanges, causing the home goal-keeper, Rowley, some anxious moments. Yet the goal which Albion threatened to score was a long time coming considering their territorial supremacy.

Woodhall twice went close, as did the forceful Pearson, and Hendry had a shot kicked off the line by Shutt, Stoke's almighty defender.

Stoke, to their credit, hit back purposefully and Albion 'keeper, Bob Roberts, had to be on his toes to keep out fine efforts from Staton and Tunnicliffe. Thus, although Albion had most of the first half, Stoke were still very much in with a chance as the 45 minutes ended.

Indeed, as the minutes ticked away in the second-half, Albion's play became sloppy and on one occasion Roberts had to be at his international best to keep out a stinging shot from Sayer.

But with only six minutes left to play, the Albion got the breakthrough they had been waiting for. Rowley was under intense pressure and was forced to clear his lines hurriedly by throwing the ball away. Joe Wilson, as quick as lightning, snapped up the ball and fired it straight back past the startled Stoke goalkeeper for Albion's first-ever goal in the Football League.

In the final minute they made absolutely certain of both points when George Woodhall headed a second goal from Billy Bassett's centre, and although it counted for little at this stage, the Throstles had the pleasure of topping the table on goal-average from Preston who, of course, were to win the Championship and the FA Cup that season.

Stoke: Rowley; Clare, Underwood, Ramsey, Shutt, Smith, Sayer, McSkimming, Staton, Edge, Tunnicliffe.
Albion: Roberts; J.Horton, H.Green, E.Horton, C.Perry, J.Bayliss, Bassett, Woodhall, Hendry, Pearson, Wilson.

Attendance: 4,524

Referee: Mr S.Swann (Sheffield)

West Bromwich Albion line up before the start of the 1888-89 season, the first Football League campaign. Back row (l to r): J.Homer, J.Dutton, H.Dawes, J.Bowen, J.Parker, W.Bisseker, Dr Rees, A.Fenn, Tom Smith (secretary). Middle: Paddock (trainer), E.Horton, J.Horton, G.Woodhall, J.Bayliss, H.Green, G.Timmins, C.Perry. Front: W.Bassett, R.Roberts, W.Hendry, T.Pearson, J.J.Wilson.

In 1891-2, however, a golden page was written in Albion's history. After three games to get rid of Nottingham Forest in the semi-final — Geddes getting a hat-trick in a fierce snowstorm at Derby — Albion met Aston Villa in the Final where they triumphed 3-0 to take the trophy for the time. Villa goalkeeper, Jim Warner returned home after the game to find all the windows in his Spring Hill Public House smashed.

Mr Louis Ford was directing Albion's fortunes in the early 1890s and his net was cast far wider than his predecessor. His team included Scots and Irish, as well as Englishmen. One 'Irishman' who deserves a special mention was John Reynolds and owing to his lack of hair, he soon become known as 'Baldy' Reynolds.

He played for Ireland five times but Albion then found out that he was an Englishman, having been born in Blackburn, and thus he went on to play for England. A player of many moods, he won a Cup-winner's medal with Albion, against Villa and later a winner's medal for Villa against Albion.

One of the Scots was Willie Groves, once Celtic's centre-forward and winner of three full caps. Two years earlier Everton protested to the Football League that Groves had signed for them, although he never played. Groves was suspended. Albion then converted him into a highly efficient half-back and he was a key figure in their 1892 FA Cup win.

Curiously enough there was again trouble when in 1893, Aston Villa signed Groves while Albion were negotiating for his transfer to Everton. Villa were fined £25 for approaching him without Albion's consent.

In 1892, Albion set a Football League scoring record by thumping Darwen 12-0, on 4 April. Tom Pearson (4) and Billy Bassett (3) led the scoring. This record still stands, although it was equalled by Leicester Fosse in 1909.

Billy Bassett, an England International and Albion 'great'.

The League had now been increased to 14 clubs, and Albion's place at the end of 1891-2 was a moderate 11th with only 18 points.

In 1894-5, Albion again fought their way through to the FA Cup Final — their fifth appearance in 11 years — but trailed after only 39 seconds. That is how long it took for Villa to score the only goal of the game. As some consolation, Albion carried off the Birmingham Senior Cup the same season, beating Aston Villa 1-0 in the Final.

WAKE MONDAY

In the closing years of the last century, a local Black Country custom allowed for celebrations on Wake Monday which was always the first Monday in November. The local pubs laid on cheap beer and free food, and Albion took advantage of the fact that most people were on holiday by arranging a home League fixture. From November 1887 to 1897, Bolton Wanderers were exclusively the visitors to Stoney Lane, winning four times, losing on six occasions and drawing one in 11 games. Everton, Sheffield United and Stoke took over the fixture until 1900, which was the last year in which Albion played a League game on Wake Monday.

As soccer — and Albion — grew in popularity, it became obvious that the club's Stoney Lane ground was not large enough. Enclosed by buildings and streets, it could not be expanded in any direction. So new, more spacious premises were sought. A keen member of the board from June 1896 had been Mr Harry Keys. Accompanied by secretary Frank Heaven, he began negotiating the lease of a 10-acre site situated on the corner of Halfords Lane and the main Birmingham Road. The area was named 'The Hawthorns' on Ordnance Survey maps and this title seemed as good as any for the new home of the 'Throstles', as Albion were now called.

Albion played their first match on their new ground against Derby County on 3 September 1900. It ended 1-1 and over 20,000 fans turned out. But Albion had a disastrous first season at The Hawthorns and they were relegated to Division Two for the first time.

Some of the more established stars were nearing the end of their playing days. Goalkeeper Joe Reader was considering retirement, and Billy Williams, one of the club's best-ever left-backs, saw his career ended by injury at the age of 24. Former Villa inside-forward Freddie Wheldon, a brilliant star in his day, was a shadow of his former self. And Tom Perry was also past his best. Albion's slump into the Second Division, plus a 4-0 FA Cup semi-final defeat by Tottenham Hotspur, meant drastic action.

New players were sought as Albion's directors decided unanimously on reorganisation. With few funds available they still managed to sign men who became some of the finest players the Albion had ever possessed.

Chief among these was Dan Nurse, a right-half from Wolverhampton Wanderers, who was immediately made club captain. A man who led by example, Nurse was to serve Albion for many years, both on and off the field.

Ike Webb, from Small Heath, took Reader's place in goal. His courageous dives at the feet of oncoming forwards were a feature of his play and after many seasons in the game, it was discovered that he had been playing with a fractured skull.

Jack Kifford, another defender of the Williams calibre, who had played for Derby County and Portsmouth, was signed from Bristol Rovers to partner Amos Adams, a local lad, who had worked at George Salters.

▲ Albion line-up, 1899-1900. Back row (left to right): W.J.Paddock (trainer), W.Walker, J.Reader, C.Simmons, T.Brennand (director), H.Powell (director), F.Heaven (secretary), H.Hadley, R.J.Roberts, B.Garfield. Centre row: A.Dunn, J.Paddock, T.Perry, W.Richards, J.Banks. Front row: A.Adams, A.Jones, W.Williams.

▼ The Albion squad for the opening of The Hawthorns, 1900. Back row: (left to right): I.Whitehouse, W.Heath, J.C.Orr, Dr I.Pitt, T.H.Sidney, H.Lockett. Third row: H.Powell, T.Harris Spencer, H.Radford, C.E.Sutcliffe, D.Haigh, J.J.Bentley, H.Keys, W.W.Hart, W.McGregor, C.Perry, J.Lones. Second row: F.Heaven, C.Keys, T.Pickering, F.Wheldon, C.Simmons, A. Jones, A.Dunn, A.Adams, J.Paddock. Front row: J.M.Bayliss, J.Chadburn, R.J.Roberts, J.Reader, W.Williams, H.Hadley.

17

Two of Albion's greatest heroes in their victory over Villa were goalkeeper Joe Reader (top), who went on to win England honours, and winger Jasper Geddes (bottom), who left for Millwall after a difference of opinion with West Brom officials.

Albion's Cup-winning team with the trophy. From the left: Bassett, Nicholson, Reynolds, McLeod, Reader, Nicholls, Perry, Pearson, Groves, McCullocn, Geddes.

Match to Remember 4   19 March 1892

Albion 3   Aston Villa 0

THE 1892 FA Cup Final was the last to be played at the Kennington Oval ground where the Surrey cricket authorities were becoming increasingly alarmed at the large crowds now being attracted to the showpiece game of the English football season. The honour of completing the end of an era fell to Midlands rivals, West Brom and Aston Villa.

Throughout the season, Albion's form had been erratic and Villa supporters felt that all their team had to do was simply turn up and the Cup was theirs for the taking. Albion, naturally, had other ideas and the result was a brilliant display by the Throstles.

Villa began brightly on a warm, sunny and cloudless day which had helped swell the attendance to almost 33,000, but Albion had an early surprise in store and after only four minutes they took the lead.

A sudden break down the right by Bassett saw the England winger end a top-speed dash by curling over a perfect centre. Geddes was correctly positioned and the Albion left-winger fired the ball past the startled Warner in the Villa goal.

Villa certainly fought back hard but they found Albion goalkeeper Joe Reader in tremendous form. The Villains' efforts to find an early equaliser were in vain and gradually the complexion of the game changed.

Albion's half-backs, Groves, Perry and Reynolds, took a tight grip on the midfield exchanges and another brilliant run by Bassett, and fine work between McLeod and Geddes, led to Sammy Nicholls making it 2-0 after 27 minutes.

Ten minutes into the second half, Villa's last hopes disappeared when Reynolds scored Albion's third with a spectacular 25-yard shot which flew past poor Warner. Thereafter, Albion's determined defenders held Villa in tight rein and the Cup was on its way to Stoney Lane for the second time.

The *Athletic News* reported that Albion's defence was 'simply superb' and praised goalkeeper Reader, saying he was 'cool, tall and calculating and 133,000 would not have upset his nerves.' Reynolds, said the newspaper, had a 'marvellous game', and Nicholls, Pearson and Geddes all played 'splendidly', as did Bassett, 'a master winger'.

Albion: Reader; Nicholson, McCulloch, Reynolds, C.Perry, Groves, Bassett, McLeod, Nicholls, Pearson, Geddes.
Aston Villa: Warner; Evans, Cox, D.Devey, Cowan, Baird, Athersmith, J.Devey, Dickson, Campbell, Hodgetts.

Attendance: 32,710 (Receipts £1,757)   Referee: Mr J.C.Clegg (Sheffield)

Albion 12   Darwen 0

THIS was the day that Albion created a little piece of football history, becoming the first team to score more than ten goals in a Football League game. And today, their achievement still holds good, being the joint biggest win in the First Division.

Against the team from the Lancashire cotton town of Darwen, Albion were quite magnificent, they attacked from the first whistle and might well have claimed another five or six goals.

Tom Pearson fired them ahead after only two minutes, his shot rocketing high past McOwen's outstretched right hand. Billy Bassett's effort struck the bar, then Nicholls chipped the ball inches over before John Reynolds steered home Jasper Geddes' corner.

Bassett netted number-three, Reynolds diverted Geddes' low cross home for the fourth goal, and on the stroke of half-time, Pearson assisted by Roddy McLeod, claimed Albion's fifth. Joe Reader made for the dressing-room to reflect that he had not been called upon to make a save in the first half.

The second half saw Albion in much the same hungry mood, although few could have forgiven them for slackening the pace in a game they had already won. Following a desperate scramble in the Darwen penalty area, Bassett made it 6-0 and the same player completed his hat-trick one minute later.

For 20 minutes Albion eased back, but the crowd were not content and urged them forward. The Throstles responded and Pearson scored their eighth. Darwen's Hunt obliged with an own-goal for the ninth and Pearson was on target again to take Albion into double figures.

Geddes made it 11-0 and in the dying moments of the game, Sammy Nicholls rounded things off with the twelfth goal to write West Brom into the record books.

Albion: Reader; J.Horton, McCulloch, Reynolds, C.Perry, Groves, Bassett, McLeod, Nicholls, Pearson, Geddes.
Darwen: McOwen; Hunt, Aspin, Entwistle, Owen, McEvoy, Wad, Nightingale, Fish, Alexander, Craven.

Attendance: 1,109

Referee: Mr S.Lockett (Derby)

Billy Bassett scored a hat-trick in Albion's record win.

Roddy McLeod (top), the former Partick Thistle forward, laid on Albion's fifth goal for Tom Pearson (bottom). A great favourite with the Albion fans, McLeod was spotted by the Throstles when playing for Glasgow against Sheffield.

Tom McCulloch played left-back for Albion against Darwen but the Throstles were in such control of the game that the defender was able to move forward at will and laid on four of his side's 12 goals.

19

Another local man, Abe Jones, the 'hard man' of the defence, who for several seasons had been a tower of strength at centre-half, had begun to put on too much weight. He was replaced by Scot Jimmy Stevenson, signed from Preston North End the previous season as a centre-forward. Harry Hadley, a polished wing-half, completed the middle trio.

The usual forward line in 1901-02 was: Jimmy McLean, a sturdy product of Walsall junior football; 'Chippy' Simmons; Billy Lee, another bustling centre-forward from Bournville; Tommy Worton, who came with Dan Nurse from Wolves; and George 'Sos' Dorsett, who was found performing admirably with Brownhills Albion. Andrew 'Scottie' Smith was the standby utility forward.

In November 1900, Albion had signed, from Stafford Rangers, a diminutive forward named Freddy Buck. He made one or two first-team appearances that season but some time was to elapse before the chant of 'Have you seen Buck?', became commonly used as an Albion war cry.

Season 1901-02 started off ominously. Glossop, the Derbyshire club who were financed by a wealthy businessman who later became identified with Arsenal, won the opening match at The Hawthorns 1-0.

But after that setback, Albion got into their stride and took the division apart with some devastating and consistent football. The next ten matches saw Albion undefeated and during this successful run Gainsborough were hammered 7-0 and Chesterfield 4-0. After a lapse at Doncaster on 23 November where they were beaten 2-0, Albion went 17 more League games without losing, to pull well clear at the head of the table.

In this undefeated sequence — a club record — Albion played some sparkling football and 14 wins were recorded. Attendances began to rise, touching 23,697 for the Christmas game against Stockport. Even a 5-1 defeat by Bury in the opening round of the FA Cup did not stop Albion's romp — and they finished off the season in tremendous style, chalking up successive wins over Burton Swifts, Woolwich Arsenal and Barnsley, to end with this record:

P	W	D	L	F	A	P
35	25	5	4	82	29	55

Albion finished four points ahead of second-placed Middlesbrough. The total of 55 points gained was then a League record, and Stoke were beaten 3-0 in the Staffordshire Cup Final.

Frank Heaven resigned as Albion secretary in 1902 — so opening the way for Fred Everiss, who was to stay with the club for 55 years. His early days were fraught with difficulties. There were internal quarrels about policy and half the board had given up their positions.

Albion, 1901-2. Back row (left to right): W.Brierley (trainer), B.Garfield, J.Lowe, I.Webb, F.Hobson, H.Cole, A.Green, Mr G.W.East (director), W.Rogers, O.Taylor, J.Westwood, W.Barber (ast. trainer). Third row: S.Brett, T.Evans, J.Stevenson, E.Smith, A.Randle, H.Hadley, G.Williams, Mr F.Heaven (secretary), Dr I.Pitt (director), Mr S.Makepeace, C.Simmons, W.Harper, J.Kifford, Mr F.Everiss (ast. secretary). Second row: P.Gollings, S.Edwards, A.Adams, W.Lee, D.Nurse, Mr H.Keys (chairman), J.Chadburn, T.Jones, W.Walker, G.Dorsett. Front row: J.McLean, A.Smith, F.Buck, T.Worton, W.Poynton, B.Appleby. Three trophies: Division Two Championship Shield, Staffordshire Cup, Birmingham & District Championship Shield.

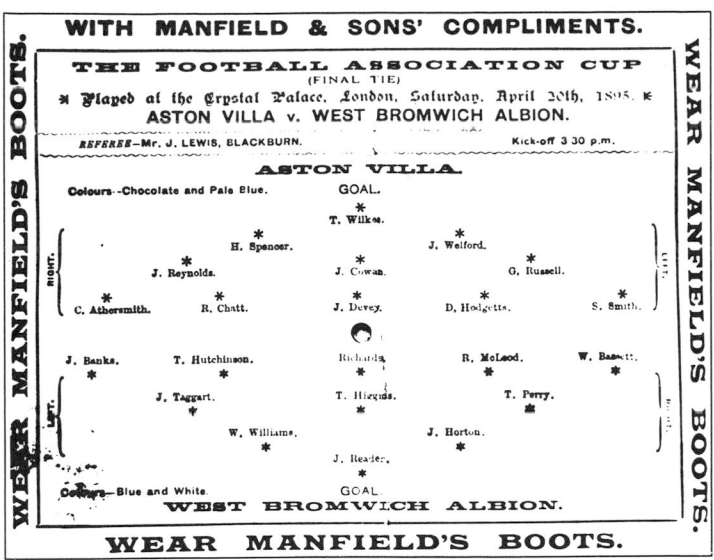

WITH MANFIELD & SONS' COMPLIMENTS.

THE FOOTBALL ASSOCIATION CUP
(FINAL TIE)
Played at the Crystal Palace, London, Saturday, April 20th, 1895.
ASTON VILLA v. WEST BROMWICH ALBION.
REFEREE—Mr. J. LEWIS, BLACKBURN.   Kick-off 3 30 p.m.

ASTON VILLA.
Colours—Chocolate and Pale Blue.   GOAL.
T. Wilkes.
H. Spencer.   J. Welford.
J. Reynolds.   J. Cowan.   G. Russell.
C. Athersmith.   R. Chatt.   J. Devey.   D. Hodgetts.   S. Smith.

Richards   R. McLeod.   W. Bassett.
J. Banks.   T. Hutchinson.
J. Taggart.   T. Higgins.   T. Perry.
W. Williams.   J. Horton.
J. Reader.
Colours—Blue and White.   GOAL.
WEST BROMWICH ALBION.

WEAR MANFIELD'S BOOTS.

(left margin) WEAR MANFIELD'S BOOTS.
(right margin) WEAR MANFIELD'S BOOTS.

Official programme line-up for the 1895 FA Cup Final, the third time in eight years that the two Midlands rivals had met in the showpiece game of the season.

Artist's impression of the collision between Higgins and Devey which left the Albion half-back groggy for the remainder of the game.

Match to Remember 6   20 April 1895

Albion 0   Aston Villa 1

ALBION were desperately unlucky to lose this superbly-fought Cup Final which was the one of the finest ever staged up to that time. Although what proved to be the match-winning goal was scored after only 39 seconds, the result was in doubt right up to the final whistle

A huge crowd of almost 43,000 packed the Crystal Palace ground at Sydenham and several thousands of them never saw the vital goal. They were still finding their places when Villa's inside-right Chatt netted.

From the kick-off the Villa forwards rushed at the Albion defence and there was a mad scramble in the Albion penalty area involving Chatt, and the Throstles' goalkeeper, Reader, and Villa's great star, John Devey. Reader got a leg to the ball but could not force it away, allowing Chatt to score one of the quickest-ever Cup Final goals.

To their great credit, Albion battled hard after that, with Higgins and Taggart doing extremely well. Reynolds, playing against his former club, steadied Villa in the centre and sent in one rocket of a shot which grazed the Albion crossbar with Reader well beaten.

In the Villa goal, Wilkes was in fine form and saved from Richards and McLeod as Albion tried to force their way back into the game. There was action at both ends as first Bassett shot wide, then Richards headed over and Chatt and Athersmith both went close for Villa.

Just before half-time, Devey and Higgins collided in midfield and the Albion player was missing when the teams came out after the interval. When he did reappear, head swathed in a bandage, he was greeted with sympathetic applause from both sets of fans.

Thereafter, Higgins played a courageous game and certainly deserved more success for his brave effort. All he had to show for it was a losers' medal and a five-pound note, given to him after the game by Colonel North, a prominent sporting figure, for his 'spirited performance'.

Albion slogged away looking for the equaliser but Villa held on to go 2-1 ahead over Albion in Cup Final victories.

Albion: Reader; J.Horton, Williams, T.Perry, Higgins, Taggart, Bassett, McLeod, Richards, Hutchinson, Banks.
Aston Villa: Wilkes; Spencer, Walford, Reynolds, Cowan, Russell, Athersmith, Chatt, Devey, Hodgetts, Smith.

Attendance: 42,652 (Receipts £1,545.10s.0d.)

Referee: Mr J.Lewis (Blackburn)

Albion 6   Newcastle United 1

NEWCASTLE, one of the finest teams in the country during the early Edwardian era, had started the 1902-03 season in style — three wins out of three games and a goals record of 9-0. Albion, newly promoted to Division One, had won two of their opening four matches and everyone at The Hawthorns was looking forward to the prospect of a cracking game.

Newcastle fielding former Albion winger Dick Roberts and the famous Scottish international Bob McColl, found themselves under intense pressure from the start and after only three minutes they were a goal down after Billy Lee netted from close-range following a mis-cued clearance from goalkeeper Kingsley.

Thereafter, Albion were in irrepressible form and after 19 minutes, Freddie Buck made it 2-0. Only 60 seconds later, Albion found themselves three goals ahead. Again Kingsley was at fault. The Magpies' goalkeeper mishandled an inswinging corner from Dorsett and there was 'Chippy' Simmons to bundle both ball and 'keeper over the line.

Before half-time, United pulled a goal back when the unmarked McColl headed Roberts' looping cross past Ike Webb, but it was only a temporary fightback and four minutes into the second half, Albion restored their three-goal advantage.

Buck raced clear to crack a scorcher over Kingsley's head from 18 yards and then another piledriver — this time from Jim Stevenson — made it 5-1.

There were still 20 minutes to go and Albion tore the Magpies' defence to shreds. They could even afford to miss a penalty — Jack Kifford was the culprit — before Jimmy McLean rounded off a fine performance by clipping in the sixth goal with barely three minutes remaining.

One report said: 'The score carries on its lop-sided face all that is necessary in the way of comment — Albion deserved to win by six goals to one. They played so manfully, skilfully, untiringly and dashingly that they would have beaten any team, past, present or to come, on the form they displayed.'

Albion: Webb; Kifford, Adams, Nurse, Stevenson, Hadley, McLean, Simmons, Lee, Buck, Dorsett.
Newcastle United: Kingsley; Agnew, Davidson, Gardner, Aitken, Carr, Stewart, Orr, McColl, Rutherford, Roberts.

Attendance: 22,160 (Receipts £520)

Referee: Mr J.Campbell (Blackburn)

Freddie Buck completed the Albion line-up that day and weighed in with two goals, the second of which was a real scorcher which gave Newcastle goalkeeper Matt Kingsley no chance.

Albion team group showing ten of the players who starred in the 6-1 win over Newcastle. Back row (l to r, players only): J.Stevenson, A.Adams, I.Webb, J.Kifford, H.Hadley. Front: A.Smith, W.Lee, D.Nurse, C.Simmons, T.Worton. On ground: J.McLean, G.Dorsett.

The club's bank balance was at a very low ebb — this despite a promotion-winning season in the Second Division — and there was an inevitable lowering in overall standards. However, under Everiss's shrewd guidance, things sorted themselves out and in time Albion became a side respected and feared by almost every team in the land.

Indeed, Albion seemed right in line for the First Division title in 1902-03. Up to mid-January they had obtained 32 points out of a possible 44 and were heading the table. Crowds were good — around the 18,000 mark — and some terrific wins had been registered. For instance, Newcastle, a fine side around this time, were slammed 6-1 at The Hawthorns, Aston Villa were clipped 3-0 at Villa Park, Blackburn Rovers were beaten 5-3, Liverpool 2-0 and Wolves 2-1.

> *Outside-left George 'Sos' Dorsett made his League debut for Albion on 4 January 1902: 12 games later (on 29 March) he was on the losing side for the first time. A club record, from debut-day to first defeat — 11 games.*

Jack Kifford was firing in penalty-kicks at a fine rate and Billy Lee was also scoring fluently, as were George Dorsett and 'Chippy' Simmons. But then everything went wrong. Poor Albion picked up a mere four points from their remaining 12 games to end in seventh position with 36 points.

The turning point could well have been their 2-0 home FA Cup defeat by Tottenham Hotspur in February. Directly after this slip Albion drew 3-3 with Sheffield United and then proceeded to lose eight League games in succession — and with them the title.

To help ease the pain, Albion carried off the 1903 Staffordshire Cup beating Stoke 2-0 in the Final at Aston, with Freddy Buck hitting both goals. And the Throstle's average home League attendance in 1902-03 was 15,657 — the fourth best in the division.

Yet Albion's next campaign was a complete disaster. They were relegated for a second time, finishing bottom of the table with 24 points out of a possible 68. It was Albion's rearguard which took most of the blame with 60 goals conceded.

Albion were back in the Second Division in 1904, with problems mounting all the time. There was little money in the bank. And on Bonfire Night that year, the old stand, transferred from Stoney Lane, joined in the activities and burned down — the cause was put down to an errant sky-rocket.

Meanwhile, Albion's creditors hammered at the door and the whole board resigned. Harry Keys returned as chairman. Billy Bassett joined the board with local businessmen, and two years' grace was obtained so that Albion could carry on.

Albion, 1904-05. Back row (left to right): F.Everiss (secretary), J.Kifford, I.Webb, R.H.Playfair, J.Pennington, Mr Dempster. Centre row: W.Barber (asst. trainer), A.Randle, L.Bell, H.Hadley, A.Lewis, J.Manners. Front row: W.Jack, H.Brown, H.Aston, G.Dorsett.

Twelve months later Albion were able to report a profit of £240 before charging depreciation, though £965 had been spent in transfer fees to strengthen the team.

One new player was Ted 'Cock' Pheasant, a half-back or centre-forward, who had rendered good service to Wolves. Another was Jack Manners, a pit lad from Morpeth Harriers in the North-East.

'Chippy' Simmons and Adam Haywood training at The Hawthorns in 1906.

Albion players out for a 'training walk' in 1905. From left to right: Fred Shinton, Eli Bradley, Bill Barber (trainer), Jim Stringer, Jesse Pennington, Jack Manners, 'Chippy' Simmons, George Young and Adam Haywood.

Dan Nurse had suffered a leg injury which eventually ended his career and to replace him, Albion introduced Arthur Randle, a talented Oldbury youngster.

Lawrie Bell, Albert Lewis — who scored a hat-trick on his debut at Burnley — Fred Haycock and Jimmy Williams were other newcomers in 1904-05, as were Jack Dawes, Llewellyn Davies — later to become a prominent Welsh international — goalkeeper Jim Stringer and centre-half Tom Hayward. Right at the end of the season Fred Shinton was signed from Hednesford Town.

Shinton was a player renowned for his aggressive all-action displays at centre-forward. His weight and strength made him a danger to any defence and he was second-highest scorer in his first full season (1905-06) with 18 goals. The following campaign he netted 28 goals in 30 matches, including four in one game on three separate occasions — against Clapton Orient, Glossop and Grimsby Town.

He suffered a nasty knock in the return game against Clapton in 1906-07 and never really recovered. He was transferred to Leicester Fosse after scoring 46 goals in only 64 League games in Albion colours.

Another player drafted into the first-team in the early 1900s was a young man called Jesse Pennington. Pennington became one of the greatest of all England left-backs, a man spoken of in high regard all over the country as 'Peerless Pennington'.

A tendency to drop points at home is not a fault that is new to Albion — they had the same trouble early in the century. For three successive seasons they finished no higher than fourth and no lower than fifth in Division Two — and each time it was dropped home points that cost them promotion.

They did keep their fans happy in 1907 when they reached the FA Cup semi-final — and the man mainly responsible was Oxford University undergraduate, Willie Jordan. Jordan, a member of a well-known Oldbury family, won a Blue and several amateur caps as a striker — and once scored six goals in a 15-0 win for England over France.

Albion could have done with a couple of those goals in 1908-09, when they missed promotion by one fifty-sixth of a goal. And Albion claimed that they were robbed by a referee's decision at Blackpool when Charlie Hewitt's shot hit the underside of the bar and rebounded out. Bill Garraty, the centre-forward, did not bother to tap it into the net because he thought Albion had scored, but the referee ruled the ball had not crossed the line and although Albion still won the match, they always reckoned that the decision cost them promotion.

It was during the years between 1906 and 1909 that several fine players first appeared for Albion, including Hubert Pearson, David Walker, Bill Davies, and a player who broke his leg four times in his career, Albert Evans. Tommy Dilly signed in 1907 and was the last Scottish-born player to join Albion for 30 years.

Season 1909-10 saw the Albion finish 11th in Division Two — their lowest position in League football — and for 1910-11 the Throstles gambled and practically rebuilt their side, many of the new players never having played League football before.

The move paid off and Albion won the Second Division Championship with one of the youngest sides they have ever fielded. The team that season usually read — Pearson; Smith, Pennington, Baddeley, Waterhouse, McNeal, Wollaston, Bowser, Pailor, Buck, Lloyd.

Jesse Pennington, Albion's great star.

Hubert Pearson served Albion for over 20 years, making more than 370 appearances and was followed into The Hawthorns team by his son, Harold. Joe Smith, who was signed from Cradley St Luke's, was capped three times for England and played 471 games for Albion. Another England player was Bobby McNeal, who was converted from an inside-forward and turned out more than 400 times for Albion. And former Wattville Road schoolboy, Sid Bowser, played for England at centre-half after starting his career as a centre-forward.

Albion clinched the title with a 1-0 win over Huddersfield in the last game of the season — the vital goal coming from a Freddie Buck penalty that went through the Huddersfield 'keeper's legs.

Back in the First Division, Albion finished a respectable ninth, but it was their Cup run that made the news, as the Throstles once more stormed through to the Final. En route they beat some good sides. Indeed only one goal had been conceded in seven matches and Albion were favourites to beat Barnsley in the Final But they failed and a row blew up over the replaying of the FA Cup Final in 1912. Albion lost the argument and lost the match too.

Albion 1908-09. Back row (left to right): Mr R.Fellows, E.Pheasant. J.Stringer, Mr H.Keys, J.Pennington, Mr F.Everiss (secretary), W.Thompson, J.Manners. Front row: R.Fielding, S.Timmins, C.Hewitt, F.Brown, A.Evans, F.Buck, W.C.Davies, G.Baddeley.

Albion team 1910. Back row (left to right): Evans, Paddock, Timmins, Richards, Pearson, Pailor, F.Everiss (secretary), Baddeley, Manners, D.Nurse (director). Centre row: Barber (trainer), Wollaston, Buck, Smith, Waterhouse. Front row: Shearman, Bowser, Pennington, Lloyd, Cook.

Albion skipper Bill Garraty (stripes) and Barnsley's Tommy Boyle tossing up before the start of a Division Two game at Oakwell on 14 April 1910.

Action from that Barnsley v Albion game in 1910.

25

Albion, Division Two champions, 1910-11. Back row (left to right): W.Barber (trainer), J.Manners, D.G.Nurse (director), R. 'Dick' Betteley, H.Pearson, W.I.Bassett (chairman), R.Pailor, S.Bowser, H.Wright, G.Baddeley, F.Everiss (secretary). Centre row: H.Keys (director), R.McNeal, F.Buck, J.Pennington, J.Smith, Major H.Ely (director). Front row: F.Waterhouse W.Wollaston, A.Lloyd.

Hubert Pearson punches clear during a raid on the Albion goal in the Division One game at White Hart Lane in September 1911.

Albion v Barnsley in the 1912 FA Cup Final at The Crystal Palace.

26

Albion 1 Aston Villa 0, Division One 4 October 1913. Top left: Hubert Pearson, Albion's goalkeeper, punching clear. Top right: Joe Smith, Albion, and Joe Bache fight for supremacy. Left: Harry Hampton, Villa, dives in but his header strikes an upright.

The original game at The Crystal Palace was drawn 0-0. When the FA announced that the replay was to be held at Sheffield, Albion protested. Their objections were overruled and the huge majority of the 38,500 crowd were Yorkshiremen urging Barnsley to victory. A 119th-minute goal by Tufnell beat Albion.

On the way to that Final there had been a crowd of 45,000 — with mounted police in attendance — when Albion beat Sunderland in the quarter-final on Wearside, and a goal by Pailor a minute from the end of extra-time won a replayed semi-final against Blackburn Rovers.

But the Cup run cost Albion dearly. They were so far behind with their League matches that they had to play 12 games in April, including one spell of seven games in ten days either side of the Final and the replay. Albion were fined by the League for fielding a weakened side in one of those games.

Albion's average League attendance of 18,042 was one of the highest in the First Division. The cash from these 'gates' allowed the

club to buy the freehold of The Hawthorns in June 1913, for £5,350. A year later they were able to finish work on the grandstand.

World War One broke out in August 1914 but League football continued for a season and was then broken down into regional competitions. One player to emerge from the conflict was Tommy Magee, the 'Pocket Hercules' who was to serve the Albion so well for 15 years. Magee, a soldier serving on the Western Front, was reccommended to Albion by one of his army colleagues, Tom Brewer.

But if the war produced a great Albion player, it took away another when Lt Harold Bache was killed in action on 15 February 1916.

Peace in 1918 was followed by the resumption of League football and that brought extra joy to Albion in the shape of their very first League Championship. They finished 1919-20 nine points clear of runners-up Burnley with 60 points from 28 wins and 104 goals. Just to cap the season Albion made a profit of £7,432.

League Champions 1919-1920

ALBION have won the First Division Championship only once, in 1919-20 — the first post-war season — when they coasted home with 60 points, nine clear of second-placed Burnley. Albion recorded 28 wins, drew only four of their 42 games, and scored a record 104 goals, conceding 47.

Albion clinched the title on Saturday, 10 April 1920 when Bradford were defeated 3-1 at The Hawthorns in front of nearly 30,000 spectators

The Throstles' season had started on 30 August 1919 with a 3-1 home win over Oldham. Freddie Morris scored twice and Tommy Magee made his League Debut.

A 2-0 win at Newcastle followed, with Pearson saving a penalty, and then Oldham turned the tables, winning the return 2-1.

Four successive wins sent Albion storming on. They triumphed 3-0 over Newcastle, beat Everton 4-3 at home and 5-2 away, and defeated Bradford City 4-1, with centre-half Sid Bowser claiming a hat-trick, including two penalties.

City, however, grabbed revenge and won the return 3-0 on the first Saturday in October.

Three more successive wins boosted Albion's confidence. Bolton were beaten 4-1 at The Hawthorns and 2-1 at Burnden Park, and an 8-0 hammering of Notts County saw Morris score five splendid goals to cheer the 36,086 crowd.

County, though, caused a major upset by beating Albion 2-0 in the return, and then Villa smashed West Brom's unbeaten home record with a 2-1 win on the 10 November. Yet that defeat was soon forgotten when Albion went to Villa Park and won the return 4-2 in front of 58,273 fans.

A second home lapse — a 3-1 defeat by Sheffield Wednesday — was followed by a great run of six consecutive victories, with the double coming over Manchester City (3-2 and 2-0), and Derby (4-0 and 3-0), plus victories over Wednesday (3-0), and Sunderland (4-0).

At the season's half-way stage Albion were one point clear at the top of the table with 32 to Burnley's 31. Newcastle were third and Sunderland fourth. At this point Albion had still to draw a game.

Into 1920 and Albion continued to prosper. After a 4-1 setback at Sunderland, they hammered Blackburn for ten goals in two games, winning 5-1 away and 5-2 at home. A 2-1 success over Manchester United saw a five-point gap open up over Burnley and the Championship prize was in sight.

Sheffield United jolted Albion by completing the double over them (2-0 and 1-0), before a run of eight games without defeat sent the Throstles' hopes soaring. They beat Middlesbrough, Manchester United, Burnley, Preston (twice) and Bradford, and drew with Middlesbrough and Burnley to pull six points clear of Burnley who had only four games left.

A 1-0 Easter defeat at Arsenal was avenged the following day when the Gunners were pipped by a Morris goal, and on 10 April, the title came to West Bromwich.

The run-in brought two draws against Liverpool (1-1 and 0-0), a 2-0 defeat at Chelsea and then a tremendous 4-0 finale against Chelsea at home when the Championship trophy was presented to Jesse Pennington, in front of 35,668 cheering supporters.

Fred Morris, with 37 goals (a new club record), topped the scoring charts. Alf Bentley (15), Howard Gregory (12), Bowser (10 including eight penalties), Jack Crisp (eight), Magee and Andy Smith (seven each), Claude Jephcott (five), Bobby McNeal (two) and an own-goal made up the total of 104.

Only McNeal was an ever-present in the side (42 games); Bowser made 41 appearances, Sam Richardson and Joe Smith each 40, followed by Hubert Pearson and Morris (39 each), Crisp (38), Pennington (37), Gregory (34), Andy Smith (29), Magee (24), Bentley (24), Jephcott (21), Cook (seven), Len Moorwood (three), Frank Waterhouse (two), Fred Reed and Sam Hatton (one each).

The average League gate at The Hawthorns in 1919-20 was 30,532, and, for the record, Albion were knocked out of the FA Cup in round one by Barnsley, but that hardly mattered.

Albion, 1919-20 Division One Champions. Back row (left to right): T.W.Barber (trainer), H.Pearson, W.Gopsill (masseur), E.Smith (ast. secretary). Third row: F.Everiss (secretary), D.Nurse (director), A.Cook, W.Bassett (chairman), H.Keys (director), A.C.Jephcott, A.Seymour (director), Lt Col Ely (director). Second row: J.Crisp, A.W.Smith, R.McNeal, J.Pennington, S.Bowser, F.Morris, H.Gregory. Front row: J.Smith, T.Magee, A.Bentley, S.Richardson.

Howard Gregory got in on the act with Albion's seventh goal.

Tommy Magee capped a fine display of creative football when he scored Albion's eighth goal.

Freddie Morris was in great form with five goals.

Match to Remember 8   25 October 1919

Albion 8   Notts County 0

ALBION had already achieved some major scoring feats before this match against Notts County at The Hawthorns in the first League season after World War One, but no one could have forseen this performance when poor Notts were slammed for eight goals without reply.

Indeed, Albion's fans were worrying about the absence of Pearson, Smith, Bowser and Jephcott, all regular first-teamers. Their fears were groundless and the Throstles' goals rained home, six of them coming in a splendid second half when County hardly got out of their own penalty area.

Freddie Morris netted twice in the first 45 minutes, both goals coming from fine moves which involved four and five players. After the interval, Morris completed his hat-trick and then Notts' Foster turned Jack Crisp's centre past his own goalkeeper, the great Albert Iremonger.

Morris added two more to put Albion 6-0 ahead and take his own personal tally to five. His fourth was laid on by a superb piece of creative football from Tommy Magee, the

'Mighty Atom', and his fifth followed some splendid wing play from Crisp.

Howard Gregory darted in to slip home goal number seven, and Magee capped a fine display by claiming the eighth when he scored from close range after Morris's shot hit the bar.

Albion's forwards had been absolutely brilliant and there had been some remarkable individual displays as well as some great team-work. Nothing seemed to go amiss and it was County's misfortune to meet Albion when the Throstles were in such rampant form.

Seven days later, however, Albion went to Meadow Lane and lost 2-0, just to underline the unpredictability of football.

Albion: Moorwood; Cook, Pennington, Richardson, Reed, McNeal, Crisp, Magee, A.W.Smith, Morris, Gregory.
Notts County: Iremonger; Tasker, Marriott, Flint, Pembleton, Foster, Cooke, Cook, McLeod, Hill, Henshall.

Attendance: 36,086

Referee: Mr J.W.D.Fowler (Sunderland)

Full-back Jesse Pennington appeared in a total of 496 competitive games for Albion (1903-22) yet never scored a goal.

Another international full-back, Joe Smith, was goalless in 471 first-class matches for Albion (1910-26) and Bob Finch and Bert Trentham failed to find the net in 234 and 272 senior outings respectively.

Albion's defensive formation of Pearson, Smith, Pennington, Richardson, Bowser and McNeal played together as a unit in 32 games and one FA Cup-tie in 1919-20 — a club record.

Yet the 'Roaring Twenties' were depressing times for Albion after such a fine first season following the war. There were only a few moments of glory as the team struggled to recapture the exciting flair and method of that Championship-winning season.

> At Warwick races on 30 March 1925, a horse called King Throstle won the opening race, while the second event was won by a colt called Top of the League. The same afternoon, Albion defeated Sheffield United 2-1 to go to the top of the First Division.

They managed to finish runners-up to Huddersfield Town in 1924-5, but two years later, finished bottom with 30 points and went back into Division Two.

It was said that a 'weakness in defence' was the cause of relegation — despite a rearguard that included Harold Pearson (in goal in place of his father), George Shaw, signed from Huddersfield Town half-way through the term, and newcomer Bob Finch.

Those years are best glossed over, but there were one or two moments to remember. Like the match in 1922-3 in which Freddie Morris scored four times in a 7-0 win over Arsenal. And the emergence of Stan Davies, the utility forward, who played in six different positions in 19 appearances for Wales.

There was also the flourishing wing partnership of Tommy Glidden and Joe Carter, who set up many chances for the goalscoring combination of George James and Charlie Wilson. James had topped the 1924-5 scoring charts with 30 goals.

Albion's forward-line during the 1924-5 season: Tommy Glidden, Joe Carter, George James, 'Tug' Wilson and Jack Byers.

Joe Smith (grounded) clears the danger as skipper Fred Reed looks on during the FA Cup game against Sheffield United at Bramall Lane in 1925.

30

Albion team 1925-6. Back row (left to right): S.Davies, P.Hunt (ast. trainer), T.Gopsill (trainer), H.Pearson, T.Sproson, G.Ashmore, S.Guest (ast. trainer), J.Evans, T.Magee. Third row: E.Smith (ast. secretary), R.McNeal, T.Glidden, J.Byers, H.Chamberlain, A.Fitton, J.Smith, J.Carter, H.Dutton, W.Adams, F.Everiss (secretary). Second row: R.Finch, E.Rooke, S.Richardson, I.Jones, W.I.Bassett (chairman), F.Reed, G.James, J.Poxton, R.Baugh. Front row: H.Smith, C.Wilson, S.Short, E.Hickman, J.Hallows, H.Gregory.

By the end of the decade there were already signs of an Albion recovery. The starting point of this resurgence in the Throstles' fortunes can be traced back to the day they signed Jimmy Cookson from Chesterfield in June 1927.

Cookson had been released by Manchester City, and Chesterfield converted him from a defender into a forward with instant success. He smashed the Chesterfield scoring record in his first season and a host of clubs chased his signature.

Albion won the race and as soon as Cookson arrived at The Hawthorns he found the net. At the end of his first season Freddie Morris' scoring record had gone as 'Cooky' netted 38 League goals, including six in the home game against Blackpool.

Indeed, three seasons in Division Two saw Albion involved in some big scorelines. They beat Grimsby 6-0 in January 1928, and the following Christmas hammered Wolves 7-3.

In 1929-30 they scored 105 League goals — a club record that still stands. Cookson scored 33 of those goals to take his tally for three seasons to 92. Tommy Glidden hit 54 over the same period and Joe Carter 46.

Other new faces had joined up now — Bert Trentham was at full-back, Len Darnell at left-half, Frank Cresswell at inside-left and Stan Wood his wing partner.

Undoubtedly the most significant arrivals shared the same name — and they were to be household names for years to come. The

Albion, 1928-9 team group. Back row (left to right): P.Hunt (ast. trainer), W.Richardson, J.Edwards, A.Parry, H.Pearson, L.Darnell, G.Ashmore, J.Carter, H.Webster, J.Evans, S.Wood, J.Hudson, Mr E.Jones (ground assistant). Third row: E.Smith (ast. secretary), F.Everiss (secretary), E.Pattison, Mr L.Nurse (director), Mr H.Keys (director), Mr W.I.Bassett (director), Dr J.Round (director), Mr W.Hackett (director), T.Glidden, S.Guest (ast. trainer), F.Reed (trainer). Second row: R.Fryer, G.James, N.Howarth, J.Rix, R.Baugh, S.Short, E.Bromage, F.Corbett, B.Cope, R.Finch. Front row: F.Leedham, F.White, J.Cookson, J.Murphy, A.Fitton, G.Shaw, A.Taylor, G.Bytheway, T.Magee.

Albion 7   Arsenal 0

WITH 18 minutes remaining in this First Division game at The Hawthorns, Albion led Arsenal 2-0 and there was a slim possibility that the Gunners might yet sneak their way back into the match. Then came a sensational finale — five goals by a vintage Albion display which produced some quite astonishing attacking play.

A week earlier, Arsenal had beaten Albion 3-1 at Highbury and for the return match in the Black Country, West Brom fielded the same team whilst Arsenal made only one change, at full-back.

In the opening quarter of the game, both goals came under threat. Jones and Morris went close for Albion — Arsenal 'keeper Dunn making two good saves — and Rutherford and Voysey had chances for the Gunners.

After 29 minutes it was Albion who drew first blood when Smith, Jones and Stan Davies combined down the right to give Davies a chance. Dunn blocked the Albion man's effort but the ball ran loose for the ever-alert Morris to slam the ball home.

Two minutes later, Morris added a second, cashing in on a slip by Turnbull. And on the stroke of half-time, Davies had a 'goal' disallowed for offside, although the Albion man disputed the decision fiercely.

Arsenal began the second half in rampant form, pressing the Throstles back, but Albion's defence held firm — one report said that the home defenders 'lay low like Brer Rabbit' as the Gunners chased the goal that would have put them back in contention.

Young and White both had half-chances but this time it was the turn of Albion goalkeeper, Pearson, to produce two fine saves. Pearson's alertness proved the turning point of the game for, after soaking up the pressure, Albion returned to the attack in no uncertain terms.

The Throstles crashed home five hammer blows in less than 15 minutes. After 71 minutes, Jack Crisp netted from Davies's clever cross; five minutes later, Morris completed his hat-trick when he cracked home a short pass from Jones; less than 60 seconds later, Crisp made it 5-0 with a close-range shot.

And so Albion continued: Morris set up Gregory for their sixth goal after 78 minutes, then Morris himself rounded off a splendid afternoon's work by grabbing his fourth and Albion's seventh goal with six minutes remaining.

In the final seconds, Davies came within inches of making it 8-0 and then the whistle blew to leave Albion only four points behind the First Division leaders, Liverpool.

Albion: Pearson; Smith, Adams, Magee, Bowser, McNeal, Crisp, Jones, Davies, Morris, Gregory.
Arsenal: Dunn; Bradshaw, Turnbull, Baker, Voysey, Graham, Rutherford, White, Young, Boreham, Dr.Patterson.

Attendance: 21,730

Referee: Mr W.F.Bunnell (Preston)

Stan Davies proved inspirational in Albion's attack. He laid on two goals, had one disallowed and in the final seconds was a coat of paint away from scoring an eighth goal.

Fred Morris rounded off a fine afternoon with his fourth goal and Albion's seventh.

Goalkeeper Hubert Pearson was another Albion hero and his alertness proved the turning point of the game.

When Manchester City transferred Jimmy Cookson to Chesterfield in 1925 they little imagined he would create a League goalscoring record that same season. Cookson, however, proved an immediate success and netted 44 goals in 38 appearances, including two games at full-back, his former position. The following season, Cookson scored 42 goals and that led to Albion's interest. Cookson did not disappoint the Throstles and was soon writing himself into the record books.

Tommy Glidden's measured pass gave Cookson his first goal in the sixth minute.

Match to Remember 10   17 September 1927

Albion 6   Blackpool 3

WHEN a useful Blackpool team visited The Hawthorns for a Second Division match at the beginning of the 1927-8 season, Albion centre-forward Jimmy Cookson turned the occasion into a personal triumph, scoring all six goals against the Seasiders.

From the first kick of the game it was evident that both teams were hungry for goals and the 20,000 crowd saw nine go into the net. Indeed, they would have been treated to a dozen or more but for some fine goalkeeping from both Ashmore and Hobbs.

Albion went ahead in the sixth minute when Cookson flicked home Glidden's measured pass. Blackpool hit back, then it was Albion's turn to counter-attack. It was action all the way and in the 33rd minute, a misunderstanding between Evans and Fryer allowed Tuffnell to nip in and equalise.

Two minutes into the second half, Albion were awarded a penalty when Thorpe handled Fitton's cross. Cookson thumped the spot kick past Hobbs and ten minutes later completed his hat-trick, cooly gliding home the ball to make it 3-1.

Tuffnell was on hand to reduce the arrears but if Blackpool then harboured thoughts of another equaliser, they were to be bitterly disappointed. Cookson, who was playing absolutely brilliantly, scored a second hat-trick, his trio of goals coming in the space on only seven minutes.

In the 63rd minute Glidden and Carter combined for Albion's hero of the day to net his fourth; his fifth came after his own initial effort had rebounded off the 'keeper; and after 70 minutes Fitton and Wilson set him up and then watched as the centre-forward lashed home a rocket of a shot from 10 yards.

Blackpool, to their credit, never gave up and ten minutes from time, Williams reduced the arrears with a long-range shot which dropped over Ashmore's head from fully 35 yards.

Right on the final whistle, Cookson thought he had scored a seventh goal but his delight was short-lived as an upraised linesman's flag robbed him. Nevertheless, Jimmy Cookson's feat went into the record books, for no other Albion player has equalled his tally of six goals in a single League or Cup game for the club.

Albion: Ashmore; Finch, Shaw, Magee, Evans, Fryer, Glidden, Carter, Cookson, Wilson, Fitton.
Blackpool: Hobbs; Thorpe, Tilford, Watson, Grimwood, Benton, Meredith, Browell, Williams, Tuffnell, Downes.

Attendance: 20,203

Referee: Mr G.N. Watson (West Bridgford)

The following unusually-named players have been associated with Albion over the years:
Willie Croot, Ernie Fancutt, Freddie Fido, Levi Howse, Reggie Kestiven-Humber, Baalaam Loviband, Jipson Peppard, Pantell Herbert Rainbow, Mountford 'Monty' Royle, Hedley Sara, Silvanius Sirnon, Lester J. Truby and Middleton Wilder. None of them were foreigners and none appeared in the club's first eleven.

In September 1927 centre-forward Jimmy Cookson, then of West Bromwich Albion, completed the quickest-ever century of Football League goals — in only his 89th match. In that very same month, Cookson, who was once a full-back, set a still-existing Albion record of scoring six League goals in one match, against Blackpool at The Hawthorns.

Albion's front line, 1928-9 (left to right): Glidden, Carter, Cookson, Chambers, Wood.

Albion's defensive trio of Bob Finch, Harold Pearson and George Shaw who played together in more than 50 matches between 1927 and 1933.

William Richardsons turned out at centre-half and centre-forward respectively in the same Albion side in the early 1930s.

The problem of identification was solved by the centre-forward's hair colouring. He was renamed 'W.G.' — for 'Ginger' Richardson.

Billy Richardson, the centre-half, was a local lad who had just won his place in the side when his namesake arrived from Hartlepools United, who were playing in the Third Division North.

'W.G.' was to lead the Albion attack for the next 16 years, achieving many scoring feats. Incredibly, he was capped only once for England — a 1-0 win over Holland in 1935.

> The first live radio broadcast of an Albion home match was their sixth round FA Cup tie against Wolverhampton Wanderers on 28 February 1931.

The team was settled and success arrived again, but there was controversy over Albion's 1931 FA Cup Final win that set up the famous 'double' of Cup success and promotion from the Second Division.

The row surrounded a 'goal that wasn't' for Birmingham. It came in the first-half when Gregg headed the ball past Harold Pearson. The linesman flagged for offside and the referee, Mr Kingscott from Derby, agreed. Blues fans maintained that their side were robbed, but a man who was close to the action, Tommy Magee, said later, "Gregg was a yard offside — he was in front of me and I was the last Albion defender apart from 'Pop' Pearson."

'W.G.' Richardson had put Albion into the lead after 25 minutes. Joe Bradford equalised for Birmingham, but it was not to last. Straight from the kick-off 'W.G.' prodded home Albion's second.

Tommy Glidden took the trophy from the Duke of Gloucester and 150,000 people lined the streets of West Bromwich when the team returned in triumph.

The Cup victory came at the end of a season that included great League wins — 4-0 and 6-3 at Charlton and Cardiff respectively, 6-1 at Nottingham Forest, 4-0 over Stoke and 5-0 against Barnsley.

The men who played in most of the matches were Harold Pearson, George Shaw, Bert Trentham, Tommy Magee, Billy Richardson, Jimmy Edwards, Tommy Glidden, Joe Carter, 'W.G.' Richardson, Teddy Sandford and Stanley Wood.

Saturday, 2 May 1931 was the proudest day in the history of Albion and the day a new page was written in the story of English football. It was the afternoon that Albion won promotion from Division Two, adding to their FA Cup win of a week before and so completing a 'double' never achieved before or since.

Cliff Bastin, Arsenal, shooting for goal as George Shaw, Albion, attempts to cover at Highbury 1931.

▲ Harry Hibbs, Birmingham, watches Tommy Glidden's cross bounce on top of his crossbar during the 1931 FA Cup Final at Wembley.

Tommy Glidden, with Cup, leads the players down the '39 steps' ▼ after Albion had beaten Birmingham 2-1 in the 1931 Final.

Albion 3   Charlton Athletic 2

WEST Bromwich Albion's defeat of Charlton ended a magnificent season for the Throstles, leaving them with the unique double of FA Cup and promotion from Division Two in the same season.

Albion went into their game against Charlton knowing that victory was the only certain way back to Division One after an absence of four years. A draw might be sufficient, but then they would have to rely on the results of other promotion contenders.

Albion also knew that their task would not be an easy one, for Charlton had given the Throstles a tough battle in three FA Cup matches on Albion's road to Wembley that season. Still, the Black Country team had the boost of an FA Cup Final victory over neighbours Birmingham, and a 1-0 win at Stoke just two days before they met Charlton.

A huge crowd saw Charlton dominate the early exchanges and it was no surprise when Dai Astley shot the Londoners in front after only eight minutes. After 37 minutes, Teddy Sandford equalised for Albion, only for Astley to restore Charlton's lead almost immediately.

Back bounced Albion once more and before half-time, skipper Tommy Glidden had levelled the scores again. The teams walked to the dressing-rooms with the game — and Albion's immediate future — still agonisingly poised.

In the 68th minute, The Hawthorns erupted when W.G.Richardson, a player not renowned for his heading ability, darted forward to nod the ball home following fine work by Glidden and Carter.

Albion hung on to that slender lead and when the whistle blew, spectators swarmed on to the pitch, overwhelming the last few Albion players to leave the stage of this great victory. They battled hard to join their colleagues in the Directors' Box to acknowledge the rapturous cheers of the fans.

Albion: Pearson; Finch, Shaw, Magee, W.Richardson, Edwards, Glidden, Carter, W.G.Richardson, Sandford, Wood.
Charlton Athletic: Robertson; Smith, Langford, Pitcairn, Pritchard, Pugsley, Wyper, McKay, Astley, McLeod, Horton.

Attendance: 52,415 (Receipts £3,155.9s.0d)

Referee: Mr W.E.Russell (Northampton)

Left: W.G.Richardson (far right) watches his header fly past Charlton goalkeeper Robertson to send Albion back to Division One.
Below left and right: Throstles' fans pour across The Hawthorns pitch to acclaim the unique double winners.

DOUBLE WINNERS 1930-31

Albion created football history in 1930-1 when they won promotion from the Second Division and also carried off the FA Cup, beating neighbours, Birmingham 2-1 in the Final at Wembley. This feat has still to be equalled.

Albion clinched a place in the First Division by winning their 42nd and last League game of the season, 3-2 at home to Charlton Athletic, before a record 52,415 crowd.

Everton won the Second Division Championship with 61 points —seven more than Albion, who had three points to spare over third-placed Tottenham Hotspur. In the Cup Final — seven days before that vital last League match — Albion went 1-0 ahead in the 25th minute with a W.G.Richardson goal. Joe Bradford equalised for the Blues 20 minutes into the second-half but within a matter of seconds, Albion were back in front with W.G.'s winning second goal.

Albion entertained wherever they went with their forceful attacking play. They netted a total of 99 goals in 52 competitive games, and five players — W.G.Richardson, Glidden, Wood, Cookson and Carter — each reached double figures in the scoring list.

Albion's 'double' winning side. Standing (left to right): Mr F.Everiss (secretary), W.Richardson, Carter, Pearson, Trentham, Sandford, F.Reed (trainer). Seated: Shaw, Magee, W.G.Richardson, Mr W.I.Bassett (chairman), Edwards, Wood, Glidden.

Medal Winners

Tommy Magee is the only player to have won an FA Cup winners' medal (1931) and a First Division Championship medal (1919-20) with Albion.

Charlie Perry, Billy Bassett and Tom Pearson all gained two FA Cup winners' medals with the club (1888 and 1892) and Doug Fraser, Graham Williams, Tony Brown, Jeff Astle, John Kaye, Graham Lovett, Bobby Hope and Clive Clark, each received a League Cup winners' tankard (1966) and an FA Cup winners' medal (1968) during their Albion careers.

Johnny Giles had in his possession when he arrived at The Hawthorns as player-manager in 1975, a wonderful collection of medals which he had won with Manchester United and Leeds. Whilst at Old Trafford he received an FA Cup winners' medal (1963) and

with Leeds he won League Championship medals in 1969 and 1974, a Division Two Championship medal in 1964, an FA Cup winners' medal in 1972, League Cup winners' tankard (1968), and Inter-Cities Fairs Cup winners' medals in 1968 and 1971. In addition he received losers' medals in the Finals of the following competitions: FA Cup 1965, 1970 and 1973; Fairs Cup 1967 and European Cup 1975. All told Giles played in eleven FA Cup semi-finals (including replays) and he shares the record for most appearances in the Final of the FA Cup — five — all at Wembley. He also played in the 1970 Final replay against Chelsea, making it six appearances collectively in that competition — a record in itself. After leaving Albion Giles gained an FAI Cup winners' medal with Shamrock Rovers. His only honour with Albion was winning promotion from Division Two in 1975-6.

Vic Watson (West Ham, centre) darts between Albion's full-back Bert Trentham and goalkeeper Harold Pearson in the League game at Upton Park on 7 November 1931.

Between 1931 and 1935, Albion were involved in some more high-scoring games. There was a 6-5 defeat by Grimsby, at home, a 4-4 draw at Blackburn, a 7-2 win at Maine Road over Manchester City, 6-5 and 6-4 scorelines against Sunderland, and a 4-4 draw with Aston Villa at Villa Park. All this brought the crowds flocking back to The Hawthorns. Attendances were averaging well over 20,000 — good figures for those days.

Chelsea against Albion at Stamford Bridge, 1933-4. 'W.G.' Richardson is foiled by the home goalkeeper, Vic Woodley.

The scenes at The Hawthorns after the victory over Charlton were never to be forgotten. Even when the players managed to reach the dressing-room they had to go out again and again to acknowledge their supporters, who refused to go home until due homage had been paid.

The historic double had a profitable spin-off for Albion. It allowed ground improvements to be carried out at The Hawthorns, including the provision of tip-up seats in the Halfords Lane stand and new surfacing on the terracing. Later that year, the Great Western Railway opened a railway station less than 200 yards from the main entrance to the ground.

Albion had arrived. More than 55,000 people turned up to see the Throstles' first match back in Division One. Arsenal were the hosts but Albion were the winners, a goal from Stan Wood earning them both points in London.

Albion's ticket allocation for the 1931 FA Cup Final against Birmingham at Wembley was a mere 7,500 — yet over 80,000 fans applied for them.

'Piggy-back' rides for George Shaw on Joe Carter (left) and Bert Trentham on Bill Richardson, 1932.

Albion had little trouble holding their own in the top flight, finishing sixth in the first season and fourth the next year. New faces arrived at The Hawthorns. Jimmy Murphy replaced Tommy Magee; Walter Robbins, the man with 'tree-trunk' legs and thumping shot, came from Cardiff; and schoolteacher Arthur Gale was appearing at either centre-forward or outside-right.

Public practice match at The Hawthorns in 1934. Albion's reserve goalkeeper, Ted Crowe, is under pressure following a corner kick.

Four years after their 1931 Wembley triumph, Albion were back at the Empire Stadium, but this time they were not successful, as the management took a gamble on the day of the 1935 FA Cup Final — and lost both the gamble and the Cup.

The right-wing pair of Tommy Glidden and Joe Carter both had knee injuries in the weeks before the Final against Sheffield Wednesday. Glidden had had a cartilage operation but was playing again before the Final. Carter was still receiving treatment right until the eve of the big game.

Secretary Fred Everiss had talks with Glidden, the captain, and after Carter had also assured him that he was fit, the board included both men in the team. After only ten minutes Carter was limping; Glidden was far from match fit and faded in the second-half when his side needed him most.

Wednesday finished 4-2 victors of a fine game in which Albion were twice behind but each time pulled back, first through Boyes and then through Sandford. Injuries apart, Albion had a good chance of pulling off a victory against the odds but 'W.G.' Richardson, of all people, missed a 'sitter' when the scores were level at 2-2.

Goalkeeper Harold Pearson punches clear from a corner-kick during an FA Cup tie against Sheffield United at The Hawthorns in 1935. The other Albion players are, left to right, Bert Trentham, George Shaw, Bill Richardson and Joe Carter.

Albion goalkeeper, Harold Pearson, tipping the ball over the bar during the 1935 FA Cup Final against Sheffield Wednesday at Wembley.

When Albion played Newcastle United at The Hawthorns in a First Division match on 4 March 1933, there were 18 players with FA Cup winners' medals on view — ten from Albion, eight from United.

Albion's bid for Central League honours in the 1930s attracted bigger crowds than some first-team matches. In March 1934, there were 22,372 people at The Hawthorns to watch Albion and Aston Villa in a Central League game. A week later, for the first-team match against Huddersfield Town, the turn-out was only just over 16,000.

In those days Albion reserves were making history. Between 1932 and 1935 they won the Central League Championship three times in succession. To mark the feat, Albion were presented with an inscribed silver salver by the League.

New faces arriving on the scene at The Hawthorns in the late 1930s included Jimmy 'Doc' Adams, the goalkeeper who was to assist Albion throughout the war, 'Sandy' McNab, a Scotsman from Sunderland, Cecil Shaw, who made 126 consecutive appearances for Wolves, and Gilbert Alsop, the hero of Walsall's sensational FA Cup win over Arsenal in 1933.

39

Albion's forwards could hardly be blamed for their side's defeat and W.G.Richardson was one who continually looked for openings to keep his side in the lead.

Stan Wood had a particularly good game on Albion's left wing but his efforts eventually counted for nought.

On the day it was Albion's defenders who let their side down. Chirbury-born left-back Bert Trentham was normally a very sound defender but he, like his colleagues in the rearguard, would quickly have wanted to forget the visit of relegated Grimsby Town.

Albion 5   Grimsby Town 6

ALBION'S 1931-32 League season came to thrilling, yet inglorious end when they lost this 11-goal tussle with Grimsby Town. It came as something of a shock to The Hawthorns fans that they could witness their side scoring five goals at home — yet still lose.

Eleven goals in one League match was indeed something of a sensation and the rapid scoring and constant see-sawing of the state of the game maintained a high pitch of excitement throughout the 90 minutes.

Without trying to minimise the merit of Grimsby's display, it must be said that Albion's defence was quite awful. The forwards could accept no responsibilty for the defeat — after all, they had scored five goals — and Stan Wood, in particular, had a fine game on the left wing. Joe Carter was also impressive and W.G.Richardson continually searched for openings.

It was 'W.G.' who began the ding-dong battle after only three minutes, shooting Albion ahead. Holmes levelled the scores after 20 minutes, then Teddy Sandford eased Albion back into the lead six minutes later.

Holmes, a clever player with a particular gift for sniffing out goals, equalised for a second time on the half-hour, and then

Dyson squeezed the Mariners 3-2 up after 36 minutes. Albion fought back and before the interval Carter had made it 3-3 with a 10-yard snap shot.

A Jimmy Edwards' penalty soon after the restart sent Albion 4-3 ahead and in the 52nd minute, Tommy Glidden netted number five. It now seemed that the Throstles were home and dry — but Grimsby were far from down and out.

Slack Albion defending allowed Dyson to reduce the arrears after 54 minutes; Holmes completed his hat-trick to level the scores on the hour; and with 16 minutes remaining, Dyson also celebrated a hat-trick with Grimsby's sixth and match-winning goal.

Victory would have left Albion in fourth position but instead they finished sixth. The real ignominy for them was that Grimsby, despite their sensational win, were still relegated, having conceded 98 goals that season.

Albion: Pearson; Shaw, Trentham, Murphy, W.Richardson, Edwards, Glidden, Carter, W.G.Richardson, Sandford, Wood.
Grimsby Town: Read; Bateman, Jacobson, Hall, Seddon, Wilson, Dyson, Bestall, Holmes, Moralee, Marshall.

Attendance: 7,796   Referee: Mr S.Boardman (Hale)

Manchester City 2   Albion 7

IT WASN'T very often that big Frank Swift conceded seven goals in one game, especially in front of his own supporters. But on the first day of 1934, 'Swifty' had backache after Albion thrashed Manchester City at Maine Road in a First Division game.

It must be said that City's defence was like a colander that season, conceding 72 goals altogether as they finished fifth in Division One, yet on New Year's Day, Albion would probably have netted a hatfull against most teams. Their performance on a pitch made treacherous by a combination of frost and heavy rain was certainly one of their very best.

City's rearguard was frequently caught square by a quite brilliant Albion forward line for whom Walter Robbins had his best game in a Throstles shirt. Outside-right Tommy Glidden, also played superbly until he was injured with 20 minutes to play.

The *Manchester Guardian* said: 'Robbins was the forward of the match; Glidden too was brilliant, and W.G.Richardson took his chances in great style. City's Gregory met his master in W.Richardson, and Pearson, in goal, maintained the family reputation with a fine performance. Full-backs Trentham and Shaw kicked with wonderful accuracy and length. Albion were a magnificent team in every department'.

Strangely, it was City who took the lead, through Herd in the 20th minute, but before the interval Robbins, with two swift efforts, pushed Albion 2-1 ahead. Then it was W.G.Richardson's turn and between the 56th and 78th minutes he scored a grand hat-trick.

Wing-half Jackie Bray, a hobbling injured passenger on the left wing, pulled a goal back for City almost immediately, but late in the game, Joe Carter and Teddy Sandford added further goals for Albion to complete the Maine Road club's humiliation.

Manchester City: Swift; Barnett, Dale, Percival, Marshall, Bray, Toseland, Herd, Gregory, Busby, Book.
Albion: Pearson; Shaw, Trentham, Murphy, W.Richardson, Edwards, Glidden, Carter, W.G.Richardson, Sandford, Robbins.

Attendance: 20,996

Referee: Mr W.R.Jennings (York)

Albion outside-left Walter Robbins had his best game in a Throstles shirt.

Joe Carter added Albion's sixth goal to extend City's humiliation.

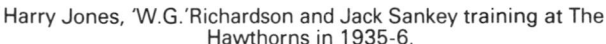
The two captains tossing up at Wembley 1935. Glidden, Albion, on the left and Starling, Sheffield Wednesday, on the right.

Harry Jones, 'W.G.'Richardson and Jack Sankey training at The Hawthorns in 1935-6.

Albion 3 Birmingham 2 at The Hawthorns in September 1936. 'W.G.'Richardson and Teddy Sandford are the Albion players.

There were goals galore in 1935-6 when Albion scored 89 and conceded 88. Among their wins was one of 7-0 at Villa Park which helped send Villa into the Second Division for the first time — 'W.G.'Richardson scored four that day.

March 1937 was a sad month for Albion. They lost an FA Cup semi-final and much more tragically also lost a grand servant in Mr William Isaiah Bassett. Billy Bassett, one-time player and long-term official of the club, died just two days before Albion took on Preston North End at Highbury. His death seemed to affect the team who were three goals down inside half-an-hour and finally lost 4-1.

The following year Albion were relegated, finishing bottom of the table and conceding 91 goals. The club's annual report stated: 'Injuries to key players at a vital period of the season undoubtedly prejudiced our position. However, we offer no excuses, and our mission is to get back to the First Division at the earliest possible moment.'

FOOTBALL LEAGUE JUBILEE TRUST FUND

On Saturday, 20 August 1938, Albion played Aston Villa in a Football League Jubilee Trust Fund match at Villa Park. A crowd of 26,640 paid £1,514 to see the 1-1 draw. Harry Jones scored for Albion and Frank Broome for Villa.

Albion fielded this team:-
Adams; Bassett, C.Shaw, Sankey, Davies, McNab, Hoyland, Heaselgrave, Jones, Burgin, Johnson.

Twelve months later, on Saturday 19 August 1939, the same two teams met again at the same venue — in a second Jubilee Trust Fund match. Once more the match ended at 1-1; W.G.Richardson (Albion) and Eric Houghton (Villa) scoring the goals. The attendance this time was 16,007 (receipts £960) and Albion lined up thus:
Adams; White, C.Shaw, Sankey, Gripton, McNab, E.Jones, Banks, W.G.Richardson, Connelly, Johnson.

That job was interrupted when League football was suspended upon the outbreak of World War Two but one of the players to emerge from the dark days of World War Two was Billy Elliott, signed from Bournemouth in 1938 after previously having a spell with Wolves.

Elliott marked his return to the Midlands with a series of dazzling wing displays that would have won him many more England caps but for the presence of Stanley Matthews. In all, Elliott played 330 senior matches for Albion and scored 157 goals. During the war alone, he scored 117 times in 148 games — including a few hat-tricks.

Elliott was the 'local' star of an Albion war-time line-up that often included famous names when players were loaned out to clubs. Some of the guests who played for Albion included George Hardwick (Middlesbrough), Gil Merrick and Don Dearson (Birmingham), Eddie Hapgood (Arsenal), Peter Doherty (Manchester City), Les Smith (Brentford) and Jack Acquaroff (Norwich City).

Arsenal's defensive plan for a corner during the match against Albion at Highbury in November 1937.

Newspaper catoonist Norman Edwards, selected highlights of Albion's story in the years leading up to World War Two

43

W.G.Richardson enjoyed many great triumphs in an Albion shirt but few could have been sweeter than his four goals at Villa Park.

Jack Sankey, Albion's left-half against Villa, also got on the scoresheet in one of the Throstles' sweetest-ever victories.

Match to Remember 14   19 October 1935

Aston Villa 0   Albion 7

VICTORY at Villa Park always tastes especially sweet for Albion fans. Whether it comes in League, Cup or even in friendly matches, the flavour is always good.

But Albion's defeat of Villa in the early days of the 1935-6 season caused a sensation. It was the talking point of Midlands soccer fans for months afterwards — and it created a record as the biggest scoreline for a match between these two old Midlands rivals.

The hero of the day was undoubtedly W.G.Richardson who scored four of Albion's seven goals, and who would have made it a double hat-trick had he accepted the two simple 'tap-in' chances in the later stages.

It should be remembered that Villa were a poor side this season and destined for relegation. Albion, on the other hand, were a useful team, having reached the FA Cup Final the previous season. Ten thousand Albion fans had made the short journey to Villa Park and they had something to celebrate as early as the seventh minute when W.G.Richardson scored from Jack Mahon's low cross.

Thus inspired, Albion struck again less than a minute later,

'W.G.' this time setting up a simple chance for Stan Wood. Playing with a gale-force wind at their backs, Villa tried to rally, but they found Albion's defence in splendid form, with goalkeeper Harold Pearson having an outstanding afternoon.

Helped by the wind, Villa were having more of the play, but after 25 minutes they found themselves 3-0 down when 'W.G.' netted a beauty from another pin-point cross from Mahon. Before the break, Mahon himself made it 4-0, after Wood had robbed Blair inside Villa's penalty area.

In the second half Albion eased up, yet still proved far too good for Villa. Further goals came from Jack Sankey (75 minutes) and 'W.G.' (77 and 78). Wood then had a goal disallowed, 'W.G.' missed those two simple chances, and Carter's shot hit the bar as Villa were swept away.

Aston Villa: Biddlestone; Beeson, Blair, Gibson, Allen, McLuckie, Houghton, Brocklebank, Broome, Astley, Cunliffe.
Albion: Pearson; Shaw, Trentham, Murphy, W.Richardson, Sankey, Mahon, Carter, W.G.Richardson, Sandford, Wood.

Attendance: 38,037   Referee: Mr G.Hewitt (St Helens)

In the mid-1930s, Albion had on their books a centre-half who 'owned' the longest string of names of any Football League player in history. He was christened Arthur Griffith Stanley Sackville Redvers Trevor Boscowan Trevis. His team-mates called him plain 'Bos'. Conversely, the shortest-named footballer ever to play for Albion is Jack Rix.

On 16 October 1907, Albion transferred to Derby County, Tommy Dilly, an outside-left. He was, in fact, the last Scot to play for Albion for more than 30 years — a League record. George Dudley, signed in 1937, ended Albion's 'No-Scot ruling' which was the idea of Billy Bassett.

44

Stoke 10   Albion 3

ALBION'S heaviest defeat in any senior competition came amidst the most amazing circumstances, with the Throstles' goalkeeper, Billy Light, literally rooted to the spot for almost all the game because of injury.

It was certainly an astonishing game and, whilst Stoke merited their victory, adapting much better to the pitch which was quite literally a quagmire, the Potters were greatly indebted to the fact that Albion persisted with the injured Light in goal.

Light's injury was sustained in the 11th minute, as Stoke took the lead. The goalkeeper hurt his ankle and was forced to leave the field. Inside-right Harry Jones donned the goalkeeper's sweater until Light returned with his ankle and foot heavily bandaged. He went back in goal, but from that moment could hardly move.

W.G.Richardson had managed to grab an equaiser whilst Albion were down to ten men, but with Light now returned, Stoke began to rain shots on his goal. By half-time they were 4-1 in front after Freddie Steele had completed a hat-trick and Turner had slotted home a penalty.

Joe Johnson made it 5-1 before Wally Boyes pulled back a goal for Albion, then Steele added two more to give Stoke a 7-2 lead with 22 minutes still to play. Johnson made it 8-2, and George Antonio scored Stoke's ninth and tenth goals before Walter Robbins flicked home Albion's third with eight minutes remaining.

Albion were left to reflect that they might have left Jones in goal, and to wonder what might have happened had centre-half Bill Richardson not been feeling unwell. Things then might have been different. As it was, the Throstles went crashing to a record defeat.

Stoke City: D.Westland; Brigham, Harbot, Tutin, Turner, Kirton, Matthews, Antonio, Steele, J.Westland, Johnson.
Albion: Light; Finch, C.Shaw, Murphy, W.Richardson, Boyes, Mahon, Jones, W.G.Richardson, Sandford, Robbins.

Attendance: 15,230   Referee: Mr H.E.Hull (Stockport)

Goalkeeper Billy Light was ill-advised to continue. Light could hardly stand as Stoke hammered Albion to their worst defeat.

Harry Jones, Albion's inside-right, replaced Light while the goalkeeper was treated for his injuries.

Joe Johnson, Stoke's left-winger who later joined Albion.

Wally Boyes scored one of Albion's consolation goals.

Albion's Jack Mahon scored twice in the Throstles' epic victory over the great Arsenal team, his second goal bringing huge relief after the Gunners had fought back to 2-1.

Ted Sandford, Albion's centre-half against Arsenal, had a fine game in blotting out the Gunners' Alf Kirchen. Sandford had started his Albion career as an inside-forward and within a year of gaining a first-team place had won an FA Cup-winners medal in 1931.

Albion 3   Arsenal 1

NEVER again will a near 65,000 crowd pack The Hawthorns. The record attendance for the ground was set in 1937 when mighty Arsenal, the team of the 1930s and one of the greatest of any era, visited West Brom for a sixth-round FA Cup tie. Gates were shut half-an-hour before kick-off and the 64,815 fans lucky enough to gain entrance saw a quite brilliant game of football, despite ice-cold conditions and a snowy pitch.

At the time Albion were languishing in the bottom five of Division One whilst Arsenal were in second place, two points behind Charlton. The odds on an Albion victory were high and a draw against the mighty Gunners was as much as most people hoped for.

But what a grand display the Throstles put on, matching Arsenal man for man, in effort, enthusiasm and, on the day, outright skill. They ran and ran, and in the end deserved their place in the semi-finals.

Albion went ahead in the tenth minute when ace goalscorer W.G.Richardson capitalised on a slip by 'keeper Frank Boulton, whipping the ball home from six yards after Mahon's effort had been initially parried.

As the snow eased, so the pitch began to churn up and soon mud was flying. This did not deter the Throstles and they stormed forward at every opportunity. One minute from the interval, Mahon grabbed a second goal when Boyes rolled a free-kick to him some 20 yards out. Mahon's shot flew into the Arsenal net off Roberts.

The Gunners looked demoralised as they trooped off and in the second half, after losing Milne just after the break, they looked dead and buried. Yet true to their great fighting tradition, Arsenal fought back with a goal from Cliff Bastin who was played through by Alex James's shrewd free-kick with Albion appealing for offside.

Jimmy Adams made three important saves in the Albion goal before Mahon relieved the tension. The outside-right rose high to head home his second goal and West Brom were victors of a memorable match they had not expected to win.

Albion: Adams; Finch, C.Shaw, Murphy, Sandford, Sankey, Mahon, Jones, Richardson, Boyes, Coen.
Arsenal: Boulton; Male, Hapgood, Crayston, Roberts, Copping, Milne, Bowden, Kirchen, James, Bastin.

Attendance: 64,815 (Receipts £3,913)   Referee: Mr J.Rennie (Oldham)

A total of 87 West Bromwich-born players have been officially registered with Albion since 1879, including the famous Perry family. In the early days virtually every member of the first-team squad came from within a 3-4 mile radius of the club's HQ; and when Albion won the 'English' Cup in 1888, each and every player in that side was a purely local-born and bred footballer.

Albion were the first Midlands club to reach a hat-trick of both FA Cup and Football League Cup Finals. Their trio of FA Cup Final appearances came in seasons 1885-6, 1886-7 and 1887-8, whilst their three League Cup Finals were in 1966, 1967 and 1970. Albion won only one of each set — the FA Cup in 1888 and the League Cup in 1966.

Albion 1946-7. Back row (left to right): D.Bradley, J.Pemberton, D.J.Walsh, W.Lunn. Third row: G.Banks, W.Gripton, L.Twigg F.Reed (trainer), J.A.Sanders, G.Tranter, L.Millard. Second row: C.Evans, I.Clarke, C.E.Shaw, W.B.Elliott, D.Witcomb, F.Hodgetts, H.Kinsell. Front row: R.A.Ryan, J.Duggan, S.Butler.

Fred Everiss was secretary of Albion for 46 years, and when he resigned in 1948 the club had over 100 applications for the new job of team manager. The man appointed was Jack Smith, who had played several games for Albion as a full-back during the years 1942 to 1944, and within nine months he had guided the team back to Division One.

In that promotion-winning side were two classy Irishmen — Dave Walsh and Jack Vernon. Walsh had been signed from Linfield in the summer of 1946 and scored at least once in each of his first six League outings for the club — a record.

Vernon came to Albion from Belfast Celtic for £9,500 in February 1947 but it was sometime before he got a first-team game. When he did, it was a day he wanted to forget — Albion were beaten 3-2 by West Ham United with the 'Hammers' centre-forward Neary scoring a hat-trick.

But Vernon went on to skipper the side, his country and to play for Great Britain against the Rest of Europe at Hampden Park in 1947. He played in 200 League and Cup games for Albion in a five-year-spell that earned him the tag from no less a judge than Fred Everiss as the best centre-half Albion ever had.

Acquaroff, in fact, helped Albion to their only major prize in almost 300 wartime matches. He scored two goals in the second leg of the Midland War Cup Final in 1944 when Albion beat Nottingham Forest 6-5 on aggregate.

But it was another Jack who was to make a bigger impact on Albion's history. Jack Smith had guested for the Throstles from Chelsea during the war and he was soon to become the club's first-ever team manager.

Albion's first manager, Jack Smith, chatting with his players and trainers in 1948. Left to right: Smith, Reg Ryan, Arthur Fitton, Jack Vernon, Dave Walsh and 'W.G.' Richardson.

47

Nottingham Forest 3   Albion 4

SENSATION followed sensation in the second leg of the Wartime Cup Final at the City Ground. It was a marathon affair, lasting only a minute short of two hours, during which time the near 14,500 crowd, which included a small but vociferous band of Albion fans who had overcome the transport difficulties, were kept in electrifying suspense.

When Forest scored their third goal late in extra-time, a large section of the crowd invaded the pitch and began to carry the home players towards the main stand where the trophy was awaiting the victors. They thought the match was over but Warwick referee Mr Dutton insisted that the police clear the pitch so that the remaining two minutes could be played.

The match restarted and from the kick-off, Albion's Jack Acquaroff sprinted away to score, so levelling the scores at 3-3 and the aggregate at 5-5.

With extra-time exhausted — and players of both sides also drained — the match continued only until another goal was scored. The match became a sudden-death affair and it was Albion who clinched it, 'Ike' Clarke netting the decisive goal after a further nine minutes. Albion were Cup winners with a 6-5 aggregate victory.

In the early stages of the game, Albion had been in a strangely subdued mood and Forest, with guest players Freddie Steele (Stoke) and goalkeeper Ray Middleton (Chesterfield), went ahead with goals from Johnston and Steele.

As half-time approached, Albion's old cup-fighting spirit began to assert itself and in the second period a dogged rally brought a goal from Acquaroff. Soon afterwards Frank Hodgetts headed a brilliant equaliser from Clarke's cross. Dulson got Forest's third and the stage was set for that thrilling finale.

West Brom skipper 'Sandy' McNab received the Cup from the Lord Mayor of Nottingham and all the players — winners and losers — were presented with savings certificates instead of medals.

Nottingham Forest: Middleton; McCall, Hutchinson, Baxter, Blagg, Elliott, Davies, Steele, Dulson, Johnston, Allen.
Albion: Heath; Southam, J.Smith, Millard, Gripton, McNab, Heaselgrave, Acquaroff, Clarke, C.Evans, Hodgetts.

Attendance: 14,438 (Receipts £1,331)

Referee: Mr G.Dutton (Warwick)

Albion skipper 'Sandy' McNab was no stranger to cup-fighting nailbiters. It was his inspiration which had rallied Sunderland after they had lost a goal to Preston in the 1937 FA Cup Final. A wing-half who often dominated the proceedings, he played his part as Albion won a sensational Midland Cup Final.

Frank Hodgetts (left) and Ike Clarke were stars of Albion's win. Hodgetts headed a brilliant equaliser and Clarke was the scorer of Albion's winning goal when the game went into 'sudden-death' extra-time.

Albion players reporting for duty at The Hawthorns (left to right): Aldridge, Hood, Richards, Elliott, 'W.G.'Richardson (asst. trainer), Tighe, Walsh, Kinsell, Hodgetts, Pemberton.

The longest game played by Albion lasted for a total of 128 minutes. It was their Midland Wartime Cup Final (second leg) against Nottingham Forest at the City Ground on 6 May 1944. (see Match to Remember 17).

So it was back to the First Division after a break of 11 years for Albion, who were watched by an average home 'gate' of well over 33,000. The biggest attendance was to see the match against other promotion candidates, Southampton, in November when 47,000 turned up.

Albion's Glyn Hood tackles Fulham's Arthur Stevens at Craven Cottage in 1948.

Frank Hodgetts (extreme right) is foiled by Brentford goalkeeper, Joe Crozier, in a League game at The Hawthorns in September 1947.

Goalkeeper Jim Sanders, who had been wounded in the war, while flying a bomber, played in all 42 League games and Len Millard and Dave Walsh 41 each. Walsh was the leading scorer with 23 League and five Cup goals.

Debates on who is the finest player Albion have had since the war go on long into the night among the fans. But the man who gets many votes is Ronnie Allen. Allen came into the side in the first season after Albion had returned to Division One after signing from Port Vale for £20,000 — then a club record fee.

He started his Albion career as an outside-right and was later converted to centre-forward. But wherever he played he scored goals. In fact, he started the habit straight away. In his first match, in front of 61,000 people at The Hawthorns against Wolves, he popped in Albion's goal in a 1-1 draw.

It was the following year that Allen switched from the right-wing to centre-forward and was an immediate success, scoring ten goals. In 1951-2 he netted 35 goals in League and Cup games, a figure bettered only by Newcastle United's George Robledo, who hit 39.

In the mid-1950s Allen, with Ray Barlow, was the king-pin of perhaps the finest side Albion have ever had. Allen's ability to elude or beat a close-marking opponent, his quickness at reading the game and his speed off the mark allowed him to play deep, well away from the defensive area and set up openings for the strikers who thrived on the gaps he created. He was capped for England only five times, but to many he was the complete footballer.

Albion's great season of 1953-4 got off to a flying start when they played the first nine League games without defeat. The highlight of

49

Dave Walsh accepted Kennedy's header to steer Albion into the lead.

Ray Barlow (left) and Joe Kennedy added further goals. Kennedy's 26th-minute effort was his first for the club.

Match to Remember 18

5 May 1949

Leicester City 0   Albion 3

WITH two games remaining of the 1948-9 season, Albion needed two points to ensure a return to Division One after a break of 11 years. Both the Throstles' remaining matches were away from home and the first, at Leicester, looked particularly difficult.

Leicester were on the brink of relegation and Albion knew they faced a side desperate for success. They also lined up against a team which, despite its lowly League position, had still been good enough to reach that season's FA Cup Final. Five days earlier they had lost 3-1 to Wolves at Wembley.

Thus, Albion needed two points to go up, City required at least one point to stay up, and the prospect attracted over 34,000 fans to Filbert Street. When the teams ran out, the atmosphere was electric.

Jack Smith, Albion's manager, gambled by playing two big men — Ray Barlow and Joe Kennedy — in the forward line either side of centre-forward Dave Walsh. Smith's gamble paid off as Barlow, Kennedy and Walsh scored the goals which put Albion back into Division One.

It was a hectic game. Albion began cautiously and then stepped up a gear so that after 26 minutes they led 2-0. Leicester refused to give up immediately and for a period in the second half Albion had to thank some fine goalkeeping by Jim Sanders for their continued two-goal lead.

Albion's first goal came after 12 minutes. Reg Ryan planted a free-kick deep into the Leicester penalty area where Kennedy rose high above 'keeper Major, nodding the ball down for Walsh to steer into an empty net.

In the 26th minute, a corner from Smith on the left was beautifully glided home by the raven-haired Kennedy. It was his first goal for the club and what an important one it proved, extending the Throstles' lead at a crucial time.

Barlow grabbed Albion's third goal in the 64th minute, striking a clean shot just inside a post from the narrowest of angles.

When the final whistle shrilled, hundreds of delighted fans ran on to the pitch and carried their heroes shoulder-high from the scene of their triumph.

Leicester City: Major; Jelly, Scott, Harrison, Plummer, Johnston, Griffiths, Lee, King, Chisholm, Adam.
Albion: Sanders; Pemberton, Millard, Ryan, Vernon, Hood, Elliott, Kennedy, Walsh, Barlow, Smith.

Attendance: 34,585

Referee: Mr E.Plinston (Warrington)

The outside-left spot has also been something of a problem position for Albion. In 1895-6 they gambled with 11 different players in the left-wing position in 34 League and Test matches. And in 1948-9, when Albion won promotion from Division Two, manager Jack Smith played nine different men at outside-left including full-back Harry Kinsell.

Ernie Shepherd, an outside-left, created a unique record by playing for three promoted sides in the 1948-9 season; Fulham and Albion (promoted from Division Two) and Hull City (promoted from Division Three North). Shepherd, in fact, played his first Football League game before the outbreak of World War Two; he played his second in 1946 — seven years later.

Albion's 1948-9 promotion squad. Back row (left to right): F.Reed (trainer), E.Wilcox, J.Kennedy, H.Kinsell, R.Barlow, R.Barker, G.Hood, J.Haines, R.Ryan, 'W.G.'Richardson (coach). Front row: L.Millard, W.Elliott, C.Williams, D.Walsh, J.Vernon, J.Sanders, J.Pemberton, A.Smith, J.Boyd.

Photo call at The Hawthorns, September 1950.

this tremendous spell was a memorable 7-3 win at St James' Park over Newcastle United, and there was also a fine 4-2 win over Sheffield Wednesday after being two goals down.

All season it was neck and neck at the top of Division One between Wolverhampton Wanderers, Albion and Huddersfield Town. At the turn of the year, with all three sides having played 26 games, Wolves had 39 points, Albion 38 points and Huddersfield 33 points.

The turning point in Albion's Championship chase came in the match against Sunderland at Roker Park. Albion were hard hit by injuries and England calls — yet their troubles had only just begun. The game was not very old before Norman Heath was injured in a goalmouth clash with Ted Purdon — so badly in fact that he never played again. Ray Barlow went into goal and played a 'blinder' but Albion went down 2-1 and with it went the real hopes of the title.

The decider was a meeting with Wolves at The Hawthorns in front of nearly 50,000 people. Wolves won 1-0 and picked up the Championship, pushing Albion into second place. With only one win in their last six League games Albion's form had taken a turn for the worst.

Albion goalkeeper, Norman Heath, gathering a centre during a game against Sheffield United at Bramall Lane in October 1953.

Sheffield Wednesday 4   Albion 5

SUPPORTERS love to see goals, preferably scored by their own team, of course. Albion's visit to Hillsborough on Boxing Day 1952 was witnessed by almost 60,000 fans who saw nine goals — six of them scored by home players — yet Albion still emerged the victors.

At this stage of the season Albion were lying second in Division One, behind neighbours Wolves. Wednesday were in a comfortable mid-table position but they began at a terrific pace and inside five minutes were a goal ahead through outside-left Denis Woodhead.

Albion bounced straight back and after ten minutes they were level when Ray Barlow, cool as you like, slotted home past Owls' goalkeeper, Capewell. Wednesday went straight back downfield to regain the lead through Redfern Froggatt. And five minutes later, Norman Curtis netted an own-goal to bring Albion level for a second time.

Before the interval Woodhead struck again for Wednesday and the teams trooped off the field to a standing ovation from both sets of supporters, appreciative of a superb, breathtaking 45 minutes football.

The second half was only two minutes old when Derek Dooley, the centre-forward who was later to tragically lose a leg, darted in to send Wednesday 4-2 ahead as Albion's defence hesitated following a dead-ball situation.

Still Albion came back and within five minutes, the Owls' lead was reduced to a single goal once more when Eddie Gannon, under pressure from Allen and Nicholls, gave away another own-goal. Albion were firmly back in the hunt.

For the next 30 minutes play swung from end to end and there were thrills and spills in front of both goals before Albion struck two killer blows, first through Johnny Nicholls (80 minutes) and then a goal from England international Ronnie Allen (87 minutes) which put the game beyond Wednesday's reach.

It was a sensational finish to a rousing match and Albion were the first to admit that the Owls had been unlucky to lose such a magnificent game of football. Twenty-four hours later, however, Wednesday had their revenge with a 1-0 victory at The Hawthorns in front of over 52,600 spectators.

Sheffield Wednesday: Capewell; Kenny, Curtis, Gannon, Turton, Witcomb, Marriott, Sewell, Dooley, Froggatt, Woodhead.
Albion: Heath; Rickaby, Millard, Dudley, Kennedy, Barlow, Griffin, Nicholls, Allen, Ryan, Lee.

Attendance: 59,398   Referee: Mr R.P.Hartley (Burnley)

Republic of Ireland international Reg Ryan was the architect of many Albion victories and he played his part as the Throstles stunned a near 60,000 Sheffield crowd.

Ronnie Allen clinched Albion's thrilling win at Hillsborough with a goal in the 87th minute. It was pressure from Allen and teammate Johnny Nicholls which forced the Owls' Eddie Gannon to give the Throstles their second own-goal of the match.

Johnny Nicholls celebrated his 50th game for Albion with a memorable hat-trick and he was applauded off by a generous Tyneside crowd.

Frank Griffin elegantly swept home Albion's seventh goal.

Match to Remember 20   16 September 1953

Newcastle United 3   Albion 7

SOME 34 years ago, in the Coronation Year of 1953, West Bromwich Albion reached the crowning glory of football perfection at Newcastle United's St James' Park.

On a mid-September evening, under a dulling Tyneside sky, Albion swept aside the famous Geordies with a remarkable display of attacking football which conjured up a 7-3 scoreline in the Throstles' favour to stun the home supporters in a massive 58,000 crowd.

One man who has special reason to remember that great occasion is former Albion favourite Johnny Nicholls who celebrated his 50th game for the club by scoring a hat-trick. And the team's overall performance was arguably the best ever given by a Throstles side.

Those who saw it will still argue that there have been few better displays — and that includes the magical Hungarians of the same period, the Tottenham of the 1960s, or the Liverpool of more recent times. On the night Albion were simply unstoppable. No wonder Nicholls remembers: 'The crowd just stood and applauded us off at the end of the game.'

Albion got off to a flying start. They had a goal disallowed inside five minutes, were denied what most people thought was an obvious penalty, and had two shots cleared off the line. They had to wait until the 32nd minute, however, for their first breakthrough when Ronnie Allen crashed home a blockbuster from 30 yards.

Nicholls made it 2-0, darting between Cowell and goalkeeper Simpson, and after 42 minutes Albion led 3-0 when another Allen thunderbolt hit the back of the net.

Newcastle stormed back after the interval and first Vic Keeble (46 minutes) and then Bobby Mitchell (60) brought the Magpies right back into the game, only to see Albion simply step up a gear to go 4-2 in front through Nicholls after 65 minutes.

With 15 minutes to go, Mitchell scored his second but Albion were now in full flood and Nicholls completed his hat-trick. Reg Ryan netted number six and with barely five minutes remaining, Frank Griffin elegantly swept home Albion's seventh goal.

In the dying seconds only a brave save by Simpson at the feet of Allen prevented Albion from scoring an eighth goal. It did not matter though as the Throstles completed one of the finest victories in their history.

Newcastle United: Simpson; Cowell, Batty, Scoular, Brennan, Crowe, Milburn, Davies, Keeble, Hannah, Mitchell.
Albion: Heath; Rickaby, Millard, Dudley, Dugdale, Barlow, Griffin, Ryan, Allen, Nicholls, Lee.

Attendance: 58,075   Referee: Mr T.Seymour (Wakefield)

Two of the most exciting matches in the club's history were the semi-final and Final of the FA Cup in 1954.

Albion had reached the last four with wins over Chelsea, Rotherham United, Newcastle United and Tottenham Hotspur and they had scored 13 goals and conceded only two.

They were favourites to beat Port Vale, from the Third Division, in front of a crowd of 68,000 packed into Villa Park. But Vale, who had given away only 19 goals in 40 League games, defied Albion's efforts for long periods. In fact, they took a half-time lead.

Goalkeeper King was Vale's hero, aided by a quick covering defence. But he missed a curling centre from Jimmy Dudley and Albion were level. In the last quarter of an hour Albion piled on even greater pressure and when George Lee was up-ended they were awarded a penalty. And the man who took it was the former Port Vale forward, Ronnie Allen, who duly knocked his former team out of the Cup.

Allen was to repeat his ice-cool kicking in the Final against Preston North End. He scored from the spot to pull Albion back to 2-2 after they had led 1-0. Allen had glided home a Lee centre to open the scoring after 21 minutes. Morrison headed an equaliser 60 seconds later and then Wayman scored a controversial second for Preston after 51 minutes as Albion appealed for offside.

The winner did not come until three minutes from time when Joe Kennedy, Reg Ryan and Frank Griffin linked down the right for Griffin to roll the ball under Thompson's body and give Albion the FA Cup for the fourth time.

Spurs against Albion at White Hart Lane, January 1954, Millard dives to head clear of goalkeeper Heath to concede a corner kick. Albion won 1-0.

Morrison, Preston's outside-left, beats Sanders, Albion's goalkeeper, to the ball but heads over the bar in the 1954 FA Cup Final.

Ronnie Allen, former centre-forward of Port Vale, Albion, Crystal Palace and England, managed three Midland League clubs whose names all began with the letter 'W' — Wolverhampton Wanderers, Walsall and West Bromwich Albion. He was also the only player to score in each of the first 20 post-war soccer seasons — 1945-6 to 1964-5 inclusive.

Albion have met Hereford United just once — in a benefit match in 1954. Albion lost 10-5 in front of a 4,500 crowd.

Former Welsh international wing-half Vic Crowe began his career as a youngster with Albion who released him as a teenager. He went on to win a total of 16 caps for his county as well as appearing in 350 League games for Aston Villa and Peterborough United (1954-67).

Frank Griffin, Albion's match-winner, celebrates FA Cup success at Wembley in 1954.

Albion 3   Newcastle United 2

ALBION had a magnificent Cup run in season 1953-4, a run which ended in style with a Wembley triumph over Preston North End, but perhaps the team's best performance in that FA Cup campaign was their fifth-round victory over those redoubtable Cup fighters, Newcastle United, at The Hawthorns.

A bumper crowd of over 61,000 squeezed into the Albion ground and gates were closed an hour before the kick-off with an estimated 20,000 locked outside. The atmosphere was electric and the 15,000 Geordie fans who had made the long journey to the Midlands made themselves heard with a rousing and continuous rendering of 'Bladon Races'.

Albion, playing in an unfamiliar change strip of red shirts, played to their full potential, as did Newcastle, and the result was a superb Cup match full of excitement. Both sides' committment to play attacking football led to many goalmouth skirmishes at both ends of the field and two of the afternoon's five goals were absolute beauties.

Albion scored twice in a thrilling first half — this after both Lee and Dudley had fluffed easy chances. Allen was Albion's scorer each time, his first coming from a classy right-foot shot that flew between Stokoe and Cowell, his second from a rebound after Nicholls had fired a shot against the crossbar.

Mitchell made it 2-1 early in the second half, and then came a goal of sheer genius. George Lee whipped over a corner from the left and Allen, moving to the edge of the box, met the ball shoulder-high with his left foot to send it screaming into the net past Simpson's right arm. It was a goal of stunning brilliance which brought the crowd to their toes and gave Allen his hat-trick.

Jackie Milburn gave United hope with a second goal but Albion were in no mood to relinquish their lead and strode further along the road to Wembley's twin towers. Stan Rickaby, Barlow — and Allen, of course — were the key figures in this dazzling Albion performance which many rated as one of the best they had ever given in front of their own fans.

Albion: Heath; Rickaby, Millard, Dudley, Dugdale, Barlow, Griffin, Ryan, Allen, Nicholls, Lee.
Newcastle United: Simpson; Cowell, McMichael, Scoular, Brennan, Stokoe, Foulkes, Broadis, Milburn, Hannah, Mitchell.

Attendance: 61,088   Referee: Mr B.M.Griffiths (Newport)

West Bromwich Albion centre-forward Ronnie Allen scores the first of his three goals against Newcastle United.

55

Albion started the 1954-5 season in great style, winning seven out of their first ten games before beginning to slide. They drew 3-3 with the eventual League Champions, Chelsea, at Stamford Bridge, then went abroad to take on the crack Hungarian club, Honved, in a challenge match in Brussels.

Honved fielded seven current internationals including goalkeeper Grosics and forwards Kocsis, Czibor and Ferenc Puskas.

Hundreds of Albion fans had travelled to Belgium to see the game and it turned out to be a real thriller — Albion losing a classic match 5-3 after they had held a 3-1 lead.

In a packed stadium, Albion were coasting to success with goals by Allen and Nicholls (2). Then Ray Barlow was hurt and the Throstles were reduced to ten men.

After this match it was back to the 'bread and butter' of the League and Albion gradually slipped down the table to finish 17th. They picked up only 40 points from a possible 84 and conceded no fewer than 96 goals — their worst deficit since 1936-7. The crowds, however, did not fade away from The Hawthorns, Albion averaged 30,732 at their 21 home League games.

Ronnie Allen was leading scorer with 32 goals in all games, Johnny Nicholls hit 14, George Lee 12 and Wilf Carter nine.

New recruits were Don Howe, a stylish young full-back from Wolverhampton Schools football, who was destined to play 23 times for England, and big Derek 'The Tank' Kevan from Bradford. He was signed by Vic Buckingham, who was once his manager at Park Avenue. Another future England international, Kevan became a tremendous hit with the Albion fans and went on to score 157 League goals in 262 outings.

Maurice Setters a tough, bandy-legged wing-half, was signed from Exeter City for £3,000; Graham Williams was brought down from Rhyl in the Welsh League; and a goalkeeper, big Fred Brown, was signed from Aldershot as cover for Jim Sanders.

Among those who left Albion were Reg Ryan, to Derby County after ten years at The Hawthorns, and Stan Rickaby, to Poole Town as player-manager.

Albion went through season 1955-6 tentatively and they eventually finished 13th. They were knocked out of the FA Cup by Birmingham City, 1-0 in front of a packed 57,381 Hawthorns crowd. Peter Murphy struck the winning goal and it helped send the Blues on to Wembley, where they lost 3-1 to Manchester City.

During this campaign, centre-half Jimmy Dugdale was transferred to Aston Villa for a reported £25,000 fee.

Albion's average home League gate in 1955-6 was 27,400, the lowest at The Hawthorns since 1946-7. Yet towards the end of the season over 55,000 turned up when Albion staged a testimonial match for their former goalkeeper, Norman Heath, who was seriously injured against Sunderland in 1954.

An All-Star International XI came to West Bromwich and drew 5-5 with Albion before an all-ticket crowd of 55,497 who paid £6,500). On the pitch that night were some great footballers including Trevor Ford, Billy Wright, Danny Blanchflower, Alf Sherwood and Charlie 'Cannonball' Fleming.

Season 1956-7 saw Albion reach their 15th FA Cup semi-final — and came within two minutes of playing in their 10th Final. They

Albion's cheerleader 'Pancho' Johnny and the team mascot John Tromans, 1957.

were joined in the last-four by West Midlands neighbours, Aston Villa and Birmingham City.

Albion were paired with Villa at Wolverhampton. Blues met Manchester United at Hillsborough. A Molineux crowd of 55,549 witnessed the Albion-Villa tie and twice Albion were in front — only for Peter McParland to pull Villa level each time. Whitehouse hit the two Albion goals, and Villa's second equaliser came two minutes from time. The replay was at St Andrew's where Albion had Ronnie Allen injured early on and lost 1-0.

In the summer of 1957 the Football Association invited Albion to visit the Soviet Union where they won two and drew one of their three matches to become the first British professional club to score a victory in Russia.

Back home there was a festival of goals in the 1957-8 season, and Albion were deeply involved.

They beat Manchester City 9-2 in the League and 5-1 in the FA Cup, hammered Nottingham Forest 5-1 in the Cup, and then hit six against Leicester City and five each against both Birmingham City and Burnley.

One of Brian Whitehouse's two goals in the 1957 FA Cup semi-final against Aston Villa at Molineux.

Albion's 1958 first team squad. Back row (left to right): V.Buckingham (manager), D.Hogg, E.Robinson, D.Howe, C.Jackman, J.Dudley, S.Williams, J.Kennedy, R.Graham (trainer). Centre: R.Allen, R.Robson, C.Drury, M.Setters, R.Barlow, D.Kevan, B.Whitehouse, F.Griffin. Front: J.Carvin, D.Burnside, J.Campbell, A.Jackson, R.Horobin. Brian Whitehouse had come in for injured England international star Ronnie Allen and he played a major role as Albion whipped Forest with only ten men.

Match to Remember 22   28 January 1958

Nottingham Forest 1   Albion 5

ALBION'S victory at the City Ground in this FA Cup match was outstanding by any measure — but the fact that it was achieved with only ten men makes the Throstles' performance that January day in 1958 even more remarkable.

Cyril Chapman (*Birmingham Post*) and Bill Holden (*Daily Mirror*) both described the win as 'a miracle' and everyone present agreed with the overall assessment of the press that Albion 'had that Wembley look written all over them'.

Brilliant Albion baffled and blinded their rivals in this fourth round replay with a display straight out of the soccer science manual. The only people who were not impressed were the thousands of Forest fans who began streaming out of the ground with some 20 minutes still to play. Those fickle Forest supporters left to Albion chants of 'We want six,' ringing in their ears.

Yet Albion, a goal down after only 12 minutes, had been reduced to ten men when tough-guy Maurice Setters was stretchered off with a suspected fractured ankle just after his team had equalised in the 24th minute. Manager Vic Buckingham came down to the touchline, sat Setters alongside him, and began to urge his team to an epic victory.

Eddie Baily crossed for Tom Wilson to head home Forest's early goal before Robson's leap to Roy Horobin's centre levelled the issue. In the 33rd minute Albion went in front when Frank Griffin fired in a cracking shot and that was the state of play as the players went off at half-time.

Brian Whitehouse, playing in place of the injured Allen, made it 3-1 in the 57th minute and a joyous Derek Kevan rapped home Albion's fourth only four minutes later, almost ripping the back out of the net with a 20-yard piledriver. A Don Howe penalty in the 70th minute ended the scoring and that was the signal for the exodus of those disgruntled Forest fans.

After the final whistle, Forest manager Billy Walker said, 'We've seen the Cup winners today — Albion were brilliant.' Alas, Albion fell at the semi-final hurdle, going down 1-0 to arch enemies Aston Villa at St Andrews, in a replay.

Nottingham Forest: Thomson; Ware, Thomas, Morley, McKinlay, Burkitt, Gray, Quigley, Wilson, Baily, Imlach.
Albion: Sanders; Howe, S.Williams, Setters, Kennedy, Barlow, Griffin, Whitehouse, Robson, Kevan, Horobin.

Attendance: 46,455 (Receipts £6,967)   Referee: Mr A.E.Ellis (Halifax)

Ray Barlow playing against Wolves at Molineux during the 1957-8 season.

Albion against Bolton Wanderers at The Hawthorns, February 1962.

The biggest goals bonanza was a rain-soaked game against the Russian Red Army that ended in a 6-5 win for Albion before 52,805 packed into The Hawthorns.

Three Albion men scored more than 20 goals that season: Ronnie Allen (28), Derek Kevan (23) and new man Bobby Robson (27). Robson was signed from Fulham for £25,000.

That 5-1 win at Forest was an incredible performance. Albion were trailing when Maurice Setters retired injured, yet they managed to score five times with ten men. Another great win with ten men was against Sheffield United in the FA Cup at The Hawthorns after Frank Griffin had broken a leg. Albion won 4-1 and that gave them a tie against Manchester United, just after the Munich air disaster had destroyed Busby's great team.

A crowd of 57,574 saw a 2-2 draw, with Albion scoring in the last two minutes. There were only 30 seconds remaining of the emotional replay at Old Trafford when Colin Webster scored the goal that knocked out Albion.

The following season of 1958-9 Albion won ten away League games including a 6-0 hammering of Birmingham City and a 6-2 win at Portsmouth. This was also the season that Aston Villa crashed back into Division Two, after Ronnie Allen's 25-yard drive earned his side a 1-1 draw against Villa in the last match of the season.

That summer Albion went to North America where they won seven of their nine games and were beaten only once. In a 15-0 win over Alberta All-Stars, Bobby Robson scored six times to equal the record set by Jimmy Cookson and 'W.G.'Richardson.

On their return to England, Vic Buckingham resigned as manager and went to Amsterdam to take charge of Ajax. Gordon Clark took over. The saddest note, however, was the sudden death of 'W.G.'Richardson who collapsed while playing in a charity match on 27 March 1959, aged 49.

> *Stanley Steele spent just three months and 17 days as a player with Albion (1961), making him the professional player who has spent the shortest time with the club.*

The 1960s were a time of constant change at The Hawthorns, both on and off the field. Gordon Clark was followed as Albion manager by Archie Macaulay, who in only a short time was succeeded by Jimmy Hagan. Hagan's period in charge is perhaps best remembered for the players' 'strike' when several of them refused to train without tracksuit trousers on a bitterly cold day.

Already Derek Kevan had moved to Chelsea for £50,000 much to the consternation of supporters, Ronnie Allen went to Crystal Palace on a free transfer, Joe Kennedy went to Chester, Bobby Robson back to Fulham, Ray Barlow to Blues, David Burnside and Stuart Williams to Southampton and Don Howe to Arsenal.

On the credit side, John Kaye arrived from Scunthorpe, for a then club record fee of £44,750. Doug Fraser came from Aberdeen for £25,000, and a similar fee was paid to Notts County for Jeff Astle.

Youngsters Tony Brown, Bobby Hope and Ken Foggo appeared in the attack and Bobby Cram and Graham Williams were the full-backs in front of goalkeeper Ray Potter. Other teenagers, Ray Wilson, Mickey Fudge, Graham Lovett, Gerry Howshall and Ian Collard, were also pressing for places as Albion rebuilt.

It was in 1962, in the FA Cup fifth round against Tottenham Hotspur, that the last crowd of over 50,000 — it was almost 55,000 — was seen on the ground. Times indeed were changing.

Cup fever broke out in a big way in the second half of the 1960s as Albion reached three Finals in four seasons, the first when they won the League Cup at the first attempt, in 1965-6, beating West Ham in a two-legged Final.

Albion 4 West Ham United 1

THIS was 'part two' of Albion's first major Cup Final for 12 years — the Football League Cup Final. In those days the competition was in its infancy. There was no sponsorship and no Wembley finale, simply a two-legged affair, the victors of which would enjoy European soccer the following season.

The first leg at Upton Park had ended in a 2-1 win for the Hammers. Now Albion knew that victory by at least two goals at The Hawthorns would mean European competition for the first time, not to mention the Throstles' first major honour since 1954.

The implications were not lost on the fans either, and over 32,000 crowded into the Albion ground on a chilly evening. They were treated to a night to remember as Albion produced some scintillating football in the first 45 minutes to demoralise and finally destroy West Ham.

John Kaye, who a week earlier had played for the Football League, was in splendid form and he levelled the aggregate score with a brilliant goal after only ten minutes, driving home Bobby Cram's measured cross in emphatic style.

After Astle and Kaye had gone close, Tony Brown netted number two in 19 minutes, inching Albion ahead over the two legs. Clive Clark grabbed a third goal after 28 minutes. The nippy winger darted forward to head home after Hammers'

goalkeeper, Jim Standen, hesitated following a shot from Kaye which was blocked by Burnett.

Astle again went close and then Brown saw his snap header saved on the line. It was all Albion as West Ham back-pedalled. In the 35th minute, Throstles' skipper Graham Williams went forward to drill home goal number four from fully 30 yards after Astle had played the ball back to him from the edge of the penalty area.

West Ham rallied a little in the second half and stole a consolation goal through Martin Peters after 75 minutes, but one minute from time Albion went back upfield and emphasized their superiority when first Kaye hit the crossbar and then Brown's header was stopped on the line.

Albion were 5-3 aggregate winners and looked forward to a place in the 1966-7 Fairs Cup competition. Throstles' manager Jimmy Hagan said afterwards: 'We won well, we played well, and I'm proud of the lads. That first-half performance was one of the best I've seen from a club side for years.'

Albion: Potter; Cram, Fairfax, Fraser, Campbell, Williams, T.Brown, Astle, Kaye, Hope, Clark.
West Ham United: Standen; Burnett, Peters, Bovington, K.Brown, Moore, Brabrook, Boyce, Byrne, Hurst, Sissons.

Attendance: 32,013 (Receipts £8,217)

Referee: Mr J.Mitchell (Whiston, Lancs.)

Throstles' manager Jimmy Hagan (extreme right) and his team proudly show off the Football League Cup after a scintillating display destroyed West Ham. 'I'm proud of the lads,' said Hagan, 'It was one of best club performances I've ever seen.'

When Tony Brown scored two goals past Manchester United's Gary Bailey in the League game at Old Trafford in December 1978 it created a little bit of footballing history because it was the first time a player had netted past father and son in senior football. Gary's dad, Roy, was in goal for Ipswich Town on 28 September 1963 when 'The Bomber' scored on his debut for Albion at Portman Road.

Tony Brown played in more First Division games than any other Albion player — 451 (plus eight as a sub). Ronnie Allen had 415 games in Division One. Jessie Pennington (214) holds the top spot for most outings for the club in Division Two. Tony Brown (281) appeared in most Football League matches for Albion at The Hawthorns (Division One & Two).

Stan Jones heading goalwards against Arsenal in the FA Cup fourth round at The Hawthorns, 1964.

Albion's first taste of competitive European soccer was in Holland when they met DOS Utrecht in the Fairs Cup, drawing 1-1 with Bobby Hope scoring their first-ever 'Euro-goal'. The second-leg saw the Throstles coast to a 5-2 victory with Brown hitting a hat-trick.

That set-up a tie with Bologna, who were much too experienced. The Italians won 3-0 in their own country and 3-1 at The Hawthorns. The second-leg defeat came four days after Albion had been beaten in the 1967 League Cup Final.

Albion lost at Wembley after they had led Third Division Queen's Park Rangers 2-0 at half-time, with both goals from Clive Clark who was playing against his old team. After the break Rangers came storming back and scored through Morgan, Marsh, and Lazarus after Albion goalkeeper Rick Sheppard had been floored in a tangle with Hunt.

Perhaps the decision to play Kaye deep alongside the inexperienced Dennis Clarke cost Albion the trophy. But whatever the reason, Bobby Cram never played for the club again and manager Jimmy Hagan left within a month.

Tears were to turn to cheers within a year, however, as Albion returned to Wembley. Their 1968 FA Cup success grew from very humble beginnings — and a referee's controversial decision.

It was at Layer Road, the home of Fourth Division Colchester United — where Leeds were later to be humbled — that the story began. Most of the crowd of just under 16,000 were convinced that referee Arthur Jones was wrong when he disallowed a goal by United's Micky Bullock only 90 seconds from the end, with the teams level at 1-1. Tony Brown's penalty had kept Albion in the game and the Throstles won the replay 4-0.

Their stuttering path to Wembley continued with two attempts to beat Southampton, with Graham Williams taking over in goal in the replay after Osborne was injured — and Astle hitting the winner in the last minute.

Alan Ashman had taken over as manager, and coached by former player Stuart Williams, Albion took a gamble by moving striker Johnny Kaye to half-back at a crucial time. It was a master-stroke, Kaye figured prominently in the sixth round tie against Liverpool.

The first two meetings were drawn, with only two goals scored after three-and-a-half hours of football. The second replay was at Maine Road, with Kaye in defence in place of Colquhoun, who broke a leg at Newcastle. Kaye took a blow on the head, but continued playing with a bandage around the wound which needed 12 stitches. Tony Hateley equalised an early goal by Astle, but Clive Clark, the winger with a reputation for scoring important Cup goals, knocked in the winner.

Kaye was ready for the semi-final at Villa Park against Birmingham City. Albion, fated for success, had only four shots at goal and scored twice — through Astle and Brown. Blues had 12 shots and did not score at all, so Albion were on the way to their tenth Final.

> The 1968 FA Cup Final between Albion and Everton lasted 120 minutes, yet just over two-fifths of the game was 'lost' through enforced stoppages of one sort or the other. Broken down, this is where the time was lost: Fouls — 17 minutes. Throw-ins — 10 minutes. Goal-kicks — 10 minutes. Injuries — 9.27 minutes. Corners — 6 minutes. Offsides — 0.27 minute. Total — 53 minutes
> The 26 minutes lost through throw-ins, goalkicks and corners was mainly due to time being spent in retrieving the ball.

The only question for manager Ashman before the Wembley meeting with Everton was who to play at outside right. The choice lay between Kenny Stephens, Dennis Clarke and Graham Lovett, the man who had suffered terrible injuries in a road accident only 17 months before. Alan Ashman and coach Stuart Williams chose Lovett.

Albion's three No 9's in 1966 — John Kaye, Jeff Astle and Ray Crawford.

A goal for Jeff Astle in the 1968 FA Cup semi-final against Birmingham City at Villa Park. Albion won 2-0.

At Wembley, Everton pinned Albion back for long periods especially in the second half, but the scoreline remained blank until the end of 90 minutes. Extra time was only two minutes old when Astle took a pass from Fraser, went past one defender and slammed a right-footed shot against Harvey. As the rebound came back to him, Astle hit it with his left and it flew high past West for the winner.

More than 250,000 people lined the streets of West Bromwich to welcome back the Cup winners and crown a great season for Ashman. To add to the Wembley victory there was an 8-1 win over Burnley and a 6-3 thrashing of Manchester United. Jeff Astle topped the First Division scoring lists with 35 goals.

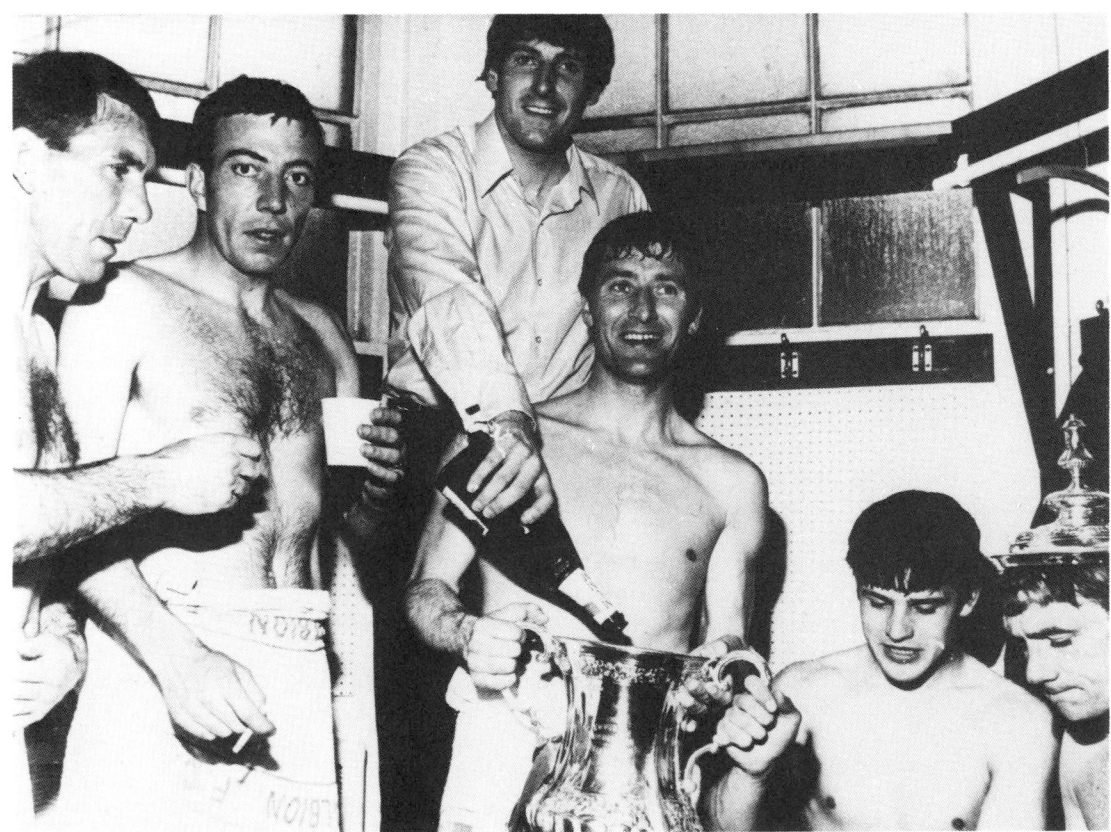

Some of the Albion players celebrating their FA Cup win in 1968.

ALBION HIT UNITED FOR 6!

Hat-trick for Astle in wonder win

WEST Bromwich Albion knocked Manchester United off the top of the First Division table last night by hammering six goals in a fantastic turn-up at the Hawthorns.

Albion's biggest crowd of the season, 55,000, saw the Cup Finalists in devastating form in a thriller that brought centre forward Jeff Astle a hat-trick. It was United's biggest defeat for years.

United had their fans roaring as they went flat out for an early goal. Centre forward Bobby Charlton burst through in the second minute to rocket a shot just wide.

Three minutes later, inside right Brian Kidd accelerated past two defenders and let fly a terrific shot which Albion goalkeeper John Osborne brilliantly tipped over the bar.

But it was Albion who went ahead in the ninth minute through a shocking mistake by United's right back Tony Dunne.

Dunne sent an intended back-pass straight to Jeff Astle. The Albion centre forward turned, brushed Denis Law aside, and hammered the ball in off a post.

United stormed back, and Osborne held a John Aston cross at the second attempt.

Then Albion's Bobby

West Bromwich	6
Man Utd	3
By PETER INGALL	

chance which two of his team-mates missed.

Law sent a header just wide, then scooped the ball over the bar from three yards—the miss of the match.

But this was Albion night. They went

Start of a massacre ... Centre forward Jeff Astle beats Denis Law before scoring the first of Albion's six goals last night.

Match to Remember 24   29 April 1968

Albion 6   Manchester United 3

JUST forty-eight hours before Manchester United were due to meet Albion in this crucial League game, the Throstles had fought through to the 1968 FA Cup Final. United were still in with a chance of taking the League Championship, and five days earlier they had taken a 1-0 lead from the first leg of their European Cup semi-final match against Real Madrid.

The stage was set for a great game at The Hawthorns — and what a game it turned out to be. Almost 46,000 fans paid to get into the ground, another 5,000 simply forced their way in free of charge, and 5,000 more were left stranded outside. It was the match everyone wanted to see.

Albion were on a 'high' following their 2-0 win over Birmingham City in the previous Saturday's FA Cup semi-final, yet their overall League form had been disappointing. Indeed, they had won only one of their last four home games and Everton had thumped them 6-2 at The Hawthorns.

On this occasion, however, the Throstles played brilliantly and destroyed this great United team in style. Every pass made by an Albion player seemed to drop into place whereas United's efforts largely went astray. Roared on by their fans, Albion, it seemed, could do no wrong.

Bobby Hope, Albion's Scottish inside-forward, remembered

later: 'The final result could have resembled a cricket score. Denis Law missed a few, including a sitter, and George Best was also way off target. We, too, spurned one or two chances — but we still managed to get six.'

Albion stormed into a 4-0 lead inside an hour through Jeff Astle (nine and 59 minutes), Ronnie Rees (39) and a Tony Brown penalty (57). Law pulled one back for United with a spot kick, but Asa Hartford and Astle again gave Albion a comprehensive 6-1 scoreline with 10 minutes to play.

United, to their credit, never gave up, such was the skill and character of that great team, and two late goals from Brian Kidd gave the scoreline a more respectable look.

Albion went on to win the FA Cup that season, whilst United became the first English team to lift the European Cup. The Reds were pipped by neighbours City for the League title and no doubt looked back to that defeat at The Hawthorns when Albion were unstoppable.

Albion: Osborne; Clarke, Williams, Brown, Talbut, Kaye, Rees, Collard, Astle, Hope, Hartford.
United: Stepney; Dunne, Burns, Crerand, Sadler, Stiles, Law, Charlton, Kidd, Aston.

Attendance: 45,992

Referee: Mr H. Davey (Verwood, Dorset)

Jeff Astle in action against RFC Bruges at The Hawthorns in the Cup-winners' Cup first round, second leg in October 1968.

Albion's second venture into Europe, in 1968-9, took them to the quarter-finals of the Cup-winners' Cup, but not before an exciting chapter in Bruges, against the Belgian Cup-holders. Albion lost 3-1 and had Jeff Astle taken to hospital after being attacked by home supporters. But that away goal, scored by Asa Hartford, helped see them through when they won 2-0 at The Hawthorns.

Yet their troubles had only just begun. In Bucharest, Hartford again scored, Ronnie Rees was sent off and players and officials had to duck a hail of stones as they left the stadium.

Albion had no problem in the second-leg — sweeping through 4-0 to win a place against Dunfermline in the last eight.

A goalless draw in Scotland made Albion favourites for The Hawthorns leg. But on a bitterley cold night, the Scots grabbed an early goal and held out to win.

Albion's defence of the FA Cup was sunk by a great goal from former Throstles supporter, Allan Clarke, with three minutes left of the semi-final against Leicester City at Hillsborough, after Albion had beaten three London clubs, Arsenal, Fulham and Chelsea, together with Norwich City, to reach that stage.

Many Albion fans believe that Jeff Astle's seventh-minute goal in the 1969-70 League Cup Final against Manchester City actually cost them yet another triumph. The goal, headed by the big England striker, tended to relax Albion and spur on City. Mike Doyle grabbed a second-half equaliser for Joe Mercer's team and when the match went into extra-time, City lasted the pace better. Glyn Pardoe hit the winner on a pitch saturated by melting snow.

In the League, Albion were away to a bad start, losing their first three home games, and it was not until the eighth match of the season, against Manchester United at home, that they managed their first victory.

A 45,120 crowd saw them win 2-1 and in the side for the first time was Alistair Robertson, one of seven new players introduced that season.

After a disappointing season in 1970-71, the Albion board replaced Alan Ashman with Don Howe. It looked the correct move when the side won their first two games of the season, but after that they began to slip down the table until they beat Liverpool and climbed back to safety.

New faces in the side included Willie Johnston, signed for a club record fee of £138,000 from Rangers, John Wile, from Peterborough United, and Ally Brown from Leicester City.

All three settled in quickly, as did Bobby Gould from Wolves. But success did not materialise and the following season Albion were relegated for the first time in 24 years. They won only eight home matches and lost their last four fixtures in a row to go down with Crystal Palace, after managing to score only 38 goals — their lowest total for 70 years.

At one stage it looked as if Albion were going to make a quick return but an FA Cup defeat by Newcastle United in the fifth round at The Hawthorns was followed by League setbacks against Hull City and Middlesbrough and from then on their form was erratic and they ended the season in eighth place. A League Cup knockout by Fourth Division Exeter City did not help morale.

One bright spot in that season was the attendance for the Boxing Day match at The Hawthorns against Aston Villa. It was the biggest Second Division attendance of the season — 43,119.

During the same season Albion were involved in an off the field

JOHN KAYE

John Kaye was 'Midland Footballer of the Year' in 1966 and 1970. He is seen here receiving his prize from J.W. Gaunt in 1970.

63

drama when Asa Hartford was due to move to Leeds United. Terms had been agreed between the club and with the player when a medical examination revealed a heart condition and Leeds backed out.

The signing of Johnny Giles as player-manager was perhaps the shrewdest deal Albion have ever pulled off. The little Irishman was persuaded to leave Leeds United in the summer of 1975, although he had plans to continue with the Yorkshire club.

He came to The Hawthorns after the sacking of Don Howe following Albion's second season in Division Two, when their promotion run-in faded in the latter half of the campaign. Successive defeats at Easter, by Villa and Blackpool, finally killed off their faint hopes.

But there was a sign of better times ahead in the young players coming through the ranks — Bob Ward, Bryan Robson, John Trewick, David Rushbury, Ian Edwards and Trevor Thompson. Joe Mayo had been signed from Walsall for £8,000, and Giles took over a side which had twice gone so close to promotion, only to fail at the last hurdle.

Giles signed Geoff Hurst, Mick Martin and Paddy Mulligan and immediately set about shaping the side into a First Division outfit. It took time though, and after 12 matches of the 1975-6 compaign Albion were just five points off the bottom of the Division.

Then Albion's fortunes began to prosper as the players started to believe in themselves. Performances were workmanlike and the support, at home and away, was tremendous. Not since 1973 had there been regular attendances of over 20,000 — and on six occasions this season that figure was topped as Albion went for promotion.

The issue was in doubt right up to the last Saturday. Sunderland and Bristol City were already up and with one promotion place remaining, Albion had to go north to Oldham on 24 April and win to regain their First Division status. Tony Brown's left-foot shot early in the second-half gave Albion victory and promotion.

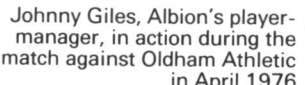
Tony Brown, Albion and England International footballer.

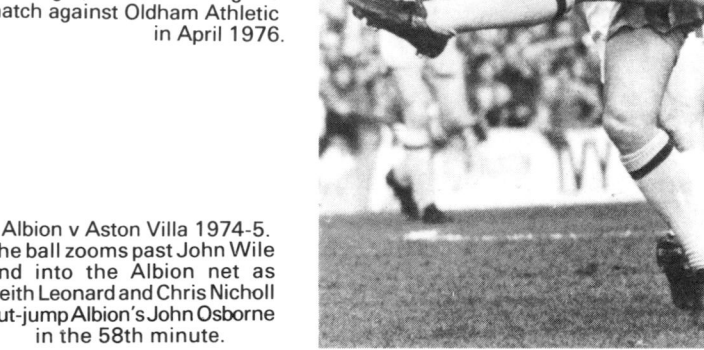
Johnny Giles, Albion's player-manager, in action during the match against Oldham Athletic in April 1976.

Albion v Aston Villa 1974-5. The ball zooms past John Wile and into the Albion net as Keith Leonard and Chris Nicholl out-jump Albion's John Osborne in the 58th minute.

Oldham Athletic 0   Albion 1

THIS was probably Albion's most vital match for six years. Consider the situation — with one game left of their Second Division programme, the Throstles had to take both points to win promotion. A draw at Oldham's Boundary Park would not be good enough. Albion had to come out fighting from the first whistle.

Upwards of 15,000 dedicated Albion fans made the 100-mile trip up the M6 to make Boundary Park look more like The Hawthorns revisited. Bolton, Albion's nearest challengers, were on their way south to meet Charlton at The Valley. The Trotters had to take four points from their remaining two matches to pip Albion at the post — if the Baggies failed to win at Oldham.

Albion arrived at the ground some 90 minutes before kick-off in order to avoid the traffic jams, and when strikers Joe Mayo and Ally Brown walked on to the pitch for a pre-match look at the surface they were astounded by the vast bank of Albion supporters behind one goal. 'It was unbelievable,' said Mayo, 'The atmosphere resembled a Cup Final.'

Oldham had former Albion favourite, David Shaw, in their ranks, while Johnny Giles was able to field a full side for what he described as a 'mini Cup Final'.

Play in the first half was somewhat restrained. Both teams had chances but nerves played their part as a taut Albion struggled to get their game together. At half-time news filtered through that Bolton were winning at Charlton. Victory for Albion was vital.

In the second half Giles began to look far more convincing and the Albion boss was soon spraying passes from midfield; Tony Brown was looking more menacing and Willie Johnston was also turning on some of his old magic.

In the 54th minute Albion found the goal they had been looking for — and appropriately it came at the end of the ground occupied by thousands of Baggies supporters.

The move developed on the right where Martin, Mulligan and Ally Brown created space. When the cross came over, it found ace striker Tony Brown some 18 yards from goal. Brown got the ball under control before hooking it wide of 'keeper Ogden. It was no more than Albion deserved and after a few heart-stopping moments near the final whistle, the Throstles celebrated their return to Division One.

Oldham Athletic: Ogden; Wood, Whittle, Bell, Edwards, Hicks, Blair, Shaw, Robins, Chapman(Branagan), Groves.
Albion: Osborne; Mulligan, Cantello, T.Brown, Wile, Robertson, Martin, A.Brown, Mayo, Giles, Johnston. Sub: Robson.

Attendance: 22,356   Referee: Mr R.Tinkler (Boston)

John Wile, one of Albion's greatest servants, had a fine game as the Baggies fought their way back to Division One.

Dave Shaw, the former Albion striker, was Oldham's main threat.

'Bomber' Brown volleys home the goal that won promotion.

John Osborne was an ever-present between the Albion posts, and he capped a grand season by keeping a blank sheet in no fewer than 22 League games, a club record. Alistair Robertson was also an ever-present in the first-team, while Tony Brown topped the scoring charts with eight goals in the League and four in the FA Cup.

The top of Division Two for 1975-6 ended thus:

	P	W	D	L	F	A	P
1 Sunderland	42	24	8	10	67	36	56
2 Bristol City	42	19	15	8	59	35	53
3 West Bromwich Albion	42	20	13	9	50	33	53
4 Bolton Wanderers	42	20	12	10	64	38	52

To crown a great season, Albion's Youth team carried off the FA Youth Cup for the first time in the club's history, beating Wolves 5-0 on aggregate in the two-legged Final, and the Central League side finished runners-up to Liverpool, failing by just four points to overtake the seemingly invincible Reds from Anfield.

Back in the First Division, Albion soon began to show their skills, picking up a creditable point in their opening game at Leeds. They hung around the middle of the table for a good four months, registering some fine wins including successive ones of — 4-2 over Tottenham (after being 2-0 down) and 4-0 over Manchester United, both at home.

After 21 games Albion were in ninth place with 22 points — 11 behind leaders Liverpool. Ten matches later, after Laurie Cunningham had been signed from Orient for £110,000 and Tony Godden had replaced John Osborne in goal, they lay seventh, one rung off a UEFA Cup place for 1978. But a tough Easter programme, coupled with 'Pop' Robson fracturing a leg for the third time in less than a year, meant that Albion had to be content with that seventh place. Yet it was indeed a happy return to the top-flight for the club, players and of course supporters, who pushed the average Hawthorns attendance for the season up from 16,000 to 24,500.

Those same fans were shocked and dismayed in the summer of 1977 when Giles left Albion. He was replaced initially by former favourite Ronnie Allen, but Allen decided to gamble on taking a job in Saudi Arabia and that left the way clear for Ron Atkinson to step into The Hawthorns.

Atkinson arrived in January 1978 and he made an immediate impact. His flamboyant approach rubbed off on everyone and in a matter of weeks Albion were again looking a useful side. Brendon Batson was signed from Atkinson's old club, Cambridge United, and with Cyrille Regis, snapped up by Allen from non-Leaguers Hayes for £5,000, plus the skills of Laurie Cunningham and the wing play of Willie Johnston, Albion were becoming a force with which to be reckoned.

They powered on in the FA Cup and after knocking out Blackpool, Manchester United, Derby County and then the favourites Nottingham Forest, a place in the Wembley Final looked a distinct possibility. At Highbury in the semi-final against Ipswich Town, however, everything went wrong. John Wile was injured early on, Johnston was carrying a damaged shoulder and then Mick Martin was sent-off as Ipswich won 3-1.

In 1977-8 Albion finished sixth in the First Division and so won a place in the UEFA Cup, their first taste of European football for ten years. Atkinson got his team geared up with some useful early season displays and they knocked out Galatasary, Braga, and the crack Spanish outfit, Valencia, before losing the first-leg of the quarter-final against Red Star, 1-0 in Belgrade. European inexperience cost Albion a place in the semi-final when they allowed the Yugoslavs a late strike and so eventually went out on that away goal.

David Mills, Britain's first £500,000 footballer, was signed from Middlesbrough, and Martyn Bennett was given his Football League debut as Albion earned a second season in European competition by finishing third in Division One in 1978-9. Indeed, they might have won the Championship had not the dreadful English winter disrupted their form and programme at a crucial time in the campaign.

Fine wins over Manchester United (5-3 at Old Trafford), Coventry (7-1 at The Hawthorns) and Manchester City (4-0 at The Hawthorns) were just three magnificent displays from Albion this season, and Tony Brown created a new club record by passing Ronnie Allen's total of 208 League goals.

Bonoff under control from Bryan Robson, Tony Godden and Ally Robertson in the UEFA Cup against Valencia in 1978-9.

Laurie Cunningham (right) put Albion 4-3 ahead and then Ally Brown (above) sent Regis away for Albion's fifth and final goal of a superb match.

Manchester United 3   Albion 5

NOT many teams have gone to Old Trafford and put five goals past Manchester United, but in December 1978, under Ron Atkinson's managership, Albion went there and whipped United 5-3 in front of a 45,000 crowd. And to rub salt into United's wounds, television cameras were there to record the action.

At the time Albion were riding on the crest of a wave, unbeaten in ten matches and pushing strongly at the top of the First Division table. United, on the other hand, were going through a bad patch, having lost three of their last six matches including two successive 3-0 defeats, one of them against struggling Bolton Wanderers.

The game itself was a magnificent advertisement for British football. A thrill-a-minute match with goalmouth action at both ends, the game also provided plenty of midfield cut and thrust — and eight goals, several of them absolute beauties.

United struck the first blow, Brian Greenhoff smashing in a shot from 20 yards following a left-wing corner. Tony Brown equalised, then Len Cantello, latching on to a deft back-heel from Cyrille Regis, scored with a classic effort which won him

ITV's 'Goal of the Season'.

Gordon McQueen headed in United's equaliser from another left wing corner, then Sammy McIlroy weaved his way through to put United 3-2 ahead. Right on the half-time whistle, Tony Brown nudged in Albion's third to make it all-square.

The action continued thick, fast and furious in the second period. Bailey made two superb saves from Regis, and then Laurie Cunningham raced away to put Albion 4-3 ahead with less than 15 minutes to play.

Regis made absolutely certain with a fantastic goal for Albion in the dying minutes, collecting Ally Brown's inside pass to rifle a fierce right-foot shot past the groping Bailey. It was a fitting end to Albion's best away performance for years.

Manchester United: Bailey; B.Greenhoff, Houston, McIlroy, McQueen, Buchan, Coppell, J.Greenhoff(Sloan), Ritchie, McCreery, Thomas.

Albion: Godden; Batson, Statham, T.Brown, Wile, Robertson, Robson, A.Brown, Regis, Cantello, Cunningham. Sub: Johnston.

Attendance: 45,091

Referee: Mr G.P.Owen (Anglesey)

Despite going out of the fifth round of the FA Cup, Albion always looked capable of finishing at least second in the table and they would have done but for a last match defeat, at home to European Cup champions, Nottingham Forest.

Nevertheless, Albion — and Atkinson — had done exceptionally well and West Bromwich was back on the footballing map.

The club's centenary season of 1979-80 was somewhat subdued. Albion took tenth place in the League, went out of the FA Cup in round three and lost to Norwich in the fourth round of the League Cup. They failed at the first hurdle in the UEFA Cup, going under to the East German club, Carl Zeiss Jena.

John Deehan (from Aston Villa), Gary Owen and Peter Barnes (from Manchester City), and Garry Pendrey (Birmingham) were added to the first-team pool as Cunningham (to Real Madrid for almost £1 million), and Johnston left The Hawthorns.

In 1980-1, Albion played some neat soccer but they still lacked that vital spark. Atkinson was being 'eyed-up' by Manchester United and as soon as the season ended he packed his bags and left The Hawthorns for Old Trafford.

Early in the 1981-2 season he paid out around £2 million and took both Bryan Robson and Remi Moses away from The Hawthorns. Their departure destroyed Albion's midfield.

Ronnie Allen returned to replace Atkinson and although he helped Albion to the semi-finals of both the FA and League Cup competitions in 1981-2, his stay was short-lived, and somewhat tempetuous. Ron Wylie the former Aston Villa and Birmingham City player, was appointed to take over from Allen in 1983 but he never really settled at The Hawthorns, despite making several changes, including the signing of Ken McNaught and Tony Morley (from Villa)

John Wile, Albion, leans on Frank Stapleton, Arsenal, at Highbury in November 1980.

West Bromwich Albion 1979-80. Back row (left to right): A.Brown, B.Batson, M.Bennett, A.Godden, C.Regis, R.Moses, P.Barnes. Front: G.Owen, J.Wile, B.Robson, D.Statham, J.Deehan.

By this time, Regis had moved to Coventry in a deal which caused quite a stir among the fans. Garrry Thompson had been bought from Coventry, Clive Whitehead from Bristol City and Peter Eastoe from Everton, along with Paul Barron from Crystal Palace and the two Dutch internationals Romeo Zondervan and Martin Jol, plus midfielder Steve Mackenzie from Manchester City. John Wile had moved on to become player-manager of Peterborough.

On paper Albion looked a useful side but their overall performances where mediocre, to say the least. Albion brought back Johnny Giles as manager in February 1984. At that time, the club was at a particularly low ebb. Home attendances had slumped to 11,000 and generally speaking the standard of play had dropped alarmingly.

Bryan Robson, the Albion player who left for over £1 million and went on to captain England.

West Bromwich Albion 1982-3. Back row (left to right): Cyrille Regis, Martin Jol, Peter Eastoe, Brendon Batson, Tony Godden, Mark Grew, Martyn Bennett, Derek Monaghan, Alistair Brown, Alistair Robertson, Richard Roberts (physiotherapist). Front row: Barry Cowdrill, Derek Statham, Alan Webb, Gary Owen, Steve Mackenzie, Ron Wylie (team manager), Clive Whitehead, Nicky Cross, Romeo Zondervan, David Mills.

Derek Statham and Steve Hunt challenge Paul Dougherty, Wolves, at Molineux in April 1984.

Albion's Worst-Ever Season – 1985-86

Without doubt 1985-6 was Albion's worst-ever League season. They started badly, deteriorated, and subsequently suffered relegation for the sixth time since the League was formed in 1888. Albion set up several unwanted records and had statistically-minded supporters thumbing through the record books.

These are the facts about the sad season of 1985-6: (Previous record totals in brackets)

- Fewest League wins — three (nine).
- Record number of defeats — 26 (23).
- Least number of away wins — just one (equalling previous low).
- Fewest home wins in season — three (six).
- Most home defeats in 21-match programme — 10 (equalling previous high).
- Least number of home points gained in season — 17 (22).
- Fewest home League goals scored — 21 (22).
- Lowest number of points gained in 42-match programme — 24 (28).
- Nine consecutive League games lost (previous record eight).
- Most players utilised in season (League & Cup games) — 34 (33).
- Most home goals conceded by a First Division club in 1985-6 — 36.
- Most away League goals conceded by a First Division club in 1985-6 — 53.
- Five goalkeepers used during season (League and Cup competitions).
- Nineteen players made their senior debuts for Albion in 1985-6.
- Albion dropped to the bottom of the First Division table after their third game — and stayed there.
- There were three managers at The Hawthorns during the season — Johnny Giles, Nobby Stiles and Ron Saunders (appointed February 1986).
- And to cap it all, Albion's reserve side suffered relegation from the Central League Division One.

Some supporters never saw Albion win a match in 1985-6. Others were so disgruntled after the first two months of the season that they stayed away for the rest of the campaign, which resulted in Albion having their lowest average League attendance (just over 12,000) for more than 70 years.

Players came and went. At the start of the season Garth Crooks and Imre Varadi were paired together to replace Garry Thompson; later, big George Reilly arrived from Newcastle. None of them sparkled although Reilly did perform a lot better during the last month of the season.

The midfield was switched around throughout the season with Steve Hunt, Mickey Thomas, Tony Grealish, Steve Mackenzie, Martin Dickinson, Andy Thompson and Darren Bradley all having spells in the team. Paul Dyson was signed from Stoke City to replace long-serving Ally Robertson in the back-four, and goalkeeper Stuart Naylor was recruited from Lincoln City to become Ron Saunders' first signing — on St Valentine's Day.

Steve Mackenzie (left) and Darren Bradley (below) were two players used by Albion as the Throstles switched the midfield around throughout the season.

Tony Godden (right) and Stuart Naylor (above) were just two of five goalkeepers used as Albion conceded more goals than any other First Division club.

	P	W	D	L	F	A	Pts
Liverpool	42	26	10	6	89	37	88
Everton	42	26	8	8	87	41	86
West Ham U	42	26	6	10	74	40	84
Manchester U	42	22	10	10	70	36	76
Sheffield W	42	21	10	11	63	54	73
Chelsea	42	20	11	11	57	56	71
Arsenal	42	20	9	13	49	47	69
Nottingham F	42	19	11	12	69	53	68
Luton T	42	18	12	12	61	44	66
Tottenham H	42	19	8	15	74	52	65
Newcastle U	42	17	12	13	67	72	63
Watford	42	16	11	15	69	62	59
Queen's Park R	42	15	7	20	53	64	52
Southampton	42	12	10	20	51	62	46
Manchester C	42	11	12	19	43	57	45
Aston Villa	42	10	14	18	51	67	44
Coventry C	42	11	10	21	48	71	43
Oxford U	42	10	12	20	62	80	42
Leicester C	42	10	12	20	54	76	42
Ipswich T	42	11	8	23	32	55	41
Birmingham C	42	8	5	29	30	73	29
West Brom A	42	4	12	26	35	89	24

West Bromwich Albion team 1984-5. Full Squad. Back row (left to right): Michael Perry, Garry Thompson, Martyn Bennett, Paul Barron, Darren Carmel, Tony Godden, Ken McNaught, Barry Cowdrill, Michael Forsyth, Gary Robson. Third row: Gary Leonard, Joe Tortolano, Clive Whitehead, Cyrille Regis, Steve Mackenzie, Nicky Cross, Wayne Ebanks, Michael Lewis. Second row: Nobby Stiles (coach), Alistair Robertson, Derek Statham, Gary Owen, John Giles (manager), Steve Hunt, Tony Grealish, Tony Morley, George Wright (physiotherapist). Front row: Carlton Palmer, Hector Wynter, Mark Housego, Wayne Dobbins, Steve Bull, Andy Thompson, Michael Icke, Ian Hathaway, Karl Addis, Philip Walker.

When Giles arrived at The Hawthorns, Albion were still in the FA Cup but his first match back in charge ended in disaster as Plymouth, from the Third Division, bundled Albion out of the competition in front of 24,000 fans at The Hawthorns.

It was now an uphill battle all the way for Giles and his back-up crew of Nobby Stiles and Norman Hunter. Albion struggled painfully on. There were regular internal disputes but Giles remained right through the 1984-5 campaign and although he signed Jimmy Nicholl, Carl Valentine, and David Cross (for a second spell) to play alongside Steve Hunt and Tony Grealish (secured on the transfer-deadline of 1984), Albion never looked a good side.

Garry Thompson was sold — to the dismay of the supporters — to Sheffield Wednesday, but when Imre Varadi, Garth Crooks, Gerry Armstrong, Colin Anderson, Paul Bradshaw and Robbie Dennison, arrived, things looked brighter.

But the promise was not sustained and Albion slumped to the foot of the First Division soon after the start of that 1985-6 campaign. Giles left following a 3-0 defeat at Coventry in September, handing over his duties to Nobby Stiles. But relegation, even at this early stage, was staring Albion in the face.

Stiles carried on, but he was fighting a losing battle. Albion needed a miracle. George Reilly signed from Newcastle but matters did not improve and the Albion board went for experience and appointed former Villa and Birmingham manager, Ron Saunders, in a last-gasp effort to prevent relegation.

Albion improved somewhat but it was too late and Second Division football became inevitable. New signings were made — Paul Dyson from Stoke, Stuart Naylor from Lincoln, Craig Madden from Bury, Darren Bradley from Aston Villa and Martin Dickinson from Leeds, all to no avail.

After such a dismal 1985-6 season — easily the worst in Albion's League history — the supporters, players and directors of the club were looking for a vast improvement in 1986-7. But, alas, things were basically unchanged and Albion were lucky not to suffer relegation for the second season running, finishing in their lowest-ever League position (15th).

They had a reasonable start to the campaign; dropped off somewhat in mid-September; had a fair October; a respectable November and a so-and-so December. But once into 1987 things started to go drastically wrong.

From 1 January to 9 May inclusive, Albion played a total of 20 Second Division games and one FA Cup tie, away to Fourth Division Swansea (lost 3-2). Out of those League fixtures they managed to win only four and plummeted deep into the relegation zone. Thankfully there were one or two other teams struggling around the same time and Albion survived the drop — and the play-offs — by the skin of their teeth.

Manager Ron Saunders' job was made more difficult by a series of injuries to key players and he began the season with Derek Statham, Darren Bradley and striker George Reilly all side-lined. During the course of the campaign Martyn Bennett, Martin Dickinson, Steve Mackenzie, Gary Robson and new-signing Robert Hopkins (from Manchester City) were also under treatment. Saunders signed strikers Bobby Williamson (from Rangers) and Stewart Evans (Wimbledon) at the start. Later on, after securing Hopkins, he snapped up Martin Singleton and Don Goodman from Bradford City, former Hawthorns apprentice Steve Lynex (from Leicester City), who returned 'home' ten years after leaving the club, and Kevin Steggles, a defender from Ipswich Town. There were also 12 players sold during the season: Irishman Jimmy Nicholl was exchanged for Williamson, going on to win a Scottish Premier Division Championship medal with Rangers; Mickey Thomas (Wichita Wings, NASL) and Gary Owen (Panionios, Greece); Tony Godden signed permanently for Chelsea; Imre Varadi and Tony Grealish both joined Manchester City; Steve Bull, Andy Thompson, Robbie Dennison and the long-serving Ally Robertson all joined Wolves, Robertson leaving Albion after 18 years service and more than 600 senior games; Craig Madden went to Blackpool (£50,000); Stewart Evans (Plymouth, £50,000) and striker Garth Crooks was sold to Charlton for £75,000.

Goalkeeper Stuart Naylor and skipper Paul Dyson were both ever-presents with Naylor being voted 'Player of the Year'. Crooks was top-scorer, closely followed by Williamson. The average League attendance at The Hawthorns was under 10,000 — the lowest figure since 1905-06.

Albion are a club with a great history. They approached 1987-8 with the knowledge that they had not won a major honour since 1968. With new secretary Gordon Bennett (from Bristol Rovers) and new Commercial Manager Alan Stevenson, the former Burnley goalkeeper, in office however, Albion look to have found at least the right blend 'behind the scenes'.

Albion also went into 1987-8 with new shirt sponsors, Apollo 2000 Limited, the largest gas and electrical-appliance retailers in the West Midlands. Apollo had agreed a three-year contract and hopes are that at the end of that period Albion will have had greater fortunes than the dismal two seasons just ended.

1888-89

Football League

Date		Opponent	Result	Scorers	Att	Roberts R	Horton J	Green H	Horton E	Perry C	Bayliss J	Bassett W	Woodhall G	Hendry W	Pearson T	Wilson J	Timmins G	Walker L	Perry W	Shaw C	Millard A	Oliver H	Haynes G	Ramsay A	Crabtree F
Sep 8	(a)	Stoke C	W 2-0	Wilson, Woodhall	4,524	1	2	3	4	5	6	7	8	9	10	11									
15	(a)	Derby C	W 2-1	Bassett, Pearson	3,700	1	2	3		5	4	8	7	9	10	11	6								
22	(a)	Blackburn R	L 2-6	Pearson, Bayliss	3,700	1	3	2	4	5		8	7	9	10	11	6								
29	(h)	Burnley	W 4-3	W.Perry, Bassett, Hendry, Shaw	2,100	1	2			5	4	7		9	10		6	3	8	11					
Oct 6	(h)	Derby C	W 5-0	W.Perry, Pearson 2, Bassett, Hendry	5,500	1	2	3		5	4	7		9	10	11	6		8						
13	(a)	Preston NE	L 0-3		10,200	1	2	3		5	4	8	7	9	10	11	6								
20	(h)	Notts C	W 4-2	Pearson 2, Wilson, Woodhall	3,448	1	3	2			4	7	8	9	10	11	6				5				
Nov 11	(h)	Accrington	D 2-2	Wilson, Bassett	3,000	1	3		4	5		8	7	9	10	11	6	2							
5	(a)	Bolton W	L 1-5	Bassett	4,000	1	3		4	5		8	7	9	10	11	6	2							
10	(a)	Burnley	L 0-2		5,000	1			4	5	2	7		9	10	11	6		8			3			
17	(a)	Bolton W	W 2-1	Hendry, Pearson	4,230	1	2			5	4	7		9	10	11	6	3	8						
24	(a)	Accrington	L 1-2	W.Perry	3,000	1	3			5	4	7		9	10		6	2	8				11		
Dec 1	(h)	Everton	W 4-1	W.Perry, Bassett 2, Hendry	5,700	1	3			5	4	7		9	10	11	6	2	8						
15	(a)	Wolves	L 1-2	Pearson	8,600	1	2			5	4	7	8		10	11	6	3	9						
22	(h)	Blackburn R	W 2-1	Bassett, Pearson	4,100	1	3			5	4	8	7	9		11	6	2					10		
26	(h)	Preston NE	L 0-5		5,150	1				5	4	8	7	9		11	6	2					10		
29	(h)	Stoke C	W 2-0	Bassett, Wilson	4,896	1				5	4	8	7	9		11	6	3					10	2	
Jan 5	(h)	Wolves	L 1-3	Woodhall	4,000	1	2			5	4	8	7	9	10	11	6	3							
12	(a)	Notts C	L 1-2	Bassett	1,500	1	2		4	5	9	7		8	10	11	6	3							
19	(a)	Aston Villa	L 0-2		10,000	1	2	3	4		9	7	8	5	10	11	6								
26	(h)	Aston Villa	D 3-3	Bassett, Pearson 2	8,515	1		3	4	5	9	7	2		10	11	6		8						
Feb 23	(a)	Everton	W 1-0	Crabtree	2,100	1		3	4	5	9		2		10	11	6		8						7
App						22	18	9	9	20	22	21	10	18	22	20	21	12	9	1	1	1	4	1	1
Goals										1	1	13	3	4	11	4			4	1					1

Bob Roberts

Tom Pearson

Joe Wilson

1889-90

Football League

Date		Opponent	Result	Scorers	Att	Roberts R	Horton J	Green H	Horton E	Perry C	Timmins G	Bassett W	Evans G	Bayliss J	Pearson T	Wilson J	Woodhall G	Millard A	Pittaway J	Walker L	Nicholls J	Reader J	Haynes G	Johnstone W	Donnachie C	Powell S	Nicholls S
Sep 14	(a)	Derby C	L 1-3	Bayliss	6,000	1	2	3	4	5	6	7	8	9	10	11											
21	(a)	Notts C	W 2-1	Pearson, Bayliss	6,200	1	2	3	4	5	6	8		9	10	11	7										
28	(h)	Aston Villa	W 3-0	Woodhall, Wilson, Bayliss	10,122	1	2	3	4	5	6	8		9	10	11	7										
Oct 5	(a)	Preston NE	L 0-5		10,000	1	2	3	4	5	6	8		9	10	11	7										
12	(a)	Burnley	W 2-1	Wilson, Pittaway	6,000	1	2	3	4	5		8			10	11	7		6	9							
19	(h)	Wolves	L 1-4	Evans	1,550	1		3	4	5			8	9	10	11	7			2	6						
26	(a)	Aston Villa	L 0-1		8,000			3	4	5			8	9	10	11	7		6	2		1					
Nov 4	(h)	Bolton W	W 6-3	Pearson 4, Bassett, Woodhall	4,813			3	4	5	6	8		9	10	11	7			2		1					
9	(h)	Derby C	L 2-3	Wilson, Bassett	5,100		2	3	4	5	6	8		9	10	11	7					1					
16	(a)	Stoke C	W 3-1	Pearson, Perry, Evans	3,900	1	2		4	5	6	7	9	8	10					3							
23	(h)	Burnley	W 6-1	Bayliss 2, Haynes, Bassett, Evans, Pearson	7,100	1	2	3	4	5	6	7	9	8	10								11				
30	(a)	Blackburn R	L 0-5		6,600	1	2	3	4	5	6	7	9	8	10	11											
Dec 7	(a)	Bolton W	L 0-7		3,500	1		3	4	5	6		8		10		7			2				11	9		
21	(h)	Accrington	W 4-1	Pearson 3, Bayliss	3,500	1	2	3	4	5		7		8	10	11								9	6		
26	(h)	Preston NE	D 2-2	Evans, Pearson	10,065	1	2	3	4	5	6	7	9	8	10	11											
28	(a)	Wolves	D 1-1	Pearson	8,500	1	2		4	5	6	7	9	8	10	11										3	
Jan 4	(h)	Notts C	W 4-2	Bayliss, Pearson 3	4,700	1	2	6	4	5		7	9	8	10	11										3	
11	(h)	Blackburn R	W 3-2	Evans 2, Bayliss	5,100	1	2	3	4	5		7	9	8	10	11					6						
Feb 8	(a)	Accrington	D 0-0		2,100	1	2		4	5		7			10	11	8					6			9	3	
Mar 8	(a)	Everton	L 1-5	Pearson	8,400	1		3	4	5		7	9	6	10	11				2							8
15	(h)	Stoke C	W 2-1	Woodhall, Bayliss	1,600		2	3	4				9	8	10	11	7				5	1			6		
22	(h)	Everton	W 4-1	Evans 2, Pearson, Wilson	4,000	1		3	4	5		7	9	6	10	11									2		8
App						18	17	18	22	21	12	19	13	19	22	20	11	2	1	6	4	4	2	3	2	4	2
Goals										1		3	8	9	17	4	3		1				1				

1890-91

Football League

Date	Venue	Opponent	Res	Scorers	Att	Reader J	Green H	Powell S	Horton E	Perry C	Bayliss J	Bassett W	Nicholls S	Dyer F	Pearson T	Roberts H	Woodhall G	Perry T	Burns J	Hortcn J	Foberts T	Haynes E	Filey J	Groves W	Timmins G	McCulloch T	McCullum W	McLeod R
Sep 6	(h)	Everton	L 1-4	Pearson	5,600	1	2	3	4	5	6	7	8	9	10	11												
13	(a)	Preston NE	L 0-3		8,500	1	2	3	4	5		8	9	6	10		7	11										
20	(h)	Sunderland	L 0-4		8,537	1	3	2		5	4		9	6	10		7	8	11									
27	(a)	Aston Villa	W 4-0	Dyer, Bayliss, Pearson, Burns	12,000	1		3	4	5	9	7		6	10			8	11	2								
Oct 4	(h)	Burnley	W 3-1	Pearson, Burns 2	6,000	1		3	4	5	9	7		6	10			8	11	2								
11	(a)	Notts C	L 2-3	T.Perry, Woodhall	4,900	1		3	4	5		7		6	10		9	8	11	2								
18	(h)	Notts C	D 1-1	Pearson	7,367	1		3	4	5	9	7		6	10		8		11	2								
25	(a)	Everton	W 3-2	Dyer, Nicholls, Burns	9,200	1		3	4	5		7	8	6	10		9		11	2								
Nov 1	(h)	Aston Villa	L 0-3		8,000	1		3	4	5		7	8	6	10		9		11	2								
3	(h)	Bolton W	L 2-4	Pearson 2	1,506	1	3		4			7	8	6	10		9		11	2	5							
8	(a)	Sunderland	D 1-1	Woodhall	3,400	1		3	4	5		7	8	6	10		9			2		11						
22	(a)	Derby C	L 1-3	Pearson	4,000	1		3	4	5		7		6	10		9	8	11	2								
29	(h)	Derby C	L 3-4	Bayliss, Pearson, Nicholls	405	1		3	4	5	9		8	6	10		7		11	2								
Dec 6	(a)	Burnley	L 4-5	C.Perry, Riley, Pearson 2	5,500	1	2	3	4	9			8	5	10		7		11			6						
13	(h)	Wolves	L 0-1		3,400	1		2		5			8	6	10		7		11	3			4	9				
20	(a)	Blackburn R	L 1-2	Pearson	5,500	1	3		4	5			8	2	10		7		11					9	6			
Jan 3	(a)	Wolves	L 0-4		9,300	1			4	5		7		3	10		8		11	2				9	6			
Feb 7	(h)	Preston NE	L 1-3	Burns	4,300	1				5	6		8	4	10		7		11					9		2	3	
Mar 7	(h)	Accrington	W 5-1	Nicholls 2, Pearson 2, Groves	800	1							8	4	11		7			3			6	9		2	5	10
9	(h)	Blackburn R	W 1-0	McLeod	2,700	1				5		7	8	6	11					2				9		3	4	10
14	(a)	Bolton W	L 1-7	Gardiner (og)	5,200	1		2	4	5		7	8	6	10									9		3		11
Apr 18	(a)	Accrington	L 0-1		3,300	1		3		5	4	7	8	6	10					2				9				
		App				22	6	16	16	20	8	17	14	22	22	1	16	6	15	15	1	2	3	8	2	4	3	3
		Goals								1	2		4	2	13		2	1	5					1				1

Charlie Perry

George Woodhall

George Timmins

1891-92

Football League

Date	Venue	Opponent	Res	Scorers	Att	Roberts R	Nicholson M	Powell S	Bayliss J	Perry C	Dyer F	Bassett W	Nicholls S	Groves W	McLeod R	Pearson T	McCulloch T	Reynolds J	Woodhall G	Reader J	Haynes E	Geddes A	Charsley C	Castle J	Horton J	Wheldon S	Millard A	Perry T
Sep 5	(h)	Everton	W 4-0	Nicholls, Groves, McLeod 2	6,000	1	2	3	4	5	6	7	8	9	10	11												
12	(a)	Aston Villa	L 1-5	Pearson	12,100	1	2	3	4	5	6	7	8	9	10	11												
19	(a)	Wolves	W 4-3	Groves 2, Nicholls, C.Perry	10,000	1	2	3		5	6	7	8	9	10	11	4											
Oct 3	(h)	Blackburn R	D 2-2	Pearson, Nicholls	4,700	1	2	3		5	6		8	9	10	11		4	7									
10	(a)	Notts C	L 0-4		4,000		2	3	4		6	7		9	10	11		5	8	1								
17	(h)	Sunderland	L 2-5	McLeod, Bassett	5,500	1	2	3	4	5	6	7	8	9	10	11												
24	(a)	Sunderland	L 0-4		6,000	1	2	3		5	6	7	8	9	10	11	4											
31	(h)	Notts C	D 2-2	Pearson 2	5,200		2		4	5	6	7	8	9		10	3			1	11							
Nov 2	(h)	Bolton W	L 0-2		6,700		2		9	5	6	7	8	4		10	3			1	11							
7	(a)	Everton	L 3-4	Bassett 2, Pearson	8,100	1	2	3		5	6	7	8	9		10	4					11						
14	(h)	Aston Villa	L 0-3		14,085	1	2		9	5		7	8	6		10	3	4				11						
21	(h)	Preston NE	L 1-2	Geddes	13,000			3		5	6	7		8		10	2	9				11	1	4				
28	(a)	Burnley	L 2-3	Bassett, Geddes	8,000					5	6	7		8		10	3	9		1		11	4	2				
Dec 5	(h)	Accrington	W 3-1	Woodhall, Pearson, Geddes	6,000		2			5		7			8	10	3	6	9	1		11		4				
12	(h)	Derby C	W 4-2	Woodhall, Pearson, Geddes 2	5,800		2			5		7			8	10	3	6	9	1		11		4				
19	(h)	Bolton W	D 1-1	McLeod	7,000		2			5	6	7		9	8	10	3	4		1		11						
26	(h)	Burnley	W 1-0	Pearson	5,000		2			5	6	7			8	10	3	4	9	1	11							
28	(a)	Wolves	L 1-2	Rose (og)	7,200		2			5	6	7			8	10	3	4	9	1		11						
Jan 9	(a)	Preston NE	L 0-1		6,400					5	6	7		9	8	10	3	4		1		11			2			
23	(a)	Accrington	L 2-4	Nicholls, Pearson	4,200						6	7	9		8	10		5		1		11			3	2	4	
Feb 6	(a)	Derby C	D 1-1	Nicholls	7,300		2			5		7	9	6	8	10	3	4		1		11						
Mar 12	(a)	Blackburn R	L 2-3	McLeod 2	6,000		2			5		7	9	6	8	10	3	4		1		11						
Apr 4	(a)	Darwen	W 12-0	Pearson 4, Reynolds 2, Bassett 3, Hunt(og), Geddes, Nicholls	1,109					5		7	9	6	8	10	3	4		1		11			2			
11	(h)	Stoke C	D 2-2	T.Perry 2	10,000	1				5	6		9		8			3	7			11			2		4	10
16	(a)	Darwen	D 1-1	Nicholls	3,000		2			5	6	7	9	10	8		3	4		1		11						
23	(a)	Stoke C	L 0-1		5,400	3				5	6	7	9	8		10		4		1		11			2			11
		App				9	19	10	7	24	19	24	17	20	20	24	19	17	7	16	3	15	1	4	6	1	2	2
		Goals								1		7	7	3	6	13		2	2			6						2

1892-93

Division 1

Date	Opponent	Result	Score	Scorers	Att	Reader J	Horton J	McCulloch T	Reynolds J	Perry C	Groves W	Bassett W	McLeod R	Bostock A	Pearson T	Geddes A	Nicholson M	Perry T	Wood H	Hadley B	Fellows E	Boyd H	Crone R	Taggart J	Neale W
Sep 10	(a) Bolton W	L	1-3	Geddes	4,100	1	2	3	4	5	6	7	8	9	10	11									
Sep 17	(h) Wolves	W	2-1	Bassett, Bostock	4,000	1		3	4	5	6	7	8	9	10	11	2								
Sep 19	(h) Aston Villa	W	3-2	McLeod, Pearson 2	11,239	1	2	3	4	5	6	7	8	9	10	11									
Sep 24	(a) Derby C	D	1-1	Pearson	7,000	1		3	4	5	6	7	8	9	10	11	2								
Oct 1	(h) Newton Heath	D	0-0		4,000	1		3	4	5	6	7	8	9	10		2	11							
Oct 8	(a) Newton Heath	W	4-2	McLeod, Bassett, Bostock 2	4,600	1		3	4	5	6	7	8	9	10	11	2								
Oct 15	(h) Everton	W	3-0	Wood, Pearson 2	4,800	1		3	4	5	6	7	8	9	10		2		11						
Oct 22	(a) Sunderland	L	1-8	Bassett	8,000	1		3	4	5	6	7	8	9	10	11	2								
Oct 29	(h) Notts C	W	4-2	Geddes, Pearson, Bassett, Bostock	3,000	1		3	4	5	6	7	8	9	10	11	2								
Nov 5	(a) Aston Villa	L	2-5	Geddes 2	12,100	1		3	4	9	6	7	8		10	11	2	5							
Nov 7	(h) Bolton W	W	1-0	Geddes	4,000	1	2	3	4	5	9	7	8		10	11		6							
Nov 12	(h) Accrington	W	4-0	Groves 2, McLeod, Bostock	4,000	1	2	3	4	5	9	7	8		10	11		6							
Nov 19	(h) Notts C	L	1-8	McLeod	8,000	1	2	3	4	5	9	7	8		10	11		6							
Nov 26	(h) Stoke C	L	1-2	Pearson	607	1		3		5	6	7	8	9	10	11	2	4							
Dec 10	(h) Preston NE	L	0-1		4,000	1		3		5	6	7	8	9	10	11	2	4							
Dec 17	(a) Accrington	L	4-5	McLeod, Pearson, Bostock 2	3,000	1	2	3		5	6	7	8	9	10	11					4				
Dec 24	(h) Sunderland	L	1-3	Bassett	8,000	1	2	3	4	5	6	7	8	9	10	11									
Dec 26	(h) Blackburn R	L	1-2	Pearson	7,000	1	2	3	4	5	6	7	8	9	10	11									
Dec 27	(a) Wolves	D	1-1	McLeod	8,000	1	2	3	4	5	6	7	8		10	11						9			
Dec 31	(a) Burnley	L	0-5		3,500	1	2	3		5	6	7	8		10	11		4				9			
Jan 2	(a) Sheffield W	L	0-6		15,000	1	2	3		5	6	7	8		10	11		4				9			
Jan 7	(h) Burnley	W	7-1	Geddes, McLeod 3, Bassett 2, Pearson	1,000	1	2	3		5	6	7	8		10	11		4				9			
Jan 14	(a) Everton	L	0-1		10,000	1	2	3		5	6	7	8		10	11		4				9			
Jan 28	(a) Blackburn R	L	1-2	Geddes	2,300	1	2	3		5	6	7	8			11		4		10		9			
Feb 11	(a) Stoke C	W	2-1	Bassett 2	6,000	1	2	3	4	5	6	7	8				10	11				9			
Mar 2	(a) Nottingham F	W	4-3	Geddes, Bassett 2, Groves	4,100	1		3	2	5	6	7	8				10	11			4	9			
Mar 18	(h) Sheffield W	W	3-0	McLeod, Pearson, Boyd	5,000	1			4	5	6	7	8		10	11	2					9	3		
Apr 1	(h) Derby C	W	3-1	C.Perry 2, Geddes	3,655	1				5		7	8		10	11	2	4					3	6	9
Apr 3	(h) Nottingham F	D	2-2	C.Perry, Reynolds (pen)	5,000	1			4	5	11	7	8		10		2	6					3		9
Apr 13	(a) Preston NE	D	1-1	C.Perry	8,200	1		3	2	4		7	8		10	11	5					9		6	
App						30	19	23	20	30	30	29	30	18	25	27	13	16	1	1	4	7	3	2	2
Goals									1	4	3	11	10	7	11	9		1	1			1			

1893-94

Division 1

Date	Opponent	Result	Score	Scorers	Att	Reader J	Nicholson M	Crone R	Perry T	Perry C	Taggart J	Norman O	McLeod R	Nicholls S	Pearson T	Geddes A	Bassett W	Hadley B	Horton J	Bostock A	Burns J	Neale W	Roberts T	Williams O	Banks J	Humpage W
Sep 2	(a) Aston Villa	L	2-3	Geddes, Cowan (og)	15,100	1	2	3	4	5	6	7	8	9	10	11										
Sep 9	(h) Newton Heath	W	3-1	Pearson, McLeod, Nicholls	4,500	1	2	3	4	5	6		8	9	10	11	7									
Sep 16	(a) Derby C	W	3-2	McLeod 2, Nicholls	7,000	1	2	3	4	5	6		8	9	10	11	7									
Sep 23	(h) Burnley	D	1-1	McLeod	3,000	1	2	3	4	5	6		8	9	10	11	7									
Sep 25	(a) Sheffield W	W	4-2	Bassett 2, Geddes 2	6,000	1		3	4	2	6		8	9	10	11	7	5								
Sep 30	(a) Nottingham F	W	3-2	McLeod 2, Bassett	5,000	1	2		4	5	6		8		10	11	7	3	9							
Oct 7	(h) Wolves	D	0-0		10,000	1	2		4	5	6	9	8		10	11	7	3								
Oct 14	(a) Newton Heath	L	1-4	Norman	8,000	1	2		4	5	6	7			10	11		3	9	8						
Oct 21	(h) Aston Villa	L	3-6	C.Perry, Geddes, McLeod	14,000	1	2		4	5	6		8		10	11	7	3	9							
Oct 28	(a) Sheffield U	W	2-0	Bassett, Neale	6,000	1	2	3	4	5	6		8		10	11	7					9				
Nov 4	(h) Stoke C	W	4-2	C.Perry 2, McLeod, Nicholls	3,000	1	2	3	4	5	6		8	9	10	11	7									
Nov 6	(h) Bolton W	W	5-2	Neale, Pearson 4	4,000	1	2	3	4	5	6		8		10	11	7					9				
Nov 11	(a) Darwen	L	1-2	Neale	2,000	1	2	3	4	5	6		8		10	11	7					9				
Nov 25	(a) Sunderland	L	1-2	Bassett	9,500	1	2	3	4	5	6		8	9	10	11	7									
Nov 27	(h) Sheffield W	D	2-2	Bostock, McLeod (pen)	4,828	1	2		4	5	6		8		10	11	7	3	9							
Dec 4	(h) Preston NE	W	2-0	Norman 2	2,000	1		3	4	2	6	9	8		10	11	7	5								
Dec 9	(a) Burnley	L	0-3		5,000	1	2	3	4	5			8	9	10	11	7				6					
Dec 16	(h) Darwen	D	2-2	McLeod, Bassett	2,000	1	2	3	4	5	6		8		10	11	7					9				
Dec 23	(h) Sunderland	L	2-3	Geddes 2	7,500	1	2	3	4	5	6		8	9	10	11	7									
Dec 26	(h) Sheffield U	W	3-1	Bassett, Pearson, Norman	7,000	1	2	3	4	5	6		8	9	10	11	7									
Dec 27	(a) Wolves	W	8-0	McLeod 3, C.Perry, Bassett 3, Williams	8,000	1	2		4	5	6		8	9		11	7	3						10		
Dec 30	(a) Everton	L	1-7	Williams	14,000	1	2	3	4	5	6		8	9		11	7							10		
Jan 6	(h) Blackburn R	W	2-1	Williams, Hadley	2,024	1	2	3			6		8	9		11	7	5						10	4	
Jan 13	(a) Blackburn R	L	0-3		6,000	1	2	3	4	5			8	9		11	7							10	6	
Jan 20	(a) Stoke C	L	1-3	Bassett	3,000	1	2	3		5			8		10		7	4				9		11	6	
Feb 3	(h) Everton	W	3-1	Williams 2, Pearson	3,000	1	2	3	4	5	6		8		10	11	7							9		
Mar 3	(a) Preston NE	L	1-3	McLeod	5,000		2	3					8			11	7					9		10	4	1
Mar 24	(h) Derby C	L	0-1		3,000	1		3	4	2	6		8			11	7	5				9		10		
Mar 26	(h) Nottingham F	W	3-0	Bostock, Williams 2	7,000	1		3	4	5	6		8			11	7			2	9			10		
Apr 7	(a) Bolton W	W	3-0	Geddes, Bostock 2	3,500	1	2	3	4	5	6	7	8	9		11								10		
App						29	24	26	27	29	27	12	29	8	23	28	27	5	7	8	1	4	1	10	4	1
Goals										4		4	14	3	7	7	11	1		4		3		7		

1894-95

Division 1

Date		Opponent	Result	Goalscorers	Att	Reader J	Williams W	Crone R	Perry T	Perry C	Taggart J	Bassett W	McLeod R	Hutchinson T	Williams O	Newall W	Richards W	Higgins T	Fellows E	Horton J	Norman O	Banks J	Rea J	Paddock J	Perry W	Parry J	Green T	Roberts F	Geddes A
Sep 1	(a)	Sheffield U	L 1-2	McLeod	12,000	1	2	3	4	5	6	7	8	9	10	11													
8	(h)	Wolves	W 5-1	McLeod, Richards, Bassett, Newall, Hutchinson	5,100	1	2	3	4	5	6	7	8	9		11	10												
15	(h)	Liverpool	W 5-0	Bassett, Williams, Richards, McLeod, Hutchinson	6,951	1	2	3	4	5	6	7	8	9		11	10												
22	(a)	Sunderland	L 0-3		7,150	1	2	3	4	5	6	7	8	9		11	10												
29	(a)	Everton*	L 1-4	Bassett	19,900	1	2	3	4	5	6	7	8	9		11													
Oct 13	(a)	Aston Villa	L 1-3	McLeod	15,000	1	2	3	4	5	6	7	8	9		11		10											
20	(h)	Derby C	D 2-2	Newall, Hutchinson	5,000	1	2	3	4	5	6	7	8	9		11		10											
27	(a)	Derby C	D 1-1	Bassett	1,990	1	2		4	5	6	7		9		11		3	8	10									
Nov 3	(h)	Sheffield U	W 1-0	Hutchinson	3,250	1	2		4	5	6	7	8	9		11		3		10									
5	(h)	Bolton W	D 1-1		3,500	1	2	3	4	5	6	7		9		11		8		10									
10	(h)	Small Heath	W 4-1	Bassett, Richards, Hutchinson, C.Perry	4,523	1	2		4	5	6	7	8	9		11	10			3									
17	(h)	Aston Villa	W 3-2	Hutchinson, Richards 2	12,000	1	2		4	5	6	7	8	9		11	10			3									
24	(a)	Burnley	L 0-2		6,000	1	2		4	5	6		8	9			10	3		7		11							
Dec 1	(h)	Everton	L 1-4	Hutchinson	6,000	1	2		4	5	6	7	8	9		11	10			3									
8	(a)	Nottingham F	L 3-5	T.Perry, McLeod, Bassett	5,800	1	2		4	5	6	7	8	9			10	3				11							
15	(h)	Stoke C	W 3-2	Hutchinson 2, Taggart	4,400	1	2	3	4	5	6	7	8	9			10					11							
22	(a)	Blackburn R	L 0-3		1,200	1	2		4	5	6	7	8	9			10	3				11							
26	(h)	Sunderland	L 0-2		15,086	1	2	3	4	5	6	7	8	9		11					10								
27	(a)	Wolves	L 1-3	Hutchinson	6,500	1	2		4	5		7	8	9				6	10	3		11							
29	(h)	Burnley	L 0-1		2,535	1	2		8		6	7			10		9	5		3		11		4					
Jan 1	(a)	Liverpool	L 0-4		19,720	1	2		4	5	6	7	8	10			9			3		11							
5	(h)	Preston NE	L 4-5	Bassett, Hutchinson 2, Richards	19,700	1	2		4	5	6	7	8	10			9			3					11				
26	(h)	Blackburn R	W 2-0	Hutchinson, Banks	3,200	1	2		4	3	6	7	8	10			9	5				11							
Feb 23	(a)	Small Heath	W 2-1	Taggart 2	8,100	1			4	2	6			10			9	5		3	7	11			8				
26	(a)	Preston NE	L 0-5		6,400	1			4	2	6			10			9	5			7	11			8	3			
Mar 25	(a)	Stoke C	D 1-1	McLeod	5,100	1	2		4		6	7	8	9	10			5		3		11							
Apr 1	(a)	Sheffield W	L 2-3	McLeod 2	14,150	1		2	4		6	7	8	10				5				11					9	3	
13	(a)	Bolton W	L 0-5		10,200	1	3		4		6	7	8	10			9	5		2									11
15	(h)	Nottingham F	W 1-0	Geddes	4,355	1	3		4		6	7	8	10			9	5		2									11
22	(h)	Sheffield W	W 6-0	Geddes 2, Green, Hutchinson, McLeod, T.Perry	8,217	1	3		4		6	7	8	10				5		2							9		11
App						30	27	11	30	24	29	27	24	30	3	14	18	11	3	17	5	13	1	1	1	1	4	2	3
Goals							1		2	1	3	7	9	15		2	6					1					1		3

* Albion played with ten players in this game.

West Bromwich Albion in 1894-5, defeated 1-0 by Aston Villa in the FA Cup but 1-0 victors over Villa in the Birmingham Cup. Back row (left to right): T.Higgins, J.Taggart, J.Reader, J.Horton, W.Williams. Front: T.Perry, W.Bassett (captain), R.McLeod, W.Richards, T.Hutchinson, J.Banks.

1895-96

Division 1

Date		Opponent	Res	Score / Scorers	Att	Reader J	Perry C	Williams W	Perry T	Higgins T	Banks J	Bassett W	McLeod R	Green T	Hutchinson T	Saunders S	Richards W	Horton J	Williams O	Paddock J	Norman O	Kelsey A	Humpage W	Fellows E	Spooner J	Richards J	Wright F	Hadley B	Hayward A	Taggart J	Flewitt A	Cave G
Sep 2	(a)	Aston Villa	L	0-1	18,000	1	2	3	4	5	6	7	8	9	10	11																
7	(h)	Burnley	L	0-2	5,000	1	2	3	4	5	6	7	8	9	10				11													
14	(h)	Preston NE	L	1-2 Hutchinson	4,250	1		3	4	5	6	7	8	9	10	11		2														
21	(a)	Stoke C	L	1-3 Green	12,000	1		3	4	5	6	7	8	9				2		11		10										
28	(h)	Nottingham F	W	3-1 Paddock 2, Bassett	3,000	1		3	4	5	6	7	8		9			2		11		10										
Oct 5	(a)	Sheffield W	L	3-5 Hutchinson 2, Richards	8,000	1		3	4	5	6		8		9		7	2		11		10										
12	(h)	Aston Villa	D	1-1 Paddock	17,510	1		3	4	5	6	7	8		9			2		11		10										
19	(a)	Everton	D	1-1 McLeod	18,900	1		3	4	5	6	7	8		9			2		11		10										
26	(h)	Sheffield W	L	2-3 Paddock, Banks	5,550	1		3	4	5	6	7	8		9			2		11		10										
Nov 2	(a)	Bury	L	0-3	8,000	1		3	4	5	6	7	8		9			2		11		10										
4	(h)	Bolton W	L	2-3 McLeod, Sutcliffe (og)	3,500	1	2	3	4	5	6	7	8		9					11		10										
9	(h)	Stoke C	W	1-0 McLeod	3,500	1		3	4	5	6	7	8		9			2				10		11								
16	(a)	Nottingham F	L	0-2	6,000	1		3	4	5	6	7	8		9			2				10		11								
23	(h)	Everton	L	0-3	3,950	1		3	4	5	6	7	8		9			2				10		11								
30	(h)	Wolves	W	2-1 Richards, McLeod	3,000	1		3	4	5	6	7	8				11	2				10				9						
Dec 14	(a)	Derby C	L	1-4 Richards	8,000	1		3	4	5	6	7	8				11	2				10				9						
21	(a)	Small Heath	D	2-2 McLeod, Banks	6,000	1		3	4	5	11	7	8					2				10				9				6		
26	(h)	Sunderland	D	1-1 Bassett	15,124	1		3	4	5	11	7	8					2				10				9				6		
Jan 4	(a)	Sheffield U	L	0-2	5,000	1		3	4	5	11	7	8					2				10				9				6		
11	(a)	Burnley	L	0-3	5,500	1		3	4	5		7	8					2				10				9			6	11		
18	(h)	Derby C	D	0-0	8,877	1		3	4	5		7	8					2				10				9			11	6		
25	(a)	Sunderland	L	1-7 McLeod	10,500	1		3	4	5		7	8					2				10				9			11	6		
Feb 17	(a)	Blackburn R	L	0-1	5,700	1		3	4	5			8		9		11	2				10				7				6		
22	(h)	Sheffield U	W	1-0 W.Richards	3,900	1		3	4	5			8				11	2				10				7				6	9	
Mar 7	(a)	Wolves	W	2-1 W.Richards, Flewitt	8,114	1		3	4	5			8				11	2				10				7				6	9	
9	(h)	Bury	L	1-3 Flewitt	4,200	1		3	4	5			8				11	2				10				7				6	9	
Apr 3	(a)	Preston NE	D	0-0	6,700	1		3	4	5			8				11	2				10				7				6	9	
4	(a)	Bolton W	L	1-2 Banks	7,000	1		3	4	5	11		8					2				10				7				6	9	
6	(h)	Small Heath	D	0-0	3,750	1		3	4	5			8				11	2				10				7				6	9	
29	(h)	Blackburn R	W	3-2 W.Richards, Hutchinson, Taggart	560	1		3	4	5	11		8		9		10	2								7				6		2
App						27	3	30	30	30	20	25	30	4	15	2	20	25	1	10	1	11	3	2	2	14	2	1	3	10	7	2
Goals											3	2	6	1	4		6			4										1	2	

TEST MATCHES

Albion, by virtue of finishing at the foot of the First Division in 1895-6, were required, along with Small Heath, to meet Liverpool and Manchester City from Division Two to contest a series of Test Matches to see who would be playing in what Division in 1896-7. Both First Division clubs had to play the Second Division clubs twice. Albion, along with Liverpool, gained five points from their four games, and thus remained in Division One. Small Heath and Manchester City each acquired three points and were forced to play in the lower Division.

Date		Opponent	Res	Score / Scorers	Att	1	2	3	4	5	6	7	8	9	10	11
Apr 18	(a)	Manchester C	D	1-1 T.Perry	8,000	Reader	J.Horton	W.Williams	T.Perry	Higgins	Taggart	J.Richards	McLeod	Flewitt	Hutchinson	W.Richards
20	(h)	Manchester C	W	6-1 Flewitt 2, Higgins, J.Richards, W.Williams, Johnson	8,000	..	..	..	..	..	..	..	..	..	Johnson	..
25	(a)	Liverpool	L	0-2	20,100	..	..	..	Banks	..	..	..	..	W.Richards	Hutchinson	
27	(h)	Liverpool	W	2-0 W.Williams (pen), W.Richards	15,000	..	..	..	T.Perry	..	..	..	..	..	..	Banks

West Bromwich Albion 1895-6 (players only, left to right): Higgins, T.Perry, Bassett, C.Perry, McLeod, Williams, W.Richards, Reader, Hutchinson, Taggart, Banks.

1896-97

Division 1

Date	Opponent	Res	Scorers	Att	Reader J	Evans T	Williams W	Perry T	Higgins T	McManus P	Bassett W	McLeod R	Ford W	Richards W	Garfield B	Banks J	Watson A	Flewitt A	Vigrow S	Cameron J	Horton J	Cave G	Dean A	Law A	Flavell A	Fellows E
Sep 1 (a) Blackburn R		W 2-1	Richards, McLeod	3,000	1	2	3	4	5	6	7	8	9	10	11											
5 (h) Aston Villa		W 3-1	Garfield 2, Williams (pen)	10,000	1	3	2	4	5		7	8	9	10	11	6										
12 (a) Sheffield W		L 1-3	Ford	6,800	1	3	2	4	5		7	8	9	10	11	6										
19 (h) Preston NE		D 1-1	Watson	9,500	1	2	3	4	5		7	8	9		11	6	10									
26 (a) Liverpool		D 0-0		15,100	1	2	3	4	5	6	7		9		11		10	8								
Oct 3 (h) Sheffield W		L 0-2		10,291	1	2	3	4	5	6	7	8	9	10	11											
10 (a) Aston Villa		L 0-2		15,500	1	2	3	4	5		7	8	9		11	6	10									
17 (h) Wolves		W 1-0	McLeod	6,000	1	2	3	4	5	6	7	8		9	11		10									
24 (h) Bury		D 0-0		5,000	1	2	3	4	5		7		9	10	11	6		8								
31 (h) Liverpool		L 0-1		6,100	1		3	2	5		7		4	9	11	6		8	10							
Nov 2 (h) Bolton W		W 1-0	Bassett	5,200	1	2	3	4	5		7		9		10	6	11	8								
14 (h) Sheffield U		L 0-1		5,700	1	2	3	4	5		7		9		10	6	11	8								
21 (a) Stoke C		D 2-2	Flewitt, Garfield	6,200	1	2	3	4	5		7	10			11	6		8		9						
28 (h) Sunderland		W 1-0	Cameron	4,000	1	2	3	4	5	6	7			10	11			8		9						
Dec 5 (a) Sheffield U		W 1-0	Bassett	6,000	1	2		4	5	6	7			10	11			8		9	3					
12 (h) Stoke C		L 1-2	Garfield	1,105	1	2	3	4	5	6	7			10	11			8		9						
19 (a) Bolton W		D 2-2	Flewitt, Cameron	7,000	1	2	3	4	5	6	7			10	11			8		9						
25 (a) Derby C		L 1-8	Flewitt	8,000	1	2	3	4	5	6	7			10	11			8		9						
26 (h) Blackburn R		W 1-0	Flewitt	9,909	1		3	4	5	6	7			10	11			8		9			2			
28 (a) Wolves		L 1-6	Bassett	11,561	1		3	4	5	6	7			10	11			8		9			2			
Jan 2 (a) Nottingham F		W 1-0	Dean	5,300	1		3	4	5	6				10	11			9					2	7		
16 (h) Everton		L 1-4	Perry	3,950	1	2	3	4	5			8		10		6	11	9		7						
23 (h) Nottingham F		W 4-0	Richards 3, Williams	2,000	1	2	3	4	5		7			10		6	11	8		9						
Feb 6 (h) Derby C		L 1-4	Garfield	6,000			3	4	5		7			10	11	6		8		9		1	2			
Mar 6 (a) Sunderland		L 1-2	Richards	4,600		2	3	4	5	6				10	11		7	8		9					1	
13 (a) Bury		L 0-3		8,000		2	3	4	5		7					6	11	8		9					1	10
Apr 3 (h) Burnley		W 3-0	McLeod, Williams, Flewitt	3,100	1		3	4		5		9		10	11	6	7	8					2			
10 (a) Burnley		L 0-5		4,900	1		3	4		5		9		10	11	6	7	8					2			
16 (a) Preston NE		D 0-0		8,000	1		3	4		5		9		10	11	6	7	8					2			
17 (a) Everton		L 3-6	Perry, Flewitt, McLeod	9,700	1		3	4		5		9		10	11	6	7	8					2			
App					27	21	29	30	26	17	23	13	12	19	22	17	22	23	1	13	4	5	2	1	2	1
Goals							3	2			3	4	1	5	5		1	6		2			1			

1897-98

Division 1

Date	Opponent	Res	Scorers	Att	Reader J	Cave G	Williams W	Perry T	McManus P	Banks J	Watson A	Flewitt A	Higgins T	McKenzie A	Garfield B	Bassett W	Richards W	Jones A	Dean A	Reid G	Knowles J	Nock J	Hadley H	Connor J	Horton J
Sep 4 (a) Aston Villa		L 3-4	McKenzie, Higgins, McManus	20,950	1	2	3	4	5	6	7	8	9	10	11										
11 (h) Nottingham F		W 2-0	Garfield 2	5,000	1	2	3	4	5	6	7	8	9	10	11										
18 (a) Derby C		L 2-3	Watson, Higgins	6,700	1	2	3	4	5	6	7	8	9	10	11										
25 (h) Stoke C		W 2-0	Flewitt, Higgins	8,200	1	2	3	4	5	6	7	8	9	10	11										
Oct 2 (a) Bury		L 2-3	Bassett, Higgins	4,500	1	2	3	4	5	6		8	9	10	11	7									
9 (h) Aston Villa		D 1-1	Garfield	12,244	1	2	3	4	5	6		8	9	10	11	7									
16 (a) Sunderland		W 2-0	McNeill (og), Bassett	6,500	1	2	3	4	5	6		8	9	10	11	7									
23 (h) Wolves		D 2-2	Flewitt, Garfield	11,750	1	2	3	4	5	6		7	8	10	11		9								
30 (h) Stoke C		D 0-0		6,400	1	2	3	4	5	6	7	8	9	10	11										
Nov 1 (h) Bolton W		W 2-0	Dean, Jones	8,200	1	2	3	4		6		8	9	10	11			5	7						
6 (h) Everton		D 2-2	Garfield, Dean	5,750	1	2	3	4		6		8	9	10	11			5	7						
13 (h) Liverpool		W 2-1	Williams, Jones	8,200	1	2	3	4		6		8		10	11			5	7	9					
20 (h) Derby C		W 3-1	Garfield, Flewitt, Reid	10,500	1	2	3	4		6		8		10	11			5	7	9					
27 (a) Everton		L 1-6	Flewitt	15,700	1	2	3	4		6		8		10	11			5	7	9					
Dec 11 (a) Nottingham F		W 1-0	Perry	10,400	1	2	3	4		6		8		10	11			5		9	7				
18 (h) Bury		W 1-0	Garfield	6,303	1	2	3	4		6		8		10	11			5		9	7				
27 (h) Blackburn R		D 1-1	Williams (pen)	5,300	1	2	3	4		6		8		10	11	7		5		9					
28 (a) Wolves		D 1-1	Reid	8,100	1	2	3	4		6		8		10	11	7		5		9					
Jan 1 (a) Liverpool		D 1-1	Flewitt	10,000	1	2	3	4		6		8		10		7		5		9	11				
15 (h) Preston NE		W 3-1	Garfield 2, Flewitt	7,000	1	2	3	4		6		8		10	11	7		5		9					
Feb 5 (a) Blackburn R		W 3-1	Reid, Flewitt, Bassett	4,000	1	2	3	4		6		8		10	11	7		5		9					
19 (h) Sunderland		D 2-2	McKenzie 2	5,000	1	2	3	4		6		8		10	11	7		5		9					
Mar 12 (h) Sheffield W		L 0-2		3,455	1	2	3	4		6		8		10	11	7	9	5							
19 (a) Notts C		D 2-2	Garfield, Jones	3,600	1	2	3	4						10	11	7	9	5					6	8	
26 (h) Sheffield U		W 2-0	Garfield, Richards	4,200	1	2	3	4		6				10	11	7	9	5						8	
31 (a) Preston NE		D 1-1	Garfield	5,900	1	2	3	4		6				10	11	7	9	5						8	
Apr 2 (a) Bolton W		L 0-2		3,650	1	2		4	5	6				10	11	7	9	3							
4 (h) Notts C		L 0-3		4,000	1	2	3	4						10		7	9	3				11	6	8	
9 (a) Sheffield W		L 0-3		3,200	1	2		4	11					10		7	9	5					6	8	3
11 (a) Sheffield U		L 0-2		2,800	1	2	3	4		6				10	11	7	9	5						8	
App					30	30	28	29	11	27	6	23	11	30	27	17	9	21	5	11	2	2	3	7	1
Goals							2	1	1		1	7	4	3	12	3	1	3	2	3					

1898-99

Division 1

Date		Opponent	Res	Scorers	Att	Reader J	Cave G	Williams W	Perry T	Jones A	Banks J	Bassett W	Flewitt A	Brett R	Richards W	Garfield B	Dunn A	Connor J	McKenzie A	Foster J	Turner J	Simmons C	Nock J	Hadley H	Brett S	Adams A	Smith A	Fellows E
Sep 3	(a)	Bolton W	D 3-3	Brett, Garfield 2	6,300	1	2	3	4	5	6	7	8	9	10	11												
10	(h)	Derby C	D 1-1	Brett	7,026	1	2	3	4	5	6	7	8	9	10	11												
17	(h)	Bury	W 2-0	Garfield, Flewitt	5,521	1	2	3	4	5	6	7	8	9	10	11												
24	(a)	Blackburn R	L 1-4	Garfield	4,600	1	2		4	5	6	7	8	9	10	11	3											
Oct 1	(h)	Sheffield W	W 2-0	Perry, McKenzie	6,767	1	2		4	5			8	9	6	11	3	7	10									
8	(a)	Sunderland	L 0-2		15,000	1	2	3	4	5					9	6	11		8	10	7							
15	(h)	Wolves	L 1-2	Bassett	6,457		2	3	4	5	6	7			9		11		8	10		1						
22	(a)	Everton	L 0-1		9,000	1	2	3	4	5	6	7		9	10	11			8									
29	(h)	Notts C	W 2-0	McKenzie, Richards	4,286	1	2	3	4	5	6	7		9	10	11			8									
Nov 5	(a)	Stoke C	L 1-2	Richards	7,500	1	2		4	5	6	7		9	10	11		3	8									
7	(h)	Everton	W 3-0	Richards 2, Brett	6,686	1	2	3	4	5	6	7		9	10	11			8									
12	(h)	Aston Villa	L 0-1		15,896	1	2	3	4	5	6	7		9	10	11			8									
19	(a)	Burnley	D 1-1	Williams (pen)	7,500	1	2	3	4		6	7		9		5			10			8	11					
26	(h)	Sheffield U	W 3-0	Nock, Thickett (og), Richards	1,999	1	2	3	4	5	6	7			10		9		8				11					
Dec 3	(a)	Newcastle U	L 0-3		16,200	1	2	3	4	5	6	7			10		9		8				11					
10	(h)	Preston NE	W 2-0	Dunn, McKenzie	2,433	1	2	3	4	5	6	7			10		9		8				11					
17	(a)	Liverpool	D 2-2	Nock 2	5,100	1	2	3	4	5	6	7			10		9		8				11					
24	(h)	Nottingham F	W 2-0	Nock 2	2,578	1	2	3	4	5		7			10		9		8				11	6				
26	(h)	Liverpool	L 0-1		8,483	1	2	3	4	5		7			10		9		8				11	6				
27	(a)	Wolves	L 1-5	McKenzie	12,052	1	2		4	3		7			10		5		8				11	6	9			
31	(h)	Bolton W	W 1-0	Nock	1,571	1	2	3	4	5		7	8		9		6		10				11					
Jan 7	(a)	Derby C	L 1-4	Richards	3,200	1	2	3	4	5		7	8		9		6		10				11					
14	(a)	Bury	D 1-1	Richards	1,500	1	2	3	4	5		7			9		6		10			8	11					
21	(h)	Blackburn R	W 6-2	Flewitt 2, McKenzie 2, Garfield, Bassett	1,957	1	2		4	3		7	9		5	11	6		10			8						
Feb 4	(h)	Sunderland	W 1-0	Richards	4,947	1	2	3	4	5	6	7			9	10	11		8									
14	(a)	Sheffield W	W 2-1	Richards 2	3,503	1	2	3	4	5		7			9	10	11	6	8									
Mar 4	(h)	Stoke C	L 0-1		1,714	1	2	3	4	5		7			9	10	11	6	8									
9	(a)	Notts C	D 0-0		2,488	1	2	3	4	5		7			10	11						8		6		9		
18	(h)	Burnley	L 0-1		2,330	1	2	3	4	5		7			9	10	11	6	8									
25	(a)	Sheffield U	L 0-5		3,996	1	2	3	4	5		7										8	11	6			9	10
Apr 1	(h)	Newcastle U	W 2-0	Smith, Bassett	2,304	1	2		8	5		7					11	4						6		3	9	10
8	(a)	Preston NE	L 0-4		2,976	1	2		8	5	6	7			10	11		4						9		3		
22	(a)	Nottingham F	L 0-3		3,015	1	2		8	5		7			10	11		4						6		3	9	
24	(a)	Aston Villa	L 1-7	Perry	10,000	1	2		9	5		7			10			4				8	11	6		3		
App						33	34	25	34	33	17	32	12	12	31	20	21	3	21	1	1	9	13	9	2	5	3	2
Goals								1	2			3	3	3	10	5	1		6				6				1	

Billy Bassett (left) who retired at the end of season 1898-9, and his England colleague Steve Bloomer, the Derby County star who scored the first League goal at The Hawthorns, in September 1900.

'Chippy' Simmons, an Albion debutant in 1898-9 and top-scorer in 1899-1900.

1899-1900

Division 1

Date	Opponent	Result	Scorers	Att.	Reader J	Cave G	Williams W	Dunn A	Jones A	Banks J	Paddock J	Perry T	Simmons C	Richards W	Garfield B	Adams A	Hadley H	Walker W	Golings P	Roberts R	Brett S	Chadburn J	Smith A
Sep 2	(h) Newcastle U	D 1-1	Simmons	6,135	1	2	3	4	5	6	7	8	9	10	11								
9	(a) Aston Villa	W 2-0	Garfield, Simmons	17,482	1	2	3	4	5	6	7	8	9	10	11								
16	(h) Liverpool	W 2-0	Garfield 2	6,431	1	2	3	4	5	6	7	8	9	10	11								
23	(a) Burnley	L 0-2		10,027	1	2	3	4	5	6	7	8	9	10	11								
30	(h) Preston NE	W 1-0	Simmons	4,684	1		3	4	5		7	8	9	10	11	2	6						
Oct 7	(a) Nottingham F	L 1-6	Perry	17,106	1		3	4	5		7	8	9		11	2	6	10					
14	(h) Glossop	D 3-3	Williams, Richards 2	5,629	1		3	4	5		7	8	9	10	11	2	6						
21	(a) Stoke C	L 0-1		3,603	1		3		5		7		9	8	11	2	6	10	4				
28	(h) Sunderland	W 1-0	Garfield	6,117	1		3	4	5	6	7	8	9		11	2		10					
Nov 4	(a) Wolves	L 0-2		10,089	1		3	4	5	6	7	8	9		11	2		10					
6	(h) Sheffield U	L 1-2	Perry	14,905	1		3	4	5	6	7	8	9		11	2		10					
11	(a) Everton	W 3-1	Paddock, Richards 2	8,996	1		5	3	6	7	4	8	9		11	2		10					
25	(a) Derby C	L 1-4	Richards	6,520	1		3	6	5		7	4	8	9	11	2		10					
Dec 2	(h) Bury	L 0-1		3,729	1		3	5	2	6		4	8	9	11			10			7		
9	(a) Notts C	W 2-1	Garfield 2	4,186	1		3	4	5	6	7	8	9		11	2		10					
16	(h) Manchester C	D 0-0		2,429	1		3	6	5		7	4	8	9	11	2		10					
23	(a) Sheffield U	D 1-1	Garfield	3,492	1		3	4	5	6	7	8	9	10	11	2							
26	(h) Everton	D 0-0		8,509	1		3	5			7	8	9		11	2	4	10	6				
30	(a) Newcastle U	L 2-4	Simmons 2	10,887	1		3	5			7	8	9	10		2	4		6	11			
Jan 6	(h) Aston Villa	L 0-2		6,575	1		3	5			7	8	9	10		2	4			11			
13	(a) Liverpool	L 0-2		12,531	1		3	5		6	7		9	10		2	4	8		11			
20	(h) Burnley	W 2-0	Hadley, Brett	3,427	1		3	4	5				9	10		2	6			11	8	7	
Feb 3	(a) Preston NE	L 2-5	Jones, Simmons	4,612	1		3	4	5			8	9	10		2	6			11	7		
Mar 3	(a) Sunderland	L 1-3	Perry	10,490	1		3	4	5			8	9	10		2	6			11	7		
10	(h) Wolves	W 3-2	Simmons 2, Richards	6,680	1		3	4	5			8	9	10		2	6			11		7	
19	(h) Stoke C	W 4-0	Jones, Brett, Chadburn, Simmons	1,717	1		3		5			4	9	10		2	6			11	8	7	
24	(a) Blackburn R	L 0-2		5,026	1		3		5			4	9	10		2	6			11	8	7	
31	(h) Derby C	D 0-0		4,603	1		3	8	5			4	9	10		2	6			11		7	
Apr 2	(h) Blackburn R	W 1-0	Roberts	3,342	1		3		5			4	9	10		2	6	8		11		7	
7	(a) Bury	L 0-1		2,978	1		3	4	5				9	10		2	6	8		11		7	
14	(h) Notts C	D 0-0		3,254	1		3	4	5				9	8		2	6	10		11		7	
16	(h) Nottingham F	W 8-0	Walker 3, Roberts 2, Simmons 2, Chadburn	5,187	1		3	4	5				9			2	6	10		11		7	8
21	(a) Manchester C	L 0-4		9,960	1		3	4	5				9			2	6	10		11		7	8
24	(a) Glossop	D 1-1	Simmons	2,025	1		3	4	5				9			2	6	10		11		7	8
	App				34	4	33	30	30	13	20	27	33	25	18	29	21	18	3	16	6	11	3
	Goals						1		2		1	3	12	6	7		1	3		3	2	2	

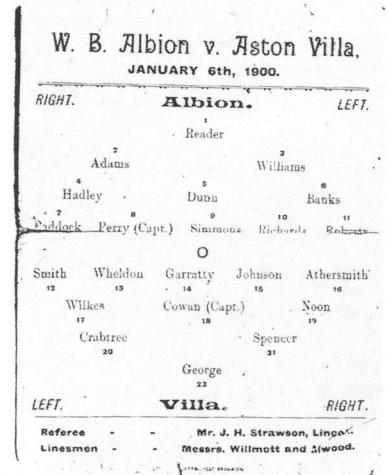

Albion's 1899-1900 team group. Back row (left to right): W.J.Paddock (trainer), H.Keys (chairman), A.Jones, A.Adams, H.Hadley, J.Reader, T.Brennand (director), W.Williams, B.Garfield, J.Banks, F.Heaven (secretary), H.Powell (director). Front: A.Dunn, J.Paddock, C.Simmons, T.Perry, W.Walker, A.Roberts, W.Richards.

1900-01

Division 1

	Date		Opponent	Res	Scorers	Att
Sep	1	(a)	Wolves	D 0-0		12,000
	3	(h)	Derby C	D 1-1	Simmons	20,104
	8	(h)	Aston Villa	L 0-1		35,417
	15	(a)	Liverpool	L 0-5		15,000
	22	(h)	Newcastle U	L 0-1		11,859
	29	(a)	Sheffield U	D 1-1	Simmons	10,000
Oct	6	(h)	Manchester C	W 3-2	Jones, Richards, Garfield	11,183
	13	(a)	Bury	L 1-6	Simmons	7,000
	20	(h)	Nottingham F	L 1-6	Adams	9,535
	27	(a)	Blackburn R	D 1-1	Smith	9,000
Nov	3	(h)	Stoke C	D 2-2	Dunn, Garfield	11,052
	5	(h)	Notts C	W 1-0	Chadburn	10,492
	10	(h)	Sheffield W	D 1-1	Stevenson	10,338
	17	(a)	Everton	L 0-1		20,000
	24	(h)	Sunderland	W 1-0	Stevenson	10,045
Dec	1	(a)	Derby C	L 0-4		11,700
	8	(h)	Bolton W	W 7-2	Banks, Roberts 3, Wheldon, Garfield, Buck	8,157
	15	(a)	Notts C	L 0-1		6,500
	22	(h)	Preston NE	L 0-1		7,997
	29	(h)	Wolves	L 1-2	Simmons	18,188
Jan	5	(a)	Aston Villa	W 1-0	Simmons	30,000
	19	(a)	Newcastle U	D 1-1	Garfield	10,500
Feb	16	(h)	Bury	L 1-2	Wheldon	9,691
Mar	2	(h)	Blackburn R	D 1-1	Wheldon	11,876
	9	(a)	Stoke C	L 0-2		12,000
	13	(a)	Nottingham F	W 3-2	Walker, Stevenson, Roberts	3,500
	16	(a)	Sheffield W	L 1-2	Roberts	9,000
	30	(a)	Sunderland	L 0-3		10,500
Apr	6	(a)	Manchester C	L 0-1		11,400
	13	(a)	Bolton W	L 2-3	Adams (pen), Smith	6,000
	15	(a)	Preston NE	W 3-2	Walker, Pickering, Perry	7,500
	22	(h)	Everton	L 1-2	Pickering	6,992
	29	(h)	Liverpool	L 0-1		8,974
	30	(h)	Sheffield U	L 0-2		1,050

Appearance grid

Match	Reader J	Adams A	Williams W	Dunn A	Jones A	Hadley H	Chadburn J	Pickering T	Simmons C	Wheldon F	Roberts R	Gollings P	Walker W	Garfield B	Richards W	Banks J	Knowles J	Perry T	Smith A	Stevenson J	Williams G	Lowe J	Cave G	Buck F
Sep 1	1	2	3	4	5	6	7	8	9	10	11													
Sep 3	1	2	3	4	5	6	7	8	9	10	11													
Sep 8	1	2	3	4	5	6	7	8	9	10	11													
Sep 15	1	2	3	4	5	6	7	8	9	10	11													
Sep 22	1	2	3	4	5	6	7	8	9	10	11													
Sep 29	1	2		3	5	6	7		9	10		4		8		11								
Oct 6	1	2		3	5	6	7			10		4		8	9	11								
Oct 13	1	2		3	5	6	7		9	10				8		11		4						
Oct 20	1	2	3	4	5	6	7		9					8		11				10				
Oct 27	1	2		3	5	6	7			10				8		11		4	9					
Nov 3	1	2		3	5	6	7			10				8		11		4		9				
Nov 5	1	2		3		6	7	8		10						11		4		9	5			
Nov 10	1	2		3		6	7	8		10	7					11		4		9	5			
Nov 17	1	2		3		6	7	8		10	11							4		9	5			
Nov 24	1	2		3	5	6	7			10	11									9	4			
Dec 1		2		3		6	7			10	11					4	1			9	5			
Dec 8	1	2				6				10	7					11		4		9	5		3	8
Dec 15	1	3				6				10	7					11		4		9	5		2	8
Dec 22	1	2				6			8	10	7					11		4	3	9	5			
Dec 29	1	2				6		10			7					11		4	3	9	5			8
Jan 5	1	2				6	3		8	10	7					11		4		5	9			
Jan 19	1	2				6	3		8	10	7					11		4			9	5		
Feb 16	1	2				6	3		8	10	7					11		4			9	5		
Mar 2	1	2				6	3		8	10	7					11		4			9	5		
Mar 9	1	2			5	6	3		8	10	7		11					4			9			
Mar 13	1	2	3		5	6					7		11					4	10	9				8
Mar 16	1	2	3		5	6					7		11					4	10	9				8
Mar 30	1	2	3		5	6					7		11						10	9	4			8
Apr 6	1	2	3		5	6					7		11						10	9	4			8
Apr 13	1	2	3			6	8				7		11					4	10	9	5			
Apr 15	1	2			5	6	3	8			7		11					4	10	9				
Apr 22	1	2			5	6	3	8			7		11					4	10	9				
Apr 29	1	2			5	6	3	8	9	10	7							4			11			
Apr 30	1	2			5	6	3	8	9	10	7							4			11			
App	33	34	8	20	20	34	24	10	20	26	27	2	14	18	1	8	1	17	8	24	15	1	2	7
Goals		2		1	1		1	2	5	3	5		2	4	1	1		1	2	3				1

Wages

Albion adopted professionalism in 1885 and have been paying their players ever since.

In those early days, certain players could earn between five shillings (25p) and 12s.6d (62p) a week — which was indeed a lot of money at the time.

By 1898-9, ten years after the League was formed, some Albion stars, including Billy Bassett, who was then in his last season as a player, were receiving as much as £4.10s (£4.50) a week. The lowest paid were on ten shillings a week.

In 1901 the Football League introduced a maximum wage rule and this stood for 60 years, up until 1961.

The first wage 'ceiling' was set at £4-a-week — but very few Albion players received the maximum immediately. Obviously as the cost of living went up, so did the players' wages, and hereunder is a chart showing the steady development of an Albion player's weekly wage:

1910 — £5 (all year round)	1951 — £14 (£10 close season)
1920 — £9 (all year round)	1953 — £15 (£12 close season)
1922 — £8 (£6 close season)	1957 — £17 (£14 close season)
1930 — £7 (£6 close season)	1958 — £20 (£17 close season)
1945 — £8 (£7 close season)	1961 — £25 (£25 close season)
1947 — £12 (£10 close season)	

Since the maximum wage restriction was lifted Albion, along with virtually every other League club, have been paying its players' wages based on service and stature. And although specific figures cannot be disclosed, it can be readily accepted that certain players have been known to earn over £1,000 a week, before bonuses.

Player-manager Johnny Giles, in 1975-6, earned between £12,000 and £15,000.

A page from the Albion wage book of 1898-99.

1901-02

Division 2

Date		Opponent	Res	Scorers	Att	Webb I	Adams A	Kifford J	Nurse D	Stevenson J	Hadley H	McLean J	Buck =	Appleby B	Worton T	Walker W	Simmons C	Smith A	Garfield B	Taylor O	Lee W	Williams G	Randle A	Harper W	Chadburn J	Dorsett G	Smith E	Poynton W
Sep 2	(h)	Glossop	L 0-1		5,064	1	2	3	4	5	6	7	8	9	10	11												
7	(h)	Preston NE	W 3-1	McLean, Garfield, Simmons	8,132	1	3	2	4	5	6	7			10		8	9	11									
9	(h)	Chesterfield	W 4-0	Simmons 2 (1 pen), Worton, Smith	10,845		3	2	4	5	6	7			10		8	9	11	1								
14	(a)	Burnley	D 0-0		4,992	1	3	2	4	5	6	7			10		8	9	11									
21	(h)	Burslem P.Vale	W 3-1	Worton 2, Smith	5,096	1	3	2	4	5	6	7			10		8	9	11									
28	(a)	Chesterfield	W 3-0	Hadley, Worton, Thacker (og)	3,201	1	3	2	4	5	6	7			10		8		11		9							
Oct 5	(h)	Gainsborough TW	7-0	Worton 2, Simmons 2, McLean, Smith, Lee	5,368	1	3	2	4	5	6	7			10		8		11		9							
12	(a)	Middlesbrough	W 2-1	Lee, Simmons	15,117	1	3	2	4	5	6	7			10		8		11		9							
19	(h)	Bristol C	D 2-2	Lee, McLean	7,829	1	3	2	4	5	6	7			10		8		11		9							
26	(a)	Blackpool	D 2-2	Nurse, Simmons	3,626	1	3	2	4	5		7			10		8		11		9	6						
Nov 9	(a)	Newton Heath	W 2-1	Simmons 2	13,029	1	3	2	4	5		7			10		8				9		6	11				
23	(a)	Doncaster R	L 0-2		8,370	1	2		4	5	6	7			10		8				9			11	3			
Dec 7	(a)	Burton U	W 3-1	Worton, Lee, Simmons	2,955	1	3	2	4	5	6	7			10		8				9			11				
9	(h)	Lincoln C	W 4-1	Simmons 2, Lee, Harper	6,224	1	3	2	4	5	6	7			10		8				9			11				
14	(h)	Middlesbrough	W 2-0	Simmons, Lee	6,868	1	3	2	4	5	6	7			10		8				9			11				
21	(h)	Barnsley	W 3-1	Worton 2, Simmons	5,577	1		2	4	5	6	7			10		8				9			11	3			
26	(h)	Stockport C	W 3-0	Simmons, Lee 2	23,697	1		2	4	5	6	7			10		8				9			11	3			
28	(a)	Leicester F	W 3-0	Simmons 2, McLean	2,034	1		2	4	5	6	7			10	11	8				9				3			
Jan 4	(a)	Preston NE	W 2-1	McLean, Lee	11,397	1	3	2	4	5	6	7			10		8				9					11		
6	(h)	Leicester F	W 1-0	Nurse	6,483	1	2		4	5	6	7			10		8				9				3	11		
11	(h)	Burnley	W 3-0	Lee 2, Dorsett	9,149	1	3	2	4	5	6	7			10		8				9					11		
18	(a)	Burslem P.Vale	W 3-2	Simmons, Lee, Worton	2,861	1	3	2	4	5	6	7			10		8				9					11		
Feb 1	(a)	Gainsborough T	D 1-1	Worton	2,016	1	3	2	4	5	6	7			10		8				9					11		
15	(a)	Bristol C	W 2-1	Worton, Simmons	14,175	1	3	2	4	5	6	7			10		8				9					11		
22	(h)	Blackpool	W 7-2	Kifford, Worton 2, Stevenson, Simmons 3	6,249	1	3	2	4	5	6	7			10		8				9					11		
Mar 1	(a)	Stockport C	W 2-0	Lee, Smith	5,049	1	3	2	4	5	6	7			10			8			9					11		
8	(h)	Newton Heath	W 4-0	Worton 3, McLean	10,206	1	3	2	4	5	6	7			10			8			9					11		
15	(a)	Glossop	W 2-1	A.Smith, E.Smith	1,658	1	3	2	4	5	6	7			10			9								11	8	
22	(h)	Doncaster R	D 2-2	Smith, Worton	6,103	1	3	2	4	5	6	7			10			8			9					11		
29	(a)	Lincoln C	L 0-1		4,460	1	3	2	4	5	6	7			10		8				9					11		
31	(a)	W Arsenal	L 1-2	Worton	15,762	1	3	2	4	5	6	7			10		8				9					11		
Apr 5	(h)	Burton U	W 2-1	Poynton, Buck	1,206	1	3	2	4	5	6		8		10						9					11		7
12	(h)	W Arsenal	W 2-1	Simmons, Lee	8,878	1	3	2	4	5	6	7			10		8				9					11		
19	(a)	Barnsley	W 2-0	Poynton, Stevenson	4,014	1	3	2	4	5	6				10		8				9					11		7
App						33	31	32	34	34	32	32	2	1	34	2	28	13	4	1	28	1	1	7	5	16	1	2
Goals								1	2	2	1	6	1		19	1	23	6	1		14					1	1	2

H.Hadley

Jimmy McLean

81

1902-03

Division 1

Date	Opp	Res	Scorers	Att	Webb I	Kifford J	Adams A	Nurse D	Stevenson J	Hadley H	McLean J	Simmons C	Lee W	Worton T	Dorsett G	Smith A	Buck F	Randle A	Hobson F	Smith E	Harper W	Taylor O	Chadburn J	Cole HJ	Elmore G	Lowe J	Smith W	Brittain J	Farrington S
Sep 1 (h) Everton		W 2-1	McLean, Simmons	16,051	1	2	3	4	5	6	7	8	9	10	11														
Sep 6 (a) Notts C		L 1-3	Kifford (pen)	12,339	1	2	3	4	5	6	7	8	9	10	11														
Sep 13 (h) Bolton W		W 2-1	Simmons, Dorsett	12,263	1	2	3	4	5	6	7	8		10	11	9													
Sep 20 (a) Middlesbrough		D 1-1	Blackett (og)	20,157	1	2	3	4	5	6	7	8	9	10	11														
Sep 27 (h) Newcastle U		W 6-1	Lee, Buck 2, Simmons, Stevenson, McLean	22,160	1	2	3	4	5	6	7	8	9		11	10													
Oct 4 (a) Wolves		W 2-1	Dorsett, Simmons	14,072	1	2	3	4	5	6	7	8	9		11	10													
Oct 11 (h) Liverpool		L 1-2	McLean	20,210	1	2	3		5	6	7	8	9		11	10	4												
Oct 18 (a) Sheffield U		W 2-1	Simmons 2	11,863	1	2	3	4	5	6	7	8	9	10	11														
Oct 25 (h) Grimsby T		W 1-0	Lee	18,047	1	2	3	4	5	6	7	8	9		11	10													
Nov 1 (a) Aston Villa		W 3-0	Kifford 2 (1 pen), Lee	35,128	1	2	3	4	5	6		8	9	10	11		7												
Nov 8 (h) Nottingham F		W 2-0	Kifford (pen), Dorsett	12,612	1	2	3	4	5	6		8	9	10	11		7												
Nov 15 (a) Bury		W 2-1	Lee, Dorsett	13,498	1	2	3	4	5	6		8	9	10	11		7												
Nov 22 (h) Blackburn R		W 5-3	Lee, Simmons, Kifford (pen), Stevenson, Worton	12,134	1	2	3	4	5	6	7	8	9	10				11											
Nov 29 (a) Sunderland		D 0-0		10,457	1	2	3	4	5	6	7		9	10	11				8										
Dec 6 (h) Stoke C		W 2-1	McLean, Smith	11,235	1	2	3	4	5	6	7		9	10						8	11								
Dec 13 (a) Everton		L 1-3	Lee	14,854	1	2	3	4	5	6	7		9	10	11		8												
Dec 20 (h) Sheffield W		L 2-3	Simmons, Dorsett	14,560	1	2	3	4	5	6	7	8	9	10	11														
Dec 27 (a) Derby C		L 0-1		21,909	1	2	3	4	5	6	7	8	9	10	11														
Jan 1 (a) Liverpool		W 2-0	Dorsett, Lee	35,731		2	3	4	5	6	7	8	9	10	11								1						
Jan 3 (h) Notts C		W 3-2	Lee 2, Worton	16,785			3	4	5	6	7	8	9	10	11								1	2					
Jan 10 (a) Bolton W		W 1-0	Lee	15,442	1	2	3	4	5	6	7		9	10	11							8							
Jan 17 (h) Middlesbrough		W 1-0	Worton	18,033	1	2	3	4	5	6	7		9	10	11							8							
Jan 24 (a) Newcastle U		L 0-1		20,156	1	2	3	4	5	6	7		9	10	11							8							
Jan 31 (h) Wolves		D 2-2	Kifford (pen), Cole	26,081	1	2	3	4	5	6	7		9	10	11							8							
Feb 14 (h) Sheffield U		D 3-3	Stevenson, Dorsett, Elmore	17,122	1	2	3	4	5		7		9	10	11					6					8				
Feb 28 (h) Aston Villa		L 1-2	Buck	28,536	1	2	3	4	5	6	7	8	9		11	10													
Mar 7 (a) Nottingham F		L 1-3	Buck	7,052	1	2	3	4	5			8	9	10	11		7	6											
Mar 21 (a) Blackburn R		L 0-1		10,354	1	2	3	4	5	6	7		9	10	11							8							
Mar 28 (h) Sunderland		L 0-3		10,517	1	2	3	4	5	6	7		9	10	11		8												
Apr 4 (a) Stoke C		L 0-3		5,540		2	3	4	5	6			9	10	11		8						1	7					
Apr 10 (a) Grimsby T		L 0-4		10,514		2	3	4	5	6		8	9	10	11		7						1						
Apr 18 (a) Sheffield W		L 1-3	Smith	19,000		2		4	5	6		8	9		11					10					7	3	1		
Apr 20 (h) Bury		L 1-3	Kifford (pen)	5,682		2		4	5	6		8	9		11					10					7	3	1		
Apr 25 (h) Derby C		W 3-0	Smith, Simmons, Farrington	4,148		2			5	6		8			11	4				10						3	1	7	9
App					27	33	31	32	34	32	25	23	32	26	32	2	13	4	1	4	1	4	3	4	3	3	3	1	1
Goals						7			3		4	9	10	3	7		4			3				1	1				1

Five fine Albion goalkeepers, Bob Roberts (1880-90), Joe Reader (1885-1901, first team from 1890), Ike Webb (1901-05), Jim Stringer (1905-10), Hubert Pearson (1904-25, first team from 1910).

1903-04

Division 1

Date		Opponent	Result	Scorers	Att	Webb I	Kifford J	Adams A	Nurse D	Stevenson J	Hadley H	Smith W	Simmons C	Lee W	Smith E	Dorsett G	Clements H	Worton T	Pennington J	Hobson F	Cole HJ	Cook F	Fenton F	Brown H	Randle A	Smith A	Corfield S	Owen A	Aston H	Folks W
Sep 2	(h)	Sheffield W	L 0-1		8,995	1	2	3	4	5	6	7	8	9	10	11														
5	(h)	Newcastle U	L 1-2	Nurse	10,352	1	2	3	4	5	6	7	8	9	10	11														
12	(a)	Aston Villa	L 1-3	Simmons	38,920	1	2	3	4	5	6		8	9		11	7	10												
19	(h)	Middlesbrough	D 0-0		14,130	1	2	3	4	5	6		8	9		11	7	10												
26	(a)	Liverpool	W 3-1	Simmons, Hobson, Dorsett	15,578	1		2	4	5	6		8			11	7	10	3	9										
Oct 3	(h)	Bury	W 3-2	Hobson 2, Cole	14,381	1		2	4	5	6					11	7	10	3	9	8									
10	(a)	Blackburn R	L 0-2		10,057	1		2	4	5	6					11	7	10	3	9	8									
17	(h)	Nottingham F	D 1-1	Stevenson	14,276	1		2	4	5	6		8			11	7	10	3	9										
24	(a)	Sheffield W	L 0-1		12,000	1		2	4	5	6		8			11	7	10	3	9										
31	(h)	Sunderland	D 1-1	Worton	10,128	1		2	4	5	6		8			11	7	10	3	9										
Nov 7	(a)	Wolves	L 0-1		12,431	1		2	4	5	6		8			11	7	10	3	9										
14	(a)	Small Heath	W 1-0	Nurse	12,563			2	4	5	6		8			11		10	3	9		1		7						
21	(h)	Everton	D 0-0		10,190			2	4	5	6		8			11		10	3	9		1		7						
28	(a)	Stoke C	L 0-5		3,724			2	4	5	6		8			11	7	10	3			1		9						
Dec 12	(a)	Manchester C	L 3-6	Fenton, Simmons, Dorsett	14,471			2	4	5	6		8		10	11	7		3			1	9							
14	(h)	Derby C	D 0-0		13,525			2		5	6		8		10	11	7		3			1	9		4					
19	(h)	Notts C	D 0-0		8,188			2	4	5	6		8		10	11	7		3			1	9							
26	(a)	Sheffield U	L 0-4		10,227		2		4	5	6	9				11	7		3		10	1		8						
28	(h)	Blackburn R	W 2-1	Brown, Simmons	19,554		2			5	6		8			11			3	9		1		10	4	7				
Jan 2	(a)	Newcastle U	L 0-1		13,376	1	2			5	6		8			11			3	9				10	4	7				
9	(h)	Aston Villa	L 1-3	Simmons	31,418	1	2			5	6		8			11			3	9				10	4	7				
16	(a)	Middlesbrough	D 2-2	Hobson, Dorsett	18,021	1	2	3			6		8			11				9				10	4	7	5			
23	(h)	Liverpool	D 2-2	Randle, Smith	10,740	1				5	6		8	9		11			3					10	4	7				
30	(a)	Bury	L 1-2	Adams	7,193	1		2		5	6			9		11			3		8			10	4	7				
Feb 20	(a)	Notts C	W 3-2	Brown, Lee, Dorsett	5,991	1	2	3			6	7	8	9		11								10	4		5			
27	(a)	Sunderland	D 1-1	Smith	5,632	1	2	3			6	7	8	9		11								10	4		5			
Mar 5	(h)	Wolves	L 1-2	Dorsett	6,338	1	2	3	4			7		9		11								10	6	8	5			
12	(h)	Small Heath	L 0-1		22,760	1	2		4			7	8	9		11			3					10	6		5			
25	(h)	Stoke C	W 3-0	Simmons, Dorsett, Brown	8,107	1	2	3			6		8			11								10	4		5	7		
30	(a)	Nottingham F	L 0-2		2,624	1	2	3			9	6		8	10	11									4		7	5		
Apr 2	(a)	Derby C	L 2-4	Simmons 2	18,140	1	2	3		5	6		8			11								10	4			7	9	
9	(h)	Manchester C	W 2-1	Aston, Owen	7,508		2	3		5	6		8			11						1		10	4			7	9	
18	(a)	Everton	L 0-4		12,025		2	3		5	6		8			11						1		10	4			7	9	
23	(h)	Sheffield U	D 2-2	Cole, Dorsett (pen)	4,467		2	3			6					11					8	1		10	4		5		9	7
					App	23	19	29	19	28	32	7	28	11	5	34	10	12	20	12	5	11	6	21	17	8	8	4	4	1
					Goals			1	2	1			8	1	1	7		1		4	2		1	3	1	1		1	1	

A.Randle

Jesse Pennington joined Albion in 1903 and served the Throstles for 19 years.

83

1904-05

Division 2

Date		Opponent	Result	Scorers	Att	Webb I	Kifford J	Adams A	Randle A	Manners J	Hadley H	Bell L	Jack W	Brown H	Lewis A	Dorsett G	Pennington J	Davies A	Bowden J	Aston H	Miller J	Edwards S	Pheasant E	Davies L	Smith W	Cook F	Dawes F	Brittain J	Turner I	Owen A	Haycock F	Bradley C	Bamford A	Burton E	Haywood T	Williams J	Stringer J	Shinton F
Sep 3	(a)	Burnley	W 4-1	Lewis 3, Dorsett	5,389	1	2	3	4	5	6	7	8	9	10	11																							
10	(h)	Grimsby T	L 0-2		4,123	1	2	3	4	5	6	7	8	9	10	11																							
17	(a)	Blackpool	D 0-0		3,852	1		2	4	5	6		8	9	10	11		3	7																			
24	(h)	Doncaster R	W 6-1	Dorsett 3, Lewis, Jack 2	5,261	1	2	3	4		6		8		10	11			7	5	9																	
Oct 1	(a)	Gainsborough T	L 2-4	Jack, Aston	4,523	1	2	3	4		6		8		10	11			7	5	9																	
8	(h)	Burton U	W 4-0	Dorsett 3 (1 pen), Bell	4,873	1		2	4		6	8			10	11		3	7	5		9																
15	(a)	Liverpool	L 2-3	Jack, Brown	16,147	1		2	4		6		8	9	10	11		3	7	5																		
29	(a)	Brsitol C	L 1-2	Jack	10,795	1		2			6		8	9	10	11		3	7	5		4																
Nov 5	(h)	Manchester U	L 0-2		5,578	1		2	4		6		8		10	11		3	7	9			5															
7	(h)	Blackpool	W 4-2	Aston, Pheasant, Manners, Birkett (og)	4,951	1		2	4		6	8			10				11	7			9	5	3														
19	(h)	Chesterfield T	L 0-2		3,753	1	2		4						10			11	3	7			9	5	6	8												
26	(a)	Bradford C	L 1-3	Aston	11,854	1	2		4		6				10			11	3	7			9	5	8													
Dec 3	(h)	Lincoln C	W 2-0	Smith, Davies	3,124	1			4		6	2			10			11	3	7			9	5	8													
15	(a)	Leicester F	L 1-3	Aston	7,890				4		6	7	8		10	11		2		9			5	3		1												
17	(h)	Barnsley	W 4-1	Aston, Smith, Brown, Pheasant (pen)	2,675				4		6	2			10			3	7	9			5		8	1		11										
24	(a)	Bolton W	L 1-2	Bell	7,341				4		11	7			10			2	6	9			5		8	1		3										
26	(h)	Burslem P.Vale	L 0-1		7,166				4		11	7						2	6	9			5		8	1		3	10									
31	(h)	Burnley	D 1-1	Aston	7,374				4		6	10				11		2		9			5		1			3	7	8								
Jan 7	(a)	Grimsby T	W 3-1	Pheasant, Bell, Aston	6,105				4		6	7		9		11		2		10			5		8	1		3										
21	(a)	Doncaster R	W 1-0	Bell	4,761		2	3	4		6	7		10	11				5	9					8	1												
28	(h)	Gainsborough TW	W 4-3	Jack, Bell 2, Aston	2,072		2	3	4		6	7	10			11				9			5		8	1												
Feb 11	(h)	Liverpool	L 0-2		8,788		2	3	4		6	7	10			11				9			5			1												
18	(a)	Burslem P.Vale	L 2-3	Jack 2	3,550		2	3	4		6	7	10			11				9			5		8	1												
25	(h)	Bristol C	D 0-0		4,172		2	3	4		6	7	10			11				9			5			1					8							
Mar 4	(a)	Manchester U	L 0-2		9,950		2	3	4		6		10			11				9			5			1				7	8							
7	(a)	Glossop	L 1-2	Jack	2,765		2		4		6		10			11	3			9			5			1				7	8							
11	(h)	Glossop	W 1-0	Lewis	3,547		2		4		6	7	8		10		3			9			5			1										11		
18	(a)	Chesterfield T	L 0-1		3,568		2		4		6	9	8		10		3						5			1										11	7	
25	(h)	Bradford C	L 0-2		2,366		2				6		9		10		3						5			1				8		11		4	7			
Apr 1	(a)	Lincoln C	W 2-0	Jack 2	4,138		2		4		6		8		10	11	3			9						1								5	7			
8	(h)	Leicester F	W 2-0	Pheasant 2	3,104		2		4		6		8		10	11	3			9														5	7			1
15	(a)	Barnsley	D 1-1	Haycock	5,661		2		4		6				10	11	3			9										8				5	7			1
21	(a)	Burton U	W 6-0	Williams, Jack 2, Lewis, Pheasant, Haycock	2,820		2		4		6				10	11	3			9										8				5	7	1		
22	(h)	Bolton W	L 0-1		10,105		2		4		6				10	11	3													8				5	7	1		9
				App		13	12	25	33	31	4	16	25	14	27	13	23	12	8	21	1	1	24	3	11	17	1	4	1	3	7	3	3	1	6	6	4	1
				Goals				1				6	13	2	6	7		1		8			6		2						2					1		

Tom Haywood

Llewellyn Davies, the only player to oust Jesse Pennington from Albion's League side.

Freddie Haycock

1905-06

Division 2

Date		Opponent	Res	Score	Scorers	Att	Stringer J	Young G	Pennington J	Randle A	Pheasant E	Manners J	Williams J	Simmons C	Shinton F	Haywood A	Perkins E	Haycock F	Adams A	Haywood T	Peters S	Varney H	Brittain J	Nicholls F	Law W	Bradley E	Lewis A	Rankin B	Dilly T	Picken T	Buck F
Sep 2	(h)	Burnley	L	1-2	Shinton	7,223	1	2	3	4	5	6	7	8	9	10	11														
9	(a)	Leeds C	W	2-0	Haycock 2	6,802	1	2	3	4	5	6		8	9	10	11	7													
16	(h)	Burton U	W	3-0	Simmons, Shinton, Haycock	6,500	1	2	3	4	5	6		8	9	10	11	7													
23	(a)	Chelsea	L	0-1		10,123	1	2	3	4	5	6		8	9	10	11	7													
30	(h)	Gainsborough T	W	4-0	Haycock, A.Haywood 2, Shinton	5,300	1		3		5	6		8	9	10	11	7	2	4											
Oct 7	(a)	Bristol C	L	0-1		8,000	1	2	3	6	5			8	9	10	11	7		4											
14	(h)	Manchester U	W	1-0	Haywood	7,024	1	2	3	6	5			8	9	10	11				4	7									
21	(a)	Glossop	W	3-1	Shinton, Haywood 2	5,000	1	2	3	6	5			8	9	10	11				4	7									
28	(h)	Stockport C	W	3-1	Haywood, Pheasant (pen), Shinton	8,200	1	2	3	6	5			8	9	10	11				4	7									
Nov 4	(a)	Blackpool	W	3-0	Peters, Shinton, Simmons	5,000	1	2	3	6	5			8	9	10	11				4	7									
11	(h)	Bradford C	W	6-1	Shinton 3, Haywood, Simmons 2	9,000	1	2	3	6	5			8	9	10	11				4	7									
25	(a)	Leicester F	D	0-0		6,500	1			4	5	6		8	9	10	11		2				3	7							
Dec 2	(h)	Hull C	D	1-1	Pheasant (pen)	11,203	1			4	5	6		8	9	10			2				3	7	11						
9	(a)	Lincoln C	W	2-1	Pheasant, Haywood	4,000	1	2		4	5	6		8	9	10							3	7	11						
16	(h)	Chesterfield T	W	3-0	Haywood, Simmons, Shinton	12,554	1		3	4	5	6		8	9	10			2					7	11						
23	(a)	Burslem P.Vale	W	1-0	Simmons	3,500	1	2	3	4	5	6		8	9	10								7	11						
25	(h)	Clapton O	D	1-1	Simmons	18,048	1	2	3	4	5	6		8	9	10								7	11						
26	(h)	Barnsley	W	5-3	Simmons 3, Shinton 2	23,021	1	2	3	4	5	6		8	9	10								7	11						
30	(a)	Burnley	W	2-0	Simmons, Shinton	6,500	1		3	4	5	6	2	8	9	10									11	7					
Jan 5	(h)	Leeds C	W	2-1	Haywood, Pheasant (pen)	2,553	1		3	4	5	6	2	8	9	10									11	7					
20	(a)	Burton U	D	2-2	Bradley, Shinton	4,000	1		3	4	5	6	2	8	9										11	7	10				
27	(h)	Chelsea	D	1-1	Manners	5,000	1		3	4	5	6	2	8	9	10									11	7					
Feb 3	(a)	Grimsby T	L	2-3	Haywood, Simmons	5,100	1		3	4	5	6	2	8	9	10	11									7					
10	(h)	Bristol C	L	1-3	Pheasant (pen)	6,400	1		3	4	5	6	2	8		10	11									9		7			
17	(a)	Manchester U	D	0-0		8,000	1		3	4	5	6	2	8		10	11									9		7			
24	(h)	Glossop	W	6-0	Rankin, Bradley, Simmons 2, Pheasant (pen), Haywood	7,200	1		3	4	5	6	2	8		10	11									9		7			
Mar 3	(a)	Stockport C	D	2-2	Manners, Perkins	4,000	1		3	4	5	6	2	8		10	11									9		7			
10	(h)	Blackpool	W	5-0	Simmons 2, Haywood 2, Bradley	6,500	1		3	4	5	6		8		10	11		2							9		7			
17	(a)	Bradford C	W	1-0	Haywood	5,106	1		3	4	5	6		8		10	11		2							9		7			
24	(h)	Grimsby T	W	2-0	Rankin, Pheasant	7,500	1		3	4	5	6		8		10	11		2							9		7			
31	(h)	Leicester F	W	3-0	Shinton, Haycock 2	10,067	1		3	4	5	6			9	10		8	2							11		7			
Apr 7	(a)	Hull C	L	0-4		9,033	1		3	4	5	6			9	10		8	2							11		7			
13	(a)	Barnsley	L	0-3		3,120	1	2		4	5	6			9	10		8	3							11		7			
14	(h)	Lincoln C	D	1-1	Haywood	6,000	1	2		4	5	6			9	10			3							11		7	8		
16	(a)	Clapton O	W	2-0	Shinton, Haywood	3,517	1			4	5	6			9	10			2				3			11		7	8		
18	(a)	Gainsborough T	L	1-2	Haywood	4,223	1			4	5	6			9	10			2				3			11		7	8		
21	(a)	Chesterfield T	W	3-0	Manners, Haywood, Shinton	5,558			3	4	5	6			9	10			2							11		7	8	1	
28	(h)	Burslem P.Vale	W	4-1	Pheasant (pen), Shinton, Haywood 2	4,800			3	4	5	6			9	10			2							11		7		1	8
App							36	16	31	36	38	32	10	30	31	37	20	8	16	2	6	5	4	7	10	15	2	15	8	2	1
Goals											8	3		16	18	21	1	6			1					3		2			

West Bromwich Albion 1905-06. Back row (left to right): W.Bassett (director), W.Barber (trainer), Pennington, Young, Stringer, Adams, Randle, F.Everiss (secretary). Middle: Haycock, Simmons, Pheasant, Shinton, Haywood, Perkins. Front: Bradley, Law.

Jim Stringer

1906-07

Division 2

Date		Opponent	Res	Score	Scorers	Att	Stringer J	Betteley R	Pennington J	Randle A	Pheasant E	Manners J	Rankin B	Buck F	Shinton F	Haywood A	Dilly T	Perkins E	Broad T	Simmons C	Timmins S	Haywood T	Legge S	Williams J	Jones H	Bradley E	Jordan W	Bourne R	Parkes H	Adams A
Sep	1	(a) Burnley	W	1-0	Buck	7,500	1	2	3	4	5	6	7	8	9	10	11													
	8	(h) Leeds C	W	5-0	Shinton 2, Buck 2, Pheasant	15,500	1	2	3	4	5	6	7	8	9	10	11													
	10	(a) Burslem P.Vale	L	1-2	Shinton	5,500	1	2	3	4	5	6	7	8	9	10		11												
	15	(a) Barnsley	W	1-0	Shinton	6,000	1	2	3	4	5	6	7	8	9	10		11												
	22	(h) Chelsea	L	1-2	Haywood	25,562	1	2	3	4	5	6	7	8	9	10		11												
	29	(a) Wolves	W	3-0	Shinton, Haywood, Buck	25,000	1	2	3	4	5	6		8	9	10		11	7											
Oct	6	(h) Clapton O	W	5-0	Shinton 4, Buck	10,482	1	2	3	4	5	6		8	9			11	7	10										
	13	(a) Gainsborough TW	W	4-2	Shinton 3, Buck	3,500	1	2	3	4	5	6		8	9		10	11	7											
	20	(h) Stockport C	D	1-1	Buck (pen)	12,300	1	2	3	4	5	6		8	9	10		11	7											
	27	(a) Hull C	W	1-0	Buck	6,140	1	2	3	4	5	6		8	9	10		11	7											
Nov	3	(h) Glossop	W	5-1	Shinton 4, Buck	13,000	1	2	3	4	5	6		8	9	10		11	7											
	10	(a) Blackpool	L	1-2	Pheasant	5,772	1	2	3	4	5			8	9	10		11	7		6									
	17	(h) Bradford C	W	3-0	Buck 3	9,000	1	2	3	4				8	9		10	11	7		6			5						
	24	(h) Chesterfield T	W	5-2	Rankin, Dilly 3, Shinton	11,335	1	2	3	4			7	8	9		10	11			6			5						
Dec	1	(a) Leicester F	L	0-3		19,820	1	2	3	4			7	8	9		10	11			6			5						
	8	(h) Nottingham F	W	3-1	Rankin, Shinton, Legge	17,000	1	2	3	4	5		7	8	9	10					6		11							
	15	(a) Lincoln C	L	1-2	Haywood	5,240	1	2	3	4			7		9	10				8	6		11	5						
	22	(h) Burton U	W	5-1	Legge, Simmons 2, Shinton 2	5,300	1	2	3	4	5		7		9	10				8	6		11							
	25	(h) Grimsby T	W	6-1	Dilly, Haywood, Shinton 4	19,047	1	2	3	4	5		7		9	8	10				6		11							
	26	(h) Burslem P.Vale	W	3-0	Rankin, Dilly, Shinton	17,000		2	3	4	5		7		9	8	10				6		11		1					
	29	(h) Burnley	W	3-2	Dilly (pen), Shinton, Legge	12,000		2	3	4	5		7		9	8	10				6		11		1					
Jan	5	(a) Leeds C	L	2-3	Shinton 2	10,330	1	2	3	4	5			7	9	8	10				6		11							
	26	(a) Chelsea	L	0-2		41,168	1	2	3	4	5	6	11	8			10	7						9						
Feb	9	(a) Clapton O	D	1-1	Dilly	3,700	1	2	3	4	5	6			9		10	11	7	8										
	16	(h) Gainsborough TW	W	5-0	Buck 2, Jordan 3	8,112	1	2	3	4	5	6		8		10						7					9	11		
Mar	2	(h) Hull C	W	3-0	Jordan 2, Buck	10,130	1		3	4	5	6		8		10	11		7			2					9			
	16	(h) Blackpool	W	3-0	Buck 2, Jordan	5,500	1		3	4				8		10	11				6	2		5			9		7	
	29	(a) Grimsby T	L	1-2	Jordan	8,202	1		3	4	5	6		8	9							2					10	11	7	
	30	(a) Chesterfield T	D	2-2	Bradley, Buck	8,000	1		3	4				8	9	10					6			5		11			7	2
Apr	1	(h) Wolves	D	1-1	Buck	22,000	1		3	4				8		10										9	11		7	2
	6	(h) Leicester F	L	0-1		5,034	1			4	5	6		8		10		11			3					9			7	2
	8	(a) Stockport C	W	1-0	Parkes	5,623	1			4		6		8		10					3			5		9	11		7	2
	13	(a) Nottingham F	L	1-3	Bradley	7,174	1		3	4		6		8	9			11			2			5		10			7	
	16	(a) Glossop	D	0-0		3,121	1		3	4		6		8	9			11			2	10		5					7	
	20	(h) Lincoln C	W	2-1	Parkes, Bourne	6,995	1			4		6		8						10	3	5				9	11		7	2
	23	(a) Bradford C	L	0-4		6,220	1		3	4		6		8	9	10				2	5						11		7	
	25	(h) Barnsley	W	3-1	Parkes, Jordan, Buck	5,100	1		3	4		6		8	10		11				5					9			7	2
	27	(a) Burton U	L	0-2		3,580	1			4		6		8	9		11			10	3					5			7	2
						App	36	26	33	38	25	25	14	32	30	24	21	13	11	6	20	7	7	5	2	7	10	7	12	7
						Goals					2		3	20	28	4	7			2			3			2	8	1	3	

West Bromwich Albion 1906-07, defeated 2-1 in the FA Cup semi-final by Everton at Burnden Park, Bolton. Back row (left to right): H.A.Parkes, A.Randle, F.Buck, J.Manners. Middle: H.Bell (asst.trainer), J.Williams, W.Barber (trainer), J.Stringer, W.Bassett (director), J.Pennington, F.Everiss (secretary). Front: W.C.Jordan, E.Pheasant, H.Keys (director), A.Haywood, T.Dilly.

1907-08

Division 2

Date		Opponent	Result	Scorers	Att	Stringer J	Betteley R	Pennington J	Timmins S	Pheasant E	Manners J	Garratt G	Buck F	Jordan W	Walker D	Brocks J	Williams J	Evenson I	Shirton F	Dilly T	Bowser W	Randle A	Haywood A	Adams A	Bradley E	Parkes H	Bourne R	Evans A	Young W	Wright H	Wilcox H	Owen's E	Fearson H	Thompson W	Hewitt C
Sep 2	(a)	Wolves	W 2-1	Buck (pen), Walker	24,000	1	2	3	4	5	6	7	8	9	10	11																			
7	(h)	Burnley	W 5-0	Buck 2, Pheasant, Garratt, Jordan	16,032	1		3	4	5	6	7	8	9	10	11	2																		
14	(a)	Oldham A	L 1-2	Garratt	11,000	1		3	4	5		7	8	9	10	11	2	6																	
21	(h)	Clapton O	W 3-0	Jordan, Walker, Buck	12,336	1		3	4	5	6	7	8	9	10	11	2																		
28	(a)	Leeds C	L 0-1		19,058	1		3	4	5	6	7	8	9	10	11	2																		
Oct 5	(h)	Wolves	W 1-0	Brooks	30,026	1	2	3	4	5	6	7	8		10	11			9																
12	(a)	Gainsborough TW	2-1	Dilly 2	4,900	1	2	3	4	5	6	7	8		10	11				9															
19	(h)	Stockport C	W 2-0	Walker 2	14,000	1	2	3	4	5	6	7	8	9	10	11																			
26	(a)	Glossop	L 1-2	Buck (pen)	1,828	1		3	2	5	6	7	8		9	11					4	10													
Nov 2	(h)	Leicester F	D 1-1	Bradley	17,000	1		3	4	5	6	7	8		10	11						2			9										
4	(a)	Oldham A	L 1-2	Walker	10,500	1		3	4	5	6		8		10							2	9	7	11										
9	(a)	Blackpool	W 1-0	Buck (pen)	9,145	1		2	6	5			8		10	11		9								7		3	4						
16	(h)	Stoke C	W 1-0	Young	10,000	1		2	6	5		7	8		10	11												3	4	9					
23	(a)	Grimsby T	D 2-2	Walker, Buck	4,552	1		2	6	9		7	8		10	11			5									3	4						
30	(a)	Bradford C	D 0-0		18,025	1		2	9	5		7	8		10	11			6									3	4						
Dec 7	(h)	Hull C	W 1-0	Buck	15,500	1		2	4	5		7	8		10	11			6									3	9						
14	(a)	Derby C	L 0-2		8,000	1	2	3	6	5		7	8		10	11												4		9					
21	(h)	Lincoln C	W 5-2	Buck (pen), Walker 2 (1 pen), Jordan, Wilcox	7,000	1	2	3	6			7	10	9		11		5										4			8				
25	(h)	Chesterfield T	W 4-0	Walker 2, Buck, Wilcox	12,478	1	2	3	6	5		7	8		10	11						4									9				
26	(a)	Barnsley	W 3-1	Buck 3 (1 pen)	5,520	1		2	6	5		7	8		10	11						4						3			9				
28	(a)	Fulham	D 1-1	Wilcox	20,063	1	2	3	6	5		7	8		10	11												4			9				
Jan 4	(a)	Burnley	D 1-1	Walker	10,146	1	2			5	6	7	8		10	11												3	4		9				
18	(a)	Clapton O	D 2-2	Buck, Evenson	15,252		2			5	6			11	9	10		8								7		3	4				1		
25	(h)	Leeds C	W 1-0	Young	8,000		2	3			6		8		10			5								7	11	4	9				1		
Feb 8	(h)	Gainsborough T	L 0-1		7,500	1	2			5	6			11	10											7		3	4	8	9				
15	(a)	Stockport C	W 2-1	Walker, Garratt	4,000		2			5	6	7	8		10											11		3	4		9		1		
22	(h)	Glossop	D 1-1	Parkes	4,140			3		5	6	7	8		10			2								11		4	9				1		
29	(a)	Leicester F	L 0-3		6,337	1		3		5	6	7	8		10	11		2										4	9						
Mar 7	(h)	Blackpool	W 3-0	Walker 2, Timmins	7,000		2		8	5	6			11	10											7		3	4		9		1		
17	(a)	Stoke C	D 1-1	Jordan	3,224		2		8	5	6			11	9											7		3	4		10		1		
21	(h)	Grimsby T	L 1-2	Pheasant	5,400		2		8	5	6			11	9	10										7		3	4				1		
28	(h)	Bradford C	W 3-2	Wilcox, Buck, Walker	7,000	1	2			5	6	7		11	9	10		4										3			8				
Apr 4	(a)	Hull C	L 2-4	Pheasant, Timmins	6,080		2	9		5	6	7		11	10													3	4		8		1		
11	(h)	Derby C	W 1-0	Wilcox	10,000		2		4	5	6	7		11	9	10												3			8		1		
17	(a)	Chesterfield T	L 0-1		5,539		2		4	5	6	7		11	10													3			8	9	1		
18	(h)	Lincoln C	W 2-0	Buck 2	6,850	1	2		4	5	6	7		11	9	10												3			8				
20	(h)	Barnsley	D 1-1	Buck (pen)	10,000	1	2		4		6	7		11	9	10								5				3			8				
25	(h)	Fulham	W 3-1	Jordan, Wright, Thompson	6,990	1		3	4	5	6			11	9			2										7						8	10
App						28	12	35	30	35	27	29	38	14	36	21	10	8	2	1	1	3	1	2	3	7	2	19	18	3	17	4	10	1	1
Goals									2	3		3	18	5	15	1		1		2					1	1			2	1	5			1	

West Bromwich Albion 1907-08. Back row (left to right): T.Dilly, S.Timmins, J.Stringer, H.Keys (director), I.Evenson, J.Pennington, F.Everiss (secretary). Front: G.Garratt, J.Williams, F.Buck, E.Pheasant, W.C.Jordan, D.Walker, J.Brooks.

1908-09

Division 2

Date		Opponent	Res	Score	Scorers	Att.	Pearson H	Pennington J	Evans A	Baddeley G	Pheasant E	Timmins S	Davies W	Thompson W	Jordan W	Legge S	Buck F	Manners J	Hewitt C	Stringer J	Brown F	Fielding R	Wright H	Betteley R	Dorsett J	Garraty W	Bowser S	Harris G	Pailor R	Hancock H	Burton H	Simpson G
Sep 5	(a)	Grimsby T	D	1-1	Buck (pen)	6,000	1	2	3	4	5	6	7	8	9	10	11															
7	(h)	Wolves	L	0-2		28,600	1	2	3		5	4	7	8	9	10	11	6														
12	(h)	Fulham	D	1-1	Skene (og)	14,529		2	3		5	4	7	8			11	6	10	1	9											
15	(a)	Bolton W	D	1-1	Buck (pen)	5,500		2	3	4	5	6					11		10	8	1	9	7									
19	(a)	Burnley	W	2-0	Buck, Hewitt	11,340		2	3	4	5	6					11		10	8	1	9	7									
26	(h)	Bradford	W	1-0	Hewitt	21,496		2	3	4	5	6					11		10	8	1	9	7									
Oct 3	(a)	Wolves	W	1-0	Davies	20,000		2	3	4	5		11					6	10	8	1	9	7									
10	(h)	Oldham A	W	1-0	Hewitt	18,190		2	3	4	5		11	7				6	10	8	1	9										
17	(a)	Clapton O	L	0-1		10,500		2	3		5	4	11	7				6	10	8	1	9										
24	(h)	Leeds C	W	2-1	Thompson, Buck	13,554			3	4	5			9				6	10	8	1			7	2	11						
31	(a)	Barnsley	W	2-0	Hewitt, Dorsett	7,000		2	3	4	5			7				6	10	8	1				11	9						
Nov 2	(h)	Chesterfield T	D	2-2	Garraty, Buck (pen)	9,540		2	3	4	5			7				6	10	8	1				11	9						
7	(h)	Tottenham H	W	3-0	Hewitt 2, Garraty	27,224		2	3	4	5			7				6	10	8	1				11	9						
14	(a)	Hull C	D	2-2	Garraty 2	10,000		2	3	4	5			7				6	10	8	1				11	9						
21	(h)	Derby C	W	2-0	Buck, Thompson	13,241		2	3	4	5			7			11	6	10	8	1					9						
28	(a)	Blackpool	W	2-0	Buck (pen), Timmins	5,500		2	3	4	5			7			11	6	10	8	1					9						
Dec 12	(a)	Glossop	W	3-1	Buck 2, Hewitt	3,074		2	3	4	5			7			11	6	10	8	1					9						
19	(h)	Stockport C	W	2-0	Hewitt, Garraty	6,240		2	3	4	5			7			11	6	10	8	1					9						
25	(h)	Gainsborough TW	2-0	Thompson, Buck		18,250		2	3	4	5			7			11	6	10	8	1					9						
26	(h)	Birmingham	D	1-1	Buck (pen)	38,049			3	4	5			7			11	6	10	8	1				2	9						
28	(a)	Birmingham	D	0-0		30,035			3	4	5			7	10		11	6		8	1				2	9						
Jan 2	(h)	Grimsby T	W	7-0	Bowser 2, Garraty 2, Buck, Manners, Thompson	5,177			3	4	5			7			11	6		8	1				2	9	10					
9	(a)	Fulham	L	0-2		25,000				4	5			7			11	6		8	1				2	9	10	3				
23	(h)	Burnley	D	0-0		18,220		2		4	5			7			11	6		8	1					9	10	3				
30	(a)	Bradford	D	0-0		17,600		2		4	5			7			11	6		8	1						10	3	9			
Feb 13	(a)	Oldham A	L	0-2		22,000			3	4	5			7			11		10		1				2	8	6	9				
20	(h)	Clapton O	W	1-0	Davies	14,565				4	5		11					6		8	1		7		2	9		3	10			
27	(a)	Leeds C	D	1-1	Garraty	12,140				4	5		11					6		8	1		7		2	9			10			
Mar 13	(a)	Tottenham H	W	3-1	Garraty, Hewitt 2 (1 pen)	35,532			3	4	5		11					10	8		1	7			2	9	6					
20	(h)	Hull C	W	1-0	Buck	17,602			3	4	5		11	7				10	8		1				2	9	6					
24	(h)	Barnsley	D	1-1	Hewitt	4,982			3	4	5		11	7				10	8		1				2	9	6					
Apr 3	(h)	Blackpool	W	5-1	Hewitt 2 (1 pen), Miller (og), Fielding, Garraty	17,426				4	5		11					10	8		1	7			2	9	6			3		
9	(a)	Gainsborough T	L	0-2		7,149			3	4	5	7					10	8		1					9	6				2	11
10	(a)	Chesterfield T	D	2-2	Davies, Garraty	5,033			3	4		11					10	6	8		1	7			2	9	5				
12	(h)	Bolton W	W	2-0	Jordan, Hewitt	34,012			3	4		11					10	6	8		1	7			2	5				2	
17	(h)	Glossop	W	1-0	Hewitt	18,344			3	4		11	7	9				10	8		1					5	6				2	
24	(a)	Stockport C	D	0-0		7,424			3	4		11		9			10	6	8		1	7					5				2	
26	(a)	Derby C	L	1-2	Garraty	6,508			3	4	5	11	7	9			10	6		1						8					2	
App							2	35	18	35	9	32	33	27	7	2	38	27	27	36	7	9	2	14	5	26	4	13	2	2	5	1
Goals									1		1	3	4		1		13	1	15			1				11	2					

West Bromwich Albion 1908. Back row (left to right): S.Timmins, H.Pearson, J.Pennington, W.Thompson. Third row: W.Barber (trainer), E.Owers, S.Legge, G.Baddeley, J.Stringer, T.Robson, R.Betteley, R.Crone (asst.trainer). Second row: W.Bassett, W.C.Davies, E.Pheasant, A.Evans, J.Manners, F.Everiss (secretary). Front: W.Young, G.Young, F.Buck, C.Hewitt.

Tom Picken, Albion's reserve goalkeeper between 1905 and 1910.

1909-10

Division 2

Date		Opponent	Result	Scorers	Att	Pearson H	Burton H	Pennington J	Baddeley G	Garraty W	Harris G	Dorsett J	Hewitt C	Rouse F	Buck F	Simpson G	Thompson W	Stringer J	Betteley R	Timmins S	Manners J	Davies W	Pheasant E	Dicken H	Young W	Bowser S	Waterhouse F	Pailor R	Corbett R	Crump A	Price G	Brown F
Sep 1	(a)	Stockport C	W 2-0	Rouse, Hewitt	6,000	1	2	3	4	5	6	7	8	9	10	11																
4	(h)	Bradford	W 1-0	Rouse	18,990	1	2	3	4	5	6		8	9	10	11	7															
6	(h)	Stockport C	L 0-1		14,883	1	2	3	4	5	6		8	9	10	11	7															
11	(a)	Oldham A	W 2-1	Manners, Garraty	12,000		3		4	9			8		10		7	1	2	5	6	11										
18	(h)	Barnsley	W 4-3	Garraty, Hewitt 2, Buck	10,520		3		4	9			8		10		7	1	2	5	6	11										
25	(a)	Fulham	W 2-0	Thompson, Buck	18,100		3		4	9			8		10		7	1	2		6	11	5									
29	(a)	Lincoln C	W 3-0	Pheasant, Buck, Garraty	6,500		3		4	9			8		10		7	1	2		6	11	5									
Oct 2	(h)	Burnley	L 1-2	Garraty	15,175		3		4	9			8		10		7	1	2		6	11	5									
9	(a)	Leeds C	W 1-0	Buck (pen)	17,500		3		4	9			8		10		7	1	2		6	11		5								
16	(a)	Wolves	L 1-3	Buck	24,000		3		4	9	5		8		10		7	1	2		6	11										
23	(a)	Gainsborough T	L 1-3	Buck (pen)	3,500		3		5	9		11	8		10		7	1	2		6				4							
30	(h)	Grimsby T	W 4-3	Hewitt 2, Buck 2 (1 pen)	7,225		3		4	8		11	9		10		7	1	2	5	6											
Nov 6	(a)	Manchester C	L 2-3	Hewitt, Dorsett	29,800		3		4			11	9	8			7	1	2		6		5			10						
13	(h)	Leicester F	L 1-2	Hewitt	9,040		3		4			11	9	8			7	1	2				5			10	6					
27	(h)	Clapton O	W 3-0	Davies, Buck, Hewitt	12,167		3		4	8			9		10		7	1	2		6	11	5									
Dec 4	(a)	Blackpool	L 1-2	Hewitt	7,700		3		4	8			9		10		7	1	2		6	11	5									
11	(h)	Hull C	L 0-2		8,208	2	3		4	8			9		10		7	1			6	11	5									
18	(a)	Derby C	L 1-2	Bowser	10,400	2	3		4	8					10	11	7	1		5	6					9						
25	(h)	Wolves	L 0-1		24,899	2	3		4	8					10	11	7	1		5	6					9						
27	(h)	Birmingham	W 3-1	Simpson, Bowser, Manners	12,104	2	3					10	8			11		1	4		6	7	5			9						
Jan 1	(a)	Birmingham	W 1-0	Simpson	15,500	2	3		4	8					10	11		1		5	6	7				9						
8	(a)	Bradford	L 0-1		7,980	2	3		4						10	11		1		5	6	7				8	9					
22	(h)	Oldham A	D 1-1	Pailor	7,901		3		4						10	11		1	2	5	6	7				8	9					
Feb 12	(a)	Burnley	W 3-2	Garraty 3	6,000	1	2	3	4	9		7			10						6	11				8	5					
Mar 5	(h)	Gainsborough T	W 5-0	Bowser, Simpson 2, Buck, Garraty	10,155	1	2	3	4	9		7			10	11					6					8	5					
7	(h)	Leeds C	W 3-1	Buck 2, Bowser	6,664	1	2	3	4	9		7			10	11					6					8	5					
12	(a)	Grimsby T	L 0-3		5,800	1	2	3	4	9		7			10	11					6					8	5					
19	(h)	Manchester C	D 0-0		13,042	1	2	3	4			7			10	11					6					8	5	9				
26	(a)	Leicester F	L 1-2	Bowser	7,000	1		3	4				8		10	11			2		6	7				9	5					
28	(h)	Glossop	D 0-0		12,360	1		3	4			11	8		10						6	7				9	5	2				
29	(h)	Fulham	W 3-2	Waterhouse, Buck, Hewitt	11,714	1		3	4	9		11	7		10						6					8	5	2				
Apr 2	(h)	Lincoln C	D 1-1	Garraty	12,150	1			4	9		11	7		10						6					8	5	3	2			
9	(a)	Clapton O	W 3-1	Dorsett, Buck, Hewitt	15,000	1		3	4	8	6	7	9			11			2	5						10						
14	(a)	Barnsley	L 1-2	Buck (pen)	16,105	1		3	4	8	6	7			10	11			2	5										9		
16	(h)	Blackpool	L 0-3		6,103	1		3	4	9				8		11			2		6	7				10	5					
23	(a)	Hull C	L 1-5	Simpson	18,744	1		3	4				9	7		11			2		6					10	5					8
26	(a)	Glossop	L 2-3	Bowser, Buck (pen)	5,225	1		3	4			11	8		10				2		6	7				9	5					
30	(h)	Derby C	D 0-0		9,098	1		3	4	8					10	11			2		6	7				9	5					
App						18	27	24	33	27	6	13	32	5	37	18	18	20	21	22	21	20	9	1	1	22	14	3	3	1	1	1
Goals										9		2	11	2	16	5	1				2	1	1			16	1	1				

West Bromwich Albion 1909-10. Back row (left to right). H. Burton, H. Pearson, W. Bassett (director), F. Everiss (secretary), J. Pennington, S. Timmins. Front: G. Baddeley, J. Dorsett, C. Hewitt, W. Garraty, F. Buck, G. Simpson, F. W. Rouse, G. Harris.

89

1910-11

Division 2

Date		Opponent	Res	Score	Scorers	Att	Pearson H	Betteley R	Timmins S	Baddeley G	Waterhouse F	Manners J	Wollaston W	Bowser S	Pailor R	Buck F	Lloyd A	Richards A	Smith J	Pennington J	Nevin J	McNeal R	Hibbert J	Wright H	Deacey C	Walker W	Moorwood L	Thompson W
Sep	3	(a) Hull C	D	1-1	Buck	10,400	1	2	3	4	5	6	7	8	9	10	11											
	5	(a) Bolton W	L	1-3	Buck	8,500	1		6	4	5		7	8	9	10	11	2	3									
	10	(h) Fulham	W	2-1	Bowser 2	10,144	1	2	6	4	5		7	8	9	10	11			3								
	17	(a) Bradford	D	3-3	Bowser, Pailor 2	9,500	1	2		4	5	6	7	8	9	10	11			3								
	24	(h) Burnley	W	2-1	Waterhouse, Wollaston	15,280	1	2		4	5	6	7	8	9	10	11			3								
Oct	1	(a) Gainsborough T	D	1-1	Bowser	3,600	1	2		4	5		7	8	9	10	11			3	6							
	8	(h) Leeds C	W	2-0	Bowser, Pailor	13,149	1	2	6	4	5		7	8	9		11			3		10						
	15	(a) Stockport C	W	1-0	Bowser	6,000	1	2	6	4	5		7	8	9		11			3		10						
	22	(h) Derby C	D	1-1	Pailor	18,488	1	2	6	4	5		7	8	9		11			3		10						
	29	(a) Barnsley	D	1-1	Lloyd	10,000	1			4	5		7	8	9		11	2		3	6	10						
Nov	5	(h) Leicester F	W	5-1	Bowser, Lloyd 2, Wollaston, Buck (pen)	15,200	1			4	5		7	8	9	10	11		2	3		6						
	12	(a) Wolves	W	3-2	Pailor 2 (1 pen), Bowser	18,500	1			4	5			8	9	10	11		2	3		6	7					
	19	(h) Chelsea	L	1-3	Bowser	21,305	1			4	5			8	9	10	11		2	3		6	7					
	26	(a) Clapton O	D	0-0		7,000	1			4	5			8		10	11		2	3		6	7	9				
Dec	3	(h) Blackpool	L	0-1		8,840	1			4	5			8		10	11		2	3		6	7	9				
	10	(a) Glossop	W	2-0	Baddeley, Pailor	4,000	1			4	5		7	8	9	10	11		2	3		6						
	17	(h) Lincoln C	W	3-0	Buck 2 (1 pen), Walker	3,577	1			4	5		7	8		10	11		2	3		6				9		
	24	(a) Huddersfield T	W	2-0	Waterhouse, Bowser	20,700	1			4	5		7	8	9	10	11		2	3		6						
	26	(h) Bolton W	W	2-0	Bowser, Lloyd	20,301	1			4	5		7	8	9	10	11		2	3		6						
	27	(a) Birmingham	D	1-1	Pailor	37,520	1			4	5		7	8	9	10	11		2	3		6						
	31	(h) Hull C	L	0-2		11,790	1			4	5		7	8	9	10	11		2	3		6						
Jan	7	(a) Fulham	W	1-0	Lloyd	16,000	1			4	5		7	8	9	10	11		2	3		6						
	21	(h) Bradford	W	3-0	Buck, Pailor, Lloyd	6,952	1			4	5		7	8	9	10	11		2	3		6						
	28	(a) Burnley	L	0-2		8,300	1			4	5			8	9	10	11		2	3		6	7					
Feb	11	(a) Leeds C	L	1-3	Wright	10,700		2		4	5			10	9		11			3		6		8	1	7		
	18	(h) Stockport C	W	4-2	Buck 2 (1 pen), Bowser 2	6,107				4	5			8	9	10	11		2	3		6			1	7		
Mar	1	(a) Derby C	W	3-1	Bowser, Pailor, Wright	21,640				4	5			8	9		11		2	3		6		10	1	7		
	4	(h) Barnsley	D	3-3	Bowser, Wright, Pailor	7,770		2	7	4	5	6		8	9		11			3				10	1			
	11	(a) Leicester F	W	3-2	Bowser 2, Wright	10,547	1			4	5	6		8	9	10	11		2	3				7				
	18	(h) Wolves	W	2-1	Buck (pen), Pailor	20,303	1			4	5			8	9	10	11		2	3		6		7				
	29	(a) Chelsea	L	1-2	Wright	12,640	1			4	5			8		10	11		2	3		6		9		7		
Apr	1	(h) Clapton O	W	3-0	Waterhouse, McNeal, Wright	12,852	1	2		4	5	6		8		10	11			3		9		7				
	8	(a) Blackpool	D	0-0		6,100	1			4	5	6		8		10	11		2	3		9		7				
	15	(h) Glossop	W	3-1	Lloyd, Wright, Bowser	13,404	1				5	6		9		10	11		2	3		4		8			7	
	17	(h) Birmingham	W	1-0	Bowser	27,042	1				5	6		8	9	10	11		2	3		4		7				
	18	(h) Gainsborough T	W	2-1	Bowser 2	23,788	1				5	6		9		10	11		2	3		4		7				8
	22	(a) Lincoln C	W	2-1	Lloyd, Bowser	8,000	1				5	6		9		10	11		2	3		4		7				8
	29	(h) Huddersfield T	W	1-0	Buck (pen)	30,135	1				5	6		9			11		2	3		4		7				8
					App		34	11	7	33	38	12	19	38	28	34	35	1	30	33	2	29	1	18	2	1	4	8
					Goals					1	3		2	22	12	10	8					1		7		1		

Albion's goalscoring outside-left Howard Gregory (1911-26).

England international left-half Bobby McNeal who spent 16 years at The Hawthorns.

Centre-forward Bob Pailor left Albion for Newcastle shortly before World War One.

1911-12

Division 1

Date		Opponent	Result	Scorers	Att	Pearson H	Smith J	Pennington J	Badceley G	Waterhouse F	McNeal R	Wright H	Bowser S	Allar S	Euck F	Shearman B	Manners J	Failor R	Wollaston W	Jephcott C	Cook A	Moorwood L	Ceacey C	Lloyd A	Hibbert J	Morris F	Wood M	Gregory H	Betteley R
Sep 2	(h)	Notts C	W 2-1	Buck, Shearman	26,638	1	2	3	4	5	6	7	8	9	10	11													
4	(a)	Aston Villa	W 3-0	Allan, Shearman, Bowser	31,884	1	2	3	4		6	7	8	9	10	11	5												
9	(a)	Tottenham H	L 0-1		31,100	1	2	3	4		6	7	8	9	10	11	5												
16	(h)	Manchester U	W 1-0	Allan	34,921	1	2	3	4		6	7	8	9	10	11	5												
23	(a)	Liverpool	W 3-1	Shearman, Bowser, Allan	18,000	1	2	3	4		6	7	8	9	10	11	5												
30	(h)	Aston Villa	D 2-2	Shearman 2	46,203	1	2	3	4		6	7	8	9	10	11	5												
Oct 7	(a)	Newcastle U	D 0-0		28,000	1	2	3	4		6	7	8	9	10	11	5												
14	(h)	Sheffield U	L 0-1		18,595	1	2	3	4	5	6	7	8	9	10	11													
21	(a)	Oldham A	L 1-3	Pailor	13,000	1	2	3	4	5	6	7	8		10	11		9											
28	(h)	Bolton W	D 0-0		14,377	1	2	3	4	5	6	7	8	9	10	11													
Nov 4	(a)	Bradford C	L 1-4	Allan	19,800	1	2	3	4		6	7	10	8		11	5	9											
11	(h)	W Arsenal	D 1-1	Shearman	13,900	1	2	3	4		6		8		10	11	5	9	7										
18	(a)	Manchester C	W 2-0	Bowser 2	12,000	1	2	3	4		6		8		10	11	5	9	7										
25	(h)	Everton	W 1-0	Pailor	12,240	1	2	3	4		6		8		10	11	5	9	7										
Dec 2	(a)	Preston NE	D 1-1	Bowser	19,000	1	2	3	4		6		8		10	11	5	9	7										
9	(a)	Sunderland	L 2-3	Pailor 2	10,000	1	2	3	4		6		8		10	11	5	9	7										
16	(h)	Blackburn R	W 2-0	Bowser, Pailor	13,176	1	2	3			6		8	4	10	11	5	9	7										
23	(a)	Sheffield W	L 1-4	Bowser	13,000	1	2	3			6		8	4	10	11	5	9		7									
26	(h)	Bury	W 2-0	Wright, Pearson (pen)	10,133	1	2	3		5	6		8	4	10	11		9		7									
30	(a)	Notts C	L 0-2		10,000	1		3		5	6		8	9	10	11	4		7	2									
Jan 1	(a)	Bury	L 0-1		12,000			3		5	6	7	8	4	10	11		9		2	1								
20	(a)	Manchester U	W 2-1	Wright 2	11,000	1		3	4		6		8		10	11	5	9		7	2								
27	(h)	Liverpool	W 1-0	Wright	16,057	1	2		4		6		8		10	11	5	9		7				3					
Feb 10	(h)	Newcastle U	W 3-1	Pailor 3	30,252	1	2		4		6		8		10	11	5	9		7				3					
17	(a)	Sheffield U	D 1-1	Pailor	15,000	1	2		4		6		8		10	11	5	9		7				3					
Mar 2	(a)	Bolton W	L 0-2		12,000	1		3	4		6		8		10		5			7	2				9	11			
13	(h)	Tottenham H	W 2-0	Jephcott 2	17,406	1	2		4		6		8		10	11	5	9		7				3					
16	(a)	W Arsenal	W 2-0	Bowser, Pailor	15,000	1		3	4		6		8		10	11	5	9		7	2								
23	(h)	Manchester C	D 1-1	Shearman	12,331	1	2		4		6		8		10	11	5	9		7				3					
Apr 5	(a)	Middlesbrough	L 0-1		12,000	1	2	3	4		6		8		10	11	5			7			9						
8	(h)	Middlesbrough	W 3-1	Pearson (pen), Jephcott 2	25,027	1		3	4		6		8		10	11	5			7	2		9						
9	(h)	Preston NE	L 0-2		8,240	1	2	3			6		8		10	11	5			7			9		4				
13	(h)	Sunderland	W 1-0	Morris	20,117	1	2		4		6		8			11	5			7			9	3		10			
22	(a)	Everton	L 0-3		7,000		2			5			8								6	7	1	3		9	11	4	10
25	(a)	Blackburn R	L 1-4	Morris	12,000	1	2	3	4		6		8			11	5	9		7						10			
26	(h)	Bradford C	D 0-0		10,663	1	2	3	4		6		8			11	5	9		7						10			
27	(h)	Sheffield W	L 1-5	Morris	9,405	1	2		4		6		8			11	5			7						9	3	10	
29	(h)	Oldham A	D 0-0		3,122	1		3	4		6		8			5			7						11	9		10	2
App						36	32	29	28	11	37	34	27	19	30	34	18	20	6	20	12	2	6	3	2	6	2	3	1
Goals						2						4	8	4	1	7		10		4						3			

Albion goalkeeper Hubert Pearson in action against Aston Villa at The Hawthorns in September 1911.

1912-13

Division 1

Date		Opponent	Res	Scorers	Att	Pearson H	Cook A	Pennington J	Baddeley G	Buck F	McNeal R	Jephcott C	Wright H	Pailor R	Bowser S	Shearman B	Waterhouse F	Smith J	Moorwood L	Gregory H	Morris F	Varty J	Wood M	Deacey C	Jackson W	Lloyd A
Sep 4	(h)	Middlesbrough	W 2-0	Buck (pen), Pailor	15,085	1	2	3	4	5	6	7	8	9	10	11										
7	(a)	Notts C	D 1-1	Wright	13,000	1	2	3	4		6	7	8	9	10	11		5								
14	(h)	Manchester U	L 1-2	Bowser	26,140	1	2	3		5	6	7	8	9	10	11		4								
21	(a)	Aston Villa	W 4-2	Wright, Pailor 3	55,064	1		3		5	6	7	10	9	8	11	4	2								
28	(h)	Liverpool	W 3-1	Pailor, Shearman, McNeal	21,908	1		3		5	6	7	10	9	8	11	4	2								
Oct 5	(a)	Bolton W	L 1-2	Morris	24,000			3		5	6	7	10			11	4	2	1	8	9					
12	(h)	Sheffield U	W 3-1	Morris 2, Wright	18,040	1		3		5	6	7	10	9		11	4	2			8					
19	(a)	Newcastle U	D 1-1	Bowser	30,000	1		3		5	6	7	10		8	11	4	2			9					
26	(h)	Oldham A	L 2-3	Wright, Shearman	15,101	1		3		5	6	7	10	9	8	11	4	2								
Nov 2	(h)	Chelsea	W 2-0	Jephcott, Pailor	35,100	1		3		5	6	7	10	9	8	11	4	2								
9	(h)	W Arsenal	W 2-1	Morris 2	15,980	1		3		5		7	10		8	11	4	2		9	6					
16	(a)	Bradford C	D 1-1	Torrance (og)	13,000	1		3		5		7	10		8	11	4	2		9	6					
23	(h)	Manchester C	L 0-2		16,799	1		3		5		7	10		8	11	4	2		9	6					
30	(h)	Sunderland	W 3-1	Morris, Pailor, Buck (pen)	13,529				4	5		7	10	9		11	6	2	1		8	3				
Dec 7	(a)	Everton	W 3-1	Pailor 2, Jephcott	25,000			3	4	5		7	10	9		11	6	2	1		8					
14	(h)	Sheffield W	D 1-1	Pailor	15,258			3	4	5		7	10	9		11	6	2	1		8					
21	(a)	Blackburn R	W 4-2	Pailor 3, Morris	22,000			3		5	6	7		9		11	4	2	1		8					
25	(a)	Derby C	W 2-1	Buck, Shearman	21,000			3	4	5		7		9	10	11	6	2	1		8					
26	(h)	Derby C	D 0-0		22,567			3	4	5	6	7	8		10	11		2	1		9					
28	(h)	Notts C	W 2-0	Gregory, Morris	21,041			3			6	7			10	11	4	2	1	8	9			5		
Jan 1	(a)	Middlesbrough	L 1-3	Buck	18,000					5	6	7		9	10	11	4	2	1		8	3				
4	(a)	Manchester U	D 1-1	Bowser	15,000			3		5	6	7	8		10	11	4	2	1		9					
18	(h)	Aston Villa	D 2-2	Morris, Gregory	40,589			3	4	5	6	7			10	11		2	1	8	9					
25	(a)	Liverpool	L 1-2		30,400			3	4	5	6	7			10	11		2	1	8	9					
Feb 8	(h)	Bolton W	D 2-2	Waterhouse, Shearman	18,225	1		3		5	6	7	8		10	11	4	2			9					
15	(a)	Sheffield U	L 0-1		12,000	1		3		5	6	7	8		10	11	4	2			9					
Mar 1	(a)	Oldham A	D 0-0		10,500	1		3		5	6	7	8		10	11	4	2					9			
8	(h)	Chelsea	L 0-1		16,293	1		3	4	8		7					6	2		10			5	9	11	
15	(a)	W Arsenal	L 0-1		6,800	1		3		5	6	7		9	10	11	4	2		8						
21	(a)	Tottenham H	L 1-3	Shearman	31,500	1		3		5	6	7		9	10	11	4	2		8						
22	(h)	Bradford C	D 1-1	Pailor	6,565	1		3		5	6	7		9	10	11	4	2		8						
24	(h)	Tottenham H	W 4-1	Bowser, Shearman, Pailor 2	13,882			3		5	6	7		9	10	11	4	2	1	8						
29	(a)	Manchester C	L 1-2	Bowser	21,500			3		5	6	7		9	10	11	4	2	1	8						
Apr 5	(a)	Sunderland	L 1-3	Gregory	33,700			3		5	6	7		9	10	11	4	2	1	8						
9	(h)	Newcastle U	W 1-0	Shearman	8,277			3		5	6	7		9	10	11	4	2	1	8						
12	(h)	Everton	D 0-0		10,795			3		5	6	7		9	8	11	4	2	1					10		
19	(a)	Sheffield W	L 2-3	Shearman, Gregory	11,400			3		5	6	7		9	10	11	4	2	1	8						
26	(h)	Blackburn R	D 1-1	Waterhouse	11,834			3		5	6	7		9	10	11	4	2	1	8						
					App	19	8	31	10	36	30	38	20	24	32	37	34	35	19	13	19	3	2	4	3	1
					Goals					4	1	2	4	16	6	8	2			4	9					

West Bromwich Albion 1912-13. Back row (left to right): A.Lloyd, J.Steer, L.Moorwood, G.Snead, J.Varty, M.Wood, C.Crutchley, B.Millward, S.Jones, A.Graham, J.Mann. Third row: E.Smith (asst.secretary), T.Fletcher, G.Baddeley, H.Pearson, S.Bowser, J.Manners, W.I.Bassett (chairman), F.Waterhouse, C.Deacey, R.Pailor, F.Morris, H.Lane, F.Everiss (secretary). Second row: D.Nurse (director), A.Cook, H.Keys (director), J.Pennington, R.McNeal, Sir E.J.Spencer (president), F.Buck, W.Barber (trainer). Front row: C.Jephcott, W.Jackson, B.Shearman, J.Smith, H.Wright, J.Smart, J.Donald, H.Gregory.

1913-14

Division 1

Date	Result	Scorers	Att	Pearson H	Smith J	Pennington J	Waterhouse F	Buck F	McNeal R	Jephcott C	Morris F	Bentley A	Lewis A	Shearman B	Newall T	Gregory H	Baddeley G	Deacey C	Pailor R	Wright H	Edwards E	Cook A	Nicholls H	Swift A	Bowser S	Wood M	Lloyd A
Sep 6 (h) Burnley	W 4-1	Bentley 4	27,014	1	2	3	4	5	6	7	8	9	10	11													
Sep 8 (a) Chelsea	D 1-1	Morris	21,000	1	2	3	4	5	6	7	8	9	10	11													
Sep 13 (a) Preston NE	W 2-0	Lewis, Morris	15,000	1	2	3	4	5	6	7	8	9	10	11													
Sep 20 (h) Newcastle U	D 1-1	Newall	29,147	1	2	3	4	5	6	7	8		10	11	9												
Sep 27 (a) Liverpool	D 0-0		25,000	1	2	3	4	5	6	7	8		10	11	9												
Oct 4 (h) Aston Villa	W 1-0	Lewis	48,057	1	2	3	4	5	6	7	8	9	10	11													
Oct 11 (a) Middlesbrough	L 0-3		15,000	1	2	3	4	5	6	7	8	9		11	10												
Oct 18 (h) Sheffield U	W 2-1	Morris, Bentley	15,282	1	2	3		5	6	7	8	9	10	11		4											
Oct 25 (a) Derby C	W 2-1	Morris, Bentley	12,000	1	2	3		5	6	7	8	9	10	11		4											
Nov 1 (h) Manchester C	D 0-0		17,443	1	2	3		5	6	7	8		10	11	9	4											
Nov 8 (a) Bradford C	L 0-1		10,000	1	2	3	4		6	7	8		10	11				5	9								
Nov 15 (h) Blackburn R	W 2-0	Shearman, Buck	32,524	1	2	3	4	5	6	7	8	9	10	11													
Nov 22 (a) Sunderland	D 0-0		39,700	1	2	3	4	5	6	7	8	9	10	11													
Nov 29 (h) Everton	D 1-1	Lewis	16,627	1	2	3	4	5	6	7		9	10	11						8							
Dec 6 (a) Tottenham H	L 0-3		26,000	1	2	3	4	5	6	7			10	11	9					8							
Dec 13 (a) Sheffield W	W 4-1	Edwards 2, Morris, Pailor	17,000	1	2	3	4	5	6	7	10			11					9		8						
Dec 20 (h) Bolton W	D 1-1	McNeal	21,311	1	2	3	4	5	6	7	10	9		11							8						
Dec 25 (a) Oldham A	L 0-2		12,000	1	2	3	4	5	6	7	10	9		11							8						
Dec 26 (h) Oldham A	D 2-2	Bentley 2 (2 pens)	30,294	1		3	4		6	7	10	9		11				5			8	2					
Dec 27 (a) Burnley	D 0-0		15,100	1		3	4		6	7	10	9						5			8	2	11				
Jan 1 (a) Manchester U	L 0-1		16,400	1		3	4		6	7	10	9						5			8	2	11				
Jan 3 (h) Preston NE	W 1-0	Buck (pen)	13,659	1	2		4	5	6	7	8		10	11								3	9				
Jan 17 (a) Newcastle U	D 3-3	Edwards, Shearman, Bentley	18,200	1	2	3	4		6	7	10	9		11				5			8						
Jan 24 (h) Liverpool	L 0-1		13,582	1	2	3	4		6	7	10	9		11	8			5									
Feb 7 (a) Aston Villa	L 0-2		48,000	1	2	3	4	5	6	7	8	9		11										10			
Feb 14 (h) Middlesbrough	W 2-1	McNeal, Bentley	15,692	1	2		4	5	6	7		9	10	11										8	3		
Feb 28 (h) Derby C	W 2-1	Bentley, Swift	14,746	1	2	3	4		6	7		8	10											9	5		11
Mar 7 (a) Bolton W	L 0-1		20,000	1	2	3	4		6	7		8	10											9	5		11
Mar 12 (h) Bradford C	W 2-1	Bentley 2	12,057	1	2	3	4		6	7	10	8												9	5	11	
Mar 19 (a) Sheffield U	D 1-1	Morris	10,120	1	2		4		6	7	10	8												9	5	3	11
Mar 21 (a) Blackburn R	L 0-2		22,126	1	2				6	7		8	10	11			4							9	5	3	
Mar 25 (a) Manchester C	W 3-2	Swift, Bentley, Gregory	16,700	1	2		4		6	7		8				10							11	9	5	3	
Mar 28 (h) Sunderland	W 2-1	Gregory 2	23,366	1	2	3	4		6	7		8				10							11	9	5		
Apr 4 (a) Everton	L 0-2		21,000	1	2				6	7	10	8		11			4							9	5	3	
Apr 11 (h) Tottenham H	D 1-1	Swift	13,627	1	2	3	4		6	7		8		11						10				9	5		
Apr 13 (h) Manchester U	W 2-1	Wright, Bentley	16,907	1	2	3	4		6	7		8		11						10				9	5		
Apr 14 (h) Chelsea	W 3-1	Jephcott 2, Swift	16,479	1	2	3	4		6	7		8	10											9	5		11
Apr 18 (h) Sheffield W	D 1-1	Bentley	14,134	1	2	3			6	7	10	8					4							9	5		11
App				38	35	32	37	19	36	37	26	31	18	27	7	5	6	6	2	4	7	4	4	13	13	5	6
Goals								2	2	2	6	16	3	2	1	3			1	1	3			4			

Action from Albion's home game against Blackburn Rovers, 15 November 1913. Left: Albert Lewis (stripes) heading for goal and (right) Bobby McNeal (stripes), sandwiched between Walmsley and the great England defender, Bob Crompton.

1914-15

Division 1

Date	Opponent	Result	Scorers	Att	Pearson H	Smith J	Pennington J	Waterhouse F	Bowser S	McNeal R	Wright H	Bentley A	Poulton A	Bache H	Bookman L	Shearman B	Moorwood L	Swift A	Morris F	Wood M	Newall T	Mann J	Jephcott C	Crisp J	Richardson S	Parkes H	Shore E	Bowen W	Gregory H	Reed F
Sep 2	(a) Newcastle U	W 2-1	Bentley, Bookman	15,000	1	2	3	4	5	6	7	8	9	10	11															
5	(a) Middlesbrough	L 0-2		14,500	1	2	3	4	5	6	7	8	9	10		11														
12	(h) Sheffield U	D 1-1	Poulton	6,481	1	2	3	4	5	6	7	8	9	10	11															
19	(a) Aston Villa	L 1-2	Swift	29,000		2	3	4	5	6		8		10	11			7	1	9										
26	(h) Liverpool	W 4-0	Bentley 2, Morris 2	18,026	1	2	3	4	5	6		8		9	11			7	10											
28	(a) Tottenham H	L 0-2		22,000	1	2	3	4	5	6		8			11			7	9	10										
Oct 3	(a) Bradford	W 4-1	Bentley, Bache, Morris 2	19,000	1		3	4	5	6		8		9	11			7	10	2										
10	(h) Oldham A	D 0-0		15,768	1	2	3	4	5	6		8			11			7	10	9										
17	(a) Manchester U	D 0-0		13,200	1	2	3	4	5	6			9		11			7	10			8								
24	(h) Bolton W	W 3-0	Bentley, Shearman, Bache	7,817	1	2	3	4	5	6		8		9		11			10				7								
31	(a) Blackburn R	L 1-2	Morris	8,005	1	2		4	5	6		8		9		11			10	3			7								
Nov 7	(h) Notts C	W 4-1	Morris 2, Bentley, Bache	10,368	1	2		4	5	6		8		9		11			10	3			7								
14	(a) Sunderland	W 2-1	Jephcott, Bentley	15,000	1	2	3	4	5	6		8		9		11			10				7								
21	(h) Sheffield W	D 0-0		11,254	1	2	3	4	5	6		8		9		11			10				7								
28	(h) Manchester C	L 0-1		9,398	1	2	3	4	5	6		8	9			11			10				7								
Dec 5	(a) Everton	L 1-2	Crisp	22,000	1	2	3	4	5	6		8	9			11			10					7						
12	(h) Chelsea	W 2-0	Jephcott, Swift	6,421	1	2	3	4	5	6						11		9	10				7	8						
19	(a) Bradford C	L 0-5		5,300	1	2	3	4	5	6						11		9	10				7	8						
25	(a) Burnley	W 2-0	Morris, Swift	10,000	1	2	3	4	5	6						11		9	10				7	8						
26	(h) Burnley	W 3-0	Swift 2, Crisp	15,853	1	2	3	4	5	6						11		9	10				7	8						
Jan 2	(h) Middlesbrough	W 1-0	Bache	10,914	1	2	3	4	5	6				9		11			10				7	8						
16	(a) Sheffield U	L 0-2		7,800	1	2	3		5	6						11		9	10				7	8	4					
23	(h) Aston Villa	W 2-0	Swift, Morris	19,492	1	2	3	4	5	6						11		9	10				7	8						
Feb 6	(h) Bradford	W 1-0	Bowser (pen)	7,466	1	2	3	4	5	6						11		9	10				7	8						
20	(h) Manchester U	D 0-0		10,169	1	2	3	4	5	6						11		9	10				7	8						
27	(a) Bolton W	D 1-1	Crisp	8,900	1	2	3	4	5	6						11		9	10					8		7				
Mar 6	(h) Blackburn R	D 0-0		15,168	1	2	3	4	5	6		8				11		9	10							7				
9	(a) Oldham A	D 1-1	Crisp	11,400	1	2	3	4	5	6			9			11			10					8		7				
13	(a) Notts C	D 1-1	Morris	28,000	1	2	3	4	5	6			9			11			10					8		7				
20	(h) Sunderland	L 1-2	Morris	10,233	1	2	3	4	5				9			11			10				8	6		7				
24	(a) Liverpool	L 1-3	Newall	16,000	1		3	4		6						11				9	8					7	2	5	10	
27	(a) Sheffield W	D 0-0		9,000	1		3		5	6			9			11				8	4					7	2		10	
Apr 3	(a) Manchester C	L 0-4		8,400	1				5	6			9			11				8	3	4	7				2		10	
5	(h) Newcastle U	W 2-0	Bentley 2	11,858	1			3	5	6		9				11				2	4		7	8					10	
6	(h) Tottenham H	W 3-2	Gregory 3	5,813			3			6				10		11	1	9		2	4		7						8	5
10	(h) Everton	L 1-2	Swift	8,748	1		4	3		6				10		11		9		2			7	8						5
17	(a) Chelsea	L 1-4	McNeal	6,000	1		3			6						11		9			4					7	2		10	5
24	(h) Bradford C	W 3-0	Gregory, Newall, McNeal	4,410	1			4	5	6		8				11				3	9					7	2		10	
App					36	29	30	35	35	37	7	19	9	12	16	28	2	15	28	8	8	2	18	18	2	8	5	1	7	3
Goals									1	2		9	1	4	1	1		7	11		2		2	4					4	

Newspaper pictures of a snow-bound Hawthorns in 1914.

1919-20

Division 1

Joe Smith

Date		Opponent	Result	Scorers	Att	Pearson H	Smith J	Pennington J	Richardson S	Bowser S	McNeal R	Crisp J	Magee T	Smith A	Morris F	Gregory H	Jephcott C	Moorwood L	Cook A	Reed F	Bentley A	Hatton S	Waterhouse F
Aug 30	(h)	Oldham A	W 3-1	Morris 2, Gregory	19,058	1	2	3	4	5	6	7	8	9	10	11							
Sep 3	(a)	Newcastle U	W 2-0	Magee, Gregory	50,000	1	2	3	4	5	6	7	8	9	10	11							
6	(a)	Oldham A	L 1-2	Bowser (pen)	16,000	1	2	3	4	5	6	7	8	9	10	11							
8	(h)	Newcastle U	W 3-0	A.Smith, Bowser (pen), Morris	20,082	1	2	3	4	5	6	7	8	9	10	11							
15	(h)	Everton	W 4-3	Magee, Morris, Gregory, Crisp	31,245	1	2	3	4	5	6	7	8	9	10	11							
20	(a)	Everton	W 5-2	Jephcott, Crisp 2, A.Smith 2	25,000	1	2	3	4	5	6	11	8	9	10		7						
27	(h)	Bradford C	W 4-1	Bowser 3 (2 pens), Morris	29,680	1	2	3	4	5	6	11	8	9	10		7						
Oct 4	(a)	Bradford C	L 0-3		17,000	1	2	3	4	5	6	11	8	9	10		7						
11	(h)	Bolton W	W 4-1	Magee, Bowser (pen), Crisp, A.Smith	35,227	1	2	3	4	5	6	11	8	9	10		7						
18	(a)	Bolton W	W 2-1	Morris, Gregory	24,000			3	4	5	6	11	8		9	10	7	1	2				
25	(h)	Notts C	W 8-0	Morris 5, Foster (og), Gregory, Magee	36,086			3	4		6	7	8	9	10	11		1	2	5			
Nov 1	(a)	Notts C	L 0-2		12,050		2	3	4	5	6	7	8	9	10	11		1					
10	(h)	Aston Villa	L 1-2	Gregory	43,121	1	2	3	4	5	6	7	8	9	10	11							
15	(a)	Aston Villa	W 4-2	Gregory 2, Morris 2	58,273	1	2	3	4	5	6		8	9	10	11	7						
22	(h)	Sheffield W	L 1-3	A.Smith	22,193	1	2	3	4	5	6		8	9	10	11	7						
29	(a)	Sheffield W	W 3-0	Bowser (pen), Bentley, Morris	25,000	1	2	3	4	5	6	11	8		10		7				9		
Dec 6	(a)	Manchester C	W 3-2	Bowser (pen), Morris 2	26,000	1	2	3	4	5	6	11	8		10		7				9		
13	(h)	Manchester C	W 2-0	Morris 2	25,040	1	2	3	4	5	6	7	8		10	11					9		
20	(a)	Derby C	W 4-0	Bentley, Morris 2, Gregory	21,000	1	2	3	4	5	6	7	8		10	11					9		
26	(h)	Sunderland	W 4-0	Magee, Morris 2, Bentley	43,579	1	2	3	4	5	6	7	8		10	11					9		
27	(h)	Derby C	W 3-0	Morris 2, Magee	34,167	1	2	3	4	5	6	7	8		10	11					9		
Jan 1	(a)	Sunderland	L 1-4	Morris	32,500	1	2	3	4	5	6	7	8		10	11					9		
3	(a)	Blackburn R	W 5-1	Bentley 3, Morris, Gregory	18,000	1	2	3	4	5	6	7	8		10	11					9		
17	(a)	Blackburn R	W 5-2	Magee, Bentley, Morris, Crisp, Gregory	23,360	1	2	3	4	5	6	7	8		10	11					9		
24	(h)	Manchester U	W 2-1	Bowser, Morris	30,192	1	2	3	4	5	6	7	8	9	10	11							
Feb 7	(h)	Sheffield U	L 0-2		28,975	1	2	3	4	5	6	7	8		10	11						9	
14	(a)	Sheffield U	L 0-1		39,850	1	2	3	4	5	6		8		10	11	7				9		
21	(h)	Middlesbrough	W 4-1	Bentley 2, Morris 2	24,955	1	2	3	4	5	6		8		10	11	7				9		
25	(a)	Manchester U	W 2-1	Bentley 2	21,000	1	2		4	5	6	11	8		10		7		3		9		
28	(a)	Middlesbrough	D 0-0		16,500	1	2	3		5	6	11	8		10		7				9		4
Mar 6	(a)	Burnley	D 2-2	Jephcott, Crisp	30,200	1	2	3		5	6		8		10	11	7				9		4
13	(h)	Burnley	W 4-1	Bentley, Morris 2, Crisp	32,213	1	2	3	4	5	6		8		10	11	7				9		
20	(a)	Preston NE	W 1-0	Crisp	20,000	1	2		4	5	6	11	8		10		7		3		9		
27	(h)	Preston NE	W 4-1	Jephcott 2, Morris 2	24,186	1	2	3	4	5	6	11	8		10		7				9		
Apr 3	(a)	Bradford	W 4-0	Bentley, Morris, McNeal (pen), A.Smith	9,000	1	2	3	4	5	6		8		10	11	7				9		
5	(a)	Arsenal	L 0-1		38,000	1	2	3	4	5	6		8		10	11	7				9		
6	(h)	Arsenal	W 1-0	Morris	39,397	1	2		4	5	6		8	9	10	11			3				
10	(h)	Bradford	W 3-1	Jephcott, Bentley, Bowser (pen)	29,414	1	2		4	5	6	11	8		10		7		3		9		
17	(a)	Liverpool	D 0-0		45,100	1	2	3	4	5	6	7	8		10	11					9		
24	(h)	Liverpool	D 1-1	Morris	33,349	1	2		4	5	6	7	8		10	11			3		9		
26	(a)	Chelsea	L 0-2		39,902	1	2	3	4	5	6	7	8		10	11					9		
May 1	(h)	Chelsea	W 4-0	McNeal, Gregory, A.Smith, Bentley	35,668	1	2	3	4	5	6	7	8		10	11					9		
App						39	40	37	40	41	42	38	24	29	39	34	21	3	7	1	24	1	2
Goals										10	2	8	7	7	37	12	5				15		

Claude Jephcott

Tommy Magee

1920-21

Division 1

Date		Opponent	Result	Scorers	Att	Pearson H	Smith J	Pennington J	Richardson S	Bowser S	McNeal R	Crisp J	Smith A	Bentley A	Morris F	Gregory H	Jephcott C	Magee T	Cook A	Taylor H	Adams W	James R	Ashmore G	Hatton S	Clark B	Long W	Newall T	Reed F	Blood R	Bedford L
Aug 28	(a)	Newcastle U	D 1-1	Morris	61,080	1	2	3	4	5	6	7	8	9	10	11														
Sep 1	(h)	Liverpool	D 1-1	Gregory	32,475	1	2	3	4	5	6	11	9			10	7	8												
4	(h)	Newcastle U	D 0-0		29,202	1	2	3	4	5	6	11	9			10	7	8												
6	(a)	Liverpool	D 0-0		27,550	1		3	4	5	6	11	9			10	7	8	2											
11	(a)	Bolton W	L 0-3		18,000	1		3	4	5	6	11		9		10	7	8	2											
18	(h)	Bolton W	W 2-1	Crisp, Bentley	34,865	1	2	3	4	5	6	7		8	10	11				9										
25	(a)	Derby C	D 1-1	Morris	18,300	1	2		4	5		7		8	10	11				9	3	6								
Oct 2	(h)	Derby C	W 3-0	McNeal, Morris, Bowser (pen)	26,893	1	2		4	5	6			8	10	11	7			9	3									
9	(a)	Blackburn R	L 1-5	Taylor	15,300		2		4	5				8	10		7			9	3		1	6	11					
16	(h)	Blackburn R	D 1-1	Morris	35,025	1	2		4	5				8	10		7			9	3			6		11				
23	(a)	Huddersfield T	L 1-5	Taylor	25,100	1	2		4	5			8		10	11				9	3			6		7				
30	(h)	Huddersfield T	W 3-0	Bowser (pen), A.Smith, Morris	44,049	1	2	3	4	5	6		8		10	11	7			9										
Nov 6	(a)	Aston Villa	D 0-0		66,094	1	2	3	4	5	6		8		10	11	7			9										
13	(h)	Aston Villa	W 2-1	A.Smith, Bowser (pen)	42,334	1	2	3	4	5	6		8		10	11	7			9										
27	(h)	Bradford C	W 2-0	Morris, Gregory	22,068	1	2	3	4	5	6		8	9	10	11	7													
Dec 4	(h)	Sunderland	W 4-1	Bentley, Gregory, Bowser 2 (1 pen)	23,726	1	2	3	4	5	6		8	9	10	11	7													
11	(a)	Sunderland	L 0-3		20,000	1	2	3	4	5	6		8	9	10	11	7													
18	(h)	Everton	L 1-2	Crisp	19,932	1	2	3	4	5	6	7	8	9	10	11														
25	(a)	Manchester C	L 0-4		22,306	1	2	3	4	5	6	7	8	9	10	11														
27	(h)	Manchester C	D 2-2	A.Smith, Morris	32,147	1	2	3	4	5	6		8	9	10	11	7													
Jan 1	(a)	Everton	D 2-2	Morris, James	59,964	1	2		4	5	6	7		8	10	11			3			9								
15	(a)	Manchester U	W 4-1	James 2, A.Smith, Morris	40,100	1	2	3		5	6		8		10	11	7				4	9								
22	(a)	Manchester U	L 0-2		26,826	1	2	3		5	6		8		10	11	7				4	9								
29	(a)	Middlesbrough	W 1-0	A.Smith	25,500	1	2	3		5	6		8		10	11	7				4	9								
Feb 5	(h)	Middlesbrough	L 0-1		24,920	1	2	3		5	6		8		10	11	7				4	9								
9	(a)	Bradford C	D 1-1	James	42,000	1	2		4	5	6	11		8	10		7		3			9								
12	(a)	Chelsea	L 0-3		15,000	1	2	3	4		6	11		8	10		7					9		5						
19	(h)	Tottenham H	W 3-1	Crisp, Bentley, Blood (pen)	31,753	1	2	3	4	5	6	11		8	10		7												9	
26	(a)	Tottenham H	L 0-1		35,000	1	2	3	4	5		11		8	10		7					6							9	
Mar 12	(a)	Oldham A	W 3-0	Blood, Morris 2	13,000	1	2	3	4	5	6			8	10	11	7												9	
14	(h)	Chelsea	D 1-1	Blood	28,140	1	2	3	4	5	6			8	10	11	7												9	
19	(h)	Oldham A	D 0-0		23,908	1	2		4	5	6			8	10	11	7		3										9	
25	(h)	Preston NE	L 0-3		23,511	1	2	3	4	5	6			8	10	11	7												9	
28	(a)	Arsenal	L 1-2	Crisp	20,152	1	2		4	5	6	11		8	10		7		3										9	
29	(h)	Arsenal	L 3-4	A.Smith, Bowser (pen), Morris	23,650	1	2	3	4	5	6	7	8		10														9	11
Apr 2	(a)	Preston NE	L 1-2	Blood	18,052	1	2	3	4	5	6	7	8		10														9	11
9	(h)	Burnley	W 2-0	Crisp, Morris	17,242		2	3	4	5	6	11	8		10		7						1						9	
16	(a)	Burnley	W 1-0	A.Smith	13,700		2	3	4	5	6	11	8		10		7						1						9	
23	(h)	Sheffield U	D 1-1	Blood	23,697		2	3	4	5	6	11	8		10		7						1						9	
30	(a)	Sheffield U	W 2-0	Morris, Blood	21,000		2	3	4	5	6	11	8		10		7						1						9	
May 2	(h)	Bradford	L 0-1		17,472		2	3	4	5	6	11	8		10		7						1						9	
7	(a)	Bradford	W 3-0	Morris 2 (1 pen), Blood	8,105		2	3	4	5	6		8		10	11		7					1						9	
		App				35	40	33	38	40	37	27	28	18	37	29	31	5	4	9	7	8	7	4	1	2	4	1	15	2
		Goals								6	1	5	7	3	16	3				2		4							7	

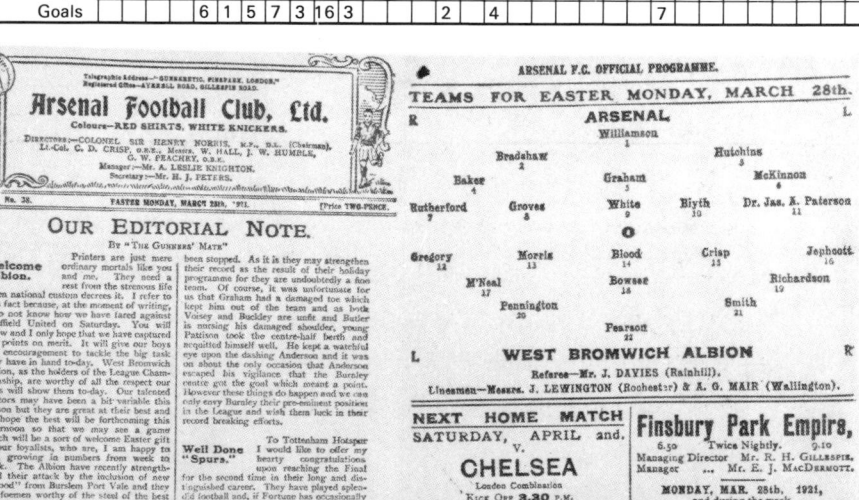

Arsenal v Albion match programme for the game at Highbury, 28 March 1921.

1921-22

Division 1

Date		Opponent	Res	Score	Scorers	Att	Ashmore G	Smith J	Adams W	Richardson S	Bowser S	McNeal R	Jephcott C	Smith A	Blood R	Morris F	Crisp J	Magee T	Bedford L	Cook A	Bentley A	Gregory H	Pennington J	Newall T	Wilson C	Blagden J	Savage G	James G	Pearson H	Hatton S	Davies S	Reed F	James R	Jones I	Watson E
Aug 27	(h)	Middlesbrough	D	0-0		24,880	1	2	3	4	5	6	7	8	9	10	11																		
29	(a)	Manchester U	W	3-2	Brett (og), Blood 2	20,000	1	2	3	4	5	6	7	8	9	10	11																		
Sep 3	(a)	Middlesbrough	L	2-3	Blood, A.Smith	15,000	1	2	3	4	5	6	7	8	9	10	11																		
7	(h)	Manchester U	D	0-0		20,557	1	2	3	4	5	6		8	9	10	11	7																	
10	(h)	Blackburn R	L	0-2		20,160	1	2	3	4	5	6		8	9	10		7	11																
17	(a)	Blackburn R	W	3-2	Crisp, Bentley	13,000	1	2		4	5	6			9	10	7			3	8	11													
24	(h)	Oldham A	L	0-1		19,840	1	2		4	5	6			9	10	7			3	8	11													
Oct 1	(a)	Oldham A	L	0-1		10,107	1	2			5	6		8		10	7					11	3	4	9										
8	(h)	Aston Villa	L	0-1		45,077	1	2		4	5	6			9	10	7				8	11	3												
15	(a)	Aston Villa	W	1-0	Blood	55,000	1	2		4	5	6		8	9	10	7			·		11	3												
22	(h)	Cardiff C	D	2-2	Gregory, A.Smith	20,969	1	2		4	5	6		8	9	10	7					11	3												
29	(a)	Cardiff C	L	0-2		16,000	1	2		4	5	6			9	10		7			8	11	3												
Nov 5	(h)	Bolton W	L	0-1		15,502	1	2			5	6			9			7		3		11		4		8	10								
12	(a)	Bolton W	L	0-2		13,514	1	2		4	5	6		8				7				11	3				10	9							
19	(a)	Manchester C	L	1-6	Bentley	18,000		2			5	6			9			7			10	11	3			8		4	1						
26	(h)	Manchester C	W	2-0	Blagden, Morris	14,145		2		4	5	6				10		7				11	3			8			1		9				
Dec 3	(a)	Everton	W	2-1	Morris, Reed	21,000		2		4		6				10		7				11	3			8			1		9	5			
10	(h)	Everton	D	1-1	Morris	16,606		2		4	5	6				10		7				11	3			8			1		9				
17	(h)	Sunderland	W	2-1	Morris, Davies	18,251		2		4	5	6				10		7				11	3			8			1		9				
24	(a)	Sunderland	L	0-5		10,522		2		4	5	6				10		7				11	3			8			1		9				
26	(h)	Birmingham	W	1-0	Davies	49,488		2		4		6				10		7				11	3			8			1		9	5			
27	(a)	Birmingham	W	2-0	Magee, Morris	44,500		2		4		6				10		7				11	3			8			1		9	5			
31	(h)	Huddersfield T	W	3-2	Morris, Blagden, Gregory	25,036		2		4		6				10		7				11	3			8			1		9	5			
Jan 14	(a)	Huddersfield T	L	0-2		6,000		2		4	10	6			11			7					3			8			1		9	5			
21	(h)	Tottenham H	W	3-0	Davies 2, Magee	21,498		2		4		6				10	11	7					3			8			1		9	5			
30	(a)	Tottenham H	L	0-2		20,400		2	3	4						10	11	7								8			1		9	5	6		
Feb 4	(h)	Bradford C	D	1-1	Crisp	15,170		2		4		6			9	10	11	7					3			8			1			5			
25	(a)	Preston NE	W	3-0	Morris, A.Smith, Davies	16,000		2		4	5	6		8		10		7				11	3						1		9				
Mar 4	(h)	Chelsea	D	2-2	Davies 2	11,026		2		4	5	6		8		10		7				11	3						1		9				
8	(a)	Bradford C	D	1-1	A.Smith	10,400		2		4		6		8		10	11	7					3						1		9	5			
11	(a)	Chelsea	D	1-1	Morris	20,000		2		4		6		8		10	11	7					3						1		9	5			
18	(a)	Sheffield U	D	0-0		10,900		2		4		6		5	9	10	11	7					3						1		8				
25	(h)	Sheffield U	W	3-0	A.Smith, Richardson, Davies	12,113		2		4		6		8		10	11	7					3						1		9	5			
29	(h)	Preston NE	W	2-0	Morris, Davies	12,585		2		4	5	6		8		10	11	7					3						1		9				
Apr 1	(h)	Burnley	W	2-0	Morris 2	13,304		2		4	5	6				10						11	3			8			1	7	9				
8	(a)	Burnley	L	2-4	Davies 2	8,900		2	3	4	5	6		8		10		7				11							1		9				
15	(a)	Newcastle U	L	0-3		28,000		2	3	4	5	6				10		7				11							1		9			8	
17	(h)	Arsenal	L	0-3		23,997		2	3	4	5	6		8		10		7				11							1		9				
18	(a)	Arsenal	D	2-2	Hutchins (og), Davies	23,663		2	3	4		6				10		7				11				8			1		9	5			
22	(h)	Newcastle U	L	1-2	Davies	32,063		2		4	5	6	7			10						11	3						1		9			8	
29	(a)	Liverpool	W	2-1	Gregory 2	20,551		2		4	5	6				10		7				11	3			8			1		9				
May 6	(h)	Liverpool	L	1-4	Davies	23,247		2			5	6				10		7				11	3			8			1		9				4
App							14	42	10	38	30	41	4	19	14	38	19	31	1	3	5	28	29	2	4	16	2	2	28	1	25	12	1	2	1
Goals										1				5	4	11	2	2			3	4				2					14	1			

Jack Crisp

Charlie 'Tug' Wilson made his debut for Albion at Oldham on 1 October 1921. He was only 16 years and 63 days old and is still Albion's youngest League debutant.

Lewis Bedford

1922-23

Division 1

Date		Opponent	Result	Scorers	Att.	Pearson H	Smith J	Adams W	Magee T	Bowser S	McNeal R	Jephcott C	Jones I	Davies S	Morris F	Gregory H	Crisp J	Smith A	Chamberlain H	Fitton A	Glidden T	Carter J	Blood R	Ashmore G	Richardson S	Dutton H	Spencer J	Wilson C	Ford E
Aug 26	(a)	Burnley	L 0-3		30,000	1	2	3	4	5	6	7	8	9	10	11													
28	(h)	Preston NE	D 2-2	Davies, Morris	25,343	1	2	3	4	5	6	7	8	9	10	11													
Sep 2	(h)	Burnley	W 2-1	Davies 2	23,561	1	2	3	4	5	6	7	8	9	10	11													
4	(a)	Preston NE	D 0-0		30,200	1	2	3	4	5	6	7	8	9	10		11												
9	(a)	Aston Villa	L 0-2		40,000	1	2	3	4	5	6	7	8	9	10		11												
16	(h)	Aston Villa	W 3-0	Davies 2, Morris	39,576	1	2	3	4	5	6			9	10	11	7	8											
23	(a)	Stoke C	W 2-0	Davies, A.Smith	20,000	1	2	3	4	5	6			9	10	11	7	8											
30	(h)	Stoke C	L 0-1		20,385	1	2	3	4	5	6			9	10	11	7	8											
Oct 7	(a)	Arsenal	L 1-3	Gregory	32,500	1	2	3	4	5	6		8	9	10	11	7												
14	(h)	Arsenal	W 7-0	Morris 4, Crisp 2, Gregory	21,730	1	2	3	4	5	6		8	9	10	11	7												
21	(a)	Tottenham H	L 1-3	Gregory	35,000	1		2	4	5	6		8	9	10	11	7		3										
28	(h)	Tottenham H	W 5-1	Jones, Davies 2, Gregory, Crisp	20,150	1	2	3	4	5	6		8	9	10	11	7												
Nov 4	(h)	Manchester C	W 2-0	Davies, Morris	17,124	1	2	3	4	5	6		8	9	10	11	7												
11	(a)	Manchester C	D 1-1	Davies	25,000	1	2	3	4	5	6		8	9	10		7			11									
18	(h)	Everton	D 0-0		18,539	1	2	3	4	5	6		8	9	10		7			11									
25	(a)	Everton	W 1-0	Morris	35,000	1	2	3	4	5	6		8	9	10					11	7								
Dec 2	(h)	Bolton W	D 1-1	Davies	16,527	1	2		4	5	6		8	9	10				3	11	7								
9	(a)	Bolton W	L 0-3		20,000	1	2		4	5	6			9	10	11			3		7	8							
16	(a)	Sunderland	L 2-3	Morris, Gregory	10,000	1	2	3	4	5	6		8		10	11					7		9						
23	(h)	Sunderland	D 1-1	Morris	23,092	1	2	3	4	5	6		8		10	11					7		9						
26	(a)	Cardiff C	L 0-3		39,000	1	2	3	4	5	6		8		10	11					7		9						
27	(h)	Cardiff C	W 3-0	Davies (pen), Morris, Spencer	14,898		2	3		5			8	9	10	11								1	4	6	7		
30	(a)	Blackburn R	L 1-5	Morris (pen)	7,000	1	2	3		5			8	9	10	11									4	6	7		
Jan 6	(h)	Blackburn R	W 3-0	Gregory, Davies, Morris (pen)	17,024	1	2	3	4	5	6		8	9	10	11											7		
20	(a)	Birmingham	W 2-0	Davies, Gregory	32,180	1	2	3	4	5	6		8	9	10	11											7		
27	(h)	Birmingham	W 1-0	Morris	25,123	1	2	3	4	5	6		8	9	10	11											7		
Feb 7	(a)	Liverpool	L 0-2		26,000	1	2	3	4	5	6		8	9	10	11											7		
10	(h)	Liverpool	D 0-0		20,464	1	2	3	4	5	6		8	9	10	11											7		
14	(a)	Newcastle U	L 0-2		10,000	1	2	3	4	5	6		8	9	10	11											7		
Mar 3	(a)	Nottingham F	W 4-0	Bowser, Blood 3	17,134	1	2	3	4	5	6		8		10	11			7				9				7		
10	(h)	Nottingham F	D 0-0		15,990	1	2	3	4	5	6		8		10	11							9				7		
14	(h)	Newcastle U	W 2-1	Jones, Blood	5,520	1	2	3	4	5	6		8		10	11							9				7		
17	(h)	Chelsea	D 0-0		12,242	1	2	3	4	5	6						11					8	9				7	10	
31	(h)	Sheffield U	W 4-0	Carter, Davies 3	15,147	1	2	3	4	5	6		10	9								8					7		11
Apr 2	(h)	Huddersfield T	L 0-2		24,291	1	2	3	4	5	6		10	9	11							8					7		
3	(a)	Huddersfield T	L 1-4	Carter	13,000	1	2	3	4	5	6		10	9	11							8					7		
7	(a)	Sheffield U	L 1-3	Davies	10,000	1	2	3	4	5	6		10	9	11							8					7		
14	(h)	Oldham A	W 1-0	Carter	8,405	1	2	3	4	5	6			9	10						11	8					7		
21	(a)	Oldham A	D 0-0		4,700	1	2	3	4	5	6		8	9	10						11						7		
25	(a)	Chelsea	D 2-2	Spencer, Jones	15,000		2	3	4	5	6		8	9	10						11			1			7		
28	(h)	Middlesbrough	W 1-0	Davies	10,021		2	3	4	5	6		8	9	10						11			1			7		
May 5	(a)	Middlesbrough	W 1-0	Davies	9,000		2	3	4	5	6			9	10						11	8		1			7		
App						38	41	40	40	42	40	5	31	37	40	27	13	3	3	4	11	8	9	4	2	2	20	1	1
Goals										1			3	20	14	7	3	1				3	4				2		

West Bromwich Albion 1922-3. Back row (left to right): Adams, Pennington, Jones, Guest (asst. trainer), Richardson, Pearson, Ashmore, Reed, Gopsill (trainer), Dutton. Middle: Bowser, McNeal, J.Smith, Morris, Magee, Gregory, Crisp. Front: Blood, Wilson, Davies, James.

1923-24

Division 1

Date		Opponent	Res	Score	Scorers	Att	Ashmore G	Smith J	Adams W	Magee T	Bowser S	McNeal R	Spencer J	Jones I	Davies S	Morris F	Fitton A	Glidden T	Richardson S	Carter J	Pearson H	Blood R	Smith H	Perry A	Reed F	Gregory H	Chamberlain H	Byers J	Dutton H	James G	Wilson C
Aug 25	(h)	Liverpool	W	2-0	Davies, Fitton	25,121	1	2	3	4	5	6	7	8	9	10	11														
27	(a)	Nottingham F	D	1-1	Davies	21,000	1	2	3	4	5	6	7	8	9	10	11														
Sep 1	(a)	Liverpool	D	0-0		40,000	1	2	3	4	5	6	7	8	9	10	11														
3	(h)	Nottingham F	W	3-2	Davies 2, Jones	26,909	1	2	3	4	5	6	7	8	9	10	11														
8	(a)	Arsenal	W	4-0	Jones, Davies 2 (2 pens), Fitton	35,233	1	2	3	4	5	6	7	8	9	10	11														
15	(a)	Arsenal	L	0-1		36,004	1	2	3	4	5	6		8	9	10	11	7													
22	(h)	Blackburn R	D	3-3	Morris 2, Jones	21,238	1	2	3	4	5	6		8	9	10	11	7													
29	(a)	Blackburn R	L	0-4		20,209	1	2	3		5	6		8	9	10	11	7		4											
Oct 6	(h)	Huddersfield T	L	2-4	Davies, Carter	17,041	1	2	3	4	5	6	7	10	9		11			8											
13	(a)	Huddersfield T	D	0-0		19,000	1	2	3	4	5	6			9	10	11	7		8											
20	(h)	Aston Villa	W	1-0	Morris	42,096	1	2	3	4	5	6			9	10	11	7		8											
27	(a)	Aston Villa	L	0-4		52,550	1	2	3	4	5	6			9	10	11	7		8											
Nov 3	(a)	Cardiff C	L	0-3		20,600	1	2	3	4	5	6			9	10	11	7		8											
10	(h)	Cardiff C	L	2-4	Blood 2 (1 pen)	15,143		2	3	4	5	6	7			10				8	1	9	11								
17	(a)	Everton	L	0-2		28,700	1	2	3	4	5	6	7			10				8		9	11								
24	(h)	Everton	W	5-0	Blood 3, Morris, Gregory	14,387	1	2		4		6	7			10				8		9		3	5	11					
Dec 1	(a)	Tottenham H	D	0-0		28,100	1	2		4		6	7			10				8		9		3	5	11					
8	(h)	Tottenham H	W	4-1	Carter 4	15,048	1	2		4		6	7			10				8		9		3	5	11					
15	(h)	Birmingham	D	0-0		24,786	1	2		4		6	7			10				8		9		3	5	11					
22	(a)	Birmingham	D	0-0		32,000	1	2		4		6	7		9	10				8				3	5	11					
25	(a)	Bolton W	L	0-2		20,000	1	2		4		6	7			10				8		9		3	5	11					
26	(h)	Bolton W	L	0-5		12,148	1	2		4		6	7	8		10						9		3	5	11					
29	(a)	Manchester C	D	3-3	Carter 2, Bowser	16,402	1	2		4	9	6	7			10				8					5	11	3				
Jan 5	(h)	Manchester C	W	2-1	Bowser, Morris	11,991	1	2		4	9	6	7			10				8				3	5	11					
19	(h)	Burnley	L	0-3		8,527	1	2		4		6	8	7		10	11			9				3	5						
26	(a)	Burnley	L	0-4		12,000	1	2				6	7		9	10			4	8				3	5			11			
Feb 9	(a)	Middlesbrough	W	1-0	Spencer	15,000	1	2				6	7		9	10			4	8				3	5			11			
16	(h)	Preston NE	L	1-2	Carter	10,024	1	2				6	7		9	10			4	8				3	5	11					
Mar 1	(h)	Chelsea	D	2-2	Byers, James	11,485		2					7	8					4		1			3	5			11	6	9	10
12	(a)	Chelsea	D	0-0		17,900		2		4						10		7			1			3	5			11	6	9	8
15	(a)	Newcastle U	D	1-1	Reed	20,000		2		4				8				7			1			3	5			11	6	9	10
19	(a)	Preston NE	W	2-1	Wilson, Dutton	12,100		2		4				8				7			1			3	5			11	6	9	10
22	(h)	Newcastle U	D	0-0		16,053		2				6		8				7			1			3	5			11	4	9	10
29	(a)	West Ham U	L	0-1		18,112		2		4				8				7			1			3	5			11	6	9	10
Apr 5	(h)	West Ham U	D	0-0		13,248	1	2		4			7	8								9		3	5			11	6		10
9	(h)	Middlesbrough	D	1-1	Blood	14,473	1	2		4			7	8								9		3	5			11	6		10
12	(h)	Notts C	W	5-0	James 2, Wilson 2 (1 pen), Jones	8,003	1	2		4			7	8										3	5	11			6	9	10
18	(a)	Sunderland	L	0-2		13,000	1	2		4			7	8										3	5	11			6	9	10
19	(a)	Notts C	L	0-1		20,000	1	2		4			7	8										3	5			11	6	9	10
21	(h)	Sunderland	W	3-1	James, Wilson, Gregory	12,033	1	2	3	4			7												5	10		11	6	9	8
26	(a)	Sheffield U	L	0-2		10,500	1	2		4			7	8										3	5			11	6	9	10
May 3	(h)	Sheffield U	W	3-1	Blood 3 (1 pen)	10,023	1	2		4			7	8		10						9		3	5	11			6		
App							35	42	16	36	17	29	27	21	21	30	14	12	5	19	7	11	2	25	27	14	1	13	14	11	13
Goals									2		1	4	7	5	2					8		9			1	2		1	1	4	4

Albion skipper Fred Reed (striped shirt) greets Wolves captain Jack Mitton before an FA Cup match in 1924.

Albion's classy outside-left Howard Gregory was nearing the end of his career with the club in 1923-4.

1924-25

Division 1

Date		Opponent	Res	Scorers	Att	Ashmore G	Smith J	Perry A	Magee T	Reed F	Dutton H	Spencer J	Jones I	Blood R	Wilson C	Byers J	McNeal R	Carter J	James G	Glidden T	Richardson S	Fitton A	Davies S	Rooke E	Baugh R	Gregory H	Pearson H	Adams W
Aug 30	(h)	Notts C	L 1-2	Blood	21,572	1	2	3	4	5	6	7	8	9	10	11												
Sep 1	(a)	Bolton W	D 1-1	Jones	25,000	1	2	3	4	5	6	7	8	9	10	11												
6	(a)	Everton	L 0-1		24,700	1	2	3	4	5		7	8	9	10	11	6											
8	(h)	Tottenham H	W 2-0	Blood, Wilson	20,880	1	2	3	4	5		7		9	10	11	6	8										
13	(h)	Sunderland	W 2-1	Wilson, James	24,166	1	2	3	4	5		7			10	11	6	8	9									
20	(a)	Cardiff C	W 1-0	Carter	21,000	1	2	3	4	5		7			10	11	6	8	9									
22	(a)	Tottenham H	W 1-0	James	37,000	1	2	3	4	5		7			10	11	6	8	9									
27	(h)	Preston NE	D 1-1	Wilson	30,183	1	2	3	4	5		7			10	11	6	8	9									
Oct 4	(a)	Burnley	W 1-0	Carter	30,000	1	2	3	4	5		7			10	11	6	8	9									
11	(h)	Leeds U	W 3-1	James 2, Carter	21,332	1	2	3	4	5					10	11	6	8	9	7								
18	(h)	Birmingham	D 1-1	James	35,617	1	2	3	4	5		7			10	11	6	8	9									
25	(a)	Aston Villa	L 0-1		48,126	1	2	3	4	5		7			10	11	6	8	9									
Nov 1	(h)	Huddersfield T	W 1-0	James	15,683	1	2	3	4	5			7		10	11		8	9		6							
8	(a)	Blackburn R	L 0-1		16,000	1	2	3	4	5			7		10			8	9		6	11						
15	(h)	West Ham U	W 4-1	Carter, Wilson 3	23,959	1	2	3	4	5					10	11		8		7	6	9						
22	(a)	Sheffield U	L 0-2		15,100	1	2	3	4	5					10	11	6	8		7		9						
29	(h)	Newcastle U	W 2-0	Carter, Byers	13,141	1	2	3	4	5	6				10	11		8	9	7								
Dec 6	(a)	Liverpool	D 1-1	James	18,000	1	2	3	4	5	6				10	11		8	9	7								
13	(h)	Nottingham F	W 5-1	James 4, Carter	16,227	1	2	3	4	5	6				10	11		8	9	7								
20	(a)	Bury	W 2-0	James 2	12,000	1	2	3	4	5	6				10	11		8	9	7								
25	(a)	Manchester C	W 2-1	James, Carter	20,000	1	2	3	4	5	6				10	11		8	9	7								
26	(h)	Manchester C	W 3-1	James 2, Carter	41,990	1	2	3	4	5					10	11		8	9	7	6							
27	(a)	Notts C	W 2-0	James, Smith (og)	12,000	1	2	3							10	11	6		9	7	4		8	5				
Jan 3	(h)	Everton	W 3-0	James 2, Wilson	21,773	1	2	3	4	5					10	11		8	9	7	6							
17	(a)	Sunderland	L 0-3		33,000	1	2	3	4	5					10	11		8	9	7	6							
24	(h)	Cardiff C	W 1-0	Wilson	22,508	1	2	3	4	5					10	11		8	9	7	6							
Feb 7	(h)	Burnley	L 1-4	James	24,492	1	2	3	4	5					10	11		8	9	7	6							
12	(a)	Preston NE	W 2-1	Carter, Wilson	16,000	1	2		4	5					10	11		8	9	7	6				3			
14	(a)	Leeds U	W 1-0	Carter	18,500	1	2		4	5					10	11		8	9	7	6				3			
28	(h)	Aston Villa	W 4-1	Davies, James 3	22,123	1	2		4	5					10	11			9	7	6		8		3			
Mar 11	(a)	Huddersfield T	D 1-1	Carter	21,000	1	2		4	5					10			8	9	7	6				3	11		
14	(h)	Blackburn R	D 1-1	James	21,858	1	2		4	5	6				10			8	9	7					3	11		
16	(a)	Birmingham	D 0-0		30,000	1	2		4	5			10					8	9	7	6	11			3			
21	(a)	West Ham U	L 1-2	Wilson	10,900		2		4	5			10					8	9	7	6	11			3		1	
30	(h)	Sheffield U	W 2-1	Glidden, Davies	9,892	1	2		4									8	9	7	6	11	10	5	3			
Apr 4	(a)	Newcastle U	W 1-0	Carter	25,400	1	2			5	4				10	11		8	9	7	6				3			
11	(h)	Liverpool	D 0-0		13,157	1	2		4	5					10	11		8	9	7	6				3			
13	(h)	Arsenal	W 2-0	Glidden, Wilson	23,285	1	2		4	5					10	11		8	9	7	6				3			
14	(a)	Arsenal	L 0-2		21,000	1	2		4	5					10	11		8	9	7	6				3			
18	(a)	Nottingham F	W 1-0	Carter	6,000	1	2		4	5					10			8	9	7	6	11						3
25	(h)	Bury	D 1-1	James	15,277	1	2		4	5					10	11		8	9	7	6				3			
May 2	(h)	Bolton W	D 0-0		13,383	1	2		4	5					10	11		8	9	7	6				3			
				App		41	42	27	40	40	9	11	6	4	40	34	12	37	36	29	23	6	5	2	14	2	1	1
				Goals									1	2	11	1		13	25	2			2					

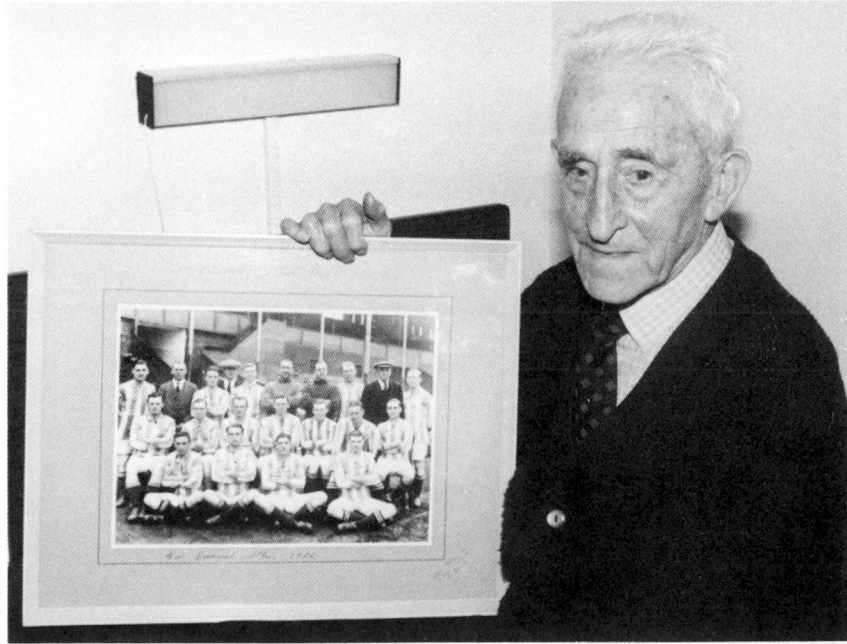

Bobby Blood, Albion's goalscoring centre-forward of the 1920s, pictured (left) in his playing days and (right) as he was in 1987, a hail and hearty 93.

1925-26

Division 1

Date		Opponent	Result	Scorers	Att	Ashmore G	Smith J	Baugh R	Magee T	Reed F	Richardson S	Glidden T	Carter J	James G	Wilson C	Byers J	Adams W	Dutton H	Jones I	Davies S	Rooke E	Parry A	Fitton A	Scroson T	Spencer J	Finch R	Evans J	Darnell L
Aug 29	(a)	Huddersfield T	D 1-1	James	30,000	1	2	3	4	5	6	7	8	9	10	11												
Sep 2	(h)	Everton	D 1-1	Wilson	29,856	1	2	3	4	5	6	7	8	9	10	11												
5	(h)	Sunderland	L 2-5	Wilson, Jones	21,520	1		3		5	4	7			10	11	2	6	8	9								
12	(a)	Blackburn R	W 2-1	Dutton, Davies	25,000	1	2	3			4	7		9		11		6	8	10	5							
16	(a)	Everton	L 0-4		40,000	1	2	3			4	7		9		11		6	8	10	5							
23	(h)	Manchester C	W 4-1	Davies 2, Wilson 2	8,287	1	2			5	4	7		9	8			6		10		3	11					
26	(a)	Birmingham	L 0-3		34,850	1	2			5	4	7		9	8			6		10		3	11					
Oct 3	(h)	Aston Villa	D 1-1	Davies	52,332	1	2	3		5	4	7	8		10			6		9			11					
10	(h)	Sheffield U	W 2-0	Wilson, Davies	15,973	1	2	3		5	4	7	8		10			6		9			11					
17	(a)	Leicester C	L 0-3		20,500	1	2	3		5	4	7	8		10			6		9			11					
24	(h)	West Ham U	W 7-1	Davies 3 (1 pen), Glidden, Wilson, Carter 2	20,851	1	2	3		5	4	7	8		10			6		9			11					
31	(a)	Bolton W	D 2-2	Carter, James	16,000		2	3		5	4	7	8	9	10			6					11	1				
Nov 7	(h)	Notts C	D 4-4	Carter 2, Davies, Wilson	10,406	1	2	3		5	4	7	8		10			6		9			11					
9	(h)	Bury	W 4-0	Davies 2, Fitton, Carter	10,922	1	2	3		5	4	7	8		10			6		9			11					
14	(a)	Liverpool	L 0-2		40,000	1	2	3		5	4	7	8		10			6		9			11					
21	(h)	Burnley	W 5-3	Davies 2, Carter, Glidden, Wilson	15,133	1	2	3		5	4	7	8		10			6		9			11					
28	(a)	Leeds U	W 1-0	Glidden	15,200	1	2			5	4	7	8	9	10		3	6					11					
Dec 5	(h)	Newcastle U	W 4-0	Davies 2, Wilson, Fitton	11,260	1	2			5	4	7	8		10		3	6		9			11					
12	(a)	Arsenal	L 0-1		35,000	1	2			5	4	7	8		10		3	6		9			11					
19	(h)	Manchester U	W 5-1	Carter, Glidden, Davies 2, James	16,554	1	2			5	4	7	8	9			3	6		10			11					
25	(a)	Cardiff C	L 2-3	Davies 2	15,225	1	2			5	4	7	8	9			3	6		10			11					
26	(h)	Cardiff C	W 3-0	Carter 2, James	31,554	1	2			5	4	7	8	9			3	6		10			11					
Jan 1	(a)	Manchester C	L 1-3	Carter	23,030	1	2			5	4	7	8	9			3	6		10			11					
2	(h)	Huddersfield T	D 2-2	Reed, Glidden (pen)	15,000	1	2			5	4	7	8	9			3	6		10			11					
16	(a)	Sunderland	L 0-4		20,000	1		2	4	5		7	8	9	10	11	3	6										
23	(h)	Blackburn R	D 1-1	Byers	11,105	1		2	4	5			8		10	11	3	6		9							7	
Feb 6	(h)	Birmingham	W 5-1	James 2, Wilson 3	23,104	1		2	7	5	4		8	9	10	11	3	6										
13	(a)	Aston Villa	L 1-2	Byers	46,200	1	2	3	7	5	4		8	9	10	11		6										
20	(a)	Sheffield U	L 2-3	Carter 2	11,400		2	3	7	5	4		8		10	11		6		9				1				
24	(a)	Bury	L 0-2		10,000	1	2	3	7	5	4		8		10	11		6		9								
27	(h)	Leicester C	W 3-1	Glidden (pen), James, Byers	19,532	1		3	4	5	6	7	8	9		11				10		2						
Mar 6	(a)	West Ham U	L 0-3		25,000	1		3	4		6	7	8	9		11				10		2			5			
13	(h)	Bolton W	L 0-3		14,388	1		3	4	5		7	8	9		11		6		10		2						
20	(a)	Notts C	D 0-0		12,000	1		3	4	5		7	8	9		11					6	2						10
27	(h)	Liverpool	L 0-3		10,503	1		3	4	5		7	8	9		11					6	2						10
Apr 2	(a)	Tottenham H	L 2-3	James, Wilson	45,000	1		3	4	5		7	8	9	10	11					6	2						
3	(a)	Burnley	W 4-3	James 2, Wilson, Reed	21,700	1		3	4	5	6	7	8	9	10	11						2						
5	(a)	Tottenham H	W 1-0	Wilson (pen)	10,180	1		3	4	5	6	7	8	9	10	11										2		
10	(h)	Leeds U	W 3-0	Hart (og), Carter, Wilson	13,065	1		3	4	5	6	7	8	9	10	11										2		
17	(a)	Newcastle U	L 0-3		12,500	1		3	4	5	6	7	8	9	10	11										2		
24	(h)	Arsenal	W 2-1	James, Wilson	16,802	1		3	4	5	6	7	8	9	10	11										2		
May 1	(a)	Manchester U	L 2-3	James, Magee	11,198	1		3	4	5	6	7	8	9	10	11										2		
App						40	26	32	20	39	36	37	37	28	30	23	12	29	3	26	5	9	19	2	1	5	1	2
Goals									1	2		6	14	12	17	3		1	1	19			2					

Albion's half-back line of Tommy Magee, skipper Fred Reed and Sammy Richardson played together 24 times in League and Cup games in 1924-5, and on nine occasions in 1925-6.

1926-27

Division 1

Date		Opponent	Result	Scorers	Att	Ashmore G	Perry A	Baugh R	Magee T	Reed F	Howarth N	Glidden T	Carter J	Davies S	Wilson C	Byers J	James G	Dutton H	Short S	Adams W	Fitton A	Sproson T	Rooke E	Richardson S	Evans J	Finch R	Corbett F	Ashurst W	Shaw G	Poxton J
Aug 28	(h)	Sunderland	W 3-0	Davies, Carter, Byers	31,132	1	2	3	4	5	6	7	8	9	10	11														
Aug 30	(a)	Huddersfield T	L 1-4	Wilson	32,500	1	2	3	4	5	6	7	8	9	10	11														
Sep 4	(a)	Cardiff C	D 1-1	Byers	18,000	1	2	3	4	5	6	7	8	10		11	9													
Sep 6	(h)	Everton	W 3-2	Davies 2, Carter	35,330	1	2	3	4	5	6	7	8	10		11	9													
Sep 11	(a)	Bury	L 3-7	Carter, James 2	15,000	1	2	3	4	5	6	7	8	10		11	9													
Sep 15	(a)	Everton	D 0-0		42,000	1	2	3	4	5	6	7		10	8	11	9													
Sep 18	(h)	Birmingham	L 1-2	Jones (og)	26,803	1	2	3	4	5		7		8	10	11		6	9											
Sep 25	(a)	Tottenham H	L 0-3		40,003	1	2		4	5	6	7		8	10	11	9		3											
Oct 2	(h)	West Ham U	L 1-3	Fitton	24,737	1	2		4	5	6	7	8		10		9			3	11									
Oct 9	(a)	Sheffield W	L 1-2	Glidden	18,000	1		2	4	5	6	7	8	9	10					3	11									
Oct 16	(h)	Bolton W	D 1-1	Glidden	24,246	1		2	4	5	6	7	8	9	10	11				3										
Oct 23	(a)	Aston Villa	L 0-2		49,952		3	2	4		6	9	8	7	10	11						1	5							
Oct 30	(h)	Burnley	W 4-2	Carter 2, Byers, Magee	20,957		3	2	7		6	9	8		10	11						1		4	5					
Nov 6	(a)	Newcastle U	L 2-5	Glidden, Wilson	30,000		3	2	7		6	9		8	10	11						1		4	5					
Nov 13	(h)	Leeds U	L 2-4	James 2	15,103		3	2	7		6				10	11	9					1		4	5					
Nov 20	(a)	Liverpool	L 1-2	Wilson	21,000	1			7		6	8		10	11	9	4							5	2		3			
Nov 27	(h)	Arsenal	L 1-3	Carter	16,351	1			7		6	9	8		10	11		4						5		3	2			
Dec 4	(a)	Sheffield U	L 1-2	James	20,000	1			4	5	6	7	8	10			9		11									2	3	
Dec 11	(h)	Derby C	W 3-1	Davies 2, Magee	19,557	1			4	5		7	8	10			9		11				6					2	3	
Dec 18	(a)	Manchester U	L 0-2		21,489	1			4	5			8	7	10		9		11				6					2	3	
Dec 25	(a)	Leicester C	L 0-5		25,017	1			4	5		7	8	10			9		11				6					2	3	
Dec 27	(h)	Leicester C	L 0-1		31,286	1			4		6	7	8	9				10	2	11				5					3	
Jan 1	(h)	Huddersfield T	D 2-2	Short 2	30,998	1			4		6	7	8	9				10	2	11				5					3	
Jan 15	(a)	Sunderland	L 1-4	Wilson	28,500	1			4		6	7	8	9	10				11					5				2	3	
Jan 29	(h)	Bury	W 3-1	Davies 2, Carter	10,043	1			4		6	7	8	9	10				11					5				2	3	
Feb 5	(a)	Birmingham	L 0-1		34,000	1			4		6	7	8	9	10				11					5				2	3	
Feb 12	(h)	Tottenham H	W 5-0	Davies 2, Carter 2, Short	15,998	1			4			7	8	9					11				10	5	6			2	3	
Feb 19	(h)	West Ham U	W 2-1	Rooke, Short	19,849	1			4			7	8	9					11				10	5	6			2	3	
Feb 21	(h)	Cardiff C	L 1-2	Glidden	10,068	1			4			7	8	9					11				10	5	6			2	3	
Feb 26	(h)	Sheffield W	D 2-2	Carter, Short	12,006	1			4			7	8	9					11				10	5	6			2	3	
Mar 5	(a)	Bolton W	D 1-1	Carter	13,076	1			4		6	7	8	9					11				10	5				2	3	
Mar 12	(h)	Aston Villa	W 6-2	Glidden 2, Carter, Davies 2, Short	50,392	1			4		6	7	8	9					11				10	5				2	3	
Mar 19	(a)	Burnley	L 1-2	Davies	11,408	1			4		6	7	8	9					11				10	5				2	3	
Mar 26	(h)	Newcastle U	W 4-2	Byers, Davies, Carter, Short (pen)	22,135	1			4		6	7	8	9					11				10	5				2	3	
Apr 2	(a)	Leeds U	L 1-3	Carter	14,898	1			4		6	7	8			11	9						10	5				2	3	
Apr 9	(h)	Liverpool	L 0-1		20,268	1			4		6	7	8	9		11							10	5				2	3	
Apr 16	(a)	Arsenal	L 1-4	Davies	27,000	1			4		6	7	8	10		11	9							5				2	3	
Apr 18	(h)	Blackburn R	W 2-0	Byers, Ashurst	14,383	1			4		6	7	8	10		11	9							5				2	3	
Apr 19	(a)	Blackburn R	D 0-0		9,965	1			4		6	7	8			11	9						10	5			3	2		
Apr 23	(h)	Sheffield U	W 1-0	James (pen)	13,104	1			4		6	7	8			11	9						10	5			3	2		
Apr 30	(a)	Derby C	L 1-2	Carter	9,000	1			4		6	7	8			11	9						10	5				2	3	
May 7	(h)	Manchester U	D 2-2	Magee, Davies	11,022	1			4		6	7	8	9									10	5				2	3	11
App						38	13	13	42	15	34	41	36	33	18	29	17	3	18	6	12	4	25	7	5	1	4	22	25	1
Goals							3				6	15	15	4	5	6		7		1		1	1						1	

Albion skipper Fred Reed (right) shaking hands with Sheffield United captain Billy Gillespie.

Stan Davies

1927-28

Division 2

Date		Opponent	Res	Scorers	Att	Sproson T	Baugh R	Shaw G	Magee T	Evans J	Howarth N	Glidden T	Carter J	Cookson J	Wilson C	Byers J	Finch R	Ashmore G	Fitton A	James G	Rooke E	Poxton J	Bytheway G	Pearson H	Short S	Chambers H	Bromage E	Corbett F	Edwards J	Rix J
Aug 27	(a)	Oldham A	L 1-3	Cookson	13,600	1	2	3	4	5	6	7	8	9	10	11														
31	(h)	Stoke C	L 2-4	Cookson, Byers	20,329	1	2	3	4	5	6	7	8	9	10	11														
Sep 3	(h)	Grimsby T	W 3-1	Carter 2, Wilson	16,615	1		3	4	5		7	8	9	10	11	2	6												
5	(a)	Stoke C	D 1-1	Cookson	20,000			3	4	5		7	8	9	10		2	6	1	11										
10	(a)	Reading	W 4-1	Cookson, Fitton, Glidden, Wilson	14,000			3	4	5		7	8	9	10		2	6	1	11										
17	(h)	Blackpool	W 6-3	Cookson 6 (1 pen)	20,203			3	4	5		7	8	9	10		2	6	1	11										
24	(a)	Chelsea	D 1-1	Carter	40,098			3	4	5		7	8	9	10		2	6	1	11										
Oct 1	(h)	Clapton O	W 4-1	Fitton, Carter, Glidden, Cookson	21,324			3	4	5		7	8	9	10		2	6	1	11										
8	(a)	Wolves	L 1-4	Evans	41,000			3	4	5		7	8		10		2	6	1	11	9									
15	(a)	Bristol C	W 1-0	Glidden	25,000			3	7	5		9	8		10		2	6	1	11	4									
22	(h)	Swansea T	W 5-2	Fitton, Carter 2, Cookson, Wilson	22,779			3	4	5		7	8	9	10		2	6	1	11										
29	(a)	Fulham	L 1-3	Cookson	20,500			3	4	5		7	8	9	10		2	6	1	11										
Nov 5	(h)	Barnsley	D 1-1	Wilson	18,350			3	4	5		7	8	9	10		2		1				6	11						
12	(a)	Preston NE	D 3-3	Cookson, Glidden 2	11,895			3	4	5		7	8	9	10		2		1				6	11						
19	(h)	Hull C	D 1-1	Glidden	8,116			3	4	5		7	8	9	10		2	6	1				11							
26	(a)	Leeds U	W 2-1	Carter 2	20,014			3	4	5		9	8		10		2	6	1				11	7						
Dec 3	(h)	Nottingham F	L 2-3	Carter, Glidden	10,205			3	4	5		9	8		10		2	6	1				11	7						
10	(a)	Manchester C	L 1-3	Glidden	40,000			3	4	5		10	8	9			2	6	1				11	7						
17	(h)	South Shields	W 3-0	Glidden, Evans, Cookson	11,376			3	4	5		10	8	9		11	2	6					7	1						
24	(a)	Port Vale	L 1-4	Cookson	13,560			3	4	5		10	8	9		11	2	6					7	1						
26	(h)	Notts C	D 2-2	Cookson, Poxton	28,038			3	4	5	6	10	8	9			2						11	7	1					
27	(a)	Notts C	L 0-3		16,000			3		5	6	7	8	9	10		2	4					11		1					
31	(h)	Oldham A	D 0-0		9,203			3	4	5	6	10	8	9			2		1	11			7							
Jan 7	(a)	Grimsby T	W 6-0	Cookson 4, Short, Bytheway	10,000			3	4	5	6		8	9			2		1	11			7		10					
21	(h)	Reading	W 5-3	Inglis (og), Cookson 4	15,014			3	4	5	6		8	9			2		1	11			7		10					
28	(a)	Blackpool	L 3-4	Cookson 2, Short	12,500			3	4	5	6		8	9			2		1	11			7		10					
Feb 4	(h)	Chelsea	W 3-0	Short 2, Carter	25,865			3	4	5	6	7	8	9			2		1	11					10					
11	(a)	Clapton O	D 0-0		11,600			3	4	5	6	7	8	9			2		1	11					10					
18	(a)	Wolves	W 4-0	Cookson 2, Carter, Wilson	37,342			3	4	5	6	7	8	9	10		2		1	11										
25	(h)	Bristol C	D 0-0		32,115			3	4	5	6	7	8	9			2			11				1	10					
Mar 3	(a)	Swansea T	L 2-3	Cookson 2	16,000			3	4	5	6	7	8	9			2			11				1	10					
10	(h)	Fulham	W 4-0	Cookson, Chambers, Glidden 2	17,029			3	4	5	6	7	8	9			2		1	11						10				
17	(a)	Barnsley	W 4-2	Carter, Cookson 2, Glidden	10,109			3	4	5	6	7	8	9			2		1							10	11			
24	(h)	Preston NE	L 2-4	Carter, Cookson	28,055			3	4	5	6	7	8	9			2		1							10	11			
31	(h)	Hull C	D 1-1	Bromage	20,000			2	4	5	6	7		9					1							10	11	3	8	
Apr 7	(h)	Leeds U	L 0-1		25,180			3	4	5	6	7	8	9			2		1							10	11			
9	(a)	Southampton	L 2-3	Glidden, Carter	16,800			3	4		6	7	8	9			2		1			5				10	11			
10	(h)	Southampton	W 2-1	Cookson, Short	20,046			3	4		6	7	8	9			2					5		1	10		11			
14	(a)	Nottingham F	W 2-0	Cookson, Carter	7,000			3	4		6		8	9			2					5	7	1		10	11			
21	(h)	Manchester C	D 1-1	Chambers	14,238			3	4		6	7	8	9			2					5		1		10	11			
28	(a)	South Shields	W 3-2	Bromage, Dunn (og), Cookson	10,700			3	4		6		8	9			2					5	7	1		10	11			
May 5	(h)	Port Vale	D 0-0		10,095			3	4		6		8	9			2					5	7	1		10	11			
App						3	2	42	41	36	23	39	38	38	19	5	39	17	28	19	1	9	8	13	11	10	8	10	1	1
Goals										2		13	15	38	5	1			3			1	1		5	2	2			

George Shaw signed from Huddersfield Town for a record fee in 1926.

Jack Rix, 'tough-nut' wing-half from 1927-39.

1928-29

Division 2

Date		Opponent	Res	Score	Scorers	Att	Pearson H	Finch R	Shaw G	Magee T	Evans J	Howarth N	Glidden T	Carter J	Cookson J	Chambers H	Fitton A	Ashmore G	Wood S	Darnell L	James G	Corbett F	Rix J	Fryer E	Short S	Bytheway G	Leedham F	Dale R	Richardson W	Webster H	Edwards J
Aug 25	(h)	Clapton O	W	3-1	Chambers, Glidden, Carter	19,756	1	2	3	4	5	6	7	8	9	10	11														
27	(a)	Notts C	L	1-3	Howarth	12,000	1	2	3	4	5	6	7	8	9	10	11														
Sep 1	(a)	Stoke C	L	1-4	Glidden	20,103		2	3	4	5	6	7	8	9	10	11	1													
3	(h)	Notts C	L	1-3	Cookson	15,221		2	3	4	5	6	7	8	9	10		1	11												
8	(h)	Grimsby T	W	1-0	Glidden (pen)	15,132		2	3	4	5		7	8		10		1	11	6	9										
15	(a)	Bradford	L	1-4	Glidden	9,014		2		4	5		7	8		10		1	11		9	3	6								
22	(h)	Swansea T	W	5-1	Carter 2, Short, James 2	12,333		2	3	4			7	8		5		1	11		9				6	10					
29	(a)	Blackpool	W	2-0	Short, Wood	10,516		2	3	4			7	8		5		1	11		9				6	10					
Oct 6	(h)	Chelsea	W	3-0	Bytheway, Short, Glidden	16,447		2	3	4			7	8		5		1	11		9				6	10					
13	(a)	Barnsley	L	0-2		8,689		2	3	4			7	8		5		1	11		9				6	10					
20	(a)	Millwall	D	2-2	Short, Glidden	10,600		2	3	4			7	8		5		1	11	6	9				10						
27	(h)	Port Vale	W	3-1	James, Glidden, Short	12,725		2	3	4			7	8		5		1	11	6	9				10						
Nov 3	(a)	Hull C	L	1-4	James	10,007		2	3	4			7	8		5		1	11	6	9				10						
10	(h)	Wolves	L	0-2		24,902		2	3	4			7	8		5		1	11	6	9				10						
17	(a)	Reading	L	3-5	Cookson 3	10,715		2	3	4				8	9	5		1	11	6					7	10					
24	(h)	Preston NE	D	1-1	Glidden	8,048		2	3	4			7	8	9	5		1	11	6						10					
Dec 1	(a)	Middlesbrough	D	1-1	Glidden	8,200		2	3	4			7	8	9	10		1	11	6									5		
8	(h)	Oldham A	W	1-0	Cookson	6,994		2	3	4				8	9	10		1	11	6							7		5		
15	(a)	Southampton	D	1-1	Carter	13,530		2	3	4				8	9	10		1	11	6							7		5		
22	(h)	Tottenham H	W	3-2	Shaw (pen), Cookson, Carter	11,565		2	3	4			7	8	9	10		1	11	6									5		
25	(h)	Bristol C	D	1-1	Glidden	11,303		2	3	4			7	8	9	10		1	11	6									5		
26	(a)	Bristol C	W	3-2	Wood 2, Cookson	10,812		2	3	4			7	8	9	10		1	11	6									5		
29	(a)	Clapton O	W	2-0	Cookson, Glidden	6,400		2	3	4			7	8	9	10		1	11	6									5		
Jan 5	(h)	Stoke C	L	2-3	Magee, Cookson	20,067		2	3	4			7	8	9	10		1	11	6									5		
19	(a)	Grimsby T	L	1-3	Cookson	9,727		2	3	4			7	8	9	10		1	11	6									5		
Feb 2	(a)	Swansea T	L	1-6	Carter	10,000		2	3	4			7	8	9	10		1	11	6									5		
9	(h)	Blackpool	D	2-2	Carter 2	12,094		2	3	4			7	8	9	10		1	11	6									5		
23	(h)	Barnsley	W	6-2	Shaw (pen), Glidden 2, Carter, Cookson 2	13,810		2	3	4			7	8	9	10		1	11	6									5		
Mar 9	(a)	Port Vale	L	1-8	James	8,000		2	3	7				8		10		1	11	4	9							6	5		
11	(h)	Bradford	L	1-2	Cookson	9,952			3				7	9	8		11			6		2					10	4	5	1	
16	(h)	Hull C	W	2-0	Cookson, Chambers	7,138	1		3		5		7		9	10	11			6		2							4		8
23	(a)	Wolves	W	1-0	Cookson	21,000	1	2	3		5		7	8	9	10	11			6									4		
29	(a)	Nottingham F	W	2-1	Cookson 2	12,289	1	2	3	4	5		7	8	9		11			6											10
30	(h)	Reading	W	5-0	Cookson 2, Fitton, Edwards, Glidden	10,382	1	2	3	4			7	8	9		11			6									5		10
Apr 1	(h)	Nottingham F	W	3-0	Glidden, Cookson, Fitton	12,130	1	2	3				7	8	9		11			6								5	4		10
6	(a)	Preston NE	D	1-1	Edwards	13,100	1	2	3		5		7	8	9		11			6									4		10
10	(h)	Millwall	W	3-2	Edwards, Glidden, Carter	13,532	1	2	3		5		7	8	9		11			6									4		10
13	(a)	Middlesbrough	D	1-1	Glidden	14,068	1	2	3		5		7	8	9		11			6									4		10
17	(a)	Chelsea	W	5-2	Glidden 3, Carter, Evans	20,000	1	2	3		5		7	8	9		11			6									4		10
20	(a)	Oldham A	L	0-3		16,000	1	2	3		5		7	8	9		11			6									4		10
27	(h)	Southampton	W	3-1	Cookson, Glidden, Carter	10,024	1	2	3		5		7	8	9		11			6									4		10
May 4	(a)	Tottenham H	L	0-2		17,233	1	2	3		5		7	8	9		11			6									4		10
App							14	39	42	31	16	4	40	36	31	32	14	27	27	27	11	3	1	4	11	2	4	10	24	1	11
Goals									2	1	1	1	21	12	21	2	2		3		5				5	1					3

Tommy Glidden

George Shaw

104

1929-30

Division 2

Date		Opponent	Result	Scorers	Att.	Pearson H	Finch R	Shaw G	Richardson W	Evans J	Darnell L	Glidden T	Carter J	Cookson J	Cresswell F	Wood S	Ashmore G	Magee T	Edwards J	Adams J	Fitton A	Boston H	Corbett F	Richardson WG	Trentham H	Dale R	Murphy J	Rix J
Aug 31	(a)	Wolves	W 4-2	Cookson 2, Carter, Shaw	25,961	1	2	3	4	5	6	7	8	9	10	11												
Sep 2	(h)	Oldham A	L 0-3		25,221	1	2	3	4	5	6	7	8	9	10	11												
7	(h)	Bradford	W 5-0	Cresswell, Cookson 3, Evans	22,997	1	2	3	4	5	6	7	8	9	10	11												
9	(a)	Southampton	L 2-3	Cookson 2	20,035	1	2	3	4	5	6	7	8	9	10	11												
14	(a)	Barnsley	D 2-2	Wood, Glidden	9,804	1	2	3	4	5	6	7	8	9	10	11												
21	(h)	Blackpool	W 5-1	Carter 2, Cookson 2, Glidden	16,515	1	2	3	4	5	6	7	8	9	10	11												
28	(a)	Bury	L 2-3	Cookson, Shaw (pen)	9,000	1	2	3	4	5	6	7	8	9	10	11												
Oct 5	(h)	Chelsea	W 2-0	Cookson, Glidden	19,317	1	2	3	4	5	6	7	8	9	10	11												
12	(a)	Nottingham F	W 2-0	Cookson, Glidden	16,000	1	2	3	4	5	6	7	8	9	10	11												
19	(a)	Bradford C	D 2-2	Glidden 2	12,000	1	2	3	4	5	6	7	8	9	10	11												
26	(h)	Swansea T	W 6-2	Glidden 4, Cresswell, Carter	21,070	1	2	3	4	5	6	7	8	9	10	11												
Nov 2	(a)	Cardiff C	L 2-3	Carter, Cresswell	15,027		2	3	4	5	6	7	8	9	10	11	1											
9	(h)	Preston NE	W 2-0	Carter 2	18,869		2	3		5	6	7	8	9	10	11	1	4										
16	(a)	Bristol C	L 1-2	Shaw (pen)	20,000		2	3	4	5	6	7	8	9		11	1		10									
23	(h)	Notts C	W 4-2	Carter, Glidden, Evans, Cookson	15,118		2	3	4	5	6	7	8	9	10	11	1											
30	(a)	Reading	D 2-2	Cookson 2	10,201		2	3	4	5	6	7	8	9	10	11	1											
Dec 7	(h)	Charlton A	D 1-1	Cookson	10,886		2	3	4	5	6	7	8	9	10	11	1											
14	(a)	Hull C	L 2-3	Cookson, Carter	16,000		2	3	4	5	6	7	8	9								10	1	11				
21	(h)	Stoke C	L 2-3	Boston, Cookson	11,809		2	3		5	6		8	9		11		4			7	10	1					
25	(a)	Millwall	L 1-2	Carter	18,000		2	3		5	6	7	8	9	10	11		4					1					
26	(h)	Millwall	W 6-2	Carter 2, Glidden 2, Richardson, Wood	24,032		2	3		5	6	7	8			11		4				10	1	9				
28	(h)	Wolves	W 7-3	Evans, Cresswell 2, Glidden, Carter 2, Shaw (og)	20,211		2	3		5	6	7	8		10	11		4		1				9				
Jan 1	(a)	Oldham A	L 0-5		11,000		2	3		5	6	7	8		10	11		4		1				9				
4	(a)	Bradford	L 1-5	Carter	10,450		2	3		5	6	7	8	9	10	11		4		1								
18	(h)	Barnsley	W 4-2	Shaw (pen), Richardson, Cresswell, Carter	8,138		2	3	4	5	6	7	8	9	10	11	1											
Feb 1	(h)	Bury	W 5-1	Fitton, Evans, Glidden, Carter 2	10,445		2	3	4	5	6	7	8	9	10		1				11							
8	(a)	Chelsea	L 0-2		20,000		2	3	4	5	6	7	8	9	10		1				11							
22	(h)	Bradford C	W 4-2	Carter, Glidden, Cookson 2	11,770		2	3	4	5	6	7	8	9	10		1				11							
Mar 1	(a)	Swansea T	L 0-1		8,000		2	3	4	5	6		8	9	10		1				11			7				
5	(a)	Blackpool	L 0-1		7,000		2	3		5	6	7	8	9	10	11		4		1								
8	(h)	Cardiff C	L 0-2		5,889		2	3		5	6	7	8	9	10	11		4		1								
15	(a)	Preston NE	D 2-2	Wood, Glidden	5,389	1	2	3		5	6	7	8	9	10	11									4			
19	(h)	Nottingham F	L 1-3	Wood	1,495	1	2	3		5	6	7	8	9	10	11		4										
22	(h)	Bristol C	W 2-0	Cookson, Evans	5,060	1	2	3		5	6		8	9		11		4			7	10						
29	(a)	Notts C	L 1-2	Cookson	6,000	1	2	3			6		8	9		11		4			7	10				5		
Apr 5	(h)	Reading	W 1-0	Edwards	8,020	1	2	3			6		8	9		11		4	10		7					5		
12	(a)	Charlton A	W 1-0	Wood	12,106	1	2	3			6		8	9		11		4	10		7					5		
18	(a)	Tottenham H	W 2-0	Wood, Boston	12,000	1	2	3			6		8	9		11		4			7	10				5		
19	(h)	Hull C	W 7-1	Glidden 2, Cookson 4, Boston	10,036	1	2	3			6		8	9		11		4			7	10				5		
21	(h)	Tottenham H	W 4-3	Cookson, Wood, Reddish (og), Glidden	12,908	1	2	3		5	6		8	9		11		4	10		7							
26	(a)	Stoke C	W 3-0	Cookson 2, Edwards	8,012	1	2	3		5			8	9		11		4	10		7						6	
May 3	(h)	Southampton	W 5-1	Cookson 4, Edwards	14,685		2	3		5			8	9		11	1	4	10		7						6	
					App	21	38	41	42	30	28	41	27	34	30	35	12	17	12	9	7	11	4	9	1	9	2	2
					Goals			4	5			20	19	33	6	7			3		1	3		2				

Jimmy 'Iron' Edwards, whose 12 games at inside-left produced three goals.

England international inside-right Joe Carter scored 19 goals in 27 League games.

105

1930-31

Division 2

Date		Opponent	Result	Scorers	Att	Pearson H	Finch R	Shaw G	Magee T	Richardson W	Rix J	Boston H	Glidden T	Cookson J	Edwards J	Wood S	Trentham H	Carter J	Richardson WG	Sandford E	Fitton A	Raw H	Murphy J	Bytheway G
Aug 30	(h)	Bristol C	W 3-0	Glidden 2, Edwards	11,037	1	2	3	4	5	6	7	8	9	10	11								
Sep 1	(a)	Charlton A	W 4-0	Cookson, Wood, Pitcairn (og), Boston	13,141	1		2	4	5	6	7	8	9	10	11	3							
6	(a)	Cardiff C	W 6-3	Cookson 4, Carter, Boston	12,088	1		2	4	5		7	8	9	6	11	3	10						
8	(h)	Wolves	W 1-0	Shaw (pen)	18,126	1		2	4	5		7	8	9	6	11	3	10						
13	(h)	Everton	L 1-2	Cookson	23,517	1	2	3	4	5		7	8	9	6	11		10						
17	(a)	Bradford C	W 3-2	Cookson, Glidden, Boston	15,120	1	2	3		5	4	7	8	9	6	11		10						
20	(a)	Bury	D 2-2	Carter 2	7,270	1	2	3		5	4	7	8	9	6	11		10						
27	(h)	Plymouth A	L 1-2	Cookson	15,938	1	2	3		5	4	7	8	9	6	11		10						
Oct 4	(a)	Swansea T	D 1-1	Carter	19,988	1		2		5	4	7	8	9	6	11	3	10						
11	(h)	Wolves	W 2-1	Carter, Cookson	40,065	1		2		5	4	7	8	9	6	11	3	10						
18	(a)	Southampton	D 1-1	Carter	12,138	1		2		5	4	7	8	9	6	11	3	10						
25	(h)	Reading	W 1-0	Wood	19,112	1		2		5	4	7	8	9	6	11	3	10						
Nov 1	(a)	Millwall	L 0-2		11,875	1		2		5	4	7	8	9	6	11	3	10						
8	(h)	Oldham A	W 2-0	Cookson, Carter	12,880	1		2	4	5			7	9	6	11	3	10	8					
15	(a)	Preston NE	W 3-2	Wood, Cookson, Sandford	15,064	1		2	4	5			7	9	6	11	3		8	10				
22	(h)	Tottenham H	L 0-2		18,078	1		2	4	5			7	9	6	11	3		8	10				
29	(a)	Nottingham F	W 6-1	Wood 2, Carter, Richardson 2, Sandford	15,207	1		2	4	5			7		6	11	3	8	9	10				
Dec 6	(h)	Burnley	W 2-0	Wood, Richardson	17,197	1		2	4	5			7		6	11	3	8	9	10				
13	(a)	Bradford	L 1-3	Richardson	9,005	1		2	4	5			7		6	11	3	8	9	10				
20	(h)	Stoke C	W 4-0	Richardson, Glidden 2, Magee	15,629	1		2	4	5		7	8		6	11	3		9	10				
25	(a)	Barnsley	D 0-0		10,052	1		2	4	5		7	8		6	11	3		9	10				
26	(h)	Barnsley	W 5-0	Richardson, Wood, Glidden 2, Shaw (pen)	22,981	1		2	4	5			7		6	11	3	8	9	10				
27	(a)	Bristol C	D 1-1	Richardson	20,996	1		2	4	5			7		6	11	3	8	9	10				
Jan 3	(h)	Cardiff C	W 3-2	Sandford, Carter, Richardson	24,028	1		2	4	5			7		6	11	3	8	9	10				
17	(a)	Everton	L 1-2	Glidden	33,199	1		2	4	5			7		6	11	3	8	9	10				
26	(h)	Bury	W 2-0	Glidden, Sandford	20,160	1		2	4	5			7		6	11	3	8	9	10				
31	(a)	Plymouth A	L 1-5	Wood	9,560	1		2	4	5		7			6	11	3	8	9	10				
Feb 7	(h)	Swansea T	D 0-0		15,977	1		2	4	5	6		7				3	8	9	10	11			
18	(a)	Wolves	W 4-1	Wood 2, Richardson 2	36,054	1		2	4	5			7	9	6	11	3		8	10				
21	(h)	Southampton	L 1-2	Richardson	20,682	1		2	4	5			7	9	6	11	3		8	10				
Mar 7	(h)	Millwall	D 0-0		17,763	1		2	4	5					6	11	3	8	9	10		7		
21	(h)	Preston NE	W 2-0	Glidden 2	26,558	1		2	4	5			7		6	11	3	8	9	10				
23	(a)	Oldham A	D 2-2	Raw, Glidden	6,305	1		2	4	5			7		6	11	3		9	10		8		
28	(a)	Tottenham H	D 2-2	Sandford, Glidden	56,012	1		2		5			7		6	11	3	8	9	10			4	
Apr 3	(a)	Port Vale	L 0-1		13,128	1		2		5			7		6	11	3	8	9	10			4	
4	(h)	Nottingham F	W 2-1	Wood 2	19,054	1		2	4	5			7		6	11	3	8	9	10				
6	(h)	Port Vale	W 4-1	Richardson 2, Glidden, Wood	23,806	1		2	4	5			7		6	11	3	8	9	10				
11	(h)	Burnley	L 1-2		24,133	1		2	4	5					6	11	3		9	10		8		7
15	(a)	Reading	W 3-0	Richardson 2, Sandford	10,510	1	2	3	4	5			7		6	11		8	9	10				
18	(h)	Bradford	D 1-1	Shaw (pen)	21,176	1	2	3	4	5			7		6	11		8	9	10				
30	(a)	Stoke C	W 1-0	Richardson	35,181	1		2	4	5			7		6	11	3	8	9	10				
May 2	(h)	Charlton A	W 3-2	Sandford, Glidden, Richardson	52,415	1	2	3	4	5			7		6	11		8	9	10				
					App	42	8	42	32	42	11	16	39	18	41	41	34	32	29	28	1	3	2	1
					Goals			3	1			3	15	11	1	13		9	18	7		1		

Bert Trentham, flanked by a policeman, shows the FA Cup to Albion fans before Albion's final League game of 1930-31.

1931-32

Division 1

Date	Opponent	Result	Scorers	Att	Pearson H	Shaw G	Trentham H	Magee T	Richardson W	Edwards J	Glidden T	Carter J	Richardson WG	Sandford E	Wood S	Foulkes H	Raw H	Murphy J	Boyes W	Cockson J	Rix J	Gale A	Adams J	Finch R	Robbins W
Aug 29	(a) Arsenal	W 1-0	Wood	55,380	1	2	3	4	5	6	7	8	9	10	11										
Sep 2	(a) Sunderland	L 1-2	Richardson	29,500	1	2		4	5	6	7	8	9	10	11	3									
5	(h) Blackpool	W 4-0	Richardson 2, Longden (og), Glidden	18,506	1	2	3	4	5	6	7	8	9	10	11										
7	(h) Sunderland	W 1-0	Wood	24,950	1	2	3	4	5	6	7	8	9	10	11										
12	(a) Sheffield W	L 0-1		16,700	1	2	3	4	5	6	7	8	9	10	11										
14	(h) Manchester C	D 1-1	Richardson	19,042	1	2	3	4	5	6	7	8	9	10	11										
19	(h) Blackburn R	W 4-1	Edwards, Sandford, Glidden 2	25,885	1	2	3	4	5	6	7	8	9	10	11										
23	(a) Manchester C	W 5-2	Richardson, Wood, Raw 2, Glidden	25,000	1	2	3	4	5	6	7		9	10	11		8								
26	(a) Portsmouth	W 1-0	Glidden (pen)	17,937	1	2	3	4	5	6	7		9	10	11		8								
Oct 3	(h) Derby C	W 4-0	Shaw (pen), Glidden, Sandford, Richardson	33,192	1	2	3	4	5	6	7		9	10	11		8								
10	(a) Huddersfield T	D 2-2	Richardson 2	25,000	1	2	3	4	5	6	7		9	10	11		8								
17	(h) Liverpool	L 1-2	Glidden	30,065	1	2	3	4	5	6	7		9	10	11		8								
24	(a) Bolton W	L 0-1		19,852	1	2		4	5	6	7		9	10	11	3	8								
31	(h) Sheffield W	D 1-1	Richardson	31,334	1	2	3	4	5	6	7		9	10	11		8								
Nov 7	(a) West Ham U	W 5-1	Richardson 4, Sandford	18,134	1	2	3	4	5		7		9	10	11		8	6							
14	(h) Aston Villa	W 3-0	Glidden, Richardson, Raw	59,674	1	2	3	4	5	6	7		9		11		8		10						
21	(a) Newcastle U	L 1-5	Glidden	36,000	1	2	3	4	5		7		9	10	11		8	6							
28	(h) Middlesbrough	D 1-1	Sandford	17,824	1	2	3	4	5		7		9	10	11		8	6							
Dec 5	(a) Leicester C	W 3-2	Richardson, Glidden, Wood	30,000	1	2	3	4	5		7		9	10	11		8	6							
12	(h) Chelsea	W 4-0	Richardson 2, Boyes, Glidden	24,186	1	2	3	4	5		7		9	10	11			6	8						
19	(a) Grimsby T	D 0-0		12,000	1	2	3	4	5		7		9	10	11			6	8						
25	(h) Birmingham	L 0-1		38,053	1	2	3	4	5		7		9	10	11			6	8						
26	(a) Birmingham	L 0-1		57,806	1	2	3		5	6	7	8		10	11			4		9					
Jan 2	(h) Arsenal	W 1-0	Glidden	25,790	1	2	3		5	6	7	8	9	10	11			4							
16	(a) Blackpool	W 2-1	Richardson, Sandford	16,000	1	2	3		5		7		9	10	11		8	4			6				
25	(h) Sheffield U	L 0-1		11,382	1	2	3		5		7	8	9	10	11			4			6				
30	(a) Blackburn R	L 0-2		12,502	1	2	3				7		9	5	11		8	4	10		6				
Feb 6	(h) Portsmouth	W 3-0	Glidden 2, Richardson	21,065	1	2	3		5		7		9	6	11		8	4	10						
17	(a) Derby C	L 1-3	Glidden	15,000	1	2			5		7		9	6	11	3	8	4	10						
20	(h) Huddersfield T	W 3-2	Richardson, Raw, Glidden	20,105	1	2			5		7		9	6	11	3	8	4	10						
Mar 2	(a) Liverpool	L 1-4	Richardson	21,000	1	2			5		7	10	9	3	11		8	4	6						
5	(h) Bolton W	W 3-0	Richardson, Glidden, Wood	16,050	1	2	3		5		7	8	9	10	11			4	6						
12	(a) Sheffield W	W 5-2	Carter, Glidden, Richardson, Sandford, Wood	13,389	1	2	3		5		7	8	9	10	11			4	6						
19	(h) West Ham U	W 3-1	Wood, Carter, Richardson	19,271	1	2	3		5		7	8	9	10	11			4	6						
25	(a) Everton	L 1-2	Richardson	20,000	1	2	3		5	6	7	8	9	10	11			4							
26	(a) Aston Villa	L 0-2		51,000	1	2	3		5		7	8	9	10	11			4	6						
28	(h) Everton	D 1-1	Carter	31,486	1	2	3		5		7	8	9	10	11			4	6						
Apr 2	(h) Newcastle U	W 2-1	Davidson (og), Glidden	18,614	1	2	3		5	6	7		9	10				4	11			8			
9	(a) Middlesbrough	L 0-1		18,000			3		5	6	7		9		11			4	10			8	1	2	
16	(h) Leicester C	L 1-2	Sandford	15,014	1	2	3		5		7	8		10	11			4			6	9			
23	(a) Chelsea	W 2-0	Carter, Richardson	29,000	1	2	3		5	6	7	8	9	10				4							11
30	(h) Grimsby T	L 5-6	Richardson, Sandford, Carter, Edwards (pen), Glidden	7,796	1	2	3		5	6	7	8	9	10	11			4							
App					41	41	37	22	41	22	42	20	40	40	40	4	18	27	17	1	3	3	1	1	1
Goals						1			2		20	5	27	8	7		4		1						

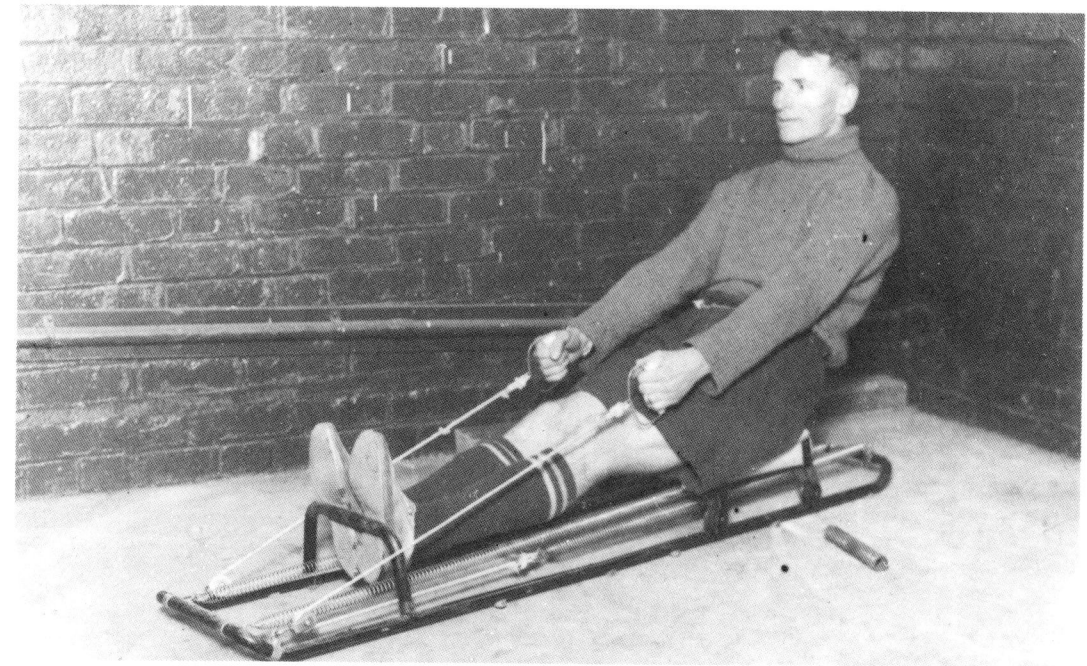

Joe Carter exercising in The Hawthorns gymnasium.

1932-33

Division 1

Date		Opponent	Result	Scorers	Att.	Pearson H	Shaw G	Trentham H	Magee T	Richardson W	Edwards J	Glidden T	Carter J	Richardson WG	Sandford E	Wood S	Finch R	Gale A	Robbins W	Murphy J	Rix J	Raw H	Ridyard A
Aug 27	(h)	Everton	W 3-1	Sandford, Carter, Richardson	31,922	1	2	3	4	5	6	7	8	9	10	11							
31	(a)	Arsenal	W 2-1	Glidden, John (og)	40,200	1	2	3	4	5	6	7	8	9	10	11							
Sep 3	(a)	Blackpool	W 4-2	Glidden 3, Richardson	21,563	1	2	3	4	5	6	7	8	9	10	11							
10	(h)	Derby C	W 2-0	Richardson, Glidden	30,715	1	2	3	4	5	6	7	8	9	10	11							
14	(h)	Arsenal	D 1-1	Carter	45,038	1	2	3	4	5	6	7	8	9	10	11							
17	(h)	Blackburn R	D 4-4	Carter 2, Glidden, Wood	18,400	1	2	3	4	5	6	7	8	9	10	11							
24	(h)	Leeds U	L 0-1		26,497	1	2	3	4	5	6	7	8	9	10	11							
Oct 1	(a)	Sheffield W	L 1-3	Robbins	21,900	1	3		4	5	6	7	8		10		2	9	11				
8	(h)	Wolves	W 4-1	Richardson 2, Glidden, Sandford	30,058	1	2	3		5	6	7	8	9	10	11				4			
15	(h)	Birmingham	W 1-0	Sandford	29,145	1	2	3		5	6	7	8	9	10	11				4			
22	(a)	Newcastle U	L 0-3		25,580	1	2	3		5	6	7	8	9	10				11	4			
29	(h)	Aston Villa	W 3-1	Robbins, Carter, Richardson	42,093	1	2	3		5	6	7	8	9	10				11	4			
Nov 5	(a)	Portsmouth	L 0-3		26,000	1	2	3		5	6	7	8	9	10				11	4			
12	(h)	Chelsea	W 3-2	Wood, Robbins, Sandford	21,569	1	2	3		5	6	7			10	11			9	4			
19	(a)	Huddersfield T	L 1-2	Richardson	27,500	1	2	3				7		9	5	11			10	4	6	8	
26	(h)	Sheffield U	L 0-1		16,882	1	2	3		5		7	8		10	11			9	4	6		
Dec 3	(a)	Middlesbrough	L 1-3	Raw	16,700	1	2	3	4	5		7			10	11			9		6	8	
10	(h)	Bolton W	W 4-0	Raw, Robbins 2, Richardson	12,662	1	2	3		5		7		9	6	11			10	4		8	
17	(a)	Liverpool	L 0-2		32,500	1	2	3		5		7		9	6	11			10	4		8	
24	(h)	Leicester C	W 4-3	Richardson 3, Sandford	15,905	1	2	3		5	6	7		9	8	11			10	4			
26	(h)	Sunderland	W 5-1	Richardson 3, Carter, Robbins	26,113	1	2	3		5	6	7	8	9		11			10	4			
31	(a)	Everton	W 2-1	Glidden, Robbins	34,700	1	2	3		5		7	8	9		11			10	4	6		
Jan 2	(a)	Sunderland	D 2-2	Richardson, Wood	29,850	1	2	3		5		7	8	9		11			10	4	6		
7	(h)	Blackpool	W 2-1	Richardson, Wood	17,280	1	2	3		5	6	7		9	8	11			10	4			
21	(a)	Derby C	D 2-2	Glidden, Carter	21,000	1	2	3			6	7	8	9	10	11				4			5
Feb 4	(a)	Leeds U	D 1-1	Richardson	24,440	1	2	3			6	7	8	9	10	11				4			5
8	(h)	Blackburn R	L 1-3	Richardson	10,775	1	2	3			6	7	8	9	10	11				4			5
11	(h)	Sheffield W	W 2-0	Richardson, Sandford	20,863	1	2	3		5	6	7	8	9	10	11				4			
18	(a)	Wolves	D 3-3	Glidden, Richardson, Wood	29,400	1	2	3		5	6	7	8	9	10	11				4			
Mar 4	(h)	Newcastle U	W 3-2	Richardson 2, Wood	21,847	1	2	3		5	6	7	8	9	10	11				4			
11	(a)	Aston Villa	L 2-3	Richardson 2	50,600	1	3			5	6	7	8	9	10	11	2			4			
18	(h)	Portsmouth	W 4-2	Richardson 2, Sandford 2	16,356	1	2	3		5	6		8	9	10	11		7		4			
25	(a)	Chelsea	W 2-1	Gale, Richardson	21,600	1	2	3		5	6		8	9	10			7	11	4			
Apr 1	(h)	Huddersfield T	W 2-1	Richardson, Carter	17,610	1	2	3		5	6		8	9	10			7	11	4			
8	(a)	Sheffield U	D 1-1	Robbins	20,528	1	2	3		5	6	7	8	9	10				11	4			
14	(a)	Manchester C	L 0-1		28,200	1	2	3		5	6	7	8	9	10				11	4			
15	(h)	Middlesbrough	L 0-1		17,530	1	2	3		5	6	7	8	9	10				11	4			
17	(h)	Manchester C	W 4-0	Robbins, Carter 3	18,988	1	2	3		5	6	7	8	9	10				11	4			
22	(a)	Bolton W	D 2-2	Robbins, Carter	14,000	1	2	3		5	6	7	8	9	10				11	4			
26	(a)	Birmingham	D 1-1	Richardson	27,000	1	2	3		5	6	7	8	9	10				11	4			
29	(h)	Liverpool	W 2-1	Carter, Richardson	8,933	1	2	3		5		7	8	9	10				11	4	6		
May 6	(a)	Leicester C	L 2-6	Carter, Sandford	19,000	1	2	3		5		7	8	9	10				11	4	6		
App						42	42	40	9	38	33	39	36	38	39	28	2	4	25	34	6	4	3
Goals												10	14	30	9	6		1	10			2	

Albion's great half-back line of the early 1930s — Magee, Richardson and Edwards.

108

1933-34

Division 1

Date	Venue/Opponent	Result	Scorers	Att.	Pearson H	Shaw G	Trentham H	Murphy J	Richardson W	Edwards J	Glidden T	Carter J	Richardson WG	Sandford E	Wood S	Ricyard A	Finch R	Robbins W	Boyes W	Gale A	Crowe E	Magee T	Sankey J	Rix J	Green T	Foulkes H	Trevis B
Aug 26	(a) Everton	L 0-1		25,760	1	2	3	4	5	6	7	8	9	10	11												
Sep 2	(h) Middlesbrough	W 3-0	Glidden, Richardson 2	21,152	1	2	3	4	5	6	7	8	9	10	11												
6	(a) Arsenal	L 1-3	Wood	34,083	1	2	3	4		6	7	8	9	10	11	5											
9	(a) Blackburn R	L 0-4		20,595	1		3	4		6	7	8	9	10	11	5	2										
13	(h) Arsenal	W 1-0	Carter	29,398	1		3	4		6	7	8	9	10	11		2										
16	(h) Newcastle U	D 1-1	Glidden	24,481	1		3	4		6	7	8	9	10	11	5	2										
23	(a) Leeds U	L 0-3		21,119	1	2	3	4	5	6	7	8	9	10	11												
30	(h) Derby C	W 5-1	Richardson 4, Glidden	24,570	1	2	3	4	5	6	7	8	9	10				11									
Oct 7	(a) Wolves	D 0-0		37,287	1	2	3	4	5	6	7	8	9	10				11									
14	(a) Birmingham	W 1-0	Richardson	29,103	1	2	3	4	5	6	7	8	9	10				11									
21	(h) Stoke C	W 5-1	Beachill (og), Richardson, Sandford 2, Wood	22,771	1	2	3	4	5	6	7		9	10	11				8								
28	(a) Huddersfield T	L 1-3		28,531	1	2	3	4	5	6	7		9	10	11				8								
Nov 4	(h) Tottenham H	L 1-2	Wood	32,276	1	2	3	4	5	6	7		9	10	11				8								
11	(a) Sunderland	D 2-2	Glidden, Carter	27,434	1	2	3	4	5	6	7	8	9	10	11												
18	(h) Chelsea	W 3-1	Richardson, Sandford, Glidden	12,325	1	2	3	4	5	6	7	8	9	10	11												
25	(a) Liverpool	D 1-1	Carter	33,089	1	2	3	4	5	6	7	8	9	10	11												
Dec 2	(h) Sheffield U	W 3-0	Wood, Richardson, Sandford	10,493	1	2	3	4	5	6	7	8	9	10	11												
9	(a) Leicester C	W 1-0	Carter	20,614	1	2	3	4	5	6	7	8	9	10	11												
16	(h) Aston Villa	W 2-1	Richardson, Glidden	25,503	1	2	3	4	5	6	7	8	9	10	11												
23	(a) Portsmouth	D 2-2	Richardson, Wood	15,113	1	2	3	4	5	6	7	8	9	10	11												
26	(a) Sheffield W	L 1-3	Glidden	34,905	1	2	3	4	5	6	7	8	9	10	11												
27	(h) Sheffield W	D 1-1	Carter	32,660	1	2	3		5	6	7	8	9	4	11		10										
30	(h) Everton	D 3-3	Gale, Richardson, Sandford	18,876	1	2	3		5	6	7	8	9	4	11					10							
Jan 1	(a) Manchester C	W 7-2	Robbins 2, Richardson 3, Carter, Sandford	20,996	1	2	3	4	5	6	7	8	9	10				11									
6	(a) Middlesbrough	L 0-3		13,927	1	2	3	4	5	6	7	8	9	10				11									
20	(h) Blackburn R	L 0-1		16,297			3		5		7	8	9	10	11						1	4	6				
27	(a) Newcastle U	W 2-1	Gale, Sandford	21,824		2	3		5		7	8		10				11		9	1	4	6				
Feb 3	(h) Leeds U	L 0-3		13,343		2	3	4	5		7			10					11	9	1		6	8			
10	(a) Derby C	D 1-1	Richardson	20,887					5		7	8	9	10			2		11		1	4	6			3	
17	(h) Wolves	W 2-0	Richardson, Sandford	24,892				4	5		7	8	9	10			2		11		1		6			3	
24	(h) Birmingham	L 1-2	Glidden	24,525		2		4	5		7	8	9	10					11		1		6			3	
Mar 8	(a) Stoke C	L 1-4	Carter	16,420		2		4	5		7	8	9	10					11		1		6			3	
10	(h) Huddersfield T	L 2-3	Richardson, Sankey	16,280					5		7	8	9	10			2		11		1	4	6			3	
17	(a) Tottenham H	L 1-2	Boyes	25,150			3	4			7	8	9	10		5	2		11		1		6				
24	(h) Sunderland	W 6-5	Richardson, Boyes, Glidden 2, Carter, Sandford (pen)	11,889			3	4			7	8	9	10		5	2		11		1		6				
31	(a) Chelsea	L 2-3	Richardson, Boyes	20,851			3	4	5		7	8	9	10			2		11		1		6				
Apr 2	(h) Manchester C	W 4-0	Carter, Boyes, Richardson 2	22,198	1	2	3	4	5		7	8	9	10					11				6				
7	(h) Liverpool	D 2-2	Carter, Sandford (pen)	15,730	1	2	3		5		7	8	9	10					11				6		4		
14	(a) Sheffield U	W 1-0	Boyes	10,402	1	2	3	4	5		7	8	9	10					11				6				
21	(h) Leicester C	W 2-0	Richardson, Boyes	11,309	1	2	3	4	5		7	8	9	10					11				6				
28	(a) Aston Villa	D 4-4	Glidden 2, Richardson, Green	20,050	1	2	3	4	5		7		9	10					11				6		8		
May 5	(h) Portsmouth	W 2-1	Glidden, Green	10,679	1	2	3	4	5		7		9	10					11				6		8		
			App		31	32	37	35	37	25	42	36	40	42	21	5	10	6	19	3	11	4	16	1	3	5	1
			Goals								13	10	26	10	5			2	6	2			1		2		

Skipper Tommy Glidden leads out Albion, followed by 'W.G.' Richardson.

Tommy Green pictured in 1986.

1934-35

Division 1

Date	V	Opponent	Res	Scorers	Att.	Pearson H	Shaw G	Trentham H	Murphy J	Richardson W	Sankey J	Glidden T	Carter J	Richardson WG	Sandford E	Robbins W	Boyes W	Edwards J	Wood S	Crowe E	Ridyard A	Whitehead N	Gale A	Jones H	Screen J	Finch R	Rawlings S
Aug 25	(h)	Manchester C	D 1-1	Richardson	24,480	1	2	3	4	5	6	7	8	9	10		11										
29	(h)	Birmingham	L 1-2	Richardson	22,025	1	2	3	4	5	6	7	8	9	10		11										
Sep 1	(a)	Middlesbrough	D 0-0		15,800	1	2	3	4	5		7	8	9	10		11	6									
3	(h)	Birmingham	W 2-1	Richardson 2	25,000	1	2	3	4	5		7	8	9	6		10			11							
8	(h)	Blackburn R	D 2-2	Richardson, Glidden	19,063	1	2	3	4	5		7	8	9	10		11	6									
15	(a)	Arsenal	L 3-4	Richardson 2, Boyes	30,100		2	3	4	5		7	8	9	10		11	6	1								
22	(h)	Portsmouth	W 4-2	Richardson 2, Glidden, Sandford	11,396	1	2	3	4	5		7	8	9	10		11	6									
29	(a)	Liverpool	L 2-3	Sandford 2	16,500	1	2	3		5	4	7	8	9	10		11	6									
Oct 6	(h)	Leeds U	W 6-3	Richardson 4, Boyes, Carter	15,843	1	2	3	4	5	6	7	8	9	10		11										
13	(a)	Wolves	L 2-3	Sandford 2 (1 pen)	45,066	1	2	3	4	5	6	7	8	9	10		11										
20	(h)	Huddersfield T	W 4-1	Boyes 2, Glidden, Richardson	19,250	1	2	3	4	5	6	7	8	9	10		11										
27	(a)	Everton	L 0-4		27,154	1	2	3	4	5	6	7	8	9	10		11										
Nov 3	(h)	Aston Villa	D 2-2	Boyes 2	44,503	1	2	3	4	5	6	7	8	9	10		11										
10	(a)	Chelsea	W 3-2	Boyes 2, Sandford	25,828	1	2	3	4	5	6	7	8	9	10		11										
17	(h)	Tottenham H	W 4-0	Sandford, Boyes 2, Richardson	20,397	1	2	3	4	5	6	7	8	9	10		11										
24	(a)	Sunderland	W 1-0	Carter	31,223	1	2	3	4	5	6	7	8	9	10		11										
Dec 1	(h)	Leicester C	W 4-1	Boyes 2, Glidden 2	17,174	1	2	3	4	5	6	7	8	9	10		11										
8	(a)	Derby C	L 3-9	Richardson, Sandford (pen), Glidden	14,308	1	2	3	4	5	6	7	8	9	10		11										
15	(h)	Grimsby T	W 4-2	Boyes 2, Sandford 2	17,098	1	2	3	4			7	8	9	10		11	6			5						
22	(a)	Preston NE	W 2-1	Richardson, Boyes	15,835	1	2	3	4			7	8	9	10		11	6			5						
25	(h)	Stoke C	W 3-0	Carter 2, Richardson	38,531	1	2	3	4	5		7	8	9	10		11	6									
26	(a)	Stoke C	L 0-3		18,334	1	2	3	4	5			8	9	10		11	6				7					
29	(a)	Manchester C	L 2-3	Gale, Sandford	23,545	1	2	3	4	5			8	9	10		11	6					7				
Jan 1	(a)	Sheffield W	L 1-2	Gale	17,636	1	2	3	4	5			8	9			11	6					7	10			
5	(h)	Middlesbrough	W 6-3	Richardson, Boyes, Gale, Sandford 2, Carter	18,582	1		3	4	5	6		8	9	10		11						7		2		
19	(a)	Blackburn R	L 0-3		15,320	1	2	3	4	5	6		8	9	10		11						7				
30	(h)	Arsenal	L 0-3		30,667	1	2	3	4	5	6		8	9	10		11						7				
Feb 2	(a)	Portsmouth	W 2-0	Sandford, Richardson	18,048	1	2	3	4	5			8	9	10		11	6					7				
9	(h)	Liverpool	D 1-1	Sandford	20,182	1	2	3	4	5			8	9	10		11	6					7				
20	(a)	Leeds U	L 1-4	Sandford	20,242	1	2	3	4	5	7		8	9	10		11	6									
23	(h)	Wolves	W 5-2	Sandford, Boyes 2, Richardson 2	31,494	1	2	3	4	5			8	9	10		11	6					7				
Mar 6	(a)	Huddersfield T	L 0-3		24,176	1		3	4	5	7						11	6					10				2
9	(h)	Everton	L 0-1		20,002	1	2	3	4	5	10		8	9			11	6					7				
23	(h)	Chelsea	D 2-2	Sandford, Jones	13,721	1	2	3	4	5				9	10		11	6						8		7	
30	(a)	Tottenham H	W 1-0	Richardson	30,144	1	2	3	4	5				9	10		11	6						8		7	
Apr 3	(a)	Aston Villa	W 3-2	Gibson (og), Boyes, Richardson	55,067	1		3	4	5				9	10		11	6						8		2	7
6	(h)	Sunderland	D 1-1	Sandford (pen)	24,510	1		3	4	5				9	10		11	6						8		2	7
13	(a)	Leicester C	D 0-0		21,508	1	2	3	4	5				9	10		11	6						8			7
20	(h)	Derby C	W 4-3	Sandford, Richardson, Glidden, Jones	16,464	1	2	3	4			7		9	10		11	6			5			8			
22	(h)	Sheffield W	D 1-1	Boyes	33,540	1	2	3	4		6			9		10	11				5		7	8			
May 1	(a)	Grimsby T	L 0-3		16,239	1	2	3	4	5	7			9	8	10	11	6									
4	(h)	Preston NE	D 0-0		10,420	1	2	3	4	5	7			9	8	10	11	6									
App						41	38	42	41	38	20	24	33	42	38	4	41	25	1	1	4	1	10	9	1	3	5
Goals												7	5	25	20		20						3	2			

'Order of the boot' — George Shaw, Teddy Sandford, Bill Richardson, Joe Carter and Jimmy Edwards pictured in season 1934-5.

110

1935-36

Division 1

Date		Opponent	Result	Scorers	Att	Pearson H	Shaw G	Trentham H	Murphy J	Richardson W	Edwards J	Glidden T	Green T	Richardson WG	Sandford E	Boyes W	Rawlings S	Finch R	Robbins W	Sankey J	Wood S	Gale A	Rix J	Mahon J	Jones H	Carter J	Crowe E	Alsop G	Ridyard A	Adams J	Light W	Foulkes H
Aug 31	(a)	Manchester C	L 0-1		23,200	1	2	3	4	5	6	7	8	9	10	11																
Sep 4	(h)	Sunderland	L 1-3	Rawlings	24,385	1	2	3	4	5	6		8	9	10	11	7															
Sep 7	(h)	Stoke C	W 2-0	Green, Richardson	24,060	1	2	3	4	5	6		8	9	10	11	7															
Sep 11	(h)	Sunderland	L 1-6	Richardson	29,530	1	2	3	4	5	6		8	9	10	11	7															
Sep 14	(a)	Blackburn R	L 1-3	Boyes	16,421	1		3	4	5	6			9	8	11	7	2	10													
Sep 18	(h)	Birmingham	D 0-0		18,083	1		3	4	5				9	10	8	7	2		6	11											
Sep 21	(h)	Chelsea	L 1-2	Gale	17,183	1		3	4	5		7		10	8			2		6	11	9										
Sep 28	(a)	Liverpool	L 0-5		28,301	1	2	3		5				9	10	11			4				6	7	8							
Oct 5	(h)	Grimsby T	W 4-1	Richardson, Mahon, Carter 2	20,787	1	2	3		5				9	10	11			4				6	7		8						
Oct 12	(a)	Leeds U	D 1-1	Richardson	16,560	1	2	3		5				9	10	11			4				6	7		8						
Oct 19	(a)	Aston Villa	W 7-0	Richardson 4, Wood, Mahon, Sankey	38,037	1	2	3	4	5				9	10					6	11			7		8						
Oct 26	(h)	Wolves	W 2-1	Richardson, Sandford	42,402	1	2	3	4	5				9	10					6	11			7		8						
Nov 2	(a)	Sheffield W	W 5-2	Wood 2, Sandford, Mahon, Richardson	15,100	1	2	3	4	5				9	10					6	11			7		8						
Nov 9	(h)	Portsmouth	W 2-0	Richardson 2	23,055	1	2	3	4	5				9	10					6	11			7		8						
Nov 16	(a)	Preston NE	L 0-3		20,146	1	2	3	4	5				9	10					6	11			7		8						
Nov 23	(h)	Huddersfield T	L 1-2	Richardson	24,324		2	3	4	5				10		11				6				7		8	1	9				
Nov 30	(a)	Derby C	L 0-2		18,600	1	2	3		5				9	10					4	11		6	7		8						
Dec 7	(h)	Everton	W 6-1	Richardson 2, Mahon 2, Sandford, Carter	17,151	1	2	3		5				9	10					4	11		6	7		8						
Dec 14	(a)	Bolton W	L 1-3	Sandford	13,400	1	2	3		5				9	10					4	11		6	7		8						
Dec 21	(h)	Brentford	W 1-0	Mahon	14,265	1	2	3		5				9	10					4	11		6	7		8						
Dec 26	(h)	Middlesbrough	W 5-2	Shaw (pen), Richardson 4	26,049	1	2	3	4	5				9					10		11		6	7		8						
Dec 28	(h)	Manchester C	W 5-1	Mahon, Robbins, Glidden, Richardson 2	31,012	1	2	3				8		9					10	4	11		6	7					5			
Jan 1	(a)	Middlesbrough	L 1-3	Richardson	18,055	1	2	3				8		9					10	4	11		6	7					5			
Jan 4	(a)	Stoke C	L 2-3	Richardson, Mahon	13,200	1	2	3						9					10	4	11		6	7	8				5			
Jan 18	(h)	Blackburn R	W 8-1	Richardson 3, Mahon 3, Robbins, Sankey	16,464		2	3		5				9	8				10	4	11		6	7						1		
Feb 1	(h)	Liverpool	W 6-1	Richardson 3, Mahon, Wood 2	23,080			3		5				9	10			2		4	11		6	7		8				1		
Feb 8	(a)	Grimsby T	L 2-4	Richardson 2	10,247			3					10	9	8			2		4	11		6	7					5	1		
Feb 19	(h)	Leeds U	W 3-2	Sandford 2, Wood	7,893			3						9	8			2	10	4	11		6	7					5	1		
Feb 29	(a)	Portsmouth	L 1-3	Richardson	15,100			3	6					9	8			2	10	4	11			7					5	1		
Mar 7	(h)	Derby C	L 0-3		18,408		2	3		5			8	9					10	4	11		6	7							1	
Mar 11	(a)	Chelsea	D 2-2	Mahon, Richardson	20,400		2	3	6				8	9					10	4	11			7					5		1	
Mar 14	(a)	Wolves	L 0-2		25,253		2	3	4				8	9					10	6	11			7					5		1	
Mar 21	(h)	Preston NE	L 2-4	Richardson, Mahon	19,665		2	3		5			8	9						4	11		6	7	10						1	
Mar 28	(a)	Huddersfield T	W 3-2	Richardson 2, Boyes	25,307					5				9	10			2		4	11		6	7		8					1	3
Apr 1	(h)	Aston Villa	L 0-3		28,821					5				9	10			2		4	11		6	7		8					1	3
Apr 4	(h)	Sheffield W	D 2-2	Jones 2	17,604			3		5				9		11		2		4			6	7	10	8					1	
Apr 10	(a)	Arsenal	L 0-4		30,176					5				9	10			2		4	11		6	7		8					1	3
Apr 11	(a)	Everton	L 3-5	Jones, Mahon	24,008			3	4	5	6			9		11		2		8				7	10		1					
Apr 13	(h)	Arsenal	W 1-0	Jones	42,286		2	3		5	6	7	8	9		11				4					10						1	
Apr 18	(h)	Bolton W	D 2-2	Glidden, Richardson	27,398		2	3		5	6	7	8	9		11				4					10						1	
Apr 25	(a)	Brentford	D 2-2	Wood, Richardson	25,692		2	3		5	6			9	10					4	11			7		8					1	
May 2	(a)	Birmingham	W 3-1	Mahon, Richardson, Boyes	28,124		2	3		5				9	10	11				4			6	7		8	1					
App						23	32	37	16	35	11	9	7	41	23	21	5	12	11	36	29	1	22	33	8	19	3	1	8	5	11	3
Goals							1					2	1	39	6	3	1		2	2	7	1		17	4	3						

All dressed up and nowhere to go. Albion staff (left to right): Fred Reed (trainer), George Shaw, Jack Sankey, Bill Richardson, Jimmy Edwards, Jimmy Murphy, Wally Boyes, Joe Carter and Harold Pearson. They are pictured after a training session at The Hawthorns in 1935.

1936-37

Division 1

Fixture	Result	Scorers	Att	Light W	Shaw G	Trentham H	Murphy J	Richardson W	Sankey J	Mahon J	Sandford E	Richardson WG	Robbins W	Wood S	Swinden S	Jones H	Edwards J	Boyes W	Finch R	Pearson H	Prew J	Brockhurst W	Green T	Ridyard A	Gale A	Foulkes W	Shaw C	Adams J	Rix J	Coen L	Heaselgrave S
Aug 29 (h) Derby C	L 1-3	Richardson	30,149	1	2	3	4	5	6	7	8	9	10	11																		
Sep 2 (h) Birmingham	W 3-2	Jones, Richardson, Wood	26,013	1		3	4	5	6	7	10	9		11	2	8																
Sep 5 (a) Manchester C	L 2-6	Boyes, Richardson	25,070	1		3	5	4		7	10	9			2	8	6	11														
Sep 9 (a) Birmingham	D 1-1	Jones	34,135	1		3	5	4		7	10	9		11	2	8	6															
Sep 12 (h) Portsmouth	W 3-1	Wood, Richardson, Sandford	12,224	1		3	5	4		7	10	9		11	2	8	6															
Sep 19 (a) Chelsea	L 0-3		25,100	1		3	5	4		7	10	9		11		8		6	2													
Sep 26 (h) Stoke C	D 2-2	Richardson, Mahon	27,086	1		3	5	4		7	10	9		11		8		6	2													
Oct 3 (a) Charlton A	L 2-4	Sandford, Jones	37,430	1		3	5	4		7	10	9		11		8		6	2													
Oct 10 (h) Grimsby T	W 4-2	Richardson 3 (1 pen), Sandford	24,445			3	5	4			10	9		11		8		6	2	1	7											
Oct 17 (h) Wolves	W 2-1	W.Richardson, Prew	33,962			3	5	4			10	9		11		8		6	2	1	7											
Oct 24 (a) Sunderland	L 0-1		28,700			3	5	4			10	9		11		8		6	2	1	7											
Oct 31 (h) Huddersfield T	W 2-1	Jones, Wood	20,605			3	5	4			10	9		11		8		6	2	1	7											
Nov 7 (a) Everton	L 2-4	Richardson, Wood	20,901			3	5	4			10	9		11		8		6	2	1	7											
Nov 14 (h) Bolton W	L 0-2		20,110			3	4					9		11		10		6	2	1	7	5	8									
Nov 21 (a) Brentford	L 1-2	Jones	18,044			3	4	7						11		10		6	2	1			8	5	9							
Nov 28 (h) Arsenal	L 2-4	Gale, Wood	27,609	1		3	4	7						11		10		6	2				8	5	9							
Dec 5 (a) Preston NE	L 2-3	Mahon 2	20,203			3	4	7			10	9		11		8		6	2	1				5								
Dec 19 (a) Manchester U	D 2-2	Mahon, Wood	25,107			3	4	7			10	9		11		8		6	2	1				5								
Dec 25 (h) Liverpool	W 3-1	Jones 2, Wood	23,697				4	7			10	9		11		8		6	2	1				5			3					
Dec 26 (a) Derby C	L 0-1		18,993				5	4		7	10	8		11		9		6	2	1							3					
Dec 28 (a) Liverpool	W 2-1	Sandford, Robbins	26,500				4	5		7	8	9	10	11				6	2	1							3					
Jan 1 (a) Middlesbrough	L 1-4	Robbins	20,099				4	5		7	8	9	10	11				6	2	1							3					
Jan 2 (h) Manchester C	D 2-2	Wood, Mahon	18,004				4	5		7	10	9		11		8		6		1							3	2				
Jan 9 (a) Portsmouth	L 3-5	Jones, Richardson 2	14,405				4	5		7	10	9		11		8		6	2	1							3					
Jan 23 (h) Chelsea	W 2-0	Jones, Sandford	9,642	1			4	5	6		10	9		11		8			2		7						3					
Feb 4 (a) Stoke C	L 3-10	Richardson, Boyes, Robbins	15,230	1			4	5		7	10	9		11		8		6	2								3					
Feb 6 (h) Charlton A	L 1-2	Mahon	26,459					5		7	10	9				8		6	2								3	1	4	11		
Feb 13 (a) Grimsby T	W 3-2	Richardson, Jones 2	12,000				4		6	7	5	9				8		10	2								3	1		11		
Feb 27 (h) Sunderland	W 6-4	Richardson, Boyes, Coen, Shaw (pen), Jones 2	25,267				4		6	7	5	9				8		10	2								3	1		11		
Mar 10 (a) Huddersfield T	D 1-1	Boyes	23,102				4		6	7	5	9		11		8		10	2								3	1				
Mar 13 (h) Everton	W 2-1	Shaw (pen), Richardson	26,283				4		6	7	5	9		11		8		10	2								3	1				
Mar 20 (h) Bolton W	L 1-4	Jones	12,035				4	5	6	7		9		11		8		10	2								3	1				
Mar 22 (h) Preston NE	D 0-0		9,068		2		4		6	7		9		11		8		10								5	3	1				
Mar 27 (h) Brentford	W 1-0	Coen	29,858		2		4		6	7		9						10								5	3	1		11	8	
Mar 29 (h) Leeds U	W 3-0	Jones, Mahon, Richardson	31,251		2		4		6	7		9				8		10								5	3	1		11		
Mar 30 (a) Leeds U	L 1-3	Coen	16,548		2		4		6	7		9						10								5	3	1		11	8	
Apr 3 (a) Arsenal	L 0-2		24,600				4			7		9	10?	11				10	2							5	3	1	6		8	
Apr 14 (a) Wolves	L 2-5	Robbins 2	28,486				4		6	7		9	10	11		8			2							5	3	1				
Apr 17 (a) Sheffield W	W 3-2	Robbins 2, Mahon	12,719	1	2		4		6	7		9	10			8		11								5	3					
Apr 21 (h) Sheffield W	L 2-3	Robbins 2	10,826	1	2		4		6	7		9	10			8		11								5	3					
Apr 24 (h) Manchester U	W 1-0	Jones	16,245		2		4		6	7		9	10			8		11								5	3	1				
May 1 (h) Middlesbrough	W 3-1	Jones, Coen, Mahon	7,022		2		4		6	7			10			8		11								5	3	1		9		
App				13	9	18	21	22	37	35	28	39	16	23	4	35	1	39	28	15	7	5	3	11	2	3	22	14	2	7	3
Goals								1		9	5	16	9	8		17		4			1				1		2			4	

Albion pre-season training in August 1936.

1937-38

Division 1

Date		Opponent	Result	Scorers	Att.	Adams J	Shaw G	Shaw C	Murphy J	Sandford E	Sankey J	Mahon J	Jones H	Richardson WG	Robbins W	Boyes W	Rix J	Clarke I	Wood S	Male N	Finch R	Light W	Johnson J	Heaselgrave S	Lowery H	McNab A	Harris W	Baldwin H	Bassett I	Davies C
Aug 28	(a)	Portsmouth	W 3-2	Richardson, Mahon	25,703	1	2	3	4	5	6	7	8	9	10	11														
30	(h)	Stoke C	L 0-1		22,113	1	2	3	4	5	6	7	8	9	10	11														
Sep 4	(h)	Chelsea	W 4-0	Mahon, Robbins 2, Richardson	23,097	1	2	3	4	5	6	7	8	9	10	11														
6	(a)	Stoke C	L 0-4		16,520	1	2	3	4	5		7	8	9	10	11	6													
11	(a)	Charlton A	L 1-3	Sankey	25,570	1	2	3	4	5	6	7		9	10			8					11							
13	(h)	Middlesbrough	W 3-1	Richardson, Clarke, Jones	8,028	1	2	3	4	5		7	8	9			6	10					11							
18	(h)	Preston NE	D 1-1	Mahon	23,469	1	2	3	4	5	6	7	8	9				10					11							
25	(a)	Grimsby T	W 4-1	Jones 2, Male, Clarke	9,713	1		3	4	5		7	8	9			6	10		11	2									
Oct 2	(h)	Leeds U	W 2-1	Mahon, Robbins	25,619	1		3	4	5		7		9	10		6	8			2		11							
9	(a)	Liverpool	W 1-0	Wood	26,505	1		3	4	5		7		9	10		6		8		2		11							
16	(a)	Leicester C	L 1-4	Robbins	18,772	1		3	4	5		7		9	10		6	8			2		11							
23	(h)	Sunderland	L 1-6	Wood (pen)	27,705	1		3	4	5		7		9	10		6		8		2		11							
30	(a)	Derby C	L 3-5	Robbins, Mahon, Jones	18,450			3	4	5		7	8	9	10		6				2	1	11							
Nov 6	(h)	Bolton W	L 2-4	Sankey, Jones	20,281			3	4	5	6	7	8	9	10						2	1	11							
13	(a)	Arsenal	D 1-1		25,790	1		3	4	5		7	10	9			6	8			2		11							
20	(h)	Everton	W 3-1	Mahon 2, Boyes	20,800	1		3	4	5	6	7	10	9		11		8			2									
27	(a)	Brentford	W 2-0	Richardson 2	16,100	1		3	4	5	6	7	10	9		11		8			2									
Dec 11	(a)	Huddersfield T	L 1-2	Richardson	20,669	1		3	4	5		7	10	9			6	8			2			11						
18	(h)	Blackpool	L 1-2	Jones	18,077	1		3	4	5		7	10	9			6	8			2			11						
27	(h)	Wolves	D 2-2	Clarke 2	55,444	1		3	4	5		7		9	10		6	8			2			11						
Jan 1	(h)	Portsmouth	L 1-2	Clarke	19,442	1		3	4	5		7		9	10		6	8			2			11						
15	(a)	Chelsea	D 2-2	Richardson, Johnson	23,533	1		3	4	5	6	7		9				8			2		10	11						
26	(a)	Charlton A	D 0-0		9,579	1		3	4	5			7	9			6				2		10	11	8					
29	(a)	Preston NE	D 1-1	Smith (og)	10,604	1		3		5		7		9			6				2		10	11	8	4				
Feb 5	(h)	Grimsby T	W 2-1	Johnson, Mahon	19,648	1		3		5		7		9			6				2		10	11	8	4				
12	(a)	Leeds U	L 0-1		10,509	1		3		5		7		9			6				2		10	11	8	4				
19	(h)	Liverpool	W 5-1	Richardson 3, Clarke, Johnson	17,565	1		3		5		7		9			6	8			2		10	11		4				
26	(h)	Leicester C	L 1-3	Johnson	21,563	1		3		5		7		9			6	8			2		10	11		4				
Mar 9	(a)	Sunderland	L 0-3		20,887	1		3		5		7		9	10		6	8			2			11		4				
12	(h)	Derby C	W 4-2	Richardson 2, Johnson, Heaselgrave	25,439	1		3		5		7	10	9			6	8			2			11		4				
16	(h)	Manchester C	D 1-1	Shaw (pen)	10,792	1		3		5		7		9			6	8			2		10	11		4				
19	(a)	Bolton W	L 0-3		13,150	1		3		5		7		9	10		6	8			2			11		4				
26	(h)	Arsenal	D 0-0		33,944	1		3		5		7	10	9	11		6	8			2					4				
Apr 2	(a)	Everton	L 3-5	Mahon, Shaw (pen), Jones	24,395			3		5		7	10	9	11		6	8			2	1				4				
9	(h)	Brentford	W 4-3	Mahon, Heaselgrave, Johnson 2	23,642			3		5		7		9			6	8			2	1	10	11		4				
15	(a)	Birmingham	L 1-2	Jones	25,008			3		5		7	10	9			6	8			2	1		11		4				
16	(a)	Manchester C	L 1-7	Shaw (pen)	16,700			3	4	5		7		9	11		6	8			2	1					10			
18	(h)	Birmingham	W 4-3	Richardson 2, Shaw (pen), Jones	34,406			3		5		7	10	9	11		6	8			2					4		1		
23	(h)	Huddersfield T	W 5-1	Heaselgrave 2, Jones 2, Richardson	27,530			3		5		7	10	9	11		6	8			2					4		1		
30	(a)	Blackpool	L 1-2	Mahon	20,000			3		5		7	10	9	11		6	8			2					4				
May 2	(a)	Wolves	L 1-2	Sandford	39,024			3	4	5		7	10	9	11		6	8											1	2
7	(a)	Middlesbrough	L 1-4	Heaselgrave	18,025			3	4	5		7	10	9	11		6	8											1	2
App						31	7	42	23	42	16	40	33	29	18	14	15	27	11	3	30	4	18	19	17	12	2	5	2	2
Goals								4		1	2	13	11	15	5	1		6	2	1			7	5						

Albion squad for season 1937-8. Back row (left to right): J.S.Carpenter (groundstaff), T.Glidden (coach), A.Everiss (clerk), G.Hewitt, W.G.Richardson, W.Tudor, L.Coen, J.Adams, W.Light, W.Harris, A.Newman, W.Robbins, J.Murphy, J.Rix, G.Shaw, H.Jones. Third row: F.Reed (trainer), E.Smith (asst.secretary), S.Guest (asst.trainer), R.Finch, I.Bassett, J.Lewis, H.Lowery, W.Brockhurst, A.Ridyard, C.Davies, N.Male, H.Kinsell, J.Screen, J.Mahon, T.J.Powell (groundstaff), S.Short (trainer). Second row (seated): C.Shaw, H.W.Keys (director), J.Prew, N.W.Bassett (director), I.Clarke, J.S.Round (vice-chairman), E.Sandford, L.J.Nurse (chairman), W.Boyes, W.H.Thursfield (director), H.Ashley, A.C.Jephcott (director), S.Wood, F.Everiss (secretary). Front row (on ground): T.Edmunds, T.Lewis, S.Heaselgrave, C.S.Morgan, B.Clift, G.Spencer, J.Sankey, D.Lapworth.

1938-39

Division 2

Date		Opponent	Result	Scorers	Att	Adams J	Bassett I	Shaw C	Sankey J	Davies C	McNab A	Mahon J	Heaselgrave S	Jones H	Burgin M	Johnson J	White H	Robbins W	Tudor W	Hoyland E	Sandford E	Murphy J	Witcomb D	Spencer G	Clarke I	Dudley G	Richardson WG	Elliott W	Saunders W	Pike R	Gripton W	Butler S	Banks G
Aug 27	(h)	Luton T	W 3-0	Jones 2, Burgin	24,377	1	2	3	4	5	6	7	8	9	10	11																	
Sep 1	(a)	Norwich C	W 3-2	Burgin 2, Jones	20,537	1	2	3	4	5	6	7	8	9	10	11																	
Sep 3	(a)	Plymouth A	L 1-2	Jones	15,166	1	2	3	4	5	6	7	8	9	10	11																	
Sep 7	(h)	Newcastle U	W 5-2	Burgin, Heaselgrave 2, Jones 2	17,016	1	2	3	4	5	6	7	8	9	10	11																	
Sep 10	(h)	Sheffield U	L 3-4	Heaselgrave 3	25,866	1		3	4	5	6	7	8		9	11	2	10															
Sep 14	(a)	Newcastle U	L 1-5	Jones	31,054	1		3	4		6		8	9		11	2		5	7	10												
Sep 17	(a)	Burnley	W 3-0	Heaselgrave, Jones, Spencer	19,222	1		3					8	9		11	2		5		10	4	6	7									
Sep 24	(h)	Tottenham H	W 4-3	Jones 3, Heaselgrave	25,041	1		3					8	9		11	2		5		10	4	6	7									
Oct 1	(a)	Southampton	L 1-2	Clarke	15,204	1		3		10				9		11	2		5			4	6	7	8								
Oct 8	(h)	Coventry C	W 3-1	Sandford, Johnson, McNab	30,943	1		3			6			9		11	2		5		10		4	7	8								
Oct 15	(h)	Chesterfield	W 1-0	Johnson	23,702	1		3			6			9		11	2		5		10		4	7	8								
Oct 22	(a)	Tranmere R	L 1-3	Johnson	12,184	1		3			6		8	9		11	2		5		10		4	7									
Oct 29	(h)	Manchester C	W 3-1	Clarke 3, Johnson	22,274	1		3			6		9	8		11	2		5				4	7	10								
Nov 5	(a)	Bury	D 3-3	Dudley, Shaw (pen), Clarke	10,109	1		3			6		9	8			2		5				4	7	10	11							
Nov 12	(h)	Sheffield W	W 5-1	Spencer, Burgin 2, Clarke, Witcomb	18,297	1		3			6			9	8		2		5				4	7	10	11							
Nov 19	(a)	Fulham	L 0-3		15,200	1		3			6			9	8		2		5				4	7	10	11							
Nov 26	(h)	Blackburn R	W 2-0	Burgin, Richardson	22,127	1		3			6	7			8	11	2		5				4		10		9						
Dec 3	(a)	Millwall	W 5-1	McNab, Clarke, Jones 2, Heaselgrave	35,140	1		3			6		7	9	8	11	2		5				4		10								
Dec 10	(h)	West Ham U	W 3-2	Clarke 2, Jones	23,909	1		3			6		7	9	8	11	2		5				4		10								
Dec 17	(a)	Bradford	D 4-4	Burgin 2, Clarke, Witcomb	10,664	1		3			6		7	9	8	11	2		5				4		10								
Dec 24	(a)	Luton T	L 1-3	Johnson	11,700	1		3			6		8	9		11	2		5				4		10			7					
Dec 27	(a)	Swansea T	L 2-3	Jones, Elliott	12,532			3			6		8	9		11	2		5				4		10			7	1				
Dec 31	(h)	Plymouth A	W 4-2	Clarke, Heaselgrave, Shaw (pen), Jones	19,833	1		3			6		8	9		11	2		5				4		10			7					
Jan 14	(a)	Sheffield U	D 1-1	Richardson	16,490	1		3			6		8			11	2		5				4		10		9	7					
Jan 28	(a)	Tottenham H	D 2-2	Johnson 2	38,868	1		3			6		8	9		11	2		5				4		10			7					
Feb 1	(h)	Burnley	L 1-2	Jones	7,781	1		3	8		6			9		11	2		5				4		10			7					
Feb 4	(h)	Southampton	W 2-0	Johnson, Elliott	21,757	1		3			6		8			11	2		5				4		10		9	7					
Feb 11	(a)	Coventry C	D 1-1	Johnson	25,086			3			6		8			11	2		5				4		10		9	7	1				
Feb 18	(a)	Chesterfield	L 1-3	Heaselgrave	18,135	1		3			6		10	8		11	2		5				4				9	7					
Feb 25	(h)	Tranmere R	W 2-0	Elliott, Shaw (pen)	17,193	1		3	4		6		8	9		11	2		5						10			7					
Mar 4	(a)	Manchester C	D 3-3	Johnson 2, Clarke	18,479	1		3	4		6		8	9		11	2		5						10			7					
Mar 11	(h)	Bury	W 6-0	Clarke, Heaselgrave, Johnson 4	17,062	1	2	3	4		6		8	9		11			5						10			7					
Mar 18	(h)	Sheffield W	L 1-2	Shaw (pen)	28,034	1	2	3			6		8	9		11			5				4		10			7					
Mar 25	(h)	Fulham	W 3-0	Jones, Clarke, Dudley	19,541	1		3	4		6		8	9			2		5						10	11		7					
Apr 1	(a)	Blackburn R	L 0-3		11,407	1		3	4		6			9			2	11	5						10			8		7			
Apr 7	(a)	Nottingham F	L 0-2		21,056	1		3	4		6					11	2	10	5						8			7			9		
Apr 8	(h)	Millwall	D 0-0		19,895	1		3	4	10						11	2						6	7	8	9					5		
Apr 10	(h)	Nottingham F	D 0-0		16,058	1		3	4	10						11	2						6	7	8	9					5		
Apr 15	(a)	West Ham U	L 1-2	Clarke	15,022	1		3	4				8				2						6		10		9	7			5	11	
Apr 19	(h)	Swansea T	D 0-0		5,162	1		3	4				8				2						6		10	11	9	7			5		
Apr 22	(h)	Bradford	L 0-2		6,885	1		3	4				8				2						6	7	10	11	9				5		
Apr 29	(h)	Norwich C	W 4-2	Banks 2, Richardson 2	3,109	1		3	4		6		7			11	2								10		9				5		8
App						40	6	42	19	5	37	5	27	32	14	34	36	3	31	1	6	3	29	13	32	6	13	17	2	1	6	1	1
Goals								4			2		11	18	9	15						1	2	2	14	2	4	3					2

Bill Tudor

Meynell Burgin

Billy Elliott

1946-47

Division 2

Date		Opponent	Result	Score	Scorers	Att.	Sanders J	Pemberton J	Kirsell H	Witcomb D	Tranter G	Millard L	Elliott W	Clarke I	Walsh D	Duggan J	Hodgetts F	Hood G	Shaw C	Edwards C	Barlow R	Butler S	Evens C	Drury G	Grimley T	Richards G	Gripton W	Tighe J	Vernon J	Ryan R	Lunn W	Aldridge N	Finch R	Rowley A
Aug 31	(a)	Swansea T	W	3-2	Walsh 2, Hodgetts	29,186	1	2	3	4	5	6	7	8	9	10	11																	
Sep 2	(a)	Coventry C	L	2-3	Walsh 2	26,204	1	2	3	4	5	6	7	8	9	10	11																	
Sep 7	(h)	Tottenham H	W	3-2	Clarke, Walsh, Hodgetts	38,670	1	2	3	4	5	6	7	8	9	10	11																	
Sep 14	(a)	Burnley	W	2-0	Walsh, Clarke	20,881	1	2	3	4	5	6	7	8	9	10	11																	
Sep 18	(h)	Birmingham C	W	3-0	Walsh, Elliott 2	42,031	1	2	3	4		6	7	10	9	8	11	5																
Sep 21	(h)	Barnsley	L	2-5	Duggan, Walsh	24,965	1	2		4		6	7	10	9	8	11	5	3															
Sep 25	(a)	Birmingham C	L	0-1		50,535	1	2	3	4	5		7	10	9	8	11			6														
Sep 28	(a)	Newport C	W	7-2	Southam (og), Barlow, Elliott, Clarke 4	20,521	1	2	3	4	5	6	7	9		8					10	11												
Oct 5	(h)	Southampton	W	2-0	Clarke, Duggan	27,122	1	2	3	4	5	6	7	9		8					10	11												
Oct 12	(a)	Nottingham F	D	1-1	Witcomb	25,272	1	2	3	4	5	6	7	9		8						11	10											
Oct 19	(a)	Millwall	W	2-1	Duggan, Walsh	20,167	1	2	3		5	6	7		9	8	11		4	10														
Oct 26	(h)	Bradford	D	1-1	Duggan	20,028	1	2	3	4	5	6	7		9	10	11						8											
Nov 2	(a)	Manchester C	L	0-5		38,821	1	2	3	4	5	6	7	10	9		11						8											
Nov 9	(h)	West Ham U	L	2-3	Walsh, Millard	18,076	1	2	3	4	5	6	7		9		11			10			8											
Nov 16	(h)	Sheffield W	D	2-2	Walsh 2	19,245	1	2	3	4	5	6	7	8	9		11			10														
Nov 23	(h)	Fulham	W	6-1	Clarke 2, Walsh, Barlow 2, Hodgetts	20,243		2		4	5	6	7	8	9		11		3	10					1									
Nov 30	(a)	Bury	L	0-4		11,146		2		4	5	6	7	8	9		11		3	10					1									
Dec 7	(h)	Luton T	L	1-2	Richards	19,867		2	3	4	5	6		8	9		11			10					1	7								
Dec 14	(a)	Plymouth A	L	1-2	Walsh	27,495		2	3			6	7	8	9	10	11		5						1									
Dec 21	(h)	Leicester C	W	4-2	Duggan 2, Millard, Walsh	18,820	1	2	3	4		6	7	8	9	10	11		5															
Dec 25	(a)	Newcastle U	W	4-2	Walsh 2, Duggan, Elliott	44,722	1	2	3	4		6	7	8	9	10	11		5															
Dec 26	(h)	Newcastle U	W	3-2	Walsh 2, Clarke	31,794	1	2	3	4		6	7	8	9	10	11		5															
Dec 28	(h)	Swansea T	W	2-1	Hodgetts, Elliott	24,998	1	2	3	4		6	7	8	9	10	11		5															
Jan 4	(a)	Tottenham H	L	0-2		40,050	1	2	3	4		6	7	8	9	10	11		5															
Jan 18	(h)	Burnley	D	1-1	Duggan	40,082	1	2	3	4		6	7		9	8	11				10							5						
Feb 1	(h)	Newport C	D	2-2	Walsh 2	15,104		2	3	4		6	7		9	8	11		5	10					1									
Feb 8	(a)	Southampton	W	1-0	Elliott	10,095		2	3	4		6	7	8	9		11		5					10	1									
Mar 15	(a)	West Ham U	L	2-3	Hodgetts, Elliott	25,136		2	3			6	7	8	9		11		4					10	1				5					
Mar 22	(h)	Sheffield W	W	2-1	Drury, Clarke	35,448		2	3			6	7	8	9		11		4					10	1				5					
Mar 29	(a)	Fulham	W	1-0	Hodgetts	22,078		2	3			6	7	8	9	10	11		4						1				5					
Apr 4	(a)	Chesterfield	D	1-1	Walsh	16,044		2	3			6	7	8	9	10	11		4						1				5					
Apr 5	(h)	Bury	W	3-0	Clarke 3	27,745		2	3			6	7	8	9	10	11		4						1				5					
Apr 7	(h)	Chesterfield	W	3-2	Walsh 2, Hodgetts	21,180		2	3					8	9	10	7		4						1				5		6		11	
Apr 12	(a)	Luton T	L	0-2		20,990		2				3	11	8	9	10	7		4						1				5		6			
Apr 19	(h)	Plymouth A	L	2-5	Walsh, Clarke	25,068							7	8	9		11		3	4					1				5		6	2	10	
Apr 26	(a)	Leicester C	D	1-1	Clarke	30,017		2	3			6	7	8	9		11		4						1				5				10	
May 3	(h)	Coventry C	D	1-1	Hodgetts	23,807		2	3			6	7	8			11		4						1				5				10	9
May 10	(h)	Millwall	L	2-4	Elliott, Clarke	10,663		2	3			6	7	8	9		11		4						1				5	5				10
May 17	(h)	Nottingham F	W	5-1	Lunn, Millard, Walsh, Elliott, Clarke	10,506		2	3			6	7	8	9		11		4						1				5		10			
May 26	(a)	Barnsley	L	1-2	Edwards	15,070		2	3			6	7	8	9		11		4						1				5		10			
May 27	(a)	Bradford	W	4-2	Walsh (pen), Lunn 2, Elliott	9,990		2				3	7	8	9		11		4						1				5	6	10			
May 31	(h)	Manchester C	W	3-1	Walsh, Clarke, Williams (og)	21,281		2				3	7	8	9		11		4						1				5	6	10			
					App		21	41	35	26	16	39	40	37	38	25	39	2	4	25	10	3	1	6	20	1	2	1	14	5	5	1	3	2
					Goals					1		3	10	19	28	8	8			1	3			1		1						3			

Winger Frank Hodgetts had joined Albion from works team Accles and Pollock in 1939.

George Drury, an inside-forward signed from Arsenal in 1946, made only 29 League appearances before moving to Watford in 1948.

Centre-half Billy Gripton, signed from Brownhills Albion in 1935, was another player whose career was interrupted by war. He moved to Luton in 1948, after 16 League games for Albion.

115

1947-48

Division 2

Date			Result	Scorers	Att.	Grimley T	Pemberton J	Millard L	Edwards C	Vernon J	Hood G	Elliott W	Clarke I	Walsh D	Drury G	Hodgetts F	Sanders J	Williams G	Lunn W	Kinsell H	Ryan R	Gripton W	Evans A	Smith D	McKennan P	Heath N	Rowley A	Finch R	Gordon D	Haines J	Richards G	Taylor A
Aug 23	(h)	Tottenham H	W 1-0	Walsh	32,521	1	2	3	4	5	6	7	8	9	10	11																
27	(h)	Fulham	W 2-1	Walsh 2 (1 pen)	23,064	1	2	3	4	5	6	7	8	9	10	11																
30	(a)	Barnsley	W 1-0	Walsh	24,989	1	2	3	4	5	6	7	8	9	10	11																
Sep 3	(a)	Fulham	W 1-0	Drury	21,065	1	2	3	4	5	6	7	8	9	10	11																
6	(h)	Plymouth A	D 1-1	Drury	31,427	1	2	3	4	5	6	7	8	9	10	11																
10	(h)	Coventry C	W 3-1	Walsh 2, Drury	21,421		2	3	4	5	6	7	8	9	10	11										1						
13	(a)	Luton T	D 1-1	Drury	26,155		2	3		5	6	7	8	9	10	11			4							1						
15	(a)	Coventry C	L 0-1		30,048		2	3		5	6	7	8	9	10	11			4							1						
20	(h)	Brentford	W 3-2	Drury 2, Walsh	29,445		2	3		5	6	7		9	8	11			4	10						1						
27	(a)	Leicester C	D 1-1	Elliott	30,266		2	3		5	6	7		9	8	11			4	10						1						
Oct 4	(h)	Leeds U	W 3-2	Lunn 2, Elliott	30,479		2	6		5		7		9	8	11			10		3		4			1						
11	(h)	Millwall	W 2-1	Walsh 2	32,661		2	6		5		7	8	9		11				10	3		4			1						
18	(a)	Chesterfield	W 2-0	Elliott, Walsh	15,400		2	6		5		7	8	9							3		4	10	11	1						
25	(h)	West Ham U	L 1-2	Walsh	37,764		2	6		5		7	8	9							3		4	10	11	1						
Nov 1	(a)	Bury	W 2-1	Walsh 2	24,179		2	3	4	5	6	7		9						8				10	11	1						
8	(h)	Southampton	W 1-0	Smith	45,985		2	3	4	5	6	7		9						8				10	11	1						
15	(a)	Doncaster R	L 1-2	Walsh	21,774	1	2	3	4		6	7		9						8		5		10	11							
22	(h)	Nottingham F	W 3-2	Elliott, Drury, McKennan	28,568	1	2	6	5		4	7		9	10	11					3				8							
26	(a)	Bradford	L 1-3	McKennan	17,480	1	2	6	5		4	7		9	10	11					3				8							
Dec 6	(h)	Cardiff C	L 2-3	Walsh, McKennan	38,914	1	2	3	4	5		7		9	10	11					6				8							
13	(a)	Sheffield W	W 2-1	Walsh, Elliott	31,553		2	3	4			7		9	8	11					6	5				1	10					
20	(a)	Tottenham H	D 1-1	Walsh	52,071		2	3	4			7		9	8	11					6	5				1	10					
26	(h)	Newcastle U	L 0-1		48,322		2	3	4			7		9	8	11	1				6	5					10					
Jan 1	(a)	Newcastle U	L 1-3	Walsh	61,301		2	3	4			7		9	8	11	1				6	5					10					
3	(a)	Barnsley	L 0-2		25,045	1	2	3	4	5		7		9	8	11					6						10					
17	(a)	Plymouth A	L 1-2	Walsh	18,050		2	3		5		7		9	8		1			10	6		4				11					
31	(h)	Luton T	W 1-0	Walsh	26,979		2		4	5		7		9			1			10	6		3				11	8				
Feb 7	(a)	Brentford	L 0-1		22,140		2		4	5		7		9			1			10	6		3				11	8				
14	(h)	Leicester C	L 1-3	McKennan	29,322		2		4	5				9			1			10	6		3		7		11	8				
21	(a)	Leeds U	L 1-3	Rowley	22,096		2		4	5				9			1			10	6		3		7		11	8				
28	(a)	Millwall	D 1-1	Walsh	17,995		2		4	5				9			1			10	6		3		7		11	8				
Mar 6	(h)	Chesterfield	W 1-0	Hodgetts	25,242		2		4	5		7		9		8	1				6		3		10		11					
13	(a)	West Ham U	W 2-0	Haines, Elliott	25,133		2		4	5		7		9		8	1				6		3				11			10		
20	(h)	Bury	D 3-3	Walsh, Hodgetts, Rowley	28,638		2		4	5		7		9		8	1				6		3				11			10		
27	(a)	Southampton	D 1-1	Rowley	27,330		2		4	5		7		9		8	1				6		3				11			10		
29	(a)	Birmingham C	L 0-4		43,168		2		4	5		7		9		8	1				6		3				11			10		
30	(a)	Birmingham C	D 1-1	Elliott	51,945		2	3		5		7		9			1				6		4	8			11			10		
Apr 3	(h)	Doncaster R	L 1-3	Squires (og)	22,076		2	3		5		7		9			1				6		4	8			11			10		
10	(a)	Nottingham F	L 1-3	Taylor	19,713		2		4	5	6	7					1						3				11	8		10		9
17	(h)	Bradford	W 6-0	Haines 3, Taylor 2, Finch	13,349		2	3		5	6	7					1						4				11	8		10		9
24	(a)	Cardiff C	W 5-0	Taylor 2, Haines 2 (1 pen), Rowley	25,032		2	3		5	6	7					1						4				11	8		10		9
May 1	(h)	Sheffield W	D 1-1	Elliott	24,818		2	3		5	6	7					1						4				11	8		10		9
App						10	42	42	15	35	20	39	12	35	23	23	19	7	5	18	14	5	18	7	11	13	21	9	3	10	2	4
Goals												8		22	7	2			2					1	4		4	1		6		5

Albion's Jack Vernon shakes hands with West Ham skipper Sam Small before the start of the Second Division match on 25 October 1947.

1948-49

Division 2

Date		Opponent	Result	Scorers	Att.	Sanders J	Pemberton J	Kinsell H	Millard L	Vernon J	Hood G	Elliott W	Haines J	Walsh D	Barlow R	Smith A	Hodgetts F	Williams C	Finch R	Ryan R	Boyd J	Barker R	Cox S	Rowley A	Morrow H	Wilcox E	Shepherd E	Kennedy J
Aug 21	(a)	Nottingham F	W 1-0	Walsh	32,110	1	2	3	4	5	6	7	8	9	10	11												
25	(h)	Chesterfield	D 0-0		29,041	1	2	3	4	5	6	7	8	9	10	11												
28	(h)	Bury	L 2-3	Barlow, Walsh	31,904	1	2	3	4	5	6		8	9	10	11	7											
Sep 1	(a)	Chesterfield	D 0-0		30,799	1	2	3	4	5	6	7	10	9				8		11								
4	(a)	West Ham U	L 0-1		26,528	1	2	3	4	5	6	7	10	9				8		11								
8	(h)	Lincoln C	W 5-0	Haines 2, Walsh 3	13,009	1	2	3	6		5	7	10	9				8	4	11								
11	(h)	Tottenham H	D 2-2	Haines, Walsh	32,279	1		3	6		5	7	10	9			11	8	4		2							
15	(a)	Lincoln C	W 3-0	Walsh, Barker, Ryan	17,232	1	2	3	6		5	7	10	9				8		4		11						
18	(a)	Brentford	D 0-0		33,145	1		3	2	5	6	7	10	9				8		4		11						
25	(h)	Leicester C	W 2-1	Williams, Walsh	32,517	1		3		5	6	7	10	9				8		4		11	2					
Oct 2	(a)	Leeds U	W 3-1	Williams 2, Walsh	30,068	1		3		5	6	7	10	9				8		4		11	2					
9	(a)	Fulham	W 2-1	Haines, Barker	22,103	1	2	3	6		5	7	10		4			8				11		9				
16	(h)	Plymouth A	W 3-0	Williams, Haines, Walsh	32,849	1	2	3	4	5	6	7	10	9				8				11						
23	(a)	Blackburn R	D 0-0		28,186	1	2	3	4	5	6	7	10	9				8				11						
30	(h)	Cardiff C	W 2-0	Haines, Williams	46,036	1	2	3	4	5	6	7	10	9				8				11						
Nov 6	(a)	Queen's Park R	W 2-0	Walsh, Hodgetts	24,200	1	2	3	4	5	6	7	10	9			11	8										
13	(h)	Luton T	W 2-1	Williams, Elliott	32,589	1	2	3	4	5	6	7	10	9			11	8										
20	(h)	Bradford	L 1-4	Haines	18,064	1	2	3	4	5	6	7	10	9			11	8										
27	(h)	Southampton	W 2-0	Millard, Elliott	47,028	1	2	3	4	5	6	7	10	9				8							11			
Dec 4	(a)	Barnsley	L 0-2		20,864	1	2	3	4	5	6	7		9	10			8								11		
11	(h)	Grimsby T	W 5-2	Williams 3, Haines (pen), Walsh	22,664	1	2	3	4	5	6	7	10	9				8								11		
18	(h)	Nottingham F	W 2-1	Haines, Elliott	32,583	1	2	3	4	5	6	7	10	9				8									11	
25	(h)	Sheffield W	W 1-0	Vernon	34,881	1	2	3	4	5	6	7	10	9				8									11	
27	(a)	Sheffield W	L 1-2	Westlake (og)	32,513	1	2	3	4	5	6	7	10	9				8									11	
Jan 1	(a)	Bury	L 0-4		16,861	1	2	3	4	5	6	7	10	9				8									11	
15	(h)	West Ham U	W 2-1	Walsh 2	33,100	1	2	3	4	5	6	7	11	9	10			8										
22	(a)	Tottenham H	L 0-2		62,556	1	2	3	4	5	6	7	11	9	10			8										
Feb 5	(h)	Brentford	W 2-0	Walsh, Smith	39,482	1	2		3	5	6	7	10	9	4	11		8										
Mar 5	(h)	Fulham	L 1-2	Elliott	27,595	1	2	11	3	5	6	7	10	9	4			8										
12	(a)	Plymouth A	W 2-1	Walsh, Elliott	26,011	1	2		3	5	6	7	10	9	4			8				11						
19	(h)	Blackburn R	W 2-1	Elliott, Haines	36,053	1	2		3	5	6	7	10	9	4			8				11						
26	(a)	Cardiff C	D 2-2	Haines, Walsh	55,177	1	2	3	6		5	7	10	9	4			8				11						
Apr 2	(a)	Queen's Park R	D 1-1	Elliott	35,093	1	2	3	6	5		7	10	9	4			8				11						
6	(h)	Leeds U	W 1-0	Barlow (pen)	28,562	1	2		3	5		7	10	9	4			8		6		11						
9	(a)	Luton T	W 1-0	Morrow	16,651	1	2		3	5			10	9				8		6		11			7			4
16	(h)	Bradford	W 7-1	Walsh 4 (1 pen), Haines 2, Morrow	39,241	1	2		3	5		7	10	9				8		6					11			4
18	(h)	Coventry C	W 1-0	Haines	42,488	1	2		3	5		7	10	9				8		6					11			4
19	(a)	Coventry C	L 0-1		39,480	1	2		3	5		7	10	9				8		6					11			4
23	(a)	Southampton	D 1-1	Smith	30,856	1	2		3	5		7	8	9	10	11				6								4
30	(h)	Barnsley	W 2-0	Barlow, Walsh	31,966	1	2	3		5	6	7		9	10	11			4									8
May 5	(a)	Leicester C	W 3-0	Walsh, Kennedy, Barlow	34,585	1	2	3		5	6	7		9	10	11			4									8
7	(a)	Grimsby T	L 0-1		16,056	1	2	3		5	6	7		9	10	11			4									8
				App		42	38	30	41	38	34	40	38	41	22	8	5	31	3	14	1	14	2	1	5	2	4	8
				Goals					1	1		7	14	23	4	2	1	9		1		2			2			1

Southampton's Ian Black foils eager Albion forwards in the Second Division match on 23 April 1949.

Dave Walsh scored 23 League goals in 1948-9.

117

1949-50

Division 1

Date		Opponent	Res	Score	Scorers	Att	Sanders J	Pemberton J	Millard L	Kennedy J	Vernon J	Barlow R	Elliott W	Williams C	Walsh D	Haines J	Lee G	Hood G	Ryan R	Smith A	Wilcox E	Horne L	Inwood G	Dudley J	Gordon G	Betteridge M	Allen R	Rickaby S
Aug 20	(h)	Charlton A	W	1-0	Williams	49,596	1	2	3	4	5	6	7	8	9	10	11											
24	(a)	Birmingham C	L	0-2		50,027	1	2	3	4	5		7	8	9	10	11	6										
27	(a)	Manchester U	D	1-1	Williams	44,655	1	2	3	4	5		7	8	9	10	11	6										
31	(h)	Birmingham C	W	3-0	Haines 2, Walsh	50,299	1	2	3	4	5		7	8	9	10	11	6										
Sep 3	(h)	Chelsea	D	1-1	Williams	45,337	1	2	3	4	5		7	8	9	10	11	6										
7	(h)	Arsenal	L	1-2	Elliott	43,663	1	2	3		5		7	8	9	10		6	4	11								
10	(a)	Stoke C	W	3-1	Haines, Williams 2	30,021	1	2	3		5		7	8		10		6	4	11	9							
14	(a)	Arsenal	L	1-4	Walsh	48,073	1	2	3		5		7	8	9	10		6	4	11								
17	(h)	Burnley	W	3-0	Elliott (pen), Walsh, Williams	37,091	1	2	3		5		7	8	9	10		6	4	11								
24	(a)	Sunderland	L	1-2	Elliott	50,896	1	2	3		5		7	8	9	10		6	4	11								
Oct 1	(h)	Liverpool	L	0-1		44,219	1	2	3				7	8	9	10	11	6	4		5							
8	(h)	Aston Villa	D	1-1	Wilcox	53,690	1	2	3	4	5		7	8			11	6	10		9							
15	(a)	Wolves	D	1-1	Elliott	56,661	1	2	3	4	5		7	8	9			6	10			11						
22	(h)	Portsmouth	W	3-0	Walsh, Williams, Elliott	40,808	1	2	3	4	5		7	8	9			6	10			11						
29	(a)	Huddersfield T	D	1-1	Walsh	22,461	1	2	3	4	5		7	8	9			6	10			11						
Nov 5	(h)	Everton	W	4-0	Walsh 2, Smith, Williams	29,309	1	2	3	4	5		7	8	9			6	10			11						
12	(a)	Middlesbrough	L	0-3		28,014	1	2	3	4	5		7	8	9			6	10			11						
26	(a)	Newcastle U	L	1-5	Walsh	32,415	1	2	3	4	5	10	7	8	9			6				11						
Dec 3	(h)	Fulham	W	4-1	Walsh 2, Elliott, Barlow	30,883	1	2	3	4	5	10	7	8	9			6				11						
10	(a)	Manchester C	D	1-1	Elliott	29,544	1	2			5	10	7	8	9		3	6				11	4					
17	(a)	Charlton A	W	2-1	Walsh 2	20,369	1	2	3	4	5	10		8	9		11	6						7				
24	(h)	Manchester U	L	1-2	Walsh	44,885	1	2	3	4	5	10	7	8	9		11	6										
26	(a)	Bolton W	L	0-3		38,122	1		2	4	5	10			9		11	6	3					8	7			
27	(h)	Bolton W	W	2-1	Walsh, Barlow	41,746	1	2	3	4	5	10		8	9			6				11		7				
31	(a)	Chelsea	L	1-2	Gordon	41,610	1	2	3	4	5	10		8	9			6				11			7			
Jan 14	(h)	Stoke C	D	0-0		34,840	1	2	3	8	5	10			9			6	11				4	7				
21	(a)	Burnley	D	0-0		26,193	1	2	3	8	5	10			9			6	11				4	7				
Feb 4	(h)	Sunderland	L	0-2		36,101	1	2	3	8	5	10			9		11	6					4	7				
18	(a)	Liverpool	L	1-2	Lee	46,634	1	2	3	4	5	6		8	9		11		10					7				
25	(a)	Aston Villa	L	0-1		40,132	1	2	3	4	5	6			9		11		10					7	8			
Mar 4	(h)	Wolves	D	1-1	Allen	60,945	1	2	3	4	5	10					11	6	8	9							7	
11	(a)	Blackpool	L	0-3		23,088	1	2	3	4		10					11	6	8	9	5						7	
18	(h)	Newcastle U	D	1-1	Walsh	33,469	1	2	3	4	5	10			9		11	6	8								7	
29	(a)	Everton	W	2-1	Allen, Barlow	18,345	1	2	3		5	10			9		11	6	8				4				7	
Apr 1	(h)	Middlesbrough	L	0-3		32,942	1	2	3	4	5	10			9		11	6	8								7	
7	(a)	Derby C	L	1-3	Allen	25,198	1	2	3	4	5				9		11	6						10	7		8	
8	(a)	Portsmouth	W	1-0	Ryan	33,903	1	2	3	4	5				9		11	6	8					10	7			
10	(h)	Derby C	W	1-0	Lee	31,516	1	2	3	4	5	10			9		11	6						8	7			
15	(h)	Huddersfield T	D	0-0		28,240	1	2	3	4	5	10			9		11	6						8	9		7	
22	(a)	Fulham	W	1-0	Allen	34,909	1	2	3	4	5	6			9		11							10	8		7	
26	(h)	Blackpool	W	1-0	Allen	28,858	1	2	3	4	5	6			9		11							10	8		7	
29	(h)	Manchester C	D	0-0		16,780	1		3	4	5	6			9		11							10	8		7	2
App							42	40	41	34	40	23	21	26	37	11	25	13	34	21	4	2	10	13	11	2	11	1
Goals												3	7	8	15	3	2		1	1	1				1		5	

Jack Vernon, Albion's skipper, missed only two League games in 1949-50.

Les Horne was a solid centre-half and Vernon's understudy. His first-team chances were limited and he eventually left for Plymouth Argyle.

1950-51

Division 1

Date	V	Opponent	Result	Scorers	Att	Sanders J	Pemberton J	Millard L	Kennedy J	Vernon J	Barlow R	Elliott W	Williams C	Walsh D	Allen R	Lee G	Rickaby S	Richardson F	Smith A	Gordon D	Ryan R	Betteridge M	Heath N	Dudley J	Wilcox E	Guy H	Horne L	McCall A	Griffin F
Aug 19	(a)	Aston Villa	L 0-2		65,036	1	2	3	4	5	6	7	8	9	10	11													
23	(a)	Newcastle U	D 1-1	Elliott	48,720	1		3	4	5	6	7	8	9	10	11	2												
26	(h)	Stoke C	D 1-1	Elliott	33,215	1		3	4	5	6	7	8	9	11		2	10											
30	(h)	Newcastle U	L 1-2	Walsh	29,377	1		3	4	5	6	7	8	9	11		2	10											
Sep 2	(a)	Everton	W 3-0	Barlow, Allen, Smith	46,602	1		3	4	5	6	7	8	9	11		2		10										
6	(a)	Middlesbrough	L 1-2	Walsh	28,000	1		3	4	5	6		8	9	11		2		10	7									
9	(h)	Portsmouth	W 5-0	Walsh, Elliott, Williams, Smith 2	34,460	1		3	4	5	6	7	8	9	11		2		10										
13	(h)	Middlesbrough	L 2-3	Elliott, Allen	31,530	1		3	4	5	6	7	8	9	11		2		10										
16	(a)	Chelsea	D 1-1	Walsh	39,570	1		3	4	5	6	7	8	9	11		2		10										
23	(h)	Burnley	W 2-1	Lee, Walsh	32,638	1		3	4	5	10		8	9	7	11	2				6								
30	(a)	Arsenal	L 0-3		53,700	1		3	4	5	10	7		9	8	11	2				6								
Oct 7	(a)	Derby C	D 1-1	Williams	28,042	1		3	5		6		8	9	7	11	2		10		4								
14	(h)	Liverpool	D 1-1	Walsh	35,030	1		3	4	5	6		8	9	7	11	2				10								
21	(a)	Blackpool	L 1-2	Allen	32,142	1		3	4	5	6		8		7	11	2	9			10								
28	(h)	Tottenham H	L 1-2	Barlow	44,543	1		3	4	5	6	7	8		11		2	9			10								
Nov 4	(a)	Fulham	W 1-0	Richardson	25,076			3	4	5	6				7	11	2	9		8	10		1						
11	(h)	Bolton W	L 0-1		28,816			3	4	5	6				7	11	2	9		8	10		1						
18	(a)	Charlton A	W 3-2	Richardson, Allen, Croker (og)	21,876			3		5	6				7	11	2	9		8	10		1	4					
25	(h)	Manchester U	L 0-1		28,146			3		5	6				7	11	2	9		8	10		1	4					
Dec 2	(a)	Wolves	L 1-3	Ryan	44,937			3		5	6				7	11	2	9		8			1	4	10				
9	(h)	Sunderland	W 3-1	Richardson 2, Wilcox	26,666			3	4	5	6				7	11	2	9		8			1		10				
16	(h)	Aston Villa	W 2-0	Richardson, Wilcox	28,796			3	4	5	6				11		2	9		7	10		1		8				
23	(a)	Stoke C	D 1-1	Allen	19,198			3	4	5	6				11		2	9		7	10		1		8				
25	(h)	Sheffield W	L 1-3	Ryan	28,023					5	6				7	11	2	9			10		1	4	8	3			
26	(a)	Sheffield W	L 0-3		44,819					5	6			8	7	11	2	9			10		1	4			3		
30	(h)	Everton	L 0-1		17,912	1		3		5	6				7	11	2	9			10			4	8				
Jan 13	(a)	Portsmouth	D 2-2	Richardson, Allen	23,642	1		3	4	5	8				7	11	2	9			10			6					
20	(h)	Chelsea	D 1-1	Lee	30,985	1		3	4	5	8				7	11	2	9			6							10	
Feb 3	(a)	Burnley	W 1-0	Allen	19,104	1		3	4	5	6				7	11	2	9						8				10	
17	(h)	Arsenal	W 2-0	Richardson 2	35,999	1		3	4	5	6				7	11	2	9						8				10	
24	(h)	Derby C	L 1-2	Dudley	33,702	1		3	4	5	6				7	11	2	9						8				10	
Mar 3	(a)	Liverpool	D 1-1	McCall	33,654	1		3		5	6				7	11	2	9			4			8				10	
17	(a)	Tottenham H	L 0-5		45,180	1		3	4	5	6				7	11	2	9						8				10	
24	(h)	Fulham	D 0-0		23,803	1		3	4	5	6				7	11	2	9						8				10	
26	(h)	Huddersfield T	L 0-2		24,360	1		3	4	5	6				7	11	2	9						8				10	
27	(a)	Huddersfield T	W 2-1	Barlow 2	32,401	1		3	4	5	9				11		2			7	6			8				10	
31	(a)	Bolton W	W 2-0	Barlow, Gordon	24,898	1		3	4	5	9				11		2			7	6			8				10	
Apr 4	(h)	Blackpool	L 1-3	Barlow (pen)	39,591	1		3	4	5	9				11		2			7	6			8				10	
7	(h)	Charlton A	W 3-0	Allen, McCall, Ryan	26,083	1		3	4	5	9	7		8	11		2				6							10	
14	(a)	Manchester U	L 0-3		24,764	1		3	4	5	9	7		8	11		2				6							10	
21	(h)	Wolves	W 3-2	Barlow 2, Allen	39,066	1		3	4	5	9	7		10	11		2				6							8	
28	(a)	Sunderland	D 1-1	Allen	20,149			3	4	5	9			10	11		2				6		1					8	7
App						31	1	40	35	41	42	13	14	14	40	31	41	24	6	11	24	3	11	16	6	1	1	15	1
Goals											8	4	2	6	10	2		8	3	1	3			1	2			2	

Arthur Smith, Dave Walsh, Ronnie Allen, Cyril Williams, Denis Gordon and Billy Elliott training at The Hawthorns in August 1950.

1951-52

Division 1

Date		Opponents	Result	Scorers	Att	Sanders J	Rickaby S	Millard L	Dudley J	Vernon J	Ryan R	Allen R	Smith A	Richardson F	McCall A	Lee G	Gordon D	Kennedy J	Heath N	Barlow R	Carter W	Griffin F	Horne L	Williams S	Nicholls J	Cutler R	Corbett G
Aug 18	(h)	Manchester U	D 3-3	Allen, Smith 2	29,897	1	2	3	4	5	6	7	8	9	10	11											
20	(a)	Stoke C	D 1-1	Smith	19,122	1	2	3	4	5	6	7	8	9	10	11											
25	(a)	Tottenham H	L 1-3	Allen	51,544	1	2	3	4	5	6	7	8	9	10	11											
29	(h)	Stoke C	W 1-0	Allen	18,903	1	2	3	4	5	6	7	8		10	11	9										
Sep 1	(h)	Preston NE	D 1-1	Allen	27,645	1	2	3	4	5	6	7	8		10	11	9										
5	(h)	Newcastle U	D 3-3	McMichael (og), McCall, Lee	29,311	1	2	3	4		6	7	8	9	10	11		5									
8	(a)	Burnley	L 1-6	Smith	23,868	1	2	3	4		6	7	8	9	10	11		5									
15	(h)	Charlton A	D 1-1	Allen	23,197		2	3		5	6	7	8		10	11		4	1	9							
22	(a)	Fulham	L 0-1		30,025		2	3		5	6	7			10	11		4	1	9	8						
29	(h)	Middlesbrough	L 2-3	Smith, Allen	28,961		2	3		5	10	9	8			11		4	1	6		7					
Oct 6	(h)	Huddersfield T	D 0-0		24,236		2	3	4			9	8		10	11		5	1	6		7					
13	(a)	Chelsea	W 3-1	Carter, Allen 2	34,917		2	3		5	10	9				11		4	1	6	8	7					
20	(h)	Portsmouth	W 5-0	Griffin 2, Smith, Kennedy, Allen (pen)	26,736		2	3		5	10	9	8			11		4	1	6		7					
27	(a)	Liverpool	W 5-2	Ryan, Lee, Griffin 2, Allen	34,891		2	3		5	10	9	8			11		4	1	6		7					
Nov 3	(h)	Blackpool	D 1-1		43,214		2	3		5	10	9	8			11		4	1	6		7					
10	(a)	Arsenal	L 3-6	Allen 2, Griffin	53,432		2	3		5	10	9	8			11		4	1	6		7					
17	(h)	Manchester C	W 3-2	Lee, Griffin, Allen	32,126	1	2	3		5	10	9			8	11		4		6		7					
24	(a)	Derby C	L 1-2	Lee	21,811	1	2	3		5	10	9			8	11		4		6		7					
Dec 1	(h)	Aston Villa	L 1-2	Allen	47,782	1	2	3		5	10	9			8	11		4		6		7					
8	(a)	Sunderland	D 3-3	Lee, Allen, Hall (og)	26,774	1	2	3		5	10	9			8	11		4		6		7					
15	(a)	Manchester U	L 1-5	Allen	27,548	1	2	3	6	5	10	9			8	11		4				7					
22	(h)	Tottenham H	W 3-1	Dudley 2, Allen	30,094	1	2	3	8	5	10	9				11		4		6		7					
25	(a)	Bolton W	L 2-3	Dudley, Rickaby	33,005	1	2	3	8	5	10	9				11		4		6		7					
26	(h)	Bolton W	W 3-2	Allen 3	37,822	1	2	3	8	5	10	9				11		4		6		7					
29	(a)	Preston NE	L 0-1		31,979		2	3	8		10	9				11		4	1	6		7	5				
Jan 5	(h)	Burnley	D 1-1	Lee	26,115		2	3	8		10	9				11		4	1	6		7	5				
19	(a)	Charlton A	D 3-3	Lee, Allen, Griffin	18,126		2	3	8		10	9				11		4	1	6		7	5				
26	(h)	Fulham	L 0-2		24,375		2	3	8		10	9				11		4	1	6		7	5				
Feb 9	(a)	Middlesbrough	W 1-0	Lee	20,123		2	3	8		10	9				11		4	1	6		7	5				
16	(a)	Huddersfield T	L 0-3		17,250		2	3	4		8					11		10	1	6		7	5		9		
Mar 1	(h)	Chelsea	L 0-1		24,431		2		8	5	10					11		4	1			7	3	6	9		
12	(a)	Portsmouth	D 1-1	Nicholls	22,991		2	3			10	9				11		4	1	6		7	5		8		
15	(h)	Liverpool	D 3-3	Ryan, Allen 2	27,183		2	3			10	9				11		4	1	6		7	5		8		
22	(a)	Blackpool	L 0-2		20,128		2	3			10	9				11		4	1	6		7	5		8		
Apr 5	(a)	Manchester C	W 2-1	Nicholls, Allen	13,842		2	3	4		10	9				11		5	1	6		7			8		
12	(h)	Derby C	W 1-0	Allen	27,733		2	3	4		10	9						5	1	6		7			8	11	
14	(h)	Wolves	W 2-1	Griffin, Nicholls	33,429		2	3	4		10	9						5	1	6		7			8	11	
15	(a)	Wolves	W 4-1	Allen 3, Nicholls	48,120		2	3	4		10	9						5	1	6		7			8		11
19	(a)	Aston Villa	L 0-2		50,137		2	3	4		10	9				11		5	1	6		7			8		
21	(h)	Arsenal	W 3-1	Allen, Lee, Ryan	29,618		2	3	4		10	9				11		5	1	6		7			8		
23	(a)	Newcastle U	W 4-1	Ryan, Nicholls, Allen, Lee	31,188		2	3	4		10	9				11		5	1	6		7			8		
26	(h)	Sunderland	D 1-1	Allen (pen)	31,154		2	3	4		10	9				11		5	1	6		7			8		
					App	15	42	41	26	22	42	40	14	5	16	39	2	36	27	33	2	33	10	2	12	2	1
					Goals		1		3		4	32	6		1	10		1			1	8			5		

Arsenal's Alex Forbes and Albion's Ray Barlow go for a high ball at Highbury in November 1951.

Outside-left Reg Cutler was George Lee's understudy. He made only two appearances in 1951-2 and eventually signed for Bournemouth in 1956, having managed only five League games in six years with Albion.

1952-53

Division 1

Date	Ven	Opponent	Result	Scorers	Att	Heath N	Rickaby S	Millard L	Dudley J	Kennedy J	Barlow R	Griffin F	Nicholls J	Allen R	Ryan R	Lee G	Evans E	Williams S	Cutler R	Dugdale J	Gallagher M	Mountford D	Sanders J	Carter W	Hodgkisson K
Aug 23	(a)	Tottenham H	W 4-3	Clarke (og), Allen 2, Lee	56,552	1	2	3	4	5	6	7	8	9	10	11									
27	(h)	Newcastle U	W 1-0	Lee	46,206	1	2	3	4	5	6	7	8	9	10	11									
30	(h)	Burnley	L 1-2	Allen	31,543	1	2	3	4	5	6	7	8	9	10	11									
Sep 6	(a)	Preston NE	L 0-1		34,072	1	2	3	4	5	6	7	8	9	10	11									
10	(h)	Cardiff C	W 1-0	Barlow	23,494	1	2	3	4	5	6	7		9	10	11	8								
13	(h)	Stoke C	W 3-2	Griffin, Ryan, Allen	27,409	1	2	3	4	5	6	7		9	10	11	8								
17	(a)	Cardiff C	W 2-1	Dudley, Allen	32,156	1	2	3	4	5	6	7		9	10	11	8								
20	(a)	Manchester C	W 1-0	Allen	33,043	1	2	3	4	5	6	7		9	10	11	8								
27	(h)	Liverpool	W 3-0	Griffin 2, Allen	33,142	1	2	3	4	5	6	7		9	10	11	8								
Oct 4	(a)	Middlesbrough	L 2-4	Allen, Evans	27,065	1	2	3	4		6	7		9	10	11	8	5							
11	(a)	Sunderland	L 0-1		40,756	1	2	3	4	5	6	7		9	10	11	8								
18	(h)	Wolves	D 1-1	Lee	54,480	1	2	3	4	5	6	7		9	10	11	8								
25	(a)	Charlton A	D 0-0		24,550	1	2	3	4	5	6	7	8	9	10	11									
Nov 1	(h)	Arsenal	W 2-0	Lee, Ryan	43,041	1	2	3	4	5	6	7	8	9	10	11									
8	(a)	Derby C	D 1-1	Lee	26,234	1	2	3	4	5	6	7	8	9	10	11									
15	(h)	Blackpool	L 0-1		33,869	1	2	3	4	5	6	7	8	9		11					10				
22	(a)	Chelsea	W 2-0	Allen, Nicholls	34,142	1	2	3	4	5	6	7	8	9	10	11									
29	(h)	Manchester U	W 3-1	Allen, Lee, Griffin	23,617	1	2	3	4	5	6	7	8	9	10	11									
Dec 6	(a)	Portsmouth	W 2-1	Griffin, Allen	27,365	1	2	3	4	5	6	7	8	9	10	11									
13	(h)	Bolton W	L 0-1		16,250	1	2	3	4		6	7	8		10	11	9			5					
20	(a)	Tottenham H	W 2-1	Ryan, Allen	18,816	1	2	3	4	5	6	7	8	9	10	11									
26	(a)	Sheffield W	W 5-4	Curtis (og), Barlow, Gannon (og), Nicholls, Allen	59,398	1	2	3	4	5	6	7	8	9	10	11									
27	(h)	Sheffield W	L 0-1		52,681	1	2	3	4	5	6	7	8	9	10	11									
Jan 1	(a)	Newcastle U	W 5-3	Ryan, Lee, Nicholls, Griffin, Barlow	48,944	1	2	3	4	5	6	7	8	9	10	11									
3	(a)	Burnley	L 0-5		35,780	1	2	3	4	5		7	8	9	10		6		11						
17	(h)	Preston NE	W 2-1	Ryan, Nicholls	44,763	1	2	3	4	5	6	7	8	9	10	11									
24	(a)	Stoke C	L 1-5	Nicholls	35,226	1	2	3	4	5	6	7	8	9	10	11									
Feb 7	(h)	Manchester C	W 2-1	Allen, Barlow	27,932	1	2	3	4	5	6	7	8	9	10	11									
14	(a)	Liverpool	L 0-3		24,981	1	2		4		6			9	10	11	8	3		5		7			
21	(h)	Middlesbrough	W 3-0	Allen 2, Lee	24,433	1	2	3	4		6			9	10	11	8			5		7			
28	(h)	Sunderland	D 1-1	Ryan	31,831	1	2	3	4		6			9	10	11	8			5		7			
Mar 7	(a)	Wolves	L 0-2		48,247	1	2	3	4		6			9	10	11	8			5		7			
14	(h)	Charlton A	W 3-1	Evans, Griffin 2	26,944	1	2	3	4		6	7		9	10	11	8			5					
21	(a)	Arsenal	D 2-2	Evans, Lee	50,078	1	2	3	4		6	7		9	10	11	8			5					
28	(h)	Derby C	D 2-2	Ryan, Lee	17,686	1	2	3	4		6	7		9	10	11	8			5					
Apr 4	(a)	Blackpool	L 0-2		30,502	1	2	3	4		6	7		9	10	11	8			5					
6	(h)	Aston Villa	W 3-2	Allen 2 (1 pen), Griffin	34,310		2	3	4		6	7		9	10	11				5			1	8	
7	(a)	Aston Villa	D 1-1	Allen	49,510		2	3	4		6	7		9	8	11				5			1		10
11	(h)	Chelsea	L 0-1		32,703		2	3	4		6	7		9	8	11				5			1		10
18	(a)	Manchester U	D 2-2	Hodgkisson, Ryan	31,380		2	3	4		6		7	9	10	11				5			1		8
22	(a)	Bolton W	W 1-0	Allen	28,547		2	3	4		6		7	9	10	11				5			1		8
25	(h)	Portsmouth	W 2-0	Hodgkisson 2	24,879		2	3	4		6		7	9		11				5			1	8	10
App						36	42	41	42	26	41	35	23	41	40	41	17	3	1	15	1	4	6	2	5
Goals									1		4	9	5	20	8	10	3								3

Jimmy Dudley clears his lines against West Ham United at Upton Park in the FA Cup, 1952-3.

Ken Hodgkisson spent six years with Albion (1949-55). In 1952-3 he managed five League games.

1953-54

Division 1

Date		Opponent	Result	Scorers	Att	Heath N	Rickaby S	Millard L	Dudley J	Dugdale J	Barlow R	Griffin F	Hodgkisson K	Allen R	Nicholls J	Lee G	Ryan R	Williams S	Cox F	Brookes W	Kennedy J	Carter W	Sanders J	Jones G	Cutler R	Davies R
Aug 19	(h)	Arsenal	W 2-0	Nicholls 2	41,812	1	2	3	4	5	6	7	8	9	10	11										
22	(h)	Bolton W	D 1-1	Barlow	29,122	1	2	3	4	5	6	7	8	9	10	11										
26	(a)	Manchester U	W 3-1	Dudley, Nicholls, Lee	42,000	1	2	3	4	5	6	7	8	9	10	11										
29	(a)	Preston NE	W 2-0	Nicholls 2	32,000	1	2	3	4	5	6	7	8	9	10	11										
Sep 2	(h)	Manchester U	W 2-0	Allen, Hodgkisson	29,036	1	2	3	4	5	6	7	8	9	10	11										
5	(h)	Tottenham H	W 3-0	Allen, Nicholls, Ramsey (og)	43,168	1	2	3	4	5	6	7		9	10	11	8									
9	(h)	Newcastle U	D 2-2	Ryan, Barlow	32,953	1	2	3	4	5	6	7		9	10	11	8									
12	(a)	Burnley	W 4-1	Nicholls 2, Allen, Ryan	38,948	1	2	3	4	5	6	7		9	10	11	8									
16	(a)	Newcastle U	W 7-3	Nicholls 3, Allen 2, Griffin, Ryan	58,075	1	2	3	4	5	6	7		9	10	11	8									
19	(h)	Charlton A	L 2-3	Barlow, Griffin	43,809	1	2	3	4	5	6	7		9	10	11	8									
26	(a)	Sheffield W	W 3-2	Griffin, Nicholls, Lee	45,503	1	2		4	5	6	7		9	10	11	8	3								
Oct 3	(h)	Middlesbrough	W 2-1	Nicholls, Lee	37,042	1	2	3	4	5	6	7		9	10	11	8									
10	(h)	Huddersfield T	W 4-0	Allen 3, Nicholls	47,043	1	2	3	4	5		7		9	10	11	8			6						
17	(a)	Sheffield U	W 2-1	Allen, Nicholls	35,114	1	2	3	4	5	6	7		9	10	11	8									
24	(h)	Chelsea	W 5-2	Allen 3, Nicholls, Lee	35,443	1	2	3	4	5	6	7		9	10	11	8									
31	(a)	Blackpool	L 1-4	Allen	27,104	1	2	3	4	5	6	7		9	10	11	8									
Nov 7	(h)	Sunderland	W 2-0	Barlow, Lee	37,704	1	2	3	4		6	7		9	8	11	10				5					
14	(a)	Wolves	L 0-1		56,590	1	2	3	4		6	7		9	8	11	10				5					
21	(h)	Cardiff C	W 6-1	Allen 4, Nicholls 2	39,618	1		3	4		6	7		9	10	11	8	2			5					
28	(a)	Manchester C	W 3-2	Lee, Allen, Nicholls	40,753	1	2	3	4		6	7		9	10	11	8				5					
Dec 5	(h)	Portsmouth	L 2-3	Nicholls, Allen	29,623	1	2	3	4		6	7		9	10	11	8				5					
12	(a)	Arsenal	D 2-2	Nicholls 2	55,269	1	2	3	4		6	7		9	10	11	8				5					
19	(a)	Bolton W	L 1-2	Ryan	27,198	1	2	3	4		6	7		9	10	11	8				5					
25	(h)	Liverpool	W 5-2	Nicholls, Griffin 2, Barlow, Allen	30,390	1	2	3	4		6	7		9	10	11	8				5					
26	(a)	Liverpool	D 0-0		51,167	1	2	3	4		6	7		9	10	11	8				5					
Jan 2	(h)	Preston NE	W 3-2	Allen 2, Nicholls	20,306	1	2	3	4		6	7		9	10	11	8				5					
16	(a)	Tottenham H	W 1-0	Allen	48,812	1	2	3	4	5	6	7		9		11	8					10				
23	(h)	Burnley	D 0-0		42,850	1	2	3	4	5	6	7		9	10	11	8									
Feb 6	(a)	Charlton A	D 1-1	Allen	27,553	1	2	3	4	5	6	7		9		11	8					10				
13	(h)	Sheffield W	W 4-2	Nicholls, Butler (og), Rickaby, Ryan	38,475	1	2	3	4	5		7		9	10	11	8			6						
24	(a)	Middlesbrough	D 1-1	Allen	15,389	1	2	3	4	5	6	7		9	10	11	8									
27	(a)	Huddersfield T	W 2-0	Ryan, Nicholls	48,237		2	3	4	5	6	7		9	10	11	8						1			
Mar 6	(h)	Sheffield U	D 2-2	Nicholls, Lee	37,650		2	3	4	5	6	7		9	10	11	8						1			
17	(a)	Chelsea	L 0-5		46,089	1	2	3	4	5	6	7		9	10	11	8									
20	(h)	Blackpool	W 2-1	Allen, Ryan	53,210	1		3	4	5	6	7		9	10	11	8	2								
31	(a)	Sunderland	L 1-2	Cox	48,060	1			4	5	6					11	8	3	9		2	10		7		
Apr 3	(h)	Wolves	L 0-1		49,884			3	4	5		9					8	2	7		6	10	1			11
10	(a)	Cardiff C	L 0-2		50,967			3	4	5				9	10	11	8	2	7		6		1			
17	(h)	Manchester C	W 1-0	Allen (pen)	38,742			3	4	5	6	7		9	10	11	8	2					1			
19	(h)	Aston Villa	D 1-1	Nicholls	45,972			3	4	5	6	7		9	10	11	8	2					1			
20	(a)	Aston Villa	L 1-6	Griffin	45,557			3	4	5	6	7		9	10	11	8	2					1			
24	(a)	Portsmouth	L 0-3		28,004			3	4	5	6				10	11	8	2	9					7	1	
App						34	33	40	42	32	39	38	5	39	38	41	36	10	4	2	13	5	7	2	1	1
Goals							1		1		5	6	1	27	28	7	7		1							

Goalmouth action at Bramall Lane in October 1953.
Albion's Len Millard and Jimmy Dugdale, and United's
Alf Ringstead wait for a break.

Jimmy Dugdale foils Spurs outside-left George Robb in the
League game at White Hart Lane in January 1954.

1954-55

Division 1

Date	Venue	Opponent	Result	Scorers	Att	Sanders J	Rickaby S	Millard L	Dudley J	Dugdale J	Barlow R	Griffin F	Ryan R	Allen R	Nicholls J	Lee G	Kennedy J	Carter W	Williams S	Davies R	Jackson A	Crowshaw A	Barnsley G	Hodgkisson K	Brookes W	Cutler R
Aug 21	(a)	Sunderland	L 2-4	Ryan, Nicholls	56,827	1	2	3	4	5	6	7	8	9	10	11										
25	(a)	Newcastle U	L 0-3		58,548	1	2	3	4		6	7	8	9	10	11	5									
28	(h)	Arsenal	W 3-1	Allen, Ryan, Nicholls	46,247	1	2	3	4		6	7	8	9	10	11	5									
Sep 1	(h)	Newcastle U	W 4-2	Nicholls 2, Allen, Ryan	36,414	1	2	3	4		6	7	8	9	10	11	5									
4	(a)	Sheffield U	W 2-1	Carter, Allen	28,005	1	2	3	4		6	7	8	9		11	5	10								
8	(a)	Everton	W 2-1	Griffin, Allen	55,147	1	2	3	4		6	7	8	9		11	5	10								
11	(h)	Preston NE	W 2-0	Lee, Allen	41,125	1	2	3	4		6	7	8	9		11	5	10								
15	(h)	Everton	D 3-3	Allen 2, Lee	32,442	1	2	3	4		6	7	8	9		11	5	10								
18	(a)	Burnley	W 2-0	Allen 2	29,726	1	2	3	4		6	7	8	9		11	5	10								
25	(h)	Leicester C	W 6-4	Allen, Griffin, Nicholls 3, Lee	48,422	1	2	3	4		6	7	8	9	10	11	5									
Oct 2	(a)	Chelsea	D 3-3	Allen, Lee, Millard	67,440	1	2	3	4	5		7	8	9		11	6			10						
9	(a)	Tottenham H	L 1-3	Nicholls	45,547	1	2	3	4	5		7	8	9	10	11	6									
16	(h)	Sheffield W	L 1-2	Lee	35,407	1	2	3	4			7	6	9	10	11	5		8							
23	(a)	Wolves	L 0-4		55,374	1	2	3	4		6	7	8	9	10	11	5									
30	(h)	Aston Villa	L 2-3	Allen, Lee	51,833		2	3	4			7	8	9	10	11	5			6						1
Nov 6	(a)	Charlton A	W 3-1	Jackson, Allen 2	36,074	1	2	3	4			7		9			5		8	6	10	11				
13	(h)	Bolton W	D 0-0		35,136	1	2	3	4			7	8	9		11	5	6			10					
20	(a)	Huddersfield T	D 3-3	Nicholls, Lee 2	28,372	1	2	3	4			7	8	9	10	11	5	6								
27	(h)	Manchester U	W 2-0	Nicholls, Allen	33,267	1	2	3	4			7	8	9	10		5	11	6							
Dec 4	(a)	Portsmouth	L 1-6	Allen	28,027	1	2	3	4			7	8	9	10		5	11	6							
11	(h)	Blackpool	L 0-1		33,792	1	2	3	4			7	8	9	10	11	5	6								
18	(a)	Sunderland	D 2-2	Williams, Nicholls	27,989	1	2	3	4	5	6			9	10	11		7	8							
25	(a)	Cardiff C	L 2-3	Carter, Allen	25,044	1	2	3	4	5	6			9	10	11		7	8							
27	(h)	Cardiff C	W 1-0	Millard	51,051	1	2	3	4	5	6	7	10	9				8				11				
Jan 1	(a)	Arsenal	D 2-2	Allen, Nicholls	40,246	1	2	3	4	5	6	7		9	10			8				11				
22	(a)	Preston NE	L 1-3	Williams	23,464		2	3	4	5	6	7		9	10	11			8					1		
Feb 5	(h)	Burnley	D 2-2	Ryan, Allen	22,896		2	3	4	5	6	7	10	9		11			8					1		
12	(a)	Leicester C	L 3-6	Carter 2, Lee	28,786			3	4	5	6	7	10	9		11		8	2					1		
Mar 5	(a)	Blackpool	L 1-3	Carter	20,430	1	2	3	4	5	6	7		9		11		8			10					
9	(h)	Chelsea	L 2-4	Allen 2	7,764	1	2	3	4	5	6	7		9		11		8					10			
12	(h)	Sheffield U	D 3-3	Carter 2, Barlow	22,249	1	2	3	4	5	10	7		9		11		8							6	
16	(h)	Wolves	W 1-0	Lee	28,573	1		3	4		10	7		9		11	5	8	2						6	
19	(a)	Aston Villa	L 0-3		40,175	1		3	4		10	7		9		11	5	8	2						6	
26	(h)	Charlton A	W 2-1	Griffin, Lee	8,191	1		3	4		10	7		9		11	5	8	2						6	
Apr 2	(a)	Bolton W	W 4-2	Allen 2, Lee, Carter	16,714	1		3	4		10	7		9		11	5	8	2						6	
8	(a)	Manchester C	L 0-4		57,226	1		3	4		10	7		9		11	5	8	2						6	
9	(h)	Portsmouth	W 3-1	Carter, Allen, Griffin	27,696	1		3	4		10	7		9		11	5	8	2						6	
11	(h)	Manchester C	W 2-1	Griffin, Lee	30,303	1		3	4		10	7		9		11	5	8	2						6	
16	(a)	Manchester U	L 0-3		24,785	1		3	4		10	7		9		11	5	8	2						6	
23	(h)	Huddersfield T	W 2-1	Allen 2	18,661	1		3	4		10	7		9		11	5	8	2						6	
27	(h)	Tottenham H	L 1-2	Allen	16,743	1		3	4		10	7		9		11	5	8	2						6	
30	(a)	Sheffield W	L 0-5		16,684	1		3	4		10			9		11	5	8	2						6	7
App						38	30	42	42	13	32	36	25	42	17	37	32	26	25	3	2	3	1	3	12	1
Goals								2			1	5	4	27	12	13		9	2		2					

Reg Ryan, Ronnie Allen and Johnny Nicholls training at The Hawthorns in 1954.

Goalkeeper Jim Sanders and fullback Len Millard in action against Sheffield Wednesday in 1954.

1955-56

Division 1

Date	Opponent	Res	Scorers	Att	Sanders J	Williams S	Millard L	Dudley J	Kennedy J	Barlow R	Griffin F	Carter W	Allen R	Nicholls J	Lee G	Howe D	Kevan D	Jackson A	Hodgkisson K	Perkins E	Dugdale J	Brown F	Brookes W	Crowshaw A	Williams G	Setters M	Summers G	Robson R	Horobin R	Whitehouse B
Aug 20	(h) Wolves	D 1-1	Nicholls	45,306	1	2	3	4	5	6	7	8	9	10	11															
24	(h) Everton	W 2-0	Kevan 2	24,402	1		3	4	5	6	7	8		10	11	2	9													
27	(a) Manchester U	L 1-3	Kevan	31,994	1		3	4	5	6	7	8		10	11	2	9													
31	(a) Everton	L 0-2		38,559	1		3	4	5	6	7	8		10	11	2	9													
Sep 3	(h) Sheffield U	W 2-1	Kevan, Nicholls	20,061	1	2	3	4	5	6	7	8		10	11		9													
7	(h) Newcastle U	D 1-1	Jackson	20,555	1	2	3	4	5	6	7			8	11			9	10											
10	(a) Preston NE	W 1-0	Docherty (og)	28,202	1	2	3	4	5	6	7			8	11			9	10											
17	(h) Burnley	W 1-0	Nicholls	23,510	1	2	3	4	5	6	7		9	8	11				10											
24	(a) Luton T	W 2-0	Griffin, Allen (pen)	24,440	1	2	3	4	5	6	7		9	8	11				10											
Oct 1	(h) Charlton A	D 3-3	Allen 2 (1 pen), Kennedy	31,168	1	2		4	5	6	7		9	8	11				10	3										
8	(h) Aston Villa	W 1-0	Nicholls	37,395	1	2	3	4	5	6	7		9	8	11				10											
15	(a) Sunderland	L 1-2	Allen (pen)	47,094	1	2	3	4	5	6	7		9	8	11				10											
22	(h) Cardiff C	W 2-1	Allen 2	22,286	1		3	4		6	7		9	8	11	2			10		5									
29	(a) Manchester C	L 0-2		25,081		2	3	4	5		7		9	8	11				10	1	6									
Nov 5	(h) Bolton W	W 2-0	Allen 2	23,808	1	2	3	4	5				9	10	11				8				6							
12	(a) Chelsea	L 0-2		41,898	1	2	3	4	5			7	8	9	10	11							6							
19	(h) Blackpool	L 1-2	Allen	38,294	1	2	3	4	5	6		8	9	10										7	11					
26	(a) Huddersfield T	L 0-1		18,731	1	2	3	4	5	6	7		9	10										11	8					
Dec 3	(h) Portsmouth	W 4-0	Setters 2, Griffin, Lee	22,949	1	2	3	4	5	6	7	10	9		11											8				
10	(a) Arsenal	L 0-2		33,217	1	2	3	4	5	6	7	10	9		11											8				
17	(a) Wolves	L 2-3	Allen, Carter	31,068	1	2	3	4	5	6	7	10	9		11											8				
24	(h) Manchester U	L 1-4	Lee	25,286	1	2	3	4	5		8		9	10	11									7			6			
26	(a) Tottenham H	L 1-4	Allen (pen)	32,061	1		3	4	5		8		9	10	11	2								7			6			
27	(h) Tottenham H	W 1-0	Lee	31,522	1		3	4			8		9	10	11	2					5			7			6			
31	(a) Sheffield U	D 2-2	Allen, Lee	23,973	1		3	4			8		9	10	11	2					5			7			6			
Jan 2	(a) Newcastle U	W 3-0	Allen 3 (1 pen)	50,768	1		3	4	5		7		9	10	11	2										8	6			
14	(h) Preston NE	W 3-2	Crowshaw 2, Lee	22,471	1			4	5				9	10	11	2					3			7		8	6			
21	(a) Burnley	W 2-1	Lee, Griffin	23,749	1		3	4	5		7		9	10	11	2										8	6			
Feb 4	(h) Luton T	W 3-1	Griffin, Lee, Williams	25,310	1	10	3	4	5		7		9		11	2										8	6			
11	(a) Charlton A	L 1-5	Nicholls	13,573	1		3	4	5		7	8	9	10	11	2											6			
25	(h) Sunderland	W 3-0	Barlow, Griffin, Lee	23,620	1		3	4	5	6	7		9	10	11	2											6			
Mar 3	(a) Blackpool	L 1-5	Allen (pen)	19,763	1		3	4	5				9	10	11	2							7			8	6			
10	(h) Manchester C	L 0-4		32,680	1		3		5					10	11	2	9						4	7			6	8		
17	(a) Bolton W	L 0-4		23,393	1		3	4	5		7		9		11	2	10										6	8		
24	(h) Chelsea	W 3-0	Nicholls 2, Griffin	20,219	1		3	4	5		7		9	10	11	2											6	8		
31	(a) Cardiff C	W 3-1	Allen, Robson, Nicholls	40,126	1		3	4	5				9	10	11	2											6	8	7	
Apr 2	(a) Birmingham C	L 0-2		38,892	1		3	4	5				9	10	11	2											6	8	7	
3	(h) Birmingham C	L 0-2		35,986	1		3	4	5		7		9	10	11	2									6			8		
7	(h) Huddersfield T	L 1-2	Horobin	16,141	1	10	3	4	5				9		11	2											6	8	7	
14	(a) Portsmouth	D 1-1	Lee	17,520	1		3	4	5				9		11	2											6	8	7	10
21	(h) Arsenal	W 2-1	Lee, Goring (og)	22,392	1		3	4	5		7		9		11	2											6	8		10
28	(a) Aston Villa	L 0-3		45,120	1		3	4	5		7		9		11	2											6	8		10
App					41	20	40	41	31	38	31	13	34	24	40	24	7	2	8	2	3	1	4	8	2	11	20	10	4	3
Goals						1			1	1	6	1	17	8	10		4	1						2		2		1	1	

Burnley goalkeeper Colin McDonald takes the ball off George Lee's toe in the League match at The Hawthorns on 17 September 1955.

Billy Brookes, Barlow's deputy in the 1950s.

124

1956-57

Division 1

Date		Opponent	Result	Scorers	Att	Sanders J	Howe D	Williams S	Dudley J	Barlow R	Summers G	Griffin F	Robson R	Allen R	Whitehouse B	Lee G	Brookes W	Kennedy J	Millard L	Kevan D	Setters M	Nicholls J	Horobin R	Carter W	Lee M	Brown F	Jackson A
Aug 18	(a)	Sheffield W	L 2-4	Lee, Allen	22,586	1	2	3	4	5	6	7	8	9	10	11											
22	(h)	Aston Villa	W 2-0	Robson, Whitehouse	37,255	1	2	3	4	6		7	8	9	10	11	5										
25	(h)	Manchester U	L 2-3	Allen, Lee	26,516	1	2	3	4	6		7	8	9	10	11		5									
27	(a)	Aston Villa	D 0-0		33,052	1	2	3	4	6		7	8	9	10	11		5									
Sep 1	(a)	Arsenal	L 1-4	Whitehouse	39,973	1	2	3	4	6		7	8	9	10	11		5									
5	(h)	Portsmouth	W 2-1	Robson, Kevan	15,059	1	2		4	6		7	8		10	11		5	3	9							
8	(h)	Burnley	D 2-2	Allen, Griffin	23,746	1	2		4	6		7	8	10		11		5	3	9							
15	(a)	Preston NE	L 2-3	Robson 2	28,380	1	2		4	6		7	8	10		11		5	3	9							
22	(h)	Chelsea	W 2-1	Griffin, Kevan	24,684	1	2			6		7	8		11			5	3	9	4	10					
29	(a)	Cardiff C	D 0-0		28,115	1	2			6			8		11			5	3	9	4	10	7				
Oct 6	(h)	Wolves	D 1-1	Allen	34,379	1	2			6		7	8		11			5	3	9	4	10					
13	(a)	Bolton W	D 1-1	Griffin	24,969	1	2			6		7	10		11			5	3	9	4	8					
20	(h)	Sunderland	W 2-0	Robson, Allen (pen)	33,075	1	2			6		7	10		11			5		9	4	8	3				
27	(a)	Luton T	W 1-0	Kevan	16,786	1	2			6		7	10		11			5	3	9	4	8					
Nov 3	(h)	Everton	W 3-0	Robson, Allen 2	23,810	1	2			6		7	8		11			5	3	9	4	10					
10	(a)	Blackpool	W 1-0	Robson	18,839	1	2		4	6		7	8		11			5	3	9		10					
17	(h)	Manchester C	D 1-1	Griffin	26,082	1	2		4	6		7	8		11			5	3	9		10					
24	(a)	Charlton A	L 2-3	Barlow, Kevan	16,361	1	2		4	6		7	8		11			5	3	9		10					
Dec 1	(h)	Leeds U	D 0-0		29,135	1	2		4	6		7	8		11			5	3	9		10					
8	(a)	Tottenham H	D 2-2	Kevan 2	38,140	1	2		4	6		7	8		11			5	3	9		10					
15	(h)	Sheffield W	L 1-4	Kevan	17,150	1	2		4	6		7	8					5	3	9		10	11				
25	(h)	Newcastle U	W 1-0	Barlow	13,780	1	2		4	6		7	10		11			5		9		8		3			
26	(a)	Newcastle U	L 2-5	Kevan, Williams	20,319	1	2	10	4	6		7			11			5		9		8		3			
29	(h)	Arsenal	L 0-2		26,162	1	2		4	6		7	10		11			5		9		8		3			
Jan 12	(a)	Burnley	L 0-1		24,249	1	2		4	6		7	10		11			5		9		8		3			
19	(h)	Preston NE	D 0-0		24,304	1	2		4	6		7	10		8			5		9			11	3			
Feb 2	(a)	Chelsea	W 4-2	Kevan 2, Allen (pen), Robson	29,361	1	2		4	6		7	8	9				5		10			11	3			
9	(h)	Cardiff C	L 1-2	Kevan	23,662	1	2		4	6			8	9	11			5		10			7	3			
23	(h)	Luton T	W 4-0	Dudley, Whitehouse, Griffin, Kevan	21,934		2		4	6		7		9	8			5	3	10			11			1	
Mar 9	(h)	Tottenham H	D 1-1	Whitehouse	30,739	1	2		4	5		7		9	8				3	10	6		11				
13	(a)	Sunderland	W 4-1	Kevan 2, Whitehouse, Allen	26,336	1	2		4	5		7		9	8				3	10	6		11				
16	(a)	Everton	W 1-0		32,606	1	2		4	5		7		9	8				3	10	6		11				
30	(a)	Manchester C	L 1-2	Robson	26,351	1	2		4	6		7	9		8			5	3	10			11				
Apr 3	(h)	Blackpool	L 1-3	Whitehouse	6,397		2			6		7	9		8			5	3		4		11			1	
6	(h)	Charlton A	D 2-2	Setters, Carter (pen)	15,055	1	2		4			7	8		11			5		9	6	10		3			
13	(a)	Leeds U	D 0-0		20,535	1	2			6			8	9				5	3	10	4	11	7				
15	(a)	Wolves	L 2-5	Robson 2	27,942	1	2	3		6			8	9				5		10	4	11	7				
20	(h)	Bolton W	W 3-2	Whitehouse, Kevan, Robson	18,465		2			6		7	8	9				5	3	10	4		11			1	
22	(h)	Birmingham C	D 0-0		18,828		2		4	6		7	8	9				5	3	10			11			1	
23	(a)	Birmingham C	L 0-2		33,301		2		4	6		7	8	9				5	3	10			11			1	
27	(a)	Portsmouth	W 1-0	Allen	24,055		2		4	5		7	8	9					3	10	6		11			1	
May 1	(a)	Manchester U	D 1-1	Millard (pen)	20,357	1	2		4	5		7	8	9					3	10	6		11				
		App				36	41	13	24	40	2	34	39	37	15	9	1	35	28	35	21	17	18	9	1	6	1
		Goals						1	1	2		5	12	10	7	2			1	16	1			1			

Goalkeeper Jim Sanders

Don Howe missed only one League game in 1956-7.

Derek Kevan, Albion's leading League scorer this season.

125

1957-58

Division 1

Date		Opponent	Res	Score	Scorers	Att	Brown F	Howe D	Williams S	Setters M	Kennedy J	Barlow R	Griffin F	Robson R	Allen R	Kevan D	Lee G	Horobin R	Jackson A	Whitehouse B	Sanders J	Dudley J	Millard L	Burnside D	Drury C	Jackman C	Campbell J	Williams G	Robinson E
Aug 24	(h)	Newcastle U	W	2-1	Robson, Allen	31,064	1	2	3	4	5	6	7	8	9	10	11												
27	(a)	Arsenal	D	2-2	Allen 2 (1 pen)	45,988	1	2	3	4	5	6	7	8	9	10		11											
31	(a)	Burnley	D	2-2	Setters, Lee	24,003	1	2	3	4	5	6	7	8	9		11			10									
Sep 4	(h)	Arsenal	L	1-2	Allen	26,117	1	2	3	4	5	6	7	8	9				11	10									
7	(h)	Preston NE	W	4-1	Allen, Kevan, Griffin, Horobin	29,903		2	3	4	5	6	7	8	9	10		11			1								
11	(a)	Chelsea	D	2-2	Allen, Horobin	29,824		2	3	4	5	6	7	8	9	10		11			1								
14	(a)	Sheffield W	W	2-1	McEvoy (og), Allen (pen)	27,933		2	3	4	5	6	7	8	9	10		11			1								
18	(h)	Chelsea	D	1-1	Allen (pen)	36,835		2	3	4	5	6	7	8	9	10		11			1								
21	(h)	Manchester C	W	9-2	Griffin 3, Howe 2 (1 pen), Robson, Horobin, Whitehouse, Kevan (pen)	26,222		2	3		5	6	7	9		10		11		8	1	4							
28	(a)	Nottingham F	W	2-0	Robson 2	41,675		2	3	4	5	6	7	8	9	10		11			1								
Oct 1	(h)	Birmingham C	D	0-0		39,909		2	3	6	5		7	8	9	10		11			1	4							
5	(h)	Portsmouth	W	3-1	Allen 2, Robson	32,030		2	3	4	5	6	7	8	9	10		11			1								
12	(h)	Bolton W	D	2-2	Kevan, Allen (pen)	31,522		2	3	4	5	6	7	8	9	10		11			1								
19	(a)	Leeds U	D	1-1	Allen	25,507		2			5		7	6	9			11		8	1	4	3	10					
26	(h)	Manchester U	W	4-3	Robson 2, Allen, Kevan	52,839		2	3		5	6	7	8	9	10		11			1	4							
Nov 2	(a)	Everton	D	1-1	Griffin	53,679		2	3	4	5	6	7	8	9	10		11			1								
9	(h)	Aston Villa	W	3-2	Robson, Allen (pen), Horobin	41,454		2	3	4	5	6	7	8	9	10		11			1								
16	(a)	Wolves	D	1-1	Kevan	55,418		2	3	4	5	6	7	8	9	10		11			1								
23	(h)	Sunderland	W	3-0	Kevan, Robson, Setters	32,682		2	3	4	5	6	7	8	9	10		11			1								
30	(a)	Leicester C	D	3-3	Robson 2, Allen	33,855		2	3	4	5	6	7	8	9	10		11			1								
Dec 7	(h)	Blackpool	D	1-1	Robson	28,236		2	3	4	5	6	7	8	9	10		11			1								
14	(a)	Luton T	L	1-5	Robson	15,365		2	3	4	5	6	7	8	9	10		11			1								
21	(a)	Newcastle U	L	0-3		31,699		2	3	4	5	6	7	8	9	10	11				1								
26	(a)	Birmingham C	W	5-3	Robson 2, Kevan 2, Allen	48,396		2	3	4	5	6	7	8	9	10	11				1								
28	(h)	Burnley	W	5-1	Robson 4, Kevan	38,386		2	3	4	5	6	7	8	9	10	11				1								
Jan 11	(a)	Preston NE	L	1-3	Kevan	25,003		2	3	4	5	6	7	8	9	10		11			1								
18	(h)	Sheffield W	W	3-1	Griffin 2, Setters	28,963		2	3	4	5	6	7	8	9	10		11			1								
Feb 1	(a)	Manchester C	L	1-4	Kevan	38,702		2	3		5	6	7	9		10		11		8	1	4							
8	(h)	Nottingham F	W	3-2	Kevan 2, Robson	32,868		2	3		5	6	7	9		10		11		8	1	4							
22	(a)	Bolton W	D	2-2	Kevan 2	19,132		2	3			5		8	9	10		11		7	1	4			6				
Mar 8	(a)	Manchester U	W	4-0	Allen 2, Greaves (og), Kevan	63,278		2	3		5	6		8	9	10		11		7	1	4							
12	(h)	Leeds U	W	1-0	Charlton (og)	16,518		2	3			5		8	9	10		11		7	1	4			6				
15	(h)	Everton	W	4-0	Robson, Kevan 2, Allen (pen)	28,915		2	3			5		8	9	10		11		7	1	4			6				
19	(a)	Portsmouth	D	2-2	Horobin, Allen	24,731		2	3		5	6		8	9	10		11				4				1	7		
22	(a)	Sunderland	L	0-2		38,323		2	3		5	6		8	9	10		11				4				1	7		
29	(h)	Wolves	L	0-3		56,904		2	3		5	6		8	9	10		11				4				1	7		
Apr 4	(a)	Tottenham H	D	0-0		56,166		2	3			5		8	11	9		10				4			6	1	7		
5	(a)	Aston Villa	L	1-2	Allen	32,010		2				5		10	11	9			7	8		4			6	1		3	
7	(h)	Tottenham H	L	0-2		26,672		2	3			5		9	11	10				8		4			6	1	7		
12	(h)	Leicester C	W	6-2	Robson 3, Whitehouse 2, Kevan	25,389		2				5		8	9	10		11		7		4			6	1		3	
19	(a)	Blackpool	L	0-2		17,442		2			5	6			9			11		7		4		10		1		3	8
26	(h)	Luton T	W	4-2	Lee 2, Howe, Allen (pen)	20,289		2		6	5			8	9	10	11			7		4				1		3	
App							4	39	38	27	34	40	29	41	39	38	8	32	2	14	29	19	1	2	7	9	5	4	1
Goals								3		3			7	24	22	19	3	5		3									

Albion's Joe Kennedy gets in a sliding tackle on Blackpool's South African-born outside-left Bill Perry at The Hawthorns in 1957.

1958-59

Division 1

Date		Opponent	Res	Score	Scorers	Att	Jackman C	Howe D	Williams S	Setters M	Barlow R	Drury C	Campbell J	Robson R	Allen R	Kevan D	Hogg D	Dudley J	Burnside D	Whitehouse B	Williams G	Potter F	Forrester A	Jackson A	Kennedy J	Griffin F
Aug 23	(a)	Luton T	D	1-1	Kevan	24,425	1	2	3	4	5	6	7	8	9	10	11									
27	(h)	Birmingham C	D	2-2	Hogg, Allen (pen)	46,468	1	2	3	4	5	6	7	8	9	10	11									
30	(h)	Bolton W	D	1-1	Allen	37,244	1	2	3	6	5		7	8	9	10	11	4								
Sep 3	(a)	Birmingham C	W	6-0	Burnside 2, Campbell 2, Allen, Kevan	35,915	1	2	3	6	5		7		9	8	11	4	10							
6	(a)	Burnley	W	3-1	Burnside 2, Campbell	22,789	1	2	3	6	5		7		9	8	11	4	10							
10	(h)	Portsmouth	L	1-2	Campbell	34,445	1	2	3	6	5		7		9	8	11	4	10							
13	(h)	Preston NE	D	1-1	Dudley	36,525	1	2	3	6	5				9	8	11	4	10	7						
17	(a)	Portsmouth	W	6-2	Allen 2(1 pen), Burnside 2, Kevan, Hayward(og)	32,972	1	2	3	6	5		7		9	10	11	4	8							
20	(a)	Leicester C	D	2-2	Allen, Kevan	38,751	1	2	3	4	5		7		9	10	11	4	8							
27	(h)	Everton	L	2-3	Campbell, Burnside	30,721	1	2	3	4	5		7		9	8	11	4	10							
Oct 4	(a)	Arsenal	L	3-4	Kevan 3	57,770	1		2	4	5			8	7	9	11	6	10		3					
11	(h)	Aston Villa	W	4-1	Burnside, Hogg, Robson, Howe (pen)	47,124	1	2	3	4	5			7	8	9	11	6	10							
18	(h)	West Ham U	W	2-1	Campbell, Howe (pen)	36,991		2		4	5			7	8	9	11	6	10		3	1				
25	(a)	Manchester U	W	2-1	Robson, Kevan	51,960		2	3	4	5			7	8	9	11	6	10			1				
Nov 1	(h)	Wolves	W	2-1	Campbell, Kevan	48,898		2	3	4	5			7	8	9	11	6	10			1				
8	(a)	Blackpool	D	1-1	Burnside	18,664		2	3	4	5			7	9	8	11	6	10			1				
15	(h)	Blackburn R	L	2-3	Burnside, Dudley	31,679		2	3	4	5			7	9	10	11	6	8			1				
22	(a)	Newcastle U	W	2-1	Kevan, Robson	51,636		2	3	4	5			7	8	9	10	11	6			1				
29	(h)	Tottenham H	W	4-3	Howe, Kevan, Forrester, Allen (pen)	21,861		2	3	4	5	6			8	9	10	11				1	7			
Dec 6	(a)	Nottingham F	D	1-1	Allen (pen)	34,634		2	3	4	5	6			8	9	10	11				1	7			
13	(h)	Chelsea	W	4-0	Forrester 2, Allen, Kevan	19,856		2	3	4	5	6			8	9	10	11				1	7			
26	(h)	Leeds U	L	1-2	Gibson (og)	35,020		2	3	4	5	6			8	9	10	11				1	7			
27	(a)	Leeds U	W	1-0	Kevan	44,998		2	3	4	5	6				9	10	11				1	7	8		
Jan 3	(a)	Bolton W	L	1-2	Allen	27,847		2	3	4	5	6			8	9		11				1	7	10		
31	(a)	Preston NE	W	4-2	Kevan 2, Griffin, O'Farrell (og)	23,138		2	3	4		6		9	11	10						1		8	5	7
Feb 7	(h)	Leicester C	D	2-2	Kevan, Allen	25,375		2	3	4	5	6			9	10	11					1		8		7
18	(a)	Everton	D	3-3	Setters, Kevan, Allen	32,629		2	3	4	5	6			11	9					10	1		8		7
21	(h)	Arsenal	D	1-1	Kevan	32,706		2	3	4	5	6		7		10	11				8	1		9		
Mar 7	(a)	West Ham U	L	1-3	Robson	30,157		2	3	4	5	6		9	7	10	11					1		8		
11	(h)	Burnley	L	2-4	Setters, Hogg	18,824		2	3	6	5			9	7	10	11					1		8		4
14	(h)	Manchester U	L	1-3	Kevan	35,608		2	3	4	5			8	7	9	11				10	1		6		
21	(a)	Wolves	L	2-5	Kevan 2	44,280		2	3	4	5			8	7	9	11				10	1		6		
28	(h)	Blackpool	W	3-1	Kevan 2, Allen	29,803		2	3	4				7	6	9	10	11				1			5	
30	(a)	Manchester C	W	2-0	Kevan, Allen	25,551		2	3	4				7	6	9	10	11				1			5	
31	(h)	Manchester C	W	3-0	Campbell, Allen (pen), Hogg	32,076		2	3	4			7		9	10	11	6	8			1			5	
Apr 4	(a)	Blackburn R	D	0-0		27,200		2	3	4			7		9	10	11	6	8			1			5	
11	(h)	Newcastle U	D	2-2	Kevan 2	23,750			2	4			7		6	9	10	11	8		3	1			5	
15	(h)	Luton T	W	2-0	Burnside, Allen	19,293		2	3	4	5			7	6	9	10	11	8			1				
18	(a)	Tottenham H	L	0-5		35,790		2	3	4	5			7	6	9	10	11	8			1				
22	(a)	Chelsea	W	2-0	Burnside, Hogg	31,948		2			4	5	11		6	9	10	7	8		3	1				
25	(h)	Nottingham F	W	2-0	Campbell, Allen	17,071		2	3		4	5	11		6	9	10	7	8			1				
29	(h)	Aston Villa	D	1-1	Allen	48,281		2	3			6		11	4	9	10	7				1			8	5
		App					12	40	40	41	36	13	26	29	36	41	40	18	27	1	4	30	6	9	10	3
		Goals						3		2			9	4	17	27	5	2	12				3			1

Almost 49,000 fans saw the Albion-Wolves local 'derby' at The Hawthorns in November 1958. Here Jimmy Campbell scores Albion's 76th minute equaliser. Derek Kevan hit the winner two minutes from time.

Goalkeeper Clive Jackman's career was terminated by a back injury.

127

1959-60

Division 1

Date	Opponent	Res	Scorers	Att	Potter R	Howe D	Williams S	Setters M	Kennedy J	Barlow R	Allen R	Burnside D	Robson R	Kevan D	Dixon R	Hogg D	Dudley J	Jackson A	Aitken A	Styles A	Wallace J	Cram R	Williams G	Whitehouse B	Drury C	Smith K	Bannister J	Hope R	Carter G
Aug 22 (h)	Manchester U	W 3-2	Burnside 2, Foulkes (og)	40,733	1	2	3	4	5	6	7	8	9	10	11														
26 (a)	Tottenham H	D 2-2	Robson, Kevan	54,114	1	2	3	4	5	6	7	8	9	10		11													
29 (a)	Preston NE	D 1-1	Kevan	24,876	1	2	3	4	5	6		8	9	10	11	7													
Sep 2 (h)	Tottenham H	L 1-2	Hogg	35,924	1	2	3		5	6			9	10	11	7	4	8											
5 (h)	Leicester C	W 5-0	Dixon, Kevan, Jackson, Robson 2	27,259	1	2	3	4	5				9	10	11	7		8											
9 (h)	Newcastle U	D 2-2	Hogg, Kevan	27,570	1	2	3	4	5		9		6	10	11	7		8											
12 (a)	Burnley	L 1-2	Robson	23,807	1	2	3	4	5		7	8	6	9	11			10											
16 (a)	Newcastle U	D 0-0		39,266	1	2	3	4	5	6	7	8	9	10		11													
19 (h)	Leeds U	W 3-0	Robson, Allen 2	26,369	1	2	3	4	5		9		6	10		11	8	7											
26 (a)	West Ham U	L 1-4	Burnside	30,570	1	2	3	4	5		9	8	6	10	7	11													
Oct 3 (h)	Chelsea	L 1-3	Jackson	27,784	1	2	3	4	5			8	9	10		11	6	7											
10 (h)	Fulham	L 2-4	Setters 2	20,395	1	2	3	4	5		9	8		10		11		7		6									
17 (a)	Bolton W	D 0-0		22,581				4	5		9		6	10		11		7	8		1	2	3						
24 (h)	Luton T	W 4-0	Allen 2, Whitehouse, Kevan	22,445		2	3	4	5		9		6	10		7		11			1			8					
31 (a)	Sheffield W	L 0-2		26,178		2	3	4	5		9		6	10		7		11			1			8					
Nov 7 (h)	Blackpool	W 2-1	Whitehouse, Jackson	30,568		2	3	4	5		9		6	10		7		11			1			8					
14 (a)	Blackburn R	L 2-3	Burnside, Whitehouse	18,396		2	3	4	5		9		6	10		7		11			1			8					
21 (h)	Manchester C	W 2-0	McTavish (og), Burnside	24,219		2	3	4	5		9	8	6	10		11		7			1								
28 (a)	Arsenal	W 4-2	Allen 2 (1 pen), Robson, Kevan	41,147		2	3	4	5		9	8	6	10		11		7			1								
Dec 5 (h)	Wolves	L 0-1		40,739		2	3	4	5		9	8	6	10		11		7			1								
12 (a)	Everton	D 2-2	Kevan, Burnside	25,769		2	3		5		9	8	6	10		11		7			1				4				
19 (a)	Manchester U	W 3-2	Hogg, Allen, Burnside	33,677		2	3		5		9	8	6	10		11		7			1				4				
26 (h)	Nottingham F	L 2-3	Kevan 2	28,817		2	3	4	5		9	8	6	10		11		7			1								
28 (a)	Nottingham F	W 2-1	Hogg, Jackson	34,608		2			5		9	8	6	10		11		7			1		3		4				
Jan 2 (h)	Preston NE	W 4-0	Richardson (og), Jackson, Kevan, Allen	23,917		2			5		9	8	6	10		11		7			1		3		4				
16 (a)	Leicester C	W 1-0	Jackson	23,802		2			5		9	8	6	10		11		7			1		3		4				
23 (h)	Burnley	D 0-0		23,512		2			5		9	8	6	10		11		7			1		3		4				
Feb 6 (a)	Leeds U	W 4-1	Burnside 2, Hogg, Kevan	23,546		2			5		9	8	6	10		11		7			1		3		4				
24 (a)	Chelsea	D 2-2	Kevan, Allen	26,222		2			5		9	8	6	10		11		7			1		3		4				
27 (a)	Wolves	L 1-3	Jackson	49,791		2		4	5		9	8	6	10		11		7			1		3						
Mar 5 (h)	Bolton W	D 1-1	Kevan	23,857		2			5		9	8	6	10		7		11			1		3						
9 (h)	West Ham U	W 3-2	Kevan 2, Allen (pen)	12,204		2			5		9	8	6	10		7		11			1		3		4				
12 (a)	Luton T	D 0-0		18,825		2			5		9	8	6	10		7		11			1		3		4				
19 (h)	Everton	W 6-2	Kevan 5, Burnside	24,887		2			5		9	8	6	10		11		7			1		3		4				
26 (a)	Blackpool	L 0-2		16,190		2			5		9	8	6	10		11		7			1		3		4				
Apr 2 (h)	Blackburn R	W 2-0	Kevan, Allen	24,180		2			5		9		6	10		11		7			1		3		4	8			
9 (a)	Manchester C	W 1-0	Jackson	24,342		2			5		9			10		11		7			1		3		4	8	6		
16 (h)	Sheffield W	W 3-1	Burnside, Kevan, Jackson	27,899		2			5		9	8	6	10		11		7			1		3		4				
18 (a)	Birmingham C	W 7-1	Allen 3 (1 pen), Jackson, Kevan 3	28,865		2			5		9	8	6	10		11		7			1		3		4				
19 (h)	Birmingham C	D 1-1	Kevan	37,937		2			5		9	8	6	10		11		7			1		3		4				
23 (a)	Fulham	L 1-2	Allen	23,631		2			5		9		6	8		7					1		3		4				
30 (h)	Arsenal	W 1-0	Jackson	26,380		2			5		9		6	8		7					1		3		4			10	11
App					12	41	23	20	41	7	36	31	41	42	7	31	2	31	16	1	30	1	20	4	20	2	1	1	1
Goals								2			15	11	6	26	1	5		11						3					

Jimmy Greaves scores for Chelsea at The Hawthorns on 30 October 1959.

Brian Whitehouse, third from right, nets for Albion against Blackpool at The Hawthorns on 7 November 1959.

128

1960-61

Division 1

Date		Opponent	Result	Scorers	Att	Wallace J	Howe D	Williams G	Drury C	Kennedy J	Robson R	Jackson A	Burnside D	Allen F	Kevan C	Hope R	Billingham P	Jones S	Hogg C	Potter R	Williams S	Smith K	Bannister J	Aitken A	Carter G	Cram R	Macready B	Clark C	Lovatt J	Steele S
Aug 20	(a)	Sheffield W	L 0-1		34,177	1	2	3	4	5	6	7	8	9	10	11														
24	(h)	Birmingham C	L 1-2	Jackson	32,102	1	2	3	4	5	6	7	10	9	8	11														
27	(h)	Fulham	L 2-4	Jackson, Burnside	20,609	1	2	3	4	5	6	7	10	9	8	11														
31	(a)	Birmingham C	L 1-3	Kevan	37,740	1	2	3			6	7	8	9	10		4	5	11											
Sep 3	(a)	Preston NE	L 1-2	Hogg	18,476		2	3	6		9	7	8		10		4	5	11	1										
5	(h)	Newcastle U	W 6-0	Jackson 3, Robson, Kevan, Burnside	22,548		2		4	5	6	7	8	9	10					1	11		3							
10	(h)	Burnley	L 0-2		26,407		2		4	5	6	7	8	9	10					1	11		3							
14	(a)	Newcastle U	L 2-3	Smith, Burnside	16,107		2		4	5	6	7	8	9						1	11	10	3							
17	(a)	Nottingham F	W 2-1	Allen, Kevan	22,791		2	3	4	5	6	7	8	9	10					1	11									
24	(h)	Manchester C	W 6-3	Allen 3, Kevan 2, Burnside	25,163		2	3	4	5	6	7	8	9	10					1	11									
Oct 1	(a)	Arsenal	L 0-1		27,176		2	3	4	5	6	7	8	9	10					1	11									
8	(a)	Bolton W	W 1-0	Allen	18,672		2	3		5		10	8	9		4				1	11			7	6					
15	(h)	West Ham U	W 1-0	Robson	22,009		2	3		5	6	10	8	9		4				1	11			7						
22	(a)	Leicester C	D 2-2	Burnside, Aitken	20,770		2			5	6		8	9	10	4				1			3	7	11					
29	(h)	Aston Villa	L 0-2		41,903		2	3	4	5	6	7	8	9	10					1					11					
Nov 5	(a)	Everton	D 1-1	Jackson	40,705		2	3	4	5	8	7	10	9						1				6	11					
12	(h)	Blackburn R	L 1-2	Burnside	18,701		2	3	6	5	8	7	10	9		4				1					11					
19	(a)	Manchester U	L 0-3		32,756	1	2	3	4	5	6	7	8	9	10										11					
26	(h)	Tottenham H	L 1-3	Howe	39,017	1	8	11	4	5	6	7		9	10						3					2				
Dec 3	(a)	Chelsea	L 1-7	Jackson	19,568	1	8	11	4	5	6	7		9	10						3					2				
10	(h)	Blackpool	W 3-1	Kevan 2, Jackson	15,099	1	2	3	6	5	4	8	10		9									11			7			
17	(h)	Sheffield W	D 2-2	Aitken, Burnside	17,862	1	2	3	6	5	4	8	10		9									11			7			
26	(a)	Cardiff C	L 1-3	Macready	30,103	1	2	3	6	5	4	8	10		9									11			7			
27	(h)	Cardiff C	D 1-1	Kevan	30,131		2	3		5	4	10		11	9					1	8	6					7			
31	(a)	Fulham	W 2-1	Kevan, Burnside	18,080		2	3	6	5	4	11	8	9	10					1							7			
Jan 14	(h)	Preston NE	W 3-1	Jackson 2, Howe (pen)	19,639		2	3	6	5	4	9	8		10					1							7	11		
21	(a)	Burnley	W 1-0	Kevan	15,305		2	3	6	5	4	9	8		10					1							7	11		
28	(a)	Wolves	L 2-4	Kevan, Burnside	31,385		2	3	6	5	4	9	8		10					1							7	11		
Feb 4	(h)	Nottingham F	L 1-2	Burnside	24,927	1	2	3	6	5	4	9	8		10												7	11		
11	(a)	Manchester C	L 0-3		21,382		2	3	6	5	4	9	8							1	10						7	11		
18	(h)	Arsenal	L 2-3	Jackson, Robson	21,962		8	3	6	5	4	7		9	10					1						2		11		
25	(h)	Bolton W	W 3-2	Allen, Hope, Burnside	15,171	1	2		6		4	7	8	9	10			5			3							11		
Mar 4	(a)	West Ham U	W 2-1	Lovatt, Hope	21,607	1	2		6		4	7	8			10		5			3							11	9	
11	(h)	Leicester C	W 1-0	Clark	25,168	1	2		6		4	7	8			10		5			3							11	9	
25	(h)	Everton	W 3-0	Kevan 2, Jackson	20,590	1	2	3	6		4	7	8		10			5										11	9	
28	(a)	Aston Villa	W 1-0	Lovatt	42,800	1	2	3	6		4	7	8		10			5										11	9	
Apr 1	(a)	Blackpool	W 1-0	Lovatt	20,809	1	2		6		4	7	8		10			5			3							11	9	
3	(h)	Wolves	W 2-1	Kevan, Burnside	34,108	1	2		6		4	7	8		10			5			3							11	9	
8	(h)	Manchester U	D 1-1	Howe	28,033	1	2	3	6		4	7	8		10			5										11	9	
15	(a)	Blackburn R	L 1-2	Kevan	14,600	1	2	3	6			7			10	4		5										11	9	8
22	(h)	Chelsea	W 3-0	Kevan 2, Robson	17,691	1	2		6		4	7	8		10			5			3							11	9	
29	(a)	Tottenham H	W 2-1	Kevan, Robson	52,054	1	2		6		4	7	8		10			5			3							11	9	
App						22	42	31	37	29	40	41	35	20	32	12	7	13	10	20	13	5	5	6	6	3	9	15	10	1
Goals							3				5	12	12	6	18	2			1			1		2			1	1	3	

Albion's 1960-61 squad.

1961-62

Division 1

Date	Opponent	Result	Scorers	Att	Wallace J	Howe D	Williams S	Robson R	Jones S	Drury C	Jackson A	Burnside D	Lovatt J	Kevan D	Clark C	Hope R	Smith K	Potter R	Millington A	Carter G	Cram R	Bannister J	Williams G
Aug 19	(h) Sheffield W	L 0-2		25,464	1	2	3	4	5	6	7	8	9	10	11								
23	(h) Everton	W 2-0	Robson, Kevan	21,594	1	2	3	4	5	6	7	8	9	10	11								
26	(a) Leicester C	L 0-1		20,899	1	2	3	4	5	6	7	8	9	10	11								
30	(a) Everton	L 1-3	Robson	36,586	1	2	3	4	5	6	7		9	10	11	8							
Sep 2	(h) Ipswich T	L 1-3	Jackson	19,016	1	2	3	4	5	6	7			10	11	8	9						
6	(h) Birmingham C	D 0-0		20,541	1	2	3	4	5	6	7			10	11	8	9						
9	(a) Burnley	L 1-3	Burnside	21,809		2	3	4	5	6	7	9		10	11	8			1				
16	(h) Arsenal	W 4-0	Clark, Jackson, Burnside, Kevan	20,298	1	2	3	4	5	6	7	9		10	11	8							
20	(a) Birmingham C	W 2-1	Burnside, Kevan	22,902	1	2	3	4	5	6	7	9		10	11	8							
23	(a) Bolton W	L 2-3	Kevan, Hope	14,155	1	2	3	4	5	6	7	9		10	11	8							
30	(h) Manchester C	D 2-2	Kevan 2	20,820		2	3	4	5	6	7	9		10	11	8			1				
Oct 7	(h) Manchester U	D 1-1	Kevan	25,645		2	3	4	5	6	7	9		10	11	8			1				
18	(a) Cardiff C	D 2-2	Williams, Smith	20,009		2	3	4	5	6	7	8		10	11		9		1				
21	(h) Aston Villa	D 1-1	Jackson	39,071		2	3	4	5	6	7	8		10	11		9		1				
28	(a) Nottingham F	D 4-4	Howe (pen), Clark, Kevan, Smith	20,424		2	3	4	5	6	7	8		10	11		9		1				
Nov 4	(h) Blackburn R	W 4-0	Kevan, Jackson, Smith 2	17,298		2	3	4	5	6	7	8		10	11		9		1				
11	(a) West Ham U	D 3-3	Jackson, Howe (pen), Kevan	18,213		2	3	4	5	6	7	8		10	11		9		1				
18	(h) Sheffield U	W 3-1	Kevan 3	19,392		2	3	4	5	6	7	8		10			9		1	11			
25	(a) Chelsea	L 1-4	Smith	25,025		2	3	4	5	6	7	8		10	11		9		1				
Dec 2	(h) Tottenham H	L 2-4	Kevan, Smith	28,701		2	3	4	5	6	7	8		10	11		9		1				
9	(a) Blackpool	D 2-2	Burnside, Kevan	13,076		2	3	4	5	6	7	8		10	11		9		1				
16	(a) Sheffield W	L 1-2	Smith	25,168		2	3	4	5	6	7	8		10	11		9		1				
23	(h) Leicester C	W 2-0	Kevan, Smith	14,286		2	3	4	5	6	7	8		10	11		9		1				
26	(h) Wolves	D 1-1	Kevan	24,778	1	2	3	4	5	6	7	8		10	11		9						
Jan 13	(a) Ipswich T	L 0-3		18,378	1	2	3	4	5	6	7	8		10	11		9						
20	(h) Burnley	D 1-1	Smith	22,141	1	2	3	4	5	6	7	8		10	11		9						
Feb 3	(a) Arsenal	W 1-0	Clark	29,597	1	2	3	4	5	6	7	8		10	11		9						
10	(h) Bolton W	W 6-2	Smith 2, Hope, Williams, Kevan 2	20,226	1	2	3	4	5	6	7	8		10		11	9						
21	(a) Manchester C	L 1-3	Kevan	17,225	1	4	3	6	5		7	8		10			9	11			2		
24	(a) Manchester U	L 1-4	Jackson	31,456		4	3		5	6	7	8		10		11	9		1		2		
Mar 3	(h) Cardiff C	W 5-1	Kevan 2, Clark, Smith, Howe (pen)	13,894		4	3		5		7	8		10	11		9		1		2	6	
4	(a) Aston Villa	L 0-1		35,104	1	2	3	4	5	6	7	8		10	11		9						
17	(h) Nottingham F	D 2-2	Smith 2	16,794	1	2	3	4	5	6	7	8		10	11		9						
24	(a) Blackburn R	D 1-1	Jackson	11,576		4	3		5	6	7			10	11	8	9		1		2		
28	(a) Wolves	W 5-1	Robson, Drury, Smith, Kevan, Thomson (og)	20,058		2		4	5	6	7			10	11	8	9		1				3
31	(h) West Ham U	L 0-1		16,937		2		4	5	6	7			10	11	8	9		1				3
Apr 7	(a) Sheffield U	D 1-1	Smith	18,697		2		4	5	6	7			10	11	8	9		1				3
14	(h) Chelsea	W 4-0	Kevan 2, Smith, Howe	14,573		2		4	5	6	7			10	11	8	9		1				3
21	(a) Tottenham H	W 2-1	Kevan 2	53,512		2		4	5	6	7			10	11	8	9		1				3
23	(a) Fulham	W 2-1	Lovatt, Jackson	29,322		2		4	5	6	7		9	10	11	8			1				3
24	(h) Fulham	W 2-0	Kevan 2	22,022		2		4	5	6	7		9	10	11	8			1				3
28	(h) Blackpool	W 7-1	Kevan 4, Lovatt, Robson, Howe	17,462		2		4	5	6	7		9	10	11	8			1				3
App					17	42	34	39	42	40	42	30	7	42	39	20	29	1	24	1	4	1	8
Goals						5	2	4		1	8	4	2	33	4	2	17						

A rare goal for Albion's Stuart Williams, against Bolton at The Hawthorns, 10 February 1962.

1962-63

Division 1

Date		Opponent	Res	Score	Scorers	Att	Millington A	Howe D	Williams G	Williams S	Jones S	Drury C	Jackson A	Burnside D	Smith K	Kevan D	Clark C	Potter R	Hope R	Cram R	Foggo K	Carter G	Lovatt J	Bannister J	Murray M	Fenton R	Bradley R	Macready B	Fairfax R
Aug 18	(a)	Manchester U	D	2-2	Kevan, Smith	51,685	1	2	3	4	5	6	7	8	9	10	11												
22	(h)	Leyton O	W	2-1	Smith, Kevan	22,409	1	2	3	4	5	6	7	8	9	10	11												
25	(h)	Burnley	L	1-2	Smith	24,040		2	3	4	5	6	7		9	10	11	1	8										
29	(a)	Leyton O	W	3-2	Lewis (og), Jackson, Clark	17,284		2	3	4	5	6	7		9	10	11	1	8										
Sep 1	(a)	Sheffield W	L	1-3	Jackson	23,042		2	3	4	5	6	7		9	10	11	1	8										
8	(h)	Fulham	W	6-1	Kevan 4, Smith 2	19,304	1	2	3		5	6	7		9	10	11			4	8								
12	(h)	Birmingham C	W	1-0	Jackson	25,499	1	2	3		5	6	7		9	10	11			4	8								
15	(a)	Leicester C	L	0-1		21,517	1	2	3		5	6	7		9	10	11			4	8								
19	(a)	Birmingham C	D	0-0		28,625	1	2	3		5	6	7		9	10				4	8			11					
22	(h)	Bolton W	W	5-4	Kevan 3, Foggo, Howe (pen)	18,670	1	2	3		5	6	7		9	10				4	8			11					
29	(a)	Everton	L	2-4	Harris (og), Jackson	45,471	1	2	3		5	6	7		9	10	11			4	8								
Oct 6	(a)	Aston Villa	L	0-2		43,613	1	2	3		5		7			10	11				8	4		9	6				
13	(h)	Tottenham H	L	1-2	Jackson	32,450	1	2	3		5		7		9	10				8	4			11	6				
20	(a)	Ipswich T	D	1-1	Kevan	19,142		2	3		5	6			9	10		1	8	4	7			11					
27	(h)	Liverpool	W	1-0	Kevan	17,852	1	2	3		5	6	7		9	10	11		8	4									
Nov 3	(a)	Blackpool	W	2-0	Jackson, Hope	12,865	1	2	3		5	6	7		9	10	11		8	4									
10	(h)	Blackburn R	L	2-5	Carter, Hope	14,103	1	2	3		5	6	7		9	10			8	4		11							
17	(a)	Sheffield U	L	0-1		17,895	1	2	3		5	6	7		9	10	11		8	4									
24	(h)	Nottingham F	L	1-4	Jackson	18,670	1	2	3		5	6	7			10	11		8	4					9				
Dec 1	(a)	West Ham U	D	2-2	Smith 2	20,391		2	3		5	6	7		9	10	11	1		4						8			
8	(h)	Manchester C	W	2-1	Smith 2	12,402		2	3		5		7		9	10	11	1		4						8	6		
15	(h)	Manchester U	W	3-0	Cram, Smith, Jackson	17,595		2	3		5	6	7		9	10	11	1		4						8			
Jan 12	(h)	Sheffield W	L	0-3		15,712		2	3		5	6	7		9	10	11	1		4						8			
Mar 2	(a)	Tottenham H	L	1-2	Fenton	40,590		2	3		5	6				10	11	1		4					9	8	7		
9	(h)	Ipswich T	W	6-1	Kevan 3, Jackson, Clark, Smith	10,759		2	3		5	6	7		9	10	11	1		4						8			
16	(a)	Wolves	L	0-7		22,618	1	2	3		5				9		11		10	4	7					8	6		
20	(a)	Liverpool	D	2-2	Fenton, Smith	43,987		2			5				9		11	1	10	4	7					8	6	3	
23	(h)	Blackpool	L	1-2	Jones	15,202		2	3		5				9		11	1	10	4	7					8	6		
25	(a)	Bolton W	W	2-1	Cram, Hope	14,895			3		5				9		11	1	10	4	7					8	6		2
Apr 3	(h)	Wolves	D	2-2	Cram, Hope	15,517		2			5				9		11	1	10	4	7					8	6		3
6	(h)	Sheffield U	L	1-2	Cram	12,497			3		5				9		11	1	10	4	7					8	6		2
12	(a)	Arsenal	L	2-3	Hope, Jackson	28,219		2	3		5		8				11	1	10	4	7	6		9					
13	(a)	Blackburn R	L	1-3	Hope	11,525			3		5		8		9		11	1	10	4	7						6		2
15	(h)	Arsenal	L	1-2	Fenton	16,597			3		5		8				11	1	10	4	7					9	6		2
20	(h)	West Ham U	W	1-0	Jackson	11,192		2	3		5		8					1	10	4	7		11			9	6		
27	(a)	Manchester C	W	5-1	Fenton, Foggo 2, Clark, Jackson	14,995		2	3		5		8				11	1	10	4	7					9	6		
30	(a)	Burnley	L	1-2	Fenton	15,971		2	3		5		8				11	1	10	4	7					9	6		
May 4	(h)	Leicester C	W	2-1	Fenton, Howe (pen)	20,564		2	3		5		8				11	1	10	4	7					9	6		
7	(h)	Everton	L	0-4		24,730		2	3		5		8				11	1	10	4	7					9	6		
11	(h)	Aston Villa	W	1-0	Jackson	25,617		2	3		5	6	8				11	1	10	4	7					9			
14	(a)	Nottingham F	D	2-2	Clark 2	13,048		2	3		5	6	8				11	1	10	4	7					9			
18	(a)	Fulham	D	2-2	Jackson, Fenton	17,481		4	3		5	6	8				11	1	10		7					9			2
						App	16	38	40	5	40	27	35	2	27	25	36	26	28	36	25	6	1	4	3	21	13	1	7
						Goals		2			1		14		12	14	5		6	4	3	1				7			

Derek Kevan's match-winning goal against Liverpool at The Hawthorns on 27 October 1962 — the only goal he ever scored against the Merseysiders.

131

1963-64

Division 1

Date		Opponent	Result	Scorers	Att.	Potter R	Howe D	Williams G	Cram R	Jones S	Simpson T	Foggo K	Fenton R	Kaye J	Hope R	Clark C	Jackson A	Readfern E	Crawford C	Fraser D	Brown T	Fairfax R	Drury C	Macready B	Carter G	Fudge M	Howshall G
Aug 24	(h)	Leicester C	D 1-1	Fenton	23,078	1	2	3	4	5	6	7	8	9	10	11											
27	(a)	Arsenal	L 2-3	Clark, Kaye	31,381	1	2	3	4	5	6	7		10	9	11	8										
31	(a)	Bolton W	W 2-1	Williams, Fenton	14,170	1	2	3	4	5	6	7		10	9	11	8										
Sep 4	(h)	Arsenal	W 4-0	Foggo 2, Kaye, Clark	20,258	1	2	3	4	5	6	7		10	9	11	8										
7	(h)	Fulham	W 3-0	Jackson, Clark, Foggo	17,995	1	2	3	4	5	6	7		10	9	11	8										
11	(a)	Birmingham C	W 1-0	Foggo	34,666	1	2	3	4	5	6	7		10		11	8	9									
14	(a)	Manchester U	L 0-1		50,453	1	4	3	8	5	6	7		10		11			9	2							
18	(h)	Birmingham C	W 3-1	Foggo, Clark, Jackson	29,662	1	2	3		5	6	7		10		11	8	9		4							
21	(h)	Burnley	D 0-0		24,591	1	2	3		5	6	7		10		11	8	9		4							
28	(a)	Ipswich T	W 2-1	Brown, Clark	13,765	1	2	3		5	6	7			9	11	10			4	8						
Oct 2	(a)	Wolves	D 0-0		37,038	1	2	3		5	6	7		10	9	11	8			4							
5	(h)	Sheffield W	L 1-3	Clark	21,145	1		3		5	6	7		10	9	11	8		2	4							
12	(h)	Aston Villa	W 4-3	Cram, Jackson, Brown, Foggo	28,602	1			9	5	6	7				11	10		2	4	8	3					
19	(a)	Liverpool	L 0-1		43,009	1		3	9	5	6	7				11	10			4	8	2					
26	(h)	Stoke C	L 2-3	Williams, Foggo	23,973	1		3	9	5	6	7				11	10			4	8	2					
Nov 2	(a)	West Ham U	L 2-4	Foggo, Cram	22,888	1	2	3	9	5	6	7				11	10			4			8				
9	(h)	Chelsea	D 1-1	Simpson	16,267	1		3	9	5	6	7	8			11	10		2	4							
16	(a)	Blackpool	L 0-1		11,047	1	2	3		5	6	7	8	9	10	11				4							
23	(h)	Blackburn R	L 1-3	Fenton	16,441	1	2	3		5	6		8	9	10	7				4				11			
30	(a)	Nottingham F	W 3-0	Fenton, Clark, Carter	19,025	1	2	3		5	6		8	9	10	7				4					11		
Dec 7	(h)	Sheffield U	W 2-0	Kaye, Clark	14,149	1	2	3		5	6		8	9		7				4				11	10		
14	(a)	Leicester C	W 2-0	Fraser, Foggo	17,740	1	2	3		5	6	7	8	9		11				4						10	
21	(a)	Bolton W	D 1-1	Kaye	10,715	1	2	3		5	6	7	8	9		11				4						10	
26	(h)	Tottenham H	D 4-4	Kaye, Clark, Fudge, Howe	37,189	1	2	3		5	6	7	8	9		11				4						10	
28	(a)	Tottenham H	W 2-0	Fenton, Foggo	47,325	1	2	3		5	6	7	8	9		11				4						10	
Jan 11	(a)	Fulham	D 1-1	Clark	16,398	1	2	3		5	6	7	8	9		11				4						10	
18	(h)	Manchester U	L 1-4	Simpson	25,624	1	2	3		5	6		8	9		7				4				11		10	
Feb 1	(a)	Burnley	L 2-3	Brown, Clark	15,840	1	2	3		5	6	7		9		11	10			4	8						
8	(h)	Ipswich T	W 2-1	Kaye, Fenton	13,476	1	2	3		5	6		10	9		11	8			4		7					
15	(a)	Sheffield W	D 2-2	Clark, Williams	19,582	1	2	3		5	6	7				11	10			4	9	8					
22	(a)	Aston Villa	L 0-1		27,663	1	2	3		5	6	7		9		11					10		8			4	
29	(h)	Wolves	W 3-1	Kaye, Clark, Fenton	19,829	1	2	3		5	6	7	8	9		11	10							4			
Mar 7	(a)	Stoke C	D 1-1	Kaye	25,012	1	2	3		5	6	7		9		11	10			4	8						
13	(h)	Blackpool	W 2-1	Kaye, Clark	13,694	1	2	3		5	6	7		9		11	10			4	8						
21	(a)	Chelsea	L 1-3	Kaye	19,829	1	2	3		5	6	7		9		11	10			4	8						
27	(a)	Everton	D 1-1	Simpson	61,187	1	2	3		5	6	7	8	9		11	10			4							
28	(h)	West Ham U	L 0-1		15,444	1	2	3		5	6	7	8	9		11	10			4							
31	(h)	Everton	W 4-2	Williams, Fudge 3	27,194	1	2	3		5	6	7		9		11	8			4						10	
Apr 4	(a)	Blackburn R	W 2-0	Fenton, Clark	12,052	1	2	3		5	6	7		9		11	8			4						10	
11	(h)	Nottingham F	L 2-3	Brown, Foggo	14,442	1	2	3		5	6	7		9		11	8			4	10						
18	(a)	Sheffield U	L 1-2	Brown	16,605	1		3	2	5	6	7		9		11				4	8					10	
25	(h)	Liverpool	D 2-2	Kaye, Clark	17,833	1		3	2	5	6	7		9		11				4	8					10	
				App		42	35	41	14	42	42	37	31	27	4	42	27	4	4	33	13	1	2	4	4	11	2
				Goals			1	4	2		3	11	8	11		16	3			1	5				1	4	

Leicester City centre-half Ian King gets in a tangle with Albion's Bobby Cram in the opening League game of 1963-4 season.

Mickey Fudge, hat-trick hero against Everton in 1964.

1964-65

Division 1

Date	Opponent	Res	Scorers	Att	Potter R	C'ram R	Williams G	Fraser D	Jones S	Simpson T	Foggo K	Brown T	Kaye J	Hope R	Clark C	Collard I	Howshall G	Astle J	Fairfax R	Fenton R	Carter G	Lovett G	Krzywicki R	Fudge M	Williams W	Crawford R
Aug 22	(a) Manchester U	D 2-2	Brown, Foulkes (og)	52,007	1	2	3	4	5	6	7	8	9	10	11											
26	(h) Sunderland	W 4-1	Brown 3, Clark	26,139	1	2	3	4	5	6	7	8	9	10	11											
29	(h) Fulham	D 2-2	Williams, Clark	18,702	1	2	3	4	5	6	7	8	9	10	11											
Sep 2	(a) Sunderland	D 2-2	Brown, Clark	52,177	1	2	3	4	5	6	7	8	9	10	11											
5	(a) Nottingham F	D 0-0		28,334	1	2	3	4	5	6	7	8	9	10	11											
9	(a) Birmingham C	D 1-1	Foggo	26,485	1	2	3	4	5	6	7	8	9	10	11											
12	(h) Stoke C	W 5-3	Foggo, Cram 3 (2 pens), Brown	24,505	1	2	3	4	5	6	7	8	9	10	11											
16	(h) Birmingham C	L 0-2		26,013	1	2	3	4	5	6	7	8	9	10	11											
19	(a) Tottenham H	L 0-1		36,525	1	2	3	4	5	6	7	8	9	10	11											
26	(h) Burnley	L 1-2	Cram (pen)	15,009	1	2	3	4	5	6	7		9		10	11	8									
30	(a) Leicester C	L 2-4	Cram (pen), Williams	17,218	1	2	3		5	6	7	8	9		11		4	10								
Oct 3	(a) Sheffield U	D 1-1	Carter	17,592	1	2			5	6	7	8					4	9	3	10	11					
10	(h) Wolves	W 5-1	Astle 2, Kaye 2, Cram (pen)	23,006	1	2	3		5	6		8	10	7	11		4	9								
17	(a) Aston Villa	W 1-0	Howshall	28,030	1	2	3		5	6		8	10	7	11		4	9								
24	(h) Liverpool	W 3-0	Clark 2, Astle	22,045	1	2	3		5	6		8	10	7	11		4	9								
31	(a) Sheffield W	D 1-1	Clark	19,004	1	2	3		5	6		8	10	7	11		4	9								
Nov 7	(h) Blackpool	L 1-3	Kaye	17,504	1	2			5	6		8	10	7	11		4	9	3							
14	(a) Blackburn R	L 2-4	Foggo, Brown	13,828	1	2	3		5	6	7	8			11		4	9		10						
21	(h) Arsenal	D 0-0		18,489	1	2	3		5	6		8		11	7		4	9		10						
28	(a) Leeds U	L 0-1		29,533	1	2	3	4	5	6	7			10	11			9	8							
Dec 5	(h) Chelsea	L 0-2		15,518	1		3	4	5		7			10	11			9	2	8	6					
12	(h) Manchester U	D 1-1	Kaye	28,504	1		3	4	5	6	7		8	10	11			9	2							
19	(a) Fulham	L 1-3	Jones	10,390	1		3	4	5			10	8		11			9	2		6	7				
26	(a) Everton	L 2-3	Fenton, Clark	46,719	1	2	3	4	5	6				10	11			9		7		8				
Jan 2	(h) Nottingham F	D 2-2	Fudge, Clark	16,040	1	2	3	4		6				10	11			9		7			8	5		
16	(a) Stoke C	L 0-2		25,405	1	2	3	4	5	6	7			10	11		8	9								
23	(h) Tottenham H	W 2-0	Cram, Clark	24,233	1	2	3	4	5	6	7			10	11		8	9								
Feb 6	(a) Burnley	W 1-0	Foggo	12,902	1		3	4	5	6	7			10	11		8	9	2							
13	(h) Sheffield U	L 0-1		10,511	1	2	3	4	5	6	7			10	11		8	9								
27	(h) Aston Villa	W 3-1	Astle, Cram (pen), Hope	24,040	1	2	3	6	5		7			10	11		4	8								9
Mar 13	(h) Leicester C	W 6-0	Astle 2, Howshall, Clark, Foggo, Williams	15,162	1	2	3	6	5		7			10	11		4	8								9
15	(a) Wolves	L 2-3	Foggo, Harris (og)	26,722	1	2	3	6	5		7		9	10	11		4	8								
20	(a) Blackpool	L 0-3		11,168	1	2	3	6	5	4	7		9		11		8	10								
23	(h) Everton	W 4-0	Astle 2, Foggo, Cram (pen)	13,013	1	2	3	6	5		7		9	10	11		4	8								
26	(h) Blackburn R	D 0-0		17,045	1	2	3	6	5		7		9	10	11		4	8								
Apr 3	(a) Arsenal	D 1-1	Hope	18,797	1	2	3	6	5		7		9	10	11		4	8								
7	(a) Liverpool	W 3-0	Kaye, Hope, Clark	34,152	1	2	3	6	5		7		9	10	11		4	8								
10	(h) Leeds U	L 1-2	Foggo	22,010	1	2	3	6	5		7		9	10	11		4	8								
16	(a) West Ham U	L 1-6	Astle	27,706	1	2	3	6	5		7		9	10	11		4	8								
17	(a) Chelsea	D 2-2	Crawford, Howshall	30,792	1	2	3	6	5		7			10			4	8							11	9
19	(h) West Ham U	W 4-2	Foggo, Astle, Brown 2	14,018	1	2	3	6	5		7	11		10			4	8								9
24	(h) Sheffield W	W 1-0	Crawford	16,002	1	2	3	6	5		7	11		10			4	8								9
App					42	38	40	33	41	28	33	17	25	37	38	1	26	32	6	7	7	2	1	2	1	5
Goals						9	3		1		9	9	5	3	11		3	10		1	1			1		2

Clive Clark heads towards the Aston Villa goal in 1965.

133

1965-66

Division 1

Date		Opponent	Res	Score	Scorers	Att	Potter R	Cram R	Williams G	Lovett G	Jones S	Fraser D	Foggo K	Astle J	Kaye J	Hope R	Clark C	Fairfax R	Howshall G	Brown T	Wilson R	Sheppard R	Crawford R	Collard I	Crawford C	Krzywicki R	Campbell D
Aug 21	(h)	West Ham U	W	3-0	Clark 2, Astle	19,956	1	2	3	4	5	6	7	8	9	10	11										
25	(a)	Newcastle U	W	1-0	Kaye	43,901	1		3	4	5	6	7	8	9	10	11	2									
28	(a)	Nottingham F	L	2-3	Astle, Foggo	27,366	1		3	4	5	6	7	8	9	10	11	2									
Sep 1	(h)	Newcastle U	L	1-2	Kaye	22,043	1		3	4	5	6	7	8	9	10	11	2									
4	(h)	Sheffield W	W	4-2	Astle 3, Kaye	15,229	1	2	3		5	6	7	8	9	10	11		4								
7	(a)	Everton	W	3-2	Brown, Kaye, Astle	43,468	1	2	3		5	6	7	8	9	10			4	11							
10	(a)	Northampton T	W	4-3	Hope, Astle 3	18,528	1	2	3	12	5	6	7*	8	9	10			4	11							
15	(h)	Everton	D	1-1	Astle	25,513	1	2	3	10	5	6		8	9		11		4	7							
18	(h)	Stoke C	W	6-2	Setters (og), Kaye 3, Cram (pen), Brown	24,374	1	2	3	4	5	6		8	9	10	11			7							
25	(a)	Burnley	L	0-2		20,489	1	2		4	5	6		8	9	10	11	3		7							
Oct 2	(h)	Chelsea	L	1-2	Fraser	23,049	1	2		4	5	6		8	9	10		3		7	11						
9	(h)	Sunderland	W	4-1	Kaye, Cram (pen), Brown 2	19,617		2		4	5	6		8	9	10	11	3		7		1					
16	(a)	Aston Villa	D	1-1	Astle	41,455		2		4	5	6		8	9	10		3		7		1					
23	(h)	Liverpool	W	3-0	Brown, Kaye, Clark	29,669		2		4	5	6			9	10	11	3		7		1	8				
30	(a)	Tottenham H	L	1-2	Crawford	43,512		2		4	5	6			9	10	11	3		7		1	8				
Nov 6	(h)	Fulham	W	6-2	Wilson, Brown 2, Lovatt 2, Clark	19,858		2		4	5	6			9	10	11	3		8	11	1					
13	(a)	Blackpool	D	1-1	Brown	12,642		2		4	5	6		8	9	10	11	3		7		1					
20	(h)	Blackburn R	W	2-1	Cram (pen), Brown	17,189		2		4	5	6		8	9	10	11	3		7		1					
27	(a)	Leicester C	L	1-2	Crawford	21,124		2		4	5	6			9	10	11	3		7		1*	8	12			
Dec 4	(h)	Sheffield U	D	1-1	Brown	15,607		2		4	5	6		8	9	10	11	3		7		1					
11	(a)	Leeds U	L	0-4		33,140		2		4	5	6	7		9	10	11	3				1	8				
27	(a)	Manchester U	D	1-1	Crawford	54,102	1	2		4	5	6			9	10	11	3					8				
Jan 1	(a)	Sunderland	W	5-1	Kaye, Hope, Brown 2, Crawford	34,938	1	2		4	5	6	12		9	10*	11	3		7			8				
8	(h)	Leeds U	L	1-2	Wilson	24,900	1	2		4	5	6			9	10		3		7	11		8				
15	(a)	Liverpool	D	2-2	Brown, Kaye	46,687	1	2		4	5	6			9	10	11	3		7			8				
29	(a)	West Ham U	L	0-4		25,500	1		3	4	5	6			9	10	11			8					2	7	
Feb 5	(h)	Nottingham F	W	5-3	Clark, Kaye, Cram (pen), Brown, Hope	14,054	1	2		4	5	6	7	9*	10	11		3	12	8							
11	(h)	Aston Villa	D	2-2	Kaye, Brown	17,089	1	2		4	5	6*	7	9	10	11		3	12	8							
19	(a)	Sheffield W	W	2-1	Clark, Mobley (og)	18,358	1		3	4	5	6			9	10	11	2		8			7				
26	(h)	Northampton T	D	1-1	Clark	18,923	1		3	4	5	6			9	10	11	2		8*			7	12			
Mar 12	(a)	Stoke C	D	1-1	Clark	23,261	1	2		6	10	4		8	9		11	3		7							5
19	(h)	Burnley	L	1-2	Brown	18,747	1	2		6	10	4		8	9		11	3		7							5
Apr 2	(a)	Fulham	L	1-2	Astle	20,426	1	2		4		6		8	9	10	11	3		7							5
5	(a)	Arsenal	D	1-1	Cram (pen)	8,738	1	2		4		6		8	9	10	11	3		7							5
9	(h)	Blackpool	W	2-1	Brown, Foggo	13,079	1	2		4	5	6	7		9	10*	11	3		8				12			
11	(h)	Arsenal	D	4-4	Cram 2 (2 pens), Astle, Lovett	16,094	1	2		4	10	5	6	8	9		11	3		7							
16	(a)	Blackburn R	W	1-0	Astle	7,637	1	2		4	10	5	6	8	9		11	3		7							
22	(h)	Leicester C	W	5-1	Kaye 2, Sjoberg 2 (2 og's), Astle	15,229	1	2	4		5	6		8	9	10	11	3		7							
25	(a)	Chelsea	W	3-2	Clark, Astle 2	22,804	1	2	4	12	5	6*		8	9	10	11	3		7							
30	(a)	Sheffield U	W	2-0	Kaye 2	16,022	1		3	4	5	6		8	9	10	11	2		7							
May 4	(h)	Manchester U	D	3-3	Clark, Lovett, Kaye	22,609	1		3	4	5	6		8	9	10	11	2		7							
7	(h)	Tottenham H	W	2-1	Hope, Astle	22,586	1	2	4		5	6		8	9	10	11	3		7							
App							32	34	22	36	38	42	12	27	42	37	37	34	6	35	3	10	9		1	1	4
Sub app										2			1							2				3			
Goals								7		4		1	2	18	18	4	10			17	2		4				

Clive Clark beats Martin Peters' outstretched leg to score Albion's first League goal of the 1965-6 season, against West Ham United.

1966-67

Division 1

Date		Opponent	Result	Scorers	Att.	Potter R	Cram R	Fairfax R	Williams G	Jones S	Fraser D	Brown T	Astle J	Kaye J	Hope R	Clark C	Sheppard R	Collard I	Lovett G	Foggo K	Campbell D	Crawford C	Krzywicki R	Stephens K	Treacy R	Simpson T	Howshall G	Clarke D	Talbut J	Osborne J	Colquhoun E
Aug 20	(a)	Manchester U	L 3-5	Hope, Clark 2	41,343	1	2	3	4	5	6	7	8	9	10	11															
24	(a)	Leeds U	L 1-2	Astle	35,102	1	2	3	4	5	6	7	8	9	10	11															
27	(h)	Burnley	L 1-2	Lovett	21,732		2			5	6	7	8	9	10	11	1	3	4												
31	(h)	Leeds U	W 2-0	Clark, Brown	22,072		2			5	6	7	8	9	10	11	1	3	4												
Sep 3	(a)	Nottingham F	L 1-2	Brown	21,871		2			5	6	7	8	9	10	11	1	3	4												
7	(a)	Newcastle U	W 3-1	Clark 2, Kaye	24,748		2			5	6	7	8	9	10	11	1	3	4												
10	(h)	Fulham	W 5-1	Clark 2, Hope 2, Astle	17,160		2			5	6	7	8	9	10	11	1	3	4												
17	(a)	Everton	L 4-5	Astle, Fraser, Cram (pen), Kaye	45,165		2			5	6		8	9	10	11	1	3	4	7											
24	(h)	Stoke C	L 0-1		24,865		2			5	6		8	9	10	11	1	3	4	7											
Oct 1	(a)	Sheffield U	L 3-4	Astle, Fraser, Clark	15,313		2		4		6		8	9	10	11	1	3		7	5										
8	(a)	Sunderland	D 2-2	Treacy, Clark	26,632	1			4						10	11		3	6		5	2	7	8	9						
15	(h)	Aston Villa	W 2-1	Astle, Krzywicki	31,128	1			4	5	6		8	9	10*	11		3	12			2	7								
22	(a)	Arsenal	W 3-2	Hope 2, Clark	31,036	1				5	6		8	9	10	11		3	4			2	7								
29	(h)	Sheffield W	L 1-2	Astle	19,335	1			7	5	6		8	9	10	11		3	4				2								
Nov 5	(a)	Aston Villa	L 2-3	Kaye, Lovett	24,018	1		3	7	5	6		8	9	10	11			4												
12	(h)	Chelsea	L 0-1		28,151	1		2	4	5	6	7	8	9	10	11		3													
19	(a)	Leicester C	L 1-2	Foggo	25,003			2	4	5	6*	10	8	9		11	1	3		7						12					
26	(h)	Liverpool	W 2-1	Brown, Clark	25,931		2	3		5	6	8		9	10	11	1		4	7											
Dec 3	(a)	West Ham U	L 0-3		22,961		2	3		5	6	8		9	10	11	1		4	7											
10	(h)	Manchester C	L 0-3		17,299			3		5	6	7	8	9	10	11	1		4							2					
17	(h)	Manchester U	L 3-4	Astle 2, Kaye	32,080	1		2	12	5	6	7	8	9	10	11		3*									4				
26	(h)	Tottenham H	W 3-0	Brown 3 (1 pen)	37,969	1		3			6	7	8	9	10	11											4	2	5		
27	(a)	Tottenham H	D 0-0		39,002	1		3		5	6	7	8	9	10	11											4	2			
31	(a)	Burnley	L 1-5	Astle	18,904	1		3			6	9	8		10	11								7			4	2	5		
Jan 7	(h)	Nottingham F	L 1-2	Clark	21,795			3			6	7	8	9	10	11											4	2	5	1	
14	(a)	Fulham	D 2-2	Collard, Cram	20,680		2	3			6	7	8	9	10	11		4											5	1	
21	(h)	Everton	W 1-0	Clark	26,104		2	3			6		8	9	10	11		4						7					5	1	
Feb 4	(a)	Stoke C	D 1-1	Astle	26,212		2	3			6	7	8	9	10	11		4										12	5*	1	
11	(h)	Sheffield U	L 1-2	Cram	20,354		2	12	3	5	6	8	9*	10		11		4		7										1	
25	(h)	Sunderland	D 2-2	Fraser, Astle	22,296					5	6	7	8	9	10	11		3	4									12		1	2*
Mar 18	(a)	Arsenal	L 0-1		16,832			2	3	5	6		8	9		11	1	10		7											4
25	(a)	Manchester C	D 2-2	Kaye, Fraser	22,780			2	3		4		8	9	10	11	1			7							6				5
27	(h)	Southampton	W 3-2	Brown, Clark, Astle	19,732			2	3		6	4	8	9	10	11	1			7											5
28	(a)	Southampton	D 2-2	Astle, Clark	28,870			2	3		6	4	8	9	10	11	1			7											5
Apr 1	(h)	Blackpool	W 3-1	Clark, Williams, Brown	19,441			2	3			4	8	9	10	11		6		7										1	5
10	(a)	Chelsea	W 2-0	Clark, Foggo	18,448			2	3			4	8	9	10	11		6		7										1	5
15	(h)	Leicester C	W 1-0	Clark	22,872			2	3			10	8	9		11		6		7								4		1	5
19	(a)	Sheffield W	L 0-1		23,056			2	3			10	8	9		11		6		7								4		1	5
22	(a)	Liverpool	W 1-0	Astle	39,883			2	3			10	8	9		11		6		7								4		1	5
28	(h)	West Ham U	W 3-1	Brown 2 (2 pens), Astle	23,210			2	3			6	8	9	10	11				7								4		1	5
May 6	(a)	Blackpool	W 3-1	Astle, Williams, Brown (pen)	9,986			2	3	12		6	8	9*	10	11				7								4		1	5
13	(h)	Newcastle U	W 6-1	Foggo, Brown 3, Williams, Clark	20,035			2	3			6	8	9		11				7								4	5	1	
App						12	11	25	30	23	34	31	38	40	36	42	14	26	15	19	2	5	3	3	1	1	6	5	12	16	12
Sub app							1	1		1									1							1		2			
Goals							3		3		4	14	16	5	5	19		1	2	3			1		1						

Jeff Astle's headed goal against Aston Villa at The Hawthorns in October 1966.

135

1967-68

Division 1

Date		Opponent	Result	Scorers	Att	Osborne J	Fraser D	Williams G	Howshall G	Colquhoun E	Talbut J	Foggo K	Astle J	Kaye J	Brown T	Clark C	Collard I	Clarke D	Hope R	Fairfax R	Stephens K	Sheppard R	Campbell D	Treacy R	Krzywicki R	Lovett G	Hartford A	Martin D	Rees R
Aug 19	(h)	Chelsea	L 0-1		33,283	1	2	3	4	5	6*	7	8	9	10	11	12												
23	(a)	Wolves	D 3-3	Foggo, Kaye, Brown	52,438	1	2	3	4	5	6	7	8	9	10	11													
26	(a)	Southampton	L 0-4		22,714	1	6	3	4	5			8	9	7	11				2	10								
30	(h)	Wolves	W 4-1	Astle, Clark, Stephens, Kaye	38,373	1	4	3		5*	6		9	12	8	11			10	2	7								
Sep 2	(h)	Liverpool	L 0-2		32,159		4	3		5	6		9	12	8*	11			10	2	7	1							
6	(h)	Arsenal	L 1-3	Clark	20,153	1	4	3		5	6		9	8		11			10	2	7								
9	(a)	Stoke C	D 0-0		21,036	1	2	3		5	6		12	9	8	11	4		10		7*								
16	(h)	Nottingham F	W 2-1	Hope, Stephens	21,136	1	2	3		5					11	4			10		7*	6	8						
23	(a)	Coventry C	L 2-4	Astle, Clark	31,258	1		3		2	5		9	8	11	4*			10	6	7		12						
30	(h)	Sheffield U	W 4-1	Astle 3, Brown	15,186	1	6	3		2	5		9	8	4	11			10		7								
Oct 7	(a)	Fulham	W 2-1	Astle, Brown	17,758	1	6	3		2	5		9	8	4	11			10		7								
14	(h)	Leeds U	W 2-0	Astle 2	21,024	1	6	3		2	5		9	8	4	11			10		7*					12			
21	(a)	Everton	L 1-2	Kaye	44,092	1	6			2	5		9*	8	4			3	10		11				12	7			
28	(h)	Leicester C	D 0-0		20,961	1	6	3		2	5		9	8	4	11			10						12	7*			
Nov 11	(h)	Burnley	W 8-1	Hope 2, Clark 2, Brown, Colquhoun, Kaye, Astle	18,952	1	6	3		2	5		9	8	4	11			10		7								
18	(a)	Sheffield W	D 2-2	Clark, Astle	28,256	1	6	3		2	5		9	8	4	11			10		7								
25	(h)	Tottenham H	W 2-0	Clark, Hope	29,033	1	6	3		2	5		9	8	4	11			10		7								
Dec 2	(a)	Manchester U	L 1-2	Kaye	52,568	1	6	3		2	5		9	8	4	11			10						7				
11	(a)	West Ham U	W 3-2	Krzywicki, Astle, Hope (pen)	18,340	1	6	3		2	5		9	8	4	11			10						7				
16	(a)	Chelsea	W 3-0	Clark, Astle, Krzywicki	27,739	1	6	3		2	5		9	8	4	11			10						7				
23	(h)	Southampton	D 0-0		24,082	1	6	3		2	5		9	8	4	11			10						7				
26	(h)	Manchester C	W 3-2	Astle 2, Brown	44,897	1	6	3		2	5		9	8	4	11*			10						7	12			
30	(a)	Manchester C	W 2-0	Krzywicki, Brown	45,754	1	6	3		2	5		9	8	4	11			10						7				
Jan 6	(a)	Liverpool	L 1-4	Brown (pen)	51,092	1	6	3		2	5		9	8	4	11			10						7				
20	(a)	Nottingham F	L 2-3	Clark 2	34,298	1	6	3		2	5		9	8	4	11			10						7				
Feb 3	(h)	Coventry C	L 0-1		28,231		6	3		2	5		9	8	4	11			10		12	1			7*				
10	(a)	Sheffield U	D 1-1	Astle	19,281		6	3		2	5		9	8	4	11			10			1		7					
24	(h)	Fulham	W 2-1	Astle, Brown (pen)	17,969	1	6	3			5		9	8	7	11*	4			2	10				12				
Mar 2	(a)	Tottenham H	D 0-0		31,318	1	6	3		2	5		9	8	7	11	4		10										
13	(h)	Stoke C	W 3-0	Astle 2 (1 pen), Collard	20,621	1	6	3		2	5		9	8			4				7				10	12			11*
16	(h)	Everton	L 2-6	Collard 2	26,481	1	6	3		2	5		9	8			4				7*				10	12			11
23	(a)	Leicester C	W 3-2	Clark 2, Astle	23,097		6	3		2*	5		9	8		11	4		10		12	1							7
Apr 2	(h)	Sunderland	D 0-0		15,490	1		3			6		9	8		11	10			2									7
6	(a)	Burnley	D 0-0		12,204	1		3			6		9	8		11	10			2									7
12	(a)	Newcastle U	D 2-2	Rees 2	40,308	1		3			6*		9	8		11	10			2			12						7
13	(h)	Sheffield W	D 1-1	Astle	20,677	1	4	3			5		9	6	8				10	2	7								11
15	(h)	Newcastle U	W 2-0	Brown 2	22,194	1	4	3			5		9	6	8		12		2		10	7							11*
20	(a)	Leeds U	L 1-3	Lovett	38,334	1	6	3			5			4					10	2	7				9	8			11
29	(h)	Manchester U	W 6-3	Astle 3, Rees, Brown (pen), Hartford	45,992	1	6	3			5		9		4		8		2	10					12		11		7*
May 1	(h)	West Ham U	W 3-1	Astle 3	25,686	1				5	6		9	8				3	10	2						11	4		7
4	(a)	Sunderland	D 0-0		31,892	1	4			5	6		9			11	10	3		2					12	8			7*
11	(a)	Arsenal	L 1-2	Fraser	24,896		2	3		5	6		9			11	4		10			1				8			7
		App				37	40	35	3	33	42	2	40	37	35	34	17	10	32	6	18	5	2	1	11	7	4	1	10
		Sub app										1	2				3				1	1			3	2	3	2	
		Goals					1	1			1		26	5	11	12	3		5		2				3	1	1		3

Another goal for Jeff Astle — this header goes in against Sheffield Wednesday at The Hawthorns on 13 April 1968.

1968-69
Division 1

Date		Opponent	Res	Score	Scorers	Att	Sheppard R	Fraser D	Williams G	Brown T	Talbut J	Kaye J	Krzywicki R	Hartford A	Astle J	Hope R	Rees R	Collard I	Wilson R	Clarke D	Osborne J	Lovett G	Clark C	Colquhoun E	Merrick A	Potter R	Hughes L	Martin D	Reed H	Cantello L
Aug 10	(h)	Sheffield W	D	0-0		25,031	1	2	3	4	5	6	7	8	9	10	11													
14	(h)	Manchester U	W	3-1	Astle 2, Brown	38,299	1	2	3	4	5	6	7		9	10	11	8												
17	(a)	Chelsea	L	1-3	Brown	33,766	1	2	3*	4	5	6	7		9	10	11	8	12											
21	(a)	Tottenham H	D	1-1	Astle	35,746	1		3	4	5	6	7		9	10	11	8	12											
24	(h)	Burnley	W	3-2	Astle 2, Collard	21,882			3	4	5	6	7		9	10	11	8*	12	2	1									
27	(a)	Coventry C	L	2-4	Rees, Brown	36,678	1	4	3	8	5	6	7		9		11		2			10								
31	(a)	West Ham U	L	0-4		29,708	1		3	8	5	6			9	10	7		2			4	11							
Sep 7	(h)	Nottingham F	L	2-5	Astle, Brown	23,377	1	2	3	4	5	8			9	10	7						11	6						
14	(a)	Newcastle U	W	3-2	Astle 2, Hartford	35,128	1	2	3	4	5	6		8	9	10	7						11							
21	(h)	Wolves	D	0-0		35,175		2	3	4	5	6	9*	10			7			1		8	11	12						
28	(a)	Everton	L	0-4		47,712		2	3	4	5	6		9	10*		7			1		8	11		12					
Oct 5	(h)	Queen's Park R	W	3-1	Hartford, Rees, Astle	22,944		2	3	4	5			8	9	10	7	6		1			11*		12					
9	(h)	Coventry C	W	6-1	Rees, Brown (pen), Astle 2, Hartford, Tudor (og)	29,255		2		4	5	6		11	9	10	7	8	3	1										
12	(a)	Leicester C	W	2-0	Astle, Hartford	26,348		2		4	5	6		11	9	10	7	8	3	1										
19	(h)	Arsenal	W	1-0	Brown	29,324		2	12	4	5	6		11	9*	10	7		3	1							8			
26	(a)	Leeds U	D	0-0		33,926		2		4	5	6		11		10	7	8	3	1								9		
Nov 2	(h)	Liverpool	D	0-0		34,805		2		4	5	6		11	9	10	7	8	3	1										
9	(a)	Southampton	L	0-2		19,885		2		4	5	6		11	9	10	7	8	3*	1						12				
16	(h)	Stoke C	W	2-1	Fraser, Hartford	21,026		2		4	5	6		11	9	10	12	8	3	1							7*			
23	(a)	Manchester C	L	1-5	Brown	24,667	1	2	12	4	5	6		11	9	10	7	8*	3											
30	(h)	Sunderland	W	3-0	Brown, Rees, Hartford	19,411		2	12	4	5			10	9		7		3		1	8	11*		6					
Dec 7	(a)	Ipswich T	L	1-4	Rees	20,725		2		4*	5	6		11	9		7	10	3		1	8							12	
14	(h)	Leicester C	D	1-1	Brown (pen)	16,483		2		4	5	6		11	9	10	7	8	3		1									
21	(a)	Arsenal	L	0-2		30,765		2		4	5	6			9	10		8	3		1	7					11			
28	(a)	Queen's Park R	W	4-0	Collard 2, Martin, Rees	18,649		2		4	5	6		11	9	10			3		1	8						7		
Jan 11	(a)	Liverpool	L	0-1		45,587		2		4	5	6		11	9		7	10	3		1	8								
18	(h)	Southampton	L	1-2	Brown (pen)	22,856		2		4	5			12	9	7	11	10*	3		1	8			6					
Feb 1	(a)	Stoke C	D	1-1	Astle	20,567				4		6	8	11	9		7		3		1	10			5	2				
Mar 5	(a)	Sheffield W	L	0-1		18,690	1	2		4	5	6*	12		9	10			3			8	11				7			
8	(h)	Chelsea	L	0-3		25,137				4	5	6	8	11	9	10			3		1					2	7			
10	(a)	Sunderland	W	1-0	Brown	15,769		2	8	4					10				3		1	11			6	5	9			7
15	(a)	Burnley	D	2-2	Brown 2	12,218		2		4	5			10					3	6*	1	8	11				9	12		7
22	(a)	Nottingham F	L	0-3		20,546		2		4	5				9	10			3		1	8	11		6		7			
Apr 2	(a)	Manchester U	L	1-2	Astle	38,846		2		4	5	6	7		9	10			3		1	8	11							
5	(h)	Everton	D	1-1	Astle	23,156		2		4	5	6	7	12	9	10*			3		1	8	11							
7	(h)	Tottenham H	W	4-3	Hope, Astle 2, Brown	24,173		2		4	5	6	7	11	9	10			3		1	8								
9	(h)	Leeds U	D	1-1	Krzywicki	28,186		2		4	5	6	7	11	9	10			3		1	8								
12	(a)	Wolves	W	1-0	Clark	37,920		2		4	5	6	7	11*		10			3		1	8	12				9			
14	(h)	West Ham U	W	3-1	Astle 2, Brown	19,780		2	3	4	5	6			9	10					1	8	11				7			
16	(h)	Manchester C	W	2-0	Krzywicki, Book (og)	22,717		2	3	4	5		7	12	9	10*					1	8	11		6					
19	(h)	Newcastle U	W	5-1	Kaye, Hartford, Brown (pen), Clark, Astle	22,481		2		4	5	6	7	10	9				3		1	8	11							
23	(h)	Ipswich T	D	2-2	Astle, Brown	21,426		2		4	5	6	7		9	10			3		1	8	11							
App							10	34	17	42	42	34	17	23	37	35	24	19	27	4	32	23	17	1	4	2	5	10	1	2
Sub app								3					1	3		1	2					1			1	1	2		1	1
Goals								1		17		1	2	7	21	1	6	3					2					1		

Jeff Astle scores his second goal in Albion's 3-1 win over Manchester United at The Hawthorns in August 1968. The Throstles scored nine goals in two home games against United that year.

1969-70

Division 1

Date		Opponent	Result	Scorers	Att.	Osborne J	Williams G	Wilson R	Brown T	Talbut J	Kaye J	Hegan D	Suggett C	Krzywicki R	Hope R	Freeman P	Nisbet G	Astle J	Fraser D	Cumbes J	Hartford A	Merrick A	Hughes L	Potter R	Cantello L	Robertson A	Martin D	Glover A	Lovett G
Aug 9	(a)	Southampton	W 2-0	Suggett 2	22,093	1	2	3	4	5	6	7	8	9	10	11													
12	(a)	Coventry C	L 1-3	Krzywicki	37,025		2	3*	4	5	6	7	8	11	10		1	9	12										
16	(h)	Arsenal	L 0-1		32,215			3	4	5	6	7	8	11	10	9			2	1									
20	(h)	Coventry C	L 0-1		33,933			3	4	5	6	7	8	9	10				2	1	11								
23	(a)	West Ham U	W 3-1	Suggett, Brown, Krzywicki	29,156			3	4	5		7	8	9					2	1	11	6	10						
26	(a)	Nottingham F	L 0-1		22,909			3	4	5	6	7*	8	9					2	1	11	12	10						
30	(h)	Derby C	L 0-2		34,173				4	5	6	7	8	9	10				2	1	11	3							
Sep 6	(a)	Sunderland	D 2-2	Suggett, Brown	14,410				4	5	6	7*	8	9	10				2	1	11	3							
13	(h)	Ipswich T	D 2-2	Astle 2	21,173		2	3	4		6	10*	8	7	11			9		1	12		5						
17	(h)	Stoke C	L 1-3	Astle	24,472			3	4		6		8	7	11			9	2	1	10		5						
20	(a)	Crystal P	W 3-1	Hegan, Hope, Astle	27,684			3		7	5	6	10	8	11			9	2	1		4							
27	(h)	Liverpool	D 2-2	Astle, Hegan	34,295			3		7	5	6	10	8	11			9	2	1		4							
Oct 4	(a)	Manchester C	L 1-2	Pardoe (og)	34,329	1	12			7	5	6	8	2	11			9	3		10	4*							
7	(a)	Arsenal	D 1-1	Astle	21,165			3			5	6	8	7	11			9	2		10			4					
11	(h)	Leeds U	D 1-1	Astle	33,037	1		3			5	6	12	8	7	11		9	2		10			4*					
18	(a)	Chelsea	L 0-2		34,810			3		7	5	6	8		11			9	2	1	10			4					
25	(h)	Manchester U	W 2-1	Brown, Hope	45,120	1		3	4	5		7	8	12	11			9	2		10*				6				
Nov 1	(a)	Wolves	L 0-1		39,832	1		3	4	5	6	7	8		11			9*	2		10				12				
8	(h)	Everton	W 2-0	Astle, Krzywicki	34,288	1		3	4	5	6		8	7	11			9	2		10								
15	(a)	Tottenham H	L 0-2		28,340	1		3	4	5	6		8	7	11			9*	2		10				12				
22	(h)	Sheffield W	W 3-0	Hope, Suggett, Astle	20,382			3	4	5	6*		8	7	11			9	2	1	10				12				
Dec 6	(h)	Burnley	L 0-1		18,512	1		3	4				8	7*	11			9	2		10		5	12	6				
13	(a)	Ipswich T	W 1-0	Astle	18,364	1	12	3	4		6		8		11			9*			10	2	5		7				
26	(h)	West Ham U	W 3-1	Suggett 2, Astle	32,246	1		3	4		6		8		11*			9	2		10	12	5		7				
27	(a)	Derby C	L 0-2		35,581	1	2	3	4			7	8	12				9			10	6	5		11*				
Jan 10	(h)	Crystal P	W 3-2	Astle 3	19,234	1		3	4	5	6		8	7	11			9	2		10								
17	(a)	Liverpool	D 1-1	Brown	43,526	1		3	4	5	6		8	9	11*				2		10	7			12				
28	(a)	Sunderland	W 3-1	Astle 2, Brown	19,024	1			4	5	6		8		11			9	2		10	3	7						
31	(h)	Manchester C	W 3-0	Suggett, Astle, Hartford	30,341	1		3	4	5	6		8		11			9	2		10				7				
Feb 6	(a)	Newcastle U	L 0-1		32,054			3	4	5	6		8		11			9	2	1	10				7				
10	(a)	Leeds U	L 1-5	Astle	31,515			3	4	5			8		11			9	2	1	10	6			7				
20	(h)	Southampton	W 1-0	Suggett	19,453	1		3	4	5	6		8		11*			9	2	1	10				7	12			
28	(h)	Wolves	D 3-3	Astle, Suggett 2	37,391			3	4	5	6		8		11			9	2	1	10				7*		12		
Mar 10	(a)	Sheffield W	L 0-2		21,990	1		3	4	5			8		11			9			10	2			7	6			
14	(h)	Newcastle U	D 2-2	Astle 2	19,322	1		3	4	5			8		11			9	2*		10				7	6		12	
21	(a)	Burnley	L 1-2	Brown	12,821	1		3	4*				8		11			9			12	6	2		10	5		7	
28	(h)	Tottenham H	D 1-1	Astle	24,890	1		3	4				8		11			9			12	6	2		10*	5		7	
30	(h)	Chelsea	W 3-1	Brown 2, Astle	31,207	1		3	4				8		11			9			10	6	2		7	5			
Apr 1	(a)	Everton	L 0-2		58,523	1		3	10				8		11			9	4			6	2		7	5			
4	(h)	Nottingham F	W 4-0	Brown 2, Astle, Glover	20,691	1		3	10				8			12		9	4			6	2		11*	5		7	
8	(a)	Manchester U	L 0-7		29,396	1		3	10				8		11			9	4		7	6	2			5			
15	(a)	Stoke C	L 2-3	Astle, Suggett	11,804	1		3	10	5			8		11			9	4		7	6	2						
				App		26	14	28	40	30	28	13	42	18	38	2	1	34	33	15	32	11	20	6	15	10	3	1	2
				Sub app			2					1		3	1				1		3	1	3		2		2	1	1
				Goals					10			2	12	3	3			25			1							1	

1970-71

Division 1

Date		Opponent	Result	Scorers	Att.	Osborne J	Hughes L	Wilson R	Merrick A	Talbut J	Kaye J	Reed H	Brown T	Astle J	Suggett C	Hope R	Cantello L	Robertson A	Johnson G	Cumbes J	McVitie G	Hartford A	Minton R	Fraser J	Lovett G	Wile J
Aug 15	(h)	Crystal P	D 0-0		25,127	1	2	3	4	5	6	7	8	9	10	11										
18	(a)	Nottingham F	D 3-3	Brown 2, Astle	24,423	1	2	3	4	5	6	7	8	9	10	11										
22	(a)	Blackpool	L 1-3	Astle	22,162	1*	2		3	5		7	8	9	10	11	4	6	12							
26	(h)	Stoke C	W 5-2	Astle 2, Brown 2, Reed	22,015		2	3	4	5		12	8	9	10	11*	7	6		1						
29	(h)	Liverpool	D 1-1	Astle	31,474		2	3	4	5		12	8	9	10	11	7*	6		1						
Sep 2	(h)	Newcastle U	L 1-2	Astle	25,112		2	3	4	5	6		8	9	10	11				1	7					
5	(a)	Manchester C	L 1-4	Hope	30,549		2	3		5	6		8*	9	10	11	4	12		1	7					
12	(h)	West Ham U	W 2-1	Suggett 2	24,606		2	3		5	6		8	9	10	11	4			1	7					
19	(a)	Arsenal	L 2-6	Reed, Brown	33,326		2		3	5		7	8	9			4	6		1	11	10				
26	(h)	Derby C	W 2-1	McVitie, Brown	31,216			3	2	5	6		8	9	10	4				1	7	11				
Oct 3	(a)	Ipswich T	D 2-2	Brown, Astle	17,027			3		5	6		8	9	10	4				1	7	11			2	
10	(h)	Leeds U	D 2-2	Suggett, McVitie	37,124			3		5	6		8	9	10	4				1	7	11			2	
17	(a)	Crystal P	L 0-3		28,330			3		5	6		8	9	10	4				1	7	11			2	
24	(a)	Manchester U	L 1-2	Brown	43,278			3		5	6		8	9	10*	4			12	1	7	11			2	
31	(h)	Everton	W 3-0	Astle, Brown, McVitie	29,628					5	6		8	9	10		3			1	7	11		4	2	
Nov 7	(a)	Wolves	L 1-2	Lovett	39,670					5	6		8	9	10		3			1	7	11		4	2	
14	(h)	Southampton	W 1-0	Hartford	17,824					5*	6		8	9	10	12	3			1	7	11		4	2	
21	(a)	Huddersfield T	L 1-2	Brown	18,209					5	6		8	9	10	12	3			1	7	11		4	2*	
28	(h)	Chelsea	D 2-2	Suggett, Astle	29,374					5	6		8	9	10	4	3			1	7	11		12	2*	
Dec 5	(a)	Burnley	D 1-1	Brown	12,437				12	5	6		8	9	10	4	3*			1	7	11			2	
12	(h)	Tottenham H	W 3-1	Brown 3 (1 pen)	26,584					5	6		8	9	10	4	3			1	7	11			2	
19	(h)	Blackpool	D 1-1	Suggett	17,909			3			6		8	9	10	4				1	7	11			2	5
26	(a)	Coventry C	D 1-1	Brown (pen)	27,526			3			6		8	9	10	4				1	7	11			2	5
Jan 9	(a)	Nottingham F	L 0-1		20,015			3			6		8	9	10	4				1	7	11			2	5
16	(a)	Stoke C	L 0-2		20,882			3			6		8	9	10	4				1	7	11			2	5
30	(a)	Chelsea	L 1-4	Astle	26,874			3			6		8	9	10	4				1	7	11			2	5
Feb 6	(h)	Burnley	W 1-0	Brown	16,982		2	3			6		8	9	10					1	7	11			4	5
17	(a)	Tottenham H	D 2-2	Brown 2	22,650			3	2		6		8	9	10					1	7	11			4	5
20	(h)	Huddersfield T	W 2-1	Brown 2	18,254	1		3	2		6		8	9	10						7	11			4	5
27	(a)	Everton	D 3-3	Astle, Brown, Wile	35,965			3	2		6		8	9	10					1	7	11			4	5
Mar 6	(h)	Manchester U	W 4-3	Brown 3, Wile	41,134			3	2		6		8	9	10					1	7	11			4	5
13	(a)	Southampton	L 0-1		19,008			3	2		6		8	9	10					1	7	11			4	5
20	(h)	Wolves	L 2-4	McVitie, Brown	36,754			3	2		6		8	9	10					1	7	11			4	5
27	(h)	Manchester C	D 0-0		20,363		2	3			6		8	9	10		4			1	7	11				5
Apr 2	(a)	Liverpool	D 1-1	Brown	43,580		2	3			6		8	9	10		4			1	7	11				5
9	(a)	West Ham U	L 1-2	Astle	34,981		2	3			6		8	9	12	10	4			1	7*	11				5
10	(h)	Coventry C	D 0-0		18,726		2	3			6		8	9	10		4			1	7	11				5
12	(h)	Ipswich T	L 0-1		12,684		2	3			6		8	9	10		4			1	7	11				5
17	(a)	Leeds U	W 2-1	Brown, Astle	36,812		2	3			6		8	9	7	10				1		11			4	5
24	(h)	Arsenal	D 2-2	Hartford, Brown	36,621		2	3			6		8	9	7	10				1		11			4	5
28	(a)	Newcastle U	L 0-3		18,310		2	3			6		8	9	7	10*	12			1		11			4	5
May 1	(a)	Derby C	L 0-2		33,651		2	3			6		8	9	7		4			1		11	10			5
		App				4	18	19	34	17	37	4	42	41	30	34	23	3		38	33	34	3	6	21	21
		Sub app						1		2						3	1	1	1					1	1	
		Goals								2			28	13	5	1					4	2			1	2

George McVitie, Albion's outside-right, scores his first goal for the Baggies, against Derby County at The Hawthorns on 26 September 1970.

139

1971-72

Division 1

Date	Opponent	Res	Scorers	Att	Cumbes J	Hughes L	Wilson R	Cantello L	Wile J	Kaye J	Hope R	Suggett C	Astle J	Brown T	Merrick A	Hartford A	Minton R	MacLean H	Gould R	McVitie G	Osborne J	Robertson A	Johnson G	Glover A	Smith G	Nisbet G	Brown A
Aug 14	(a) West Ham U	W 1-0	Brown	27,420	1	2	3	4	5	6	7	8	9	10	11												
18	(h) Everton	W 2-0	Wile, Brown	29,055	1	2	3	4	5	6	10	7	9	8		11											
21	(h) Coventry C	D 1-1	Brown	24,692	1	2	3	4	5	6	10	7	9	8		11											
23	(a) Manchester U§	L 1-3	Brown	23,146	1	2	3	4	5	6	10	7	9	8		11											
28	(h) Sheffield U	D 0-0		32,768	1	2	3	4	5	6	10	7	8	9		11											
Sep 1	(a) Chelsea	L 0-1		29,931	1	2	3	4	5	6	10	7	8	9		11											
4	(h) Arsenal	L 0-1		29,809	1	2	3	4	5	6	10	7*	9	8	12	11											
11	(a) Huddersfield T	L 0-1		9,938	1	2		4	5	6	12	7	8	10	11		3	9*									
18	(h) Ipswich T	L 1-2	Brown	18,885	1	2	3	4	5	6		7		8		10			9	11							
25	(a) Derby C	D 0-0		30,628	1	2	3	4	5	6		10		8		11			9	7							
Oct 2	(h) Manchester C	L 0-2		25,834	1	2	3	4	5	6	10*	12		8		11			9	7							
9	(a) Crystal P	W 2-0	Brown, Gould	22,399		2	3	4	5			12	10	8		11			9	7*	1	6					
16	(h) West Ham U	D 0-0		20,620		2	3	4	5			12	9	8		11		7*	10		1	6					
23	(h) Leicester C	L 0-1		23,088			3	4	5			7*	9	8		11	2		10		1	6	12				
30	(a) Southampton	D 1-1	Hartford	16,972			3	4	5						11	8	2		9		1	6	10	7			
Nov 6	(h) Stoke C	L 0-1		19,204			3	4	5			8				11	2		9		1	6	10	7			
13	(a) Nottingham F	L 1-4	Astle	20,024			3	4	5				10		11	8	2		9		1	6		7			
20	(a) Tottenham H	L 2-3	Gould, Brown	31,895			3	4	5	12			9*		11	8	2		10		1	6		7			
27	(h) Wolves	L 2-3	Brown (pen), Gould	37,696			3	4	5				9		11	8	2		10		1	6		7			
Dec 4	(a) Leeds U	L 0-3		32,521			3	4	5				9	11	7	8	2		10			6			1		
11	(h) Newcastle U	L 0-3		18,142			3	4	5	12			9	11		8	2		10			6	7*		1		
18	(a) Arsenal	L 0-2		28,177			3	4	5			8	9	10		11				7		6			1	2	
27	(h) Liverpool	W 1-0	Brown	43,785			3	4	5			10		8		11			9	7		6			1	2	
Jan 1	(a) Ipswich T	W 3-2	Brown, Gould, McVitie	17,085			3	4	5			10		8		11			9	7		6			1	2	
8	(h) Sheffield U	D 2-2	Brown 2	21,225			3	4	5			10		8		11			9	7		6			1	2	
22	(a) Everton	L 1-2	Gould	36,413			3	4	5			10		8		11			9	7*	1	6		12		2	
29	(h) Manchester U	W 2-1	Gould, Astle	46,992			3	4	5			10	9	8		11				7	1	6				2	
Feb 12	(a) Leicester C	W 1-0	Brown	24,225			3	4	5			10	9	8		11				7	1	6				2	
19	(h) Southampton	W 3-2	Gould, Cantello, Brown	17,875			3	4	5			10	9	8		11				7	1	6				2	
Mar 1	(a) Manchester C	L 1-2	Brown (pen)	25,677			3	4	5			10	9	8		11				7	1	6				2	
4	(a) Nottingham F	W 1-0	Wile	16,702			3	4	5			10	9	8		11				7	1	6				2	
11	(h) Crystal P	D 1-1	A.Brown	17,105			3	4	5			10	9	8		11					1	6				2	7
17	(a) Coventry C	W 2-0	Wile, A.Brown	22,424			3	4	5				9	8		11				7	1	6				2	10
25	(h) Huddersfield T	D 1-1	Gould	18,373			3	4	5				9	8		11				7	1	6				2	10
Apr 1	(a) Liverpool	L 0-2		46,564			3	4*	5				9	8		11				7	1	6		12		2	10
5	(h) Derby C	D 0-0		32,439			3		5	7	4		9	8		11					1	6				2	10
8	(h) Tottenham H	D 1-1	Hope (pen)	20,862			3		5	7	4		9			11			8		1	6				2	10
15	(a) Wolves	W 1-0	T.Brown	30,619			3		5	7	4		9			11			8		1	6				2	10
22	(h) Leeds U	L 0-1		40,675			3		5	7	4		9			11			8		1	6				2	10
27	(h) Chelsea	W 4-0	T.Brown, Gould, A.Brown, Cantello	18,413				11	5	7	4		9	3					8		1	6				2	10
May 3	(a) Newcastle U	L 2-4	Gould 2	20,052			3	4	5	12	7		9			11			8		1	6				2	10*
5	(a) Stoke C	D 1-1	Gould	16,206	12		3	4*	5		7		9			11			8		1	6				2	10
App					11	13	40	38	42	11	17	30	22	40	6	39	9	2	31	9	25	31	2	6	6	21	11
Sub app					1				1	5	1						1							1	2		
Goals								2	3		1		2	17		1			12	1							3

§ Played at Victoria Ground, Stoke

Jeff Astle heads Albion's second goal against Manchester United at The Hawthorns on 29 January 1972.

140

1972-73

Division 1

Date		Opponent	Result	Scorers	Att	Smith G	Nisbet G	Wilson R	Cantello L	Wile J	Robertson A	Brown T	Brown A	Gould R	Suggett C	Hartford R	Latchford P	MacLean H	Merrick A	Hughes L	Woolgar S	Johnston W	Glover A	Astle J	Shaw D	Osborne J	Minton R
Aug 12	(h)	West Ham U	D 0-0		22,234	1	2	3	4	5	6	7	8	9	10	11											
16	(h)	Tottenham H	L 0-1		19,175	1	2	3	4	5	6	7	8	9	10	11											
19	(a)	Leeds U	L 0-2		36,555	1	2	3	4	5	6	7	8	9	10	11											
23	(a)	Newcastle U	D 1-1	A.Brown	29,010	1	2	3	4	5	6	7	8	9	10	11											
26	(h)	Sheffield U	L 0-2		15,559		2	3	4	5	6	7	8	9*	10	11	1		12								
30	(h)	Birmingham C	D 2-2	Gould, Suggett	37,108		2	3		5	6		8	9	10	11	1		4	7							
Sep 2	(a)	Everton	L 0-1		36,269		2	3		5	6		10	9	7	11	1			8	4						
9	(h)	Derby C	W 2-1	Gould, T.Brown	17,262		2	3	4	5	6	8	10	9	7	11	1										
16	(a)	Crystal P	W 2-0	Gould, Robertson	17,858		2	3	4	5	6	8	10	9	7	11	1										
23	(h)	Coventry C	W 1-0	Suggett	15,373		2		4	5	6	8	10	9	7	11	1		3								
30	(a)	Manchester C	L 1-2	T.Brown	27,332		2	3	4	5	6	8	10	9	7	11	1										
Oct 7	(h)	Manchester U	D 2-2	A.Brown 2	39,209		2	3	4*	5	6	8	10	9	7	11	1					12					
14	(a)	Chelsea	L 1-3	T.Brown (pen)	28,998		2	3	4	5	6	8	10	9	7	11	1										
21	(h)	Wolves	W 1-0	Gould	30,121		2		4*	5	6	8	10	9	7	11	1		3			12					
28	(a)	Southampton	L 1-2	Hartford	15,810		2			5	6	8	10	9	7	11	1		3			4					
Nov 4	(h)	Newcastle U	L 2-3	Suggett, Gould	14,668		2	3		5	6	8	10	9	7	11	1		4								
11	(a)	Tottenham H	D 1-1	T.Brown	25,875		2	3		5	6	8	10	9	7	11	1		4								
18	(a)	Norwich C	L 0-2		21,874		2	3	4	5		8	10	9	7	11	1		6								
25	(h)	Stoke C	W 2-1	T.Brown 2 (1 pen)	13,332		2	3	4	5		8	7	9		10	1	11	6								
Dec 2	(a)	Leicester C	L 1-3	Gould	15,307		2	3	4*	5	6	8	10	9		11	1	12	7								
9	(h)	Liverpool	D 1-1	T.Brown	27,258		2	3	4*	5	6	8	7	9	12	10	1					11					
16	(a)	Arsenal	L 1-2	T.Brown	27,119		2	3	4	5		8	9*		7	10	1		6			11	12				
23	(h)	Ipswich T	W 2-0	Glover, Hartford	12,215		2	3	4	5		8	7			10	1		6			11	9				
26	(a)	Coventry C	D 0-0		31,493		2	3	4	5	6	8	9			10	1		7			11					
Jan 6	(a)	Sheffield U	L 0-3		16,231		2		4	5	3	8	9			10	1		6			11	7				
27	(a)	Derby C	L 0-2		28,833		2	3	4	5		8	9		7	10	1		6			11					
Feb 10	(h)	Crystal P	L 0-4		15,163		2	3	4	5	9	8	12	7*		10	1		6			11					
17	(a)	West Ham U	L 1-2	T.Brown	26,071		2	3	4	5	9	8				10	1		6		7	11*	12				
28	(h)	Arsenal	W 1-0	T.Brown	23,308		2	3	4	5	6	8	12			10	1		7			11		9*			
Mar 3	(a)	Manchester U	L 1-2	Astle	46,735		2	3	4	5	6	8				10	1		7			11*		9	12		
10	(h)	Chelsea	D 1-1	T.Brown	21,466		2	3	4	5	6	8				10			7*			11		9	12	1	
17	(a)	Ipswich T	L 0-2		17,619		2	3	4	5	6	8				7*	12					11		9	10	1	
20	(a)	Wolves	L 0-2		33,520		2	3	4	5	6	8				10			7			11		9		1	
24	(h)	Southampton	D 1-1	T.Brown	12,559		3	2		5	6	8				10			7			11		9	4	1	
28	(h)	Leeds U	D 1-1	Shaw	32,804		3	2		5	6	4				10			7			11		9	8	1	
31	(a)	Stoke C	L 0-2		21,296		3	2		5	6	4*				10			7			11	12	9	8	1	
Apr 7	(h)	Leicester C	W 1-0	Astle	15,235			3	4	5		7				10			6			11		9	8	1	2
11	(h)	Everton	W 4-1	Astle, Hartford, Shaw 2	21,375			3	4	5		7				10			6			11		9	8	1	2
14	(a)	Liverpool	L 0-1		43,853			3	4	5		7				10			6			11		9	8	1	2
21	(h)	Norwich C	L 0-1		23,263			3	4	5	12	7				10			6			11		9	8	1	2*
25	(h)	Manchester C	L 1-2	Astle	21,480			3	4	5		7	12			10			6			11*		9	8	1	2
28	(a)	Birmingham C	L 2-3	Astle, Wile	36,784			3	4	5		7	12			10			6			11		9	8	1	2*
App						4	33	38	37	40	35	38	26	21	21	41	26	2	30	2	2	22	2	14	10	12	6
Sub app													1	1	3		1		2	1		2		3	2		
Goals										1	1	12	3	6	3	3							1	5	3		

Albion goalkeeper John Osborne dives at the feet of Ipswich striker Trevor Whymark in the League game at Portman Road in March 1975. Three and a half years later, Whymark scored four goals past Osborne as Albion crashed 7-0 to the Suffolk club.

141

1973-74

Division 2

Date		Opponent	Result	Scorers	Att	Latchford P	Minton R	Merrick A	Hughes L	Wile J	Robertson A	Cantello L	Shaw D	Glover A	Brown T	Johnston W	Hartford A	Brown A	Donaghy B	Nisbet G	Mayo J	Wilson R	Thompson T	Astle J
Aug 25	(a)	Blackpool	W 3-2	T.Brown 2, Glover	14,328	1	2	3	4	5	6	7	8	9	10	11								
Sep 1	(h)	Crystal P	W 1-0	Glover	17,898	1	2	3	4	5	6	7	8	9	10	11								
8	(a)	Swindon T	L 0-1		11,583	1	2*	3		5	6	4	8	7	10	11	9	12						
12	(a)	Sheffield W	L 1-3	T.Brown	15,927	1	2	3	9	5	6	4	10	7	8	11*	12							
15	(h)	Nottingham F	D 3-3	A.Brown, Minton, T.Brown	14,779	1	2	3	4*	5	6	7		12	10		8	9	11					
18	(h)	Preston NE	L 0-2		11,722	1	2	3*	8	5	6		12	7	10		4	9	11					
22	(a)	Hull C	D 0-0		7,089	1		3	4*	5	6		11	7	10		8	9		2	12			
29	(h)	Sunderland	D 1-1	A.Brown	17,024	1		3		5	6		9	7	10		4	8	11	2				
Oct 1	(a)	Preston NE	L 1-3	T.Brown	15,419	1		3		5	6		11	4	9	7	8	10		2				
6	(a)	Bristol C	D 1-1	T.Brown	14,326	1		3		5	6	4	10		8	11	7	9		2				
13	(h)	Carlisle U	D 1-1	T.Brown	12,556	1		3		5	6	4	11		9	7	10	8		2				
20	(a)	Middlesbrough	D 0-0		18,997	1		3		5	6	4	10		8	11	7	9		2				
24	(h)	Sheffield W	W 2-0	Shaw 2	12,667	1		3		5	6	4	11		9	7	10	8		2				
27	(h)	Bolton W	D 0-0		16,148	1		3		5	6	4	11		9	7	10	8		2				
Nov 3	(a)	Cardiff C	W 1-0	T.Brown	10,668	1				5	6	4	11		8	7	10			2	9	3		
10	(h)	Notts C	W 2-1	T.Brown, Shaw	15,564	1				5	6	4	12	11	8*	7	10			2	9	3		
17	(a)	Orient	L 0-2		11,981	1				5	6	4	12	11*	8	7	10			2	9	3		
24	(h)	Fulham	W 2-0	Glover, Hartford	12,606	1				5	6	4	12	11	8	7	10			2	9*	3		
Dec 1	(a)	Luton T	W 2-0	Shaw, Hartford	10,192	1				5	6	4	12	11	8	7	10			2	9*	3		
8	(h)	Oxford U	W 1-0	Shaw	12,277	1				5	6	4	12	11	8	7	10			2	9*	3		
15	(h)	Portsmouth	L 1-2	Cantello	11,574	1				5	6	4	9	11	8	7	10			2		3		
22	(a)	Sunderland	D 1-1	Shaw	18,389	1	12			5	6	4	9	11*	8	7	10			2		3		
26	(h)	Aston Villa	W 2-0	T.Brown 2	43,119	1	10			5	6	4	9	11	8	7				2		3		
29	(h)	Swindon T	W 2-0	Merrick, Johnston	14,969	1	10			5	6	4	9	11	8	7				2		3		
Jan 1	(a)	Crystal P	L 0-1		23,338	1	12			5	6	4	9	11	8	7	10			2		3*		
12	(a)	Nottingham F	W 4-1	T.Brown 4	15,501	1				5	6	4	9	11	8	7	10			2		3		
19	(h)	Blackpool	D 1-1	Wile	17,808	1				5	6	4	9	11	8	7	10			2		3		
Feb 3	(a)	Portsmouth	D 1-1	Glover	19,769	1				5	6	4	9	11	8	7	10			2		3		
23	(h)	Bristol C	D 2-2	Wile, Astle	18,928	1				5	6	4		11	8	7	10						3	9
25	(a)	Carlisle U	W 1-0	Johnston	6,407	1				5	6	4		11	8	7	10*		12	2			3	9
Mar 2	(a)	Aston Villa	W 3-1	Wile, T.Brown 2 (1 pen)	37,323	1	10			5	6	4	12	11	8	7				2			3	9*
9	(a)	Bolton W	D 1-1	T.Brown	17,760	1	10			5	6	4	12	11	8	7				2			3	9*
16	(h)	Middlesbrough	L 0-4		24,178	1				5	6	4	12	11	8	7	10			2*			3	9
19	(h)	Hull C	L 2-3	Shaw, A.Brown	13,712	1	10			5	6	4	7	11	8			9		2			3	
23	(a)	Notts C	L 0-1		9,667	1	10			5	6	4	7	8				11	9	2			3	
30	(h)	Cardiff C	D 2-2	Murray (og), Shaw	11,528	1				5	6	4	7	10	9*		8		11	2			3	12
Apr 6	(a)	Fulham	D 0-0		9,494	1	6			5		4	8	7	9	11	10			2			3	
12	(a)	Millwall	L 0-1		8,752	1			6	5		4	8	9	7	11	10			2			3	
13	(h)	Orient	W 1-0	Hartford	11,456	1				5	6	4*	9	11	8	7	10			2	12		3	
17	(h)	Millwall	D 1-1	Glover	12,346	1				5	6		8	11	4	7	10			2	9		3	
20	(a)	Oxford U	L 0-1		9,256	1				5	6		9	11	8	7	10				4	3	2	
27	(h)	Luton T	D 1-1	T.Brown (pen)	13,164	1				4	5	6	11	8	7		10				9	3	2	
				App		42	6	21	8	42	40	35	28	36	41	35	33	13	4	34	9	22	8	5
				Sub app			2						9	1				2	1		2			1
				Goals			1	1		3		1	8	5	19	2	3	3						1

Albion during their Second Division days, 1973-4. Back row (left to right): L.Hughes, D.Shaw, G.Nisbet, A.Glover, A.Brown, B.Donaghy. Middle: G.Wright (physiotherapist), T.Thompson, R.Minton, P.Latchford, A.Robertson, J.Osborne, J.Mayo, R.Wilson, B.Whitehouse (coach). Front: A.Merrick, W.Johnston, J.Wile, D.Howe (manager), T.Brown, L.Cantello, A.Hartford.

1974-75

Division 2

Date		Opponent	Result	Scorers	Att.	Latchford P	Nisbet G	Wilson R	Cantello L	Robertson A	Merrick A	Glover A	Brown T	Shaw D	Hughes L	Johnston W	Wile J	Mayo J	Donaghy B	Osborne J	Rushbury D	Trewick J	Thompson T	Ward R	Edwards I	Minton R	Brown A	Robson B
Aug 17	(h)	Fulham	L 0-1		11,425	1	2	3	4	5	6	7	8	9	10	11												
24	(a)	Hull C	L 0-1		7,864	1	2	3	4	5	6	7	8	9	10	11												
31	(h)	Sunderland	W 1-0	Glover	12,501	1	2	3	4	5		7	8	9	10	11	6											
Sep 7	(a)	Portsmouth	W 3-1	Johnston, Shaw, Merrick	9,158	1	2	3	4	5	10	7	8	9		11	6											
14	(h)	Manchester U	D 1-1	Merrick	28,666	1	2	3	4	6	10	7	8	9		11	5											
18	(h)	Hull C	D 2-2	Shaw 2	10,038	1	2	3	4	6	10	7	8	9		11	5											
21	(a)	Notts C	D 0-0		10,004	1	2	3	4	6	10	7	8	9		11	5											
25	(a)	Sheffield W	D 0-0		12,333	1	2	3	4	6	10	7	8	9*	12	11	5											
28	(h)	Oxford U	W 3-0	T.Brown, Merrick, Cantello	9,667	1	2	3	4	6	10*	7	8		12	11	5	9										
Oct 5	(h)	York C	W 2-0	Johnston, Merrick	11,846	1	2	3	4	6	10	7	8			11	5	9										
12	(a)	Cardiff C	W 2-0	Mayo, Donaghy	6,723	1	2	3	4	6	10*	7	8			11	5	9	12									
19	(h)	Nottingham F	L 0-1		13,948	1	2	3	4	6	10*	7	8	12		11	5	9										
22	(a)	Bristol R	L 1-2	Shaw	12,101	1	2	3	4	6	10	7	8	9		11	5											
26	(a)	Millwall	D 2-2	Hughes, Kitchener (og)	8,179		2	3	4		10	7	8	9*	11		5	12		1	6							
Nov 2	(h)	Norwich C	D 1-1	Shaw	12,064		2	3			10	7	8	9*	4	11	5	12		1	6							
6	(h)	Bristol R	D 2-2	T.Brown, Glover	8,849		2	3	4		10	7	8	9		11	5			1	6							
9	(a)	Southampton	L 0-1		15,638		2	3	4*		10	7	8	9	12	11	5			1	6							
16	(h)	Bristol C	W 1-0	Mayo	11,936		2	3				7		9	10	11	5	8		1	6	4						
23	(a)	Orient	W 2-0	Hughes, Johnston	6,766		2	3	4			7		9	10	11	5	8		1	6							
30	(h)	Oldham A	W 1-0	T.Brown	11,399		2	3	4			7	11	9	10		5	8		1	6							
Dec 7	(a)	Bolton W	W 1-0	Mayo	12,315		2	3	4	12		7	11*	8	10		5	9		1	6							
14	(a)	Fulham	L 0-1		6,730		2	3	4	12		7	11	9	10		5	8*		1	6							
21	(h)	Aston Villa	W 2-0	Johnston, Mayo	29,614		2		4			7	8		10	11	5	9		1	6			3				
26	(a)	Manchester U	L 1-2	Cantello	51,104		2	3	4			7	8		10	11	5	9		1	6							
28	(h)	Blackpool	W 2-0	Johnston, Mayo	14,839		2	3	4			7*	12	8	10	11	5	9		1	6							
Jan 18	(a)	Oldham A	D 0-0		11,355		2	3	4			7	8		10	11	5	9		1	6							
Feb 1	(h)	Southampton	L 0-3		15,763		2	3	4	12		7	8*		10	11	5	9		1	6							
8	(a)	Norwich C	L 2-3	Mayo, Hughes	34,509		2*		4			7	8	12	10	11	5	9		1	6			3				
15	(h)	Orient	W 1-0	Johnston	9,388		2		4			7*	8	12	10	11	5	9		1	6			3				
22	(h)	Bristol C	L 1-2	Shaw	14,180			3	4	5		8	7	10	11		9*			1	6	12	2	3				
Mar 1	(a)	Sunderland	L 0-3		28,867		2		4	5		7	12	8	10	11		9		1*	6			3				
8	(h)	Sheffield W	W 4-0	T.Brown 2 (1 pen), Wile, Edwards	10,330		2	3	4			7	8		10	11	5			1	6				9			
15	(a)	Oxford U	D 1-1	T.Brown	7,212		2	3	4			7	8	12	10	11	5			1	6				9*			
22	(h)	Portsmouth	W 2-1	T.Brown, Wilson	10,017		2	3	4			7	8	12		11	5			1	6	10*			9			
29	(a)	Aston Villa	L 1-3	T.Brown	47,574		2		4		10	7	8			11	5			1	6			3	9			
31	(a)	Blackpool	L 0-2		11,611		2		4			7	8		10	11	5			1	6		12	3*	9			
Apr 2	(h)	Notts C	W 4-1	Edwards, T.Brown 2 (1 pen), Cantello	7,812		2		4	6		7	8		10	11	5			1				3	9			
5	(h)	Millwall	W 2-1	T.Brown 2	8,130		2		4	6		7	8	12	10*	11	5			1				3	9			
8	(h)	Bolton W	L 0-1		7,957		2	3	4	6		7	8			11	5			1		10			9			
12	(a)	York C	W 3-1	Johnston, Mayo 2	7,566		2	3	4	6		7				11	5	9		1							8	10
19	(h)	Cardiff C	W 2-0	Robson, Robertson	10,071		2	3		6		7	4			11	5	9		1							8	10
26	(a)	Nottingham F	L 1-2	Robson	11,721		2	3		6		7	4			11	5	9		1							8	10
App						13	41	34	37	21	24	35	32	27	23	38	38	21		22	26	2	7	7	7		4	3
Sub app											2	1	2	6	3			2	1			1				1		2
Goals								1	3	1	4	2	12	6	3	7	1	8	1						2			2

Lyndon Hughes

John Trewick

Trevor Thompson

1975-76

Division 2

Date		Opponent	Result	Scorers	Att	Osborne J	Nisbet G	Wilson R	Cantello L	Wile J	Robertson A	Trewick J	Brown A	Mayo J	Merrick A	Johnston W	Brown T	Hurst G	Giles J	Robson B	Thompson T	Rushbury D	Glover A	Martin M	Mulligan P	Edwards I
Aug 16	(a)	Southampton	L 0-3		15,246	1	2	3	4	5	6	7	8	9*	10	11	12									
20	(h)	Chelsea	D 0-0		17,962	1	2	3	4	5	6	7				11	8	9	10							
23	(h)	Luton T	W 1-0	Trewick	14,062	1	2	3		5	6	7				11	8	9	10	4						
30	(a)	Fulham	L 0-4		9,910	1	2	3	4							11	8*	9	10	12						
Sep 6	(h)	York C	D 2-2	T.Brown, Hurst	10,904	1	2		4	5	6	7				11	8	9	10	3						
13	(a)	Sunderland	L 0-2		25,159	1	2		4	5	6	7				11*	8	9	10	12	3					
20	(h)	Charlton A	D 1-1	Hurst	10,496	1		3	4		5		12			11	8*	9	10	2	6	7				
27	(a)	Carlisle U	D 1-1	A.Brown	6,625	1		3	4	5	6		8			11	12	9*	10	2		7				
Oct 4	(h)	Oldham A	D 1-1	Johnston	10,668	1		3	4	5	6		8			11	12	9*		2		7	10			
11	(a)	Blackburn R	D 0-0		9,973	1		3	4	5	6		8			11		9	10					7	2	
18	(h)	Plymouth A	W 1-0	A.Brown	10,970	1		3	4	5	6		8			11		9	10					7	2	
25	(a)	Bristol C	W 2-0	A.Brown, T.Brown	19,132	1		3	4	5	6		9			11	8		10					7	2	
Nov 1	(h)	Notts C	D 0-0		12,670	1		3	4	5	6		9			11	8		10					7*	2	12
4	(a)	Bristol R	D 1-1	Edwards	13,105	1		3	4	5	6		9			11	8		10*					7	2	12
8	(a)	Blackpool	W 1-0	Johnston	8,271	1		3	4*	5	6	12		9		11	8		10					7	2	
12	(a)	Oxford U	W 1-0	Mayo	5,685	1		3		5	6	4		9			8		10					7	2	11
15	(h)	Hull C	W 2-0	Martin, T.Brown	14,469	1		3		5	6	4		9			8		10					7	2	11
22	(a)	Plymouth A	L 1-2	Giles	17,380	1		3		5	6	4*	9	11			8		10					7	2	12
29	(a)	Bolton W	W 2-1	Mayo, Robson	18,710	1		3		5	6		8	9		11	7		10	4					2	
Dec 6	(h)	Portsmouth	W 3-1	A.Brown 2, T.Brown	15,325	1		3			6		8	9		11	4		10	5				7	2	
13	(a)	Luton T	L 1-2	Martin	10,203	1		3			6		8	9		11	4		10	5				7	2	
19	(h)	Southampton	L 0-2		16,780	1			4		6	10	9			11	8			5	3			7	2	
26	(a)	Nottingham F	W 2-0	Giles, Johnston	19,393	1			4	5	6			9		11	8		10	3				7	2	
27	(h)	Orient	D 1-1	Mayo	20,601	1			4	5	6			9		11	7		10	3				8	2	
Jan 10	(h)	Sunderland	D 0-0		24,383	1			4	5	6			9		11	7		10	3				8	2	
17	(a)	York C	W 1-0	A.Brown	5,628	1			4	5	6		9			11	7		10	3				8	2	
31	(a)	Chelsea	W 2-1	Martin, T.Brown	15,896	1				5	6			9		11	7		10	4	3			8	2	
Feb 7	(h)	Bristol R	W 3-0	Cantello, Mayo, A.Brown	16,732	1			8	5	6			9		11	4		10	3				7	2	
21	(a)	Hull C	L 1-2	Johnston	6,137	1			8*	5	6		12	9		11	4		10	3				7	2	
25	(h)	Oxford U	W 2-0	T.Brown, Robertson	14,412	1		3			6		8	9		11	4		10	5				7	2	
Mar 6	(a)	Notts C	W 2-0	Mayo, Johnston	20,032	1			8	5	6			9		11	4		10	3				7	2	
13	(h)	Blackburn R	D 2-2	Mayo, Wile	16,969	1			8	5	6			9		11	4		10	3				7	2	
17	(h)	Bristol C	L 0-1		26,640	1			8*	5	6		12	9		11	4		10	3				7	2	
20	(h)	Bolton W	W 2-0	Mayo, Wile	25,650	1			8	5	6		12	9		11	4		10*	3				7	2	
27	(a)	Portsmouth	W 1-0	Cantello	10,617	1			8	5	6			9		11	4		10	3				7	2	
31	(h)	Blackpool	D 0-0		20,257	1			8	5	6		12	9		11	4		10	3*				7	2	
Apr 3	(h)	Carlisle U	W 3-0	A.Brown, Martin, Mayo	17,133	1			3	5	6		8	9		11	4		10					7	2	
9	(a)	Charlton A	L 1-2	T.Brown (pen)	14,252	1			3	5	6		8	9		11	4		10					7	2	
14	(h)	Fulham	W 3-1	A.Brown 2, Cantello	18,237	1			3	5	6		8	9		11	4		10					7	2	
17	(h)	Nottingham F	W 2-0	Martin, Johnston	26,580	1			3	5	6		8	9		11	4		10					7	2	
20	(a)	Orient	D 0-0		10,857	1			3	5	6		8	9		11	4		10					7	2	
24	(a)	Oldham A	W 1-0	T.Brown	22,356	1			3	5	6		8	9		11	4		10					7	2	
					App	42	6	19	34	37	42	10	26	28	1	39	37	10	38	14	5	2	3	34	33	2
					Sub app								1	5				3			2					3
					Goals				3	2	1	1	10	8		6	8	2	2	1				5		1

Joe Mayo (No.9) scores an excellent goal against Bolton Wanderers at Burnden Park in Albion's 1975-6 promotion-winning season.

1976-77

Division 1

Date		Opponent	Result	Scorers	Att	Osborne J	Mulligan P	Cantello L	Brown T	Wile J	Robertson A	Martin M	Brown A	Mayo J	Giles J	Johnston W	Robson B	Edwards I	Treacy R	Trewick J	Ward R	Cross C	Statham D	Glover A	Godden A	Cunningham L	Hughes W
Aug 21	(a)	Leeds U	D 2-2	A.Brown, T.Brown	40,248	1	2	3	4	5	6	7	8	9	10	11											
25	(h)	Liverpool	L 0-1		29,735	1	2	3	4	5	6	7	8	9	10	11											
28	(h)	Norwich C	W 2-0	A.Brown, T.Brown (pen)	16,434	1	2	3	4	5	6	7	8	9	10	11											
Sep 4	(a)	Queen's Park R	L 0-1		18,876	1	2	3	4	5	6	7	8	9	10*	11	12										
11	(a)	Birmingham C	W 1-0	T.Brown	38,448	1	2	3*	4	5	6	7		9	12	11	8	10									
17	(h)	Coventry C	D 1-1	Wile	24,474	1	2		4	5	6	7		9	10	11	3	8									
25	(a)	Derby C	D 2-2	Treacy 2	24,278	1	2		4	5	6	7	11	9	10		3		8								
Oct 2	(h)	Tottenham H	W 4-2	T.Brown (pen), Martin 2, Treacy	23,461	1	2	9	4	5	6	7			12	10	11	3*	8								
6	(a)	Newcastle U	L 0-2		28,757	1	2	3	4	5	6	7	12	9*	10	11			8								
16	(h)	Manchester U	W 4-0	Giles, A.Brown, Cantello, Treacy	36,615	1	2	3	4	5	6	7	9		10	11			8								
23	(a)	Middlesbrough	L 0-1		23,169	1	2	3	4	5	6	7	9		10	11			8								
30	(h)	West Ham U	W 3-0	Martin, A.Brown 2	20,396	1	2	3	4	5	6	7	9		10	11*			8	12							
Nov 6	(a)	Ipswich T	L 0-7		26,706	1	2	3	4	5	6	7	9		10				8	11							
10	(h)	Aston Villa	D 1-1	Wile	41,867		2	3	4	5	6	7	11	9	10				8						1		
20	(a)	Manchester C	L 0-1		36,656	1	2	3	4	5	6	7	11		10				8			9					
27	(h)	Everton	W 3-0	T.Brown, Cross, Treacy	21,078	1	2	3	4	5	6	7	12		10*	11			8			9					
Dec 11	(h)	Leicester C	D 2-2	Treacy, Cross	19,049	1	2	3	4	5	6	7			10	11			8			9					
18	(a)	Stoke C	W 2-0	Statham, Trewick	15,989		2		4	5	6	7				11			8	10	1	9	3				
27	(h)	Bristol C	D 1-1	Cross	30,497	1	2		4	5	6	7	12			11	3		8	10		9*					
Jan 3	(a)	West Ham U	D 0-0		25,236	1	2		4	5	6	7				11	3		8	10		9					
15	(a)	Liverpool	D 1-1	Cross	39,195	1	2*	3	4	5	6	7				11	12		8	10		9					
22	(h)	Leeds U	L 1-2	T.Brown (pen)	25,958	1	2		4	5	6	7			10	11	3		8			9					
Feb 5	(a)	Norwich C	L 0-1		19,613	1	2	7	4	5	6				10	11*	3		8	12		9					
12	(h)	Queen's Park R	D 1-1	Wile	18,342	1	2	3	4	5	6				10		7					9		11			
22	(a)	Sunderland	L 1-6	Robson	30,317	1	2	3	4	5	6				10	11	7		8			9					
28	(h)	Birmingham C	W 2-1	Robson, A.Brown	28,639	1	2		4	5	6		8		10	11	7					9	3				
Mar 5	(h)	Derby C	W 1-0	Robson	19,280	1	2	3	4	5	6		8		10	11	7					9					
8	(a)	Arsenal	W 2-1	Cross 2	19,517	1	2		4	5	6		8		10	11	7*				12	9	3				
12	(a)	Tottenham H	W 2-0	Robson, Cross	28,834		2		4	5	6				10	11	7					9	3		1	8	
16	(h)	Ipswich T	W 4-0	Robson 3, Cunningham	23,054		2		4*	5	6		12		10	11	7					9	3		1	8	
19	(a)	Newcastle U	D 1-1	Cunningham	23,843		2			5	6	4			10	11	7					9	3		1	8	
23	(a)	Manchester U	D 2-2	Cross, Robson	51,053		2			5	6	4			10	11	7					9	3		1	8	
Apr 2	(h)	Middlesbrough	W 2-1	Cunningham, Johnston	18,519		2			5	6	4			10	11	7					9	3		1	8	
5	(a)	Bristol C	W 2-1	Hunter (og), Cross	23,752		2			5	6	4			10	11	7					9	3		1	8	
9	(h)	Arsenal	L 0-2		24,242	1	2			5	6	4			10	11	7					9	3			8	
16	(h)	Manchester C	L 0-2		24,899	1	2	12		5	6	4			10	11	7*					9	3			8	
19	(a)	Coventry C	D 1-1	Wile	19,136	1	2	7		5	6	4	9		10	11							3			8	
30	(h)	Sunderland	L 2-3	Cunningham, Cross	21,859	1	2	7		5	6	4			10	11						9	3			8	
May 7	(a)	Leicester C	W 5-0	Martin 2, Cross, Cunningham, T.Brown	18,139	1	2	7	5*		6	4	11		10					12		9	3			8	
14	(h)	Stoke C	W 3-1	Martin, Cunningham, Cross	22,754	1	2	7		5	6	4			10	11						9	3			8	
16	(a)	Everton	D 1-1	T.Brown	20,102	1		7		5	6	2	4		10	11						9	3			8	
23	(a)	Aston Villa	L 0-4		42,532	1	2	7		5	6*	3	4		10	11			8			9					12
				App		34	40	21	36	42	42	34	19	9	36	34	21	4	20	5	2	27	16	1	6	13	
				Sub app				1					4	1	1			2	1	3							1
				Goals				1	8	4		6	6		1	1	8		6	1		12	1			6	

Dave Cross scores for Albion against Tottenham Hotspur at White Hart Lane on 12 March 1977. Albion won 2-0.

1977-78

Division 1

Date		Opponent	Result	Scorers	Att	Godden A	Mulligan P	Statham D	Brown T	Wile J	Robertson A	Cantello L	Cunningham L	Cross D	Robson B	Johnston W	Trewick J	Regis C	Martin M	Hughes W	Brown A	Batson B
Aug 20	(h)	Chelsea	W 3-0	T.Brown 2 (1 pen), Cross	20,146	1	2	3	4	5	6	7	8	9	10	11						
24	(a)	Leeds U	D 2-2	Cunningham, Cross	21,846	1	2	3	4	5	6	7	8	9	10	11						
27	(a)	Liverpool	L 0-3		48,525	1	2	3	4	5	6	7	8	9*	10	11		12				
Sep 3	(h)	Middlesbrough	W 2-1	Robson, Regis	19,044	1	2	3		5	6	7	8		10	11	4*	9	12			
10	(a)	Newcastle U	W 3-0	Regis, Cunningham, Robson	23,351	1	2	3	4	5	6	7	8*		10	11		9		12		
17	(h)	Wolves	D 2-2	T.Brown (pen), Cross	30,395	1	2	3	4	5	6	7		8	10	11		9				
24	(h)	Birmingham C	W 3-1	T.Brown 2 (1 pen), Regis	29,115	1	2	3	4	5	6	7			10	11		9			8	
Oct 1	(a)	Coventry C	W 2-1	T.Brown 2	25,707	1	2	3	4	5	6	7*			10	11		9	12		8	
4	(a)	Everton	L 1-3	T.Brown (pen)	34,582	1	2	3	4	5	6	7	8		10	11		9				
8	(h)	Ipswich T	W 1-0	Robson	22,970	1	2	3	4	5	6	7	8		10	11		9				
15	(a)	Derby C	D 1-1	Regis	28,397	1	2	3	4	5	6	7	8		10	11		9				
22	(h)	Manchester U	W 4-0	Cross 2, Wile, Cunningham	27,649	1	2	3	4	5	6	7	8	9	10							
29	(a)	Queen's Park R	L 1-2	Johnston	18,880	1	2	3	4	5	6	7*	8	9	10	11	12					
Nov 5	(h)	Leicester C	W 2-0	T.Brown, Cross	20,082	1	2	3	4	5	6	7	8	9	10	11						
12	(a)	West Ham U	D 3-3	Wile 2, Cunningham	23,601	1	2	3	4	5	6	7	8	9	10	11						
19	(h)	Manchester C	D 0-0		26,953	1	2	3	4	5	6		8	9	10	11		7				
26	(a)	Nottingham F	D 0-0		31,908	1	2	3	4	5	6		8	9	10	11		7				
Dec 3	(h)	Norwich C	D 0-0		18,137	1	2	3	4	5	6			11	9	10		8	7			
10	(a)	Aston Villa	L 0-3		43,196	1	2	3	4	5	6	7	11*		10			8	12	9		
17	(h)	West Ham U	W 1-0	A.Brown	18,896	1	2	3	4	5	6				10	11		8	7	9		
26	(h)	Bristol C	L 1-3	T.Brown	29,292	1	2	3	4	5	6		12		10	11	9*	7		8		
27	(h)	Arsenal	L 1-3	Cunningham	27,876	1	2	3	4	5	6		12		10*	11		9	7	8		
31	(h)	Leeds U	W 1-0	T.Brown (pen)	24,206	1	2		4	5	6			3	11	10	8	7		9		
Jan 2	(a)	Chelsea	D 2-2	A.Brown, T.Brown	30,302	1	2*		4	5	6			3	11	10	8	7	12	9		
14	(h)	Liverpool	L 0-1		36,067	1	2	3	4	5	6		9		11	10	8*	7		12		
21	(a)	Middlesbrough	L 0-1		19,172	1	2	3	4	5	6		8		11	10	9	7				
Feb 25	(h)	Coventry C	D 3-3	Trewick 2, Wile	25,269	1		3	4	5	6		12	2*	11	10	9	7		8		
28	(a)	Birmingham C	W 2-1	T.Brown, A.Brown	26,633	1		3	4	5	6				11	10	9	7		8		2
Mar 4	(a)	Ipswich T	D 2-2	T.Brown 2 (1 pen)	20,130	1		3	4	5	6		12		11	10	9	7*		8		2
14	(a)	Wolves	D 1-1	Trewick	29,757	1	2	3	4	5	6		8		11	10	9	7				
18	(a)	Manchester U	D 1-1	Robertson	46,329	1	2	3	4	5	6		8		7	11	10	9				
22	(h)	Queen's Park R	W 2-2	A.Brown, Regis	19,536	1	2	3	4	5	6				7	11	10	9		8		
25	(a)	Arsenal	L 0-4		36,763	1	2	3	4	5	6		11		7		10	9		8		
27	(h)	Bristol C	W 2-1	Johnston, T.Brown	23,741	1	2	3	4	5	6		8		11	10	9	7				
Apr 1	(a)	Leicester C	W 1-0	T.Brown	14,637	1	2	3	4	5	6				11	10	9	7		8		
12	(a)	Newcastle U	W 2-0	Regis, Mulligan	17,053	1	2	3	4		6	7	11		5			10	9		8	
15	(a)	Manchester C	W 3-1	Regis, Cunningham, A.Brown	36,521	1	2	3	4		6	7	11		5			10	9		8	
18	(h)	Derby C	W 1-0	T.Brown (pen)	20,961	1	2	3	4		6	7	11		5			10	9		8	
22	(h)	Aston Villa	L 0-3		35,112	1	2*	3	4	12	6	7	11		5			10	9		8	
25	(h)	Everton	W 3-1	Regis 2, Hughes	20,247	1		3	4	5	6	7	11		8			9		10		2
29	(a)	Norwich C	D 1-1	Regis	17,302	1		3	4	5	6	7	11		8			9		10		2
May 2	(h)	Nottingham F	D 2-2	T.Brown, Hughes	23,523	1		3	4	5	6	7	11		8			9		10		2
				App		42	36	40	41	38	42	23	29	11	35	32	18	33	16	3	18	5
				Sub app				1					4					1	4	2	1	
				Goals			1		19	4	1		6	6	3	2	3	10		2	5	

Albion are back in Division One in 1977-8. Back row (left to right): D.Statham, R.Ward, A.Godden, J.Osborne, T.Thompson. Middle: G.Wright (physiotherapist), L.Cunningham, M.Martin, A.Brown, J.Trewick, B.Whitehouse (coach). Front: P.Mulligan, L.Cantello, J.Wile, R.Allen (manager), B.Robson, W.Johnston, D.Cross.

1978-79

Division 1

Date	Opponent	Res	Scorers	Att	Godden A	Batson B	Statham D	Brown T	Wile J	Robertson A	Robson B	Brown A	Regis C	Cantello L	Cunningham L	Johnston W	Trewick J	Martin M	Mills D	Summerfield K	Bennett M
Aug 19	(h) Ipswich T	W 2-1	A.Brown, T.Brown	23,738	1	2	3	4	5	6	7	8	9	10	11						
22	(a) Queen's Park R	W 1-0	Howe (og)	15,481	1	2	3	4	5	6	7	8	9	10	11						
26	(h) Bolton W	W 4-0	A.Brown 2, Cunningham, Regis	23,095	1	2	3	4	5	6	7	8	9	10	11*	12					
Sep 2	(a) Nottingham F	D 0-0		28,239	1	2	3		5	6	7	8	9	4	10	11					
9	(h) Norwich C	D 2-2	Cunningham, Robson	21,893	1	2	3		5	6	7	8	9	10	4	11					
16	(a) Derby C	L 2-3	Regis, Cunningham	23,697	1	2	3		5	6	7	8	9	4	11	10					
23	(h) Liverpool	D 1-1	Cunningham	33,772	1	2	3		5	6	7	8	9	10	4		11				
30	(a) Chelsea	W 3-1	Regis, Wile, T.Brown	21,022	1	2	3	11*	5	6	7	8	9	10	4		12				
Oct 7	(h) Tottenham H	L 0-1		33,068	1	2	3	11	5	6	7	8	9	4			10				
14	(a) Leeds U	W 3-1	T.Brown, Regis 2	25,931	1	2	3*	11	5	6	7	8	9	10	4		12				
21	(h) Coventry C	W 7-1	Cantello, Cunningham 2, Regis 2, T.Brown, Statham	27,409	1	2	3	11	5	6	7	8	9	10*	4		12				
28	(a) Manchester C	D 2-2	Regis, Robson	40,521	1	2	3	11	5	6	7	8	9	10	4						
Nov 4	(h) Birmingham C	W 1-0	Trewick	32,130	1	2		4	5	6	7	8	9	10	11		3				
11	(a) Ipswich T	W 1-0	A.Brown	20,938	1	2		4	5	6	7	8	9	10	11		3				
18	(a) Bolton W	W 1-0		22,298	1	2		4	5	6	7	8		10	11		3	9			
25	(h) Aston Villa	D 1-1	T.Brown (pen)	35,166	1	2	3	4	5	6	7	8	9	10	11						
Dec 9	(h) Middlesbrough	W 2-0	Regis, Cantello	19,949	1	2	3	4	5	6	7	8	9	10	11						
16	(a) Wolves	W 3-0	A.Brown 2, T.Brown	29,117	1	2	3	4	5	6	7	8	9	10	11						
26	(a) Arsenal	W 2-1	Robson, A.Brown	40,055	1	2	3	4	5	6	7	8	9	10	11						
30	(a) Manchester U	W 5-3	T.Brown 2, Cantello, Cunningham, Regis	45,091	1	2	3	4	5	6	7	8	9	10	11						
Jan 1	(h) Bristol C	W 3-1	A.Brown 2, Wile	31,738	1	2	3	4	5	6	7	8	9	10	11						
13	(a) Norwich C	D 1-1	Regis	20,972	1	2	3	4	5	6	7	8	9		11	10					
Feb 3	(a) Liverpool	L 1-2	A.Brown	52,211	1	2	3	4	5	6	7	8	9	10*	11			12			
24	(h) Leeds U	L 1-2	T.Brown	27,846	1	2	3	4	5	6	7	8*	9	10	11			12			
Mar 3	(a) Coventry C	W 3-1	Robson, A.Brown, Mills	25,795	1	2	3		5	6	7	8	9		11		4		10		
14	(h) Chelsea	W 1-0	A.Brown	20,472	1	2	3	4	5	6		8	9*		11	12	7		10		
24	(h) Queen's Park R	W 2-1	A.Brown, Cunningham	23,678	1	2	3	4*	5	6	7	8		10	11	12			9		
26	(h) Derby C	W 2-1	Cunningham, A.Brown	20,010	1	2	3		5	6	7	8*		10	11		4		9	12	
Apr 4	(h) Manchester C	W 4-0	Trewick, Power (og), Mills, Summerfield	22,314	1	2*	3		5	6	7		9	10	11		4		8	12	
7	(h) Everton	W 1-0	A.Brown	29,689	1		3		5	6	7	8	9		11		4		10		2
13	(a) Southampton	D 1-1	Regis	22,063	1	2	3	12	5	6	7	8	9		11		4		10*		
14	(h) Arsenal	D 1-1	T.Brown	28,623	1	2	3	10	5	6	7	8	9		11		4				
17	(a) Bristol C	L 0-1		30,191	1	2	3		5	6	7	8	9	10	11		4				
21	(h) Wolves	D 1-1	Robson	32,386	1	2	3	4	5	6	7	8	9	10	11						
24	(a) Birmingham C	D 1-1	Robson	19,895	1	2	3	4	5	6	7	8*	9	10	11			12			
28	(a) Middlesbrough	D 1-1	A.Brown	18,063	1	2	3	4	5	6	7	8	12	10	11*				9		
May 1	(a) Everton	W 2-0	Mills, Robson	30,083	1	2	3	4	5	6	7	8	9	10					11		
5	(h) Manchester U	W 1-0	Regis	28,060	1	2	3	4*	5	6	7	8	9			12	10		11		
8	(h) Southampton	W 1-0	A.Brown	17,499	1	2	3	12	5	6	7	8	9			4	10*		11		
11	(a) Aston Villa	W 1-0	Trewick	35,991	1	2	3		5		7	8	9	6	4		10		11		
14	(a) Tottenham H	L 0-1		24,789	1	2	3		5		7	8	9	10	11		4		6		
18	(h) Nottingham F	L 0-1		28,210	1	2	3	4	5		7	8	9	10			11		6		
App					42	41	39	29	42	39	41	41	38	32	39	3	19	1	15		1
Sub app								2					1			4	3	3		2	
Goals							1	10	2		7	18	13	3	9		3		3	1	

Albion's trio of Laurie Cunningham, Cyrille Regis and Brendon Batson, pictured in 1978-9.

1979-80

Division 1

Date		Opponent	Res	Scorers	Att	Godden A	Batson B	Statham D	Trewick J	Wile J	Robertson A	Robson B	Brown A	Brown T	Owen G	Barnes P	Mills D	Summerfield K	Deehan J	Pendrey G	Regis C	Bennett M	Moses R	Monaghan D	Cowdrill B
Aug 18	(h)	Derby C	D 0-0		24,727	1	2	3	4	5	6	7	8	9	10	11									
22	(a)	Manchester U	L 0-2		53,377	1	2	3		5	6	7	8	4	10	11	9								
25	(a)	Liverpool	L 1-3	Barnes	48,021	1	2	3		5	6	7	8	4	10	11	9*		12						
Sep 1	(h)	Nottingham F	L 1-5	Owen	26,405	1	2	3	12	5	6	7		4	10	11	9*		8						
8	(h)	Bolton W	D 0-0		17,033	1	2	3	4	5	6	7	8	9	10	11									
15	(h)	Manchester C	W 4-0	A.Brown, Owen, Summerfield, Robson	22,267	1	2	3	4	5	6	7	8	9	10	11*		12							
22	(a)	Tottenham H	D 1-1	A.Brown	29,914	1	2	3	4	5	6	7	8	12	10*	11			9						
29	(h)	Brighton & HA	D 2-2	Robson, A.Brown	22,225	1	2	3	4	5	6	7	8		10	11			9						
Oct 6	(a)	Middlesbrough	L 1-2	Owen	16,312	1	2	3		5	6	7	8	12	10*	11	4		9						
10	(h)	Manchester U	W 2-0	Robson, Deehan	27,811	1	2	3		5	6	7	8		10	11	4		9						
13	(a)	Aston Villa	D 0-0		36,007	1	2	3		5	6*	7	8	12	10	11	4		9						
20	(h)	Southampton	W 4-0	Deehan, Owen, Robson, A.Brown	22,766	1	2	3	12	5		7	8	11	10*		4		9	6					
27	(h)	Coventry C	W 4-1	A.Brown 2, T.Brown 2 (1 pen)	22,746	1	2	3		5	6	7	8	11	10		4		9						
Nov 3	(a)	Derby C	L 1-2	Robson	21,408	1	2	3		5	6	7	8	11*	10		4		9		12				
10	(h)	Norwich C	W 2-1	Wile, Robson	20,028	1	2			5	6	7	8		10	11	4		9	3					
17	(a)	Leeds U	L 0-1		17,481	1	2			5	6	7	8		10	11	4		9	3					
24	(a)	Wolves	D 0-0		32,564	1	2			5	6	7	8		10		4		9	3	11				
Dec 1	(h)	Everton	D 1-1	Regis	21,227	1	2			5	6	7	8	4	10	11				3	9				
8	(a)	Stoke C	L 2-3	Regis, Barnes (pen)	18,865	1	2		7	5	6		8		10*	11	4	12		3	9				
15	(h)	Arsenal	D 2-2	Robson, Trewick	18,820	1	2		10	5		7	8			11	4			3	9	6			
26	(h)	Bristol C	W 3-0	Owen, Barnes 2	19,590	1	2		4	5	6	7			10	11			8	3	9				
29	(h)	Liverpool	L 0-2		35,093	1	2		4	5	6	7	12		10*	11			8	3	9				
Jan 1	(a)	Ipswich T	L 0-4		22,511	1	2		4	5	6	7*	8		10	11			9	3	12				
12	(a)	Nottingham F	L 1-3	Regis	27,724	1	2	3	4	5	6				12	10	11*	7	8		9				
26	(a)	Crystal P	D 2-2	Robertson, Regis	23,869	1	2	3*		5	6	7	12		10	11			8		9		4		
Feb 2	(a)	Manchester C	W 3-1	Regis, Barnes 2	32,904	1	2			5	6	7	8		10	11				3	9		4		
9	(h)	Tottenham H	W 2-1	Regis 2	26,860	1	2			5		7	8		10	11				3	9	6	4		
16	(h)	Brighton & HA	D 0-0		22,633	1	2*			5		7	8			11	12		10	3	9	6	4		
23	(h)	Aston Villa	L 1-2	Robson	33,658	1	2			5	6	7	8			11			10	3	9		4		
Mar 1	(a)	Southampton	D 1-1	Regis	22,138	1	2			5	6*	7			10	12			8	3	9		4	11	
8	(a)	Coventry C	W 2-0	Barnes 2 (1 pen)	23,287	1	2			5	6	7			10	11			8	3	9		4		
14	(h)	Middlesbrough	D 0-0		15,955	1	2			5	6	7			10	11			8	3	9		4		
18	(h)	Bolton W	D 4-4	Barnes 3 (2 pens), Moses	11,735	1				5	6	7			10	11	12		8	3	9*	2	4		
22	(a)	Norwich C	D 1-1	Bond (og)	14,811	1	2			5	6	7	8		10	11					9		4	3	
29	(h)	Leeds U	W 2-1	Barnes (pen), Deehan	19,188	1	2			5	6	7*			10	11			8		9		4	12	3
Apr 1	(h)	Crystal P	W 3-0	Trewick, Barnes 2	17,723	1	2		7	5	6				10	11			8		9		4		3
5	(a)	Bristol C	D 0-0		15,677	1	2			5	6	7			10	11			8		9		4		3
7	(h)	Ipswich T	D 0-0		19,888	1	2		12	5	6	7			10	11			8*		9		4		3
19	(h)	Wolves	D 0-0		30,010	1	2		7	5	6		8		10	11					9		4		3
26	(a)	Arsenal	D 1-1	Barnes	30,326	1	2		7	5	6		8		10	11					9		4		3
28	(a)	Everton	D 0-0		20,356	1	2		7	5	6				10	11					9		4	8	3
May 3	(h)	Stoke C	L 0-1		18,920	1	2		7	5	6				10	11					9		4	8	3
App						42	40	16	17	42	38	35	27	12	37	37	15	1	27	18	24	4	18	3	9
Sub app									3				2				4	1	2	2	1		2	1	
Goals									2	1	1	8	6	2	5	15		1	3		8		1		

Garry Pendrey, loyal servant to Birmingham City before joining Albion.

Barry Cowdrill, left-back stand-in for Derek Statham.

1980-81

Division 1

Date		Opponent	Result	Scorers	Att	Golden A	Trewick J	Statham D	Moses R	Wile J	Robertson A	Robson B	Deehan J	Regis C	Owen G	Barnes P	Batson B	Brown A	Monaghan D	Mills D	Benjamin I	Cowdrill B	Bennett M	Cross N
Aug 16	(h)	Arsenal	L 0-1		22,360	1	2	3	4	5	6	7	8	9	10	11								
20	(a)	Stoke C	D 0-0		14,085	1	2	3	4	5	6	7	8	9	10	11								
23	(h)	Wolves	D 1-1	Regis	25,409	1		3	4	5*	6	7	8	9	10	11	2	12						
30	(a)	Brighton & HA	W 2-1	Regis, Owen	18,162	1	2	3	4	5	6	7		9	10	11		8						
Sep 6	(h)	Norwich C	W 3-0	Barnes (pen), Owen, Brown	15,414	1	2	3	4	5	6	7*	12	9	10	11		8						
13	(a)	Liverpool	L 0-4		36,792	1	12	3	4	5	6	7		9	10*	11	2	8						
20	(a)	Birmingham C	D 1-1	Brown	22,016	1	10	3	4	5	6	7		9		11	2	8						
27	(h)	Southampton	W 2-1	Brown 2	20,845	1	7	3	4	5	6			9	10	11	2	8						
Oct 4	(a)	Crystal P	W 1-0	Regis	16,081	1	7	3	4	5	6			9	10	11	2	8						
8	(h)	Coventry C	W 1-0	Barnes	16,377	1	12	3	4*	5	6	7			10	11	2	8	9					
11	(h)	Manchester C	W 3-1	Regis, Robson, Trewick	19,515	1	4	3		5	6	7		9	10	11	2	8						
18	(a)	Nottingham F	L 1-2	Moses	25,096	1	12	3	4	5	6	7		9	10	11*	2	8						
21	(a)	Everton	D 1-1	Wile	24,076	1	10	3	4	5	6	7		9			2	8	11					
25	(h)	Middlesbrough	W 3-0	Regis 2, Brown	16,162	1	10	3	4	5	6	7		9			2	8	11*	12				
Nov 1	(a)	Ipswich T	D 0-0		23,043	1	2	3*	4	5	6	7		9				8	11	10	12			
8	(h)	Aston Villa	D 0-0		34,195	1				4	5	6	7		9	10	11	2	8			3		
15	(a)	Arsenal	D 2-2	Barnes, Owen (pen)	25,855	1				4	5	6	7		9	10	11*	2	8		12	3		
22	(h)	Leicester C	W 3-1	Robson, Moses, Owen (pen)	17,752	1				4	5	6	7		9	10	11	2	8			3		
25	(h)	Stoke C	D 0-0		15,922	1				4	5	6	7		9	10	11	2	8			3		
29	(a)	Tottenham H	W 3-2	Brown, Robson, Barnes	27,371	1	3			4	5		7		9	10	11	2	8				6	
Dec 6	(h)	Leeds U	L 1-2	Moses	17,771	1				4	5		7		9	10	11	2	8*		12	3	6	
13	(a)	Coventry C	L 0-3		16,027	1				4	5	6	7	12	9	10	11*	2	8			3		
26	(a)	Sunderland	D 0-0		28,296	1				4	5		7		9	10	11	2	8			3	6	
27	(h)	Manchester U	W 3-1	Owen (pen), Barnes, Regis	30,326	1				4	5		7		9	10	11	2	8			3	6	
Jan 10	(a)	Leicester C	W 2-0	Bennett, Deehan	17,778	1				4	5		7	9		10	11	2	8			3	6	
17	(h)	Brighton & HA	W 2-0	Regis, Barnes	15,643	1				4	5	2	7		9	10	11		8			3	6	
31	(a)	Wolves	L 0-2		29,764	1		3	4	5		7		9	10	11	2	8					6	
Feb 7	(h)	Liverpool	W 2-0	Robson, Regis	27,905	1		3	4	5		7*	8	9	10	11	2			12			6	
14	(a)	Norwich C	W 2-0	Regis, Owen (pen)	15,218	1		3	4	5		7	8	9	10	11	2						6	
21	(a)	Southampton	D 2-2	Robson, Regis	21,910	1		3	4	5		7	8	9	10	11	2						6	
28	(h)	Birmingham C	D 2-2	Moses, Brown	24,843	1		3	4	5		7	8	9*	10	11	2			12			6	
Mar 7	(h)	Crystal P	W 1-0	Robson	15,599	1		3	4	5		7		9	10	11	2*	8		12			6	
14	(a)	Manchester C	L 1-2	Robson	36,581	1		3	4	5	2	7	9		10*	11		8		12			6	
21	(h)	Nottingham F	W 2-1	Gunn (og), Deehan	19,269	1		3	4	5		7	8	9		11	2			10			6	
28	(a)	Middlesbrough	L 1-2	Robson	13,288	1		3	4	5		7	8*	9		11	2		12	10			6	
31	(h)	Everton	W 2-0	Robson, Brown	14,833	1		3	4	5		7	8	9		11	2		12	10			6*	
Apr 4	(h)	Ipswich T	W 3-1	Brown, Batson, Barnes	22,216	1		3	4	5	6	7		9	10	11	2	8						
8	(a)	Aston Villa	L 0-1		47,998	1		3	4	5	6	7		9	10	11	2	8						
18	(a)	Manchester U	L 1-2	Regis	44,442	1		3	4	5	6	7		9	10	11	2	8*						12
20	(h)	Sunderland	W 2-1	Regis 2	15,243	1		3	4	5	6	7		9	10	11	2	8						
May 2	(h)	Tottenham H	W 4-2	Brown, Barnes, Robson, Cross	20,429	1		3	4	5	6	7		9	10*	11	2	8						12
6	(a)	Leeds U	D 0-0		17,218	1		3	4	5	6	7		9		11	2	8		10				
				App		42	12	31	41	42	28	40	13	38	34	39	35	31	4	5	1	10	16	
				Sub app			3						2						5	5	1			2
				Goals			1		4	1		10	2	14	6	8	1	10					1	1

Peter Barnes scoring from the penalty spot in Albion's 3-0 home win over Norwich City on 6 September 1980.

149

1981-82

Division 1

Date		Opponent	Res	Score	Scorers	Att	Godden A	Batson B	Statham D	Moses R	Wile J	Bennett M	Robson B	Mills D	Deehan J	Lowery A	Mackenzie S	Cross N	Robertson A	Owen G	Regis C	Brown A	Arthur D	King A	Summerfield K	Jol M	Grew M	Whitehead C	Monaghan D	Lewis M	Childs G	Webb A	Zondervan R	Cowdrill B
Aug 29	(a)	Manchester C	L	1-2	Mills (pen)	36,187	1	2	3	4	5	6	7	8	9	10*	11	12																
Sep 2	(h)	Arsenal	L	0-2		17,104	1	2	3	4*	5		7	8	9		11	12	6	10														
Sep 5	(h)	Swansea C	W	4-1	Regis 3, Mackenzie	18,063	1	2	3	4	5		7	8			11		6	10	9													
Sep 12	(a)	Nottingham F	D	0-0		22,618	1	2	3	4	5		7	8			11		6	10	9													
Sep 19	(h)	West Ham U	D	0-0		19,516	1	2	3		5		7	8			11	12	6	10*	9	4												
Sep 22	(a)	Ipswich T	L	0-1		20,542	1	2	3		5			8	7		11	10	6*		9	4	12											
Sep 26	(a)	Everton	L	0-1		23,871	1	2	3		5			8	7		11		6	10	9	4												
Oct 3	(h)	Middlesbrough	W	2-0	Summerfield, Regis	12,849	1	2	3		5						11	7	6	10	9	4			8									
Oct 10	(h)	Brighton & HA	D	0-0		13,704	1	2	3		5	12					11	7*	6	10	9	4			8									
Oct 17	(a)	Leeds U	L	1-3	Mills	19,164	1	2	3		5			8	7		11		6	10	9	4												
Oct 24	(h)	Southampton	D	1-1	Brown	15,730	1	2	3		5	12					11		6	10	9	4*	7		8									
Oct 31	(a)	Birmingham C	D	3-3	Regis 3	21,301	1	2	3		5						11		6	10	9	4		8		7								
Nov 7	(a)	Tottenham H	W	2-1	Hughton (og), Jol	32,436		2*	3		5						11		6	10	9			8	12	7	1	4						
Nov 14	(h)	Stoke c	L	1-2	Smith (og)	15,787		2*	3		5						11		6	10	9			8	12	7	1	4						
Nov 21	(h)	Liverpool	D	1-1	Regis	20,871		2	3		5						11		6	10	9			8*	12	7	1	4						
Nov 28	(a)	Sunderland	W	2-1	Brown, Regis	15,897		2	3		5						11		6	10	9			8		7	1	4						
Dec 5	(h)	Wolves	W	3-0	Regis 2, Whitehead	23,378		2	3		5						11		6	10	9			8	12	7*	1	4						
Dec 26	(a)	Coventry C	W	2-0	Owen, Regis	15,053		2	3		5						11		6	10*	9	4		8		7	1							
Jan 30	(a)	West Ham U	L	1-3	King	24,423		2	3		5						11	12	6	10	9	4		8*		7	1							
Feb 6	(h)	Nottingham F	W	2-1	Bennett, Summerfield	15,006		2			5	6					11		3	10	9				8	7	1	4						
Feb 20	(h)	Everton	D	0-0		14,819		2	3		5						11	12	6	10	9			8*		7	1	4						
Feb 27	(a)	Brighton & HA	D	2-2	Cross, Bennett	14,553		2	3		5	6					11	12		10	9			8		7	1	4*	2					
Mar 9	(a)	Middlesbrough	L	0-1		9,884		2	3		5						11	12	6	10*	9			8		7	1	4						
Mar 13	(a)	Southampton	D	0-0		21,376		2			5						11		6	10	9			8		7	1	4						3
Mar 16	(a)	Arsenal	D	2-2	King, Cross	15,799		2*	3		5							12	6	10	9			8		7	1	4					11	
Mar 20	(h)	Birmingham C	D	1-1	Robertson	21,160		2	3		5								6	10	9			8		7	1	4					11	
Mar 24	(h)	Notts C	L	2-4	Regis, King	12,759		2	3*		5							12	6	10	9			8		7	1	4					11	
Mar 27	(h)	Tottenham H	W	1-0	Regis	20,275		2			5								6	10	9			8		7	1	4					11	3
Mar 30	(a)	Aston Villa	L	1-2	King	28,440		2			5						11		6	10	9			8		7	1	4						3
Apr 6	(a)	Swansea C	L	1-3	Mackenzie	15,744		2	3		5						11		6	10	9			8	12	7	1	4*						
Apr 10	(a)	Coventry C	L	1-2	Mackenzie	12,718			3		5						11		6	10	9			8*	12	7	1	4						
Apr 12	(a)	Manchester U	L	0-1		38,717		2	3		5						11	12	6	10	9	8				7*	1	4						
Apr 17	(a)	Liverpool	L	0-1		34,286		2	3		5		7				11	12	6	10	9			8*			1	4						
Apr 21	(h)	Manchester C	L	0-1		11,733		2	3		5						11		6	10*	9	8				7	1	4	12					
Apr 24	(h)	Sunderland	L	2-3	Brown, Owen (pen)	13,298		2	3		5	6					11*			10	9	4		8		7	1		12					
May 1	(a)	Wolves	W	2-1	Regis, Monaghan	19,813	1	2			5						11		6	10	9	4		8		7*			12					3
May 5	(h)	Ipswich T	L	1-2	Owen	12,564	1	2			5						11*		6	10	9	4		8		7			12					3
May 8	(h)	Aston Villa	L	0-1		19,650	1	2	3		5								6	10	9	4		8								7	11	
May 12	(h)	Manchester U	L	0-3		19,772	1	2	3		5				7	12				10	9	4		8*							6		11	
May 15	(a)	Notts C	W	2-1	Mackenzie, Regis	8,734	1	2	3		5				7	12	11*			10	9	4		8							6			
May 18	(h)	Leeds U	W	2-0	Regis, Mackenzie	23,118	1	2	3		5						11			10	9	4		8							6	7		
May 20	(a)	Stoke C	L	0-3		19,698	1	2	3		5				7					10	9	4		8					12	9	6*		11	
App							19	39	35	4	42	23	5	9	4	1	37	11	33	39	37	22	2	21	4	9	23	8	5	3	2	6	13	6
Sub app												2						11				3	1	4		3	1						1	2
Goals												2		2			5	2	1	3	17	3		4	2	1		1	1				

John Deehan, the striker Albion bought from Aston Villa and sold to Norwich City.

Remi Moses was sold to Manchester United in 1981, in a seven-figure 'package deal' along with Bryan Robson.

150

1982-83

Division 1

Date		Opponent		Result	Scorers	Att.	Grew M	Batson B	Cowdrill B	Zondervan R	Bennett M	Robertson A	Jol M	Brown A	Eastoe P	Mackenzie S	Whitehead C	Webb A	Owen G	Cross N	Regis C	Statham D	Godden A	Wile J	Mills D	Barron P	Lewis M	Thompson G	Perry M	Luke N	Robson G
Aug 28	(a)	Liverpool		L 0-2		35,652	1	2	3	4	5	6*	7	8	9	10	11	12													
Sep 1	(h)	Brighton & HA		W 5-0	Cross, Brown 2, Jol, Eastoe	11,546	1	2		4	5	6	7	8	9		3		10	11											
4	(h)	Manchester U		W 3-1	Bennett, Eastoe, Brown	25,014	1	2		4	5	6	7	8	11		3		10		9										
8	(a)	Stoke C		W 3-0	Regis, Eastoe, Brown	17,446	1	2		4	5	6	7	8	11		3		10		9										
11	(a)	Watford		L 0-3		17,603	1	2		4	5	6	7	8	11		3		10		9										
18	(h)	West Ham U		L 1-2	Eastoe	15,321	1	2		4	5	6	7	8*	11		3		10	12	9										
25	(a)	Norwich C		W 3-1	Regis 3	15,130	1	2		4	5	6	7	8	11		3		10		9										
Oct 2	(h)	Aston Villa		W 1-0	Cross	25,331	1	2		4	5	6	7	8	11		3		10		9										
9	(h)	Nottingham F		W 2-1	Regis, Owen	13,718	1	2		4	5	6	7	8	11*		3		10	12	9										
16	(a)	Arsenal		L 0-2		21,666	1	2		4	5	6	7	8			3		10	11*	9	12									
23	(h)	Luton T		W 1-0	Whitehead	16,345		2		4	5	6	7	8			11		10		9	3	1								
30	(a)	Ipswich T		L 1-6	Regis	20,011		2*		4		6	7	8			11		10	12	9	3	1	5							
Nov 6	(a)	Birmingham C		L 1-2	Eastoe	18,520				2	4*	6	7		8		11		10	12	9	3	1	5							
13	(h)	Swansea C		D 3-3	Cross, Jol, Eastoe	12,432				4		6	7		11			2	10	8	9	3	1	5							
20	(a)	Everton		D 0-0		16,001				4		6	7		11			2	10	8	9	3	1	5							
27	(h)	Coventry C		W 2-0	Robertson, Regis	12,115				4		6	7		11			2	10	8	9	3	1	5							
Dec 4	(a)	Tottenham H		D 1-1	Mills	26,208				4		6	7		11*			2	10	8	9	3	1	5	12						
11	(h)	Sunderland		W 3-0	Robertson, Owen, Zondervan	11,137				4		6	7		11			2	10	8*	9	3	1	5	12						
18	(a)	Southampton		L 1-4	Regis	16,896				4		6	7		11			2	10	8	9	3	1	5							
27	(h)	Notts C		D 2-2	Eastoe, Owen	17,768				4		6	7		11			2	10	8	9	3	1	5							
28	(a)	Manchester C		L 1-2	Brown	25,172				4*	12	6	7	8	11			2	10		9	3	1	5							
Jan 1	(h)	Everton		D 2-2	Zondervan, Owen	15,194				4		6	7		11			2	10	8*	9	3	1	5	12						
3	(a)	Manchester U		D 0-0		39,123				4	8	6	7		11			2	10		9	3		5		1					
15	(h)	Liverpool		L 0-1		24,560				4	8	6	7		11			2	10		9	3		5		1					
22	(a)	West Ham U		W 1-0	Eastoe	19,887				4	8	6	7		11			2	10	12	9*	3		5		1					
Feb 5	(h)	Stoke C		D 1-1	Cross	11,486				4	2	6	7	8	11				10	9		3		5		1					
12	(a)	Brighton & HA		D 0-0		9,902				4		6	7	8	11			2		9		3		5	10	1					
19	(a)	Nottingham F		D 0-0		14,507				4		6	7	8	11			2		9		3		5	10	1					
26	(h)	Arsenal		D 0-0		16,923				4	2*	6	7		11	12			10	8	9	3		5		1					
Mar 5	(a)	Luton T		D 0-0		10,852				4	2	6	7		11				10	8	9	3		5		1					
12	(h)	Ipswich T		W 4-1	Thompson 2, Statham, Gernon (og)	12,892				4	6				12	7	2		10	11	9*	3		5		1		8			
19	(h)	Birmingham C		W 2-0	Regis, Thompson	20,794				4	6					7	2		10	11	9	3		5		1		8			
26	(a)	Swansea C		L 1-2	Thompson	11,222				4		6	7			11*	2		10	12	9	3		5		1		8			
Apr 2	(h)	Manchester C		L 0-2		13,654				4		6	7			11	2		10*	9		3		5		1		12	8		
4	(a)	Notts C		L 1-2	Thompson	8,692						6	7		9	4	2			11		3		5		1		10	8		
9	(a)	Watford		L 1-3	Jol	11,828			3	4		6	7		9		2		10	11				5		1		8			
16	(a)	Aston Villa		L 0-1		26,921				4		6	7			2	9		10	11		3		5		1		8			
23	(h)	Tottenham H		L 0-1		14,940				4		6	7			11*	2		10		9	3		5		1		8	12		
30	(a)	Coventry C		W 1-0	Perry	9,410				12		6	7*			4	2		10	11		3		5		1		8	9		
May 2	(h)	Norwich C		W 1-0	Thompson	9,221				4		6					2		10	11		3		5		1	7*	9	8	12	
7	(h)	Southampton		W 1-0	Statham	11,241				4		6	7*				2		10	11		3		5		1		9	8	12	
14	(a)	Sunderland		D 1-1	Thompson	16,375				4			7				2	6	10	11		3		5		1		9	8*	12	
		App					10	12	2	40	22	37	39	16	30	1	35	12	38	26	26	31	12	31		20	4	12	6		
		Sub app						1	1		1				1	1		6		1					3			1	1	2	
		Goals								2	1	2	3	5	8		1		4	4	9	2			1			7	1		

Garry Thompson scoring his first goal for Albion, against Ipswich Town at The Hawthorns on 12 March 1983. Albion won 4-1 — their first home win in six League games.

Peter Eastoe, secured from Everton in 1982.

151

1983-84

Division 1

Date	Opponent	Result	Scorers	Att	Barron P	Webb A	Whitehead C	Zondervan R	McNaught K	Bennett M	Jol M	Thompson G	Regis C	Owen G	Cross N	Robson G	Robertson A	Cowdrill B	Perry M	Lewis M	Childs G	Luke N	Monaghan D	Forsyth M	Mackenzie S	Morley A	Ebanks W	Statham D	Kent K	Hunt S	Grealish A
Aug 27	(a) Aston Villa	L 3-4	Zondervan, Thompson, Regis	29,522	1	2	3	4*	5	6	7	8	9	10	11	12															
29	(a) Stoke C	L 1-3	Cross	16,156	1		3		5	6	7	8	9	10	11	4	2														
Sep 3	(h) Leicester C	W 1-0	Whitehead	12,016	1		3	2	5	6	7	8	9	10	11	4															
7	(h) Tottenham H	D 1-1	Regis	14,889	1		2	4	5	6	7*	8	9	10	11			3	12												
10	(a) Everton	D 0-0		15,543	1		2	4	5	6		8	9	10	12	7*		3		11											
17	(h) West Ham U	W 1-0	Thompson	15,161	1		2	4	5	6		8	9	10	11*			3	12	7											
24	(a) Ipswich T	W 4-3	Zondervan, Regis, Perry, Thompson (pen)	16,611	1		2	4	5	6		8	9	10*	11			3	12	7											
Oct 1	(h) Watford	W 2-0	Regis, Thompson	14,456	1	2	7	4	5	6		8	9		11*			3	10	12											
15	(a) Manchester U	L 0-3		42,221	1		2	4	5	6		8	9	10	11			3		7											
22	(a) Coventry C	W 2-1	Regis, Perry	13,441	1		2	7	5	6		8	9*	10		12		3	11	4											
29	(h) Birmingham C	L 1-2	Perry	20,224	1		2	4	5	6*		8	9	10	12			3	11	7											
Nov 5	(h) Notts C	W 2-0	McNaught, Luke	10,821	1		2	4	5			8		10		6		3	9	7		11									
12	(a) Southampton	L 0-1		16,450	1		2	4*	5			8		10	12	7	6	3	9			11									
19	(a) Norwich C	L 0-2		13,368	1		2	4	5		7	8		10	12	6		3	9*			11									
26	(h) Wolves	L 1-3	Thompson	17,947	1		2	4	5		7	8		10		6		3	9*			11	12								
Dec 3	(a) Arsenal	W 1-0	Monaghan	22,271	1	2		4	5			8		10				3				7	9	6	11						
10	(h) Queen's Park R	L 1-2	Morley	11,717	1	2		4	5	6		8		10				3	12				9		11*	7					
18	(a) Luton T	L 0-2		11,566	1		2		5		7		9	10				3	8			4	6			11					
26	(h) Liverpool	L 1-2	Morley	25,139	1	2		4	5		7		9		8*			3	12	10		6				11					
27	(a) Sunderland	L 0-3		17,968	1			4	5			8	9	10	12			3	7			6				11	2*				
31	(a) Leicester C	D 1-1	Thompson	15,128	1		2	4	5	6	7	8	9	10				3								11					
Jan 2	(h) Ipswich T	W 2-1	Owen, Thompson	11,199	1		2	4*	5	6		8	9	10	12			3	7							11					
14	(h) Aston Villa	W 3-1	Thompson 2, Regis	20,399	1		2	7	5	6		8	9	10				3				4				11					
21	(a) West Ham U	L 0-1		17,213	1		2	7	5		12	8	9	10*		6		3				4				11					
Feb 4	(a) Watford	L 1-3	Zondervan	14,240	1		2	4	5		7	8	9					3	10			6				11					
8	(h) Nottingham F	L 0-5		11,020	1		2	4	5		7	8*	9						10			6			12	11		3			
11	(h) Everton	D 1-1	Perry	10,313	1		2	4	5		7				12				9			6*			10	11		3	8		
25	(h) Coventry C	D 1-1	Cross	10,929	1			4	5	6	7	8			9										10	11	2	3			
28	(a) Birmingham C	L 1-2	Mackenzie	16,780	1			4	5	6	7	8			9										10	11	2	3			
Mar 3	(a) Notts C	D 1-1	Cross	7,373	1		2	4	5	6	7	8			9										10	11		3			
17	(a) Tottenham H	W 1-0	Regis	22,385	1		2		5	6		8	9												10	11		3		4	7
24	(h) Stoke C	W 3-0	Mackenzie, Hunt, Morley	13,681	1		2		5	6*		8	9												10	11	12	3		4	7
31	(h) Manchester U	W 2-0	Mackenzie, Regis	27,954	1		2		5	6		8	9												10	11		3		4	7
Apr 7	(a) Nottingham F	L 1-3	Thompson	15,245	1		2		5	6		8	9												10	11		3		4	7
14	(a) Norwich C	D 0-0		11,572	1				5	6		8	9												10	11	2	3		4	7
21	(a) Liverpool	L 0-3		35,320	1		2		5	6		8	9												10	11		3		4	7
23	(h) Sunderland	W 3-1	Regis, Hunt, Thompson	11,252	1		2		5	6		8	9		12										10	11		3*		4	7
28	(a) Wolves	D 0-0		13,208	1		2		5	6		8	9												10	11		3		4	7
May 5	(h) Arsenal	L 1-3	Thompson	13,566	1		2		5	6		8	9		12										10	11		3		4	7*
7	(a) Queen's Park R	D 1-1	Thompson	14,418	1		2		5			8	9									6			10	11	7	3		4	
12	(h) Luton T	W 3-0	Morley, Regis, Mackenzie	12,417	1		2		5				9		8										10	11		3		4	7
14	(h) Southampton	L 0-2		10,365	1		2		5	6		8													10	11		3*	12	4	7
App					42	5	34	29	42	29	15	37	30	20	16	5	6	22	8	14		8	2	8	18	26	6	16	1	12	11
Sub app										1				9	2			5		1		1	1	1		1		1		1	
Goals							1	3	1			13	10	1	3				4			1	1		4	4				2	

Albion in 1984. Back row (left to right): M.Perry, G.Thompson, M.Bennett, P.Barron, A.Godden, K.McNaught, B.Cowdrill, M.Forsyth, G.Robson. Middle: G.Leonard, J.Tortolano, C.Whitehead, C.Regis, S.Mackenzie, N.Cross, W.Ebanks, M.Lewis. Front: N.Stiles (coach), A.Robertson, D.Statham, G.Owen, J.Giles (manager), S.Hunt, A.Grealish, A.Morley, G.Wright (physiotherapist).

1984-85

Division 1

Date		Opponent	Result	Scorers	Att.	Godden A	Whitehead C	Statham D	Hunt S	Bennett M	Robertson A	Grealish A	Thompson G	Regis C	Mackenzie S	Cross N	Morley A	Robson G	Forsyth M	Valentine C	Cross D	Lewis M	Nichol J	Barron P	Owen G	Cowdrill B
Aug 25	(a)	Queen's Park R	L 1-3	Mackenzie	12,802	1	2	3	4	5	6	7	8	9	10	11										
27	(h)	Everton	W 2-1	Hunt, Thompson	13,464	1	2	3	4	5	6	7*	8	9	10	12	11									
Sep 1	(h)	Luton T	W 4-0	Hunt, Regis, Cross, Thompson	11,720	1	2	3	4	5	6	7	8	9*	10	12	11									
5	(a)	Norwich C	L 1-2	Grealish	14,234	1	2	3	4	5	6	7	8	9	10		11									
8	(a)	Sunderland	D 1-1	Thompson	18,206	1	2	3	4	5	6	7	8	9	10		11									
15	(h)	Sheffield W	D 2-2	Thompson 2	16,439	1	2	3	4	5	6	7	8	9	10		11									
22	(a)	Leicester C	L 1-2	Cross	11,960	1	2	3	4	5	6	7	8		10	9	11									
29	(h)	Manchester U	L 1-2	Thompson (pen)	26,401	1	2	3	4	5	6*	7	8	9	10	12	11									
Oct 6	(a)	Liverpool	D 0-0		29,346	1	2	3	4	5	6	7	8		10	9		11*	12							
13	(h)	Nottingham F	W 4-1	Mackenzie, Thompson 3	12,991	1	2	3	4	5	6	7	8		10	9		11								
20	(a)	Ipswich T	L 0-2		14,154	1	2	3	4	5	6	7	8	9	10			12		11*						
27	(h)	Southampton	D 0-0		12,454	1	2	3*	4	5	6	7	8	9	12					10	11					
Nov 3	(a)	Tottenham H	W 3-2	Statham (pen), Cross, Mackenzie	24,494	1	2	3	4	5	6	7	8	9				12		11*	10					
10	(h)	Stoke C	W 2-0	Hunt, Mackenzie	12,828	1	12	3	4	5	6	7*	8	9				11			10		2			
17	(a)	Chelsea	L 1-3	Thompson	17,573	1	11	3	4*	5	6	7	8	9	12						10		2			
24	(h)	Coventry C	W 5-2	Thompson, Valentine, Mackenzie, Hunt, Statham	12,742	1		3	4	5	6	7	8	9	12					11	10*		2			
Dec 1	(a)	West Ham U	W 2-0	Hunt, Thompson	15,572	1		3	4	5	6	7	8	9						11	10		2			
8	(h)	Watford	W 2-1	Thompson, Cross	13,581	1		3	4		6	7	8	9					5	11	10		2			
15	(a)	Arsenal	L 0-4		23,728	1	4	3		5	6	7	8	9	12					11	10*		2			
18	(a)	Luton T	W 2-1	Thompson, Statham (pen)	7,286	1	4	3		5	6	7	8	9	10					11			2			
26	(h)	Newcastle U	W 2-1	Hunt, Thompson	20,248	1		3	4	5	6	7	8	9						11	10		2			
29	(h)	Norwich C	L 0-1		13,406	1	12	3	4	5	6	7*	8	9						11	10		2			
Jan 1	(a)	Aston Villa	L 1-3	Statham (pen)	31,710	1	7	3	4	5	6*		8	9	12					11	10		2			
12	(a)	Sheffield W	L 0-2		24,345	1	12	3	4	5*	6	7	8	9						11	10		2			
26	(h)	Queen's Park R	D 0-0		9,324	1	4	3		5		7	8	9				6		11	10		2			
Feb 2	(a)	Manchester U	L 0-2		36,681		10	3	4	5		7	8	9*				6		11			2	1	12	
23	(h)	Tottenham H	L 0-1		17,002	1	10		4	5	6		8	9				3		11			2		7	
Mar 2	(a)	Southampton	L 3-4	Valentine, Thompson 2	15,567	1	12	3	4	5	6		8	9*						11	10		2		7	
12	(a)	Stoke C	D 0-0		6,885	1	3*		4	5		12	8	9				6		11	10		2		7	
16	(a)	Nottingham F	W 2-1	Cross, Owen	12,663	1	3		4	5		12	8	9	10			6		11			2		7*	
23	(h)	Liverpool	L 0-5		20,847	1	12	3	4	5	6	7	8	9*	10					11			2			
30	(h)	Leicester C	W 2-0	Hunt 2	9,347	1	2	3	4		6	12	8		10	9*		5		11					7	
Apr 3	(a)	Ipswich T	L 1-2	Hunt	8,112	1	2	3	4		6	12	8		10*	9		5		11					7	
6	(a)	Newcastle U	L 0-1		22,690	1			4	5	6	12	8			9				11	10		2		7*	3
8	(h)	Aston Villa	W 1-0	Valentine	21,044	1			4	5	6	10	8	12		9*				11			2		7	3
16	(a)	Everton	L 1-4	Grealish	29,750	1	12		4	5	6*	10	8	7		9				11			2			3
20	(h)	Chelsea	L 0-1		11,196	1			4	5		10	8	12		9*	6			11			2		7	3
24	(h)	Sunderland	W 1-0	Cross	7,423	1	12			5	6	9*	8		4	10				11			2		7	3
27	(a)	Coventry C	L 1-2	Mackenzie	10,356	1	9*			5	6	12	8		4	10				11			2		7	3
May 4	(h)	West Ham U	W 5-1	Hunt, Mackenzie, Grealish, Cross	8,878	1			4	5	6	12	8		9	10				11			2		7*	3
7	(a)	Watford	W 2-0	Thompson, Owen	14,062	1			4	5	6	12	8		9	10*				11			2		7	3
11	(h)	Arsenal	D 2-2	Valentine, Thompson	13,485	1			4	5	6		8		9	10				11			2		7	3
App						41	25	30	37	39	37	30	42	7	37	15	7	9	9	29	16	1	27	1	14	9
Sub app							7						8		1	9		2	1						1	
Goals								4	10			3	19	1	8	5				4	2				2	

Derek Statham's early penalty goal for Albion against Aston Villa on New Year's Day, 1985.

153

1985-86

Division 1

Date		Opponent	Result	Scorers	Att.	Godden A	Nicholl J	Statham D	Whitehead C	Bennett M	Robertson A	Grealish A	Varadi I	Mackenzie S	Valentine C	Crooks G	Cowdrill B	Hunt S	Forsyth M	Anderson C	Robson G	Armstrong G	Dennison R	Palmer C	Thomas M	Bradshaw P	Thompson A	Reilly G	Owen G	Grew M	Naylor S	Dickinson M	Dyson P	Bradley D	Madden C	Bull S	Burrows D	Robinson M
Aug 17	(h)	Oxford U	D 1-1	Varadi	14,626	1	2	3	4	5	6	7	8	9	10	11*	12																					
20	(a)	Everton	L 0-2		26,788	1	2	10	7	5			8	9		11		3*	4	6	12																	
24	(a)	Watford	L 1-5	Varadi	14,541	1	2	10	12	5	6*		8	9		11		3	4	7																		
26	(h)	Manchester C	L 2-3	Mackenzie 2	12,152	1	2	10		5			8	9		11			6	3	4	7																
31	(a)	Chelsea	L 0-3		15,376	1	5	10	2				8	9		11			6	3	4	7																
Sep 4	(h)	Aston Villa	L 0-3		17,077	1	2	3			5*	10	8	9		11			6	12	4	7																
7	(h)	Ipswich T	L 1-2	Crooks	7,733	1	2	3				7	8	9	10	11			6	12	4*	5																
14	(a)	Newcastle U	L 1-4	Mackenzie	21,855	1	2	3	5					9		11			6	7	4	8	10*	12														
21	(h)	Manchester U	L 1-5	Crooks	25,068	1	2	3		5				9	10	11			4	6		8	7															
28	(a)	Coventry C	L 0-3		10,295	1	2	3		5	6	12	8	9*	7	11				4					10													
Oct 5	(h)	Tottenham H	D 1-1	Valentine	12,040		2	3*	12	5	6	4		9		7		11		8					10	1												
12	(a)	Leicester C	D 2-2	Crooks 2	7,236		2	3	4	5	6		8	9		7		11							10	1												
19	(h)	Birmingham C	W 2-1	Varadi, Valentine	14,576			3	4	5	6		8	9		7		11					2		10	1												
26	(h)	Sheffield W	L 0-1		19,873		2	3	8*	5	6			9		7		11		4				12	10	1												
Nov 3	(a)	Nottingham F	L 1-2	Hunt	19,610		2	3		5	6		8	9		7		11		4					10	1												
9	(h)	Queen's Park R	L 0-1		9,016		6	3	2	5			8	9		7		11		4				12	10*	1												
16	(a)	Liverpool	L 1-4	Crooks	28,407	1	2	3	5*	6				9		11				4		7	12		10			8										
23	(h)	Arsenal	D 0-0		9,165		3*		8	5	6			9		11				4	12	7	2		10	1												
30	(a)	West Ham U	L 0-4		16,325		2		8*	5	6	7		9	12	11		3	4						10	1												
Dec 7	(h)	Everton	L 0-3		12,206	1	2			5	6*		8	7		11		3	4					12	10			9										
14	(h)	Oxford U	D 2-2	Hunt, Varadi	9,020	1	2	3		5	6	11	8	7					4						10			9										
22	(h)	Watford	W 3-1	Hunt (pen), Dennison, Varadi	11,092	1	2	3		5	6	11*	8	7					4				12		10			9										
26	(h)	Luton T	L 1-2	Varadi	12,508	1	2	3		5	6	11*	8	7					4				12		10			9										
28	(a)	Aston Villa	D 1-1	Hunt	18,796	1	2*	3		5	6		8	7					4				12		10		11	9										
Jan 1	(a)	Southampton	L 1-3	Varadi	13,154	1	2	3		5	6		8	7					4*				12		10		11	9										
11	(h)	Newcastle U	D 1-1	Varadi	9,106	1	2	3		5	6		8	7*											10		11	12	9	4								
18	(h)	Chelsea	L 0-3		11,275		2	3						8*			11	4		6				9	5			10	7		1		12					
Feb 1	(a)	Manchester C	L 1-2	Grealish	20,540	1	2	3	6			7	8					4							5			10					9	11				
8	(a)	Birmingham C	W 1-0	Bennett	11,514	1	2	3	6			7	12	8*				4							5			10					9	11				
22	(a)	Manchester U	L 0-3		45,193		2	3	6			12	8			11		4			7			10*	5						1		9					
Mar 8	(a)	Tottenham H	L 0-5		10,841	1	2	3	7					8*	10				4		5	11				12		9				6						
15	(h)	Leicester C	D 2-2	Varadi, Mackenzie	8,337		2	3						8	10				4									7	9		1	6	5		11			
19	(h)	Coventry C	D 0-0		8,831		2	3						8	10				4									7	9		1	6	5		11			
22	(a)	Ipswich T	L 0-1		12,121		2	3							10	12			4									7	9		1	6	5		11*	8		
29	(h)	Southampton	W 1-0	Thompson	7,325		2	3							10				4									7	9		1	6	5		11	8		
Apr 1	(a)	Luton T	L 0-3		9,226		2	3					12	9*	10				4									7			1	6	5		11	8		
5	(h)	Nottingham F	D 1-1	Bennett	7,901		2	3	6						10				4				12					7*	9		1		5		11	8		
12	(a)	Queen's Park R	L 0-1		11,866		2								10					6	3	9		4				7*			1		5		11	8		12
19	(h)	Liverpool	L 1-2	Madden	22,010		2	3						9						6	12	7		4				8			1		5	10	11*			
22	(h)	Sheffield W	D 1-1	Reilly	6,021		2							9						4	12	7		6				8			1		5		10		3	11
26	(a)	Arsenal	D 2-2	Reilly 2	14,843		2	3	8					9						4	3	12		6*				7			1		5	10	11			
May 3	(h)	West Ham U	L 2-3	Madden, Reilly (pen)	17,831		2	3	8*					9						4	12			6				7			1		5	10	11			
				App		21	29	37	22	25	20	14	30	30	15	18	9	19	11	7	9	7	7	16	20	8	13	20	3	1	12	7	11	10	9		1	1
				Sub app			2			2	2	1			1				4	5	1	5	4		2		1								1			
				Goals						2		1	9	4	2	5		4					1				1	4							2			

Albion 1985-6. Back row (left to right): M.Forsyth, J.Nicholl, M.Bennett, A.Godden, P.Bradshaw, B.Cowdrill, C.Palmer. Middle: G.Wright (physiotherapist), T.Brown (coach), G.Robson, C.Anderson, N.Cross, C.Whitehead, D.Statham, S.Hunt, N.Stiles (coach). Front: C.Valentine, S.Mackenzie, A.Robertson, J.Giles (manager), G.Crooks, I.Varadi, A.Grealish.

1986-87

Division 2

Date		Opponent	Result	Scorers	Att	Naylor S	Whitehead C	Burrows D	Bennett M	Dyson P	Dickinson M	Palmer C	Evans S	Mackenzie S	Williamson R	Madden C	Thompson A	Dennison R	Dobbins W	Bull S	Cowdrill B	Anderson C	Robinson M	Crooks G	Hopkins R	Singleton M	Statham D	Steggles K	Bradley D	Reilly G	Robson G	Lynex S	Goodman D
Aug 23	(a)	Hull C	L 0-2		8,658	1	2	3	4	5	6	7	8	9	10	11*	12																
25	(h)	Sheffield U	W 1-0	Evans	9,102	1		3	4	5	6	7	8	9	10		2	11*	12														
30	(h)	Huddersfield T	W 1-0	Bennett	9,252	1	2	3	4	5	6	7	8	9	10*	11	12																
Sep 2	(a)	Stoke C	D 1-1	Palmer	8,664	1	2	3	4	5	6	7	8	9	10	11																	
6	(a)	Reading	D 1-1	Madden	7,537	1	2	3	4	5	6	7			10	12	11*				9	8											
13	(h)	Ipswich T	L 3-4	Bull 2, Williamson	9,034	1	2	3	4	5	6	7		9	10	12					8	11*											
20	(a)	Brighton & HA	L 0-2		8,766	1	2	3	4	5	6	7	8	9	10			11*	12														
27	(h)	Derby C	W 2-0	Mackenzie 2	10,847	1	2			5	6	4	8	9	10		12				7	3		11*									
Oct 4	(h)	Oldham A	W 2-0	Whitehead, Crooks	9,351	1	2			5	6	4	8	9	10						7	3		11									
11	(a)	Blackburn R	W 1-0	Dyson	5,701	1	2			5		4	8	9	10		12	6			7	3*		11									
18	(h)	Grimsby T	D 1-1	Hopkins	8,851	1	2			5		4	8	9	10		6				3			11	7								
25	(a)	Portsmouth	L 1-2	Crooks	11,608	1	2	9*		5	6	4	12		10			8			3			11	7								
Nov 1	(h)	Birmingham C	W 3-2	Williamson 2, Crooks	15,329	1	2			5	6	4		9	10						3	8		11	7								
8	(a)	Sunderland	W 3-0	Dickinson, Crooks, Williamson	16,162	1	2			5	6	4		9	10		12				3	8*		11	7								
15	(a)	Plymouth A	L 0-1		14,697	1	2			5	6	4		9	10						3	8		11	7								
22	(h)	Millwall	L 0-1		8,035	1	2			5	6	4		9*	10			12			3	8		11	7								
29	(a)	Barnsley	D 2-2	Williamson, Crooks	5,750	1	2			5	6	4		9	10			12			3	8*		11	7								
Dec 6	(h)	Leeds U	W 3-0	Whitehead 2, Crooks	10,433	1	2			5	6	4		9	10						3	8		11	7								
12	(a)	Bradford C	W 3-1	Abbott (og), Williamson, Hopkins	4,580	1	2	12		5	6*	4		9	10						3	8		11	7								
19	(h)	Reading	L 1-2	Crooks	7,888	1	2			5	12	4		9	10						3	8*		11	7		6						
26	(a)	Shrewsbury T	L 0-1		9,281	1	2			5	6			10	9		12				3	8		11*	7			4					
27	(h)	Plymouth A	D 0-0		12,879	1	2			5	6			9	10*			12			3	8		11	7			4					
Jan 1	(h)	Crystal P	L 1-2	Hopkins	8,424	1	2			5	6*	4		10	9						3	8		11	7	12							
3	(a)	Sheffield U	D 1-1	Crooks	9,240	1	2	6		5		4		9	10						3			11	7	8							
24	(h)	Hull C	D 1-1	Reilly	6,785	1	2			5		4	8	10	7*						3	11				12			6	9			
Feb 7	(a)	Huddersfield T	L 1-2	Reilly	5,218	1	12			5		4	2	8*	10							11			7		3		6	9			
14	(h)	Stoke C	W 4-1	Crooks 2, Reilly 2 (1 pen)	12,452	1	4			5		2		10								8		11	7		3		6	9			
21	(a)	Derby C	D 1-1	Anderson	16,237	1	2			5				7							10	8		11			3	4	6	9			
28	(h)	Brighton & HA	D 0-0		8,395	1	2			5		8		7*							12	10		11			3	4	6	9			
Mar 3	(a)	Ipswich T	L 0-1		9,704	1	2			5		8		12							10*			11	7		3	4	6		9		
14	(a)	Grimsby T	L 1-3	Crooks	5,024	1		3		5		8		2							10			11	7			4	6	9			
21	(h)	Blackburn R	L 0-1		8,998	1	3	12		5		8		2	11						10				7			4	6	9*			
28	(a)	Oldham A	L 1-2	Bradley	6,944	1			4	5		2			11						3				7	10	6		12	8	9*		
Apr 4	(h)	Sunderland	D 2-2	Lynex, Bennett	6,198	1			6	5		2									3	11			7			4		9		10	8
12	(a)	Birmingham C	W 1-0	Reilly	11,158	1			4	5		2			11						3				7				6	9		10	8
18	(h)	Crystal P	D 1-1	Goodman	7,127	1				5		2			11						3				7			4	6	9		10	8
20	(a)	Shrewsbury T	L 1-2	Williamson	7,567	1				5		2*			11	9					3	12			7			4	6			10	8
25	(a)	Millwall	W 1-0	Williamson	3,912	1	2		4	5					9						3	6				11			7			10	8
29	(h)	Portsmouth	W 1-0	Hopkins	10,018	1	2		4	5	3				9							11			7				6			10	8
May 2	(h)	Barnsley	L 0-1		6,496	1	2	12	4	5	3			9*	7							11							6			10	8
4	(a)	Leeds U	L 2-3	Dyson, Burrows	24,688	1		3	4	5	2			7	11														6		9	10	8
9	(h)	Bradford C	D 2-2	Robson, Goodman	8,559	1	2	3	4	5				7							6	11									9	10	8
App						42	33	12	15	42	26	36	13	30	30	1	5	2	3	2	28	27	1	21	25	5	6	10	14	9	4	10	10
Sub app							1	3			1	1	1				1	2	4	2	3	1	1	1		2					1		
Goals							3	1	2	2	1	1	1	2	8	1			2		1			11	4				1	5	1	1	2

Barry Cowdrill and Paul Dyson in action against Birmingham City at St Andrew's on 12 April 1987. Martyn Bennett is the other Albion player.

Stuart Naylor was an ever-present in the Albion side in 1986-7 and was voted Player of the Year.

Albion's two post-war FA Cup-winning teams. Top: The side which beat Preston in 1954. Back row (left to right): Kennedy, Dugdale, Barlow, Sanders, Dudley, Millard, Lee. Front: Ryan, Allen, Griffin, Nicholls. Bottom: Albion's 1968 line-up which defeated Everton at Wembley. Back row (left to right): S.Williams (trainer), Astle, Talbut, Osborne, Kaye, Lovatt, Fraser. Front: Collard, T.Brown, G.Williams, A.Ashman (manager), Hope, Clark.

Albion in the FA Cup

1883-4
Round 1
Nov 10 v Wednesbury Town (h) 0-2
Roberts; H.Bell, Stanton, E.Horton, Bunn, Swallow, Whitehouse, Aston, Bisseker, Timmins, G.Bell.
Att: 5,129

1884-5
Round 1
Oct 25 v Junction Street School, Derby (a) 7-1
Bayliss 2, G.Bell 2, Aston 2, Loach
Roberts, H.Bell, H.Green, E.Horton, Bunn, Stanton, Woodall, Aston, Bayliss, Loach, G.Bell.
Att: 4,000
Round 2
Dec 6 v Wednesbury Old Athletic (h) 4-2
Aston 2, Woodhall, Taylor (og)
Roberts, J.Horton, H.Green, E.Horton, Bunn, Stanton, Woodhall, Aston, Bayliss, Loach, G.Bell.
Att: 4,497
Round 3
Jan 3 v Aston Villa (a) 0-0
Roberts, H.Bell, H.Green, E.Horton, Bunn, Stanton, Woodhall, Aston, Bayliss, Loach, G.Bell.
Att: 22,088
Replay
Jan 10 v Aston Villa (h) 3-0
Loach 2, Bayliss
Roberts, H.Bell, H.Green, E.Horton, Bunn, Stanton, Woodhall, Aston, Bayliss, Loach, G.Bell.
Att: 10,021
Round 4
Jan 24 v Druids (h) 1-0
Loach
Roberts, H.Bell, H.Green, E.Horton, Bunn, Stanton, Woodhall, Aston, Bayliss, Loach, G.Bell.
Att: 5,537
Round 5
Albion received a bye
Round 6
Feb 21 v Blackburn Rovers (h) 0-2
Matthews; H.Bell, H.Green, E.Horton, Bunn, Timmins, Woodhall, Aston, Bayliss, Loach, G.Bell.
Att: 16,393

1885-6
Round 1
Oct 31 v Aston Unity (h) 4-1
T.Green 2, Woodhall 2
Roberts; H.Green, H.Bell, E.Horton, Bunn, Timmins, Woodhall, T.Green, Bayliss, Loach, G.Bell.
Att: 4,027
Round 2
Nov 21 v Wednesbury Old Athletc (h) 3-2
Loach 2, G.Bell
Roberts; H.Green, H.Bell, E.Horton, Bushell, Timmins, Woodhall, T.Green, Bayliss, Loach, G.Bell.
Att: 3,578
Round 3
Albion received a bye
Round 4
Jan 2 v Wolverhampton Wanderers (h) 3-1
G.Bell, T.Green, Loach
Roberts; H.Green, H.Bell, E.Horton, Bunn, Timmins, Woodhall, Bayliss, T.Green, Loach, G.Bell.
Att: 5,196
Round 5
Jan 23 v Old Carthusians (h) 1-0
T.Green
Roberts; H.Green, H.Bell, E.Horton, Bunn, Timmins, Woodhall, Bayliss, T.Green, Loach, G.Bell.
Att: 8,137

Round 6
Feb 13 v Old Westminsters (h) 6-0
Bayliss 3, G.Bell 2, Woodhall
Roberts; H.Green, H.Bell, E.Horton, Bunn, Timmins, Woodhall, Bayliss, T.Green, Loach, G.Bell.
Att: 5,884
Semi-final
Mar 6 v Small Heath (at Aston) 4-0
Loach 2, Woodhall 2
Roberts; H.Green, H.Bell, E.Horton, Bunn, Timmins, Woodhall, Bayliss, T.Green, Loach, G.Bell.
Att: 4,100

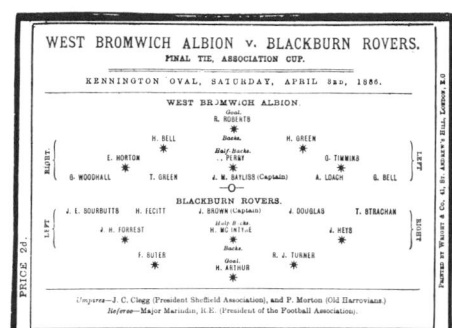

Programme from Albion's first appearance in an FA Cup Final. The 1886 match was replayed at Derby where the Throstles lost to Blackburn.

Final
Apr 3 v Blackburn Rovers (at The Oval) 0-0
Roberts; H.Green, H.Bell, E.Horton, C.Perry, Timmins, Woodhall, T.Green, Bayliss, Loach, G.Bell.
Att: 15,156
Replay
Apr 10 v Blackburn Rovers (at Derby) 0-2
Roberts; H.Green, H.Bell, E.Horton, C.Perry, Timmins, Woodhall, T.Green, Bayliss, Loach, G.Bell.
Att: 16,144

1886-7
Round 1
Oct 30 v Burton Wanderers (home) 6-0
T.Green 2, Bayliss 2, Holden, Paddock
Roberts; Aldridge, H.Green, E.Horton, C.Perry, Timmins, Woodhall, T.Green, Bayliss, Holden, W.Paddock.
Att: 5,107
Round 2
Nov 20 v Derby Junction (a) 2-1
G.Bell, Roberts*
Roberts; Aldridge, Walker, E.Horton, J.Horton, Bayliss, Woodhall, Holden, T.Green, W Paddock, G.Bell.
Att: 2,100
* 'Roberts, the goalkeeper, punted the ball downfield and, following a scrimmage in the Derby goalmouth, the ball suddenly passed between the posts.'
Round 3
Albion received a bye
Round 4
Jan 15 v Mitchell's St George (at Aston) 1-0
T.Green
Roberts; H.Green, Aldridge, E.Horton, C.Perry, Timmins, Woodhall, Holden, Bayliss, T.Green, W.Paddock.
Att: 4,061
Round 5
Jan 29 v Lockwood Brothers, Sheffield (a) 1-0*
Woodhall
Roberts; H.Green, Aldridge, E.Horton, C.Perry, Timmins, Woodhall, T.Green, Bayliss, Holden, W.Paddock.
Att: 6,029
* Following a protest about the goal, the tie was replayed as follows:
Feb 12 v Lockwood Brothers, Sheffield (at Derby) 2-1
T.Green, Paddock
Roberts; Aldridge, H.Green, E.Horton, C.Perry, Timmins, Woodhall, Holden, Bayliss, T.Green, W.Paddock.
Att: 2,120
Round 6
Feb 19 v Notts County (a) 4-1
Bayliss 2, T.Green, Woodhall
Roberts; Aldridge, H.Green, E.Horton, C.Perry, Timmins, Woodhall, T.Green, Bayliss, Pearson, W.Paddock.
Att: 15,067

Although subsequently 'retouched' this is the earliest photograph of an FA Cup Final. It shows Albion's 'Jem' Bayliss heading towards the Villa goal in the 1887 Final at The Oval. Warner is the Villa goalkeeper and note he is also wearing a striped shirt.

Semi-final
Mar 5 v Preston North End (at Nottingham) 3-1
Pearson 2, Paddock
Roberts; Aldridge, H.Green, E.Horton, C.Perry, Timmins, Woodhall, T.Green, Bayliss, Pearson, W.Paddock.
Att: 16,068
Final
Apr 2 v Aston Villa (at The Oval) 0-2
Roberts; Aldridge, H.Green, E.Horton, C.Perry, Timmins, Woodhall, T.Green, Bayliss, Pearson, W.Paddock.
Att: 15,534

1887-8
Round 1
Oct 15 v Wednesbury Old Athletic (h) 7-1
Bayliss 3, Wilson 2, Pearson, Horton
Roberts; Aldridge, H.Green, E.Horton, C.Perry, Timmins, Woodhall, Bassett, Bayliss, Wilson, Pearson.
Att: 2,484
Round 2
Nov 5 v Mitchell's St George (a) 1-0
Bayliss
Roberts; Aldridge, H.Green, E.Horton, C.Perry, Timmins, Woodhall, Bassett, Bayliss, Pearson, Wilson.
Att: 7,800
Round 3
Nov 26 v Wolverhampton Wanderers (h) 2-0
Bassett, Wilson
Roberts; Aldridge, H.Green, E.Horton, C.Perry, Timmins, Bassett, Woodhall, Bayliss, Askin, Wilson.
Att: 7,429
Round 4
Albion received a bye
Round 5
Jan 7 v Stoke (h) 4-1
Bayliss 4
Roberts; Aldridge, H.Green, E.Horton, C.Perry, Timmins, Woodhall, Bassett, Bayliss, Pearson, Wilson.
Att: 9,093
Round 6
Jan 28 v Old Carthusians (h) 4-2
Pearson 2, Wilson 2
Roberts; Aldridge, H.Green, E.Horton, C.Perry, Timmins, Bassett, Woodhall, Bayliss, Pearson, Wilson.
Att: 8,818
Semi-final
Feb 18 v Derby Junction (at Stoke) 3-0
Bayliss, Wilson, Woodhall
Roberts; Aldridge, H.Green, E.Horton, C.Perry, Timmins, Bassett, Woodhall, Bayliss, Pearson, Wilson.
Att: 5,996
Final
Mar 24 v Preston North End (at The Oval) 2-1
Bayliss, Woodhall
Roberts; Aldridge, H.Green, E.Horton, C.Perry, Timmins, Woodhall, Bassett, Bayliss, Pearson, Wilson.
Att: 18,904

PLAYER'S CIGARETTES
ASSOCIATION CUP WINNERS WEST BROMWICH ALBION, 1888

1888-9
Round 1
Feb 2 v Small Heath (a) 3-2
W.Perry, Wilson, Pearson
Roberts; Robinson, H.Green, E.Horton, C.Perry, Timmins, Bassett, W.Perry, Bayliss, Pearson, Wilson.
Att: 3,034
Round 2
Feb 16 v Burnley (h) 5-1
Bayliss 2, Bassett, Wilson, W.Perry
Roberts; Robinson, H.Green, E.Horton, C.Perry, Timmins, Bassett, W.Perry, Bayliss, Pearson, Wilson.
Att: 5,104
Round 3
Mar 2 v Chatham (a) 10-1
Wilson 3, Bayliss 2, Bassett 2, Timmins, W.Perry, Conquer (og)
Roberts; J.Horton, H.Green, E.Horton, C.Perry, Timmins, Bassett, W.Perry, Bayliss, Pearson, Wilson.
Att: 17,000
Semi-final
Mar 16 v Preston North End (at Sheffield) 0-1
Roberts; Robinson, H.Green, E.Horton, C.Perry, Timmins, Bassett, W.Perry, Bayliss, Pearson, Wilson.
Att: 22,688

1889-90
Round 1
Jan 18 v Accrington (a) 1-3*
Wilson
Roberts; J.Horton, H.Green, E.Horton, C.Perry, J.Nicholls, Bassett, Bayliss, Evans, Pearson, Wilson.
Att: 3,400
* Albion protested about the ground and the tie was replayed as follows:
Jan 25 v Accrington (a) 0-3
Roberts; J.Horton, Powell, E.Horton, C.Perry, J.Nicholls, Bassett, Bayliss, Evans, Pearson, Wilson.
Att: 5,300

1890-91
Round 1
Albion received a bye
Round 2
Jan 31 v Mitchell's St George (a) 3-0
Nicholls, Dyer, C.Perry
Reader; J.Horton, Powell, Bayliss, C.Perry, Dyer, Woodhall, S.Nicholls, Groves, Pearson, J.Burns.
Att: 7,000
Round 3
Feb 14 v Sheffield Wednesday (a) 2-0
Groves, Pearson
Reader; Powell, McCulloch, Bayliss, C.Perry, Dyer, Bassett, S.Nicholls, Groves, Pearson, McLeod.
Att: 16,871
Semi-final
Feb 28 v Blackburn Rovers (at Stoke) 2-3
Groves, Pearson
Reader; Robinson, Powell, Bayliss, C.Perry, Dyer, Bassett, S.Nicholls, Groves, Pearson, J.Burns.
Att: 21,774

1891-2
Round 1
Jan 16 v Old Westminsters (a) 3-2
McLeod, Pearson, Reynolds
Reader; Nicholson, McCulloch, Reynolds, C.Perry, Dyer, Bassett, McLeod, Groves, Pearson, Geddes.
Att: 10,000
Round 2
Jan 30 v Blackburn Rovers (h) 3-1
Pearson 2, Geddes
Reader; Nicholson, McCulloch, Reynolds, C.Perry, Dyer, Bassett, McLeod, S.Nicholls, Pearson, Geddes.
Att: 12,135
Round 3
Feb 13 v Sheffield Wednesday (h) 2-1
C.Perry, Nicholls
Reader; Nicholson, McCulloch, Reynolds, C.Perry, Dyer, Bassett, McLeod, S.Nicholls, Pearson, Geddes.
Att: 10,477

158

Semi-final
Feb 27 v Nottingham Forest (at Molineux) 1-1
Geddes
Reader; Nicholson, McCulloch, Reynolds, C.Perry, Groves, Bassett, McLeod, S.Nicholls, Pearson, Geddes.
Att: 21,076
Replay
Mar 5 v Nottingham Forest (at Molineux) 1-1
Bassett
Reader; Nicholson, McCulloch, Reynolds, C.Perry, Groves, Bassett, S.Nicholls, Bayliss, Pearson, Geddes.
Att: 15,930
Second replay
Mar 9 v Nottingham Forest (at Derby) 6-2
Geddes 3, Bassett, Groves, Perry
Reader; Nicholson, McCulloch, Reynolds, C.Perry, Groves, Bassett, McLeod, S.Nicholls, Pearson, Geddes.
Att: 8,024
Final
Mar 19 v Aston Villa (at The Oval) 3-0
Geddes, Nicholls, Reynolds
Reader; Nicholson, McCulloch, Reynolds, C.Perry, Groves, Bassett, McLeod, S.Nicholls, Pearson, Geddes.
Att: 32,710

PLAYER'S CIGARETTES
ASSOCIATION CUP WINNERS WEST BROMWICH ALBION, 1892

1892-3
Round 1
Jan 21 v Everton (a) 1-4
Pearson
Reader; McCulloch, J.Horton, T.Perry, C.Perry. Groves, Bassett, McLeod, Boyd, Pearson, Geddes.
Att: 23,867

1893-4
Round 1
Jan 27 v Blackburn Rovers (h) 2-3
McLeod 2
Reader; Nicholson, Crone, T.Perry, C.Perry, Taggart, Bassett, McLeod, Neale, Williams, Geddes.
Att: 10,243

1894-5
Round 1
Feb 2 v Small Heath (a) 2-1
McLeod, Banks
Reader; C.Perry, Williams, T.Perry, Higgins, Taggart, Bassett, McLeod, W.Richards, Hutchinson, Banks.
Att: 10,203
Round 2
Feb 16 v Sheffield United (a) 1-1
Bassett
Reader; C.Perry, Williams, T.Perry, Higgins, Taggart, Bassett, McLeod, W.Richards, Hutchinson, Banks.
Att: 14,559
Replay
Feb 20 v Sheffield United (h) 2-1
Hutchinson, Foulke (og)
Reader; C.Perry, Williams, T.Perry, Higgins, Taggart, Bassett, McLeod, W.Richards, Hutchinson, Banks.
Att: 10,025

Round 3
Mar 2 v Wolverhampton Wanderers (h) 1-0
McLeod
Reader; C.Perry, Williams, T.Perry, Higgins, Taggart, Bassett, McLeod, Hutchinson, W.Richards, Banks.
Att: 20,977
Semi-final
Mar 16 v Sheffield Wednesday (at Derby) 2-0
Hutchinson, Williams (pen)
Reader; C.Perry, Williams, T.Perry, Higgins, Taggart, Bassett, McLeod, W.Richards, Hutchinson, Banks.
Att: 25,013
Final
Apr 20 v Aston Villa (at The Crystal Palace) 0-1
Reader; J.Horton, Williams, T.Perry, Higgins, Taggart, Bassett, McLeod, W.Richards, Hutchinson, Banks.
Att: 42,652

1895-6
Round 1
Feb 1 v Blackburn Rovers (a) 2-1
J.Richards, W.Richards
Reader; J.Horton, Williams, T.Perry, Higgins, Taggart, Bassett, McLeod, Hutchinson, W.Richards, J.Richards.
Att: 10,035
Round 2
Feb 15 v Grimsby Town (a) 1-1
McLeod
Reader; J.Horton, Williams, T.Perry, Higgins, Taggart, Bassett, McLeod, Hutchinson, W.Richards, J.Richards.
Att: 7,108
Replay
Feb 20 v Grimsby Town (h) 3-0
McLeod, W.Richards 2
Reader; J.Horton, Williams, T.Perry, Higgins, Taggart, Bassett, McLeod, Hutchinson, W.Richards, Johnson.
Att: 8,443
Round 3
Feb 29 v Derby County (a) 0-1
Reader; J.Horton, Williams, T.Perry, Higgins, Taggart, Bassett, McLeod, Hutchinson, W.Richards, Banks.
Att: 14,117

1896-7
Round 1
Jan 30 v Luton Town (a) 1-0
Flewitt
Reader; J.Horton, Williams, T.Perry, Higgins, Banks, McLeod, Flewitt, Cameron, W.Richards, Watson.
Att: 6,898
Round 2
Feb 13 v Liverpool (h) 1-2
Watson
Reader; Evans, Williams, T.Perry, Higgins, Banks, Dean, Flewitt, Cameron, W.Richards, Watson.
Att: 16,147

1897-8
Round 1
Jan 29 v New Brighton Tower (h) 2-0
Garfield, Flewitt
Reader; Cave, Williams, T.Perry, Jones, Banks, Bassett, Flewitt, W.Richards, McKenzie, Garfield.
Att: 15,897
Round 2
Feb 12 v Sheffield Wednesday (h) 1-0
Flewitt
Reader; Cave, Williams, T.Perry, Jones, Banks, Bassett, Flewitt, Reid, McKenzie, Garfield.
Att: 16,012
Round 3
Feb 26 v Nottingham Forest (h) 2-3
Williams, Bassett
Reader; Cave, Williams, T.Perry, Jones, Banks, Bassett, Flewitt, Reid, McKenzie, Garfield.
Att: 17,483

1898-9
Round 1
Jan 28 v South Shore, Blackpool (h) 8-0
Bassett 3, Jones 2, W.Richards, Garfield, Barrow (og)
Reader; Cave, Williams, T.Perry, Jones, Dunn, Bassett, Simmons, Flewitt, W.Richards, Garfield.
Att: 5,870
Round 2
Feb 11 v Bury (h) 2-1
W.Richards 2
Reader; Cave, Williams, T.Perry, Jones, Dunn, Bassett, Simmons, Flewitt, W.Richards, Garfield.
Att: 14,094
Round 3
Feb 25 v Liverpool (h) 0-2
Reader; Cave, Williams, T.Perry, Jones, Dunn, Bassett, Simmons, Richards, McKenzie, Garfield.
Att: 17,124

1899-1900
Round 1
Jan 27 v Walsall (a) 1-1
Roberts
Reader; Adam, Williams, Dunn, Jones, Hadley, S.Brett, T.Perry, Simmons, W.Richards, Roberts.
Att: 9,106

Replay
Feb 1 v Walsall (h) 6-1
Jones 2, Brett, Roberts, Richards, Simmons
Reader; Adams, Williams, Dunn, Jones, Hadley, S.Brett, T.Perry, Simmons, W.Richards, Roberts.
Att: 4,892
Round 2
Feb 17 v Liverpool (a) 1-1
Simmons
Reader; Adams, Williams, Dunn, Jones, Hadley, Chadburn, T.Perry, Simmons, W.Richards, Roberts.
Att: 15,116
Replay
Feb 21 v Liverpool (h) 2-1
Dunn, Chadburn
Reader; Adams, Williams, Dunn, Jones, Hadley, Chadburn, T.Perry, Simmons, W.Richards, Roberts.
Att: 8,994
Round 3
Feb 24 v Southampton (a) 1-2
Simmons
Reader; Adams, Williams, Dunn, Jones, Hadley, Chadburn, T.Perry, Simmons, W.Richards, Roberts.
Att: 10,067

1900-01
Round 1
Jan 26 v Manchester City (h) 1-0
Garfield
Reader; Adams, Chadburn, T.Perry, G.Williams, Hadley, Roberts, Simmons, Stevenson, Wheldon, Garfield.
Att: 10,026
The above was the first FA Cup match to be played at The Hawthorns.
Round 2
Feb 23 v Woolwich Arsenal (a) 1-0
Garfield
Reader; Adams, Chadburn, T.Perry, G.Williams, Hadley, Roberts, Simmons, Stevenson, Wheldon, Garfield.
Att: 11,024
Round 3
Mar 23 v Middlesbrough (a) 1-0
Buck
Reader; Adams, Dunn, T.Perry, Jones, Hadley, Roberts, Buck, Stevenson, Smith, Walker.
Att: 24,769
Semi-final
Apr 8 v Tottenham Hotspur (at Villa Park) 0-4
Reader; Adams, Dunn, T.Perry, Jones, Hadley, Roberts, Smith, Stevenson, Wheldon, Walker.
Att: 34,979

159

1901-02
Round 1
Jan 25 v Bury (a) 1-5
Simmons
Webb; Kifford, Adams, Nurse, Stevenson, Hadley, McLean, Simmons, Lee, Worton, G.Dorsett.
Att: 5,622
1902-03
Round 1
Feb 7 v Tottenham Hotspur (a) 0-0
Webb; Kifford, Adams, Nurse, Stevenson, Hadley, McLean, Buck, Lee, Worton, G.Dorsett.
Att: 26,125
Replay
Feb 11 v Tottenham Hotspur (h) 0-2
Webb; Kifford, Adams, Nurse, Stevenson, Hadley, McLean, Elmore, Lee, Worton, G.Dorsett.
Att: 32,097

Albion's Jim Stevenson (centre) heads clear during the goalless FA Cup match at Tottenham in February 1903.

1903-04
Round 1
Feb 6 v Nottingham Forest (h) 1-1
Simmons
Webb; Adams, Pennington, Randle, Stevenson, Hadley, A.Smith, Simmons, Lee, Hobson, G.Dorsett.
Att: 10,367
Replay
Feb 13 v Nottingham Forest (a) 1-3
Smith
Webb; Adams, Pennington, Randle, Stevenson, Hadley, A.Smith, Simmons, Lee, Hobson, G.Dorsett.
Att: 15,084

1904-05
Intermediate Round
Jan 14 v Leicester Fosse (h) 2-5
Aston*, Pheasant
Cook; Pennington, Brittain, Randle, Pheasant, Manners, Bell, W.Smith, Jack, Aston, H.Brown.
Att: 5,230
* Some reports give Smith as the scorer.

1905-06
Round 1
Jan 13 v Everton (a) 1-3
Haywood
Stringer; Williams, Pennington, Randle, Pheasant, Manners, Bradley, Simmons, Shilton, Haywood, Law.
Att: 18,023

1906-07
Round 1
Jan 13 v Everton (a) 1-3
Haywood
Stringer; Williams, Pennington, Randle, Pheasant, Manners, Bradley, Simmons, Shinton, Haywood, Law.
Att: 18,023
Jan 17 v Stoke (a) 2-2 (a.e.t.)
Rankin, Randle
Stringer; Betteley, Pennington, Randle, Pheasant, Manners, Broad, Buck, Shinton, Dilly, Rankin.
Att: 13,545
Second replay
Jan 21 v Stoke (at Villa Park) 2-0
Pheasant, Dilly (pen)
Stringer; Adams, Pennington, Randle, Pheasant, Manners, Broad, Buck, Bradley, Dilly, Rankin.
Att: 32,050

Round 2
Feb 2 v Norwich City (h) 1-0
Simmons
Stringer; Betteley, Pennington, Randle, Pheasant, Manners, Broad, Simmons, Shinton, Dilly, Perkins.
Att: 25,388
Round 3
Feb 23 v Derby County (h) 2-0
Jordan, Buck
Stringer; Betteley, Pennington, Randle, Pheasant, Manners, J.Williams, Buck, Jordan, Haywood, Dilly.
Att: 35,529
Round 4
Mar 9 v Notts County (h) 3-1
Jordan 2, Buck
Stringer; J.Williams, Pennington, Randle, Pheasant, Manners, Parkes, Buck, Jordan, Haywood, Dilly.
Att: 27,474
Semi-final
Mar 23 v Everton (at Bolton) 1-2
Haywood
Stringer; J.Williams, Pennington, Randle, Pheasant, Manners, Parkes, Buck, Jordan, Haywood, Dilly.
Att: 32,381.

1907-08
Round 1
Jan 11 v Birmingham (h) 1-1
Wilcox
Stringer; Pennington, Evans, Young, Pheasant, Timmins, Garratt, Buck, Wilcox, Walker, Brookes.
Att: 36,727
Replay
Jan 15 v Birmingham (a) 2-1
Wilcox, Jordan
Pearson; Pennington, Evans, Young, Pheasant, Manners, Parkes, Buck, Wilcox, Jordan, Walker.
Att: 24,895
Round 2
Feb 1 v Southampton (a) 0-1
Pearson; Pennington, Evans, Young, Pheasant, Manners, Parkes, Wilcox, Wright, Walker, Buck.
Att: 18,728

1908-09
Round 1
Jan 16 v Bolton Wanderers (h) 3-1
Garraty, Harris (pen), Buck
Stringer; Pennington, Harris, Baddeley, Timmins, Manners, Thompson, Buck, Garraty, Bowser, Davies.
Att: 19,164
Round 2
Feb 6 v Bradford City (h) 1-2
Garraty
Stringer; Pennington, Harris, Baddeley, Timmins, Manners, Thompson, Buck, Garraty, Bowser, Davies.
Att: 32,105

1909-10
Round 1
Jan 15 v Clapton Orient (h) 2-0
Pailor 2
Stringer; Burton, Pennington, Garraty, Timmins, Manners, Davies, Hewitt, Pailor, Bowser, Simpson.
Att: 7,339
Round 2
Feb 5 v Bristol City (a) 1-1
Pailor
Pearson; Burton, Pennington, Garraty, Waterhouse, Manners, Hewitt, Bowser, Pailor, Buck, Simpson.
Att: 16,885
Replay
Feb 9 v Bristol City (h) 4-2
Hewitt 2, Pailor, Simpson
Pearson; Burton, Pennington, Garraty, Waterhouse, Manners, Hewitt, Bowser, Pailor, Buck, Simpson.
Att: 14,870
Round 3
Feb 19 v Barnsley (a) 0-1
Pearson; Burton, Pennington, Garraty, Waterhouse, Manners, Hewitt, Bowser, Pailor, Buck, Simpson.
Att: 19,121

1910-11
Round 1
Jan 14 v Fulham (h) 4-1
Bowser 2, Wollaston, Lloyd
Pearson; Smith, Pennington, Baddeley, Waterhouse, McNeal, Wollaston, Bowser, Pailor, Buck, Lloyd.
Att: 18,034
Round 2
Feb 4 v Derby County (a) 0-2
Pearson; Smith, Pennington, Baddeley, Waterhouse, McNeal, Thompson, Bowser, Pailor, Buck, Simpson.
Att: 20,242

1911-12
Round 1
Jan 13 v Tottenham Hotspur (h) 3-0
Bowser, Deacey, Wright
Pearson; Cook, Pennington, Baddeley, Buck, McNeal, Jephcott, Wright, Deacey, Bowser, Shearman.
Att: 21,947

Round 2
Feb 3 v Leeds City (a) 1-0
Bowser
Pearson; Cook, Pennington, Baddeley, Buck, McNeal, Jephcott, Wright, Pailor, Bowser, Shearman.
Att: 21,320
Round 3
Feb 21 v Sunderland (a) 2-1
Pailor 2
Pearson; Pennington, Cook, Baddeley, Buck, McNeal, Jephcott, Wright, Pailor, Bowser, Shearman.
Att: 43,383
Round 4
Mar 9 v Fulham (h) 3-0
Bowser 2, Wright
Pearson; Cook, Pennington, Baddeley, Buck, McNeal, Jephcott, Wright, Pailor, Bowser, Shearman.
Att: 41,880
Semi-final
Mar 30 v Blackburn Rovers (at Liverpool) 0-0
Pearson; Pennington, Cook, Baddeley, Buck, McNeal, Jephcott, Wright, Pailor, Bowser, Shearman.
Att: 30,063

Replay
Apr 3 v Blackburn Rovers (at Sheffield) 1-0 (a.e.t.)
Pailor
Pearson; Pennington, Cook, Baddeley, Buck, McNeal, Jephcott, Wright, Pailor, Allan, Shearman.
Att: 20,050
Final
Apr 20 v Barnsley (at The Crystal Palace) 0-0 (a.e.t.)
Pearson; Cook, Pennington, Baddeley, Buck, McNeal, Jephcott, Wright, Pailor, Bowser, Shearman.
Att: 55,213
Replay
Apr 24 v Barnsley (at Sheffield) 0-1 (a.e.t.)
Pearson; Cook, Pennington, Baddeley, Buck, McNeal, Jephcott, Wright, Pailor, Bowser, Shearman.
Att: 38,555

Albion's 1912 FA Cup Final side. Players only (back row, left to right): G.Baddeley, H.Pearson, S.Bowser, R.Pailor. Seated: A.Cook, J.Pennington, R.McNeal, F.Buck. On ground: C.Jephcott, B.Shearman, H.Wright.

1912-13
Round 1
Jan 13 v West Ham United (h) 1-1
Wright
Moorwood; Smith, Cook, Waterhouse, Buck, McNeal, Jephcott, Morris, Wright, Bowser, Shearman.
Att: 19,958
Replay
Jan 16 v West Ham United (a) 2-2 (a.e.t.)
Gregory, Bowser
Moorwood; Smith, Cook, Waterhouse, Buck, McNeal, Jephcott, Gregory, Morris, Bowser, Shearman.
Att: 14,762
Second replay
Jan 22 v West Ham United (at Chelsea) 0-3
Moorwood; Smith, Cook, Waterhouse, Buck, McNeal, Jephcott, Gregory, Morris, Bowser, Shearman.
Att: 26,689

1913-14
Round 1
Jan 10 v Grimsby Town (h) 2-0
Edwards, Morris
Pearson; Smith, Pennington, Waterhouse, Buck, McNeal, Jephcott, Edwards, Bentley, Morris, Shearman
Att: 13,976

Round 2
Jan 31 v Leeds City (a) 2-0
Bentley, Jephcott
Pearson; Smith, Pennington, Waterhouse, Buck, McNeal, Jephcott, Morris, Bentley, Lewis, Shearman.
Att: 29,733
Round 3
Feb 21 v Aston Villa (a) 1-2
Bowser
Pearson; Smith, Pennington, Waterhouse, Buck, McNeal, Jephcott, Bowser, Bache, Bentley, Shearman.
Att: 57,293

1914-15
Round 1
Jan 9 v Hull City (a) 0-1
Pearson; Smith, Pennington, Waterhouse, Bowser, McNeal, Jephcott, Crisp, Bache, Morris, Shearman.
Att: 12,142

1919-20
Round 1
Jan 10 v Barnsley (a) 0-1
Pearson; Smith, Pennington, Richardson, Bowser, McNeal, Crisp, Magee, Bentley, Morris, Gregory.
Att: 32,327

1920-21
Round 1
Jan 8 v Notts County (a) 0-3
Pearson; Smith, Cook, Richardson, Bowser, McNeal, Crisp, Bentley, A.W.Smith, Morris, Gregory.
Att: 32,995

1921-2
Round 1
Jan 7 v Chelsea (a) 4-2
Blagden 2, Davies, Crisp
Pearson; Smith, Pennington, Richardson, Reed, McNeal, Magee, Blagden, Davies, Morris, Crisp.
Att: 36,365
Round 2
Jan 28 v Liverpool (a) 1-0
Davies
Pearson; Smith, Pennington, Richardson, Reed, Bowser, Magee, Blagden, Davies, Morris, Crisp.
Att: 42,118
Round 3
Feb 18 v Notts County (h) 1-1
Davies (pen)
Pearson; Smith, Pennington, Richardson, Reed, McNeal, Magee, Blagden, Davies, Morris, Crisp.
Att: 43,853
Replay
Feb 22 v Notts County (a) 0-2
Pearson; Smith, Pennington, Richardson, Reed, McNeal, Magee, Blagden, Davies, Morris, Crisp.
Att: 24,278

1922-3
Round 1
Jan 13 v Stalybridge Celtic (h) 0-0
Pearson; Smith, Adams, Magee, Bowser, McNeal, Spencer, Jones, Davies, Morris, Gregory.
Att: 24,008
Replay
Jan 17 v Stalybridge Celtic (a) 2-0
Davies, Morris
Pearson; Smith, Adams, Magee, Bowser, McNeal, Spencer, Jones, Davies, Morris, Gregory.
Att: 9,753
Round 2
Feb 3 v Sunderland (h) 2-1
Morris, Jones
Pearson; Smith, Adams, Magee, Bowser, McNeal, Spencer, Jones, Davies, Morris, Gregory.
Att: 56,474
Round 3
Feb 24 v Charlton Athletic (a) 0-1
Pearson; Smith, Adams, Magee, Bowser, McNeal, Spencer, Jones, Davies, Morris, Gregory.
Att: 31,489

1923-4
Round 1
Jan 12 v Millwall (a) 1-0
Carter
Ashmore; Smith, Perry, Magee, Reed, McNeal, Glidden, Carter, Bowser, Morris, Fitton.
Att: 30,922
Round 2
Feb 2 v The Corinthians (h) 5-0
Morris, Reed, Carter, Davies 2 (1 pen)
Ashmore; Smith, Perry, Richardson, Reed, McNeal, Spencer, Carter, Davies, Morris, Gregory.
Att: 49,005
Round 3
Feb 23 v Wolverhampton Wanderers (h) 1-1
Wilson
Ashmore; Smith, Perry, Richardson, Reed, McNeal, Spencer, Carter, G.James, Wilson, Gregory.
Att: 53,649
Replay
Feb 27 v Wolverhampton Wanderers (a) 2-0
Wilson, Gregory
Ashmore; Smith, Perry, Richardson, Reed, Dutton, Spencer, Morris, G.James, Wilson, Gregory.
Att: 40,283
Round 4
Mar 8 v Aston Villa (h) 0-2
Ashmore; Smith, Perry, Magee, Reed, McNeal, Davies, Wilson, G.James, Morris, Gregory.
Att: 43,743

1924-5
Round 1
Jan 10 v Luton Town (h) 4-1
James 3, Wilson
Ashmore; Smith, Perry, Magee, Reed, Richardson, Glidden, Carter. James, Wilson, Byers.
Att: 30,287
Round 2
Jan 31 v Preston North End (h) 2-0
James, Wilson
Ashmore; Smith, Perry, Magee, Reed, Richardson, Glidden, Carter, James, Wilson, Byers.
Att: 39,752
Round 3
Feb 21 v Aston Villa (h) 1-1
Carter
Ashmore; Smith, Baugh, Magee, Reed, Richardson, Glidden, Carter, James, Wilson, Byers.
Att: 64,612
Replay
Feb 25 v Aston Villa (a) 2-1
Gregory, James
Ashmore; Smith, Baugh, Magee, Reed, Richardson, Glidden, Carter, James, Gregory, Byers.
Att: 60,015
Round 4
Mar 7 v Sheffield United (a) 0-2
Ashmore; Smith, Baugh, Magee, Reed, Richardson, Glidden, Carter, James, Wilson, Byers.
Att: 57,197

1925-6
Round 3
Jan 9 v Bristol City (h) 4-1
Glidden 2 (1 pen), Carter, Byers
Ashmore; Smith, Adams, Magee, Reed, Dutton, Glidden, Carter, James, Davies, Byers.
Att: 33,293
Round 4
Jan 29 v Aston Villa (h) 1-2
Carter
Ashmore; Baugh, Adams, Richardson, Reed, Dutton, Glidden, Carter, James, Wilson, Byers.
Att: 52,160

1926-7
Round 3
Jan 8 v Hull City (a) 1-2
Howarth
Ashmore; Ashurst, G.Shaw, Magee, Rooke, Howarth, Glidden, Carter, Short, Davies, Fitton.
Att: 24,909

1927-8
Round 3
Jan 14 v Arsenal (a) 0-2
Ashmore; Finch, Shaw, Magee, Evans, Howarth, Taylor, Glidden, Cookson, Short, Fitton.
Att: 41,298

1928-9
Round 3
Jan 12 v Grimsby Town (a) 1-1
Cookson
Ashmore; Finch, Shaw, Magee, W.Richardson, Dale, Glidden, Carter, Cookson, Chambers, Wood.
Att: 12,516
Replay
Jan 16 v Grimsby Town (h) 2-0
Cookson, Chambers
Ashmore; Finch, Shaw, Magee, W.Richardson, Dale, Glidden, Carter, Cookson, Chambers, Wood.
Att: 20,381
Round 4
Jan 26 v Middlesbrough (h) 1-0
Cookson
Ashmore; Finch, Shaw, Magee, W.Richardson, Darnell, Glidden, Carter, Cookson, Chambers, Wood.
Att: 33,466
Round 5
Feb 16 v Bradford (h) 6-0
Cookson 4 Glidden, Carter
Ashmore; Finch, Shaw, Magee, W.Richardson, Darnell, Glidden, Carter, Cookson, Chambers, Wood.
Att: 30,307
Round 6
Mar 2 v Huddersfield Town (h) 1-1
Glidden
Ashmore; Finch, Shaw, Magee, W.Richardson, Darnell, Glidden, Carter, Cookson, Chambers, Wood.
Att: 52,333
Replay
Mar 6 v Huddersfield Town (a) 1-2
Wood
Ashmore; Finch, Shaw, Magee, W.Richardson, Darnell, Glidden, Carter, Cookson, Chambers, Wood.
Att: 36,779

1929-30
Round 3
Jan 11 v Wrexham (a) 0-1
Ashmore; Finch, Shaw, W.Richardson, Evans, Darnell, Glidden, Carter, Cookson, Cresswell, Wood.
Att: 16,570

1930-31
Round 3
Jan 10 v Charlton Athletic (h) 2-2
Wood, Sandford
Pearson; Shaw, Trentham, Magee, W.Richardson, Edwards, Glidden, Carter, W.G.Richardson, Sandford, Wood.
Att: 27,249
Replay
Jan 14 v Charlton Athletic (a) 1-1 (a.e.t.)
Carter
Pearson; Shaw, Trentham, Magee, W.Richardson, Edwards, Glidden, Carter, W.G.Richardson, Sandford, Wood.
Att: 18,703
Second replay
Jan 19 v Charlton Athletic (at Villa Park) 3-1
Carter, Wood, W.G.Richardson
Ashmore; Shaw, Trentham, Magee, W.Richardson, Edwards, Glidden, Carter, W.G.Richardson, Sandford, Wood.
Att: 27,764

Spurs goalkeeper Spiers punches clear from Albion's Tommy Glidden in the fourth round tie at The Hawthorns in January 1931.

Round 4
Jan 24 v Tottenham Hotspur (h) 1-0
Wood
Pearson; Shaw, Trentham, Magee, W.Richardson, Edwards, Glidden, Carter, W.G.Richardson, Sandford, Wood.
Att: 40,850
Round 5
Feb 14 v Portsmouth (a) 1-0
W.G.Richardson
Pearson; Shaw, Trentham, Magee, W.Richardson, Edwards, Glidden, W.G.Richardson, Cookson, Sandford, Wood.
Att: 30,891
Round 6
Feb 28 v Wolves (h) 1-1
W.G.Richardson
Pearson; Shaw, Trentham, Magee, W.Richardson, Edwards, Glidden, Carter, W.G.Richardson, Sandford, Wood.
Att: 52,285
Replay
Mar 4 v Wolves (a) 2-1
Wood, W.G.Richardson
Pearson; Shaw, Trentham, Magee, W.Richardson, Edwards, Glidden, Carter, W.G.Richardson, Sandford, Wood.
Att: 46,860
Semi-final
Mar 14 v Everton (At Old Trafford) 1-0
Glidden
Pearson; Shaw, Trentham, Magee, W.Richardson, Edwards, Glidden, Carter, W.G.Richardson, Sandford, Wood.
Att: 69,241
Final
Apr 25 v Birmingham (at Wembley) 2-1
W.G.Richardson 2
Pearson; Shaw, Trentham, Magee, W.Richardson, Edwards, Glidden, Carter, W.G.Richardson, Sandford, Wood.
Att: 90,368

1931-2
Round 3
Jan 9 v Aston Villa (h) 1-2
W.G.Richardson
Pearson; Shaw, Trentham, Murphy, W.Richardson, Edwards, Glidden, Raw, W.G.Richardson, Sandford, Wood.
Att: 49,232

1932-3
Round 3
Jan 14 v Liverpool (h) 2-0
Wood, W.G.Richardson
Pearson; Shaw, Trentham, Murphy, W.Richardson, Edwards, Glidden, Carter, W.G.Richardson, Sandford, Wood.
Att: 29,329
Round 4
Jan 28 v West Ham United (a) 0-2
Pearson; Shaw, Trentham, Murphy, Ridyard, Edwards, Glidden, Carter, W.G.Richardson, Sandford, Wood.
Att: 37,222

W.G.Richardson scores Albion's winner in the 1931 Final against Birmingham.

1933-4
Round 3
Jan 13 v Chelsea (a) 1-1
Robbins
Pearson; Shaw, Trentham, Murphy, W.Richardson, Sankey, Glidden, Carter, W.G.Richardson, Sandford, Robbins.
Att: 51,451
Replay
Jan 17 v Chelsea (h) 0-1 (a.e.t.)
Pearson; Shaw, Trentham, Murphy, W.Richardson, Sankey, Glidden, Carter, W.G.Richardson, Sandford, Robbins.
Att: 20,061

1934-5
Round 3
Jan 12 v Port Vale (h) 2-1
Gale, W.G.Richardson
Pearson; Shaw, Trentham, Murphy, W.Richardson, Sankey, Gale, Carter, W.G.Richardson, Sandford, Boyes.
Att: 18,989
Round 4
Jan 26 v Sheffield United (h) 7-1
W.G.Richardson 3, Sandford 2, Carter, Gale
Pearson; Shaw, Trentham, Murphy, W.Richardson, Sankey, Gale, Carter, W.G.Richardson, Sandford, Boyes.
Att: 34,908
Round 5
Feb 16 v Stockport County (a) 5-0
W.G.Richardson 2, Carter, Gale, Boyes
Pearson; Shaw, Trentham, Murphy, W.Richardson, Edwards, Gale, Carter, W.G.Richardson, Sandford, Boyes.
Att: 24,684

Arthur Gale's superb goal against Preston in the 1935 quarter-final at The Hawthorns.

Round 6
Mar 2 v Preston North End (h) 1-0
Gale
Pearson; Shaw, Trentham, Murphy, W.Richardson, Edwards, Gale, Carter, W.G.Richardson, Sandford, Boyes.
Att: 56,227
Semi-final
Mar 16 v Bolton Wanderers (at Leeds) 1-1
W.G.Richardson
Pearson; Shaw, Trentham, Murphy, W.Richardson, Edwards, Gale, Carter, W.G.Richardson, Sandford, Boyes.
Att: 49,605
Replay
Mar 20 v Bolton Wanderers (at Stoke) 2-0
W.G.Richardson, Sandford (pen)
Pearson; Shaw, Trentham, Murphy, W.Richardson, Edwards, Gale, Carter, W.G.Richardson, Sandford, Boyes.
Att: 49,110
Final
Apr 27 v Sheffield Wednesday (at Wembley) 2-4
Sandford, Boyes
Pearson; Shaw, Trentham, Murphy, W.Richardson, Edwards, Glidden, Carter, W.G.Richardson, Sandford, Boyes.
Att: 93,204

Wally Boyes' scores for Albion against Sheffield Wednesday but the Owls won the 1935 Wembley game 4-2.

1935-6
Round 3
Jan 11 v Hull City (h) 2-0
Wood, W.G.Richardson
Pearson; Finch, Trentham, Sankey, W.Richardson, Rix, Mahon, Sandford, W.G.Richardson, Robbins, Wood.
Att: 27,505
Round 4
Jan 29 v Bradford (a) 1-1
Robbins
Crowe; Shaw, Trentham, Sankey, W.Richardson, Rix, Mahon, Sandford, W.G.Richardson, Robbins, Wood.
Att: 14,958
Replay
Feb v Bradford (h) 1-1 (a.e.t.)
Sandford (pen)
Adams; Finch, Trentham, Sankey, W.Richardson, Rix, Mahon, Glidden, W.G.Richardson, Sandford, Wood.
Att: 27,503
Second replay
Feb 10 v Bradford (at Old Trafford) 0-2
Adams; Finch, Trentham, Sankey, Ridyard, Rix, Mahon, Sandford, W.G.Richardson, Robbins, Wood.
Att: 11,685

1936-7
Round 3
Jan 16 v Spennymoor United (h) 7-1
Sandford 2, W.G.Richardson 2, Wood, Jones, Mahon
Light; Finch, C.Shaw, Murphy, W.Richardson, Boyes, Mahon, Jones, W.G.Richardson, Sandford, Wood.
Att: 23,746
Round 4
Jan 30 v Darlington (h) 3-2
W.G.Richardson 3
Light; Finch, C.Shaw, Murphy, W.Richardson, Sankey, Mahon, Jones, W.G.Richardson, Sandford, Boyes.
Att: 15,917

Round 5
Feb 20 v Coventry City (a) 3-2
Boyes, Mahon 2
Adams; Finch, C.Shaw, Murphy, Sandford, Edwards, Mahon, Jones, W.G.Richardson, Boyes, Coen.
Att: 44,492
Round 6
Mar 6 v Arsenal (h) 3-1
Mahon 2, W.G.Richardson
Adams; Finch, C.Shaw, Murphy, Sandford, Sankey, Mahon, Jones, W.G.Richardson, Boyes, Coen.
Att: 64,815
Semi-final
Apr 10 v Preston North End (at Highbury) 1-4
Robbins
Adams; Finch, C.Shaw, Murphy, Ridyard, Sankey, Mahon, Jones, W.G.Richardson, Boyes, Robbins.
Att: 42,636

1937-8
Round 3
Jan 8 v Newcastle United (h) 1-0
W.G.Richardson
Adams; Finch, C.Shaw, Murphy, Sandford, Sankey, Mahon, Clarke, W.G.Richardson, Boyes, Johnson.
Att: 33,932
Round 4
Jan 22 v York City (a) 2-3
W.G.Richardson, Pinder (og)
Adams; Finch, C.Shaw, Murphy, Robbins, Sankey, Jones, Clarke, W.G.Richardson, Boyes, Johnson.
Att: 18,795

1938-9
Round 3
Jan 7 v Manchester United (h) 0-0
Adams; White, C.Shaw, Witcomb, Tudor, McNab, Heaselgrave, Wilkes, Jones, Clarke, Johnson.
Att: 23,899

Replay
Jan 11 v Manchester United (a) 5-1
Jones 2, Witcomb, Clarke, W.G.Richardson
Adams; White, C.Shaw, Witcomb, Tudor, McNab, W.G.Richardson, Heaselgrave, Jones, Clarke, Johnson.
Att: 17,641
Round 4
Jan 21 v Portsmouth (a) 0-2
Adams; White, C.Shaw, Witcomb, Tudor, McNab, W.G.Richardson, Heaselgrave, Jones, Clarke, Johnson.
Att: 36,661

1945-6
Round 3 (1st leg)
Jan 5 v Cardiff City (a) 1-1
Connelly
Sanders; C.Shaw, Kinsell, Witcomb, Tranter, Millard, Elliott, Clarke, Newsome, Connelly, Saunders.
Att: 28,928
Round 3 (2nd leg)
Jan 9 v Cardiff City (h) 4-0 (agg 5-1)
Clarke 2, Newsome 2
Twigg; C.Shaw, Kinsell, Witcomb, Tranter, Millard, Elliott, Clarke, Newsome, Connelly, Hodgetts.
Att: 18,025
Round 4 (1st leg)
Jan 26 v Derby County (a) 0-1
Sanders; C.Shaw, Kinsell, Witcomb, Tranter, Millard, Elliott, Clarke, Newsome, Connelly, Butler.
Att: 31,440
Round 4 (2nd leg)
Jan 30 v Derby County (h) 1-3 (agg 1-4)
Clarke
Sanders; C.Shaw, Kinsell, Witcomb, Tranter, Millard, Elliott, Clarke, Newsome, Connelly, Butler.
Att: 35,882

1946-7
Round 3
Jan 11 v Leeds United (h) 2-1
Barlow, Walsh
Sanders; Pemberton, Kinsell, Witcomb, C.Edwards, Millard, Elliott, Duggan, Walsh, Barlow, Hodgetts.
Att: 31,007
Round 4
Jan 25 v Charlton Athletic (h) 1-2
Elliott
Sanders; Pemberton, Kinsell, Witcomb, C.Edwards, Millard, Elliott, Duggan, Walsh, Barlow, Hodgetts.
Att: 29,996

Action from the fourth round match against Charlton at The Hawthorns in January 1947.

1947-8
Round 3
Jan 10 v Reading (h) 2-0
Finch, Drury
Sanders; Pemberton, Millard, G.Williams, Vernon, Ryan, Gordon, Finch, Drury, A.Evans, Elliott.
Att: 30,241
Round 4
Jan 24 v Tottenham Hotspur (a) 1-3
Rowley
Sanders; Pemberton, Millard, G.Williams, Vernon, Ryan, Elliott, McKennan, Walsh, Drury, Rowley.
Att: 71,853

1948-9
Round 3
Jan 8 v Lincoln City (a) 1-0
Barlow
Sanders; Pemberton, Kinsell, Millard, Vernon, Hood, Elliott, C.Williams, Walsh, Barlow, Haines.
Att: 19,602
Round 4
Jan 29 v Gateshead (a) 3-1 (a.e.t.)
Walsh 2, A.Smith
Sanders; Pemberton, Kinsell, Millard, Vernon, Hood, Elliott, C.Williams, Walsh, Barlow, A.Smith.
Att: 16,885
Round 5
Feb 12 v Chelsea (h) 3-0
Walsh 3
Sanders; Pemberton, Millard, Barlow, Vernon, Hood, Elliott, C.Williams, Walsh, Haines, A.Smith.
Att: 57,843
Round 6
Feb 26 v Wolverhampton Wanderers (a) 0-1
Sanders; Pemberton, Millard, Barlow, Vernon, Hood, Elliott, C.Williams, Walsh, Haines, A.Smith.
Att: 55,684

1949-50
Round 3
Jan 7 v Cardiff City (a) 2-2
C.Williams, Inwood
Sanders; Pemberton, Millard, Kennedy, Vernon, Ryan, Gordon, C.Williams, Walsh, Barlow, Inwood.
Att: 39,980

Replay
Jan 11 v Cardiff City (h) 0-1
Sanders; Pemberton, Millard, Kennedy, Vernon, Ryan, Gordon, C.Williams, Walsh, Barlow, Inwood.
Att: 37,358

1950-51
Round 3
Jan 6 v Derby County (a) 2-2
Lee, Barlow
Sanders; Rickaby, Millard, Kennedy, Vernon, Dudley, Allen, Barlow, F.Richardson, Ryan, Lee.
Att: 24,807
Replay
Jan 10 v Derby County (h) 0-1
Sanders; Rickaby, Millard, Kennedy, Vernon, Dudley, Allen, Barlow, F.Richardson, Ryan, Lee.
Att: 33,223

1951-2
Round 3
Jan 12 v Bolton Wanderers (h) 4-0
Lee 2, Allen, Griffin
Heath; Rickaby, Millard, Kennedy, Horne, Barlow, Griffin, Dudley, Allen, Ryan, Lee.
Att: 38,428
Round 4
Feb 6 v Gateshead (at Newcastle) 2-0
Allen 2
Heath; Rickaby, Millard, Kennedy, Horne, Barlow, Griffin, Dudley, Allen, Ryan, Lee.
Att: 38,681
Round 5
Feb 23 v Blackburn Rovers (a) 0-1
Heath; Rickaby, Millard, Kennedy, Horne, Ryan, Griffin, Dudley, Nicholls, McCall, Lee.
Att: 51,177

1952-3
Round 3
Jan 10 v West Ham United (a) 4-1
Lee, Ryan, Allen, Nicholls
Heath; Rickaby, Millard, Dudley, Kennedy, S.Williams, Griffin, Nicholls, Allen, Ryan, Lee.
Att: 35,150
Round 4
Jan 31 v Chelsea (a) 1-1
Nicholls
Heath; S.Williams, Millard, Dudley, Dugdale, Barlow, Mountford, Nicholls, Allen, Ryan, Lee.
Att: 58,912

Replay
Feb 4 v Chelsea (h) 0-0 (a.e.t.)
Heath; S.Williams, Millard, Dudley, Kennedy, Barlow, Griffin, Nicholls, Allen, Ryan, Lee.
Att: 37,974
Second replay
Feb 9 v Chelsea (at Villa Park) 1-1 (a.e.t.)
Dudley
Heath; Rickaby, Millard, Dudley, Dugdale, Barlow, Griffin, Nicholls, Allen, Ryan, Lee
Att: 33,534
Third replay
Feb 11 v Chelsea (at Highbury) 0-4
Heath; Rickaby, S.Williams, Dudley, Dugdale, Barlow, Griffin, Nicholls, Allen, Ryan, Lee.
Att: 27,997

1953-4
Round 3
Jan 9 v Chelsea (h) 1-0
Greenwood (og)
Heath; Rickaby, Millard, Dudley, Dugdale, Barlow, Griffin, Ryan, Allen, Nicholls, Lee.
Att: 35,294
Round 4
Jan 30 v Rotherham United (h) 4-0
Nicholls 2, Allen, Ryan
Heath; Rickaby, Millard, Dudley, Dugdale, Barlow, Griffin, Ryan, Allen, Nicholls, Lee.
Att: 48,242
Round 5
Feb 20 v Newcastle United (h) 3-2
Allen 3
Heath; Rickaby, Millard, Dudley, Dugdale, Barlow, Griffin, Ryan, Allen, Nicholls, Lee.
Att: 61,088
Round 6
Mar 13 v Tottenham Hotspur (h) 3-0
Barlow, Nicholls 2
Heath; Rickaby, Millard, Dudley Dugdale, Barlow, Griffin, Ryan, Allen, Nicholls, Lee.
Att: 51,049
Semi-final
Mar 27 v Port Vale (at Villa Park) 2-1
Dudley, Allen (pen)
Heath; Rickaby, Millard, Dudley, Dugdale, Barlow, Griffin, Ryan, Allen, Nicholls, Lee.
Att: 68,221

Jimmy Dudley's equaliser against Port Vale in the 1954 semi-final at Villa Park.

Frank Griffin kisses the boot which scored the winning goal over Preston in the 1954 Final. Ray Barlow and Ronnie Allen share his joy.

Final
May 1 v Preston North End (at Wembley) 3-2
Allen 2 (1 pen) Griffin
Sanders; Kennedy, Millard, Dudley, Dugdale,
Barlow, Griffin, Ryan, Allen, Nicholls, Lee.
Att: 99,852

1954-5
Round 3
Jan 8 v Bournemouth (a) 1-0
Williams
Sanders; Rickaby, Millard, Dudley, Dugdale,
Barlow, Jones, S.Williams, Allen, Nicholls, Lee.
Att:19,498
Round 4
Jan 29 v Charlton Athletic (h) 2-4
Williams 2
Davies; Rickaby, Millard, Dudley, Dugdale, Barlow,
Griffin, S.Williams, Allen, Nicholls, Lee.
Att: 36,264

1955-6
Round 3
Jan 7 v Wolverhampton Wanderers (a) 2-1
Griffin, Lee
Sanders; Howe, Millard, Dudley, Kennedy,
Summers, Griffin, Setters, Barlow, Allen, Lee.
Att: 55,564

Round 4
Jan 28 v Portsmouth (h) 2-0
Lee, Allen (pen)
Sanders; Howe, Millard, Dudley, Kennedy,
Summers, Griffin, Setters, Barlow, Allen, Lee.
Att: 59,448
Round 5
Feb 18 v Birmingham City (h) 0-1
Sanders; Howe, Millard, Dudley, Kennedy,
Summers, Griffin, Setters, Barlow, Allen, Lee.
Att: 57,213

1956-7
Round 3
Jan 5 v Doncaster Rovers (a) 1-1
Robson
Sanders; Howe, Carter, Dudley, Kennedy, Barlow,
Griffin, Setters, Kevan, Robson, Allen
Att: 25,627
Replay
Jan 9 v Doncaster Rovers (h) 2-0
Allen 2
Sanders; Howe, Carter, Dudley, Kennedy, Barlow,
Griffin, Setters, Kevan, Robson, Allen.
Att: 18,043

Round 4
Jan 26 v Sunderland (h) 4-2
Kevan 2, Horobin, Allen (pen)
Sanders; Howe, Carter, Dudley, Kennedy, Barlow,
Griffin, Horobin, Allen, Kevan, Lee
Att: 42,406
Round 5
Feb 16 v Blackpool (a) 0-0
Sanders; Howe, Millard, Dudley, Kennedy, Barlow,
Griffin, Whitehouse, Allen, Kevan, Lee.
Att: 32,707
Replay
Feb 20 v Blackpool (h) 2-1
Kevan, Allen
Sanders; Howe, Millard, Dudley, Kennedy, Barlow,
Griffin, Whitehouse, Allen, Kevan, Horobin.
Att: 48,054
Round 6
Mar 2 v Arsenal (h) 2-2
Allen, Wills (og)
Sanders; Howe, Millard, Dudley, Kennedy, Barlow,
Griffin, Whitehouse, Allen, Kevan, Horobin
Att: 53,459
Replay
Mar 5 v Arsenal (a) 2-1
Whitehouse, Kevan
Sanders; Howe, Millard, Dudley, Barlow, Setters,
Griffin, Whitehouse, Allen, Kevan, Horobin.
Att: 58,757

Aresnal's Jack Kelsey watches the ball flash wide during an Albion attack in the drawn quarter-final game at The Hawthorns in March 1957.

Semi-final
Mar 23 v Aston Villa (at Molineux) 2-2
Whitehouse 2
Sanders; Howe, Millard, Dudley, Kennedy, Barlow,
Griffin, Whitehouse, Allen, Kevan, Horobin.
Att: 55,549
Replay
Mar 28 v Aston Villa (at St Andrew's) 0-1
Sanders; Howe, Millard, Dudley, Kennedy, Barlow,
Griffin, Whitehouse, Allen, Kevan, Horobin.
Att: 58,067

1957-8
Round 3
Jan 4 v Manchester City (h) 5-1
Allen 2, Griffin, Barlow, Ewing (og)
Sanders; Howe, S.Williams, Setters, Kennedy,
Barlow, Griffin, Robson, Allen, Kevan, Horobin.
Att: 49,669
Round 4
Jan 25 v Nottingham Forest (h) 3-3
Allen, Kevan, Robson
Sanders; Howe, S.Williams, Setters, Kennedy,
Barlow, Griffin, Robson, Allen, Kevan, Horobin.
Att: 58,163
Replay
Jan 28 v Nottingham Forest (a) 5-1
Kevan, Whitehouse, Griffin, Robson, Howe (pen)
Sanders; Howe, S.Williams, Setters, Kennedy,
Barlow, Griffin, Whitehouse, Robson, Kevan,
Horobin.
Att: 46,455
Round 5
Feb 15 v Sheffield United (a) 1-1
Allen
Sanders; Howe, S.Williams, Dudley, Kennedy,
Barlow, Griffin, Robson, Allen, Kevan, Horobin.
Att: 55,847
Replay
Feb 19 v Sheffield United (h) 4-1
Kevan 2, Allen (pen), Robson
Sanders; Howe, S.Williams, Dudley, Kennedy, Barlow,
Griffin, Robson, Allen, Kevan, Horobin.
Att: 57,503

Round 6
Mar 1 v Manchester United (h) 2-2
Allen, Horobin
Sanders; Howe, S.Williams, Dudley, Kennedy,
Barlow, Whitehouse, Robson, Allen, Kevan, Horobin
Att: 57,574
Replay
Mar 5 v Manchester United (a) 0-1
Sanders; Howe, S.Williams, Dudley, Kennedy,
Barlow, Whitehouse, Robson, Allen, Kevan, Horobin.
Att: 60,523

1958-9
Round 3
Jan 19 v Sheffield Wednesday (a) 2-0
Jackson, Hogg
Potter; Howe, S.Williams, Setters, Barlow, Drury,
Griffin, Jackson, Allen, Kevan, Hogg
Att: 50,455
Round 4
Jan 24 v Brentford (h) 2-0
Kevan 2
Potter; Howe, S.Williams, Setters, Barlow, Drury,
Griffin, Jackson, Allen, Kevan, Hogg
Att: 41,948
Round 5
Feb 14 v Blackpool (a) 1-3
Robson
Potter; Howe, S.Williams, Setters, Barlow, Drury,
Griffin, Robson, Allen, Jackson, Hogg.
Att: 30,415

1959-60
Round 3
Jan 9 v Plymouth Argyle (h) 3-2
Kevan 3
Wallace; Howe, G.Williams, Drury, Kennedy,
Robson, Jackson, Burnside, Allen, Kevan, Hogg.
Att: 27,548
Round 4
Jan 30 v Bolton Wanderers (h) 2-0
Jackson, Burnside
Wallace; Howe, G.Williams, Drury, Kennedy,
Robson, Jackson, Burnside, Allen, Kevan, Hogg.
Att: 36,411

Round 5
Feb 20 v Leicester City (a) 1-2
Kennedy
Wallace; Howe, G.Williams, Drury, Kennedy,
Robson, Jackson, Burnside, Allen, Kevan, Hogg.
Att: 37,753

1960-61
Round 3
Jan 7 v Lincoln City (a) 1-3
Burnside
Potter; Howe, G.Williams, Robson, Kennedy,
Drury, Macready, Burnside, Allen, Kevan, Jackson.
Att: 14,025

1961-2
Round 3
Jan 6 v Blackpool (a) 0-0
Wallace; Howe, S.Williams, Robson, Jones, Drury,
Jackson, Burnside, Smith, Kevan, Clark.
Att: 19,560
Replay
Jan 10 v Blackpool (h) 2-1
Burnside, Smith
Wallace; Howe, S.Williams, Robson, Jones, Drury,
Jackson, Burnside, Smith, Kevan, Clark.
Att: 27,781
Round 4
Jan 27 v Wolverhampton Wanderers (a) 2-1
Clark 2
Wallace; Howe, S.Williams, Robson, Jones, Drury,
Jackson, Burnside, Smith, Kevan, Clark.
Att: 46,411
Round 5
Feb 17 v Tottenham Hotspur (h) 2-4
Kevan, Smith
Wallace; Howe, S.Williams, Robson, Jones, Drury,
Jackson, Burnside, Smith, Kevan, Clark.
Att: 54,992

1962-3
Round 3
Jan 5 v Plymouth Argyle (a) 5-1
Kevan 2, Smith, Cram, Newman (og)
Potter; Howe, G.Williams, Cram, Jones, Drury,
Jackson, Fenton, Smith, Kevan, Clark.
Att: 21,915

Round 4
Mar 6 v Nottingham Forest (h) 0-0
Potter; Howe, G.Williams, Cram, Jones, Drury, Jackson, Fenton, Smith, Kevan, Clark.
Att: 21,511
Replay
Mar 11 v Nottingham Forest (a) 1-2 (a.e.t.)
Smith
Potter; Howe, G.Williams, Cram, Jones, Drury, Jackson, Fenton, Smith, Kevan, Clark.
Att: 21,540

1963-4
Round 3
Jan 4 v Blackpool (h) 2-2
Clark, Howe (pen)
Potter; Howe, G.Williams, Fraser, Jones, Simpson, Foggo, Fenton, Readfern, Fudge, Clark.
Att: 22,459
Replay
Jan 8 v Blackpool (a) 1-0
Fenton
Potter; Howe, G.Williams, Fraser, Jones, Simpson, Foggo, Fenton, Kaye, Fudge, Clark.
Att: 21,241
Round 4
Jan 25 v Arsenal (h) 3-3
Fenton, Kaye, Jones
Potter; Howe, G.Williams, Fraser, Jones, Simpson, Foggo, Fenton, Kaye, Jackson, Clark.
Att: 39,703
Replay
Jan 29 v Arsenal (a) 0-2
Potter; Howe, G.Williams, Fraser, Jones, Simpson, Foggo, Cram, Kaye, Jackson, Clark.
Att: 57,698

1964-5
Round 3
Jan 9 v Liverpool (h) 1-2
Astle
Potter; Cram, G.Williams, Fraser, Jones, Simpson, Fenton, Fudge, Astle, Hope, Clark.
Att: 29,851

1965-6
Round 3
Jan 22 v Bolton Wanderers (a) 0-3
Potter; Cram, Fairfax, Lovett, Jones, Fraser, Brown, R.Crawford, Kaye, Hope, Clark.
Att: 24,425

1966-7
Round 3
Jan 28 v Northampton Town (a) 3-1
Astle, Clark, Brown
Sheppard; Cram, G.Williams, Collard, Talbut, Fraser, Brown, Astle, Kaye, Hope, Clark.
Att: 16,899
Round 4
Feb 18 v Leeds United (a) 0-5
Sheppard; Cram, G.Williams, Collard, Jones, Fraser, Foggo, Brown, Astle, Hope, Clark.
Att: 41,329

1967-8
Round 3
Jan 27 v Colchester United (a) 1-1
Brown (pen)
Osborne; Colquhoun, G.Williams, Brown, Talbut, Fraser, Krzywicki (Lovett), Kaye, Astle, Hope, Clark.
Att: 15,981
Replay
Jan 31 v Colchester United (h) 4-0
Astle 2, Kaye, Clark
Sheppard; Colquhoun, G.Williams, Brown, Talbut, Fraser, Lovett, Kaye, Astle, Hope, Clark.
Att: 38,448
Round 4
Feb 17 v Southampton (h) 1-1
Brown
Sheppard; Clarke, Williams, Brown, Talbut, Fraser, Krzywicki, Kaye, Astle, Hope, Clark.
Att: 29,957

Replay
Feb 21 v Southampton (a) 3-2
Astle 2, Brown
Osborne* (Lovett); Clarke, Williams, Collard, Talbut, Fraser, Brown, Kaye, Astle, Hope, Clark.
Att: 26,036
* Williams went in goal for the injured Osborne.
Round 5
Mar 9 v Portsmouth (a) 2-1
Astle, Clark
Osborne; Colquhoun, Williams, Collard, Talbut, Fraser, Brown, Kaye, Astle, Hope, Clark.
Att: 42,642
Round 6
Mar 30 v Liverpool (h) 0-0
Osborne; Colquhoun, Williams, Brown, Talbut, Fraser, Krzywicki, Kaye, Astle, Collard, Clark.
Att: 43,503
Replay
Apr 8 v Liverpool (a) 1-1 (a.e.t.)
Astle
Osborne; Clarke, Williams, Fraser, Talbut, Colquhoun, Kaye, Brown, Astle, Collard (Stephens), Clark.
Att: 54,273
Second replay
Apr 18 v Liverpool (at Maine Road) 2-1
Astle, Clark
Osborne; Clarke (Stephens), Williams, Fraser, Talbut, Kaye, Brown, Collard, Astle, Hope, Clark.
Att: 56,139
Semi-final
Apr 27 v Birmingham City (at Villa Park) 2-0
Astle, Brown
Osborne; Fraser, Williams, Brown, Talbut, Kaye, Stephens, Collard, Astle, Hope, Clark.
Att: 60,831
Final
May 18 v Everton (at Wembley) 1-0 (a.e.t.)
Astle
Osborne; Fraser, Williams, Brown, Talbut, Kaye (Clarke), Lovett, Collard, Astle, Hope, Clark.
Att: 99,665

Jeff Astle's winner in the 1968 Final.

1968-9
Round 3
Jan 4 v Norwich City (h) 3-0
Rees, Astle (pen), Forbes (og)
Osborne; Fraser, Wilson, Hughes, Talbut, Kaye, Hope, Lovett, Astle, Collard, Rees.
Att: 30,004
Round 4
Jan 25 v Fulham (a) 2-1
Hartford, Rees
Osborne; Fraser, Williams, Brown (Rees), Talbut, Kaye, Hope, Lovett, Astle, Collard, Hartford.
Att: 31,204
Round 5
Feb 12 v Arsenal (h) 1-0
Brown
Osborne; Fraser, Wilson, Brown, Talbut, Kaye, Martin, Collard, Astle, Lovett, Hartford.
Att: 45,354
Round 6
Mar 1 v Chelsea (a) 2-1
Brown, Astle
Osborne; Fraser, Wilson, Brown, Talbut, Kaye, Martin, Lovett, Astle, Hope, Hartford (Krzywicki).
Att: 52,285
Semi-final
Mar 29 v Leicester City (at Hillsborough) 0-1
Osborne; Fraser, Wilson, Brown, Talbut, Kaye, Martin (Clark), Lovett, Astle, Hope, Hartford.
Att: 53,207

1969-70
Round 3
Jan 3 v Sheffield Wednesday (a) 1-2
Brown
Osborne; Fraser, Wilson, Brown, Talbut, Kaye, Krzywicki, Hughes, Suggett, Hartford, Martin.
Att: 29,174

1970-71
Round 3
Jan 2 v Scunthorpe United (h) 0-0
Cumbes; Lovett, Wilson, Brown, Talbut, Kaye, McVitie, Suggett, Astle, Cantello, Hartford.
Att; 22,844
Replay
Jan 11 v Scunthorpe United (a) 3-1
Brown 2, Astle
Cumbes; Lovett, Wilson, Brown, Talbut, Kaye, McVitie, Suggett, Astle, Hope, Hartford.
Att: 15,926
Round 4
Jan 23 v Ipswich Town (h) 1-1
Suggett
Cumbes; Lovett, Wilson, Brown, Talbut, Kaye, McVitie, Suggett, Astle, Hope (Merrick), Hartford.
Att: 27,178
Replay
Jan 26 v Ipswich Town (a) 0-3
Cumbes; Lovett, Merrick, Brown, Talbut, Kaye, McVitie, Suggett, Astle, Hope, Hartford.
Att: 27,015

1971-2
Round 3
Jan 15 v Coventry City (h) 1-2
Brown
Osborne; Nisbet, Wilson, Cantello, Wile, Robertson, McVitie, Brown, Gould, Suggett, Hartford.
Att: 26,313

1972-3
Round 3
Jan 13 v Nottingham Forest (h) 1-1
Winfield (og)
Latchford; Nisbet, Wilson, Cantello, Wile, Merrick, Suggett, T.Brown, A.Brown, Hartford, Johnston.
Att: 15,743

Replay
Jan 16 v Nottingham Forest (a) 1-1*
Hartford
Latchford; Nisbet (Robertson), Wilson, Cantello, Wile, Merrick, Suggett, T.Brown, A.Brown, Hartford, Johnston.
Att: 19,168
* Tie abandoned after 79 minutes (fog).
Replay
Jan 22 v Nottingham Forest (a) 0-0 (a.e.t.)
Latchford; Nisbet, Wilson, Cantello, Wile, Merrick, Suggett, T.Brown, A.Brown (Robertson), Hartford, Johnston.
Att: 17,069
Second replay
Jan 29 v Nottingham Forest (at Leicester) 3-1
Cantello, Hartford, Suggett
Latchford; Nisbet, Wilson, Cantello, Wile, Merrick, Suggett, T.Brown, A.Brown, Hartford, Johnston.
Att: 12,606
Round 4
Feb 3 v Swindon Town (h) 2-0
T.Brown, Cantello
Latchford; Nisbet, Wilson, Cantello, Wile, Merrick, Suggett, T.Brown, A.Brown (Robertson), Hartford, Johnston.
Att: 20,795
Round 5
Feb 24 v Leeds United (a) 0-2
Latchford; Nisbet (A.Brown), Wilson, Cantello, Wile, Robertson, Merrick, T.Brown, Astle, Hartford, Johnston.
Att: 39,229

1973-4
Round 3
Jan 5 v Notts County (h) 4-0
T.Brown 3, Johnston
Latchford; Nisbet, Wilson, Cantello, Wile, Robertson, Johnston, T.Brown, Shaw, Hartford, Glover.
Att: 13,123
Round 4
Jan 27 v Everton (a) 0-0
Latchford; Nisbet, Wilson, Cantello, Wile, Robertson, Johnston, T.Brown, Shaw, Hartford, Glover.
Att: 53,509
Replay
Jan 30 v Everton (h) 1-0
T.Brown
Latchford; Nisbet, Wilson, Cantello, Wile, Robertson, Johnston, T.Brown, Shaw, Hartford, Glover.
Att: 27,556
Round 5
Feb 16 v Newcastle United (h) 0-3
Latchford; Nisbet, Wilson, Cantello (Merrick), Wile, Robertson, Johnston, T.Brown, Shaw, Hartford, Glover.
Att: 42,747

1974-5
Round 3
Jan 4 v Bolton Wanderers (a) 0-0
Osborne; Nisbet, Wilson, Cantello, Wile, Rushbury, T.Brown, Shaw, Mayo, Hughes, Johnston.
Att: 17,305
Replay
Jan 8 v Bolton Wanderers (h) 4-0
Cantello, Wile, Shaw, Mayo
Osborne; Nisbet, Wilson, Cantello, Wile, Rushbury, T.Brown, Shaw, Mayo, Hughes, Johnston.
Att: 21,210
Round 4
Jan 25 v Carlisle United (a) 2-3
T.Brown (pen), Nisbet
Osborne; Nisbet, Wilson, Cantello, Wile, Rushbury, T.Brown, Shaw, Mayo, Hughes, Johnston.
Att: 14,843

1975-6
Round 3
Jan 3 v Carlisle United (h) 3-1
T.Brown 2 (1 pen), A.Brown
Osborne; Mulligan, Mayo, Cantello, Wile, Robertson, T.Brown, Martin, A.Brown, Giles, Johnston.
Att: 16,159
Round 4
Jan 24 v Lincoln City (h) 3-2
T.Brown, Martin, Robson
Osborne; Mulligan, Mayo, Robson, Wile, Robertson, T.Brown, Martin, A.Brown, Giles, Johnston.
Att: 26,878
Round 5
Feb 14 v Southampton (h) 1-1
T.Brown
Osborne; Mulligan, Mayo, T.Brown, Wile, Robertson, Martin, Cantello, A.Brown, Giles, Johnston.
Att: 36,645
Replay
Feb 17 v Southampton (a) 0-4
Osborne; Mulligan, Mayo, T.Brown, Wile, Robertson, Martin, Cantello, A.Brown (Robson), Giles, Johnston.
Att: 27,614

1976-7
Round 3
Jan 8 v Manchester City (a) 1-1
Johnston
Osborne; Mulligan, Cantello, T.Brown, Wile, Robertson, Martin, Treacy, D.Cross, Trewick, Johnston.
Att: 38,195
Replay
Jan 11 v Manchester City (h) 0-1
Osborne; Mulligan, Cantello (Robson), T.Brown, Wile, Robertson, Martin, Treacy, D.Cross, Trewick, Johnston.
Att: 27,218

1977-8
Round 3
Jan 7 v Blackpool (h) 4-1
Johnston 2, Regis, T.Brown (pen)
Godden; Martin, Statham, T.Brown, Wile, Robertson, A.Brown, Regis, Cunningham, Trewick, Johnston.
Att: 21,379
Round 4
Jan 28 v Manchester United (a) 1-1
Johnston
Godden; Mulligan, Statham, T.Brown, Wile, Robson, Martin, Regis, A.Brown, Trewick, Johnston.
Att: 57,056
Replay
Feb 1 v Manchester United (h) 3-2 (a.e.t.)
Regis 2, T.Brown
Godden; Mulligan, Statham, T.Brown, Wile (W.Hughes), Robson, Martin, Regis, A.Brown, Trewick, Johnston.
Att: 37,792
Feb 22 v Derby County (a) 3-2
Regis 2, Johnston
Godden; Mulligan (Cunningham), Statham, T.Brown, Wile, Robertson, Martin, Regis, A.Brown, Trewick, Johnston.
Att: 32,689
Round 6
Mar 11 v Nottingham Forest (h) 2-0
Martin, Regis
Godden; Mulligan, Statham, T.Brown, Wile, Robertson, Martin, Regis, A.Brown (Cunningham), Trewick, Johnston.
Att: 36,506
Semi-final
Apr 8 v Ipswich Town (at Highbury) 1-3
T.Brown (pen)
Godden; Mulligan, Statham, T.Brown, Wile (Cunningham), Robertson, Martin, A.Brown, Regis Trewick, Johnston.
Att: 50,922

1978-9
Round 3
Jan 9 v Coventry City (a) 2-2
Cunningham, A.Brown
Godden; Batson, Statham, T.Brown, Wile, Robertson, Robson, A.Brown, Regis, Trewick, Cunningham.
Att: 38,046
Replay
Jan 15 v Coventry City (h) 4-0
Batson, T.Brown 2, A.Brown
Godden; Batson, Statham, T.Brown, Wile, Robertson, Robson, A.Brown, Regis, Cantello, Cunningham.
Att: 36,175
Round 4
Feb 24 v Leeds United (h) 3-3
Cunningham, A.Brown, Regis
Godden; Batson, Statham, T.Brown, Wile, Robertson, Robson, A.Brown (Mills), Regis, Cantello, Cunningham.
Att: 32,424
Replay
Feb 26 v Leeds United (h) 2-0 (a.e.t.)
Wile, A.Brown
Godden; Batson, Statham, T.Brown (Mills), Wile, Robertson, Robson, A.Brown, Regis, Cantello, Cunningham.
Att: 31,143

Round 5
Mar 10 v Southampton (h) 1-1
A.Brown
Godden; Batson, Statham, T.Brown, Wile, Robertson, Robson, A.Brown, Regis, Mills, Cunningham.
Att: 30,789
Replay
Mar 12 v Southampton (a) 1-2 (a.e.t.)
Cunningham
Godden; Batson, Statham, Trewick, Wile, Robertson, Mills, A.Brown, Regis (Johnston), T.Brown, Cunningham.
Att: 25,755

1979-80
Round 3
Jan 5 v West Ham United (h) 1-1
Regis
Godden; Batson, Statham, Trewick, Wile, Robertson, Deehan, A.Brown, Regis, Owen, Barnes.
Att: 21,321
Replay
Jan 8 v West Ham United (a) 1-2
T.Brown
Godden; Batson, Statham, Trewick, Wile, Robertson, Deehan, A.Brown, Regis, Owen (T.Brown), Barnes.
Att: 30,869

1980-81
Round 3
Jan 3 v Grimsby Town (h) 3-0
Robson, Cowdrill, Barnes
Godden; Batson, Cowdrill, Moses, Wile, Bennett, Robson, A.Brown (Mills), Regis, Owen, Barnes.
Att: 22,477
Round 4
Jan 24 v Middlesbrough (a) 0-1
Godden; Robertson, Cowdrill, Moses, Wile, Bennett, Robson, A.Brown, Regis, Owen, Barnes.
Att: 28,285

1981-2
Round 3
Jan 2 v Blackburn Rovers (h) 3-2
Whitehead, Mackenzie, King (pen)
Grew; Batson, Statham, Whitehead, Wile, Robertson, Jol, Monaghan, Regis, King, Mackenzie.
Att: 17,892
Round 4
Jan 23 v Gillingham (a) 1-0
Statham
Grew; Batson, Statham, A.Brown, Wile, Robertson, Jol, Whitehead, Regis, Owen, Mackenzie.
Att: 16,038
Round 5
Feb 13 v Norwich City (h) 1-0
Regis
Grew; Bennett, Statham, Lewis, Wile, Robertson, N.Cross, King, Regis, Owen, Mackenzie.
Att: 18,897

Cyrille Regis scores the only goal against Norwich in the 1981-2 fifth round.

Round 6
Mar 6 v Coventry City (h) 2-0
Regis, Owen
Grew; Batson, Statham, Bennett, Wile, Robertson,
A.Brown, King, Regis, Owen, Mackenzie.
Att: 28,045
Semi-final
Apr 3 v Queen's Park Rangers (at Highbury) 0-1
Grew; Batson, Statham, Zondervan, Wile, Robertson,
Bennett, King (Owen), Regis, N.Cross, Mackenzie.
Att: 45,015

1982-3
Round 3
Jan 8 v Queen's Park Rangers (h) 3-2
Owen 2 (1 pen), Eastoe
Barron; Whitehead, Statham, Zondervan, Wile,
Robertson, Jol, Bennett, Regis, Owen, Eastoe.
Att: 16,528
Round 4
Jan 29 v Tottenham Hotspur (a) 1-2
Whitehead
Barron; Whitehead (A.Brown), Statham, Zondervan,
Wile, Robertson, Jol, Bennett, N.Cross, Owen,
Eastoe.
Att: 38,208
1983-4
Round 3
Jan 3 v Rotherham United (a) 0-0
Barron; Whitehead, Cowdrill, N.Cross, McNaught,
Bennett, Lewis, Thompson, Regis, Owen (Luke),
Morley.
Att: 8,142
Replay
Jan 11 v Rotherham United (h) 3-0
Thompson, Morley 2
Barron; Whitehead, Cowdrill, Luke, McNaught,
Bennett, Lewis, Thompson, Regis, Owen, Morley.
Att: 12,107
Round 4
Feb 1 v Scunthorpe United (h) 1-0
Forsyth
Barron; Whitehead, Cowdrill, Luke, McNaught,
Forsyth, Zondervan, Thompson, Regis, Lewis,
Morley.
Att: 18,235
Round 5
Feb 18 v Plymouth Argyle (h) 0-1
Barron; Whitehead, Statham, Zondervan, McNaught,
Bennett, Jol, Thompson, Perry (Luke), Mackenzie,
Morley
Att: 23,795

George Reilly heads Albion's first goal at Hillsborough in the 1985-6 third round.

1984-5
Round 3
Jan 5 v Orient (a) 1-2
Cross
Godden; Nicholl, Statham (Robson), Hunt, Bennett,
Forsyth, Grealish, Thompson, Mackenzie, N.Cross,
Whitehead.
Att: 7,061

1985-6
Round 3
Jan 13 v Sheffield Wednesday (a) 2-2
Reilly, Statham
Godden; Nicholl, Statham, Owen, Bennett,
Robertson, Thompson, Varadi, Reilly, Thomas,
Dennison.
Att: 17,042

Replay
Jan 16 v Sheffield Wednesday (h) 2-3
Hunt, Thomas
Godden; Nicholl, Statham, Hunt, Bennett (Owen),
Robertson, Thompson, Varadi, Reilly, Thomas,
Dennison.
Att: 11,152

1986-7
Round 3
Jan 10 v Swansea City (a) 2-3
Anderson, Lewis (og)
Naylor; Whitehead, Anderson (Singleton), Palmer,
Dyson, Burrows, Hopkins, Statham, Mackenzie,
Williamson, Crooks.
Att: 8,792

David Burrows was one of the unfortunate
Albion players humiliated by Fourth Division
Swansea City in the 1986-7 FA Cup.

Albion's full record in the FA Cup (1883-1987 inclusive)

At The Four Acres (1883-85)

P	W	D	L	F	A
5	3	0	2	8	6

At Stoney Lane (1885-1900)

P	W	D	L	F	A
26	22	0	4	82	25

At The Hawthorns (1901-87)

P	W	D	L	F	A
119	69	29	21	241	112

Totals

	P	W	D	L	F	A
Home	150	94	29	27	331	143
Away	174	71	39	64	244	227
Total	324	165	68	91	575	370

FA Cup Facts & Figures

Beaten by the FA Cup Winners

Albion have been beaten by the subsequent FA Cup winners for the season on 22 occasions:

1884-5 — Blackburn Rovers	1934-5 — Sheffield Wednesday
1885-6 — Blackburn Rovers	1938-9 — Portsmouth
1886-7 — Aston Villa	1945-6 — Derby County
1888-9 — Preston North End	1946-7 — Charlton Athletic
1890-1 — Blackburn Rovers	1948-9 — Wolverhampton W
1894-5 — Aston Villa	1956-7 — Aston Villa
1897-8 — Nottingham Forest	1961-2 — Tottenham Hotspur
1900-1 — Tottenham Hotspur	1964-5 — Liverpool
1905-6 — Everton	1975-6 — Southampton
1911-2 — Barnsley	1977-8 — Ipswich Town
1924-5 — Sheffield United	1979-80— West Ham United

Only Everton (21) have appeared in more FA Cup semi-finals than Albion who have so far reached that stage on 19 occasions.

Tony Brown became the first Albion player to appear in 50 FA Cup ties when he lined up against Leeds United at The Hawthorns in the fourth round on 24 February 1979. When he left Albion, Brown had reached a total of 54 (including one as a substitute) FA Cup outings — a club record.

Tony Brown (53) also holds the record for most consecutive FA Cup appearances for Albion (1966-79). John Wile made 42 (1972-83) and Joe Reader 39 (1891-1901).

Tony Brown (27) has scored most FA Cup goals for Albion. 'W.G.'Richardson secured 26, 'Jem' Bayliss 24 and Ronnie Allen 23.

Extra-time was first introduced to the FA Cup Final in 1912 when Albion met Barnsley.

Albion played 14 FA Cup games without defeat between 27 January 1968 (at Colchester) and 1 March 1969 (at Chelsea). The run ended in the next match, the semi-final against Leicester City at Sheffield.

When Albion met Newcastle United in a Division One match on 4 March 1933, 18 of the participating players were in possession of FA Cup winners' medals (ten were Albion men).

Albion's heaviest defeat in an FA Cup game is 5-0 — at Elland Road, Leeds, in a fourth round tie on Saturday, 18 February 1967. Albion's biggest set-back at home in the competition is 5-2, — against Leicester Fosse (intermediate round) on 14 January 1905.

7-0, at home to South Shore, on 28 January 1899, is Albion's highest half-time score in an FA Cup tie. This is also the record half-time scoreline for the club at senior level, League or Cup.

Albion's biggest victory in the Cup is 10-1 — away to Chatham in round three, 16 March 1889.

Lancashire teams knocked Albion out of the FA Cup seven times in ten seasons in the period from 1885 to 1894.

Jeff Astle is the only Albion player to score in every round of an FA Cup competition. He achieved this feat in 1967-8 when he scored thus: Round 3 v Colchester (h) two goals; Round 4 v Southampton (a) two goals; Round 5 v Portsmouth (a) one goal; Round 6 v Liverpool (a) one goal; v Liverpool (2nd Replay) one goal; Semi-final v Birmingham City (Villa Park) one goal; Final v Everton (Wembley) one goal. Total nine goals.

Albion's first FA Cup goal was scored by 'Jem' Bayliss against Junction Street (Derby) on 25 October 1884.....and this was also Albion's first FA Cup victory, winning 7-1.

Albion's 1888 FA Cup-winning team. Back row (left to right): Woodhall, Timmins, Perry, Aldridge, H.Green, Horton, Paddock. Front: Tom Green, J.Bayliss, Bob Roberts, Pearson.

Albion's 100th FA Cup goal was scored by Frank Dyer against Mitchell's St George (a) on 31 January 1891.

Albion conceded only two goals in eight FA Cup ties in season 1911-12.

The most FA Cup goals by an Albion player in one season's competition is ten — by 'Jem' Bayliss in 1887-8.

Albion lost two FA Cup matches in season 1945-6 — both to Derby County, 1-0 at home, and 3-1 away. This was the only season the tournament was played on a two-legged basis.

Albion were the first Midlands club to reach the FA Cup Final (1886).

The 1888 Final between Albion and Preston North End attracted a record crowd of 18,904 spectators, who paid £827.13s. in receipts. For the first time ever in England the gates were shut long before the kick-off.

Albion appeared in six FA Cup semi-finals in seven seasons (1885-6 — 1891-2). They missed out in 1889-90 when they lost in the first round to Accrington.

The 1886 FA Cup Final replay was the first Final played outside London. It was staged at Derby Cricket Ground, and Albion lost 2-0 to Blackburn Rovers.

Albion have played only one FA Cup tie on a Sunday. That was their fourth round match against Everton at Goodison Park on 27 January 1974, when they drew 0-0 in front of a record Sunday crowd, of 53,509. Albion won the replay 1-0.

When Albion beat Aston Villa 3-0 in the 1892 FA Cup Final it was witnessed by a then record crowd of 32,710 who paid £1,757 in receipts. It was also the last Final to be played at the famous Kennington Oval Ground. In Albion's side that day was John Reynolds. Three years later he was a Villa player in the 1895 Cup Final against Albion.

The 1912 Cup Final between Albion and Barnsley lasted for 240 minutes. The first match at The Crystal Palace ended 0-0 after two hours play. The replay at Sheffield also went to two hours before Barnsley finally won with a goal by Tuffnel in the last minute of extra-time.

Albion's longest ever FA Cup tie is their fourth round clash with Chelsea in 1952-3, which went to four games. The first meeting in London ended 1-1; The Hawthorns replay finished 0-0; the second replay at Villa Park was level at 1-1 and then at Highbury in the third replay, Chelsea won 4-0. The total time involved was 420 minutes, including two periods of extra-time.

Albion's line-up for their first-ever FA Cup tie in 1883 was: Roberts; Bell, Stanton, E.Horton, F.Bunn, Swallow, Whitehouse, Aston, Bisseker, Timmins and G.Bell — all local-born players.

In their 1885-6 FA Cup run, Albion knocked out four Midlands teams en route to the Final: Aston Unity, Wednesbury Old Athletic, Wolverhampton Wanderers and Small Heath. They repeated this action in 1886-7, ousting Burton Wanderers, Derby Junction, Mitchell's St George and Notts County, and then in 1887-8 they went one better putting out Wednesbury Old Athletic, Mitchell's St George, Wolverhampton Wanderers, Stoke and Derby Junction.

In 1968-9 Albion ko'd three London clubs on their way to the semi-final stage: Fulham, Arsenal and Chelsea.

In 1889-90 Albion lost a first round tie at Accrington by 3-1, but then protested over the state of the pitch. A replay was ordered and Accrington again came out on top, winning 3-0.

Similar circumstances surrounded Albion's tie with the Lockwood Brothers Club of Sheffield, in the fifth round of the 1886-7 competition. The match, at Sheffield, ended in a 1-0 Albion win, but Lockwood lodged a complaint about the validity of the winning goal. Their appeal was upheld and a replay arranged at Derby. Albion were victors again, this time by 2-1.

Against the Druids Club of Ruabon, Wales, in a home fourth round tie on 24 January 1885, Albion took the field and scored without their opponents being there to prevent it. The referee insisted that the Druids came out of hiding, and when they did, Albion promptly scored again to go through 'officially' by a goal to nil.

When Albion won the Cup in 1954 they had the good fortune to be drawn in the Midlands in every round up to the Final. They received home ties in rounds three, four, five and six, and then met Staffordshire rivals Port Vale in the semi-final at neutral Villa Park — just three miles from The Hawthorns.

Albion's 1935 FA Cup Final squad. Back row (left to right): F.Reed (trainer), W.H.Keys (director), H.Trentham, H.Pearson, J.Carter, J.Round (director), C.Jephcott (director). Middle: L.Nurse (director), W.Richardson, W.G.Richardson, W.I.Bassett (chairman), T.Glidden, E.Sandford, F.Everiss (secretary). Front: A.Gale, J.Edwards, G.Shaw, J.Murphy, W.Boyes, J.Sankey.

Albion's first FA Cup tie at The Hawthorns was against Manchester City on 26 January 1901. A crowd of 10,026 saw Albion win 1-0 with a goal by Ben Garfield.

Between 31 October 1885 and 5 March 1886, Albion lost only one Cup tie out of 15. They were beaten once in 26 ties between October 1885 and March 1889.

Starting on 15 October 1887 and ending on 2 March 1889, Albion won ten FA Cup games on the trot — against Wednesbury Old Athletic 7-1, Mitchell's St George 1-0, Wolves 2-0, Stoke 4-1, Old Carthusians 4-2, Derby Junction 3-0, Preston 2-1, Small Heath 3-2, Burnley 5-1 and Chatham 10-1.

When Albion won the FA Cup in 1888 each member of their side was a purely local born player: Bob Roberts (born West Bromwich), Albert Aldridge (Walsall), Harry Green (West Bromwich), Ezra Horton (West Bromwich), Charlie Perry (West Bromwich), George Timmins (West Bromwich), George Woodhall (West Bromwich), Billy Bassett (West Bromwich), 'Jem' Bayliss (Tipton), Tom Pearson (West Bromwich), Joe Wilson (Handsworth). Albion, with this team, were in fact the first side to win the trophy with an all-English XI. They repeated the feat in 1931 with another all-England side.

The winning penalty goal by Ronnie Allen, which beat Port Vale goalkeeper King and put Albion in the 1954 Final.

Albion have been playing FA Cup football since 1883 — their first tie coming against Wednesbury Town (home) in that year (0-2).

Albion have appeared in ten FA Cup Finals (12 if you add replays) — only Arsenal and Newcastle United have played in more.

Tony Brown and Jeff Astle, Albion's scorers in the 1968 FA Cup semi-final v Birmingham.

Ousted by the Minnows

Here are the instances whereby Albion were knocked out of the FA Cup by teams from lower Divisions:

1899-1900 — Southampton (SL); 1900-01 — Tottenham Hotspur (SL);
1902-03 — Tottenham Hotspur (SL); 1907-08 — Southampton (SL);
1911-12 — Barnsley (Division Two); 1912-13 — West Ham United (SL);
1914-15 — Hull City (Division Two); 1919-20 — Barnsley (Division Two);
1919-20 — Notts Co (Division Two); 1921-2 — Notts Co (Division Two);
1922-3 — Charlton Ath (Division Three S); 1926-7 — Hull City (Division Two);
1929-30 — Wrexham (Division Three N); 1932-3 — West Ham United (Division Two);
1935-6 — Bradford (Division Two); 1937-8 — York City (Division Three N);
1949-50 — Cardiff City (Division Two); 1951-2 — Blackburn Rovers (Division Two);
1960-61 — Lincoln City (Division Three); 1965-6 — Bolton Wanderers (Division Two);
1979-80 — West Ham United (Division Two); 1981-2 — Queen's Park Rangers (Division Two);
1983-4 — Plymouth Argyle (Division Three); 1984-5 — Orient (Division Three).
1986-7 — Swansea City (Division Four).

Tony Brown (54 total) has appeared in most FA Cup games for Albion. Ray Barlow had 46 outings and Ronnie Allen and John Wile 42 each.

The following all made their Albion debuts at senior level in the FA Cup:-
Joe Matthews (1884-5), George Johnson (1895-6), Alf Taylor (1927-8), Jack Sankey (1933-4), Graham Wilkes (1938-9), Dennis Gordon (1947-8), Johnny Nicholls (1951-2), Dave Mountford (1952-3).

Right-half Ezra Horton played in each of Albion's first 36 FA Cup matches — 1883 to 1890 inclusive.

Jim Sanders and Joe Kennedy both won FA Cup winners' medals in 1954 without appearing in any of the previous rounds leading up to the Final — a rare occurrence.

173

Jeff Astle, Clive Clark and Graham Williams celebrate Albion's League Cup victory over West Ham United in 1966. The Final was played over two legs.

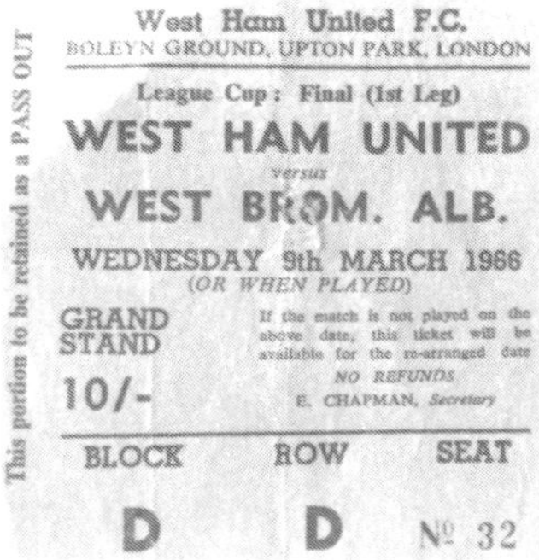

Albion in the Football League Cup

ALBION entered the Football League Cup for the first time in 1965-6 and since then they have appeared in three Finals, winning the trophy once, in their first season. In 1982-3 the competition became known as the Milk Cup and in season 1986-7 it became the Littlewoods Challenge Cup. In the following section, the competition is referred to as the League Cup throughout.

1965-6
Round 1
Bye
Round 2
Sep 22 v Walsall (h) 3-1
Brown (2), Bennett (og)
Potter; Cram, Fairfax, Lovett, Jones, Fraser, Brown, Astle, Kaye, Hope, Clark.
Att: 41,188
Round 3
Oct 13 v Leeds United (a) 4-2
Brown, Kaye, Clark, Astle
Sheppard; Cram, Fairfax, Lovett, Jones, Fraser, Brown, Astle, Kaye, Hope, Clark.
Att: 13,455
Round 4
Nov 3 v Coventry City (a) 1-1
Kaye
Sheppard; Cram, Fairfax, Lovett, Jones, Fraser, Brown, Crawford, Kaye, Hope, Clarke.
Att: 38,476
Round 4 (Replay)
Nov 10 v Coventry City (h) 6-1
Astle 3, Fraser 2, Brown
Sheppard; Cram, Fairfax, Lovett, Jones, Fraser, Brown, Astle, Kaye, Hope, Clark.
Att: 31,956
Round 5
Nov 17 v Aston Villa (h) 3-1
Kaye 2, Brown
Sheppard; Cram, Fairfax, Lovett, Jones, Fraser, Brown, Astle, Kaye, Hope, Clark.
Att: 40,694
Semi-Final (1st leg)
Dec 1 v Peterborough United (h) 2-1
Brown, Astle
Sheppard; Cram, Fairfax, Lovett, Jones, Fraser, Brown, Astle, Kaye, Hope, Clark.
Att: 20,933
Semi-Final (2nd leg)
Dec 15 v Peterborough United (a) 4-2 (agg 6-3)
Brown 3, Crawford
Potter; Cram, Fairfax, Lovett, Jones, Fraser, Brown, Crawford, Kaye, Hope, Clark.
At: 18,288
Final (1st leg)
Feb 9 v West Ham United (a) 1-2
Astle
Potter; Cram, Fairfax, Fraser, Campbell, Williams, Brown, Astle, Kaye, Lovett, Clark.
Att: 28,588
Final (2nd leg)
Feb 23 v West Ham United (h) 4-1 (agg 5-3)
Kaye, Brown, Clark, Williams
Potter; Cram, Fairfax, Fraser, Campbell, Williams, Brown, Astle, Kaye, Hope, Clark.
Att: 32,013.

1966-7
Round 1
Bye
Round 2
Sep 14 v Aston Villa (h) 6-1
Hope 3, Fraser 2, Clark
Sheppard; Cram, Collard, Lovett, Jones, Fraser, Foggo, Astle, Kaye, Hope, Clark.
Att: 25,039

Round 3
Oct 5 v Manchester City (h) 4-2
Stephens, Krzywicki, Astle, Clark
Potter; Crawford, Collard, Williams, Campbell, Fraser (Krzywicki), Stephens, Lovett, Astle, Hope, Clark.
Att: 19,016
Round 4
Oct 25 v Swindon Town (a) 2-0
Astle, Clark
Potter; Crawford, Collard, Lovett, Jones, Fraser, Williams, Astle, Kaye, Hope, Clark.
Att: 16,254
Round 5
Dec 7 v Northampton Town (a) 3-1
Brown, Simpson, Clark
Sheppard; Simpson, Williams, Lovett, Jones, Fraser, Brown, Astle, Kaye, Hope, Clark.
Att: 14,706

Semi-Final (1st leg)
Jan 18 v West Ham United (h) 4-0
Astle 3, Clark
Sheppard; Cram, Williams, Collard, Jones, Fraser, Brown, Astle, Kaye, Hope, Clark.
Att: 30,193
Semi-Final (2nd leg)
Feb 8 v West Ham United (a) 2-2 (6-2)
Hope, Clark
Sheppard; Cram, Williams, Collard, Jones, Fraser, Foggo, Brown, Kaye, Hope, Clark.
Att: 35,790
Final (Wembley)
Mar 4 v Queen's Park Rangers 2-3
Clark 2
Sheppard; Cram, Williams, I.Collard, Clarke, Fraser, Brown, Astle, Kaye, Hope, Clark.
Att: 97,952

1967-8
Round 2
Sep 13 v Reading (a) 1-3
Collard
Osborne; Fraser, Williams, Collard, Colquhoun, Talbut, Brown, Astle, Kaye, Hope, Clark.
Att: 18,910

1968-9
Round 2
Sep 3 v Nottingham Forest (at Meadow Lane) 3-2
Astle 2, Rees
Sheppard; Fraser, Williams, Brown, Talbut, Colquhoun, Rees, Kaye, Astle, Hope, Clark.
Att: 23,970
Round 3
Sep 25 v Peterborough United (a) 1-2
Brown (pen)
Osborne; Fraser, G.Williams, Brown, Talbut, Merrick, Rees, Lovett, Astle, Kaye, Clark.
Att: 16,510

1969-70
Round 2
Sep 3 v Aston Villa (a) 2-1
Suggett, Astle
Osborne; Fraser, Merrick, Brown, Talbut, Kaye, Suggett, Hughes, Astle, Hope, Hartford.
Att: 40,303

Jeff Astle flashes home Albion's winning goal at Villa Park in September 1969 to launch the Throstles on the road to Wembley.

Round 3
Sep 24 v Ipswich Town (a) 1-1
Suggett
Osborne; Fraser, Wilson, Hughes, Talbut, Kaye (Krzywicki), Brown, Hegan, Astle, Suggett, Hope.
Att: 19,261
Round 3 (Replay)
Oct 1 v Ipswich Town (h) 2-0
Hope, Astle
Osborne; Fraser, Wilson (T.Brown), Hughes, Talbut, Kaye, Krzywicki, Suggett, Astle, Hegan, Hope.
Att: 24,631
Round 4
Oct 15 v Bradford City (h) 4-0
Cantello, Hope, Brown, Krzywicki
Osborne; Fraser, Williams, Cantello, Talbut, Kaye, Krzywicki, T.Brown, Astle, Hartford, Hope.
Att: 25,343
Round 5
Oct 29 v Leicester City (a) 0-0
Osborne; Fraser, Williams, T.Brown, Talbut, Kaye, Hegan, Suggett, Astle, Hartford, Hope.
Att: 35,121

175

Astle, on ground, scores one of his two goals in the replay against Leicester in November 1969.

Replay
Nov 5 v Leicester City (h) 2-1
Astle 2
Osborne, Fraser, Williams, Brown, Talbut, Kaye, Hegan, Suggett, Astle, Hartford, Hope.
Att: 26,981
Semi-Final (1st leg)
Nov 19 v Carlisle United (a) 0-1
Osborne; Fraser, Williams, Brown, Talbut, Kaye, Krzywicki, Suggett, Astle, Hartford, Hope.
Att: 20,322
Semi-Final (2nd leg)
Dec 3 v Carlisle United (h) 4-1 (agg 4-2)
Hope, Suggett, Brown, Martin
Osborne; Fraser, Wilson, Brown, Talbut (Martin), Kaye, Krzywicki, Suggett, Astle, Hartford, Hope.
Att: 34,835

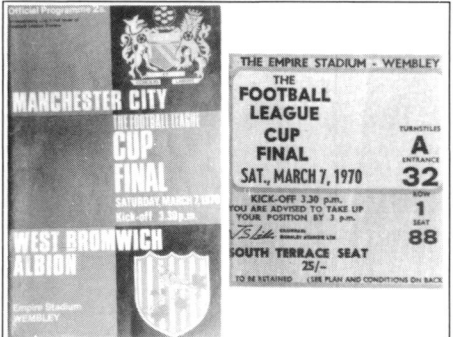

Final (Wembley)
Mar 7 v Manchester City 1-2 (a.e.t.)
Astle
Osborne; Fraser, Wilson, Brown, Talbut, Kaye, Cantello, Suggett, Astle, Hartford (Krzywicki), Hope.
Att: 97,963

1970-71
Round 2
Sep 8 v Charlton Athletic (h) 3-1
Kaye, Astle, Suggett
Cumbes; Hughes, Merrick, Robertson (Glover), Talbut, Kaye, Reed, Suggett, Astle, Hope, Cantello.
Att: 16,124
Round 3
Oct 6 v Preston North End (a) 1-0
Hartford
Cumbes; Minton, Merrick, Brown, Talbut, Kaye, McVitie, Suggett, Astle, Hope, Hartford.
Att: 18,222
Round 4
Oct 28 v Tottenham Hotspur (a) 0-5
Cumbes; Fraser, Merrick, Cantello (Lovett), Talbut, Kaye, McVitie, Suggett, Astle, Brown, Hartford.
Att: 31,598

1971-2
Round 2
Sep 8 v Tottenham Hotspur (h) 0-1
Cumbes; Hughes, Minton, Cantello, Wile, Kaye, Suggett, Brown, MacLean, Hope, Hartford.
Att: 26,185

1972-3
Round 2
Sep 6 v Queens Park Rangers (h) 2-1
Evans (og), T.Brown (pen)
Latchford; Nisbet, Wilson, Hughes, Wile, Robertson, Suggett, T.Brown, Gould, A.Brown, Hartford.
Att: 10,494
Round 3
Oct 3 v Liverpool (h) 1-1
Hartford
Latchford; Nisbet, Wilson, Cantello, Wile, Robertson, Suggett, T.Brown, Gould, A.Brown, Hartford.
Att: 17,661
Replay
Oct 10 v Liverpool (a) 1-2 (a.e.t.)
Robertson
Latchford; Nisbet, Wilson, Cantello (Woolgar), Wile, Robertson, Suggett, T.Brown, Gould, A.Brown, Hartford.
Att: 26,461

Doug Fraser leads Albion out to a snowy Wembley pitch for the 1970 League Cup Final.

1973-4
Round 2
Oct 8 v Sheffield United (h) 2-1
Shaw, Cantello
Latchford; Nisbet, Merrick, Cantello (Glover), Wile, Robertson, Johnston, A.Brown, T.Brown, Hartford, Shaw.
Att: 10,482
Round 3
Oct 31 v Exeter City (h) 1-3
Johnston
Latchford; Nisbet, Merrick, Cantello, Wile, Robertson, Johnston, A.Brown, T.Brown, Hartford, Shaw.
Att: 10,719

1974-5
Round 2
Sep 10 v Millwall (h) 1-0
Cantello
Latchford; Nisbet, Wilson, Cantello, Wile, Robertson, Glover, T.Brown, Shaw, Merrick, Johnston.
Att: 8,294
Round 3
Oct 9 v Norwich City (h) 1-1
Stringer (og)
Latchford; Nisbet, Wilson, Cantello, Wile, Robertson, Glover, T.Brown, Mayo, Merrick, Johnston.
Att: 11,625
Replay
Oct 16 v Norwich City (a) 0-2 (a.e.t.)
Latchford; Nisbet, Wilson, Cantello, Wile, Robertson, Glover, Shaw, Mayo (Donaghy), Hughes, Johnston.
Att: 18,235

1975-6
Round 2
Sep 9 v Fulham (h) 1-1
Johnston
Osborne; Mulligan, Thompson, Cantello, Wile, Robertson, Trewick, T.Brown, Hurst, Giles, Johnston.
Att: 10,912
Replay
Sep 24 v Fulham (a) 0-1
Osborne; Thompson, Wilson, Cantello, Wile, Robertson, Glover, A.Brown, Hurst, Giles, Johnston.
Att: 10,785

1976-7
Round 2
Aug 31 v Liverpool (a) 1-1
Giles
Osborne; Mulligan, Cantello, T.Brown, Wile, Robertson, Martin, A.Brown, Mayo, Giles, Johnston.
Att: 22,984
Replay
Sep 6 v Liverpool (h) 1-0
Martin
Osborne; Mulligan, Cantello, T.Brown, Wile, Robertson, Martin, Robson, Mayo, Edwards, Johnston.
Att: 22,662
Round 3
Sep 22 v Brighton & Hove Albion (h) 0-2
Osborne; Mulligan, Cantello, T.Brown, Wile, Robertson, Martin, Edwards (Robson), Mayo, Giles, Johnston.
Att: 18,728

Stringer of Norwich turns the ball into his own net at The Hawthorns in October 1974 but Albion lost the replay at Carrow Road.

1977-8
Round 2
Aug 31 v Rotherham United (h) 4-0
Regis 2 (1 pen), Wile, Martin
Godden; Mulligan (Trewick), Statham, Martin, Wile, Robertson, Cantello, Cunningham, Regis, Robson, Johnston.
Att: 15,005
Round 3
Oct 25 v Watford (h) 1-0
T.Brown
Godden; Mulligan, Statham, T.Brown, Wile, Robertson, Cantello, Cunningham, D.Cross, Robson, Johnston.
Att: 21,985
Round 4
Nov 29 v Bury (a) 0-1
Godden; Mulligan, Statham, T.Brown (Regis), Wile, Robertson, Martin, Cunningham, D.Cross, Robson, Johnston.
Att: 13,898

1978-9
Round 2
Aug 30 v Leeds United (h) 0-0
Godden; Batson, Statham, Trewick, Wile, Robertson, Robson, A.Brown (Martin), Regis, Cunningham, Johnston.
Att: 25,188
Replay
Sep 6 v Leeds United (a) 0-0 (a.e.t.)
Godden; Batson, Statham, Cunningham, Wile, Robertson, Robson, A.Brown, Regis, Cantello, Johnston.
Att: 29,316
Second Replay
Oct 2 v Leeds United (Maine Road) 0-1
Godden; Batson, Statham, Cunningham, Wile, Robertson, Robson, A.Brown, Regis, Cantello, T.Brown.
Att: 8,164

1979-80
Round 2 (1st leg)
Aug 29 v Fulham (h) 1-1
Robson
Godden; Batson, Statham, T.Brown, Wile, Robertson, Robson, A.Brown, Mills, Owen, Barnes.
Att: 14,617

Round 2 (2nd leg)
Sep 5 v Fulham (a) 1-0 (agg 2-1)
Robson
Godden; Batson, Statham, Trewick, Wile, Robertson, Robson, Mills, T.Brown, Owen, Barnes.
Att: 11,542
Round 3
Sep 26 v Coventry City (h) 2-1
T.Brown (pen), Wile
Godden; Batson, Statham, Trewick, Wile, Robertson, Robson, T.Brown, Mills, Owen, Barnes.
Att: 18,058
Round 4
Oct 31 v Norwich City (h) 0-0
Godden; Batson, Statham, Mills, Wile, Robertson, Robson, A.Brown, Regis, Owen, T.Brown.
Att: 24,251
Replay
Nov 7 v Norwich City (a) 0-3
Godden; Trewick, Statham (Barnes), Mills, Wile, Robertson, Robson, A.Brown, Regis, Owen, T.Brown.
Att: 19,677

1980-81
Round 2 (1st leg)
Aug 26 v Leicester City (h) 1-0
Barnes
Godden; Trewick, Statham, Moses, Wile, Robertson, Robson, A.Brown, Regis, Owen, Barnes.
Att: 13,810
Round 2 (2nd leg)
Sep 3 v Leicester City (a) 1-0 (agg 2-0)
Regis
Godden; Trewick, Statham, Moses, Wile, Robertson, Bennett, A.Brown, Regis, Owen, Barnes.
Att: 17,081
Round 3
Sep 24 v Everton (a) 2-1
Moses, Robertson
Godden; Batson, Statham, Moses, Wile, Robertson, Trewick, A.Brown, Regis, Owen, Barnes (Monaghan)
Att: 23,546
Round 4
Oct 29 v Preston North End (h) 0-0
Godden; Batson, Statham, Moses, Wile, Robertson, Robson, A.Brown, Regis, Trewick, Barnes (Mills).
Att: 17,579
Replay
Nov 4 v Preston North End (a) 1-1 (a.e.t.)
A.Brown
Godden; Batson, Cowdrill, Moses, Wile, Robertson, Robson, A.Brown, Regis, Owen (Trewick), Mills.
Att: 14,420
Second Replay
Nov 12 v Preston North End (h) 2-1
Regis 2
Godden; Batson, Cowdrill, Moses, Wile, Robertson, Robson, A.Brown, Regis, Owen, Barnes (Mills).
Att: 15,218
Round 5
Dec 5 v Manchester City (a) 1-2
Booth (og)
Godden; Batson, Trewick, Moses, Wile, Bennett, Robson, A.Brown, Regis, Owen, Barnes.
Att: 35,611

Tony Godden saves a penalty against Everton at Goodison Park in the 1980-81 League Cup.

1981-2
Round 2 (1st leg)
Oct 6 v Shrewsbury Town (a) 3-3
Regis, Mackenzie, N.Cross
Godden; Batson, Statham, King, Wile, Robertson, N.Cross, Summerfield, Regis, Owen, Mackenzie.
Att: 9,291
Round 2 (2nd leg)
Oct 28 v Shrewsbury Town (h) 2-1 (agg 5-4)
A.Brown, Owen
Godden; Batson, Statham, King, Wile, Robertson, Jol, A.Brown, Regis, Owen, Mackenzie.
Att: 12,596
Round 3
Nov 10 v West Ham United (a) 2-2
Regis, King
Grew; Arthur, Statham, King, Wile, Robertson, Jol, A.Brown, Regis, Owen, Mackenzie.
Att: 24,168
Replay
Nov 24 v West Ham United (h) 1-1 (a.e.t.)
Regis
Grew; Batson, Statham, King, Wile, Robertson, Jol, A.Brown, Regis, Owen, Mackenzie.
Att: 15,985
Second Replay
Dec 1 v West Ham United (a) 1-0
Regis
Grew; Batson, Statham, King, Wile, Robertson, Jol, A.Brown, Regis, Owen, Mackenzie.
Att: 24,502
Round 4
Dec 15 v Crystal Palace (a) 3-1
Regis 2, Monaghan
Grew; Batson, Bennett, King, Wile, Robertson (Lewis), Arthur, Monaghan, Regis, Owen, Mackenzie.
Att:10,311
Round 5
Jan 20 v Aston Villa (a) 1-0
Statham
Grew; Batson, Statham, A.Brown, Wile, Robertson, Jol, King, Regis, Owen, Mackenzie.
Att: 35,197
Semi-Final (1st leg)
Feb 3 v Tottenham Hotspur (h) 0-0
Grew; Batson, Statham, King, Wile, Bennett, Jol, Monaghan (N.Cross), Regis, Owen, Mackenzie.
Att: 32,166
Semi-Final (2nd leg)
Feb 10 v Tottenham Hotspur (a) 0-1 (agg 0-1)
Grew; Arthur, Statham, Bennett, Wile, Robertson, Jol, Summerfield, Regis, Owen (King), Mackenzie.
Att: 47,241

1982-3
Round 2 (1st leg)
Oct 6 v Nottingham Forest (a) 1-6
Regis
Grew; Batson, Whitehead, Zondervan, Bennett, Robertson, Jol, A.Brown, Regis, Owen, Eastoe.
Att: 11,969

Round 2 (2nd leg)
Oct 27 v Nottingham Forest (h) 3-1 (agg 4-7)
Regis, N.Cross, Whitehead
Godden; Batson, Statham, Zondervan, Wile, Robertson, Jol, A.Brown, Regis (Cowdrill), N.Cross, Whitehead.
Att: 6,536

1983-4
Round 2 (1st leg)
Oct 4 v Millwall (a) 0-3
Barron; Whitehead, Cowdrill, Zondervan, McNaught (Mackenzie), Smith, Lewis, Thompson, Regis, Robson, N.Cross.
Att: 10,721
Round 2 (2nd leg)
Oct 25 v Millwall (h) 5-1 (agg 5-4)
Thompson 2, Regis 2, Owen (pen)
Barron; Whitehead, Cowdrill, Zondervan, McNaught, Bennett, Lewis, Thompson, Regis, Owen (N.Cross), Perry.
Att: 13,331
Round 3
Nov 9 v Chelsea (a) 1-0
Thompson
Barron; Whitehead, Cowdrill, Zondervan, McNaught, Robertson, Lewis, Thompson, Perry, Owen, Luke.
Att: 22,932
Round 4
Nov 30 v Aston Villa (h) 1-2
Regis
Barron; Whitehead, Cowdrill, Zondervan, McNaught, Robertson, Jol, Thompson, Regis (Mackenzie), Owen, N.Cross.
Att: 31,114

1984-5
Round 2 (1st leg)
Sep 25 v Wigan Athletic (a) 0-0
Godden; Whitehead, Statham, Hunt, Bennett, Robertson, Grealish, Thompson, N.Cross, Mackenzie, Morley.
Att: 6,209
Round 2 (2nd leg)
Oct 10 v Wigan Athletic (h) 3-1 (agg 3-1)
Hunt, Thompson, N.Cross
Godden; Whitehead, Statham, Hunt, Bennett, Forsyth, Grealish, Thompson, N.Cross, Mackenzie, Robson.
Att: 8,133
Round 3
Oct 30 v Birmingham City (a) 0-0
Godden; Whitehead, Cowdrill, Hunt, Bennett, Robertson, Lewis, Thompson, Mackenzie, D.Cross, Robson.
Att: 17,616
Replay
Nov 7 v Birmingham City (h) 3-1
Thompson, Robertson, D.Cross
Godden; Whitehead, Statham, Hunt, Bennett, Robertson, Grealish, Thompson, Mackenzie, D.Cross, Valentine (Robson).
Att: 16,717

Round 4
Nov 20 v Watford (a) 1-4
D.Cross
Godden; Nicholl, Statham, Hunt, Bennett, Robertson, Grealish, Thompson, Mackenzie, D.Cross, Valentine.
Att: 16,378

1985-6
Round 2 (1st leg)
Sep 24 v Port Vale (h) 1-0
G.Armstrong
Godden; Nicholl, Statham, Hunt, Cowdrill, Robertson, G.Armstrong, Robson, Mackenzie (Anderson), Valentine, Crooks.
Att: 6,288
Round 2 (2nd leg)
Oct 7 v Port Vale (a) 2-2 (agg 3-2)
Varadi 2
Bradshaw; Nicholl, Statham, Grealish, Bennett, Robertson, Valentine (Whitehead), Hunt, Varadi, Thomas, Crooks.
Att: 7,895
Round 3
Oct 29 v Coventry City (a) 0-0
Bradshaw; Nicholl, Statham, Hunt, Bennett, Robertson, Valentine, Grealish, Varadi, Thomas, Crooks.
Att: 9,804
Replay
Nov 6 v Coventry City (h) 4-3
Hunt, Varadi 2, Crooks
Bradshaw; Nicholl, Statham, Hunt, Bennett, Robertson (Whitehead), Valentine, Grealish, Varadi, Thomas, Crooks.
Att: 8,987
Round 4
Nov 20 v Aston Villa (a) 2-2
Crooks, Bennett
Bradshaw; Nicholl, Statham, Hunt, Bennett, Robertson, Armstrong (Palmer), Whitehead, Varadi, Thomas, Crooks.
Att: 20,204
Replay
Nov 27 v Aston Villa (h) 1-2
Hunt
Bradshaw; Palmer, Statham, Hunt, Bennett, Robertson, Dennison (Grealish), Whitehead, Varadi, Thomas, Crooks.
Att: 18,868

1986-7
Round 2 (1st leg)
Sep 24 v Derby County (a) 1-4
Bull
Naylor; Whitehead, Anderson, Bennett (Burrows), Dyson, Dickinson, Palmer, Evans (Robinson), Bull, Williamson, Dobbins.
Att: 11,304
Round 2 (2nd leg)
Oct 7 v Derby County (h) 0-1 (agg 1-5)
Naylor; Whitehead, Anderson, Palmer, Dyson, Dickinson, Cowdrill, Evans, Mackenzie, Williamson, Bull (Thompson).
Att: 6,765

Paul Dyson (far left) and Colin Anderson (left) were members of the Albion defence which went down to Derby County in the 1986-7 Littlewoods Challenge Cup. Jimmy Nicholl (right) was a regular the previous season when Albion reached the fourth round of the Milk Cup. Nicholl missed the Villa replay, however, when the Throstles went out.

178

League Cup Facts & Figures

- Albion entered the League Cup for the first time in season 1965-6 and they won it, beating West Ham United 5-3 on aggregate in the two-legged Final.

- Tony Brown set a League Cup record in that season's competition by becoming the first player to score in every round. The 41,188 gate for the Albion v Walsall second round tie at The Hawthorns on 22 September 1965, created a new record for the competition — and it is still Albion's best home attendance in the League Cup. Incidently, this was also Albion's first ever League Cup match.

- Albion's longest League Cup tie to date is their second round clash with Leeds United in 1978-9 which went to a second replay. The first game ended 0-0 at The Hawthorns; the replay at Leeds also finished goalless, after extra-time; then in the next battle at neutral Maine Road, United won through with a goal from Paul Hart. The total playing time in these matches was 300 minutes.

- Albion won their first 13 home League Cup ties, and included in this were two 6-1 victories — against Coventry City in 1965-6, and Aston Villa the following season. That scoreline remains Albion's best in the competition, whilst Nottingham Forest inflicted Albion's heaviest defeat, in 1982-3 when they won 6-1 at the City Ground. Tottenham beat Albion 5-0 in 1970-1. Albion's heaviest home defeat was by Exeter City, who won 3-1 on 31 October 1973.

- Albion scored in every one of their first 23 Football League Cup ties — in their 24th they drew 0-0 at Leicester City on 29 October 1969. Tony Brown had the distinction of scoring Albion's first League Cup goal — against Walsall at The Hawthorns in September 1965. His League Cup goals tally for that season was ten, a club record. Clive Clark's total in 1966-7 was eight.

- Jeff Astle has scored most League Cup goals for Albion — 19. Tony Brown's total is 17 and Clive Clark's tally, 10.

- Ally Robertson made 53 League Cup appearances for Albion — a club record. Tony Brown's tally was 47 and John Wile's 42. Albion's best League Cup victory away from home is 4-2 — achieved twice — at Leeds in 1965-6 and in the second leg of the 1965-6 semi-final against Peterborough United.

- In reaching the Final in 1970, Albion became the first Midlands club to win through to this stage in the competition on three separate occasions. Jeff Astle's goal in this Final gave him the record of being the first player to score in an FA Cup Final and League Cup Final at Wembley.

- Albion's longest unbeaten sequence in the League Cup is seven matches — created on three different occasions, 1965-6, 1966-7 and 1969-70.

- The following players all made their debuts for Albion in the League Cup:
  Danny Campbell, v West Ham United (a) Final, 1st leg, 9 February 1966.
  Kenny Stephens, v Manchester City (h) Round 3, 5 October 1966.
  Hugh MacLean, v Tottenham Hotspur (h) Round 2, 8 September 1971.
  Paddy Mulligan, v Fulham (h) Round 2, 9 September 1975.
  Cyrille Regis, v Rotherham United (h) Round 2, 31 August 1977.
  John Smith, v Millwall (a) Round 2, 1st leg, 4 October 1983.
  (Stephens and Regis both scored on their debuts).

Albion's Record in the League Cup, Milk Cup and Littlewoods Challenge Cup competitions – 1965-1986

League Cup

	HOME						AWAY				
P	W	D	L	F	A	P	W	D	L	F	A
35	23	9	3	71	27	37	13	9	15	47	52

Milk Cup

	HOME						AWAY				
P	W	D	L	F	A	P	W	D	L	F	A
8	6	0	2	21	11	9	1	5	3	7	17

Littlewoods Challenge Cup

	HOME						AWAY				
P	W	D	L	F	A	P	W	D	L	F	A
1	0	0	1	0	1	1	0	0	1	1	4

FULL TABLE

	HOME						AWAY				
P	W	D	L	F	A	P	W	D	L	F	A
44	29	9	6	92	39	47	14	14	19	55	73

Jeff Astle scored most League Cup goals for Albion and his goal in the 1970 Final made him the first player to have scored in both League Cup and FA Cup Finals at Wembley.

179

Albion in Europe

Fairs Cup

1966-7
Round 1
Bye
Round 2 (1st leg)
Nov v DOS Utrecht (a) 1-1
Hope
Potter; C. Crawford, Collard, Lovett, Jones, Fraser, Williams, Astle, Kaye, Hope, Clark.
Att: 5,500
Round 2 (2nd Leg)
Nov 9 v DOS Utrecht (h) 5-2 (agg 6-3)
Brown 3 (1 pen), Kaye, Clark
Potter; C. Crawford, Collard, Williams, Jones, Fraser, Brown, Astle, Kaye, Hope, Clark.
Att: 19,170
Round 3 (1st leg)
Feb 1 v Bologna (a) 0-3
Osborne; Cram, Williams, Collard, Talbut, Fraser, Brown, Astle, Kaye, Hope, Clark.
Att: 20,100
Round 3 (2nd leg)
Mar 8 v Bologna (h) 1-3 (agg 1-6)
Fairfax
Osborne; Clarke, Fairfax, Collard, Colquhoun, Fraser, Brown, Astle, Kaye, Hope, Clark.
Att: 27,401

European Cup-winners Cup

1968-9
Round 1
Sep 18 v RFC Bruges (a) 1-3
Hartford
Osborne; Fraser, Williams, Brown, Talbut, Kaye, Rees, Hartford, Astle (Lovett), Hope, Clark.
Att: 28,000
Round 1 (2nd leg)
Oct 2 v RFC Bruges (h) 2-0 (agg 3-3)
Hartford, Brown
Osborne; Fraser, Williams, Brown, Talbut, Kaye, Rees, Hartford (Collard), Astle, Hope, Clark.
Att: 33,747
Albion through on away-goals rule.
Round 2 (1st leg)
Nov 13 v Dinamo Bucharest (a) 1-1
Hartford
Osborne; Fraser, Wilson, Brown, Talbut, Kaye (Lovett), Rees, Collard, Astle, Hope, Hartford.
Att: 15,000
Round 2 (2nd Leg)
Nov 27 v Dinamo Bucharest (h) 4-0 (agg 5-1)
Brown 2 (1 pen), Lovett, Astle
Osborne; Fraser, Wilson, Brown, Talbut, Kaye, Clark, Lovett, Astle, Hope, Hartford.
Att: 33,059
Round 3 (1st Leg)
Jan 15 v Dunfermline Ath (a) 0-0
Osborne; Fraser, Wilson, Brown, Talbut, Kaye, Hope, Lovett, Astle, Collard, Hartford (Krzywicki).
Att: 22,073
Round 3 (2nd Leg)
Feb 19 v Dunfermline Ath (h) 0-1 (agg 0-1)
Osborne; Fraser, Wilson, Brown, Talbut, Kaye, Martin, Lovett, Astle, Collard, Hartford
Att: 32,373

◀ Ian Collard looks on as the Dinamo goalkeeper punches clear from Jeff Astle in Bucharest.

UEFA Cup

1978-9
Round 1
Bye
Round 2 (1st Leg)
Sep 13 v Galatasary (a) 3-1
Cunningham 2 Robson
Godden; Batson, Statham, Cunningham, Wile, Robertson, Robson, A. Brown, Regis, Trewick, Cantello.
Att: 38,443
Round 2 (2nd Leg)
Sep 27 v. Galatasary (h) 3-1 (agg 6-2)
Cunningham (pen), Robson, Trewick
Godden (Grew); Batson, Statham, Cunningham, Wile, Robertson, Robson, A.Brown, Regis, Cantello, Trewick (T.Brown).
Att: 22,380
Round 3 (1st leg)
Oct 18 v Sporting Braga (a) 2-0
Regis 2
Godden; Batson, Statham, Cunningham, Wile, Robertson, Robson, A.Brown, Regis, Cantello, T.Brown.
Att: 31,383
Round 3 (2nd Leg)
Nov 1 v Sporting Braga (h) 1-0 (agg 3-0)
A.Brown
Godden; Batson, Statham, Cunningham, Wile, Robertson, Robson (Martin), A.Brown, Regis, Cantello (Trewick), T.Brown.
Att: 26,036
Round 4 (1st Leg)
Nov 22 v Valencia (a) 1-1
Cunningham
Godden; Batson, Statham, Trewick, Wile, Robertson, Robson, A.Brown, Regis, Cantello, Cunningham.
Att: 47,746
Round 4 (2nd leg)
Dec 6 v Valencia (h) 2-0 (agg 3-1)
T.Brown 2 (1 pen)
Godden; Batson, Statham, T.Brown, Wile, Robertson, Robson, A.Brown, Regis, Cantello (Trewick), Cunningham.
Att: 35,118
Round 5 (lst Leg)
Mar 7 v Red Star Belgrade (a) 0-1
Godden; Batson, Statham, T.Brown, Wile, Robertson, Robson, A.Brown, Regis, Trewick, Cunningham.
Att: 95,300
Round 5 (2nd Leg)
Mar 21 v Red Star Belgrade (h) 1-1 (agg 1-2)
Regis
Godden; Batson, Statham, T.Brown, Wile, Robertson, Robson, A.Brown, Regis, Cantello, Cunningham.
Att: 31,587

1979-80
Round 1
Bye
Round 2 (1st Leg)
Sep 19 v Carl Zeiss Jena (a) 0-2
Godden; Batson, Statham, Trewick, Wile, Robertson, Robson, A.Brown, T.Brown, Owen, Mills.
Att: 21,660
Round 2 (2nd Leg)
Oct 3 v Carl Zeiss Jena (h) 1-2 (agg 1-4)
Wile
Godden; Batson, Statham, Trewick (Monaghan), Wile, Robertson (Mills), Robson, A.Brown, T.Brown, Owen, Barnes.
Att: 19,204

1981-2
Round 1 (1st Leg)
Sep 16 v Grasshoppers of Zurich (a) 0-1
Godden; Batson, Statham, Moses, Wile, Robertson, Robson, Mills, Regis, Owen, Mackenzie.
Att: 8,101
Round 1 (2nd Leg)
Sep 30 v Grasshoppers of Zurich (h) 1-3 (agg 1-4)
Robertson
Godden; Batson, Statham, Robertson (Webb), Wile, Deehan, Robson, Mills (N.Cross), Regis, Owen, Mackenzie.
Att: 16,745

European Facts & Figures

- Bobby Hope scored Albion's first goal in European competition — against DOS Utrecht (away) on 2 November 1966.

- Ray Fairfax scored only one senior goal for Albion — against Bologna (home) in the second leg of the third round Fairs Cup tie on 8 March 1967.

- Ronnie Rees was sent off playing for Albion against Dinamo Bucharest in Rumania in a European Cup-winners' Cup tie on 13 November 1968.

- Against Dunfermline Athletic (home) in the European Cup-winners' Cup third round, second leg tie on 19 February 1969, several Albion players wore gloves during the match as the temperature dropped to well below freezing. Goalkeeper John Osborne wore virtually two complete strips including a woollen hat.

- Albion's finest European performance came against Valencia, in Spain, in the UEFA Cup on 22 November 1978. That evening Albion controlled the Kempes-inspired home team and were well worth the draw they achieved through a fine goal from Cunningham.

- The 95,300 attendance at the Red Star-Albion UEFA Cup tie in Belgrade on 7 March 1979, is the biggest crowd Albion have played in front of outside a Wembley Cup Final.

- Tony Brown (eight goals) has registered most European goals for Albion. Laurie Cunningham hit four and Cyrille Regis and Asa Hartford three each.

- Six players — Tony Godden, Brendon Batson, Derek Statham, John Wile, Ally Robertson and Bryan Robson — each appeared in 12 competitive European games for Albion.

- Albion's average home attendance in European competitions stands at 26,983 — aggregate 296,820 (11 games played). The biggest single turn-out was 35,118 (v Valencia in 1978) and the lowest 16,745 (v Grasshoppers of Zurich in 1981).

Albion's full record in European competition:

	P	W	D	L	F	A
Home	11	6	1	4	21	13
Away	11	2	4	5	9	14
Totals	22	8	5	9	30	27

Above: Albion defender, Brendon Batson, gets the ball away from a Valencia forward in the 1978-9 UEFA Cup match in Spain.
Left: Cyrille Regis is out-jumped by a Spanish defender in the same match.

Ally Brown (left) scored twice against Hull in the 1975-6 Anglo-Scottish Cup. Joe Mayo (right) hit three goals in the following season's competition.

Anglo-Scottish Cup

1975-6
Group 2
Aug 2 v Mansfield Town (h) 1-1
Cantello
Osborne; Nisbet, Wilson, Cantello (Mayo), Wile, Robertson, Robson, T.Brown, A.Brown, Giles, Johnston.
Att: 5,704
Aug 6 v Hull City (a) 2-1
A.Brown 2
Osborne; Nisbet, Wilson, Cantello, Robertson, Robson, Trewick, A.Brown, Mayo, Giles, Johnston.
Att: 3,094
Aug 9 v Leicester City (a) 1-2
Giles
Osborne; Nisbet, Wilson, Cantello, Wile, Robertson, Robson, A.Brown, Mayo, Giles (Trewick), Johnston.
Att: 8,219

1976-7
Midland Group
Aug 7 v Bristol C (a) 0-1
Osborne; Mulligan, Cantello, T.Brown, Wile, Robertson, Martin, A.Brown, Mayo, Giles, Johnston.
Att: 4,941
Aug 10 v Nottingham Forest (a) 2-3
Mulligan, Mayo
Ward; Mulligan, Cantello, T.Brown, Wile, Robson, Martin, Edwards, Mayo, Trewick, Johnston.
Att: 7,018
Aug 14 v Notts County (h) 3-1
Mayo 2, Johnston
Osborne; Mulligan, Robson, T.Brown, Wile, Robertson Martin, Edwards, Mayo, Giles, Johnston.
Att: 6,936

Full Members Cup

1985-6
Group 8
Oct 2 v Brighton (a) 2-1
Crooks 2
Bradshaw; Nicholl, Statham, Hunt, Bennett, Robertson, Valentine, Grealish, Varadi, Thomas, Crooks. Subs: Whitehead, Thompson.
Att: 4,649
Oct 23 v Crystal Palace (h) 2-1
Hunt, Nicholl
Powell; Nicholl, Palmer, Hunt, Bennett, Forsyth, Valentine, Grealish, Armstrong (Robson), Whitehead, Crooks (Bull).
Att: 3,914
Semi-final (Southern area)
Nov 13 v Chelsea (h) 2-2 (a.e.t)
Valentine, Crooks
Godden; Palmer (Anderson), Statham, Hunt, Bennett, Robertson, Valentine (Bull), Robson, Varadi, Thompson, Crooks.
Att: 4,070
Chelsea won 5-4 on penalties. Bull, Hunt, Varadi and Thompson scored for Albion.

1986-7
Round 1
Oct 21 v Millwall (a) 0-2
Naylor; Whitehead, Cowdrill, Palmer, Dyson, Hayward, Dennison, Evans, Bull (A.Thompson), Williamson, Crooks.
Att: 957

Watney Cup

1971-2
Round 1
July 31 v Wrexham (a) 2-1
T.Brown 2 (1 pen)
Cumbes; Hughes, Wilson, Cantello (Merrick), Wile, Kaye, Suggett, T.Brown, Astle, Hope, Hartford.
Att: 11,218
Semi-final
Aug 4 v Halifax Town (a) 2-0
Suggett 2
Cumbes; Hughes, Wilson, Cantello, Wile, Kaye, McVitie (Merrick), T.Brown, Astle, Suggett, Hartford,
Att: 12,069
Final
Aug 7 v Colchester United (h) 4-4*
Astle 2, Cantello, Suggett
Cumbes; Hughes, Wilson, Cantello, Wile, Kaye, Suggett, T.Brown, Astle, Hope, Hartford. Subs: Merrick, Robertson, MacLean.
Att: 19.009
*Colchester won 4-3 on penalties. Astle, T.Brown and Hope scored for Albion.

Rudi Krol (left) of Ajax, exchanges pennants with Albion's John Wile before the club's Centenary Match in 1979.

Centenary Match

1979-80
Aug 11 v Ajax Amsterdam (h) 1-0
Barnes
Katalinic; Batson, Statham, Trewick (Mills), Wile, Robertson, Robson, A.Brown, T.Brown, Owen, Barnes.
Att: 13,334

Opening of Floodlights

1957-8
Oct 29 v CDSA (Russian Red Army Club) (h) 6-5
Kevan 2, Allen (pen), Robson, Griffin, Howe
Sanders; Howe, Setters, Dudley, Kennedy, Barlow, Griffin, Robson, Allen, Kevan, Horobin.
Att: 52,805

Ronnie Allen's penalty goal for Albion v CDSA (Russian Army Side) at The Hawthorns in October 1957.

Festival of Britain Matches

1951
May 12 v SC Wacker (Austria) (h) 3-4
Allen 2, Barlow
Sanders; Rickaby, Millard, Kennedy, Horne, Dudley, Griffin, McCall, Barlow, Allen, Lee.
Att: 16,074
May 15 v FC Floriana (Malta) (h) 2-0
Smith, Barlow
Sanders; Rickaby, Millard, Kennedy, Vernon, S.Williams, Griffin, Smith, Barlow, Allen, Lee.
Att: 15,133

Anglo-Italian Tournament

1969-70
Group 2
May 2 v Lanerossi Vicenza (h) 0-0
Osborne; Hughes, Fraser, Lovett (Reed), Talbut, Merrick, T.Brown, Hartford, Suggett, Cantello, Hope.
Att: 17,655
May 8 v A.S. Roma (h) 4-0
T.Brown 2, Hope, Talbut
Osborne; Hughes, Fraser, Lovett (Glover), Talbut, Merrick, T.Brown, Hartford, Suggett(Martin), Cantello, Hope.
Att: 11,833
May 16 v Lanerossi Vicenza (a) 1-1*
Glover
Osborne; Hughes, Fraser, Lovett, Talbut, Merrick, T.Brown, Hartford, Suggett (Martin), Cantello (Glover), Hope.
Att: 12,000
* Game abandoned after 76 minutes due to fighting on and off the field.
May 23 v A.S. Roma (a) 1-1
Suggett
Osborne; Hughes, Fraser, T.Brown, Talbut, Merrick, Suggett, Kaye, Martin (Lovett), Hartford, Hope.
Att: 16,000
Albion failed to qualify.

1970-71
Group 2
May 26 v Inter Milan (h) 1-1
Wile
Cumbes; Hughes, Wilson, Cantello, Wile, Kaye, Suggett, T.Brown, Astle, Hope, Hartford.
Att: 17,645
May 29 v Cagliari (h) 1-2
Astle
Cumbes; Hughes, Wilson, Cantello, Wile, Kaye, Suggett, T.Brown, Astle, Hope, Hartford.
Att: 17,620
June 1 v Inter Milan (a) 0-1
Osborne; Hughes, Wilson, Lovett, Wile, Kaye, Suggett, T.Brown, Astle, Hope (MacLean), Hartford.
Att: 15,000
June 4 v Cagliari (a) 0-1
Osborne; Hughes, Wilson, Robertson, Wile, Kaye, MacLean, T.Brown, Suggett, Lovett, Merrick (Glover).
Att: 30,000
Albion failed to qualify.

Albion's defensive 'wall' holds firm as a Floriana free-kick comes in.

Jack Vernon (right) exchanges pennants with the Floriana skipper Lolly Borg before the start of the game on 15 May 1951.

United Counties League

1893-4
Group A (on League basis)
Feb 24 v Small Heath (a) 5-4
Pearson 2, McLeod 2, Geddes
Reader; Nicholson, Crone, T.Perry, C.Perry, Taggart, Bassett, McLeod, Bostock, Pearson, Geddes.
Att: 3,000
Feb 26 v Small Heath (h) 3-1
Pearson, McLeod 2
Reader. J.Horton, Crone, T.Perry, B.Hadley, Taggart, Norman, McLeod, Bostock, Pearson, Geddes.
Att: 2,700
Mar 10 v Stoke (h) 5-0
Bostock, McLeod 2, Bassett, Geddes
Reader; Nicholson, Crone, T.Perry, C.Perry, Taggart, Bassett, McLeod, Bostock, Pearson, Geddes.
Att: 3,000
Mar 19 v Stoke (a) 2-5
C.Perry, Geddes
Reader Nicholson, Crone, T.Perry, C.Perry, Taggart, Bassett, McLeod, Bostock, Pearson, Geddes.
Att: 3,000
Apr 2 v Wolves (a) 2-4
Geddes, Pearson
Reader; J.Horton, Crone, T.Perry, C.Perry, Taggart, Bassett, McLeod, O.Williams, Pearson, Geddes.
Att: 4,000
April 9 v Wolves (h) 3-1
McLeod, Bassett, Taggart
Reader, J.Horton, Crone, T.Perry, C.Perry, Taggart, Bassett, McLeod, O.Williams, Bostock, Geddes.
Att: 5,853
Albion won their group with 8 points.
Final
April 30 v Derby County (a) 1-1 (a.e.t)
Geddes
Reader; J.Horton, Crone, T.Perry, C.Perry, Taggart, Bassett, McLeod, Bostock, Pearson, Geddes.
Att: 9,000
Replay held over until 1894-5, again at Derby.
Replay
Oct 6 v Derby County (a) 1-2
McLeod
Reader; W.Williams, Crone, T.Perry, C.Perry, Taggart, Bassett, McLeod, Hutchinson, O.Williams, Newall.
Att: 6,000

International Club Match

1954
Oct 13 v Honved (in Brussels) 3-5
Nicholls 2, Allen
Sanders; Rickaby, Millard, Dudley, Kennedy, Barlow, Griffin, Ryan, Allen, Nicholls, Lee.
Att: 55,000

Championship of the World (v Scottish Cup-holders)

1888
May 19 v Renton (at Hampden Park) 1-4
Pearson
Roberts; Mason, H.Green, E.Horton, C.Perry, Timmins, Woodhall, Bassett, Bayliss, Pearson, Wilson
Att: 6,000

Texaco Cup

1970-1
Round 1 (1st leg)
Sept 14 v Morton (a) 1-2
Rankin (og)
Cumbes; Hughes, Wilson, T.Brown, Kaye, Merrick (Lovett), McVitie, Suggett, Astle, Hartford, Cantello.
Att: 7,943
Round 1 (2nd leg)
Sept 30 v Morton (h) 0-1 (agg 1-3)
Cumbes; Minton, Merrick, T.Brown, Talbut, Kaye, McVitie, Suggett, Astle, Hope, Hartford.
Att: 16,168

1974-5
Group 1
Aug 3 v Birmingham City (h) 0-0
Osborne; Nisbet, Wilson, Cantello, Wile, Robertson, Hughes, T.Brown, A.Brown (Shaw), Hartford, Johnston.
Att: 18,317
Aug 6 v Norwich City (h) 5-1
T.Brown, Shaw, A.Brown, Hughes, Johnston
Latchford; Nisbet, Wilson, Glover, Wile, Robertson, Hughes, T.Brown (A.Brown), Shaw, Hartford, Johnston.
Att: 5,393
Aug 10 v Peterborough Utd (a) 1-2
Shaw
Latchford; Nisbet, Wilson, Glover, Wile, Robertson, Hughes, T.Brown, Shaw (A.Brown), Hartford, Johnston.
Att: 8,083
Albion failed to qualify.
The 1970-1 tournament was billed as the British Isles Cup.

Lyndon Hughes (extreme left) clearing his lines for Albion in the away leg of the Texaco Cup match with Morton in 1970.

Coronation Cup

1952-3
May 4 v Wolves (h) 1-3
Lee
Sanders; Rickaby, Millard, Dudley, Dugdale, Brookes, Griffin, Hodgkisson, Allen, Ryan, Lee.
Att: 5,802

Record Victory (1st XI)
Birmingham Senior Cup

1882-3
Round 1
Nov 11 v Coseley (h) 26-0 (ht 17-0)
Aston 5, Bisseker 4, Timmins 4, G.Bell 3, Bunn 2, E.Horton 2, While 2, Whitehouse 2, H.Bell, Stanton.
Roberts; Stanton, H.Bell, E.Horton, Bunn, While, Whitehouse, Aston, Bisseker, Timmins, G.Bell.
Att: 2,500

FA Charity Shield

1920
May 15 v Tottenham Hotspur (a) 2-0
A.Smith 2
Pearson; J.Smith, Pennington, S.Richardson, Bowser, McNeal, Crisp, A.Smith, Bentley, Morris, Gregory.
Att: 58,168

1931
Oct 7 v Arsenal (at Villa Park) 0-1
Pearson; Shaw, Trentham, Magee, W.Richardson, Edwards, Glidden, Raw, W.G.Richardson, Sandford, Wood.
Att: 21,276

1954
Sept 29 v Wolves (a) 4-4
Allen 3, Ryan
Sanders; Rickaby, Millard, Dudley, Kennedy(Dugdale), Brookes, Griffin, Ryan (Hodgkisson), Allen, Carter, Lee.
Att: 45,035

1968
Aug 3 v Manchester City (a) 1-6
Krzywicki
Osborne; Fraser, Williams (Merrick), Lovett, Talbut, Kaye, Stephens, T.Brown, Krzywicki, Collard, Hartford.
Att: 35,510
Osborne retired injured in this game. Williams moved into goal and Merrick came on as substitute.

Bass Charity Vase

1892-3
Final
Feb 27 v Stoke (h) 3-3
Geddes, Boyd, Reynolds (pen)
Reader; Nicholson, McCulloch, Reynolds, C.Perry, Groves, Bassett, McLeod, Boyd, Fellows, Geddes.
Att: 5,150
Replay
Mar 9 v Stoke (a) 1-1
Bassett
Reader; Sheldon, McCulloch, Reynolds, T.Perry, Groves, Bassett, McLeod, Boyd, Fellows, Geddes.
Att: 6,000
The trophy was shared.

1893-4
Round 1
March 21 v Burton Swifts (a) 4-1
Bassett 2, Bostock, Geddes
Reader; J.Horton, Crone, T.Perry, C.Perry, Taggart, Bassett, McLeod, Bostock, Pearson, Geddes.
Att: 2,000
Semi-final
April 11 v Aston Villa (a) 2-5
O.Williams 2
Reader; J.Horton, Crone, T.Perry, Banks, Taggart, Norman, McLeod, Bostock, O.Williams, Geddes.
Att: 5,800

Ronnie Allen, scorer of a hat-trick v Wolves in the 1954 Charity Shield game.

Laurie Cunningham, star of Albion's Tennent-Caledonian Cup Final win over Rangers.

John Reynolds, a penalty, goalscorer in the Bass Charity Vase Final of 1893.

Tennent-Caledonian Cup
(all games played at Ibrox Park)

1977-8
Semi-final
Aug 6 v St. Mirren 4-3
T.Brown 2 (1pen), D.Cross, Robson
Osborne; Mulligan, Statham, T.Brown, Wile, Robertson, Robson, Cunningham, D.Cross, Cantello, Johnston.
Att: 40,404
Final
Aug 7 v Rangers 2-0
Cunningham 2
Godden; Mulligan, Statham, Martin, Wile, Robertson, Robson, Cunningham, A.Brown (D.Cross), Trewick, Johnston.
Att: 35,066

1978-79
Semi-final
Aug 5 v Southampton 1-1*
Regis
Godden; Batson, Statham, T.Brown, Wile, Robertson, Robson, A.Brown (Johnston), Regis, Trewick, Cunningham.
Att: 25,563
*Southampton won 3-1 on penalties — T.Brown scored for Albion.
Third place play-off
Aug 6 v Hearts 0-2
Godden; Batson, Statham, T.Brown, Wile, Robertson, Martin, Robson, Regis (Hughes), Trewick, Cunningham (A.Brown).
Att: 18,823

Albion in Wartime

TWO WARS have interrupted the general flow of League and Cup football in England but during each enforced break (1915-19 and 1939-45) Albion managed to participate in a number of matches, both of a competitive and friendly nature.

In 1919 they won the Midland Victory League and then in 1944 carried off the Midland War Cup — their only two honours during the hostilities.

During the World War One, Albion never travelled outside the Midlands — indeed they played relatively few matches.

Initially, when the 1914-15 season came to an end, it was decided by the four major League clubs from the West Midlnds — Albion, Aston Villa, Birmingham and Wolverhampton Wanderers — that they would take no part in wartime League football.

Villa, Albion and Wolves adhered to this arrangement but Birmingham, after season 1915-16, reconsidered the matter and decided to play in the Midland Section of the Football League.

A handful of games (some for charity) were then played between Albion, Villa and Wolves, the gate money being principally spent on comforts for soldiers. At the war's end in November 1918, the funds accumulated and were then used entirely for charitable purposes and needs.

World War Two was somewhat different. The end of League football in September 1939 was announced after only three games had been played. After a short interlude, friendly games were arranged and then the entire League was divided into 13 regional sections. These were expanded and Albion at the outset began in the Midland Region, playing later in both the League South and North Divisions. Cup competitions were introduced — based on a league qualifying basis in the early rounds and also counting towards the overall League positions — and many friendlies were played to keep the interest alive.

A full 42-match programme was re-introduced at the start of the 1945-6 transitional season when clubs prepared themselves for the resumption of the Football League in August 1946. In 1945-6, the FA Cup started up again — on a home and away basis up to and including the quarter-finals — and attendances improved tremendously.

'Sandy' McNab, Albion's left-half and regular wartime skipper.

Eric Jones scored a hat-trick against Spurs in the last 'peacetime' League game, 2 September 1939.

West Bromwich Albion 1946. Back (left to right): Kinsell, Shaw, White, Sanders, Tranter, Millard. Front: Elliott, Clarke, Newsome, Witcomb, Connelly, S.Butler.

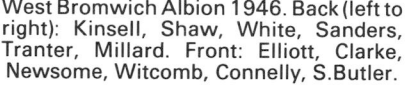

Albion in World War 1

1915-16

					1	2	3	4	5	6	7	8	9	10	11
Apr 22	(a) Aston Villa	D 1-1	Gregory	15,253	Pearson	Smith	Shore	Waterhouse	Bowser	McNeal	Wright	Morris	Newall	Gregory	Crisp
24	(h) Aston Villa	W 3-1	Wright, Mann, Reed	8,221	..	..	Pennington	..	Reed	..	Jephcott	Wright	..	Mann	Hackett

1916-17

					1	2	3	4	5	6	7	8	9	10	11
Nov 11	(n) Wolves*	L 0-1		2,000	Linden	..	..	Bowser	Attfield	Seymour	Bore	Shore	..	Gregory	Crisp
Dec 26	(h) Aston Villa	W 5-1	Mann 3, Newall, Gregory	7,145	Moorwood	..	..	Waterhouse	Bowser	McNeal	Jephcott	Mann	..	Morris	Gregory
Mar 17	(a) Birmingham	L 1-3	Newall	15,000	Pearson	..	..	..	..	..	..	..	..	Wright	Shearman
Apr 7	(a) Aston Villa	W 2-1	Gregory, McNeal	6,282	..	Bowser	..	..	Newall	..	..	Edwards	Wright	Mann	Gregory
9	(a) Wolves*	L 2-9	Jephcott, Edgley	2,200	Nicholls	Shore	..	Richardson	Harrop	..	..	York	..	Davies	Edgley
May 15	(h) Birmingham	L 0-1		7,603	Pearson	..	..	Waterhouse	Bowser	..	Wright	Edwards	Mann	Gregory	Shearman

1917-18

					1	2	3	4	5	6	7	8	9	10	11
Dec 24	(h) Aston Villa	L 1-2	Mann	6,882	..	Smith	..	..	..	..	Jephcott	..	Newall	Mann	Hackett
26	(a) Aston Villa	W 2-0	Joyce 2	7,500	..	..	..	..	..	Richardson	Elford	Joyce	..	..	Shearman
Mar 30	(h) Wolves*	L 1-3	Davies	4,500	..	..	Davison	..	Holder	Hackett	Jephcott	Wright	..	Davies	Merrick
Apr 1	(a) Wolves	D 3-3	Newall 3	3,000	..	..	Pennington	..	..	..	..	..	..	..	..

1918-19

					1	2	3	4	5	6	7	8	9	10	11
Aug 23	(h) Wolves	D 4-4	Roberts 3, Mann	5,186	Webb	..	..	Hackett	Bowser	McNeal	..	Hatton	Roberts	Mann	Gregory
5	(h) Aston Villa	L 3-4	Roberts, Mann, Bunn	8,537	..	..	..	Waterhouse	..	..	Wright	Newall	..	..	Bunn
10	(a) Wolves	D 3-3	Wright, Mann, Bowser(pen)	5,000	..	..	..	..	..	..	..	..	..	..	..
Mar 1	(h) Birmingham Wks*	W 4-1	Poulton, Hartland, Hobbs, Aston	2,000	Pearson	Robinson	Alexander	Butler	Johnston	Hackett	Poulton	Hartland	Hobbs	Gregory	Aston
22	(a) Aston Villa*	W 5-0	Magee 2, Woolley, Wright, Newall	1,500	..	Cook	..	Arch	Barwell	Wall	Jones	Wright	Magee	Newall	Woolley
29	(h) Wolves §	L 0-1		4,348	..	Smith	Cook	..	Waterhouse	Richardson	Crisp	..	Sambrook	Gregory	Shearman
Apr 5	(h) Derby C §	W 3-1	Magee, Sambrook, McNeal	7,236	..	..	..	Richardson	Reed	McNeal	Wright	Magee	..	Bentley	Gregory
12	(a) Derby C §	L 0-1		6,500	..	..	Pennington	..	Newall	..	Shearman	Wright	Magee	..	..
19	(h) Aston Villa §	W 5-1	Morris 2, Gregory 2, Magee	8,218	..	..	Cook	Waterhouse	Reed	Richardson	Wright	Magee	Morris	Gregory	Bookman
21	(a) Wolves §	D 1-1	Edwards	6,730	..	..	..	..	Bowser	..	..	Edwards	Magee	Morris	..
22	(h) RAF	W 5-3	Magee 3, Bentley, Hartland	8,056	..	..	Adams	..	Reed	..	..	Hartland	..	Bentley	Gregory
26	(a) Aston Villa §	W 3-0	Gregory, Edwards, Magee	10,000	..	..	Cook	..	..	..	..	Edwards / sub Bentley	..	Morris	..

§ Midland Victory League Matches
* Matches played with mixed teams

Summary of matches:

P	W	D	L	F	A
24	10	5	9	57	46

APPEARANCES – 1916-1919

Adams W 1, Alexander PS 2, Arch W 2, Aston A 1, Attfield W 1, Barwell R 1, Bentley A 3(1), Bookman L 2, Bore E 1, Bowser S 12, Bunn B 2, Butler E 1, Cook A 6, Crisp J 3, Davies H 3, Davison T 1, Edgley H 1, Edwards E 5, Elford W 1, Gregory H 13, Hackett W 6, Harrop J 1, Hartland H 2, Hatton S 1, Hobbs B 1, Holder H 2, Jephcott C 9, Johnston H 1, Jones A 1, Joyce S 1, Linden J 1, Magee T 7, Mann JF 10, McNeal R 13, Merrick J 2, Moorwood L 1, Morris F 5, Newall JT 14, Nicholls W 1, Pearson H 18, Pennington J 14, Poulton O 1, Reed F 5, Richardson S 9, Roberts W 3, Robinson AE 1, Sambrook C 2, Seymour C 1, Shearman B 5, Shore EW 4, Smith J 19, Wall H 1, Waterhouse F 17, Webb I 3, Woolley H 1, Wright H 18, York RE 1. Total 264(1).

GOALSCORERS – 1916-1919

8 Magee, Mann, 6 Gregory, Newall, 4 Roberts, 3 Wright, 2 Edwards, Hartland, McNeal, Morris, Joyce, 1 Aston, Bentley, Bunn, Bowser, Davies, Edgley, Hobbs, Jephcott, Poulton, Reed, Sambrook, Woolley. Total 57

MIDLAND VICTORY LEAGUE

This was arranged to give clubs competitive matches before the start of the 1919-20 season.
Four teams participated — Albion, Aston Villa, Derby County and Wolves.
The outcome was 'victory' for Albion with this record:

P	W	D	L	F	A	Pts
6	3	1	2	12	5	7

Derby finished runners-up, Wolves third, Villa fourth.

This photograph was taken at the start of World War One. Most of the players represented Albion throughout the hostilities, some of them afterwards as well. Back row (left to right): Ernie Shore, Sid Bowser, Hubert Pearson, Ted Bowen, Jim Stevenson (trainer), Len Moorwood. Standing: Bill Barber (trainer), Alonzo Poulton, Billy Hackett, Tommy Newall, Harry Wright, Matt Wood, Sam Richardson, Harry Parkes, Louis Bookman. Seated: Arthur Cook, Arthur Swift, Frank Waterhouse, Bobby McNeal, Jesse Pennington, Ben Shearman, Fred Morris, Howard Gregory. Front: Alf Bentley, Joe Smith, Claude Jephcott.
• The 'V'-styled jerseys were used as a change strip for Albion during the 1914-18 wartime period.

Albion' average home attendance for this period (1916-1919) was 7,040 — aggregate for nine competitive matches — 63,376.

Albion in World War 2

1939-40

Date		Opponent	Result	Scorers	Att.	1	2	3	4	5	6	7	8	9	10	11
Apr	19	(a) Aston Villa *	D 1-1	Richardson	16,007	Adams	White	C.Shaw	Sankey	Gripton	McNab	E.Jones	Banks	Richardson	Connelly	Johnson
	26	(a) Swansea T §	W 2-1	H.Jones 2	15,000	..	..	..	..	..	..	..	..	H.Jones	..	..
	28	(a) Coventry §	D 3-3	E.Jones, Banks, Connelly	26,000	..	..	..	..	..	..	..	..	..	..	..
Sept	2	(h) Tottenham H §	L 3-4	E.Jones 3	17,008	..	..	..	..	..	..	..	..	..	..	..
Oct	21	(h) Luton T	W 3-1	Banks 2, Johnson	5,424	Saunders	..	C.Shaw	..	..	..	..	..	..	..	..
	28	(a) Coventry C	L 3-6	Banks, H.Jones, Witcomb	3,056	..	..	..	..	Witcomb	Lowery	..	..	..	..	..
Nov	4	(a) Northampton T	D 1-1	H.Jones	4,643	..	..	..	Sankey	Gripton	Witcomb	Heaselgrave	..	..	..	..
	11	(h) Leicester C	W 1-0	H.Jones	4,265	..	..	..	..	..	McNab	Newsome	Bell	..	..	..
	18	(h) Birmingham	D 2-2	H.Jones, Sankey(pen)	8,671	..	..	..	..	..	..	..	..	..	..	..
	25	(h) Wolves	W 5-0	H.Jones 2, Bell, Newsome, Johnson	5,722	..	..	..	..	..	..	..	..	..	..	..
Dec	2	(a) Walsall	W 2-0	H.Jones, Newsome	4,815	..	..	..	..	..	..	..	..	..	..	..
	9	(a) Luton T	W 5-4	H.Jones 3, Newsome, Sankey(pen)	4,000	..	..	..	..	..	..	..	..	..	..	..
	16	(a) Coventry C	W 3-1	H.Jones 2, Johnson	3,802	..	..	..	..	..	..	..	..	..	..	..
	23	(h) Northampton T	W 4-1	H.Jones 2, Newsome, Bell	4,129	..	..	..	..	..	..	..	..	..	Banks	..
	26	(h) Birmingham	W 3-0	H.Jones, Johnson, Sankey(pen)	6,934	..	..	..	..	..	Clarke	..	..	..	Connelly	..
	30	(a) Leicester C	W 5-2	H.Jones(pen), Connelly, Johnson, Witcomb, Newsome	1,939	..	..	..	..	..	Witcomb	..	..	..	..	..
Jan	13	(a) Wolves	L 0-2		9,412	..	..	..	..	..	..	Newsome	..	..	..	..
	20	(h) Walsall	W 7-2	H.Jones 3(1 pen), Bell 2, Johnson 2	1,831	..	..	..	..	C.Davies	..	..	..	..	..	..
Feb	24	(h) Birmingham	W 6-1	H.Jones 2, Newsome, Connelly, Johnson, Bell	6,799	..	Bassett	..	..	Gripton	..	..	..	..	..	..
Mar	2	(h) Wolves	D 1-1	Johnson	8,641	..	..	..	..	..	..	..	..	..	..	..
	9	(a) Walsall	D 1-1	Connelly	3,012	..	White	..	Lowery	..	..	..	..	Richardson	..	..
	16	(a) Luton T	W 6-3	H.Jones 3, Newsome, Heaselgrave, Connelly	3,224	..	Bassett	..	Sankey	..	..	..	Heaselgrave	H.Jones	..	..
	23	(h) Coventry C	W 3-1	Sankey 2, Connelly	6,743	..	White	..	..	..	..	..	..	..	..	..
	25	(h) Birmingham	W 4-1	H.Jones 3, Newsome(pen)	9,986	..	..	..	..	..	..	..	..	..	..	..
	26	(h) Leicester C	W 5-1	H.Jones 2, Newsome 2(1 pen), Connelly	6,088	..	..	..	..	..	..	..	..	..	..	Butler
	30	(h) Northampton T	W 4-1	H.Jones 2, Heaselgrave, Butler	5,504	..	Bassett	..	..	C.Davies	..	..	..	..	..	..
Apr	6	(a) Leicester C	L 2-5	H.Jones, Heaselgrave	5,006	Adams	White	..	..	Bassett	..	..	..	..	..	..
	13	(h) Luton T	W 3-1	H.Jones 3	3,398	Saunders	..	..	..	Gripton	..	..	..	..	Clarke	Johnson
	20	(h) Portsmouth †	W 3-1	Connelly 2, Heaselgrave	11,511	..	..	..	..	..	..	..	..	..	Connelly	..
	27	(a) Portsmouth †	L 2-3	H.Jones, Summerbee(og)	9,873	..	Bassett	..	..	..	..	..	..	..	..	..
May	4	(a) Bournemouth †	W 2-1	H.Jones 2	9,665	..	..	..	..	..	..	..	..	..	..	..
	11	(a) Bournemouth †	W 3-1	H.Jones, Heaselgrave, Connelly	7,619	..	..	..	..	..	..	..	..	..	..	..
	13	(a) Wolves	L 4-5	H.Jones, Newsome 2(1 pen), Springthorpe(og)	6,014	..	..	..	..	..	..	..	..	..	..	..
	14	(h) Walsall	L 2-3	Connelly, Newsome	1,567	..	Kinsell	..	..	C.Davies	..	..	..	..	..	..
	18	(a) Coventry C †	W 1-0	(a.e.t)Sankey	8,901	Adams	Bassett	..	..	Lowery	..	..	..	Clarke	..	..
	25	(a) Blackburn R †	L 1-2	Richardson	9,742	..	..	..	Edwards	Gripton	..	Elliott	Clarke	Richardson	Chapman	E.Jones
Jun	5	(h) Northampton T	W 2-1	Newsome, Heaselgrave	1,374	..	C.Shaw	Kinsell	Sankey	Lowery	McNab	Newsome	Heaselgrave	H.Jones	Connelly	Johnson
	8	(a) Coventry C	L 0-4		3,998	..	..	..	..	..	..	..	..	..	Bell	..

OTHER MATCHES

Date		Opponent	Result	Scorers	Att.	1	2	3	4	5	6	7	8	9	10	11
Sep	23	(h) Wolves	L 3-5	C.Shaw(pen), H.Jones, Banks	5,833	Adams	White	C.Shaw	Sankey	Gripton	McNab	E.Jones	Banks	H.Jones	Connelly	Johnson
	30	(h) Stoke C	W 6-0	H.Jones 3, E.Jones 2, Johnson	3,696	Saunders	..	..	..	..	..	..	..	..	..	..
Oct	7	(a) Chester	W 2-0	H.Jones 2	3,313	..	..	..	..	..	..	..	..	..	..	..
	7	(a) Burton T	W 11-1	Richardson 4, Clarke 3, Bell 2, Newsome, Butler	1,126	Adams	Bassett	Kinsell	Lowery	C.Davies	Witcomb	Newsome	Bell	Richardson	Clarke	Butler
	14	(h) Coventry C	W 4-2	H.Jones 2(1 pen), E.Jones 2	2,350	Saunders	White	..	Sankey	Gripton	McNab	E.Jones	Banks	H.Jones	Connelly	Johnson
	14	(a) Kidderminster H	W 5-1	Richardson 2, Heaselgrave, Lowery	1,190	Adams	Pemberton	Bassett	Lowery	C.Davies	Witcomb	Elliott‡	Heaselgrave	Richardson	Clarke	Butler
	21	(a) Shrewsbury T	W 5-0	Richardson 2, Newsome, Bell, Dudley	3,847	Harris	Bassett	Kinsell	..	..	Edwards	Newsome	Burgin	..	Bell	Dudley
Nov	25	(a) Worcester C	W 5-0	Richardson 2, Bassett, Elliott, Witcomb	2,976	Adams	..	..	..	..	Witcomb	Elliott	Heaselgrave	..	Banks	..
Dec	2	(a) Shrewsbury T	W 3-1	Heaselgrave, Clarke, Witcomb(pen)	1,816	Harris	..	..	..	..	..	..	..	..	Clarke	Butler
	9	(a) Bath C	W 7-3	Heaselgrave 3, Richardson 2, Elliott, Clarke	1,403	Adams	..	..	..	..	..	..	..	..	..	..
	16	(a) Port Vale	W 4-1	E.Jones, Pike, Dudley, Burgin	2,645	..	..	..	Holder	..	Clarke	E.Jones	Burgin	Pike	Chapman	Dudley
	26	(a) Wellington T	L 2-3	Elliott 2	1,985	..	..	..	Edwards	Lowery	Dudley	Elliott	Heaselgrave	..	..	E.Jones
	30	(a) Notts C	L 0-4		2,251	..	..	..	..	..	Clarke	E.Jones	..	Richardson	Banks	Butler
Jan	6	(a) Newport C	W 3-1	Heaselgrave, Witcomb, Newsome	2,445	..	Pemberton	..	Lowery	Bassett	Witcomb	Newsome	..	..	Clarke	..
	6	(h) Sheffield W	L 0-3	Abandoned after 47 mins(fog)	1,426	Saunders	White	C.Shaw	Sankey	Gripton	McNab	E.Jones	Bell	H.Jones	Connelly	Johnson
Mar	2	(a) Chesterfield	L 0-4		3,142	Adams	Robinson	Kinsell	Lowery	Britnell	Witcomb	Elliott	Heaselgrave	Richardson	Chapman	Dudley
	9	(a) Chelmsford	L 1-3	Elliott	1,406	..	Pemberton	..	Holder	..	Edwards	..	..	Pike	..	Butler
	25	(a) Cardiff C	D 1-1	Butler	3,552	..	..	..	Lowery	Bassett	Witcomb	..	Bell	Richardson	Dudley	..
Jun	1	(a) Birmingham	D 2-2	Connelly, Johnson	5,176	..	C.Shaw	..	Sankey	Lowery	McNab	Newsome	Heaselgrave	H.Jones	Connelly	Johnson

* Jubilee Fund match.   § Division 2 matches.   † League Cup matches   ‡ Elliott was substituted by T. Bell

APPEARANCES – DIVISION 2
Adams J 3, Banks G 3, Connelly E 3, Gripton W 3, Johnson J 3, Jones E 3, Jones H 3, McNab A 3, Sankey J 3, Shaw C 3, White H 3 Total 33

GOALSCORERS – DIVISION 2
4 E.Jones, 2 H.Jones, 1 Banks, Connelly. Total 8

APPEARANCES – MIDLAND REGIONAL LEAGUE
Adams J 3, Banks G 4, Bassett I 6, Bell T 15, Butler S 3, Clarke I 2, Connelly E 25, Davies C 3, Gripton W 21, Heaselgrave S 12, Johnson J 25, Jones E 2, Jones H 27, Kinsell H 3, Lowery H 4, McNab A 25, Newsome R 25, Richardson WG 1, Sankey J 26, Saunders W 25, Shaw C 28, White H 20, Witcomb D 3. Total 308

GOALSCORERS – MIDLAND REGIONAL LEAGUE
36 H.Jones, 14 Newsome, 9 Johnson, 7 Connelly, 5 Bell, Sankey, 4 Heaselgrave, 3 Banks, 2 Witcomb, 1 Butler, Opp own goal 1. Total 87

APPEARANCES – LEAGUE CUP
Adams J 2, Bassett I 5, Chapman G 1, Clarke I 2, Connelly E 5, Edwards C 1, Elliott W 1, Gripton W 5, Heaselgrave S 5, Johnson J 5, Jones E 1, Jones H 4, Lowery H 1, McNab A 5, Newsome R 5, Richardson WG 1, Sankey J 5, Saunders W 4, Shaw C 6, White H 1, Witcomb D 1. Total 66

GOALSCORERS – LEAGUE CUP
4 H.Jones, 3 Connelly, 2 Heaselgrave, 1 Richardson, Sankey, Opp own goal 1. Total 12

1940-41

Date		Opponent	Result	Scorers	Att.	1	2	3	4	5	6	7	8	9	10	11
Aug 31	(h)	Walsall	W 3-1	Price 2, Heaselgrave	2,966	Adams	C.Shaw	Kinsell	Sankey	Gripton	Edwards	Newsome	Heaselgrave	Price	Connelly	Dudley
Sep 7	(a)	Walsall	W 2-0	Heaselgrave, Johnson	2,968	..	..	..	..	..	Witcomb	..	..	Richardson	..	Johnson
14	(h)	Northampton T	W 4-1	Richardson 2, Newsome 2(1 pen)	2,607	..	..	..	..	..	Edwards	..	Clarke	..	..	..
21	(a)	Northampton T	D 1-1	Newsome (pen)	3,200	..	..	..	..	..	..	..	..	..	..	..
28	(h)	Birmingham	L 1-2	Richardson	4,718	..	..	..	..	..	Witcomb	..	..	..	..	..
Oct 5	(a)	Birmingham	W 3-1	Newsome, Clarke, Johnson	5,394	..	Bassett	C.Shaw	..	..	Edwards	..	..	..	..	..
12	(h)	Stoke C	L 0-1		4,091	..	..	..	..	..	..	..	..	..	..	..
19	(a)	Stoke C	W 3-1	Richardson 2, Johnson	3,392	..	Kinsell	..	..	..	..	Heaselgrave	..	..	..	..
26	(h)	Notts C	W 3-1	Richardson 2, Hodgetts	2,496	..	Bassett	..	..	..	..	Hodgetts	Heaselgrave	..	..	Dudley
Nov 2	(a)	Notts C	L 2-3	Sankey 2(1 pen)	2,100	..	..	..	..	..	McNab	..	..	..	..	..
9	(h)	Coventry C	L 1-4	Sankey (pen)	978	..	C.Shaw	Kinsell	..	..	..	Newsome	..	H.Jones	..	Johnson
23	(h)	Mansfield T	W 4-2	Richardson 2, Heaselgrave, Sankey(pen)	831	..	..	..	..	..	..	..	..	Richardson	..	..
30	(a)	Mansfield T	D 3-3	Richardson 2, Elliott	2,000	..	..	..	..	..	Edwards	Elliott	..	..	..	..
Dec 7	(h)	Nottingham F	W 5-0	Richardson 3, Heaselgrave, Elliott	1,261	Goodall	..	..	Lowery	..	Sankey	..	..	..	..	Edwards
14	(a)	Leicester C	L 3-4	Heaselgrave 2, Richardson	939	Adams	..	..	Sankey	..	Edwards	E.Jones	..	..	Clarke	Johnson
21	(h)	Leicester C	L 4-5	Richardson 3, Elliott	765	..	..	..	..	..	..	Elliott	..	..	..	..
28	(h)	Nottingham F	W 5-3	Richardson 2, Elliott 2, Heaselgrave	1,839	..	Bassett	C.Shaw	..	..	..	..	..	..	Chapman	..
Jan 11	(h)	Notts C *	W 8-1	Elliott 2, Heaselgrave 2, Richardson 2, Chapman, Johnson	1,403	..	..	..	..	..	..	..	..	..	..	..
Feb 8	(a)	Walsall *	L 3-4	Johnson 2, Elliott	3,135	..	..	Kinsell	..	..	Witcomb	..	..	..	..	..
15	(h)	Notts C §	L 0-4		2,700	..	..	C.Shaw	..	..	Edwards	..	..	Clarke	..	..
22	(h)	Notts C §	W 5-0	Heaselgrave 2, Richardson 2, C.Shaw(pen)	2,581	..	..	..	..	..	..	..	..	Richardson	..	..
Mar 1	(h)	Mansfield T §	L 2-3	Richardson 2	2,132	..	..	Kinsell	..	..	..	..	..	..	..	..
8	(a)	Mansfield T §	L 2-6	Gripton 2	2,800	..	..	..	..	..	..	..	..	..	..	..
15	(h)	Stoke C	D 2-2	Richardson, Sankey	2,086	..	..	..	..	Lowery	..	..	..	H.Jones	..	..
22	(a)	Stoke C	W 2-0	Elliott 2	794	..	..	..	Lowery	Gripton	..	..	..	Chapman	..	..
29	(h)	Walsall	W 4-1	H.Jones 2, Elliott, Richardson	1,412	..	..	..	Sankey	Lowery	..	..	H.Jones	..	..	..
Apr 5	(a)	Walsall	D 3-3	Wilkes 2, Heaselgrave	1,850	..	..	..	..	Gripton	..	..	Heaselgrave	Wilkes	..	E.Jones
12	(a)	Northampton T	L 1-3	Elliott	2,141	..	..	..	..	Davies	..	..	..	H.Jones	..	Johnson
19	(h)	Northampton T	W 3-2	Chapman, Sankey, Hunter(og)	1,463	..	..	..	..	Gripton	McNab	..	..	Richardson	..	Dudley
May 3	(a)	Reading	L 3-6	Heaselgrave, Richardson, Wilkes	4,000	..	..	..	..	..	Edwards	..	..	..	Wilkes	..
17	(a)	Cardiff C	D 4-4	Elliott 2, Wilkes, C.Evans	3,009	..	Quinton	..	Lowery	..	..	..	..	Wilkes	C.Evans	..
31	(a)	Walsall	L 3-10	Johnson, Elliott, Sankey	1,512	Alderwick	Bassett	..	Sankey	Lowery	McNab	..	..	Richardson	..	Johnson

OTHER MATCHES

Date		Opponent	Result	Scorers	Att.	1	2	3	4	5	6	7	8	9	10	11
Apr 5	(h)	RAF	W 2-0	Dudley 2	513		Warrender	Poultney	Lowery	Davies		Hodgetts	Bell	Newsome	Clarke	Dudley
14	(h)	Aston Villa	W 4-3	H.Jones 3, Chapman	4,549	Sankey	Robinson	Kinsell	Edwards	Gripton		Elliott	Heaselgrave	H.Jones	Chapman	Johnson
26	(h)	Aston Villa	L 1-6	Sankey	3,700	Alderwick			Sankey							
May 3	(h)	RAF	W 4-1	Bell 2, Newsome, Clarke	601		Warrender	Robinson	Lowery	Seeley		Clift	Bell	Newsome	Clarke	A.Evans
10	(a)	Hednesford T	L 1-5	Bell	1,201			Kinsell		Lewis	Witcomb	Hodgetts		Ashley		
17	(h)	REVO Sports	L 2-6	Clarke, Atkiss	253		Robinson	Poultney	Ashley		McNab	Clift	Dutton	Chatterley		Atkiss
24	(h)	RAF	W 6-1	Richardson 6	386		Warrender	Kinsell	Sankey	Lowery		Elliott	Heaselgrave	Richardson	C.Evans	

*Midland Cup matches. § League Cup matches.

APPEARANCES – FOOTBALL LEAGUE SOUTH
Adams J 24, Alderwick J 1, Bassett I 13, Chapman G 6, Clarke I 8, Connelly E 14, Davies C 1, Dudley G 6, Edwards C 19, Elliott W 13, Evans C 2, Goodall E 1, Gripton W 22, Heaselgrave S 20, Hodgetts F 2, Johnson J 18, Jones E 2, Jones H 4, Kinsell H 21, Lowery H 6, McNab A 5, Newsome R 9, Price W 1, Quinton W 1, Richardson WG 21, Sankey J 24, Shaw C 17, Wilkes G 3, Witcomb D 2. Total 286

GOALSCORERS – FOOTBALL LEAGUE SOUTH
23 Richardson, 12 Elliott, 9 Heaselgrave, 7 Sankey, 4 Johnson, Newsome, Wilkes, 2 H.Jones, Price, 1 Clarke, Chapman, Evans, Hodgetts, Opp own goal 1. Total 72

APPEARANCES – MIDLAND CUP & LEAGUE CUP
Adams J 6, Bassett I 6, Chapman G 6, Clarke I 1, Edwards C 5, Elliott W 6, Gripton W 6, Heaselgrave S 6, Johnson J 6, Kinsell H 3, Richardson WG 5, Sankey J 6, Shaw C 3, Witcomb D 1. Total 66

GOALSCORERS – MIDLAND CUP & LEAGUE CUP
6 Richardson, 4 Heaselgrave, 3 Elliott, Johnson, 2 Gripton 1 Chapman, Shaw. Total 20

• The biggest single League turnout during World War Two was 38,077 v Wolves on 23 April 1946. The lowest was 537 v Swansea Town on 18 October 1941.
• Albion used a total of 116 players in all matches during World War Two, 42 of them being guests.

Cliff Edwards, who accumulated 60 appearances during World War Two.

1941-42

Date		Opponent	Result	Score	Scorers	Att.	1	2	3	4	5	6	7	8	9	10	11
Aug	30	(h) Cardiff C	W	6-3	H.Jones 4, Elliott, Johnson	4,462	Adams	Bassett	C.Shaw	Sankey	Gripton	Edwards	Elliott	Heaselgrave	H.Jones	Evans	Johnson
Sep	6	(a) Cardiff C	D	1-1	C.Edwards	4,647	..	..	..	..	..	Witcomb	..	..	Dudley	..	C.Edwards
	13	(h) Leicester C	W	4-1	C.Evans 2, Richardson, Johnson	3,786	..	..	..	..	..	McNab	..	..	Richardson	..	Johnson
	20	(a) Leicester C	L	2-3	Elliott, Sankey	3,526	..	..	..	Edwards	..	..	..	..	May	..	..
	27	(a) Walsall	L	1-2	Elliott	4,494	..	..	..	Sankey	..	Edwards	..	..	Banks	..	..
Oct	4	(h) Walsall	W	4-0	Elliott, Heaselgrave, Wilkes, Evans	4,135	..	..	..	Lowery	..	..	..	..	Wilkes	..	Dudley
	11	(a) Aston Villa	W	3-2	H.Jones, Elliott 2	5,500	..	..	..	..	..	..	..	..	H.Jones	..	..
	18	(h) Swansea T	W	8-0	Richardson 5, Elliott 2, Evans	537	..	..	..	Sankey	..	McNab	..	..	Richardson	..	..
Nov	8	(a) Wolves	W	8-2	Elliott 3, Evans 3, Johnson Sankey	6,000	..	..	..	..	..	Edwards	..	Clarke	..	..	Johnson
	15	(a) Wolves	W	5-3	Elliott 2, Richardson 2, Dudley	3,774	..	..	..	..	..	McNab	..	..	..	..	Dudley
	22	(h) Luton T	W	10-1	Richardson 6, Evans 2, Elliott, Johnson	2,618	..	..	..	..	..	Edwards	..	..	..	..	Johnson
	29	(a) Luton T	W	5-4	Richardson 2, Elliott 2, Clarke	2,200	..	C.Shaw	Kinsell	..	..	..	..	..	..	..	..
Dec	6	(h) Northampton T	W	7-0	McKennan 3, Elliott 2, Richardson, Sankey	1,766	..	Bassett	C.Shaw	..	..	..	..	McKennan	..	..	..
	13	(a) Northampton T	L	1-4	Richardson	2,000	..	..	..	..	..	..	..	Dudley	..	..	..
	27	(h) Wrexham §	W	6-4	Richardson 2, Elliott 2, McKennan, Evans	4,497	Willetts	..	C.Shaw	Edwards	..	McNab	..	McKennan	..	..	..
Jan	3	(a) Wrexham §	D	5-5	Richardson 2, McKennan, Dearson, Elliott	2,500	Merrick	..	..	Dearson	H.Jones	Edwards	..	..	..	..	..
	10	(h) Stoke §	W	4-0	Richardson, Elliott, McKennan, Johnson	7,335	..	..	..	Sankey	Edwards	McNab	..	..	..	..	..
	17	(a) Stoke §	L	1-2	Elliott	4,578	..	..	..	..	..	..	..	..	..	..	..
Feb	14	(h) Leicester C §	W	3-2	Richardson 2, Elliott	4,378	Adams	..	..	..	Gripton	Edwards	..	..	..	..	Dudley
	21	(h) Mansfield T §	W	3-1	McKennan 2, Richardson	1,398	..	..	..	..	Edwards	McNab	..	..	..	..	Johnson
Mar	7	(a) Northampton T §L		3-4	Elliott 2, Evans	2,000	..	Quinton	..	..	Gripton	Edwards	..	..	..	..	..
	14	(a) Northampton T§	D	2-2	McKennan, Johnson	3,706	..	Bassett	..	..	..	..	..	H.Jones	..	..	..
	21	(a) Leicester C §	L	2-4	Sankey, Gripton	5,685	..	..	Ashley	..	..	..	..	Heaselgrave	Richardson	..	..
Apr	4	(a) Stoke C §	L	3-5	Johnson, Elliott, Evans	5,000	..	..	C.Shaw	Ashley	Edwards	McNab	..	..	..	..	..
	6	(h) Stoke C §	W	6-1	Richardson 2, McKennan 2 (1 pen), Elliott, Sankey	13,400	..	..	..	Sankey	Gripton	..	..	McKennan	..	..	Edwards
	11	(a) Cardiff C §	D	1-1	Richardson	10,781	..	..	..	..	..	Witcomb	..	..	..	..	..
	18	(h) Cardiff C §	W	3-2	Richardson 2, Elliott	10,198	..	..	..	..	..	McNab	..	Edwards	..	..	Johnson
	25	(h) Everton §	W	3-1	Evans, Elliott, Edwards	19,006	..	..	..	..	..	..	..	McKennan	..	..	Edwards
May	2	(a) Everton §	W	5-1	Elliott 2 McKennan 2, Evans	34,000	..	..	..	..	..	..	..	..	..	..	..
	9	(h) Wolves §	L	0-4		35,000	..	..	..	..	..	..	..	..	..	..	..
	16	(a) Wolves §	L	0-3		29,000	Harris	..	..	Witcomb	..	..	..	..	..	..	Johnson
	23	(h) Walsall	W	3-1	Bowen, Elliott, Ashley	1,695	..	..	..	Sankey	..	Edwards	..	C.Jones	Ashley	..	Bowen

OTHER MATCHES

Date		Opponent	Result	Score	Scorers	Att.	1	2	3	4	5	6	7	8	9	10	11
Nov	1	(h) Czech Army	W	3-1	Evans, Elliott, Richardson	2,638	Adams	..	..	..	..	McNab	..	Heaselgrave	Richardson	..	Johnson
Dec	20	(h) Birmingham	W	4-1	Richardson 3, Elliott	1,270	..	..	Kinsell	..	..	Edwards	..	Duggan	..	..	..
	25	(h) Aston Villa	L	0-2		5,178	..	..	C.Shaw	Edwards	..	McNab	..	McKennan	..	..	..
Mar	28	(h) Aston Villa	L	1-2	Sankey	4,148	Harris	..	..	Sankey	Edwards	..	Hodgetts	Heaselgrave	..	..	..
May	25	(h) Aston Villa	L	3-4	Elliott 2, Evans	2,035	Adams	..	..	C.Edwards	Gripton	..	Elliott	Sankey	..	..	..
	30	(h) Birmingham	W	4-1	C.Edwards 2(1 pen), G.Edwards, Newsome(pen)	5,357	..	..	..	Witcomb	..	C.Edwards	Newsome	G.Edwards	..	..	..

§ League Cup matches

APPEARANCES – FOOTBALL LEAGUE SOUTH

Adams J 13, Ashley H 1, Banks G 1, Bassett I 13, Bowen T 1, Clarke I 4, Dudley G 5, Edwards C 11, Elliott W 14, Evans C 14, Gripton W 14, Harris W 1, Heaselgrave S 7, Johnson J 9, Jones C 1, Jones H 1, Kinsell H 1, Lowery H 1, McKennan P 1, McNab A 4, May G 1, Richardson WG 8, Sankey J 12, Shaw C 14, Wilkes G 1, Witcomb D 1. Total 154

GOALSCORERS – FOOTBALL LEAGUE SOUTH

18 Richardson, 17 Elliott, 9 Evans, 4 Johnson, H.Jones, 3 McKennan, Sankey, 1 Ashley, Bowen, Clarke, Dudley, Edwards, Heaselgrave, Wilkes. Total 65

APPEARANCES – LEAGUE CUP

Adams J 12, Ashley H 2, Bassett I 16, Dearson D 1, Dudley G 1, Edwards C 16, Elliott W 17, Evans C 17, Gripton W 12, Harris W 1, Heaselgrave S 2, Johnson J 11, Jones H 2, McNab A 11, McKennan P 14, Merrick G 3, Quinton W 1, Richardson WG 16, Shaw C 16, Sankey J 13, Willetts J 1, Witcomb D 2. Total 187

GOALSCORERS – LEAGUE CUP

14 Elliott, 13 Richardson, 10 McKennan, 5 Evans, 3 Johnson, 2 Sankey, 1 Dearson, Edwards, Gripton. Total 50

Albion v Cardiff City, 30 August 1941. Back row (left to right): H.Kinsell, H.Jones, I.Bassett, J.Adams, W.Gripton, C.Shaw, E.Jones. Front row: J.Johnson, C.Edwards, S.Heaselgrave, J.Sankey, W.Elliott, C.Evans.

- In 1939-40 Harry Jones scored in 11 successive games for Albion; Billy Elliott equalled this record in 1941-2.
- Albion scored eight goals in 32 minutes against Luton Town on 22 November 1941. They won the match 10-1.
- The Football League sanctioned a payment of 30 shillings (£1.50) per match to each player for seasons 1939-40 to 1942-3. In 1943-4 it went up to £2 and by 1945-6 it had reached £4.

1942-43

Date		Opponent	Result / Scorers	Att	1	2	3	4	5	6	7	8	9	10	11
Aug 29	(a)	Northampton T	L 0-2	4,882	Adams	Bassett	A.J.Smith	Sankey	Davies	Millard	Elliott	Heaselgrave	Richardson	C.Evans	K.Butler
Sep 5	(h)	Northampton T	W 6-3 Elliott 3, Sankey 2, Evans	1,500	..	..	..	Millard	Gripton	McNab	..	Sankey	..	..	McDonald
12	(h)	Leicester C	W 3-2 Millard 3	4,000	..	..	..	Sankey	..	..	..	E.Jones	Millard	..	..
19	(a)	Leicester C	D 0-0	4,029	..	Shaw	..	..	Brown	..	Richardson	Clarke	..	..	..
26	(a)	Wolves	L 0-2	8,382	..	Parker	Shaw	Millard	Sankey	Witcomb	Elliott	Chapman	H.Jones	..	..
Oct 3	(h)	Wolves	W 6-2 Millard 3, Elliott 2, Evans	7,813	..	Shaw	A.J.Smith	Sankey	Davies	McNab	..	Heaselgrave	Millard	..	Finch
10	(h)	Aston Villa	W 6-2 Elliott 2, Shaw, Millard, Evans, Finch	10,326	..	..	..	..	..	..	..	..	..	..	..
17	(a)	Aston Villa	L 2-8 Heaselgrave 2	12,000	..	..	..	..	..	..	Hodgetts	..	..	..	..
24	(a)	Derby C	L 0-4	7,810	..	Bassett	..	..	Gripton	Edwards	Richardson	..	..	..	Dudley
31	(h)	Derby C	D 3-3 Heaselgrave 2, Newsome (pen)	4,571	..	Shaw	..	..	..	Millard	Newsome	..	Richardson	..	Finch
Nov 7	(h)	Stoke C	D 0-0	4,564	..	Bassett	..	..	..	..	..	..	Simms	..	..
14	(a)	Stoke C	L 1-5 Clarke	3,331	..	..	Kinsell	..	..	A.Evans	..	Clarke	H.Butler	..	..
21	(h)	Walsall	D 0-0	2,783	Harris	..	A.Smith	..	..	Millard	..	McDonald	..	..	..
28	(a)	Walsall	L 0-2	3,412	Billingsley	..	..	..	..	..	Hodgetts	Burgin	..	..	..
Dec 5	(n)	Birmingham	L 0-3	3,000	J.Smith	..	..	..	Edwards	..	Elliott	..	Richardson	..	..
12	(h)	Birmingham	W 4-3 Ashley 2, Sankey, Dudley	3,393	..	..	..	..	Gripton	Ashley	..	Heaselgrave	..	Millard	Dudley
19	(a)	Coventry C	L 1-2 Ashley	5,000	Adams	..	..	..	..	Millard	Hodgetts	Walsh	Ashley	Wood	..
25	(h)	Coventry C	W 3-0 Ashley 2, Witcomb	5,199	..	..	..	Witcomb	..	McNab	..	Elliott	..	C.Evans	..
26	(h)	Leicester C §	W 5-1 Elliott 3(1 pen), Hodgetts, Dudley	8,119	..	..	..	..	..	..	..	..	..	..	..
Jan 2	(a)	Leicester C §	L 0-9	3,578	..	..	..	Millard	Sankey	..	..	..	..	..	..
9	(h)	Coventry C §	L 2-3 Elliott (pen), Sankey	3,676	Marks	Sankey	J.Smith	..	Gripton	S.Jones	..	..	..	..	Finch
16	(a)	Coventry C §	L 0-1	8,500	Adams	Bassett	..	Sankey	..	Millard	Elliott	Doherty	Richardson	..	..
23	(a)	Aston Villa §	W 5-3 Doherty 2, Green, Elliott, Evans	12,000	..	..	Hapgood	Witcomb	..	..	..	..	Green	..	..
30	(a)	Aston Villa §	W 2-1 Elliott (pen), Shaw	13,200	..	..	..	Millard	..	McNab	..	Green	Shaw	..	..
Feb 6	(n)	Birmingham §	W 1-0 Green	8,000	..	Scott	..	..	..	..	..	Heaselgrave	Green	..	..
13	(h)	Birmingham §	W 2-1 Elliott (pen), Jones	7,217	..	..	A.J.Smith	Sankey	..	Millard	..	..	H.Jones	..	Hodgetts
20	(a)	Wolves §	L 0-1	12,444	..	Bassett	..	Millard	..	McNab	..	..	Richardson	..	Finch
27	(h)	Wolves §	W 2-0 Evans, Shaw	10,138	..	..	..	..	..	..	Hodgetts	Sankey	Shaw	..	Johnson
Mar 6	(a)	Coventry C §	D 1-1 Evans	11,502	..	Shelton	..	Sankey	Smalley	Millard	Elliott	Hodgetts	Dearson	..	..
13	(h)	Coventry C §	W 3-0 Lane, Dearson, Elliott	13,332	..	..	Shaw	Millard	Gripton	McNab	..	Lane	..	..	S.Butler
20	(h)	Chesterfield §	L 2-3 Elliott 2	13,447	..	..	A.J.Smith	..	..	Millard	..	..	..	..	..
27	(h)	Chesterfield §	D 3-3 Richardson 3	13,661	..	..	Shaw	Millard	..	McNab	..	Dearson	Richardson	..	Finch
Apr 3	(n)	Birmingham	L 3-5 Richardson 3	4,000	..	..	J.Smith	..	..	Edwards	Dunkley	C.Evans	..	A.Evans	..
10	(h)	Birmingham	L 0-4	1,818	..	Parker	Ashley	Davenport	..	McNab	Elliott	..	Millard	..	..
17	(h)	Walsall	W 4-0 Richardson 2, Jones, A.Evans	1,575	..	Robinson	J.Smith	Sankey	..	Millard	Hodgetts	..	Richardson	..	E.Jones
24	(a)	Walsall	W 2-1 Richardson, Finch	1,500	..	Ashley	..	Bye	..	..	Elliott	Clarke	..	C.Evans	Finch
26	(h)	Northampton T	W 6-1 Richardson 3, Clarke 2, A.Evans	2,468	..	Shaw	..	Millard	..	McNab	Hodgetts	..	..	A.Evans	C.Evans
May 1	(a)	Aston Villa	W 6-2 Richardson 5, Jones	5,613	..	Ashley	..	Sankey	..	Millard	..	E.Jones	..	..	..

§ League Cup matches

APPEARANCES – FOOTBALL LEAGUE NORTH

Adams J 20, Ashley H 6, Bassett I 12, Billingsley G 1, Brown A 1, Burgin M 2, Butler H 1, Butler K 1, Bye J 1, Chapman G 1, Clarke I 5, Davenport A 1, Davies C 4, Dudley G 4, Dunkley M 1, Edwards C 3, Elliott W 11, Evans A 6, Evans C 22, Finch L 12, Gripton W 17, Harris W 1, Heaselgrave S 9, Hodgetts F 7, Jones E 3, Jones H 1, Kinsell H 1, McDonald J 6, McNab A 9, Millard L 22, Newsome R 4, Parker A 2, Richardson WG 11, Robinson E 1, Sankey J 19, Shaw C 7, Simms H 1, Shelton J 1, Smith AJ 21, Smith J 2, Walsh W 1, Witcomb D 2, Wood T 1. Total 264

GOALSCORERS – FOOTBALL LEAGUE NORTH

14 Richardson, 7 Elliott, Millard, 5 Ashley, 4 Heaselgrave, 3 Clarke, C.Evans, Sankey, 2 A.Evans, E.Jones, Finch, 1 Dudley, Newsome, Shaw, Witcomb. Total 56

APPEARANCES – LEAGUE CUP

Adams J 13, Ashley H 3, Bassett I 7, Butler S 2, Dearson D 4, Doherty P 2, Dudley G 2, Elliott W 13, Evans C 14, Finch L 7, Green T 3, Gripton W 12, Hapgood E 3, Heaselgrave S 3, Hodgetts F 6, Johnson J 2, Jones H 1, Jones S 1, Lane H 2, McNab A 8, Millard L 13, Marks G 1, Richardson WG 3, Sankey J 7, Scott L 2, Shaw C 4, Shelton J 4, Smalley T 1, Smith AJ 9, Witcomb D 2. Total 154

GOALSCORERS – LEAGUE CUP

10 Elliott, 3 C.Evans, Richardson, 2 Doherty, Green, Shaw, 1 Dearson, Dudley, Hodgetts, H.Jones, Lane, Sankey. Total 28

• Two Albion players — WA Darby and W Wheatley — were both tragically killed in World War Two. Six others, three of whom lost a leg, were seriously injured. Those who suffered loss of limb were goalkeeper Cliff Wright, George Dale and George Foulkes. The other three who were repatriated were Bill Harris, Dick Pike and Tommy Griffiths. George Handley, an Albion reserve in the 1930s, was killed in Sicily on 7 June 1943.

Billy Gripton, who accumulated almost 200 wartime appearances for Albion in League and Cup from the centre-half position.

1943-44

Date		Opponent		Result	Scorers	Att.	1	2	3	4	5	6	7	8	9	10	11
Aug	28	(h) Derby C	W	3-2	Richardson, Evans, Armstrong	5,926	Adams	Bassett	A.J.Smith	Millard	Gripton	McNab	Elliott	E.Jones	Richardson	Armstrong	C.Evans
Sep	4	(a) Derby C	W	5-1	Richardson 4, Jones	6,393	..	..	..	Sankey	..	Millard	..	..	..	..	Duns
	11	(h) Northampton T	D	4-4	Elliott 4 (1 pen)	6,222	..	..	..	Millard	..	McNab	..	Duns	Armstrong	A.Evans	C.Evans
	18	(a) Northampton T	L	1-2	Elliott	3,721	..	..	..	..	..	..	..	McCormick	Richardson	Armstrong	Duns
	25	(h) Wolves	W	4-1	Richardson 2, Elliott, Duns	7,363	Heath	..	..	..	..	Williams	..	..	..	C.Evans	..
Oct	2	(a) Wolves	W	3-2	Richardson 2 Duns	8,819	..	..	..	..	..	..	..	..	..	..	..
	9	(a) Leicester C	W	3-0	Richardson 2, Hodgetts	6,971	..	..	..	..	..	McNab	Hodgetts	..	..	..	Finch
	16	(h) Leicester C	D	2-2	Richardson 2	7,090	..	..	..	..	..	..	Elliott	..	..	Clarke	C.Evans
	23	(a) Aston Villa	L	1-3	Richardson	19,000	..	..	..	..	..	..	..	..	..	Armstrong	..
	30	(h) Aston Villa	W	5-4	Richardson 2, Elliott 2, Evans	23,550	..	..	..	Sankey	..	Millard	..	Ball	..	C.Evans	Hodgetts
Nov	6	(a) Stoke C	D	3-3	Richardson, Elliott (pen), Hodgetts	3,520	..	..	Southam	..	..	..	Armstrong	..	..	..	..
	13	(h) Stoke C	W	3-0	Richardson 2, C.Evans	6,912	..	..	..	Witcomb	..	..	Hodgetts	C.Evans	..	A.Evans	Russell
	20	(a) Walsall	L	0-2		4,297	..	..	..	Edwards	..	..	Elliott	..	..	..	..
	27	(h) Walsall	L	1-4	Duns	4,556	..	..	..	Millard	..	McNab	..	Edwards	Armstrong	C.Evans	Duns
Dec	4	(h) Birmingham	L	1-3	Elliott	5,494	..	Griffiths	A.J.Smith	..	..	..	..	Wilcoxson	Richardson	A.Evans	..
	11	(a) Birmingham	L	0-3		5,156	..	Southam	..	Sankey	..	Millard	Hodgetts	E.Jones	..	Armstrong	Finch
	18	(h) Coventry C	W	3-0	Elliott 2, Clarke	2,647	..	..	..	..	..	..	Elliott	Clarke	Ball	C.Evans	Duns
	25	(h) Coventry C	L	0-8		7,000	..	Ashley	..	..	..	..	..	Ball	Richardson	..	Hodgetts
	27	(h) Birmingham §	D	1-1	Elliott (pen)	14,717	..	Southam	..	Millard	..	McNab	..	Clarke	Ball	..	Finch
Jan	1	(a) Birmingham §	L	0-4		9,142	..	Millard	..	Witcomb	..	..	Duns	Heaselgrave	Richardson	..	E.Jones
	8	(a) Walsall §	D	2-2	Ball 2	5,793	Adams	Southam	..	Millard	..	..	..	Witcomb	Ball	..	Finch
	15	(h) Walsall §	W	7-1	Ball 3, Elliott 3, Witcomb	4,800	..	..	..	..	..	..	Elliott	..	..	..	Hodgetts
	22	(h) Coventry C §	D	2-2	Elliott, Witcomb	5,577	..	..	..	..	..	..	..	..	..	..	..
	29	(a) Coventry C §	D	3-3	Elliott 2, Ball	8,500	Heath	..	..	..	..	..	..	..	..	E.Jones	..
Feb	5	(a) Northampton T §L		0-2		4,381	..	..	..	..	..	..	..	..	..	..	..
	12	(h) Northampton T §W		3-1	Ball 2, Hodgetts	4,503	..	..	..	..	..	Edwards	Hodgetts	..	..	C.Evans	Russell
	19	(h) Stoke C §	L	2-8	Duns, Elliott	5,000	..	..	..	..	..	McNab	Elliott	E.Jones	Duns	..	Hodgetts
	26	(a) Stoke C §	L	4-5	Elliott 3, Duns	8,030	..	..	..	..	..	Williams	Duns	McNab	Elliott	..	..
Mar	4	(h) Nottingham F *	L	0-1		3,392	..	..	Pemberton	..	Edwards	..	..	Richardson	..	..	..
	11	(a) Nottingham F *	L	2-3	Pears, Russell	6,346	..	..	A.J.Smith	..	Gripton	McNab	Hodgetts	Heaselgrave	Pears	..	Russell
	18	(h) Wolves *	W	5-0	Elliott 3, Hodgetts, Guest	4,588	Adams	..	..	..	..	Williams	..	..	Elliott	..	Guest
	25	(h) Wolves *	D	3-3	Heaselgrave 2, Guest	6,281	..	..	Bradley	..	..	McNab	..	..	..	..	..
Apr	1	(a) Walsall *	D	2-2	Acquaroff 2	2,120	..	White	Southam	..	..	..	..	..	Acquaroff	..	Rowley
	8	(h) Walsall *	W	1-0	Acquaroff	5,588	Heath	..	A.J.Smith	..	..	..	..	..	..	..	Guest
	10	(a) Aston Villa §	L	1-4	Heaselgrave	15,000	..	Adderley	..	..	..	..	..	..	..	..	..
	15	(a) Stoke C *	D	1-1	Elliott	3,434	..	Millard	..	Williams	..	..	Elliott	..	..	..	Hodgetts
	22	(h) Stoke C *	W	3-1	Elliott, Heaselgrave, Richardson	7,202	..	Southam	..	Millard	..	..	..	Richardson	..	..	..
	29	(h) Nottingham F *	D	2-2	Richardson, Evans	8,373	..	..	..	..	..	..	Hodgetts	..	..	..	Finch
May	6	(a) Nottingham F *	W	4-3†	Acquaroff 2, Hodgetts, Clarke	14,438	..	..	..	..	..	..	Heaselgrave	Acquaroff	Clarke	..	Hodgetts

OTHER MATCHES

Date		Opponent		Result	Scorers	Att.	1	2	3	4	5	6	7	8	9	10	11
Feb	19	(a) Aston Villa	W	4-2	Heaselgrave 2, Clarke, Russell	4,067	Adams	Bradley	Pemberton	Sankey	Tranter	Williams	..	Clarke	Pears	Bowen	Russell
Mar	25	(h) Aston Villa	W	8-2	Clarke 5, Pears 3	2,155	Saunders	Ashley	Adderley	Rollason	..	Sankey	Yuell	Pears	Clarke	Bell	Ratcliffe
Apr	1	(h) Wolves	W	3-1	Clarke 2, Pears	3,266	Heath	Davenport	..	Hampton	..	Williams	..	..	..	Bowen	..
	15	(a) Wolves	W	6-1	Clarke 4, Bowen, Russell	3,008	Adams	..	..	Vincent	..	Ashley	..	..	..	..	Russell

§ League Cup matches.   * Midland Cup matches.   † After extra-time.

APPEARANCES – FOOTBALL LEAGUE NORTH
Acquaroff J 1, Adams J 4, Adderley J 1, Armstrong M 8, Ashley H 1, Ball H 3, Bassett I 14, Clarke I 2, Duns L 8, Edwards C 2, Elliott W 15, Evans A 4, Evans C 15, Finch L 2, Griffiths J 1, Gripton W 19, Guest W 1, Heaselgrave S 1, Heath N 15, Hodgetts F 7, Jones E 3, McCormick J 6, McNab A 9, Millard L 19, Richardson WG 15, Russell T 2, Sankey J 6, Smith AJ 15, Southam J 6, Wilcoxson G 1, Williams G 2, Witcomb D 1. Total 209

GOALSCORERS – FOOTBALL LEAGUE NORTH
19 Richardson, 12 Elliott, 3 Duns, C.Evans, 2 Hodgetts, 1 Armstrong, Clarke, E.Jones. Total 42

APPEARANCES – MIDLAND CUP & LEAGUE CUP
Acquaroff J 4, Adams J 6, Ball H 7, Bradley D 1, Clarke I 2, Duns L 5, Edwards C 2, Elliott W 11, Evans C 18, Finch L 3, Gripton L 19, Guest W 3, Heaselgrave S 10, Heath N 14, Hodgetts F 17, Jones E 3, McNab A 18, Millard L 20, Pears W 1, Pemberton J 1, Richardson WG 4, Rowley GA 1, Russell T 2, Smith AJ 17, Southam J 17, White H 2, Williams G 4, Witcomb D 7. Total 220

GOALSCORERS – MIDLAND CUP & LEAGUE CUP
16 Elliott, 8 Ball, 5 Acquaroff, 4 Heaselgrave, 3 Hodgetts, 2 Duns, Guest, Richardson, Witcomb, 1 Clarke, Evans, Pears, Russell. Total 48

Idris Bassett, full-back with over 90 wartime outings for Albion.

◄ *Billy Elliott, top wartime scorer.*

							1	2	3	4	5	6	7	8	9	10	11
Aug	26	(a)	Northampton T	W 4-1	Evans, Richardson, Elliott(pen), Hodgetts	5,890	Adams	Southam	Millard	Sankey	Gripton	McNab	Elliott	Heaselgrave	Richardson	Evans	Hodgetts
Sep	2	(h)	Northampton T	W 3-1	Heaselgrave 2, Hodgetts	5,998	..	..	..	Williams	..	..	..	..	..	..	..
	9	(h)	Port Vale	W 2-1	Rowley, Elliott	7,749	..	..	..	..	..	..	Hodgetts	..	Elliott	..	Rowley
	16	(a)	Port Vale	D 0-0		6,000	..	..	..	..	..	..	Jones	..	Richardson	..	Hodgetts
	23	(a)	Coventry C	D 1-1	Clarke	8,245	Heath	Sankey	..	..	..	..	..	..	Clarke	..	..
	30	(h)	Coventry C	W 4-1	Clarke 3, Hodgetts	9,512	..	..	..	..	Tranter	..	Hodgetts	..	..	..	Rowley
Oct	7	(h)	Leicester C	D 1-1	Heaselgrave	9,970	..	..	Kinsell	Millard	Gripton	..	..	..	..	..	Johnson
	14	(a)	Leicester C	W 2-0	Evans, Clarke	7,201	..	Tranter	Millard	Vincent	..	Lowery	Elliott	..	..	..	Hodgetts
	21	(a)	Aston Villa	D 2-2	Rowley (pen), Clarke	25,200	..	..	..	Williams	..	McNab	Hodgetts	..	..	..	Rowley
	28	(h)	Aston Villa	L 1-5	Clarke	25,487	..	Sankey	..	..	..	..	..	..	..	..	..
Nov	4	(h)	Stoke C	L 2-3	Elliott, Evans	18,656	Lewis	Tranter	..	..	..	..	Elliott	..	..	..	Hodgetts
	11	(h)	Stoke C	W 3-2	Clarke 3	8,067	..	..	..	..	..	..	Hodgetts	..	..	..	Johnson
	18	(a)	Wolves	L 2-3	Clarke, Johnson	12,485	..	..	..	..	..	..	..	..	..	..	..
	25	(h)	Wolves	W 3-2	Heaselgrave, Evans, Elliott	5,916	..	..	..	..	..	..	Elliott	..	..	..	Hodgetts
Dec	2	(h)	Walsall	W 3-0	Elliott 2, Clarke	8,992	..	..	..	..	..	..	..	Ball	..	..	..
	9	(a)	Walsall	W 2-1	Clarke 2	5,303	..	..	..	..	..	..	Hodgetts	..	..	..	Johnson
	16	(a)	Birmingham	L 0-2		6,796	..	..	..	..	..	..	..	..	..	..	Rowley
	23	(h)	Birmingham	L 1-4	Heaselgrave	5,000	..	Southam	Kinsell	Sankey	..	Williams	Elliott	Heaselgrave	..	..	Hodgetts
	26	(a)	Aston Villa	W 4-3	Clarke 3, McNab	5,007	..	Tranter	Millard	Williams	..	McNab	Hodgetts	..	..	..	Rowley
	30	(h)	Coventry C §	D 1-1	Heaselgrave	8,659	..	..	..	..	..	..	..	..	..	..	Jones
Jan	6	(h)	Aston Villa §	L 1-3	Ball	21,995	..	..	..	Sankey	..	..	Elliott	..	..	Ball	Hodgetts
	13	(a)	Aston Villa §	L 2-6	McNab, Heaselgrave	15,000	..	..	..	..	..	..	..	..	Ball	Clarke	..
Feb	3	(h)	Walsall §	L 0-2		6,334	..	Millard	Kinsell	Lowery	..	..	Hodgetts	Ball	Richardson	Barlow	Johnson
	10	(a)	Walsall §	D 0-0		6,376	..	Tranter	Millard	..	..	..	..	Heaselgrave	Clarke	Parkes	..
	17	(h)	Birmingham §	W 4-0	Clarke 3, Smith	12,479	..	Millard	Hardwick	..	..	..	..	..	..	..	Smith
	24	(a)	Birmingham §	D 1-1	Heaselgrave	17,727	..	..	..	Sankey	..	..	..	..	..	..	..
Mar	3	(a)	Coventry C §	W 3-0	Hodgetts 2, Smith	7,048	..	..	..	Lowery	..	..	..	..	..	..	..
	10	(a)	Northampton T §	D 2-2	Heaselgrave 2	6,200	..	Southam	Millard	..	..	..	..	..	..	..	Johnson
	17	(h)	Northampton T §	W 6-0	Clarke 3, Heaselgrave, Johnson, Coley(og)	6,938	..	Shelton	Male	..	..	..	..	..	..	..	..
	24	(a)	Bristol C §	L 2-5	Clarke, Elliott	21,371	..	Southam	Millard	..	..	..	..	..	Elliott	Clarke	..
	31	(h)	Bristol C §	D 3-3	Parker, Heaselgrave, Clarke	18,315	..	..	Millard	Parker	..	..	..	..	Clarke	Evans	Dudley
Apr	2	(h)	Aston Villa	L 2-4	Heaselgrave, Evans	14,378	Adams	Tranter	Millard	..	..	..	Bowen	..	..	..	Hodgetts
	7	(a)	Walsall	D 1-1	Clarke	5,227	W.Saunders	Millard	Kinsell	..	..	..	Elliott	..	..	Bowen	..
	14	(a)	Walsall	W 2-1	Clarke, Bowen	1,780	Lewis	..	..	..	..	..	Bowen	..	..	Finch	..
	21	(h)	Leicester C *	W 1-0	Clarke	5,002	..	..	..	..	..	Williams	Elliott	..	..	..	..
	28	(a)	Leicester C *	L 0-3		6,166	..	..	..	..	..	McNab	Bowen	..	..	..	..
May	5	(a)	Birmingham	L 1-4	Clarke	1,025	..	..	Parker	..	..	..	Jones	..	..	..	..
	12	(h)	Birmingham	L 2-3	Saunders, Evans	10,947	..	..	..	Williams	..	..	Hodgetts	..	..	Evans	D.Saunders
	19	(a)	Wolves	L 0-1		6,702	..	Southam	Millard	..	..	..	..	..	..	Finch	..
	26	(h)	Wolves	D 1-1	Hodgetts	4,742	..	..	..	..	..	..	Bowen	..	..	..	..

§ League Cup matches.　* Midland Cup matches.　**Note:** Match on 26 December v Aston Villa (a) was abandoned after 81 minutes due to fog but the result was allowed to stand.

APPEARANCES – FOOTBALL LEAGUE NORTH

Adams J 5, Ball H 3, Bowen T 4, Clarke I 22, Elliott W 9, Evans C 3, Finch R 4, Gripton W 25, Heaselgrave S 22, Heath N 6, Hodgetts F 26, Johnson J 4, Jones E 3, Kinsell H 4, Lewis E 14, Lowery H 5, McNab A 24, Millard L 25, Parker A 2, Richardson WG 3, Rowley GA 6, Sankey J 6, Saunders D 3, Saunders W 1, Southam J 7, Tranter G 12, Vincent E 1, Williams G 19. Total 286

GOALSCORERS – FOOTBALL LEAGUE NORTH

20 Clarke, 6 Elliott, Evans, Heaselgrave, 4 Hodgetts, 2 Rowley, 1 Bowen, Johnson, McNab, Richardson, D.Saunders. Total 49

APPEARANCES – MIDLAND CUP & LEAGUE CUP

Ball H 3, Barlow R 1, Bowen T 1, Clarke I 13, Dudley G 1, Elliott W 4, Evans C 4, Finch R 2, Gripton W 14, Hardwick G 3, Heaselgrave S 13, Hodgetts F 14, Johnson J 5, Jones E 1, Kinsell H 3, Lewis E 14, Lowery H 10, McNab A 13, Male N 1, Millard L 13, Parker A 1, Parkes H 6, Richardson WG 1, Sankey J 3, Shelton 1, Smith L 3, Southam J 2, Tranter G 4, Williams G 2. Total 154

GOALSCORERS – MIDLAND CUP & LEAGUE CUP

9 Clarke, 7 Heaselgrave, 2 Hodgetts, Smith, 1 Ball, Elliott, Johnson, McNab, Parker. Opp own goal 1. Total 26

• Albion's reserve XI beat Smethwick Highfield 17-0 in a friendly match in January 1945, Tommy Bowen (7) and Ray Barlow (6) were the two principal scorers.

• Forty-four hat-tricks were scored by Albion players (all games) between 1939 and 1946. Top of the list was WG Richardson with 10, Ike Clarke hit 9 and Harry Jones and Billy Elliott 8 each.

Albion's full playing record 1939-46						
1939-40	P	W	D	L	F	A
Division Two	3	1	1	1	8	8
Midland Regional League	28	18	4	6	87	51
League Cup	6	4	0	2	12	8
Jubilee Fund	1	0	1	0	1	1
1940-41						
Football League South	28	13	5	10	83	69
League Cup	4	1	0	3	9	13
1941-2						
Football League South	14	10	1	3	65	27
League Cup	17	8	3	6	50	42
1942-3						
Football League North	24	10	4	10	56	56
League Cup	14	7	2	5	28	27
1943-4						
Football League North	19	8	3	8	43	48
League Cup	10	2	4	4	24	29
Midland Cup	10	4	4	2	23	16
1944-5						
Football League North	26	11	6	9	49	48
League Cup	12	3	5	4	25	23
Midland Cup	2	1	0	1	1	3
1945-6						
Football League South	42	22	8	12	104	69
FA Cup	4	1	1	2	6	5
TOTALS	**264**	**124**	**52**	**88**	**674**	**543**

Albion also played a total of 40 'other' matches, winning 25, drawing three and losing 12, with a goal average of 138 for and 81 against.

1945-46

Date		Opponent	Result	Scorers	Att.	1	2	3	4	5	6	7	8	9	10	11
Aug 25	(h)	Swansea T	W 4-1	Clarke, Barlow, Millard, Hodgetts	18,033	Harris	White	Kinsell	Witcomb	Gripton	Millard	Hodgetts	Barlow	Clarke	Evans	Butler
29	(h)	Aston Villa	W 1-0	Millard	15,898	..	..	..	..	..	..	..	Elliott	..	Barlow	..
Sep 1	(a)	Swansea T	W 4-2	Barlow 2, Hodgetts, White (pen)	8,223	..	..	..	..	..	..	..	..	..	..	..
5	(a)	Aston Villa	D 3-3	Elliott (pen), Clarke, Saunders	36,103	..	..	..	..	..	..	..	..	..	..	D.Saunders
8	(a)	Birmingham	L 0-4		20,068	..	Southam	Bradley	..	..	..	..	Heaselgrave	..	..	Butler
12	(h)	Luton T	W 3-1	Clarke, Elliott, Barlow	14,146	..	..	Shaw	..	..	..	..	Elliott	..	..	..
15	(h)	Birmingham	D 0-0		27,745	..	White	..	..	Tranter	..	..	Barlow	Pears	Evans	..
22	(h)	Tottenham H	W 5-0	Barlow 3, Pears, Butler	26,002	..	N.Williams	..	..	..	..	..	Elliott	..	Barlow	..
29	(a)	Tottenham H	L 2-4	Barlow, Ward (og)	31,403	..	Shaw	Kinsell	..	..	..	..	..	..	..	..
Oct 6	(h)	Brentford	L 3-4	Rowley 2, Barlow	29,821	..	White	..	..	..	..	..	..	..	Rowley	..
13	(a)	Brentford	L 0-2		20,160	..	..	Shaw	..	..	..	..	Evans	..	..	..
20	(a)	Chelsea	L 4-7	Hodgetts, Elliott, Barlow, Butler	31,061	W.Saunders	..	..	..	Millard	G.Williams	..	Elliott	..	..	..
27	(h)	Chelsea	W 8-1	Clarke 4, Rowley 2, Hodgetts, Witcomb	21,905	Harris	Shaw	Kinsell	..	Hood	Millard	Elliott	Clarke	..	..	Hodgetts
Nov 3	(h)	Millwall	W 3-1	Clarke, Rowley, Hodgetts	16,046	W.Saunders	..	..	..	Tranter	..	..	..	..	..	..
10	(a)	Millwall	W 4-1	Clarke, Rowley, Barlow, Hodgetts	20,045	Sanders	..	..	..	..	Ryan	..	..	..	..	..
17	(a)	Southampton	W 2-1	Elliott, Clarke	17,116	..	..	Millard	..	..	..	..	..	..	..	..
24	(h)	Southampton	W 5-2	Elliott 3, Hodgetts, Rowley	18,768	..	White	..	..	..	..	..	..	..	..	..
Dec 1	(h)	Derby C	L 2-3	Elliott, Rowley	29,525	..	..	..	..	..	..	..	..	..	..	..
8	(a)	Derby C	D 3-3	Newsome 2, Barlow	24,138	..	Millard	Kinsell	..	..	..	..	..	Newsome	..	..
15	(a)	Leicester C	W 3-1	Elliott, Newsome, Millard	14,227	..	Shaw	..	..	..	Millard	..	..	..	..	..
22	(h)	Leicester C	W 3-2	Elliott 2, Newsome	15,107	..	..	..	..	..	..	..	..	..	..	..
24	(h)	Coventry C	D 2-2	Clarke, Newsome	18,038	..	..	..	..	..	..	..	..	..	Evans	..
26	(a)	Coventry C	L 2-3	Clarke, Newsome	19,303	..	..	..	..	..	Ryan	..	..	Gomm	Connelly	Newsome
29	(h)	Luton T	W 2-1	Connelly, Saunders	9,146	..	White	Shaw	Millard	..	..	..	..	..	..	D.Saunders
Jan 12	(a)	Arsenal	L 0-2		22,334	Twigg	Shaw	Kinsell	Witcomb	..	Edwards	..	Newsome	Millard	..	Butler
19	(h)	Arsenal	L 0-1		26,014	Sanders	..	..	..	..	Millard	Newsome	Clarke	Gomm	..	..
Feb 2	(a)	Charlton A	D 1-1	Clarke	25,083	..	White	Shaw	..	..	..	Elliott	..	Newsome	..	..
9	(a)	Fulham	W 4-1	Elliott, Newsome 2, Freeman (og)	15,139	..	..	Kinsell	..	..	..	..	..	..	..	..
16	(h)	Fulham	W 3-1	Elliott 2, Butler	20,229	..	Shaw	..	..	..	..	..	..	..	..	..
23	(h)	Plymouth A	W 5-2	Clarke 2, Elliott, Connelly, Gomm	13,117	..	..	..	Millard	..	Ryan	..	..	Gomm	..	..
Mar 2	(a)	Plymouth A	W 4-0	Newsome 2, Connelly, Butler	20,227	..	..	..	..	..	..	..	Newsome	..	..	..
9	(a)	Portsmouth	L 0-3		15,987	..	..	..	Witcomb	..	..	..	Barlow	..	..	..
16	(h)	Portsmouth	W 2-0	Elliott, Jinks	15,908	..	..	..	..	..	..	..	Jinks	Barlow	..	..
23	(h)	Nottingham F	W 1-0	Banks	19,755	..	..	..	Millard	..	..	..	Banks	..	..	..
30	(a)	Nottingham F	W 2-0	Butler, Hodgetts	21,529	..	..	..	..	..	..	Hodgetts	..	..	..	..
Apr 6	(a)	Newport C	W 3-0	Clarke, Banks, Butler	14,014	..	..	..	Witcomb	..	Millard	..	..	..	..	..
13	(h)	Newport C	W 6-0	Clarke 3, Hodgetts, Butler, Millard	18,690	..	..	..	..	..	..	..	..	..	..	..
15	(h)	Charlton A	L 2-5	Banks, Elliott	5,187	..	..	..	..	..	..	..	Elliott	..	..	Hodgetts
20	(a)	West Ham U	D 1-1	Elliott	24,630	..	Millard	..	..	..	Ryan	..	..	..	..	Butler
22	(a)	Wolves	D 0-0		36,361	..	..	..	..	..	..	..	..	..	..	..
23	(h)	Wolves	D 1-1	Banks	38,077	..	..	..	..	..	..	..	..	..	..	..
27	(h)	West Ham U	L 1-2	Elliott (pen)	11,821	..	Shaw	..	..	..	..	..	..	Newsome	..	..

1946 TOUR TO BELGIUM & LUXEMBOURG

Date		Opponent	Result	Scorers	Att.	1	2	3	4	5	6	7	8	9	10	11
May 1	(n)	Belgian XI	L 4-5	Banks, Elliott (pen), Hodgetts 2	16,212	..	Millard	..	..	..	..	..	..	Banks	..	..
4	(n)	Fola Jennesse XIW	W 5-1	Hodgetts, Clarke 2, Elliott, Butler	7,035	Twigg	Pemberton	*	..	Millard	..	..	..	..	Hodgetts	Butler
8	(n)	Anderlecht	D 1-1	Hodgetts	8,540	Sanders	Millard	..	..	..	Ryan	..	..	..	Barlow	Hodgetts §

* Substituted by Ryan.   § Substituted by Butler.

APPEARANCES – FOOTBALL LEAGUE SOUTH

Banks G 8, Barlow R 32, Bradley D 1, Butler S 25, Clarke I 35, Connelly E 10, Edwards C 1, Elliott W 34, Evans C 4, Gomm B 4, Gripton W 6, Harris W 12, Heaselgrave S 1, Hodgetts F 29, Hood G O 1, Jinks J 1, Kinsell H 31, Millard L 37, Newsome R 12, Pears W 3, Rowley GA 9, Ryan RA 17, Sanders J 27, Saunders D 2, Saunders W 2, Shaw C 29, Southam J 2, Tranter G 34, Twigg L 1, White H 13, Williams G 1, Williams N 1, Witcomb D 37. Total 462

GOALSCORERS – FOOTBALL LEAGUE SOUTH

19 Clarke, Elliott, 12 Barlow, 10 Newsome, 9 Hodgetts, 8 Rowley, 7 Butler, 4 Banks, Millard, 3 Connelly, 2 D.Saunders, 1 Gomm, Jinks, Pears, White, Witcomb. Opp own goal 2. Total 104

Players with 50 or more wartime appearances to their credit:

195	W.Gripton	100	I.Clarke
153	L.Millard	92	I.Bassett
152	W.Elliott	90	W.G.Richardson
134	A.McNab	88	J.Johnson
133	J.Sankey	71	H.Kinsell
131	C.Shaw	62	A.J.Smith
129	C.Evans	62	D.Witcomb
111	J.Adams	60	E.Connelly
111	S.Heaselgrave	60	C.Edwards
109	F.Hodgetts	59	R.Newsome
		54	G.Tranter

Totals include Division Two, FA Cup, League South and North, League Cup and Midland Cup matches, 1939-1946 inclusive.
W.Gripton also played in 13 'other' matches to total 208 in wartime football.

• The two Chelsea-Albion games in 1945-6 produced 20 goals — Albion winning 8-1 at home but losing 7-4 away.

Action from the Birmingham v Albion Football League South match on 8 September 1945. Albion lost 4-0, their heaviest defeat during 1945-6, in front of 20,068 spectators.

• At the start of 1945-6 season there was a penalty-kick awarded in each of Albion's first five matches — a club record.

• A total of 15 players scored on their debuts for Albion between September 1939 and April 1946.

• Albion's average home wartime attendance — in all major competitions — was around the 9,000 mark. In 1945-6 their average home League gate was 19,992 — aggregate 419,832.

OVERSEAS OPPOSITION

Albion have visited a number of countries since their first overseas tour was undertaken in 1909, to Sweden and Denmark. Up to end of season 1986-7 Albion had been involved in competitive and friendly matches in 35 different countries.

Sweden (1909, 1972, 1981, 1984)
Denmark (1909, 1979)
Republic of Ireland (1932, 1953, 1975)
Belgium (1946, 1954, 1968, 1974)
Luxemburg (1946)
USSR (1957)
Spain (1958, 1971, 1978, 1979, 1981, 1982)
Canada (1959, 1969, 1981)
USA (1959, 1965, 1969, 1981)
Austria (1961)
Holland (1964, 1966, 1972, 1982, 1983)
Peru (1966)

Argentina (1966)
Uruguay (1966)
Brazil (1966)
Italy (1967, 1970, 1971, 1980)
Tanzania (1968)
Uganda (1968)
Kenya (1968)
Rumania (1968)
Norway (1969)
Yugoslavia (1962, 1979, 1980)
Saudi Arabia (1977)
China (1978)

Hong Kong (1978, 1984)
Syria (1978)
Turkey (1978)
Portugal (1978)
East Germany (1979)
Abu Dhabi (1980)
Bahrain (1980)
Switzerland (1981)
Kuwait (1981)
Cyprus (1982)
Tunisia (1985)

At Stoney Lane and The Hawthorns, Albion have received visits from clubs in 18 different countries — Canada, South Africa, Czechoslovakia, Austria, Malta, USSR, Spain, Rumania, Switzerland, Holland, Italy, Belgium, Turkey, Portugal, Yugoslavia, China, East Germany and Israel, in that order.

Overseas tournaments in which Albion have particpated include the 1965 New York International Tournament, the Brussels International Tournament (v Honved) in 1954, the Palo Alto International Tournament (1969), the Anglo-Italian Tournaments of 1970 and 1971, the Orendscupen Tournament (1969), the Anglo-Italian Tournaments of 1970 and 1971, the Orendscupen Tournament (1972), the Trofeo Costa Blanca (1977), Marjan Tournament in Yugoslavia (1980), Sevilla International Tournament (1981), Barcelona International Tournament (1982).

And, of course, Albion have appeared in the Fairs Cup (1966-7), in the European Cup-Winners Cup of 1968-9, and the UEFA Cup in 1978-9, 1979-8 and 1981-2.

FACTS AND FIGURES

First match v overseas opposition: 27 October, 1888 v The Canadians (h) (1-0)
Record home win: 11-6 v The Kaffirs 22 November, 1899
Record home defeat: 3-4 v SC Wacker 12 May, 1951
Record win overseas: 15-0 v Alberta All Stars at Calgary 27 May, 1959

Record defeat overseas: 0-6 v Polonia Bytom at New York 25 July, 1965
Most goals by an Albion player overseas: 6 by Billy Garraty v Gefle in May, 1909, and by Bobby Robson v Alberta All Stars in May, 1959.

In the summer of 1957, Albion played three matches in the USSR and became the first British club to win in that country. On the Canadian-American tour of 1959 Albion scored 59 goals in nine matches. In 1968 Albion toured East Africa as FA Cup winners and were undefeated in six matches. In May, 1978, Albion became the first professional European team to visit China, winning all four games there.

The furthest Albion have played away from The Hawthorns is at Shanghai, People's Republic of China, on their Chinese tour in May, 1978, a distance of approximately 7,800 miles from West Bromwich.

In a Trofeo Costa Blanca game at Alicante on 14 August, 1977, Albion had two players, John Wile and Mick Martin, and their manager, Ronnie Allen, sent off. This was the first time in the club's history that two first-team players had been dismissed from the field in the same game.

The largest crowd to watch Albion play in an overseas match is 95,300 who attended the Crvena Zvezda (Red Star) — Albion UEFA Cup tie in Belgrade on 7 March, 1979.

Albion tour party, to USA and Canada 1959. Left to right: Ronnie Allen, Derek Hogg, Alec Jackson, Davy Burnside, Graham Williams, Clive Jackman, Archie Styles, Bobby Cram, Chuck Drury, Keith Smith, Bobby Robson, Joe Kennedy, Dick Graham, Brian Whitehouse, Ray Potter, Stuart Williams, Maurice Setters and Ray Barlow (with his daughter).

Foreign Tours and Overseas Tournaments

All matches played by Albion on overseas tours and in foreign tournaments are recorded in this section with the relevant goalscorers and attendances. Single matches played abroad can be found in the section covering friendly games, etc. Fuller details of Albion's visits to Russia and China may be found on page 200.

1908-09
Scandanavian Tour
May 18 v Newcastle United (in Copenhagen) 0-3
Att: 5,000
May 20* v Hull City (in Stockholm) 2-1
Buck, Timmins
Att: 4,000
May 21 v Gefle FC (in Gefle) 10-0
Garraty 6, Buck 2, Harris, Manners
Att: 6,500
May 23* v Stockholm Select XI (in Stockholm) 8-3
Buck 4, Davies 2, Garraty, Harris
Att: 10,200
May 24* v Hull City (in Gothenburg) 3-4
Thompson, Buck, Timmins (pen)
Att: 5,500
May 26* v Swedish Select XI (in Stockholm) 2-0
Garraty, Buck
Att: 15,000
May 28 v Danish Select XI (in Copenhagen) 1-3
Buck
Att: 12,000
*Dates of games not confirmed

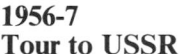

George Harris, scorer against Gefle and Stockholm during the 1909 Scandanavian tour.

1931-2
Irish Tour
May 2 v Linfield 5-1
Wood 2, W.G.Richardson, Carter, Trentham
Att: 12,500
May 4 v Shelbourne 0-0
17,000

1945-6
Tour to Belgium and Luxembourg
May 1 v Belgium XI (at Verviers) 4-5
Banks, Elliott (pen), Hodgetts 2
Att: 15,212
May 4 v Fola Jennesse XI (at Esch-sur-Alzette) 5-1
Hodgetts, Clarke 2, Elliott, Batler
Att: 7,035
May 8* v Anderlecht (in Brussels) 1-1
Hodgetts
Att: 8,540
*Benefit match for Tubentia FC. See also under Benefits & Testimonials

1952-3
Irish Tour
May 10 v Waterford Select XI 5-4
Lee 2, Hodgkisson 2, Griffin
Att: 5,136
May 13 v Bohemians Select XI 5-1
Griffin, Hodgkisson, Allen, Millard, Brookes
Att: 6,913

1954-5
Le Soir International Festival
Oct 13 v Honved (in Brussels) 3-5
Nicholls 2, Allen
Att: 55,000

Joe Kennedy clears the danger with a powerful header against FC Zenit in 1957.

1956-7
Tour to USSR
Jun 2 v Zenit 1-1
Kevan
Att: 80,000
Jun 7 v Dynamo Tbilisi 3-0
Horobin, Kevan 2
Att: 35,000
Jun 12 v CDSA (Russian Red Army) 4-2
Whitehouse, Kevan 2, Griffin
Att: 80,500

1958-9
Tour to Canada and USA
May 22 v Ontario All Stars (in Toronto) 6-1
Whitehouse 2, Allen, Hogg, Robson 2
Att: 12,000
May 24 v Dundee (at Ebbetts Field, New York) 2-2
Allen 2
Att: 21,312
May 27 v Alberta All Stars (at Calgary) 15-0
Smith 3, Whitehouse 2, Kennedy, Robson 6, G.Williams 2, Jackson
Att: 6,000
May 30 v Dundee (in Vancouver) 7-1
Jackson 2, Kevan 2, Allen, Hamilton (og), Drury
Att: 17,800
Jun 1 v British Columbia All Stars (in Vancouver) 2-3
Allen, Burnside
Att: 15,000
Jun 3 v Manitoba All Stars (at Winnipeg) 10-1
Whitehouse 2, Allen 3, Robson 2, Kevan, Smith, Kennedy
Att: 8,500
Jun 6 v Dundee (in Toronto) 4-2
Allen, Burnside 3
Att: 10,000
Jun 8 v Ottowa All Stars (in Ottowa) 9-0
Whitehouse 3, Burnside 2, Robson 2, Kevan, Jackson
Att: 25,000
Jun 10 v Montreal All Stars (in Montreal) 4-0
Allen 2, Hogg, Whitehouse
Att: 15,000
On this tour, Albion scored 59 goals in nine matches, Bobby Robson (12) and Ronnie Allen (11) were top marksmen.

Bert Trentham, scorer against Linfield in May 1932 — his only goal for Albion.

1960-61
Austrian Tour
May 22 v Lustenau 3-3
Kevan, Burnside, Kiesinger (og)
Att: 10,000
May 24 v Linz ASK 3-2
Jackson 2, Clark
Att: 12,000
May 26 v Graz 2-1
Burnside, Cram
Att: 12,500

1964-5
Tour to Holland
Aug 8 v Alkmaar 1-2
Clark
Att: 12,000
Aug 12 v ADO (The Hague) 2-1
Brown, Fraser
Att: 8,000
Aug 15 v Ajax 1-0
Hope
Att: 8,100

1965-6
South American Tour
May 13 v Alianza Lima (in Lima) 3-2
Brown 2, Cram (pen)
Att: 20,000
May 15 v Sporto Cristal (in Lima) 2-1
Brown, Kaye
Att: 10,000
May 22 v Uruguay Select XI (in Montevideo) 1-1
Collard
Att: 20,000
May 25 v Newells Old Boys (in Rosario) 0-0
Att: 15,700
May 29 v Uruguay Select XI (in Montevideo) 0-2
15,000
Jun 5 v Flamengo (in Rio de Janiero) 2-1
Cram (pen), Kaye
Att: 30,100

New York International Tournament (Section 2)
Jul 7 v Kilmarnock 0-2
Att: 2,278
11 Jul v Ferencvaros 1-1
Astle
Att: 6,387
Jul 14 v Polonia Bytom 2-2
Kaye, Foggo
Att: 4,096
Jul 18 v Kilmarnock 2-0
Kaye, Cram (pen)
Att: 10,066
Jul 21 v Ferencvaros 1-2
Clark
Att: 5,663
Jul 25 v Polonia Bytom 0-6
Att: 8,162
Albion finished third in their section and failed to qualify for the finals.

1967-8
Tour to East Africa
May 23 v Dar-Es-Salaam Select XI 1-1
Astle
Att: 20,000
May 25 v Tanzania 1-1
Astle
Att: 20,000
May 29 v Uganda 1-0
Hartford
Att: 15,000
Jun 1 v Kenya 2-1
Brown (2 pens)
Att: 11,000
Jun 5 v East African XI 2-2
Astle, Rees
Att: 22,000
Jun 8 v Kenya 4-3
Hartford, Brown, Krzywicki, Collard
Att: 16,500

1968-9
Tour to Canada and USA
May 11 v Vancouver All Stars 2-0
Brown (2 pens)
Att: 10,000
May 14 v Victoria O'Keefes 4-1
Kaye, Krzywicki, Brown, Hegan
Att: 2,351
May 18 v Dukla Prague 2-1
Krzywicki 2
Att: 5,207
May 23 v California Clippers 2-2
Brown, Hegan
Att: 3,500
May 25 v Vitoria Setubal 0-1
Att: 6,000
May 27 v Edmonton's All Stars 12-0
Martin 3, Lovett 2, Hegan 2, Hope 2, Kaye, Krzywicki, Cantello
Att: 6,500
Last four games played in Polo Alto International Tournament.

1969-70
Tour to Norway
Jul 30 v Norway Under-23 XI (in Bergen) 2-3
Hegan 2
Att: 6,000
Jul 31 v SK Lyn (Oslo) 6-0
Astle 3, Hope 2, Freeman
Att: 5,000

1971-2
Tour to Yugoslavia
May 9 v Hajduk Split (in Split) 1-2
Gould
Att: 8,000
May 11 v FK Velez (in Mostar) 3-2
Suggett, Hartford, Gould
Att: 6,000
May 15 v FK Sarajevo (in Sarajevo) 1-1
Gould (pen)
Att: 10,000

1972-3
Swedish Örenduscupen Tournament
Jul 28 v Kalmar FF 3-0
Gould 2, Nisbet
Att: 5,026
Jul 30 v Hälsingborg IFK 3-1
Gould 2, McVitie
Att: 7,995
Aug 1 v Lanskrona Bols 1-1
T.Brown
Att: 7,114

1974-5
Tour to Belgium
Jul 28 v KV Mechelen 0-1
Att: 3,559
Aug 1 v Diest 2-1
Hughes, Shaw
Att: 4,503

1975-6
Irish Tour
Jul 25 v Shamrock Rovers 1-0
Fagan (og)
Att: 2,211
Jul 28 v Finn Harps 0-1
Att: 1,753

1977-8
Spanish Trofeo Costa Blanca Tournament in Alicante
Aug 12 v Dynamo Tbilisi 1-0
D.Cross
Att: 10,000
Aug 14 v Hercules CF 1-5
Cunningham
Att: 4,000

Tour to China and Hong Kong
May 17 v Peking XI 3-1
Regis, A.Brown 2
Att: 80,000
May 19 v China 2-0
A.Brown, Regis
Att: 89,400
May 22 v Shanghai XI 2-0
Regis, Cunningham
Att: 40,000
May 26 v Kwantung Province 6-0
Regis 2, Cunningham, T.Brown, Wile, Martin
Att: 30,500
May 28 v Hong Kong 3-0
Chi-Keung (og), Regis, T.Brown
Att: 18,000

1978-9
Syrian Tour
Aug 11 v North Territory Provincial XI 1-0
A.Brown
Att: 10,000
Aug 13 v Damascus Police XI 1-1
T.Brown
Att: 12,500

Tour to Denmark
May 28 v Aalborg Fodbold-Alliancen 0-1
Att: 8,300
May 29 v Fyn Boldspil-Union Select XI 4-1
Regis 2, T.Brown 2
Att: 6,600
May 31 v IHF (Denmark) 7-0
Cunningham 2, Regis 2, A.Brown 2, T.Brown
Att: 4,200

Programme for one of Albion's games in Canada, 1969.

Kevin Summerfield scored against Portland Timbers and Edmonton Drillers in May 1981.

1979-80
Spanish Trofeo Teresa Tournament in La Coruna
Aug 14 v Sporting Gijon 0-1
Att: 25,200
Aug 15 v Honved 0-1
Att: 38,140

Tour to Abu Dhabi and Bahrain
Jan 14 v Al Amarath 3-0
A.Brown 2, Benjamin
Att: 5,000
Jan 16 v Al Hala 4-1
Regis, Moses, Deehan, Malrahti (og)
Att: 5,400

1980-81
Yugoslavian Trofej Marjan Tournament
Aug 6 v Hajduk Split 1-5
Regis
Att: 20,140
Aug 6 v FC Zurich 0-0
Att: 4,066

Tour to Canada and USA
May 11 v Vancouver Whitecaps 1-2
Regis
Att: 17,339
May 13 v Portland Timbers 1-0
Summerfield
Att: 10,140
May 15 v Edmonton Drillers 2-1
Regis, Summerfield
Att: 6,820

1981-2
X Trofeo Futbol Ciudad de Sevilla Tournament in Spain
Aug 19 v Real Betis 4-1
Owen, Mills 2, Moses
Att: 35,535
Aug 21 v Sevilla 2-0
Mackenzie, Deehan
Att: 46,723

1982-3
Spanish IX Trofeo Futbol Ciudad de Barcelona Tournament
Aug 17 v RCD Espanol 2-3
Regis, Jol
Att: 9,371
Aug 18 v C A Osasuna 1-2
Regis
Att: 5,035

1983-4
Tour to Holland
Aug 10 v FC Den Bosch '67 3-0
Robson, Jol, Thompson
Att: 1,920
Aug 13 v NAC Breda 2-2
Jol, Robson
Att: 2,034
Aug 16 v Go Ahead Eagles (Deventer) 4-3
Thompson, Regis, Jol, Cross
Att: 2,145

CHINA TOUR 1978

In May 1978 Albion visited the People's Republic of China where they played four games, thus becoming the first British professional club side to set foot in that country. All four games ended in victories for Albion who also defeated Hong Kong on the homeward journey.

May 17 v Peking XI 3-1
A.Brown 2, Regis
Godden (Grew); Batson, Statham, T.Brown, Wile, Robertson, Martin, Robson, Regis (Hughes), A.Brown (Summerfield), Cunningham (Monaghan).
Att: 80,000

May 19 v China 2-0
Regis, A.Brown
Godden; Batson, Statham, T.Brown (Hughes), Wile, Robertson, Martin (Loveridge), Robson, Regis, A.Brown, Cunningham.
Att: 89,400

May 22 v Shanghai 2-0
Regis, Cunningham
Grew; Batson, Statham, Hughes (Loveridge), Wile, Robertson, Martin (Trewick) Robson, Regis, A.Brown (Summerfield), Cunningham (Monaghan).
Att: 40,000

May 26 v Kwantung Province 6-0
Regis 2, Wile, Martin, T.Brown, Cunningham.
Godden (Grew); Batson (Hughes), Statham, T.Brown, Wile, Robertson, Martin (Loveridge), Robson, Regis (Summerfield), A.Brown, Cunningham (Monaghan).
Att: 30,500

May 28 v Hong Kong Select 3-0
Regis, T.Brown, Chi-Keung (og)
Godden; Batson, Statham, T.Brown, Wile, Robertson, Martin, Robson, Regis, A.Brown, Cunningham.
Att: 18,000

Full record: P W D L F A
              5 5 0 0 16 1

Top scorers: Regis 6, A.Brown 3, T.Brown 2, Cunningham 2.

In August 1979 China played Albion at The Hawthorns in a 'Friendship Friendly' match. A crowd of 11,382 saw Albion win 4-0, Regis, A.Brown, Barnes and an opponent (og) the scorers.

中、英足球友谊比赛名单
(一九七八年五月廿二日下午三时)

英国布朗米奇队   上 海 队
教练员: 阿特金森   教练员: 陈志华
         赖 特   王后军
运动员: 1 格 鲁   运动员: 2 2 刘文斌
        2 巴特森   1 陶 涛
        3 斯特灵姆   2 蒋炳尧
        4 休 斯   5 邵永福
        5 怀 尔   6 张卫星
        6 鲁宾逊   7 张亮阁
        7 马 丁   8 陈安康
        8 罗布森   9 吴志康
        9 里吉斯   1 1 徐国强
       10 阿.布朗   1 2 朱柏宁
       11 坎宁安   1 3 李中华
       12 布 朗   1 4 丁龙发

Not a menu from a Chinese restaurant, but the team line-ups for one of Albion's tour games.

ALBION IN RUSSIA, 1957

In June 1957, Albion visited the Soviet Union to play three matches against Russian club sides from the First Division. Albion were undefeated and won many admirers.

Jun 2 v Leningrad Zenit 1-1
Kevan
Brown; Howe, Millard, Setters, Kennedy, Barlow, Griffin, Robson, Allen, Horobin (Kevan), Lee.
Att: 80,000

Jun 7 v Dynamo Tbilisi 3-0
Kevan 2, Horobin
Sanders; Howe, S.Williams, Setters (Dudley), Kennedy, Barlow, Griffin, Robson (Whitehouse), Allen, Kevan, Horobin.
Att: 35,000

Jun 12 v CDSA (Russian Army Side) 4-2
Kevan 2, Whitehouse, Griffin
Brown; Howe, S.Williams, Setters, Kennedy, Barlow (Dudley), Griffin, Whitehouse (Robson), Allen, Kevan, Horobin.
Att: 80,500

Albion 'keeper, Fred Brown, in 'flying action' against FC Zenit, 2 June 1957.

THE THROSTLE WENT TO RUSSIA DURING THE "BRIAN CLOSE" SEASON TO SHOW 'EM THAT WEST BROMWICH HAS ITS OWN MAGNIFICENT VERSION OF "STEPPES"

RAY BARLOW

CORKSKI! ONE..TWO..STEPS.. AND HE'S IN OUR PENALTY AREAVITCH!

Abandoned-Postponed Matches

Nowadays it is very rare indeed for a club to complete a full season without having at least one match abandoned or postponed because of bad weather. Albion have been somewhat fortunate in as much that since 1888 they have had only 12 League games halted before the scheduled 90 minutes had been played. Here are those 12 games, with the score of the re-arranged fixture in brackets.

9 Mar 1895	Stoke 1 Albion 2	Abandoned 68 mins, rain	(1-1)
7 Dec 1895	Albion 0 Bury 0	Abandoned 15 mins, snow	(1-3)
18 Nov 1905	Grimsby 1 Albion 0	Abandoned 65 mins, fog	(3-2)
19 Jan 1907	Albion 0 Barnsley 0	Abandoned 80 mins, poor light	(3-1)
6 Jan 1912	Albion 0 Tottenham 0	Abandoned 52 mins, fog	(2-0)
13 Feb 1915	Oldham 0 Albion 1	Abandoned 21 mins, snow	(1-1)
19 Sep 1925	Albion 0 Bury 2	Abandoned 51 mins, rain	(4-0)
22 Feb 1936	Albion 1 Aston Villa 0	Abandoned 26 mins, snow	(0-3)
19 Nov 1949	Albion 1 Blackpool 2	Abandoned 70 mins, fog	(1-0)
20 Dec 1958	Albion 1 Luton 1	Abandoned 70 mins, rain	(2-0)
26 Dec 1962	Wolves 2 Albion 0	Abandoned 45 mins, snow	(7-0)
14 Dec 1965	Albion 0 Aston Villa 0	Abandoned 51 mins, rain	(2-2)

Nottingham Forest and Albion players are called to the centre of the field before the abandonment of the FA Cup tie at the City Ground in January 1973.

In the FA Cup, Albion have had only one tie abandoned — the third round replay against Nottingham Forest (away) on January 16 1973, when fog called an end to the proceedings in the 79th minute with the scores level at 1-1.

There have been other games involving Albion which were forced into an early finish due to the weather:

Friendlies

6 Jan 1940	Albion 0 Sheffield Wednesday 3	(47 mins)
5 Dec 1892	Albion 1 Aston Villa 1	(35 mins)
30 Mar 1889	Albion 4 Grimsby Town 0	(60 mins)
28 Dec 1885	Albion 0 Bolton Wanderers 0	(75 mins)
25 Apr 1885	Bolton Wanderers 1 Albion 0	(70 mins)
26 Jan 1884	Albion 2 Wednesbury Old Athletic 0	(15 min)
12 Nov 1883	Stoke 1 Albion 1	(80 mins)
10 Feb 1883	Albion 1 Notts Rangers 1	(60 mins)
5 Nov 1881	Milton 0 Albion 3	(35 mins)

Staffs Cup

3 Dec 1883	Albion 1 Cocknage 0	(40 mins)

Wartime game

26 Dec 1944	Aston Villa 3 Albion 4	(81 mins)

(This scoreline was allowed to stand)

On 16 May 1970, the Lanerossi-Vincenza Anglo-Italian Cup tie was called off by the referee because of crowd and player disturbances.

POSTPONED MATCHES

There have been many instances in which certain Albion games have had to be postponed due to the unforseen circumstances which surrounded the fixture itself, unfit grounds, sick players, etc.

One game — a home fourth round FA Cup tie against Nottingham Forest in season 1962-3 — was called-off no fewer than 11 times before it was finally allowed to go on 58 days late — on 6 March 1963. This is the longest-delayed Cup-tie in Albion's history.

In the Arctic winter of 1947, Albion did not play a single game between 9 February and 14 March and when similar conditions gripped England in 1962-3 Albion managed to fulfil two fixtures (one League, one FA Cup) between 16 December and 1 March.

FIRSTS

Albion were the first British professional football team to win a match in the Soviet Union — 3-0 v Dynamo Tbilisi on 7 June 1957.

During May 1978, Albion made an historic trip to The People's Republic of China, thus becoming the first European professional club side to play in that country.

Albion were the first club to head the Football League — going to the top of the table on the opening day of the competition, 8 September, 1888, after winning 2-0 at Stoke.

When Tommy Glidden collected the F.A. Cup at Wembley in 1931 (after Albion had beaten Birmingham 2-1 in the Final), he became the first outside-right to skipper an FA Cup-winning team.

Jeff Astle was the first player to score a goal in both the FA Cup Final (1968 v Everton) and in the League Cup Final (1970 v Manchester City), at Wembley.

Tony Brown was the first player to score in every round of the Football League Cup — in season 1965-6. And Clive Clark of Albion was the first footballer to score in every game of a League Cup competition — 1966-7.

Albion were the first club to reach the League Cup Final on three occasions — 1966, 1967 and 1970.

When winning the FA Cup in 1888, Albion were the first team to do so with an all-English-born team. They repeated this feat in 1931.

Albion were the first team to score more than 100 goals in Division One in a season — 104 in 1919-20. In this same championship-winning season of 1919-20 Albion also became the first team to register 60 points.

In 1886 Albion became the first Midland club to reach the F.A Cup Final (v Blackburn Rovers), and they went on to become the first Midland side to play in three successive Finals, with further appearances in 1887 (v Aston Villa) and 1888 (v. Preston North End).

Albion were the first, and so far only, side to win the FA Cup and promotion from the Second Division in the same season — 1930-1.

Albion were the first club to be relegated from the First Divisions of the Football League and the Central League in the same season — 1985-6.

Birmingham Cup

THE BIRMINGHAM CUP was first competed for in 1875-6 when Tipton FC were the winners. In December 1875, the Birmingham County FA had been formed in Birmingham at a meeting convened by the Calthorpe and Aston Unity clubs, and the Cup competition was quickly introduced by the new body. In April 1881, West Bromwich FC were defeated 2-0 in the semi-final by Aston Villa but Albion's first entry into the competition did not materialise until the following season when Calthorpe, Elwell's, Fallings Heath Rovers and Notts Rangers were beaten on the way to a semi-final meeting with Wednesbury Old Athletic.

Albion's first Birmingham Cup tie was against Calthorpe (away) on 12 November 1881, when this team brought off a surprise 3-2 victory: Eld; H.Bell, Bunn, Stanton, While, Whitehouse, Aston, Timmins, Bisseker, Kershaw, G.Bell. Albion's display was so pleasing that the referee, Mr J.H.Cofield, who was secretary of the Birmingham FA, wrote them a long letter of congratulation.

In the semi-final, at the Aston Lower Grounds on 25 March 1882, Albion were well supported as the correspondent of the *Midland Advertiser* pointed out: 'The howling, hooting, and yelling, indulged in by the West Bromwich contingent of onlookers, was simply horrible. May I be far away when next Athletic meet West Bromwich Albion in another semi-final, for I have scarcely got the din of the discordant yells out of my hearing yet.'

Unfortunately for the vociferous Albionites the 'Old 'Uns' proved just too good for their opponents in winning an exciting game by 3-2.

On 11 November 1882, Albion crushed Coseley 26-0 in a first round tie, having led 17-0 at half-time, and then defeated Wolves 4-2 away, in the first-ever clash between the two clubs, before losing once again to the 'Old 'Uns'. In 1883-4, Albion progressed to the semi-final again after a three-match marathon with Wednesbury Old Athletic. In the semis they lost to Walsall Swifts. It was during the 1885-6

season that Albion won the trophy for the first time. In the first two rounds Albion's reserve team took over the fixtures after which Albion's seniors demolished Notts Rangers, Burslem Port Vale and Walsall Swifts.

In 1894, Albion and Wolves shared the trophy for six months each. Albion were losing semi-finalists in 1881-2, 1883-4, 1890-91 and 1896-7. In nine home ties from 9 October 1886 to 17 January 1891, Albion did not concede a goal, and in 34 home Cup ties in 24 years the Baggies scored in all but two of them.

Albion's record victory was the 1882 slaughter of Coseley whilst the heaviest defeat incurred was 7-0 at Stoney Lane on 16 January 1899 when Wolverhampton Wanderers were the visitors.

Albion's record in the Birmingham Cup:-

	Home					Away				
P	W	D	L	F	A	W	D	L	F	A
80	26	3	5	141	33	22	9	15	99	76

The Birmingham Cup was one of the major competitions in the earliest days of Midlands football and was taken very seriously, as shown when Albion withdrew Billy Bassett from the Football League team to meet the Football Alliance in 1891 so that he could play in a semi-final replay against Aston Villa.

Three years earlier Albion withdrew from the Birmingham FA (and the Birmingham Cup) because the club's management did not like the attitude of the FA and the Birmingham newspapers towards the club. By the end of the century, however, the competition had lost much of its importance and in 1906-07 the Birmingham FA decreed that local clubs could field their reserve sides in the Birmingham Cup. Albion's last Birmingham Cup tie at senior level was a 5-1 home defeat by Aston Villa on 4 September 1905.

Arthur Watson, who signed from Mansfield Town in 1896, scored for Albion against Aston Villa in the 1896-7 Birmingham Cup.

Winger George Dorsett found the net when Wolves were trounced 5-1 in the 1902-03 Birmingham Cup.

1881-2
Round 1
Nov 12 v Calthorpe (a) 3-2
Att: 1,000
Round 2
Dec 10 v Elwells (a) 2-1
Att: 800
Round 3
Jan 21 v Fallings Heath Rovers (a) 3-1
Att: 1,200
Round 4
Feb 18 v Notts Rangers (a) 5-2
Stokes, Bisseker, Whitehouse, Aston 2
Att: 500
Semi-final
Mar 25 v Wednesbury Old Athletic (at Aston) 2-3
Bisseker, Aston
Att: 1,000
Scorers not listed for Rounds 1, 2 and 3.

1882-3
Round 1
Nov 11 v Coseley (h) 26-0
Aston 5, Bisseker 4, Timmins 4, G.Bell 3, Bunn 2, Horton 2, Whitehouse 2, White 2, H.Bell, Stanton.
Att: 2,500
Round 2
Albion received a bye
Round 3
Jan 20 v Wolverhampton Wanderers (a) 4-2
G.Bell, Bisseker, Biddulph, Aston
Att: 3,000
Round 4
Mar 13 v Wednesbury Old Athletic (a) 1-2
Aston
Att: 2,500

1883-4
Round 1
Oct 27 v Stourbridge Standard (h) 7-0
Bisseker 2, Timmins 2, G.Bell, F.Bunn, Aston
Att: 2,000
Round 2
Dec 8 v Walsall Alma Athletic (h) 6-0
Timmins 2, G.Bell, Aston, Smith, Loach
Att: 2,500
Round 3
Jan 5 v Wednesbury Old Athletic (h) 1-1
G.Bell
Att: 3,000
Replay
Feb 9 v Wednesbury Old Athletic (a) 3-3
Timmins 3
Att: 700
Second replay
Feb 18 v Wednesbury Old Athletic (at Aston) 3-1
G.Bell, Aston, Kent (og)
Att: 3,000
Round 4
Feb 23 v Wolverhampton Wanderers (at Aston) 1-1
Bisseker
Att: 5,000
Replay
Mar 3 v Wolverhampton Wanderers (at Wednesbury) 2-1
Aston, Bisseker
Att: 3,800
Semi-final
Mar 10 v Walsall Swifts (at Aston) 0-1
Att: 2,000

1884-5
Round 1
Oct 18 v Darlaston All Saints (h) 8-0
Aston 3, Bayliss 2, Loach 2, Jacobs (og)
Att: 1,200
Round 2
Nov 22 v Bloxwich Strollers (h) 15-0
Bayliss 6*
Att: 1,500
*No other scorers listed for this match.
Round 3
Dec 20 v St George's (h) 2-3
Loach, G.Bell
Att: 4,000

1885-6
Round 3
Dec 5 v Notts Rangers (a) 7-2
Woodhall, T.Green 3, Loach 2, G.Bell.
Att: 520
Semi-final
Jan 16 v Burslem Port Vale (at Aston) 5-0
T.Green 2, Timmins, Loach, Bunn
Att: 3,000
Final
Mar 13 v Walsall Swifts (at Aston) 1-1
T.Green
Att: 4,000
Replay
Apr 12 v Walsall Swifts (at Aston) 1-0
Woodhall
Att: 10,000
*Because of pressure of fixtures, Albion's reserve team represented the club in the first two rounds, defeating Sparkhill Alliance 6-0 and Burton Swifts 4-1 to progress into the quarter-finals.

1886-7
Round 1
Oct 9 v Aston Villa (h) 1-0
T.Green
Att: 12,000
Round 2
Nov 13 v Mitchell's St George (h) 3-0
T.Green, Woodhall 2
Att: 3,000
Round 3
Dec 11 v Derby County (h) 6-0
Paddock 2, T.Green 2, Bayliss, Woodhall
Att: 8,000
Round 4
Mar 19 v Stoke (h) 3-0
Pearson 2, Bayliss
Att: 5,100
Semi-final
Apr 30 v Burslem Port Vale (at Stoke) 5-1
Bayliss 3, Woodhall 2
Att: 4,000
Final
May 7 v Long Eaton Rovers (at Perry Barr) 0-1
Att: 5,000

1887-8
Round 1
Oct 8 v Small Heath Alliance (h) 2-0
Bayliss 2
Att: 4,000
Round 2
Oct 31 v Burslem Port Vale (a) 3-0
Askin, Bayliss, J.Horton
Att: 2,500
Round 3
Nov 19 v Aston Shakespeare (h) 3-0
G.Bell, Woodhall 2
Att: 3,500
Round 4
Dec 24 v Mitchell's St George (h) 4-0
Wilson 2, Pearson, Woodhall
Att: 4,500
Semi-final
Feb 11 v Wolverhampton Wanderers (h) 2-0
Wilson, Timmins
Att: 5,000
Final
Mar 3 v Aston Villa (at Aston Lower Grounds) 2-3
Pearson 2
Att: 12,000

1889-90
Round 1
Jan 23 v Notts Rangers (a) 4-0
Pearson, Sauve 3
Att: 3,000
Round 2
Feb 17 v Small Heath (h) 2-0
Pearson 2
Att: 1,500
Semi-final
Apr 5 v Walsall Town Swifts (at Wednesbury) 2-1
Evans 2
Att: 5,500
Final
Apr 19 v Aston Villa (a) 0-2
Att: 8,000

1890-91
Round 1
Jan 17 v Small Heath (h) 3-2
Burns, Nicholls, C.Perry
Att: 3,000
Round 2
Mar 16 v Warwick County (h) 6-0
Nicholls, T.Perry, Pearson 3, Bassett
Att: 2,600
Semi-final
Apr 11 v Aston Villa (at Edgbaston) 2-2
Dyer, Woodhall
Att: 12,000
Replay
Apr 20 v Aston Villa (at Wolverhampton) 1-1 (a.e.t.)
Haynes
Att: 5,000
Second replay
Apr 22 v Aston Villa (at Wolverhampton) 2-3
Woodhall 2
Att: 6,700

1891-2
Round 3
Jan 2 v Wednesbury Old Athletic (h) 2-2
Nicholls 2
Att: 2,500
Replay
Feb 15 v Wednesbury Old Athletic (a) 2-1
Nicholls, Groves
Att: 3,500
Round 4
Mar 28 v Small Heath (h) 4-1
C.Perry, Nicholls, McLeod, Geddes
Att: 4,000
Semi-final
Apr 9 v Aston Villa (at Wolverhampton) 2-0
Campbell (og), McLeod
Att: 8,000
Final
Apr 30 v Wolverhampton Wanderers (at Perry Barr) 2-5
Reynolds, Bassett
Att: 6,500
*Albion received a bye in Rounds 1 & 2.

1892-3
Round 1
Jan 23 v Stoke (h) 3-0
Horton, McLeod, T.Perry
Att: 3,500
Round 2
Mar 27 v Wolverhampton Wanderers (a) 1-3
McLeod
Att: 4,000

1893-4
Round 1
Jan 29 v Walsall (a) 1-0
Bassett
Att: 3,150
Round 2
Feb 12 v Burslem Port Vale (h) 3-1
McLeod, Pearson, Bostock
Att: 2,100
Semi-final
Mar 17 v Loughborough (at Aston) 6-1
Boston 2, Geddes, McLeod 3
Att: 3,000
Final
Apr 21 v Wolverhampton Wanderers (Perry Barr) 3-3
Bostock 2, Geddes, Bassett
Att: 8,000
*Trophy shared

1894-5
Round 1
Jan 19 v Walsall (h) 6-2
Hutchinson 2, Williams, Bassett 2, Taggart
Att: 5,000
Round 2
Feb 1 v Burton Wanderers (a) 1-1
Hutchinson
Att: 2,000
*Burton refused to replay
Semi-final
Mar 18 v Small Heath (at Wolverhampton) 3-2 (a.e.t.)
Hutchinson, McLeod, T.Perry
Att: 5,100
Final
Mar 30 v Aston Villa (at Small Heath) 0-0
Att: 12,000
Replay
Apr 29 v Aston Villa (at Aston) 1-0
Hutchinson
Att: 14,200

1895-6
Round 1
Jan 20 v Aston Villa (a) 0-3
Att: 7,000

1896-7
Round 2
Jan 25 v Aston Villa (h) 2-1
Cameron, Watson
Att: 4,000
Semi-final
Feb 20 v Wolverhampton Wanderers (at Perry Barr) 0-3
Att: 6,800
*Albion received a bye in Round 1.

1897-8
Round 1
Dec 13 v Burslem Port Vale (a) 0-0
Att: 6,000
Replay
Jan 17 v Burslem Port Vale (h) 0-0 (a.e.t.)
Att: 3,000
Second replay
Feb 7 v Burslem Port Vale (h) 2-1 (a.e.t.)
Richards Flewitt
Att: 3,500
*Albion withdrew from competition.

1898-9
Round 1
Dec 19 v Wellington St George (h) 5-0
Bassett 2, Hadley, Nock, S.Brett
Att: 750
Round 2
Jan 16 v Wolverhampton Wanderers (h) 0-7
Att: 2,474

1899-1900
Round 1
Dec 11 v Burslem Port Vale (a) 0-5
Att: 2,000

1900-01
Round 1
Sep 24 v Small Heath (h) 5-0
Wheldon, Chadburn, Walker, Jones, Simmons
Att: 3,600
Round 2
Oct 15 v Stoke (h) 2-3
Garfield, Walker
Att: 6,000

1901-02
Round 1
Sep 30 v Wolverhampton Wanderers (a) 0-1
Att: 3,500

1902-03
Round 1
Sep 29 v Wolverhampton Wanderers (a) 5-1
Lee, Simmons 2, Buck, Dorsett
Att: 5,000
Semi-final
Oct 13 v Walsall (a) 7-1
Buck, Simmons 4, A.Smith, Kifford
Att: 5,000
Final
Dec 8 v Aston Villa (a) 0-3
Att: 16,000

1903-04
Round 1
Sep 28 v Wolverhampton Wanderers (h) 1-2
Hadley
Att: 5,500

1904-05
Round 1
Sep 26 v Wolverhampton Wanderers (a) 2-0
Bell, Jack
At: 7,000
Semi-final
Oct 22 v Burslem Port Vale (h) 2-1
Davies, Jack
Att: 5,000
Final
Feb 20 v Small Heath (a) 2-7
Aston, Jack
Att: 8,500

1905-06
Round 1
Sep 4 v Aston Villa (h) 1-5
E.Bradley
Att: 5,000

Walsall Cup

ALBION entered their second team for the Walsall Senior Cup in 1885-6 and from then on it was almost exclusively a competition for the reserves except for two occasions when the first team took over the fixtures. On 16 October 1886 the Albion committee chose a strong team to face Crosswell's Brewery (home) because the brewers had included seven former Throstles in their ranks. Albion won 5-2 and then left the remainder of the ties to the second team who eventually lost to Walsall Town. In 1887-8 Albion reserves drew twice with Oldbury Town (formerly Crosswell's Brewery) in the first round of the Walsall Cup before the Albion first team took over the tie and sent Oldbury Town packing, 5-1 (away). The second team went on to win the trophy for the first time, overwhelming Walsall Swifts 4-1 in the Final.

In 1900-01 the reserves participated again after a long absence and were joint holders of the Cup after drawing 1-1 with Small Heath Reserves. In 1903 they became Cup winners by beating Brierley Hill Alliance 5-0 and in 1904 were losing Finalists, going down 5-0 to Small Heath after a 0-0 draw. They were again losing finalists, to Wolves, in 1906.

Results
1886-7
Round 1
Oct 16 v Crosswells (h) 5-2
Holden, Pearson, Horton 2, Moore (og)
Att: 2,500
*Remainder of fixtures completed by Albion Reserves.

1887-8
Round 1
Second replay
Dec 12 v Oldbury Town (a) 5-1
Bayliss 3, Askin, H.Green
Att: 1,000
*Albion Reserves completed the remaining fixtures, going on to win the trophy.

Liverpool Charity Cup

IN NOVEMBER 1895, Albion contested a match for the Liverpool Charity Cup on the Everton ground, as a gesture towards the Everton Football Club who had kindly played several matches at Stoney Lane in aid of West Bromwich charities. Albion and Everton met under electric light at night-time and attracted a crowd of over 5,000.

Nov 5 1895 v Everton (a) 1-4
A.Wilson
Att: 5,200

Coventry Charity Cup

ALBION have competed only the once in the Coventry Charity Cup, in 1930 when they met their neighbours Coventry City for the first time ever, in the Final at Highfield Road.

28 Apr 1930 v Coventry City (a) 2-1
Edwards, Cookson
Att: 8,000

Staffordshire Cup

THE STAFFORDSHIRE FA was created in 1877, and a year later the Staffordshire Cup was introduced. Before Albion won the trophy in their first season of entry, 1882-3, Stoke (twice), Wednesbury Old Athletic and Walsall Town had all been Staffordshire Cup winners.

Albion's first Staffordshire Cup tie was at Bloxwich Strollers on 4 November 1882 when they drew 3-3 before winning the replay 4-0 at the Four Acres a fortnight later. In the second round Albion again emerged with a 3-3 away draw, this time on the Aston Villa ground in what was the very first meeting between the clubs. Albion won the replay 1-0. In the third round Albion drew 2-2 at home with St George's but afterwards protested that the Dragons had fielded two ineligible players, one of whom was Tom Green who subsequently signed for Albion in 1885. The Staffordshire FA upheld the protest and Albion proceeded to a home semi-final where Leek White Star were dismissed 8-0.

There was great excitement in the Black Country at the prospect of the hitherto relatively unknown Albion team appearing in their very first Final and they did not let their supporters down, beating Stoke 3-2 (see *Match to Remember No 1.*).

In April 1884, Albion found themselves in the Final again after overcoming Cocknage, Walsall Town and Stoke, but this time St George's pipped them 2-1 after the Throstles had scored first through Arthur Loach. The winning goal was scored by the above mentioned Tom Green. Between 1883 and 1889 Albion appeared in the Staffordshire Cup Final six times and were losing semi-finalists in 1885.

Albion's complete record in the Staffordshire Cup (first team only):-

		Home						Away			
P	W	D	L	F	A	W	D	L	F	A
68	22	4	1	114	20	21	6	14	91	62

Bayliss scored 12 of 23 goals during the 1886-7 competition.

In all but one of 27 home Staffordshire Cup ties, Albion managed to record at least one goal. The record Staffordshire Cup victory was 23-0 against Burton Wanderers on 1 February 1890 when five players each scored three goals or more, In the first round on 10 October 1898, Albion slumped to their heaviest defeat, 6-1 away to Aston Villa.

Albion played their last Staffordshire Cup tie at senior level on 2 October 1905, away to Aston Villa where they lost 4-0. In 1906-07 the Staffordshire FA decreed that reserve teams could take part. The Albion second team won the trophy in 1923-4 (beating Stoke 3-0), 1925-6 (beating Stoke 3-1), 1931-2 (defeating Wolves 3-2), 1932-3 (beating Villa 2-0) and 1950-51 (defeating Wolves 1-0). They were also losing Finalists in 1906-07, 1907-08, 1909-10, 1924-5, 1937-8 and 1952-3. In 1968-9 the Cup was shared with Stoke City when the sides drew 0-0 in the Final which was also treated as a Central League fixture.

Official programme for the Staffordshire Cup Final, played on 21 April 1883.

Arthur Loach scored first for Albion in the Staffordshire Cup Final in 1884 but the Throstles lost to St George's.

1882-3
Round 1
Nov 4 v Bloxwich Strollers (a) 3-3
G.Bell, Aston, Timmins
Att: 650
Replay
Nov 18 v Bloxwich Strollers (h) 4-0
Biddulph 2, G.Bell, Aston
Att: 1,200
Round 2
Dec 9 v Aston Villa (a) 3-3
G.Bell 2, Aston
Att: 13,900
Replay
Dec 23 v Aston Villa (h) 1-0
Timmins
Att: 10,500
Round 3
Feb 3 v St George's (h) 2-2
Timmins, Bisseker
Att: 2,000
*St George's were subsequently disqualified for playing two ineligible players against Albion.
Semi-final
Mar 10 v Leek White Star (h) 8-0
G.Bell, Aston 3, Biddulph 2, Bisseker 2
Att: 2,000
Final
Apr 21 v Stoke (a) 3-2
Timmins, Bunn, G.Bell
Att: 6,150

1883-4
Round 1
Dec 3 v Cocknage (h) 1-0
G.Bell
Att: 600
Round 2
Dec 22 v Walsall Town (h) 4-0
Aston 4
Att: 1,400

Semi-final
Mar 15 v Stoke (at Wednesbury) 2-0
Bisseker, Timmins
Att: 3,000
Final
Apr 12 v St George's (at Stoke) 1-2
Loach
Att: 5,500

1884-5
Round 1
Nov 8 v Burton Swifts (h) 7-1
G.Bell, Loach 2, Aston 2, Bayliss 2
Att: 2,000
Round 2
Dec 13 v Leek (h) 8-0
Aston, Bayliss 2, Loach 3, Woodhall, G.Bell
Att: 2,000
Round 3
Jan 31 v Stoke (h) 6-2
Bayliss 3, Bettany (og), Aston, G.Bell
Att: 2,000
Semi-final
Feb 28 v Walsall Town (at Stoke) 0-2
Att: 6,000

205

1885-6
Round 1
Oct 24 v Stafford Rangers (h) 0-0
Att: 3,000
Replay
Nov 7 v Stafford Rangers (a) 4-0
Loach 2, G.Bell 2
Att: 2,500
Round 2
Jan 9 v Leek (h) 5-2
Loach, Woodhall 3, G.Bell
Att: 1,000
Round 3
Albion received a bye.
Round 4
Jan 30 v Stoke Free Wanderers (h) 5-0
G.Bell, Bayliss, Loach, Woodhall 2
Att: 800
Semi-final
Apr 17 v Burton Wanderers (at Stoke) 3-0
Bayliss 2, T.Green
Att: 6,000
Final
Apr 24 v Stoke (a) 0-0
Att: 9,000
Replay
May 10 v Stoke (h) 4-2
Bayliss 2, T.Green, Woodhall
Att: 5,500

1886-7
Round 1
Oct 4 v Hednesford Town (h) 8-0
Bayliss 4, G.Bell 2, T.Green 2
Att: 3,000
Round 2
Nov 6 v Stafford Rangers (h) 5-1
G.Bell, Timmins, Bayliss 2, Woodhall
Att: 2,500
Round 3
Feb 26 v Leek (h) 3-0
Bayliss 2, Woodhall
Att: 3,500
Semi-final
Mar 21 v Wolverhampton Wanderers (at Burslem) 3-0
Bayliss 2, Timmins
Att: 4,000
Final
Apr 9 v Walsall Swifts (at Stoke) 4-0
Bayliss 2, Woodhall, Paddock
Att: 4,000

1887-8
Round 1
Oct 1 v Burton Wanderers (a) 12-2
Black (og), Woodhall 3, Pearson 2, Bayliss 3, Wilson, Bassett 2
Att: 3,500
Round 2
Nov 28 v Wednesbury Old Athletic (a) 2-1
Woodhall, Bayliss
Att: 3,000
Round 3
Dec 31 v Leek (a) 3-2
Woodhall, Pearson, Wilson
Att: 2,700
Semi-final
Mar 17 v Stoke (a) 1-0
Wilson
Att: 5,500
Final
Mar 31 v Wolverhampton Wanderers (at Stoke) 0-0
Att: 8,000
Replay
Apr 14 v Wolverhampton Wanderers (at Stoke) 1-1 (a.e.t.)
Woodhall
Att: 8,500
Second replay
Apr 28 v Wolverhampton Wanderers (h) 1-2
Woodhall
Att: 7,000

1888-9
Round 4
Mar 23 v Birmingham St George's (a) 3-1
Hadley (og), Pearson, Bayliss
Att: 5,000
Semi-final
Apr 6 v Walsall Town Swifts (at Wednesbury) 5-0
Woodhall 2, Pearson 2, W.Perry
Att: 3,500
Final
Apr 20 v Leek (at Stoke) 2-0
Bayliss, Wilson
Att: 5,500
*Albion were exempt until Round 4 because of Football League commitments.

1889-90
Round 1
Feb 1 v Burton Wanderers (h) 23-0
Pearson 3, Bassett 6, Wilson 2, Woodhall 3, C.Perry 3, Roberts, Evans 3, Green, J.Horton
Att: 3,000
Round 2
Mar 31 v Stoke (h) 4-0
Woodhall 2, Evans, Bassett
Att: 5,000
Semi-final
Apr 12 v Walsall Town Swifts (at Wednesbury) 2-3
Pearson, Bassett
Att: 5,000

1890-91
Round 2
Jan 24 v Wolverhampton Wanderers (a) 1-3
Pearson
Att: 5,000

1893-4
Round 1
Jan 15 v Walsall (a) 2-4
Geddes, Neale
Att: 2,500

1894-5
Semi-final
Feb 4 v Aston Villa (a) 0-2
Att: 7,600

1895-6
Round 1
Jan 6 v Small Heath (h) 2-1
J.Richards 2
Att: 1,000
Round 2
Mar 16 v Aston Villa (a) 2-4
W.Richards, Flewitt
Att: 6,000

1896-7
Round 1
Oct 19 v Aston Villa (h) 2-1
Ford, Garfield
Att: 4,000
Round 2
Jan 11 v Wolverhampton Wanderers (a) 1-5
Watson
Att: 2,000

1897-8
Round 1
Nov 8 v Aston Villa (h) 2-1
Garfield, McKenzie
Att: 7,000
Round 3
Jan 22 v Small Heath (a) 1-0
Robertson (og)
Att: 4,500
Final
Mar 5 v Burslem Port Vale (at Stoke) 0-1
Att: 10,000
*Albion received a bye in Round 2, and semi-final stage was declared void.

1898-9
Round 1
Oct 10 v Aston Villa (a) 1-6
Jones (pen)
Att: 7,000

1899-1900
Round 1
Sep 18 v Aston Villa (a) 3-2
Paddock, Walker, Garfield
Att: 8,200
Round 2
Oct 9 v Stoke (a) 3-1
Walker, Paddock, Garfield
Att: 4,350
Semi-final
Nov 20 v Wolverhampton Wanderers (h) 3-1
Simmons, Jones, Paddock
Att: 2,150
Final
Dec 4 v Burslem Port Vale (at Stoke) 1-1
Simmons
Att: 3,500
Replay
Apr 26 v Burslem Port Vale (at Aston) 5-0
Simmons, Walker 2, Roberts 2
Att: 5,000

1900-01
Round 1
Oct 8 v Wolverhampton Wanderers (a) 1-2
Walker
Att: 5,500

1901-02
Round 1
Sep 23 v Wolverhampton Wanderers (h) 2-1
Simmons 2
Att: 3,000
Semi-final
Oct 7 v Small Heath (h) 2-1
Simmons, McLean
Att: 4,000
Final
Nov 25 v Stoke (at Burslem) 3-0
McLean, Lee, Harper
Att: 3,000

1902-03
Round 1
Sep 15 v Burton United (a) 2-0
Dorsett, Simmons
Att: 3,000
Semi-final
Oct 6 v Wolverhampton Wanderers (h) 1-1
Simmons
Att: 6,000
Replay
Oct 27 v Wolverhampton Wanderers (a) 4-0
Simmons, Stevenson, Lee 2
Att: 7,500
Final
Nov 17 v Stoke (at Aston) 2-0
Buck 2
Att: 10,000

1903-04
Round 1
Sep 14 v Burton United (h) 1-1
Cole
Att: 3,000
Replay
Oct 5 v Burton Utd (a) 1-2
Hadley (pen)
Att: 4,000

1904-05
Round 1
Oct 3 v Derby County (a) 1-3
Dorsett
Att:4,000

1905-06
Round 1
Oct 2 v Aston Villa (a) 0-4
Att: 8,500

Birmingham Charity Cup

FROM 1884 until 1933 Albion took part intermittently in the Lord Mayor of Birmingham's Charity Cup. The club's first game in the competition, on 5 April 1884, brought a 4-1 defeat at the hands of Aston Villa who repeated the scoreline the following season. The Albion team for that first Birmingham Charity Cup tie was: Roberts; H.Bell, Green, Horton, Bunn, Stanton, Woodhall, Aston, Smith, Timmins, G.Bell.

Albion's complete record in the Birmingham Charity Cup reads:-

	Home					Away				
P	W	D	L	F	A	W	D	L	F	A
41	4	1	5	26	26	9	4	18	40	72

Aston Villa were its first winners, in 1882. It was never regarded as a major local event as Albion showed by entering their second team in 1885-6 (they lost in the first round to Wednesbury Old Athletic), and by refusing to take part in 1887-8 because of pressure of fixtures. During the 1886-7 season Albion lost 3-1 to Wolves after two drawn games in the semi-final. An angry crowd of Albion fans besieged the referee after the final whistle and he had to seek refuge in the Stoney Lane grandstand before rescue came in the shape of six policemen and a number of Albion committee members.

Albion's first Birmingham Charity Cup win did not materialise until 13 September 1897 when Small Heath were overcome 7-4 at home in a first round tie. This was Albion's 12th tie at senior level in the competition and was also to be their record victory. The worst defeat came at Aston Villa in the semi-final on 10 April 1893 when Villa won 6-0.

Albion have played in the Final on 16 occasions — winning the trophy four times and sharing it once, between 1899 and 1933.

From 1910 onwards, the Birmingham Charity Cup Final was an invitation match and no preliminary rounds were contested. On 8 May 1926, Albion were due to meet Aston Villa at St Andrew's in the Final but it was postponed because of the General Strike and ultimately cancelled.

1883-4
Semi-final
Apr 5 v Aston Villa (a) 1-4
Riddell (og)
Att: 6,000

1884-5
Semi-final
Apr 18 v Aston Villa (at Wednesbury) 1-4
Bayliss
Att: 5,000

1886-7
Semi-final
Apr 18 v Wolverhampton Wanderers (a) 3-3
Pearson, Woodhall, T.Green
Att: 8,000
Replay
Apr 20 v Wolverhampton Wanderers (a) 0-0 (a.e.t.)
Att: 6,000
Second replay
Apr 25 v Wolverhampton Wanderers (h) 1-3
Paddock
Att: 7,200

1889-90
Semi-final
Apr 26 v Wolverhampton Wanderers (h) 0-1
Att: 3,000

1890-91
Semi-final
Apr 27 v Wolverhampton Wanderers (a) 1-4
Pearson
Att: 4,000

1891-2
Semi-final
Apr 27 v Wolverhampton Wanderers (a) 0-3
Att: 5,000

1892-3
Semi-final
Apr 10 v Aston Villa (a) 0-6
Att: 6,500

1893-4
Semi-final
Apr 16 v Aston Villa (a) 1-3
Pearson
Att: 7,000

1894-5
Semi-final
Apr 6 v Small Heath (a) 0-4
Att: 8,500

1897-8
Round 1
Sep 13 v Small Heath (h) 7-4 (a.e.t.)
Garfield 4, Flewitt 2, McKenzie
Att: 3,000
Semi-final
Sep 20 v Aston Villa (a) 0-3
Att: 8,500

1898-9
Round 1
Sep 12 v Small Heath (a) 4-3
Garfield 2, R.Brett, Banks
Att: 3,000
Semi-final
Sep 26 v Walsall (a) 1-3
Jones
Att: 4,000

1899-1900
Round 1
Sep 11 v Burton Swifts (h) 4-1
Richards 2, Parrett, Paddock
Att: 2,100
Semi-final
Sep 25 v Aston Villa (a) 2-2
Simmons, Richards
Att: 8,250
Semi-final
Oct 16 v Aston Villa (a) 2-1 (a.e.t.)
Jones, Walker
Att: 12,150
Final
Nov 13 v Walsall (at Aston) 1-0
Walker
Att: 8,250

1900-01
Semi-final
Sep 17 v Walsall (h) 6-1
Wheldon 2, Simmons, Chadburn, Jones, Roberts
Att: 2,500
Final
Nov 19 v Aston Villa (h) 1-1
Wheldon
Att: 10,000
Replay
Dec 17 v Aston Villa (a) 0-2
Att: 12,652

1901-02
Semi-final
Oct 28 v Small Heath (a) 1-0
Worton
Att: 3,000
Final
Nov 18 v Aston Villa (a) 0-1
Att: 10,600

1902-03
Round 1
Sep 3 v Small Heath (a) 3-1
Buck 3
Att: 5,000
Final
Nov 24 v Wolverhampton Wanderers (at Aston) 2-3
Lee, Simmons
Att: 4,500
Albion went straight into Final after opening round.

'Chippy' Simmons scored three goals for Albion in Birmingham Charity Cup games.

1903-04
Semi-final
Sep 21 v Small Heath (h) 4-5
Worton, Cole, Dorsett 2
Att: 5,000

Teams for To-day's Match, Wednesday, May 2nd, 1923.

LORD MAYOR OF BIRMINGHAM'S CHARITY CUP.

West Bromwich Albion v. Aston Villa

Kick-off at 6 p.m.

WEST BROMWICH ALBION.

Right   Left

ASHMORE (1)

SMITH (2)   ADAMS (3)

MAGEE (4)   BOWSER (5)   McNEAL (6)

SPENCER (7)   JONES (8)   DAVIES (9)   MORRIS (10)   GLIDDEN (11)

REFEREE : Mr. C. E. LINES (Bordesley Green).
LINESMEN : (1) Mr. E. BEARDS (Wolverhampton), and (2) Mr. J. H. ROPER (Edgbaston).

DORRELL (12)   CAPEWELL (13)   WALKER (14)   DICKSON (15)   KIRTON (16)

BLACKBURN (17)   BALL (18)   MOSS (19)

JONES (20)   SMART (21)

SPIERS (22)

Left   Right

ASTON VILLA.

In the event of any alteration in the above teams, a board giving particulars will be sent round the ground.

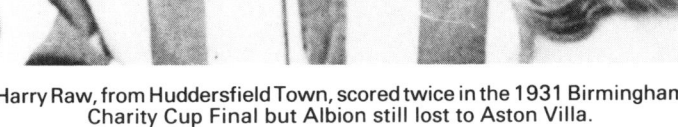

Harry Raw, from Huddersfield Town, scored twice in the 1931 Birmingham Charity Cup Final but Albion still lost to Aston Villa.

1904-05
Round 1
Sep 19 v Aston Villa (a) 0-2
Att: 6,500

1905-06
Semi-final
Sep 18 v Birmingham (h) 2-1
Randle, Broad
Att: 5,000
Final
Nov 20 v Aston Villa (at Small Heath) 3-4
Bradley, Broad, F.Nicholls
Att: 12,000

1910-11
Final
Sep 19 v Aston Villa (a) 1-2
Lloyd
Att: 5,507

1911-12
Final
Sep 18 v Aston Villa (a) 0-4
Att: 6,503

1912-13
Final
Oct 2 v Aston Villa (h) 1-5
Shearman
Att: 8,077

1913-14
Final
Oct 22 v Aston Villa (a) 1-0
Morris
Att: 6,000

1914-15
Final
Sep 23 v Aston Villa (a) 3-2
Morris, Bache 2
Att: 5,017

1920-21
Final
May 14 v Birmingham (at Aston) 2-2
Morris, Bentley
Att: 8,067
*Trophy shared

1921-2
Final
May 13 v Birmingham (at Aston) 2-0
Wilson, Morris
Att: 7,500

1922-3
Final
May 2 v Aston Villa (a) 0-2
Att: 2,300

1924-5
Final
May 9 v Birmingham (a) 3-1
James 2, Byers
Att: 10,000

1930-31
Final
May 9 v Aston Villa (h) 2-3
Raw 2
Att: 18,189

1932-3
Final
May 13 v Aston Villa (h) 0-4
Att: 8,500

West Bromwich Charity Cup

ALBION'S senior team took part in the West Bromwich Friendly Societies Charity Cup for the first time in May 1888. Although the two ties Albion contested were for the benefit of local charities, all was not particularly friendly, for when Albion mastered Wednesbury Old Athletic 4-1 in the semi-final there were skirmishes among the rival supporters and in the Final (where Albion overwhelmed Great Bridge Unity 10-1) a Unity player was ordered off for rough play, a very rare occurrence in those days.

Albion's record in the West Bromwich Charity Cup in matches played by the first team.-

	Home					Away				
P	W	D	L	F	A	W	D	L	F	A
11	6	2	2	25	11	0	0	1	0	4

During the 1890s, Everton made regular trips to Stoney Lane to play in the Final — they met Albion on six different occasions. Albion's first team won the trophy in 1888, 1895 and 1897 and shared it with Aston Villa in 1890; and the reserve team were winners in 1903, 1904, 1905, 1906, 1912, 1914, 1915, 1921, 1922 and 1923, this being the last year in which Albion competed for the Cup.

1887-8
Semi-final
May 7 v Wednesbury Old Athletic (h) 4-1
Wilson, Bayliss, Woodhall 2
Att: 5,000
Final
May 21 v Great Bridge Unity (h) 10-1
Bayliss 4, Wilson 2, Bassett 2, Woodhall, H.Green
Att: 6,500

1888-9
Final
Jun 1 v Wolverhampton Wanderers (h) 2-0
Bassett, Wilson
Att: 3,000

1889-90
Final
May 17 v Aston Villa (h) 1-1
S.Nicholls
Att: 4,000
*Trophy shared

1890-91
Final
May 30 v Wednesbury Old Athletic (h) 3-2
Pearson, C.Perry, Reynolds
Att: 5,000

1892-3
Final
Nov 21 v Everton (h) 0-2
Att: 3,500

1894-5
Final
Oct 15 v Everton (h) 1-0
C.Perry
Att: 5,000

1895-6
Final
Jan 13 v Everton (h) 1-2
Hayward
Att: 3,500

1896-7
Final
Feb 15 v Everton (h) 2-1
McManus, W.Williams
Att: 3,000

1897-8
Final
Nov 29 v Everton (h) 1-1
Garfield
Att: 5,000

Replay
Apr 18 v Everton (a) 0-4
Att: 12,000

Wednesbury Charity Cup

THIS was a short-lived competition which Albion entered for only two seasons, 1882-3 and 1883-4. By overcoming Wednesbury Strollers and Aston Unity, Albion qualified for the 1883 Final against Nottingham Forest but after leading 2-1 they lost 5-3 after captain John While had been taken off with a broken leg which ended his playing career. Albion were dismissed from the 1884 Wednesbury Charity Cup by St George's, and the first team did not participate again. In 1887-8 the reserve team accepted an invitation to enter but were removed from the first round by Wednesbury Old Athletic. Albion reserves were losing Finalists in 1889-90 but won the Cup in 1893-4 by defeating Newport 4-0 at Wellington.

Complete first team record in the Wednesbury Charity Cup:-

	Home					Away				
P	W	D	L	F	A	W	D	L	F	A
7	1	0	0	7	1	2	2	2	11	13

1882-3
Round 1
Nov 25 v Wednesbury Strollers (a) 3-3
G.Bell, Bisseker, Whitehouse
Att: 2,000
Replay
Dec 30 v Wednesbury Strollers (h) 7-1
Bisseker 2, Aston, G.Bell 2, Whitehouse 2
Att: 2,100
Semi-final
Feb 24 v Aston Unity (at Perry Barr) 1-0
Aston
Att: 4,000
Final
May 19 v Notts Rangers (at Perry Barr) 3-5
Aston 2, Bisseker
Att: 4,000

1883-4
Round 1
Nov 24 v Aston Unity (a) 3-0
G.Bell, Timmins, Aston
Att: 2,500
Semi-final
Jan 12 v St George's (at Aston) 1-1
Stevenson (og)
Att: 3,700
Replay
Mar 29 v St George's (at Wednesbury) 0-4
Att: 3,500

West Bromwich Albion 2nd XI, 1897-98. Back row (left to right): T.Brennand (director), F.Everiss (clerk), W.Moore, P.McManus, A.Flavell, W.G.Ford, T.Harris-Spencer (chairman), J.Banks, H.Powell (director), C.Perry (director), R.Brett. Front row: A.McKenzie, S.Vigrow, J.Connor, E.Fellows, J.Nock, S.Brett.

Testimonial and Benefit Matches

Albion's first team have played numerous benefit and testimonial matches for various players and causes down the years and details of these are recorded in this section except for wartime benefit matches which are under the appropriate wartime section. Attendances and goalscorers are listed from 1900 onwards.

26 Mar 1883 v Wellington (h) 4-0
(West Bromwich Hospital)

7 Apr 1883 v Calthorpe (h) 6-1
(West Bromwich Dartmouth)

16 Jun 1883 v Wednesbury Old Athletic (a) 2-3
(J.Roberts)

15 Dec 1883 v Wellington (h) 5-1
(West Bromwich Hospital)

25 Aug 1884 v Aston Villa (a) 2-3
(A.Hunter)

16 May 1885 v District XI (a) 1-2
(J.Stanton)

19 Apr 1886 v Aston Villa (a) 1-3
(Villa-WBA players)

19 July 1886 v Aston Villa (a) 5-1
(S.Richardson)

24 July 1886 v Aston Villa (a) 3-6
(S.Richardson)

27 Sept 1886 v Birmingham & District XI (h) 0-0
(Benefit match)

14 Nov 1887 v Brierley Hill Alliance (a) 3-0
(Brockmoor Colliery Relief Fund)

22 May 1888 v Walsall Town Swifts (h) 3-0
(R.Roberts)

17 Dec 1888 v WBA 2nd XI (h) 4-4
(Mrs J.While)

20 May 1889 v Hednesford Town (a) 5-0
(Hospital Benefit)

3 Mar 1890 v Birmingham & District XI (h) 4-1
(G.Timmins)

24 May 1890 v Aston Villa (a) 0-1
(J.Burton, A.Allan)

1 Nov 1890 v Stoke (a) 0-1
(A.Edge)

2 Mar 1891 v Birmingham & District XI (h) 1-1
(C.Perry)

19 Oct 1891 v Stoke (a) 1-1
(A.Underwood)

25 Apr 1892 v Birmingham & District XI (a) 2-2
(T.Pearson)

17 Oct 1892 v Birmingham & District XI (h) 2-1
(G.Woodhall)

20 Mar 1893 v Small Heath (a) 0-5
(C.Jenkins)

11 Dec 1893 v Dudley & District XI (a) 6-3
(Hart Hill Unity)

8 Oct 1894 v Small Heath (a) 3-1
(F.Wheldon)

26 Nov 1894 v Blackburn Rovers (h) 3-1
(S.Nicholls)

30 Apr 1895 v Oldbury Town (a) 1-4
(A.Matthews, C.Fluck)

16 Sept 1895 v Wolverhampton Wanderers (a) 2-2
(J.Hassall)

23 Sept 1895 v Aston Villa (a) 1-2
(A.Hunter)

18 Nov 1895 v Aston Villa (h) 1-1
(R.McLeod)

7 Apr 1896 v Stoke (h) 3-1
(J.Horton)

12 Oct 1896 v Wolverhampton Wanderers (a) 2-0
(H.Wood)

10 Nov 1896 v Grimsby Town (a) 2-5
(W.Higgins)

7 Dec 1896 v Kettering (a) 1-1
(R.Draper)

17 Mar 1897 v Stoke (at Brighton) 2-4
(Brighton Children Free Dinner Fund)

28 Apr 1897 v Aston Villa (a) 1-3
(Villa players)

27 Sept 1897 v Leicester Fosse (a) 1-4
(R.McLeod)

18 Oct 1897 v Aston Villa (h) 2-0
(J.Reader)

3 Jan 1898 v Small Heath (a) 3-8
(A.Leake)

14 Feb 1898 v Wolverhampton Wanderers (h) 1-1
(W.Williams)

5 Sept 1898 v Aston Villa (a) 1-6
(F.Burton)

31 Oct 1898 v Aston Villa (h) 4-0
(T.Perry)

17 Apr 1899 v Walsall (a) 1-1
(S.Holmes)

26 Apr 1899 v Walsall (at Dudley) 1-1
(Dudley Town FC)

30 Oct 1899 v Aston Villa (h) 3-2
(J.Banks)

29 Oct 1900 v Wolverhampton Wanderers (h) 3-3
(W.Richards)
Simmons 2, A.Smith
Att: 5,000

24 Dec 1900 v W.B.A. Past XI (h) 6-5
(Family of H.Green)
Buck 3, Garfield, Simmons 2
Att: 5,500

2 Dec 1901 v Small Heath (h) 2-0
(J Paddock)
Garfield 2
Att: 2,000

1 May 1902 v Wolverhampton Wanderers (a) 4-0
(Ibrox Park Disaster Fund)
Simmons 2, Worton 2
Att: 5,000

20 Oct 1902 v Aston Villa (h) 1-5
(H.Hadley)
Lee
Att: 8,560

29 Dec 1902 v Aston Villa (a) 1-2
(W.George)
Hadley
Att: 12,000

14 Apr 1903 v Wolverhampton Wanderer (a) 1-5
(E.Pheasant)
Tovey
Att: 5,000

29 Apr 1903 v Small Heath (h) 3-2
(Warwickshire CCC)
E.Smith, Hadley, Cole
Att: 4,000

26 Oct 1903 v Aston Villa (h) 3-3
(C.Simmons)
Dorsett, Hobson, Hadley
Att: 5,000

25 Dec 1903 v Select XI (h) 1-1
(G.Cave)
Simmons
Att: 4,500

29 Dec 1903 v Aston Villa (a) 0-3
(G.Johnson)
Att: 6,000

25 Jan 1910 v Aston Villa (a) 1-0
(Birmingham Theatrical Sports)
Bowser
Att: 3,000

4 May 1921 v Wolverhampton Wanderers (h) 2-0
(W.Barber)
Gregory, Blood
Att: 3,106

8 May 1924 v Montgomeryshire District XI (a) 2-1
(Montgomery County Infirmary)
Davies, James
Att: 2,057

4 May 1925 v Aston Villa XI (a) 5-5
(Rowley Regis Ambulance Fund)
Reed 2, Carter, James, Wilson
Att: 2,500

6 May 1925 v Lampard Vachell's XI (a) 7-4
(Dudley Guest Hospital)
James 5, Carter, Morris
Att: 3,500

3 May 1926 v Cradley Heath (a) 1-5
(Rowley Regis Ambulance Fund)
Davies
Att: 5,800

5 May 1926 v F.Morris' XI (at Tipton) 9-0
(Tipton & District Nurses Home)
James 3, Davies 2, Carter 2, Byers, H.Smith
Att: 3,000

8 May 1930 v Cardiff City (at Newtown) 2-1
(Montgomeryshire County Hospital)
Edwards, Bytheway
Att: 5,000

4 May 1931 v Winsford United (a) 3-1
(Cheshire Royal Infirmary)
Richardson 3
Att: 2,500

28 Apr 1932 v Mersey-Widnes XI (a) 4-1
(Widnes Ground Purchase Fund)
Cookson, Titley, Sankey, Raw
Att: 5,000

Tommy Magee's Albion XI line-up with a Mersey-Widnes team in April 1932. The match was in aid of the Widnes Ground Purchase Fund. Albion players (in striped shirts) left to right: J.Quantick, J.Sankey, J.Rix, R.Bragley, H.Raw, T.Magee, J.Cookson, H.Foulkes, S.Horrocks, A.Titley, E.Crowe (goalkeeper). Albion won the match 4-1 and over £200 was raised at the gate.

9 May 1932 v Mid-Cheshire XI (a) 4-2
(Cheshire Royal Infirmary)
Cookson 2, Bytheway, Sandford
Att: 3,000

8 May 1933 v Winsford & District XI (a) 8-0
(Cheshire Royal Infirmary)
Richardson 3, Spencer 2, Sankey, Robbins, Wood
Att: 3,200

7 May 1934 v Winsford & District XI (a) 5-1
(Cheshire Royal Infirmary)
Boyes, Sandford, Richardson, Raw, Sankey
Att: 2,828

20 Aug 1938 v Aston Villa (a) 1-1
(Football League Jubilee Fund)
Jones
Att: 26,640

19 Aug 1939 v Aston Villa (a) 1-1
(Football League Jubilee Fund)
Richardson
Att: 16,007

8 May 1946 v Anderlecht (a) 1-1
(Tubentia FC)
Hodgetts
Att: 8,540

23 Apr 1951 v Swindon Town (a) 5-2
(H.Martin)
Allen 2, Lee, F.Richardson 2
Att: 6,608

24 Mar 1953 v Wolverhampton Wanderers (at Hednesford) 2-4
(Hednesford Town)
Nicholls 2
Att: 7,153
• Also official opening of Hednesford's floodlights

28 Apr 1953 v King's Lynn (a) 5-4
(P.Hooper)
Nicholls 2, Hodgkisson, Ryan, S.Williams
Att: 9,200

1 Nov 1954 v Hereford United (a) 5-10
(J.Sankey & R.Bowen)
Carter 2, Lee 2, Jackson
Att: 4,500

2 May 1955 v Mansfield Town (a) 4-1
(D.Bradley and O.Fox)
Allen 3, Barlow
Att: 12,000

25 Apr 1956 v International XI (h) 5-5
(N.Heath)
Allen, Whitehouse 2, Robson 2
Att: 55,497

21 Apr 1971 v Athletic Bilbao (h) 4-2
(R.Hope)
Merrick, T.Brown 2, Johnson
Att: 14,198

4 May 1971 v Athletic Bilbao (a) 1-1
(Athletic player)
Brown
Att: 26,103

18 May 1971 v Swansea City (a) 2-2
(W.Robbins)
Maclean, Astle
Att: 3,950

George Best (centre of picture with beard) was a guest player for Albion in Jeff Astle's Testimonial Match at The Hawthorns in October 1974. Other players pictured are (left to right): George McVitie, Ken Foggo, Bobby Hope, Ian Collard, Jeff Astle, Ray Fairfax, Graham Lovett, Dennis Clarke (partly hidden), John Kaye (behind Best), John Osborne, Tony Brown, Duggie Fraser and Graham Williams.

8 May 1975 v Aston Villa (h) 2-2
(R.Wilson)
Wilson (pen), Mayo
Att: 9,133

22 Oct 1975 v Leeds United (h) 3-1
(J.Giles)
Dougan, Mulligan, A.Brown
Att: 8,652

26 Apr 1976 v Aston Villa (a) 1-0
(F.Turnbull)
Johnston
Att; 15,808

30 Apr 1976 v Walsall (a) 4-1
(C.Harrison)
T.Brown, A.Brown, Edwards 2
Att: 6,729

20 Oct 1976 v Wolves (a) 0-3
(M.Bailey)
Att: 19,733

18 May 1977 v Swansea City (a) 1-2
(A.Millington)
Johnston
Att: 4,385

5 May 1978 v Don Rogers XI (at Swindon) 4-4
(D.Rogers)
A.Brown, Regis 2, Hughes
Att: 3,103

8 May 1978 v J.Giles XI (h) 0-2
(J.Osborne)
Att: 12,302

3 Aug 1978 v Motherwell (a) 8-1
(J.Wark)
Stevens (og), A.Brown 3, Cunningham 3, T.Brown
Att: 7,401

13 Nov 1978 v Stafford Rangers (a) 2-2
(S.Chapman)
Cunningham 2
Att: 2,443

11 Dec 1978 v Exeter City (a) 2-2
(A.Beer)
Regis, Johnston
Att: 4,474

2 Feb 1979 v Nottingham Forest (at Witney Town) 0-0
(T.Stokes)
Att: 3,558

TV and film personality, Sabrina (42-28-36), in action prior to Norman Heath's Benefit Game at The Hawthorns in 1956.

1 May 1958 v Athletic Bilbao (a) 1-0
(Athletic player)
Allen
Att: 35,051

28 Apr 1965 v W.B.A. Past XI (h) 4-6
(G.Williams)
Kaye, Crawford, T.Brown, Cram
Att: 10,160

15 May 1967 v All Stars XI (h) 6-5
(R.Cram)
Clark 3, Treacy 2, Foggo
Att: 3,943

30 Nov 1971 v Bristol City (a) 0-0
(T.Bush)
Att: 4,950

6 May 1974 v Wolves-Birmingham XI (h) 2-1
(T.Brown)
Hamilton, T.Brown
Att: 11,901
(Albion-Aston Villa Combined XI opposed Wolves-Birmingham XI)

29 Oct 1974 v WBA '68 XI (h) 1-2
(J.Astle)
Foggo (og)
Att: 11,941

John Osborne (left), shakes hands with John Wile before the Albion goalkeeper's Testimonial in 1978.

Len Cantello and Cyrille Regis tossing-up prior to Cantello's Testimonial Match at The Hawthorns in 1979.

15 May 1979 v Cyrille Regis XI (h) 2-3
(L.Cantello)
A.Brown, Robson
Att: 7,023

21 May 1979 v Birmingham City (a) 0-4
(G.Pendrey)
Att: 5,963

22 May 1979 v Bristol Rovers (a) 3-2
(R.Sheppard)
A.Brown, Cowdrill 2
Att: 2,069

24 May 1979 v Kettering Town (a) 3-1
(R.Clayton)
Robson 2, Cowdrill
Att: 3,474

3 Aug 1979 v Torquay United (a) 1-0
(F.King)
A.Brown
Att: 4,718

15 Oct 1979 v Colchester United (a) 0-1
(M.Cook)
Att: 2,882

29 Jan 1980 v Oxford United (a) 1-0
(L.Bateman)
A.Brown
Att: 1,437

21 Apr 1980 v Cambridge United (a) 2-1
(T.Eades)
Trewick, Barnes
Att: 3,794

29 Apr 1980 v Wolverhampton Wanderers (h) 3-1
(A.Robertson)
Regis, Barnes, Cowdrill
Att: 5,110

13 Oct 1980 v Norwich City (at Spalding United) 3-2
(P.Kent)
Deehan 3
Att: 4,029

8 Dec 1980 v Barnett (a) 5-0
(R.Clayton)
Mills, Trewick, Regis, Deehan, T.Brown
Att: 1,001

16 Mar 1981 v Weymouth (a) 5-2
(A.Iannone)
A.Brown, Owen, Barnes, Benjamin, Deehan
Att: 3,124

14 Apr 1981 v Aldershot (a) 2-0
(M.Brodie)
Barnes 2 (1 pen)
Att: 3,991

4 May 1981 v International Select XI (h) 2-3
(J.Wile)
Deehan, M.Robertson
Att; 6,960

24 Feb 1982 v Dudley Town (a) 3-1
(J.Wile)
Pike, Owen (pen), King
Att: 5,524

15 Mar 1983 v Wigan Athletic (a) 2-1
(R.Ward)
Luke, Zondervan
Att: 784

26 Apr 1983 v Walsall (a) 3-3
(A.Caswell)
Webb, Zondervan, Eastoe
Att: 1,870

30 Apr 1984 v Aston Villa (h) 1-2
(B.Batson)
Morley
Att: 4,800

18 May 1984 v Oxford United (a) 3-3
(W.Jeffrey)
N.Cross 2, Morley
Att: 1,660

3 Aug 1984 v Newport County (a) 1-2
(J.Relish)
Hunt
Att: 1,535

8 Aug 1984 v Doncaster Rovers (a) 3-3
(W.Boyd)
G.Thompson 2, Regis
Att: 2,535

17 Sep 1984 v Grimsby Town (a) 2-1
(J.Waters)
N.Cross, Morley
Att: 1,120

5 May 1985 v WBA '78 XI (h) 1-1
(A.Godden)
Dyson
Att: 2,815

13 May 1985 v Bristol City (a) 4-2
(J.Shaw)
Whitehead, Thompson, N.Cross, Mackenzie
Att: 1,823

17 May 1985 v Aston Villa (a) 3-3
(Bradford City Fire Disaster Fund)
Mackenzie (pen), Grealish, Thompson
Att: 7,858

Football League Benefit Matches

Several Albion players have been granted home Football League matches as benefits with most of the gate receipts being presented to the player in question:

W.Bassett v Sheffield Wednesday, 27 Nov 1893.
A.Adams v Stockport County, 28 Oct 1905.
A.Randle v Stockport County, 20 Oct 1906.
J.Pennington v Leeds City, 24 Oct 1908.
F.Buck v Woolwich Arsenal, 11 Nov 1911.
H.Pearson v Bradford City, 22 Mar 1913.
G.Baddeley v Bolton Wanderers, 20 Dec 1913.
J.Pennington v Sunderland, 28 Mar 1914.

Opposition players who have been awarded home League games against Albion as benefit matches include:

H.Pike (Nottingham Forest), 2 Jan 1897.
E.Doig (Sunderland), 8 Oct 1898.
G.Davis (Derby County), 14 Dec 1907.
J.Windridge (Chelsea), 29 Mar 1911.
R. Roberts (Chelsea), 29 Mar 1911.
D.Wilson (Oldham Athletic), 21 Oct 1911.
D.Willis (Newcastle United), 19 Oct 1912.
J.McIlvenny (Bradford City), 9 Feb 1921.

John Wile's first Testimonial game in 1981 against an International XI skippered by Emlyn Hughes (right).

Friendly Matches

This section lists friendly matches played by Albion's first team from 1879 until the end of 1986-7. Excluded from this list are wartime friendlies, overseas tour games and testimonial and benefit matches which can be found in a separate section.

It should be appreciated that prior to 1883 a full record of friendly matches is not available. No official club records seem to have survived from this period and the newspapers of the time did not record every game contested by the infant Albion club. Goalscorers and attendances have been inserted from 1900 onwards, the year in which Albion moved to The Hawthorns.

Because of an increase in the number of Football League fixtures Albion's quota of friendlies decreased during the 1900s. During part of that decade and for several seasons in the 1920s no friendlies of any description were undertaken.

Harry Aston, scorer of Albion's first goal against Black Lake Victoria.

1879-80
Dec 13 v Black Lake Victoria (h) 1-0
This is Albion's first recorded game and a crowd of around 500 saw Harry Aston's goal win the match. Albion fielded 12 players: S.Biddlestone; H.Twist, H.Bell, T.Smith, J.Johnstone, J.Stanton, W.Bisseker (capt), J.Stokes, E.Smith, G.Timmins, H.Aston, G.Ball.
Dec 20 v Bullock's Club (h) 4-0
Jan 31 v St Phillip's (h) *
Apr 3 v Heart of Oak (h) 5-0
May 1 v Christ Church (h) *
Score not recorded

1880-81
Nov 6 v Summer Hill Works (h) 4-0
Dec 6 v Hockley Abbey (a) 2-0
Jan 1 v Aston Napier (a) 0-0
Jan 29 v Hockley Belmont (h) 5-0
Billy Bisseker's three goals in this match gave him the first reported hat-trick by an Albion player.
Feb 5 v Summer Hill Works (h) 4-0
Feb 12 v Hockley Abbey (a) 2-0
Feb 19 v Hockley Belmont (h) 5-0
Feb 26 v West Bromwich Royal (h) *
Mar 10 v Smethwick Windmill (h) 9-1
Mar 12 v West Bromwich Rovers (h) 8-0
Mar 26 v Oakfield (h) 14-0
Score not recorded

1881-2
Sep 10 v Oldbury (h) 5-1
Oct 1 v The Grove (a) 2-3
Oct 8 v Milton (h) 12-0
Billy Bisseker scored five goals.
Nov 5 v Milton (a) 3-0 (abandoned 35 minutes; ball burst)
Nov 19 v Walsall Unity (a) *
Nov 26 v The Grove (h) 2-4
Dec 3 v Nechells (h) 9-1
Dec 17 v Walsall Alma Athletic (h) *
Dec 24 v Wednesfield Rovers (h) *
Jan 7 v Brunswick Wheel Works (a) 2-1
Jan 14 v Fallings Heath Rangers (h) *
Jan 28 v Stourbridge (h) *
Feb 4 v West Bromwich Rovers (h) 6-1
Feb 25 v Fallings Heath Rangers (h) 5-0
Mar 4 v St Luke's (h) 10-0
George Bell scored six goals.
Mar 11 v Nechells (a) *
Apr 9 v Aston Unity (a) 2-3
Score not recorded

1882-3
Sep 23 v St George's (a) 1-7
Sep 30 Oldbury (a) *

Oct 7 v Stourbridge Standard (h) 10-0
Albion's first game at Four Acres. Billy Bisseker scored six goals.
Oct 14 v Aston Unity (h) 1-0
Oct 17 v The Grove (a) *
Oct 21 v Excelsior (a) 2-2
Dec 2 v Excelsior (h) 3-2
Dec 16 v Leek (h) 2-0
Dec 26 v Wrexham (a) 5-2
Dec 27 v Notts Rangers (a) 2-3
Jan 6 v Wellington (a) 2-2
Jan 13 v Walsall Alma Athletic (h) 4-0
Jan 22 v St John's United (h) 11-0
Jan 27 v St George's (h) 3-0
Feb 10 v Notts Rangers (h) 1-1 (abandoned)
Feb 17 v Birmingham Heath (h) 3-0
Feb 19 v Birmingham Junior Association (h) 10-1
Harry Aston scored six goals.
Mar 17 v Leek (a) 6-3
Mar 19 v The Grove (a) 2-1
Mar 31 v Wrexham (h) 3-1
Apr 25 v All Saints (h) *
Apr 28 v Walsall Swifts (a) 1-2
May 5 v Small Heath Alliance (h) 5-1
May 12 v Nechells (h) *
Score not recorded

1883-4
Sep 17 v Forwards XI (a) 3-3
Oct 1 v Wednesbury Old Athletic (h) 2-5
Oct 6 v Preston North End (a) 1-3
Last Preston goal disputed and so some reports gave the score as 1-2.
Oct 13 v Wolverhampton Wanderers (h) 4-2
Oct 20 v Stoke (h) 1-5
Nov 5 v Walsall Swifts (h) 2-2
Nov 12 v Stoke (a) 1-1 (abandoned)
Nov 17 v Blackburn Rovers (a) 0-1
Nov 19 v Bolton Wanderers (a) 1-2
Some reports give the score as 1-3 after a third Bolton 'goal' was disputed.
Dec 1 v West Bromwich Sandwell (h) 5-1
Dec 26 v Preston North End (h) 2-1
Dec 27 v Sheffield Heeley (h) 8-0
Dec 29 v Aston Unity (h) 5-0
Jan 19 v Aston Unity (h) 5-0
Jan 26 v Wednesbury Old Athletic (h) 2-0 (abandoned)
Feb 2 v Bolton Great Lever (h) 4-1
Feb 16 v West Bromwich Albion 2nd XI (h) 0-2
Feb 26 v Wednesbury Town (h) 2-0
Mar 1 v Wednesbury Old Athletic (a) 2-2
Mar 22 v Walsall Town (h) 3-2
Mar 24 v West Bromwich Sandwell (h) 7-0
Apr 19 v Burslem Port Vale (a) 6-0
Apr 26 v Wolverhampton Wanderers (a) 3-0
May 5 v Walsall Swifts (a) 0-1

1884-5
Jul 28 v Wednesbury Old Athletic (a) 1-0
Aug 23 v Small Heath Alliance (a) 2-0
Sep 22 v Walsall Swifts (a) 1-4
Oct 4 v Burslem Port Vale (h) 3-0
Oct 11 v Aston Unity (h) 3-0
Nov 1 v Stoke (a) 4-0
Nov 3 v Stafford Rangers (h) 5-0
Nov 15 v Wednesbury Town (h) 7-1
Nov 29 v Aston Villa (h) 2-4
Dec 26 v Preston North End (a) 1-1
Dec 27 v Bolton Great Lever (a) 0-3
Jan 17 v Walsall Swifts (h) 0-0
Feb 7 v Burslem Port Vale (a) 3-2
Feb 14 v Aston Unity (a) 2-0
Mar 7 v St Luke's (h) 3-2
Mar 14 v Aston Villa (a) 2-1
Mar 16 v West Bromwich Sandwell (h) 6-2

Mar 21 v Church (h) 1-1
Mar 28 v Church (a) 0-2
Apr 4 v Third Lanark Rifle Volunteers (a) 2-2
Apr 6 v Wednesbury Old Athletic (h) 3-2
Last game at the Four Acres, watched by 3,500 spectators.
Apr 11 v Stoke (a) 1-1
Apr 20 v Burslem Port Vale (a) 1-1
Apr 25 v Bolton Wanderers (a) 0-1 (abandoned)
May 25 v Wolverhampton Wanderers (a) 0-2

1885-6
(Albion's first season at Stoney Lane)
Jul 27 v Wednesbury Old Athletic (h) 0-1
Aug 22 v Small Heath Alliance (a) 7-0
Sep 5 v Third Lanark Rifle Volunteers (h) 4-1
Albion's first game at Stoney Lane. A crowd of 2,122 saw Tommy Green score a hat-trick for Albion.
Sep 12 v Aston Villa (h) 5-0
Sep 19 v Birmingham Excelsior (h) 4-2
Sep 21 v Walsall Swifts (a) 0-3
Sep 26 v Wednesbury Old Athletic (h) 2-1
Oct 3 v Northwich Victoria (a) 1-2
Oct 5 v Great Bridge Unity (a) 4-0
Oct 10 v Blackburn Olympic (a) 3-2
Oct 17 v Stoke (h) 3-1
Nov 2 v Wolves (h) 3-0
Nov 14 v Notts County (a) 3-4
Nov 23 v Burnley (h) 0-3
Nov 28 v Aston Villa (a) 5-4
Dec 12 v Derby Midland (a) 5-3
Dec 19 v Aston Unity (h) 7-0
Dec 26 v Blackburn Olympic (h) 4-0
Dec 28 v Bolton Wanderers (h) 0-0 (abandoned)
Feb 6 v Aston Villa (h) 3-2
Feb 20 v Nottingham Forest (h) 1-0
Feb 27 v Derby Junction (h) 5-0
Mar 20 v Notts County (h) 3-0
Mar 27 v Stoke (a) 3-1
Apr 26 v Halliwell (h) 7-0
May 1 v Preston North End (h) 0-7
May 8 v Blackburn Rovers (h) 2-5
May 15 v Preston North End (h) 1-0
May 22 v Bolton Wanderers (h) 1-3
May 29 v Aston Villa (h) 3-1

1886-7
Jul 26 v Wednesbury Old Athletic (h) 6-0
Sep 4 v Wolves (a) 2-0
Sep 11 v Stoke (a) 4-0
Sep 18 v Third Lanark Rifle Volunteers (a) 2-1
Sep 20 v Hibernian (a) 1-1
Sep 25 v Northwich Victoria (h) 2-1
Oct 2 v Derby Midland (h) 3-1
Oct 23 v Bolton Wanderers (a) 0-1
Nov 1 v Oxford University (h) 6-1
Nov 27 v Old Carthusians (h) 5-1
Dec 4 v Preston North End (a) 0-7
Dec 18 v Aston Villa (a) 1-1
Dec 27 v Preston North End (h) 5-1
Dec 28 v Bolton Wanderers (h) 1-2
Jan 22 v Nottingham County (a) 1-3
Feb 5 v Aston Unity (h) 5-0
Feb 7 v Oxford University (a) 3-2
Mar 12 v Wolverhampton Wanderers (h) 0-0
Mar 26 v Birmingham Excelsior (h) 3-0
Apr 11 v Third Lanark Rifle Volunteers (a) 3-1
Apr 16 v Darwen (h) 4-0
May 14 v Aston Villa (h) 3-1
May 16 v Great Bridge Unity (a) 0-0
May 21 v Stoke (h) 1-0
May 28 v Bolton Wanderers (h) 2-0
May 30 v Blackburn Rovers (h) 3-0
June 4 v Wolverhampton Wanderers (a) 0-1
June 18 South Shore (a) 3-2
June 20 Fleetwood Rangers (a) 3-1

1887-8
Aug 27 v Oldbury Town Crosswells (a) 1-0
Sep 3 v Sheffield Wednesday (h) 4-1
Sep 10 v Third Lanark Rifle Volunteers (a) 0-2
Sep 17 v Stoke (h) 4-0
Sep 24 v Bolton Wanderers (a) 1-1
Oct 3 v Nottingham County (h) 5 1
Oct 17 v Walsall Town (h) 8-0
Oct 22 v Blackburn Rovers (a) 6-7
Oct 29 v Lincoln City (h) 4-1
Nov 7 v Bolton Wanderers (h) 6-0
Nov 12 v Preston North End (a) 2-4
Nov 21 v Oxford University (a) 6-2
Dec 3 v Burnley (h) 3-0
Dec 5 v Cambridge University (h) 5-0
Dec 10 v Lincoln City (a) 6-1
Dec 17 v Long Eaton Rangers (h) 3-1
Dec 26 v Wolverhampton Wanderers (h) 1-1
Jan 14 v Nottingham County (a) 3-3
Jan 21 v Wolverhampton Wanderers (a) 5-0
Feb 4 v Oxford University (a) 5-0
Feb 25 v Aston Villa (h) 4-1
Feb 27 v Cambridge University (a) 6-1
Mar 10 v Aston Villa (h) 4-0
Apr 2 v Third Lanark Rifle Volunteers (a) 0-3
Apr 3 v Newcastle West End (a) 5-1
Apr 7 v Everton (a) 1-0
Apr 16 v Burnley (a) 1-0
Apr 21 v Preston North End (h) 2-2
May 5 v Blackburn Rovers (h) 2-1
May 12 v Third Lanark Rifle Volunteers (h) 5-2
May 19 v Renton (at Hampden Park) 1-4
Played to decide the 'Championship of the World'
(see page 13).
May 26 v Aston Villa (a) 1-1
May 28 v Preston North End (a) 0-2

1888-9
Aug 6 v Preston North End (h) 2-4
Aug 7 v Birmingham & District XI (h) 0-1
Sep 1 v Sheffield Wednesday (h) 3-1
Sep 3 v Wolverhampton Wanderers (h) 4-2
Sep 17 v Studley & District (a) 23-2
Billy Bassett (5), Bill Hendry (3) and Tom Pearson
(3) led the scoring in this game.
Sep 24 v Walsall Town Swifts (a) 2-2
(played under electric lighting)
Oct 22 v London Caledonians (a) 1-0
Oct 27 v Canadian XI (h) 1-0
Dec 3 v Cambridge University (h) 1-1
Dec 8 v Kidderminster Harriers (a) 4-1
Jan 28 v Oxford University (a) 4-2
Feb 9 v Newcastle West End (a) 2-0
Feb 11 v Sunderland Albion (a) 1-1
Feb 18 v Cambridge University (a) 2-3
Mar 9 v Birmingham St George's (a) 3-1
Mar 30 v Grimsby Town (h) 4-0 (abandoned)
Apr 13 v Small Heath (h) 4-1
Apr 15 v Kidderminster Harriers (a) 5-2
Apr 22 v Newton Heath (a) 3-1
Apr 23 v Stockton-on-Tees (a) 3-2
Apr 27 v Birmingham St George's (h) 0-3
Apr 29 v Wolverhampton Wanderers (a) 0-2
May 4 v Small Heath (a) 2-1
May 6 v Wolverhampton Wanderers (h) 3-0
May 8 v Burton & District XI (a) 7-1
May 11 v Wednesbury Old Athletic (a) 2-0
May 18 v Hurst (a) 4-0

1889-90
Sep 2 v Warwick County (a) 2-0
Sep 7 v Grimsby Town (a) 1-6
Sep 9 v Great Bridge Unity (a) 6-0
Sep 16 v Walsall Town Swifts (h) 2-1
Oct 14 v Walsall Town Swifts (a) 1-1
Nov 2 v Oxford University (h) 2-3
Feb 15 v Aston Villa (a) 1-0
Feb 22 v Chatham (a) 7-1
Mar 29 v Aston Villa (h) 2-2
Apr 7 v West Manchester (a) 3-2
Apr 8 v Middlesbrough Ironopolis (a) 4-3
Apr 14 v Bootle (a) 3-0
Apr 21 v Kidderminster Olympic (a) 1-2
May 3 v Sunderland (a) 5-3
May 10 v Hyde (a) 3-1
May 24 v Aston Villa (a) 0-1
May 26 v Warwick County (a) 2-1
May 31 v Everton (a) 1-4

1890-91
Aug 30 v Stoke (a) 2-2
Sep 8 v Wolverhampton Wanderers (a) 4-2
Sep 15 v Small Heath (h) 3-1
Sep 22 v Walsall Town Swifts (a) 2-1
Sep 29 v Burslem Port Vale (a) 2-1
Oct 6 v Chirk (a) 5-1
Oct 9 v Wolverhampton Wanderers (h) 4-1
Oct 20 v Small Heath (a) 3-3
Nov 10 v Warwick County (a) 4-0
Nov 15 v Nottingham Forest (h) 2-2
Dec 8 v Aston Villa (a) 2-4
Dec 26 v Preston North End (h) 2-0*
Jan 1 v Ardwick (a) 2-2
Jan 10 v Blackburn Rovers (h) 0-4*
Jan 12 v Brierley Hill (a) 2-1
Jan 19 v Aston Villa (h) 4-2
Over 5,000 spectators saw three Scots, McCulloch,
McCullum and McLeod make their debuts for
Albion.
Feb 11 v Oxford University (a) 1-1
Feb 21 v Bootle (a) 0-0
Mar 12 v Nottingham Forest (a) 3-2
Mar 16 v Sheffield Wednesday (a) 2-1
Mar 21 v Preston North End (h) 1-2
Mar 28 v Small Heath (a) 1-2
Mar 30 v Everton (a) 1-2
Mar 31 v Kettering (a) 1-2
Apr 4 v Wolverhampton Wanderers (a) 2-4
Apr 25 v Brierley Hill (a) 2-2
Apr 30 v Hednesford Town (a) 1-3
*Originally designated as Football League matches
but replayed after protest.*

1891-2
Sep 1 v Birmingham St George's (h) 4-0
Sep 2 v Coles Farm (a) 5-1
Sep 9 v Burton Swifts (a) 2-1
Sep 14 v Small Heath (a) 0-4
Sep 21 v Birmingham St George's (a) 4-1
Sep 26 v Royal Arsenal (a) 1-1
Sep 28 v Chatham (a) 1-2
Sep 30 v Northwich Victoria (a) 5-0
Oct 5 v Wolverhampton Wanderers (a) 3-3
Oct 26 v Wolverhampton Wanderers (a) 1-2
Nov 9 v Wednesbury Old Athletic (h) 2-0
Nov 30 v Aston Villa (a) 2-8
Dec 7 v Wednesbury Old Athletic (a) 3-1
Dec 25 v Birmingham St George's (h) 1-1
Dec 29 v Kettering (a) 2-0
Dec 30 v Luton Town (a) 4-0
Jan 1 v Ardwick (a) 2-4
Jan 11 v Aston Villa (h) 2-1
Feb 20 v Corinthians (a) 4-4
Mar 22 v Wrexham (a) 2-2
Mar 26 v Corinthians (h) 2-0
Apr 2 v Chirk (h) 3-0
Apr 6 v Everton (a) 0-7
Apr 18 v Heart of Midlothian (a) 0-2
Apr 19 v Sheffield United (a) 0-3
Apr 20 v Bristol Association (a) 7-0

1892-3
Sep 1 v Coles Farm Unity (a) 6-2
Sep 3 v Aston Villa (h) 0-1
Sep 5 v Bloxwich (a) 3-1
Sep 7 v Middlesbrough (a) 2-7
Sep 12 v Wrexham (a) 3-1
Sep 26 v Aston Villa (a) 2-3
Sep 27 v Walsall Town Swifts (a) 0-3
Nov 14 v Walsall Town Swifts (h) 2-2
Nov 28 v Wolverhampton Wanderers (h) 1-1
Dec 3 v Royal Arsenal (a) 4-2
Dec 5 v Aston Villa (h) 1-1 (abandoned)
Feb 4 v Aston Villa (h) 4-4
Feb 18 v Corinthians (a) 3-1
Mar 4 v Aston Villa (h) 2-0
Mar 11 v Burslem Port Vale (h) 2-2
Mar 25 v Heart of Midlothian (a) 0-1
Apr 8 v Bury (a) 2-1
Apr 15 v Newcastle United (a) 2-7
Apr 17 v Small Heath (a) 1-4
Apr 24 v Linfield Athletic (in Belfast) 1-3
Apr 25 v Ulster XI (in Belfast) 0-1
Apr 27 v Wolverhampton Wanderers (a) 4-2
Apr 29 v Millwall (a) 0-1

1893-4
Sep 4 v Leicester Fosse (a) 0-3
Sep 11 v Wolverhampton Wanderers (h) 1-0
Sep 14 v Coseley (a) 7-1
Sep 18 v Everton (a) 0-3
Oct 2 v Nottingham County (h) 2-0
Oct 16 v Wolverhampton Wanderers(a) 2-2
Dec 2 v Woolwich Arsenal (a) 0-5
Jan 4 v Nottingham County (a) 0-3
Jan 31 v Oxford University (a) 0-2
Feb 10 v Corinthians (a) 2-5
Feb 19 v Oldbury Town (a) 2-1
Mar 31 v Doncaster Rovers (a) 7-1
Apr 28 v Millwall Athletic (a) 0-3

1894-5
Sep 13 v Aston Villa (h) 5-4
Sep 17 v Woolwich Arsenal (a) 1-0
Sep 24 v Wolverhampton Wanderers (a) 2-1
Sep 27 v Coseley (a) 3-2
Oct 22 v Wolverhampton Wanderers (h) 0-1
Nov 20 v Oxford University (a) 4-2
Dec 3 v Walsall (a) 5-1
Jan 28 v Aberystwyth (a) 8-2
Billy Richards scored five goals.
Mar 23 v Everton (a) 2-9
Apr 8 v Wrexham (a) 2-0

1895-6
Sep 14 v Bolton Swifts (a) 1-5
Sep 24 v Walsall (a) 2-1
Sep 25 v Aberystwyth (a) 10-1

Tom Hutchinson, hat-trick hero
against Aberystwyth (10-1) in 1895.

Sep 30 v Millwall Athletic (a) 3-0
Oct 14 v Dundee (a) 1-3
Nov 11 v Cambridge University (a) 2-3
Nov 25 v Oxford University (a) 2-2
Feb 8 v Corinthians (a) 2-5
Mar 14 v Liverpool (a) 1-5
Mar 20 v Thames Ironworks (a) 4-2
(Played under electric lighting)
Mar 21 v West Norwood (a) 4-0
Mar 23 v Rev A.R.Bourke's XI (a) 4-1
Mar 24 v West Brompton (a) 9-1
Mar 25 v Wickham Wanderers (a) 4-1
Mar 28 v Llandudno (a) 2-1
Apr 13 v Preston North End (h) 2-2

Archie Bostock, a key Albion goalscorer
in the 1890s.

Tom Higgins — on target against West Norwood in March 1896.

1896-7
Sep 21 v Walsall (a) 0-2
Nov 7 v Great Marlow (a) 3-5
Nov 30 v Oxford University (a) 0-2
Jan 9 v Bolton Wanderers (a) 2-2
Feb 27 v Corinthians (a) 1-3
Mar 20 v Swindon Town (a) 1-0
Mar 27 v Dartford (a) 4-1
Mar 29 v Oldbury Town (a) 2-0
Apr 19 v Hereford Town (a) 2-1
Apr 21 v Derby County (at Bristol) 1-2
Apr 24 v Gravesend (a) 4-0
Apr 29 v Small Heath (a) 1-5

1897-8
Sep 28 v Walsall (a) 2-1
Nov 22 v Cambridge University (a) 5-3
Dec 6 v Oxford University (a) 1-1
Jan 8 v Queen's Park Rangers (a) 4-1
Apr 16 v Newcastle United (a) 1-1
Apr 23 v Bristol City (a) 1-1
Apr 25 v Chirk (a) 1-0
Apr 27 v Devon County (a) 8-0
Apr 28 v Dorset County (a) 3-0
Apr 29 v Suffolk County (a) 2-1
Apr 30 v Watford (a) 1-1

1898-9
Nov 14 v Cambridge University (a) 4-3
Mar 11 v Newton Heath (a) 0-2
Apr 3 v Small Heath (a) 0-1
Apr 4 v Northampton (a) 1-6
Apr 20 v Swansea Town (a) 13-1
One of Albion's goals was credited to the referee.
Apr 29 v Swindon Town (a) 1-2

1899-1900
Sep 16 v Burton Swifts (a) 0-0
Nov 22 v Kaffirs XI (h) 11-6
Nov 27 v Cambridge University (a) 2-2
Mar 17 v Leicester Fosse (a) 1-3
Apr 28 v Small Heath (a) 1-1

1900-01
(Albion's first season at The Hawthorns)
Nov 13 v Cambridge University (a) 2-6
Buck, A.Smith
Att: 2,500
Dec 26 v Liverpool (h) 5-2
Simmons, Stevenson, Buck, Banks, Roberts
Att: 10,000

1901-02
Nov 16 v Reading (a) 1-1
Simmons
Att: 4,133
Nov 30 v Walsall (a) 2-1
Brett, Harper
Att: 2,500
Mar 25 v New Brompton (a) 3-2
Simmons 2, A.Smith
Att: 5,000
Apr 9 v Brownhills Albion (a) 5-0
Simmons 3, Brett 2
Att: 2,000
Apr 26 v Woolwich Arsenal (at Exeter) 1-0
Stevenson
Att: 3,500
Apr 28 v West Bromwich Albion Reserves (h) 1-2
Dorsett
Att: 807
Apr 30 v Middlesbrough (a) 1-1
Lee
Att: 6,150

1902-03
Feb 21 v Belfast Distillery (a) 5-5
McLean, Dorsett 2, Lee, Worton
Att: 5,000

1903-04
Dec 3 v Northampton Town (a) 1-2
Dorsett
Att: 3,000
Apr 27 v Brighton & Hove Albion (a) 2-3
Dorsett, Aston
Att: 5,000
Apr 30 v Middlesbrough (a) 0-2
Att: 3,400

Willie Smith, scorer against Leeds City in February 1905.

◀ Andrew Smith (right) scored in Albion's away friendly against Cambridge University in 1900.

1904-05
Oct 19 v Clapton Orient (a) 1-1
Jack
Att: 3,000
Nov 12 v Plymouth Argyle (a) 2-3
Jack 2
Att: 4,350
Dec 10 v Portsmouth (a) 2-3
Brown, Bell
Att: 1,200
Feb 4 v Leeds City (a) 5-0
W.Smith, Aston, Lewis, Manners, Pheasant
Att: 2,100
Apr 29 v Shepherd's Bush (a) 3-3
Williams 3
Att: 3,250

Jimmy Williams, hat-trick against Shepherd's Bush in 1905.

1907-08
Sep 9 v Barnsley (a) 1-0
Shinton
Att: 3,000

1913-14
Apr 25 v Corinthians (h) 0-4
Att: 3,867

1919-20
Jan 31 v Corinthians (h) 4-3
A.Smith 2, Crisp, Hatton
Att: 9,265

1920-21
Mar 5 v Corinthians (h) 3-0
Gregory, Blood 2
Att: 10,134

1924-5
Mar 28 v Corinthians (h) 4-4
Carter 2, James, Davies
Att: 7,227

216

1929-30
Jan 25 v Crystal Palace (a) 2-1
Carter 2
Att: 5,000

1931-2
Jan 23 v Corinthians (h) 4-0
Carter 2, Richardson, Fitton
Att: 10,165

1954-5
Feb 19 v Leeds United (a) 1-1
Hodgkisson
Att: 16,240

1957-8
Oct 29 v CDSA (Russian Red Army) (h) 6-5
Howe, Kevan 2, Griffin, Robson, Allen (pen)
Att: 52,805
Official opening of The Hawthorns floodlights

'W.G.' Richardson was on target in Albion's ▶
4-0 win over The Corinthians in 1932.

Ken Hodgkisson netted Albion's goal at Leeds
in 1955.

Action from the game against CDSA (Russian Red Army) in 1957 which Albion won 6-5. Kevan (centre), Robson (No.8) and Allen (9) make a combined attack on the Red Army goal.

1958-9
Sep 24 v Port Vale (a) 3-5
Burnside 2, Main
Att: 18,795
Official opening of Vale Park floodlights
Nov 5 v Atletico Bilbao (h) 1-2
Allen (pen)
Att: 24,800
Dec 10 v Bucharest XI (h) 3-0
Forrester, Allen, Setters.
Att: 7,904

1959-60
Oct 5 v Grenchen (h) 0-0
Att: 10,909
May 2 v Geo.Salters Works XI (a) 13-2
Jackson 5, Burnside 3, G.Williams 2, Hope, Wallace, G.Carter
Att: 2,103
Salters' Works Bi-centennial celebration match

1960-61
Oct 4 v Canadian FA XI (h) 0-1
Att: 8,724

1962-3
Feb 20 v Aston Villa (at Stourbridge) 3-2
Jones, Kevan, Hope
Att: 1,600
Feb 22 v Charlton Athletic (a) 0-5
Att: 2,282

1963-4
Apr 7 v Alkmaar (h) 2-1
Foggo, Jones
Att: 9,411

1967-8
Aug 7 v Bristol City (a) 4-1
Clark 2, Astle, Foggo
Att: 7,719

Aug 9 v Bournemouth (a) 1-0
Brown
Att: 5,500
Aug 12 v Portsmouth (a) 1-0
Astle
Att: 8,929

1968-9
Jul 30 v Carlisle United (a) 1-1
Brown
Att: 11,607

1969-70
Jul 26 v Rotherham United (a) 4-0
Watson (og), Hegan, Glover, Astle
Att: 4,468
Jan 23 v Birmingham City (a) 2-2
Astle, Suggett
Att: 20,110
May 20 v US Triestina (a) 1-1
Suggett
Att: 12,345

1970-71
Aug 3 v Heart of Midlothian (h) 2-0
Reed, Wilson (pen)
Att: 8,024
Aug 8 v Aston Villa (a) 1-1
Wright (og)
Att: 20,893

1971-2
Feb 2 v Queen's Park Rangers (a) 2-1
T.Brown, Hartford
Att: 7,082
Feb 26 v Preston North End (a) 1-2
T.Brown
Att: 5,912

1972-3
Jul 26 v Feyenoord (a) 1-4
Gould
Att: 26,251
Aug 8 v Hibernian (a) 2-0
A.Brown, Gould
Att: 10,203
Dec 30 v Walsall (h) 1-1
Robertson
Att: 5,648

1973-4
Aug 14 v Colchester United (a) 0-3
2,840
Aug 14 v Rhyl (a) 3-1
A.Brown, Edwards, Williams (og)
Att: 1,112
Aug 16 v Wolves (a) 0-3
Att: 12,928
Aug 18 v Bournemouth (h) 0-1
Att: 4,304

1975-6
May 4 v Coventry City (h) 5-1
T.Brown 2, Johnston, A.Brown, Rushbury
Att: 5,777
Match arranged to celebrate promotion.

1976-7
Aug 2 v Crewe Alexandra (a) 6-2
A.Brown 2, Cantello, Mayo, T.Brown (pen) Nisbet
Att: 1,089
Dec 21 v Kettering Town (a) 2-3
Treacy, Mayo
Att: 1,699
Centenary Match
Jan 29 v Sheffield United (a) 0-1
Att: 3,924

1977-8
Dec 13 v Saudi Arabia (at Dhahran) 1-0
T.Brown
Att: 5,000

1978-9
Feb 6 v Portsmouth (a) 0-2
Att: 8,552
Feb 17 v Birmingham City (in Guernsey) 1-1
Regis
Att: 4,400

The China national team line-up before their friendly with Albion at The Hawthorns in August 1979.

1979-80
Aug 1 v China XI (h) 4-0
Luofeng (og), Regis, A.Brown, Barnes
Att: 11,382
Aug 6 v Bradford City (a) 1-0
Robson
Att: 4,098

Aug 11 v Ajax Amsterdam (h) 1-0
Barnes
Att: 13,334
Albion Centenary Match
Mar 3 v Barnet (a) 2-1
Moses, Mills
Att: 3,556

Cyrille Regis scored Albion's goal against Birmingham City in the 1979 friendly in Guernsey.

Peter Barnes, scorer of Albion's winning goal against Ajax at The Hawthorns in 1979. ▶

218

1980-81
Jul 26 v Reading (a) 2-4
Regis, Deehan
Att: 1,595
Jul 28 v Bradford City (a) 1-0
Owen
Att: 1,268
Aug 2 v Swindon Town (a) 3-1
Muzinic, Deehan, Mills
Att: 3,054
Aug 12 v Hapoel Tel Aviv (h) 2-1
Barnes, Mills
Att: 3,445
Sept 10 v AC Naples (a) 2-2
Mills, Owen
Att: 24,000
Feb 2 v Crvena Zvezda (Red Star) (h) 4-2
Robson, Wile, Deehan, Mills
Att: 3,217

Bryan Robson, scored in friendly games in
1979-80 and 1980-81.

Feb 23 v Poole Town (a) 4-2
Deehan, A.Brown, Regis, Batson
Att: 4,103
Mar 3 v Linfield (a) 2-0
Robson, Barnes
Att: 8,092
Apr 12 v Kuwait XI (a) 1-1
Regis
Att: 11,200
Apr 29 v Sweden XI (a) 0-2
Att: 3,969

1981-2
Aug 14 v Newcastle United (a) 2-0
Regis, N.Cross
Att: 4,340
Jan 17 v Birmingham City (in Guernsey) 1-2
A.Brown
Att: 2,658

1982-3
Aug 7 v Twente Enschede (a) 3-1
Jol 2, Mackenzie
Att: 7,894
Aug 23 v Sheffield Wednesday (a) 2-2
Eastoe, Mackenzie
Att: 4,518

Nov 10 v Limassol (a) 4-0
Eastoe 2, N.Cross, Owen (pen)
Att: 2,150
Feb 13 v Poole Town (a) 1-2
N.Cross
Att: 1,408
Apr 14 v Stourbridge (a) 3-1
Perry 2, Zondervan
Att: 1,045
May 16 v The Army XI (at Aldershot) 5-0
Kent 2, G.Thompson, G.Robson, N.Cross
Att: 1,016

1983-4
Jul 27 v Dorchester Town (a) 3-1
Perry, Eastoe, Luke
Att: 1,100
Jul 29 v Poole Town (a) 2-0
Regis, Perry
Att: 550
Aug 2 v Rangers (a) 2-4
Regis, Luke
Att: 21,566
Aug 5 v Gloucester City (a) 1-0
Thompson
Att: 400
Aug 19 v Walsall (a) 1-0
Jol
Att: 1,853
Aug 22 v Sheffield Wednesday (a) 0-1
Att: 3,331
Dec 11 v BSR (Stourbridge) (a) 9-0
N.Cross 3, Monaghan 3, Morley, Owen, Thompson
Att: 752

1984-5
Aug 7 v Walsall (a) 1-3
Lewis
Att: 200
Aug 15 v Walsall (h) 2-0
Mower (og), Hunt
Att: 150
Aug 18 v Oldham Athletic (a) 1-0
Bennett
Att: 3,000

John Deehan, scorer in Poole Town's Centenary
Match of 1981.

219

Mickey Forsyth found the net against
Orgryte in October 1984.

Aug 20 v Stockport County (a) 3-2
G.Thompson 2, McNaught
Att: 1,792
Oct 3 v Orgryte (a) 2-2
Grealish, Forsyth
Att: 2,588
Oct 23 v Hong Kong XI (a) 3-0
Grealish, G.Thompson 2
Att: 8,022
Jan 30 v Tunisian XI (in Tunis) 1-1
M.Giles
Att: 2,550
Feb 19 v Scunthorpe United (a) 0-0
Att: 387

1985-6
July 27 v Rotherham United (at Spring Road) 2-1
Crooks, Mackenzie
Att: 155
Aug 3 v Peterborough United (a) 2-0
G.Thompson, Mackenzie
Att: 1,329
Aug 10 v Doncaster Rovers (a) 3-2
Whitehead, Mackenzie, Varadi
Att: 1,226
Aug 12 v Whitby Town (a) 1-2
Valentine
Att: 908
Feb 14 v Oldham Athletic (a) 1-5
Grealish
Att: 632
Apr 28 v Swansea City (a) 2-2
Robson, Bradley
Att: 1,565

1986-7
Aug 9 v Bristol City (a) 0-1
Att: 2,227
Aug 12 v Crewe Alexandra (a) 2-0
Burke, Macowat (og)
Att: 655
Aug 15 v Moscow Torpedo (h) 0-2
Att: 2,591
Aug 18 v Walsall (a) 2-2
Evans 2
Att: 2,781

ALBION RESERVES

BIRMINGHAM & DISTRICT LEAGUE

ALBION first fielded a second team in 1882-3, playing against local opposition such as Excelsior, Handsworth Oakfield, Bloxwich Strollers, Caldmore Rovers, Stourbridge Standard, Aston Unity, Oldbury, Oak Villa, Birmingham Heath, Warley Villa, Walsall Swifts, Wellington, Pensnett and Camp Hill. In 24 matches Albion were undefeated, winning 18 of them with a highest score of ten goals against Wellington and 101 goals in all games. During the following season Albion's reserves were unstoppable, winning all 30 matches, including the Final of the Birmingham Junior Cup in which Speedwell were crushed 10-1 after they had led 1-0 at the interval. Some other emphatic successes during that season included a 15-1 victory over an Old Boys' XI, 10-1 thrashings of West Bromwich Royal and Aston Unity and a 9-0 defeat of Witton Unity. Among the heroes of the campaign were Joe Matthews (goalkeeper), Luther Walker, Jack Horton, Arthur Bradbury, Jimmy Painter and Will Lines (defenders) and William Bradley (captain), George Askin, Abraham Bunn and Dennis Smith (forwards). In March 1884 a young centre-half, Charlie Perry, made his first appearance for the reserves, against Aston Unity, and two years later he was a member of Albion's first FA Cup Final team.

During the 1884-5 season, Albion's reserves retained the Birmingham Junior Cup by defeating Walsall Swifts 1-0, and the club were permitted to keep the trophy in recognition of the feat. On 11 October 1884 the reserves suffered their first-ever defeat when they fell 5-1 to the Welsh club, Newtown; later in the season they visited Preston to play North End's second team and lost 2-0. In 1885-6 trips were made to Stoke, Newtown, Notts County and Newton Heath of Manchester with a view to discovering stronger opposition than that provided by the local junior clubs, most of whom were totally outclassed when they came up against the Albion juniors. The Albion reserves also participated in the first two rounds of the Birmingham Cup before the first team took over for the remaining rounds and in the Birmingham Charity and Walsall Cups for the first time.

In 1887-8 Albion's reserves carried off the Walsall Cup with wins over Aston Shakespeare, Wednesbury Old Athletic, Mitchell's St George and Walsall Swifts (4-1 in the Final). By the time the Birmingham and District League was formed in 1889 with the active support of Mr Joe Round, subsequently an Albion director, it was apparent that Albion's second string would be much better off playing in a regular league competition. Thus it was that Albion entered the League and for many years it was a useful proving ground for many of the young stars of the fututre. It also provided Albion with a large number of recruits, among them Tom Higgins (from Stourbridge) and Fred Morris (from Redditch). In 1921 the Albion reserve team left the Birmingham League to join the more competitive Central League.

Albion's first Championship win was not until 1901-02, thus illustrating the high standard in the Birmingham League in the earliest days of the competition. Albion finished eight points ahead of Stourbridge, the runners-up, and failed to score in only three of the 34 matches. In four consecutive games in December 1901 and January 1902, they collected 34 goals. All 17 home fixtures were won, 79 goals being scored and only five conceded. Four goals or more were recorded in 16 games, and in January 1902 Ruabon Druids were crushed 10-0 and Kidderminster Harriers 10-1. Championship medals went to John Chadburn, Platt Gollings, Oliver Taylor, Arthur Randle, Fred Buck, 'Ted' Smith, Andrew Smith, Billy Walker, Sam Edwards, William Poynton, Fred Hobson, Billy Harper, George Williams, Ben Appleby and Tom Jones.

In 1912-13 came a second Championship win by three points from the nearest challengers, Coventry City, and it was made possible by taking 19 points from the final ten fixtures. Albion had ten victories in which four or more goals were scored, including a 6-0 mauling of Worcester City and a 6-1 hammering of Kidderminster Harriers. The players who made over 16 appearances were Matt Wood, Amos Lloyd, Charles Deacy, Will Hackett, Jack Mann, Howard Gregory, Bill Jackson, Arthur Cook, Wallace Fletcher, James Varty and Fred Morris.

The third Championship success in 1919-20 coincided with the senior team winning the First Division Championship for the only time. The trainer of the reserve side was Sam Guest who looked after six Central League Championship-winning teams at The Hawthorns. Although they lost their opening match 5-1 at Hednesford on 30 August and showed indifferent early-season form, the Albion reserves remained unbeaten at home. The turning point came on 20 December when Coventry City, the League leaders, were beaten 5-0 at West Bromwich. Although Coventry revenged this upset by winning 5-1 when the two sides met a week later, Albion remained invincible at home and thoroughly deserved their third title win. Arthur Cook, George Ashmore, Tommy Newall (leading scorer with 27 goals), Roly James, Sam Hatton, Billy Adams, Tommy Magee, Fred Reed, Ernie Edwards, Matt Wood, Ben Hobbs and Albert Lea made most appearances but nearly 40 players appeared during the campaign including Billy Bassett's son, Norman, himself a right winger, who afterwards served Albion as a director.

FACTS AND FIGURES

Record victory: 13-2 v Oldbury Town (h) 9 January 1892.
Record defeat: 1-11 v Wolverhampton Wanderers (a) 26 March 1898.
Record away win: 6-0 v Kidderminster Harriers 23 September 1893.

Albion's next highest victory in the Birmingham League was a 12-2 defeat of Stafford Rangers on 9 February 1907 and the next heaviest defeat came at Bristol on 14 March 1899 when Eastville Rovers trounced Albion 10-0.

CENTRAL LEAGUE

ALBION entered the Central League in 1921, the competition having been formed in 1911. The immediate result was that the club's reserve players found themselves facing much stiffer opposition than they had encountered in the Birmingham and District League, and so it was hardly surprising that Albion finished in 14th position in 1921-2. But in the next five seasons Albion reserves won the Central League Championship on three occasions and a number of the players involved in these achievements progressed into the senior side.

Despite losing two of their first three games in 1922-3, Albion were Champions for the first time, thanks mainly to a tremendous run of 25 matches without defeat between 25 November 1922 and 28 April 1923, and an unbeaten home record which produced 61 goals in 21 games. Nine victories in which Albion collected four goals or over were recorded with centre-forward Bob Blood claiming three goals on six separate occasions. The largest victory of the campaign was a 10-0 savaging of Blackburn Rovers at The Hawthorns on 30 December 1922. Of 28 players used, 20 had already played or were to play in the Albion first team. The most regular players were Fred Reed (captain), Jonathan Blagden, Sammy Richardson, George Ashmore, Bob Blood, Harold Chamberlain, Harry Dutton, Arthur Perry, 'Tug' Wilson, Joe Carter, Tommy Glidden, Arthur Fitton and 'Ted' Rooke.

Fred Reed, captain in 1922-3.

Albion were Champions once more in 1923-4 but only because of a better goal average than their closest challengers, Huddersfield Town, who made a spirited late rally so that the issue remained in doubt until the last day. For over six months (from September until March) Albion led the Central League table and ultimately were worthy Champions. A week after clinching the Championship the reserves completed a 'double' by defeating Stoke 3-0 in the Final of the Staffordshire Cup. As many as ten, four-goal or over, victories were achieved, the largest of these being 6-4 over Bury and 6-1 v Birmingham. The stalwarts who appeared most regularly were Hubert Pearson, 'Tug' Wilson, Ivor Jones, Arthur Perry, Joe Carter, Billy Adams, Tommy Glidden, Harold Chamberlain, Bob Blood, Harry Dutton, Sammy Richardson, Arthur Fitton, George James, Fred Reed, 'Ted' Rooke and Horace Smith.

When the Albion reserves next carried off the Championship (in 1926-7) their seniors were being relegated to Division Two. Championship medals on this occasion were awarded to Tom Sproson, Joe Evans, Francis Corbett, Arthur Fitton, Jimmy Edwards, Len Darnell, Horace Smith, Bob Finch, Harry Dutton, Sammy Short, Sammy Richardson, George James, 'Tug' Wilson, Dick Baugh, Ernest Fryer and Ernest Pattison. By winning 3-0 on the very last day of the season, 7 May 1927, Albion topped the Central League for the first time, thus pipping Manchester United by one point and Sheffield United by two. Sammy Short emerged as the leading marksman with 27 goals including five against Bury at The Hawthorns on 11 September 1926. Albion scored over three goals in 11 matches including a 7-4 defeat of Derby County and six-goal drubbings of Burnley and Oldham Athletic but did not have everything their own way for Manchester United administered a 7-0 thrashing in October 1926 and Manchester City were 5-2 winners at The Hawthorns. On 5 March 1927 there was an 11-goal thriller at West Bromwich, Aston Villa coming out on top by 6-5.

The seasons from 1932-3 to 1934-5 were continually successful for the Albion second-teamers who carried off the Central League Championship three years in succession, a feat which was recognised by the award of a special commemorative shield. Aston Villa were the Baggies' chief rivals in 1932-3 but Albion pulled off a fine double over the old enemy by clinching the Championship at Villa Park (1-0) on 30 April 1933 and by defeating Villa 2-0 two days later at The Hawthorns in the Staffordshire Cup Final. In their first six fixtures Albion won only once, losing the opening game 4-1 at Everton, but a run of seven successive victories and 13 wins out of a sequence of 14 matches brought the season to a successful climax. Both Birmingham and Leeds United were humbled 7-1 at West Bromwich, and eight of Albion's wins were by four-goal scorelines or more. A record Central League attendance of 11,343, which was to last only a season, was created on 3 March 1932 at The Hawthorns when Albion played host to Sheffield United Reserves. The most frequent wearers of the navy blue and white stripes were Stan Horrocks, 'Ted' Crowe, Bob Finch, Hugh Foulkes, Wally Boyes, 'Bos' Trevis, Walter Robbins, Arthur Gale, Harry Raw, Jimmy Cookson, Jack Sankey, Tommy Magee, Jack Rix and Alf Ridyard. Cookson was the scorer of 29 of the 106 goals recorded.

▲ Albion's reserve team pictured in 1933 after winning the Central League title. They were to retain it twice before being presented with a commemorative shield to mark the achievement.

◀ Phil Griffiths, Welsh international right-winger.

221

A selection of the players who were so successful in 1932-3 were in regular action the following season, among them Foulkes, Gale, Raw, Ridyard, Trevis, Rix, Sankey, Crowe, Boyes and Robbins, but there were several newcomers including Phil Griffiths (a Welsh international winger who never played for Albion's first team), Lawrie Coen, Harry Jones, Tommy Green and Sid Swindon. Albion had a ding-dong battle with Aston Villa for the Championship with a crucial match taking place between the two clubs at The Hawthorns on 3 March 1934 before an amazing attendance of 22,372, some 6,000 more than Albion's first team attracted for the visit of Huddersfield Town the following week. The sides drew 2-2 but Albion eventually won the title by seven points from Villa in second place thanks to an unbeaten run of 20 matches (17 victories) from 6 January 1934 until the end of the season. Arthur Gale, a versatile forward, obtained 39 goals yet despite this he could not command a regular first-team place during this season. He scored five times in an eight-goal defeat of Sheffield United in October 1933; another substantial victory was an 8-0 thrashing of Newcastle United on 6 January 1934. Over three goals were netted on ten separate occasions.

◄ Bob Finch's Championship-winning medal of 1934.

▼ Albion skipper Bob Finch receiving the Central League Championship Trophy in 1935.

Despite being without their skipper, Bob Finch, for four months — he was absent through injury — the Albion reserves, under the guidance of the experienced Harry Raw, triumphed for the third season in a row in 1934-5, bringing the total of points earned during this period to a remarkable 184 out of a possible 252. Arthur Gale was in terrific scoring form with 43 goals in only 22 games and this time he did force his way into regular action at senior level. On two occasions he scored five times, against Bury (his former club) in an 8-1 success at Gigg Lane and v Burnley (h), Albion winning 7-1. Four goals or more were obtained in as many as 13 fixtures. Fifteen players recorded 15 or more appearances: Hugh Foulkes, Harry Raw, 'Ted' Crowe, Bob Finch, Stan Wood, Norman Whitehead, 'Bos' Trevis, Lawrie Coen, Arthur Gale, Tommy Green, Jack Rix, Alf Ridyard, Jack Screen, Harry Jones and Walter Robbins.

'Ted' Crowe, capable and solid goalkeeper of the 1930s.

'Bos' Trevis, a dominant centre-half of the 1930s.

Albion won the Central League Championship for the first time in 48 years by defeating Sheffield United 2-0 before a 4,150 crowd on 18 May 1983. With the Central League divided into two divisions, Albion played only 30 matches and remained unbeaten in the last ten. On 21 February 1983 the reserves drew 0-0 at Wolverhampton against the full Wolves Second Division side. The highest scoring victories were 5-0 v Stoke City (a) on 19 January 1983 and 5-2 v Bury (a) on 11 May 1983. Ebanks, Smith, Luke, Childs, Jones, Cowdrill and Lewis all made 20 appearances or over and Kent was the top goalscorer with ten. The team was captained by Barry Cowdrill.

At the end of the 1985-6 season Albion reserves suffered relegation from the First Division of the Central League, despite fielding many quality and established professionals during the course of the campaign. These included Garth Crooks, Imre Varadi, Ally Robertson and Tony Grealish. It was the first time they had suffered such a fate.

BIRMINGHAM & DISTRICT LEAGUE
Record 1892 - 1921

	P	W	D	L	F	A	Pts	Pos
1892-3	18	8	5	5	35	24	21	4th
1893-4	26	10	6	10	53	43	26	8th
1894-5	30	23	4	3	100	49	50	2nd
1895-6	30	18	5	7	100	45	41	4th
1896-7	30	11	4	15	60	68	26	11th
1897-8	30	11	1	18	56	88	23	12th
1898-9	34	14	5	15	65	81	33	8th
1899-1900	30	14	4	12	69	57	32	5th
1900-01	34	17	5	12	83	61	39	5th
1901-02	34	26	2	6	126	32	54	1st
1902-03	34	19	7	8	68	37	45	3rd
1903-04	34	15	7	12	74	52	37	6th
1904-05	34	11	5	18	47	79	27	15th
1905-06	34	21	6	7	106	51	48	3rd
1906-07	34	18	6	10	79	52	42	4th
1907-08	34	19	5	10	86	54	43	3rd
1908-09	34	18	6	10	85	43	42	4th
1909-10	34	16	5	13	75	65	37	8th
1910-11	34	13	8	13	54	58	34	9th
1911-12	34	17	6	11	75	55	40	5th
1912-13	34	21	5	8	86	32	47	1st
1913-14	34	11	11	12	67	46	33	11th
1914-15	34	23	5	6	88	39	51	2nd
1919-20	34	18	9	7	61	45	45	1st
1920-1	34	15	7	12	46	41	37	7th

Note: Albion's first season in the Birmingham and District League was that of 1889-90 when the competition was apparently unfinished. This was also the case in the following two seasons and records of the matches played were not kept by Albion.

George Williams, a Welsh international and a key figure in Albion's Birmingham and District League side of 1901-02.

CENTRAL LEAGUE
Record 1921 - 1987

	P	W	D	L	F	A	Pts	Pos		P	W	D	L	F	A	Pts	Pos
1921-2	42	17	8	17	54	52	42	14th	1957-8	42	14	11	17	72	80	39	12th
1922-3	42	26	11	5	95	33	63	1st	1958-9	42	9	10	23	71	102	28	21st
1923-4	42	25	12	5	103	46	62	1st	1959-60	42	18	6	18	83	68	42	12th
1924-5	42	25	8	9	91	35	58	3rd	1960-1	42	20	9	13	90	69	49	9th
1925-6	42	18	7	17	87	74	43	10th	1961-2	42	18	8	16	68	64	44	9th
1926-7	42	27	5	10	114	75	59	1st	1962-3	42	17	8	17	91	82	42	12th
1927-8	42	19	6	17	98	94	44	10th	1963-4	42	24	8	10	99	49	56	2nd
1928-9	42	13	9	20	82	101	35	20th	1964-5	42	22	9	11	104	57	53	5th
1929-30	42	24	8	10	128	64	56	3rd	1965-6	42	21	11	10	92	63	53	5th
1930-1	42	15	6	21	74	103	36	17th	1966-7	42	21	8	13	87	64	50	6th
1931-2	42	21	5	16	113	100	47	10th	1967-8	42	23	9	10	93	51	55	3rd
1932-3	42	26	6	10	106	61	58	1st	1968-9	42	20	12	10	62	38	52	3rd
1933-4	42	28	8	6	101	45	64	1st	1969-70	42	24	11	7	80	38	59	2nd
1934-5	42	28	6	8	121	62	62	1st	1970-1	42	15	13	14	65	59	43	10th
1935-6	42	21	10	11	108	73	52	4th	1971-2	42	18	18	6	70	43	54	3rd
1936-7	42	18	12	12	86	63	48	6th	1972-3	42	20	11	11	72	51	51	5th
1937-8	42	11	15	16	69	89	37	20th	1973-4	42	18	11	13	62	48	47	8th
1938-9	42	21	9	12	84	63	51	3rd	1974-5	42	20	15	7	58	36	55	3rd
1945-6	40	22	6	12	98	67	50	5th	1975-6	42	25	13	4	83	35	63	2nd
1946-7	42	18	5	19	86	92	41	14th	1976-7	42	15	14	13	52	49	44	8th
1947-8	42	13	6	23	66	98	32	21st	1977-8	42	18	12	12	56	46	48	6th
1948-9	42	19	8	15	71	61	46	9th	1978-9	42	18	12	12	80	51	48	6th
1949-50	42	20	7	15	58	42	47	8th	1979-80	42	18	15	9	73	49	51	5th
1950-1	42	14	14	14	58	66	42	13th	1980-1	42	22	14	6	68	31	58	2nd
1951-2	42	19	3	20	60	66	41	10th	1981-2	42	17	13	12	57	44	47	7th
1952-3	42	11	8	23	49	71	30	21st	1982-3	30	19	6	5	53	18	44	1st
1953-4	42	16	4	22	59	57	36	18th	1983-4	30	14	7	9	46	35	49	6th
1954-5	42	17	9	16	79	76	43	10th	1984-5	34	11	4	19	35	53	37	13th
1955-6	42	18	10	14	86	75	46	6th	1985-6	34	9	10	15	41	65	37	16th
1956-7	42	13	10	19	76	84	36	15th	1986-7	32	16	5	11	57	45	53	5th

FACTS AND FIGURES

First Central League match: Manchester United 1, Albion 0, 27 August 1921. Albion team: Pearson; Littlewood, Cook, Newall, Reed, Hatton, Magee, Blagden, Savage, Bentley, Gregory.

Record victory: 12-2 v Derby County (h) 2 November 1929.

Record defeat: 2-10 v Huddersfield Town (a) 20 February 1932.

Record away win: 9-1 v Burnley 22 March 1930.

Most goals in a match: Seven by Jimmy Cookson v Liverpool (10-1) 14 November 1931.

Most goals in a season: 50 in 1929-30 by WG Richardson.

Record Central League attendance: 22,372 v Aston Villa (h) 3 March 1934.

Hugh Foulkes, key member of the Central League side during the 1930s.

Albion have scored over 100 goals in the Central League on nine separate occasions, the last time being in 1964-5. The highest total of goals scored in any one season amounted to 128 in 1929-30, 12 of them coming in the record win over Derby County.

On 25 February 1956, Albion's goalkeeper, Fred Brown, was ordered off in a Central League fixture at Wolverhampton. Another goalkeeper, Jim Sanders, had a quite different experience when playing for Albion Reserves v Derby County Reserves on 7 December 1946. He was forced to go on the wing after injuring a hand but this did not prevent him from scoring direct from a corner kick.

The record number of appearances in the Central League was made by winger Arthur Fitton who accumulated 261 between 1922 and 1932. Bob Finch (231), Hugh Foulkes (229), Graham Williams (228), Roger Minton (207+1) and Bobby Cram (206) have all made over 200 appearances.

The most players used in one season of Central League football is 59 in 1945-6 when only 40 matches were contested instead of the usual 42.

Those players who have not missed a single match in a season are few and far between but include goalkeepers 'Ted' Crowe (1932-3), Norman Heath (1949-50), Bob Ward (1973-4) and Mark Grew (1980-1), defenders Terry Simpson (1965-6) and David Arthur (1979-80).

Albion's top post-war Central League victory came on New Year's Day, 1949 when Stoke City were overcome by 9-0 (h). The worst defeat during this time came at Wolverhampton on 1 May 1963 (3-8). Other large wins achieved by Albion include the folowing: 8-1 v Sheffield United (h) 1959-60; 8-1 v Chesterfield and Blackburn Rovers (h) 1960-1; 8-0 v Manchester City and Barnsley (a) 1963-4; 8-3 v Blackburn Rovers (a) 1963-4; 8-0 v Bury (h) 1964-5.

Albion's 1,000th Central League victory came on 30 April 1979 at Preston (3-1).

At the commencement of the 1939-40 season Albion's reserves played in three Central League fixtures, v Manchester United (h) (0-2), Birmingham (h) (0-2) and Sheffield United (a) (1-1), before the competition was abandoned because of the outbreak of war.

Between 17 September 1932 and 11 September 1935, Albion reserves did not lose a single Central League match at The Hawthorns.

Among the players who have scored 30 goals or more in a Central League season were Arthur Gale (39) in 1933-4 and 41 in 1934-5, Jimmy Cookson (43) in 1931-2, WG Richardson (50) in 1929-30, Stan Davies (30) in 1924-5 and Bob Blood (32) in 1923-4. Two players, Arthur Gale (146) and Sammy Short (103), have scored over a century of Central League goals, their nearest challengers being Jimmy Cookson (95), George James (87), 'WG' Richardson (83), Bob Blood (73), Brian Whitehouse (73) and 'Tug' Wilson (71).

TERRY SIMPSON

DAVID ARTHUR

ARTHUR GALE

WG RICHARDSON

Albion's Record Against Other League Clubs

Albion have played a total of 76 clubs in League competition since 1888. Some clubs have modified their names over the years (eg Small Heath to Birmingham to Birmingham City, Clapton Orient to Leyton Orient to Orient). In all cases the last name used by each club covers all games under previous appellations. Since season 1981-2 three points have been awarded for a win.

	HOME P W D L F A Pts	AWAY P W D L F A Pts	TOTAL P W D L F A Pts
Accrington	5 4 1 0 18 5 9	5 0 1 4 7 12 1	10 4 2 4 25 17 10
Arsenal	52 21 12 19 76 65 54	52 9 13 30 63 112 32	104 30 25 49 139 177 86
Aston Villa	61 28 15 18 100 83 74	61 15 7 39 74 118 37	122 43 22 57 174 201 111
Barnsley	16 9 4 3 44 27 22	16 6 5 5 21 20 17	32 15 9 8 65 47 39
Birmingham C	42 19 14 9 62 41 55	42 17 12 13 57 48 48	84 36 26 22 119 89 103
Blackburn R	44 23 12 9 89 55 58	44 9 7 28 47 98 26	88 32 19 37 136 153 84
Blackpool	36 20 6 10 83 45 46	36 12 6 18 42 58 30	72 32 12 28 125 103 76
Bolton W	53 24 16 13 100 74 64	53 13 14 26 58 102 40	106 37 30 39 158 176 104
Bradford C	14 9 4 1 32 13 22	14 3 5 6 14 28 12	28 12 9 7 46 41 34
Bradford	13 8 2 3 30 9 18	13 4 3 6 27 30 11	26 12 5 9 57 39 29
Brentford	5 5 0 0 11 5 10	5 1 2 2 5 5 4	10 6 2 2 16 10 14
Brighton & HA	5 2 3 0 9 2 8	5 1 3 1 4 5 5	10 3 6 1 13 7 13
Bristol C	14 6 6 2 21 12 18	14 5 3 6 16 17 13	28 11 9 8 37 29 31
Bristol R	2 1 1 0 5 2 3	2 0 1 1 2 3 1	4 1 2 1 7 5 4
Burnley	54 27 11 16 110 65 65	54 18 11 25 68 98 47	108 45 22 41 178 163 112
Burton U	4 4 0 0 14 2 8	4 2 1 1 11 5 5	8 6 1 1 25 7 13
Bury	18 10 3 5 40 20 23	18 3 3 12 21 47 9	36 13 6 17 61 67 32
Cardiff C	19 11 3 5 40 23 25	19 7 4 8 32 32 18	38 18 7 13 72 55 43
Carlisle U	2 1 1 0 4 1 3	2 1 1 0 2 1 3	4 2 2 0 6 2 6
Charlton A	13 5 6 2 23 17 16	13 5 3 5 24 25 13	26 10 9 7 47 42 29
Chelsea	49 21 13 15 87 53 55	49 14 13 22 71 97 41	98 35 26 37 158 150 96
Chesterfield	10 7 2 1 23 8 16	10 3 4 3 14 10 10	20 10 6 4 37 18 26
Coventry C	20 10 7 3 41 18 29	20 7 4 9 25 30 21	40 17 11 12 76 48 50
Crystal P	8 4 2 2 10 9 10	8 4 2 2 11 8 10	16 8 4 4 21 19 20
Darwen	2 1 1 0 14 2 3	2 0 1 1 2 3 1	4 1 2 1 16 5 4
Derby C	44 24 12 8 78 44 61	44 6 12 26 54 101 24	88 30 24 34 132 145 85
Doncaster R	3 1 1 1 9 6 3	3 1 0 2 2 4 2	6 2 1 3 11 10 5
Everton	66 35 17 14 135 79 88	66 14 14 38 84 147 42	132 49 31 52 219 226 130
Fulham	24 16 3 5 64 29 35	24 11 4 9 25 30 26	48 27 7 14 89 59 61
Gainsborough T	8 7 0 1 29 5 14	8 2 2 4 12 16 6	16 9 2 5 41 21 20
Glossop	9 5 3 1 20 7 13	9 4 2 3 15 11 10	18 9 5 4 35 18 23
Grimsby T	16 12 1 3 50 24 25	16 4 3 9 26 33 11	32 16 4 12 76 57 36
Huddersfield T	24 13 5 6 44 30 32	24 4 7 13 26 45 15	48 17 12 19 70 75 47
Hull C	13 6 4 3 23 13 16	13 1 4 8 12 29 6	26 7 8 11 35 42 22
Ipswich T	19 9 3 7 38 26 22	19 5 4 10 18 42 15	38 14 7 17 56 68 37
Leeds C	6 6 0 0 15 3 12	6 2 1 3 7 8 5	12 8 1 3 22 11 17
Leeds U	32 16 5 11 53 37 39	32 8 8 16 34 56 24	64 24 13 27 87 93 63
Leicester C	38 24 7 7 86 40 57	38 13 9 16 56 68 35	76 37 16 23 142 108 92

	HOME P W D L F A Pts	AWAY P W D L F A Pts	TOTAL P W D L F A Pts
Lincoln C	8 6 2 0 23 6 14	8 6 0 2 15 5 12	16 12 2 2 38 11 26
Liverpool	54 19 16 19 79 63 54	54 9 17 28 48 94 35	108 28 33 47 127 157 89
Luton T	15 12 1 2 35 9 28	15 5 4 6 13 20 15	30 17 5 8 48 29 43
Manchester C	53 28 15 10 103 56 71	53 15 6 32 82 128 36	106 43 21 42 185 184 107
Manchester U	50 26 11 13 98 72 65	50 11 13 26 65 102 35	100 37 24 39 163 174 100
Middlesbrough	32 20 6 6 59 31 47	32 5 8 19 24 53 18	64 25 14 25 83 84 65
Millwall	9 4 3 2 16 11 11	9 3 3 3 14 12 10	18 7 6 5 30 23 21
Newcastle U	47 24 14 9 98 54 63	47 14 10 23 68 98 38	94 38 24 32 166 152 101
Newport C	1 0 1 0 2 2 1	1 1 0 0 7 2 2	2 1 1 0 9 4 3
Northampton T	1 0 1 0 1 1 1	1 1 0 0 4 3 2	2 1 1 0 5 4 3
Norwich C	11 5 4 2 15 8 15	11 3 3 5 14 16 10	22 8 7 7 29 24 25
Nottingham F	50 27 9 14 107 77 66	50 19 11 20 77 82 50	100 46 20 34 184 159 116
Notts C	27 15 8 4 66 37 39	27 6 7 14 26 47 20	54 21 15 18 92 84 59
Oldham A	18 7 7 4 18 14 22	18 3 5 10 14 29 11	36 10 12 14 32 43 33
Orient	12 10 2 0 28 5 22	12 5 5 2 15 9 15	24 15 7 2 43 14 37
Oxford U	4 3 1 0 7 1 7	4 1 2 1 4 4 4	8 4 3 1 11 5 11
Plymouth A	7 3 2 2 12 10 8	7 1 0 6 7 15 2	14 4 2 8 19 25 10
Portsmouth	21 17 0 4 56 20 35	21 9 6 6 35 37 24	42 26 6 10 91 57 59
Port Vale	7 5 1 1 17 5 11	7 2 0 5 9 20 4	14 7 1 6 26 25 15
Preston NE	41 17 11 13 65 56 45	41 12 11 18 50 74 35	82 29 22 31 115 130 80
Queen's Park R	8 3 3 2 10 7 9	8 3 1 4 10 8 7	16 6 4 6 20 15 16
Reading	5 4 0 1 13 5 8	5 2 2 1 13 9 6	10 6 2 2 26 14 14
Sheffield U	39 19 8 12 66 44 47	39 8 13 18 35 57 29	78 27 21 30 101 101 76
Sheffield W	47 15 16 16 77 69 46	47 12 6 29 69 103 30	94 27 22 45 146 172 76
Shrewsbury T	1 0 0 1 1 2 0	1 0 0 1 0 1 0	2 0 0 2 1 3 0
Southampton	25 16 4 5 38 21 38	25 2 10 13 25 44 14	50 18 14 18 63 65 52
South Shields	1 1 0 0 3 0 2	1 1 0 0 3 2 2	2 2 0 0 6 2 4
Stockport C	7 5 1 1 15 5 11	7 5 2 0 10 3 12	14 10 3 1 25 8 23
Stoke C	47 26 7 14 97 56 62	47 9 16 22 50 87 35	94 35 23 36 147 143 97
Sunderland	57 31 13 13 112 81 78	57 8 16 33 59 130 34	114 39 29 46 171 211 112
Swansea C	8 5 3 0 25 10 14	8 1 1 6 11 21 3	16 6 4 6 36 31 17
Swindon T	1 1 0 0 2 0 2	1 0 0 1 0 1 0	2 1 0 1 2 1 2
Tottenham H	53 32 8 13 114 68 73	53 14 14 25 56 91 45	106 46 22 38 170 159 118
Tranmere R	1 1 0 0 2 0 2	1 0 0 1 3 3 0	2 1 0 1 3 3 2
Watford	4 3 0 1 8 5 9	4 1 0 3 4 11 3	8 4 0 4 12 16 12
West Ham U	31 20 4 7 64 32 46	31 9 4 18 41 66 24	62 29 8 25 105 98 70
Wolves	58 26 17 15 105 81 70	58 16 13 29 83 114 46	116 42 30 44 188 195 116
York C	2 1 1 0 4 2 3	2 2 0 0 4 1 4	4 3 1 0 8 3 7

Albion's Football League Record 1888-9 to 1986-7 inclusive

	Pos	P	W	D	L	F	A	Pts
	Division One							
1888-9	6th	22	10	2	10	40	46	22
1889-90	5th	22	11	3	8	47	50	25
1890-91	12th	22	5	2	15	34	57	12
1891-2	12th	26	6	6	14	51	58	18
1892-3	8th	30	12	5	13	58	69	29
1893-4	8th	30	14	4	12	66	59	32
1894-5	13th	30	10	4	16	51	66	24
1895-6	16th	30	6	7	17	30	59	19
1896-7	12th	30	10	6	14	33	56	26
1897-8	7th	30	11	10	9	44	45	32
1898-9	14th	34	12	6	16	42	57	30
1899-1900	13th	34	11	8	15	43	51	30
1900-01	18th	34	7	8	19	35	62	22
	Division Two							
1901-02	1st	34	25	5	4	82	29	55
	Division One							
1902-03	7th	34	16	4	14	54	53	36
1903-04	18th	34	7	10	17	36	60	24
	Division Two							
1904-05	10th	34	13	4	17	56	48	30
1905-06	4th	38	22	8	8	79	36	52
1906-07	4th	38	21	5	12	83	45	47
1907-08	5th	38	19	9	10	61	39	47
1908-09	3rd	38	19	13	6	56	27	51
1909-10	11th	38	16	5	17	58	56	37
1910-11	1st	38	22	9	7	67	41	53
	Division One							
1911-12	9th	38	15	9	14	43	47	39
1912-13	10th	38	13	12	13	57	50	38
1913-14	5th	38	15	13	10	46	42	43
1914-15	11th	38	15	10	13	49	43	40
	Competition abandoned (1915-19) during World War One							
1919-20	1st	42	28	4	10	104	47	60
1920-21	14th	42	13	14	15	54	58	40
1921-2	13th	42	15	10	17	51	63	40
1922-3	7th	42	17	11	14	58	49	45
1923-4	16th	42	12	14	16	51	62	38
1924-5	2nd	42	23	9	58	34	56	
1925-6	13th	42	16	8	18	79	78	40
1926-7	22nd	42	11	8	23	65	86	30
	Division Two							
1927-8	8th	42	17	12	13	90	70	46
1928-9	7th	42	19	8	15	80	79	46
1929-30	6th	42	21	5	16	105	73	47
1930-31	2nd	42	22	10	10	83	49	54
	Division One							
1931-2	6th	42	20	6	16	77	55	46
1932-3	4th	42	20	9	13	83	70	49
1933-4	7th	42	17	10	15	78	70	44
1934-5	9th	42	17	10	15	83	83	44
1935-6	18th	42	16	6	20	89	88	38
1936-7	16th	42	16	6	20	77	98	38
1937-8	22nd	42	14	8	20	74	91	36
	Division Two							
1938-9	10th	42	18	9	15	89	72	45
	Competition abandoned (1939-46) during World War Two							
1946-7	7th	42	20	8	14	88	75	48
1947-8	7th	42	18	9	15	63	58	45
1948-9	2nd	42	24	8	10	69	39	56
	Division One							
1949-50	14th	42	14	12	16	47	53	40
1950-51	16th	42	13	11	18	53	61	37
1951-52	13th	42	14	13	15	74	77	41
1952-53	4th	42	21	8	13	66	60	50
1953-54	2nd	42	22	9	11	86	63	53
1954-55	17th	42	16	8	18	76	96	40
1955-56	13th	42	18	5	19	58	70	41
1956-57	11th	42	14	14	14	59	61	42
1957-58	4th	42	18	14	10	92	70	50
1958-59	5th	42	18	13	11	88	68	49
1959-60	4th	42	19	11	12	83	57	49
1960-61	10th	42	18	5	19	67	71	41
1961-62	9th	42	15	13	14	83	67	43
1962-63	14th	42	16	7	19	71	79	39
1963-64	10th	42	16	11	15	70	61	43
1964-65	14th	42	13	13	16	70	65	39
1965-66	6th	42	19	12	11	91	69	50
1966-7	13th	42	16	7	19	77	73	39
1967-68	8th	42	17	12	13	75	62	46
1968-69	10th	42	16	11	15	64	67	43
1969-70	16th	42	14	9	19	58	66	37
1970-71	17th	42	10	15	17	58	75	35
1971-72	16th	42	12	11	19	42	54	35
1972-73	22nd	42	9	10	23	38	62	28
	Division Two							
1973-74	8th	42	14	16	12	48	45	44
1974-75	6th	42	18	9	15	54	42	45
1975-76	3rd	42	20	13	9	50	33	53
	Division One							
1976-77	7th	42	16	13	13	62	56	45
1977-78	6th	42	18	14	10	62	53	50
1978-79	3rd	42	24	11	7	72	35	59
1979-80	10th	42	11	19	12	54	50	41
1980-81	4th	42	20	12	10	60	42	52
1981-82	17th	42	11	11	20	46	57	44
1982-83	11th	42	15	12	15	51	49	57
1983-84	17th	42	14	9	19	48	62	51
1984-85	12th	42	16	7	19	58	62	55
1985-86	22nd	42	4	12	26	35	89	24
	Division Two							
1986-87	15th	42	13	12	17	51	49	51

225

Youth Football

Development

AS EARLY AS 1886-7, Albion fielded a third team but it was not until after World War Two that real strides were made in the development of youth football.

In 1950-1 the maximum weekly wage was £12 and with attendances booming Albion could afford to have over 40 professional players on their books, although not all of them were available because of National Service. Albion turned out seven teams in those days, in Division One, Central League, Midland Midweek League, Birmingham Combination, Walsall Senior League, Birmingham and West Midland Alliance and Handsworth League. In addition, Albion's nursery club, Erdington Albion, participated in the Birmingham Youth Committee.

During the 1950s the Albion Youth team entered the FA Youth Cup for the first time — they eventually won it in 1976 — and have had a very successful record in the Amsterdam Youth International Tournament. Albion won the Tournament in 1956 (beating Everton 4-2); in 1957 (defeating Racing Club de Paris 2-0) and in 1960 (beating Nottingham Forest 2-1). They were the losing Finalists in 1958 (Ajax winning 1-0).

In 1960 the Midland Intermediate League was formed with Albion secretary, 'Eph' Smith, as the first honorary secretary. By the start of the 1960-1 season, however, Albion paraded only four teams — in Division One, Central League, Warwickshire Combination and Midland Intermediate League — and by 1964 the club had withdrawn from the Combination. The reduction of Albion's playing strength and consequently their youth football activities had been brought about by the abolition of the maximum wage in 1961 which meant that football clubs could no longer afford such a large pay-roll.

Albion's Youth team continued to play overseas tournaments as the 1970s approached — they lost in the Final of the Bremen International Tournament in 1969, 3-1 to Ajax — but in 1972-3 the club's youth policy was completely reorganised with trainer Albert McPherson and scout Roy Horobin (later to become the club's first youth development officer) taking an increasing interest in affairs. The foreign trips continued — to Yugoslavia in 1972, 1974, 1975 and 1977, (Albion won the tournament there in 1974) — under the expert eye of former player and then director Cliff Edwards.

In 1972-3 Albion also reached the quarter-final stage of the Southern Junior Floodlit Cup.

Their latest successes at youth level were the winning of the Baden Youth International Tournament in West Germany in 1979, the Duisburg International Tournament in 1981, and the Phorzheim Youth Tournament in 1982.

Honours

Apart from winning the aforementioned FA Youth Cup Final and International Youth Tournaments, Albion have acquired several other honours in youth football as follows:

Midland Midweek League Champions 1937-8, 1938-9
Midland Intermediate League Champions 1971-2, 1973-4, 1976-7. Runners-up 1968-9

Midland Intermediate League Cup Winners 1969-7, 1973-4. Runners-up 1971-2

Midland Youth League Champions 1977-8, 1981-2

Midland Youth League Cup Finalists 1981-2

Youth International Honours

Players who have represented their country at youth team level while associated with Albion:

England
I.Benjamin (1979), R.J.Bradley (1955), A.(Tony) Brown (1964), P.Bunch (1956), D.G.Burnside (1956, 1957), L.Cantello (1970), G.Childs (1981, 1982), B.Cooke (1955, 1956), J.L.Crosby (1959), B.Donaghy (1973, 1974), C.Drury (1955), M.Forsyth (1983, 1984), P.Frain (1982), M.Gibson (1956), L.J.Hughes (1970), A.Jones (1961), G.A.Jones (1947), M.Lewis (1982), A.R.Merrick (1968), D.J.Monaghan (1976, 1977), B.Robson (1975), J.Rumjahn (1974), M.E.Setters (1956), D.J.Statham (1976, 1977), K.Summerfield (1976, 1977), J.Trewick (1975), A.Wileman (1957, 1958).

Scotland
R.A.Hartford (1968, 1969), J.A.Holton (1969), M.McCartney (1973), S.McLaren (1971), H.Reed (1968), A.Robertson (1968, 1970).

Wales
B.W.Hughes (1976), M.Trenter (1976).

Northern Ireland
D.Patterson (1987)

Republic of Ireland
J.Anderson (1977), R.C.Treacy (1964).

Schoolboy International Honours
The following players, who were all schoolboy internationalists, subsequently appeared in League Football for Albion:

England
M.Bennett, S.Butler, L.Cantello, H.Chambers, F.Cresswell, J.Evans, T.Glidden, L.Hughes, G.McVitie, J.Osborne, C.Suggett, J.Talbut, J.Trewick, W.Williams.

Scotland
C.Crawford, K.Foggo, R.Hope, A.Robertson.

Wales
M.Lee, J.Murphy, W.Tudor.

Northern Ireland
W.Lunn.

Republic of Ireland
J.Giles, R.Treacy.

Another schools internationalist, Fred Horne (England), did not play for Albion's first team, but became assistant-secretary of the club in 1959.

Junior Internationals
The Birmingham County FA and the Scottish Junior FA met annually between 1894 and 1939 in the 'junior' international match which preceded the annual senior England-Scotland fixture.

The England side was drawn from players associated with Midlands clubs and in later years international caps were awarded. England played three junior internationals at The Hawthorns and were victors each time — 1908 (4-0), 1925 (4-1) and 1935 (3-1).

Among the better-known Albion players who were selected for junior honours were Jesse Pennington (1903), Tommy Broad (1906), Jack Mann (1913), Arthur Perry (1923), Joe Evans (1925), Sammy Short (1926), Len Darnell (1927), Jack Rix (1928), Ted Crowe (1931), Ike Clarke (1937), Geoffrey Spencer (1937), Cyril Davies (1938), Harry Kinsell (1939) and Stan Butler (1939).

A few more Albion stars were also honoured with junior caps before they signed for The Hawthorns club, including Billy Garraty, Billy Lee, Billy Harper, Arthur Randle, George Harris, Hubert and Harold Pearson, Frank Waterhouse, Joe Smith, Billy Wollaston, Claude Jephcott, Fred Morris, Bert Trentham and Sammy Heaselgrave.

Apprentice Footballers

The apprentice scheme was initiated in 1960 and a number of outstanding Albion players have emerged from it including Len Cantello, Tony Brown, Rick Sheppard, Asa Hartford, Dick Krzywicki, Derek Statham, John Trewick and Bryan Robson.

A player must be 17 years of age before he can be registered as a professional with any club under the jurisdiction of the FA, but youths between the ages of 15 and 17 may be registered as apprentices, and they have until their 18th birthday to decide whether or not they want to join the full-time professional ranks if invited to do so by their club.

Albion have been quite successful with the scheme, although there have been exceptions. In the close season of 1974, 11 new apprentices were engaged but only one of them (Wayne Hughes) played for Albion in the Football League, although Steve Lynex subsequently made the grade with Shamrock Rovers, Birmingham City and Leicester City.

The first Albion apprentice professional to play in the first team while still a teenager was outside-right Dick Krzywicki who made his League debut at Fulham on 19 December 1964.

Youth Training Scheme

The YTS was introduced by the Government during the early 1980s and one lad who has emerged from it is utility player Carlton Palmer.

CARLTON PALMER

Youth Team Football

FA Youth Cup
Albion have been playing in the FA Youth Cup annually since 1952-3, and up to the end of season 1986-7 their full record in the competition was:

	P	W	D	L	F	A
Home	63	35	17	11	149	71
Away	64	29	9	26	124	105
TOTAL	127	64	26	37	273	176

Albion Youth Group, 1968-9. Back (left to right): Jimmy Dunn (coach), Hogg, Minton, Bell, Hughes, Nisbet, Holton, Robertson, Woolgar, Brown. Front: Findlater, Butler, Hartford, Morton, Cantello, MacLean, Collard.

Albion's first FA Youth Cup tie was against Brush Sports (Loughborough), away, on 4 October 1952. Albion won 10-1 — their best scoreline in the competition to date.

Albion's heaviest defeat is 6-0, suffered against Wolverhampton Wanderers (home) on 15 October 1955, and at Sunderland in the second leg of the 1969 Final at Roker Park on 3 May.

Albion have so far appeared in three FA Youth Cup Finals —1955, 1969 and 1976 — winning the last one.

Albion were beaten in the semi-finals of the competition in 1953-4 (by Manchester United), 1973-4 (by Huddersfield Town) and 1977-8 (by Crystal Palace).

Albion did not lose a home FA Youth Cup tie between 1974 and 1980 — a total of 19 games.

Two players have scored six goals for Albion in an FA Youth Cup tie: Richard 'Dick' McCartney, against Aston Villa (away) in 1954-5; and Ray Wilson, against Northampton Town (home) in 1964-5.

Two Albion players — Asa Hartford and Jim Holton — were sent-off against Sunderland in the second leg of the 1969 Final at Roker Park. In addition, Lyndon Hughes was booked by referee Tommy Dawes.

In 1963-4 Albion beat Coventry City 6-4 in a magnificent first-round tie at Highfield Road, and a season later Albion and Birmingham City drew 4-4 in a thrilling second-round encounter at The Hawthorns.

Albion were eliminated from the 1984-5 FA Youth Cup by non-Leaguers Hednesford Town, who won 2-1 in a replay at The Hawthorns after a goalless draw at Hednesford.

Albion's heaviest home FA Youth Cup defeat is 6-3, suffered against Leicester City in season 1985-6.

Alan Merrick, England Youth International, 1968.

227

FA Youth Cup Results

*Denotes after extra-time

1952-3
Round 1   Brush Sports (a) 10-1
Round 2   Stoke City (h) 7-0
Round 3   Wolverhampton Wanderers (a) 0-2

1953-4
Round 2   Chesterfield (a) 1-0
Round 3   Boldmere St Micheal's (h)7-2
Round 4   Sunderland (a) 1-0
Round 5   Leeds United* (h) 3-1
Semi-final   Manchester United (h) 1-3
Semi-final   Manchester United (a) 0-4

1954-5
Round 1   Hereford United (h) 2-1
Round 2   Aston Villa (a) 7-0
Round 3   Wolverhampton Wanderers (h) 4-1
Round 4   Vauxhall Motors (h) 6-1
Round 5   Bolton Wanderers (h) 3-1
Semi-final   Stoke City (h) 2-0
Semi-final   Stoke City (a) 1-0
Final   Manchester United (a) 1-4
Final   Manchester United (h) 0-3

1955-6
Round 1   Wolverhampton Wanderers (h) 0-6

1956-7
Round 1   Kidderminster Harriers (h) 5-0
Round 2   Leicester City (h) 8-1
Round 3   Sheffield United (a) 0-2

1957-8
Round 1   Wolverhampton Wanderers (h) 2-2
Replay   Wolverhampton Wanderers (a) 1-6

1958-9
Round 1   Burton Albion (a) 5-2
Round 2   Peterborough United (a) 8-1
Round 3   Wolverhampton Wanderers (a) 1-1
Replay   Wolverhampton Wanderers (h) 2-4

1959-60
Round 1   Gloucester City (h) 8-0
Round 2   Stoke City (a) 0-1

1960-61
Round 1   Shrewsbury Town (h) 5-1
Round 2   Coventry City (h) 3-3
Replay   Coventry City (a) 1-3

1961-2
Prelim Rd   Heanor Town (a) 7-1
Round 1   Peterborough United (a) 6-0
Round 2   Stoke City (a) 2-2
Replay   Stoke City (h) 1-2

1962-3
Round 1   Walsall (h) 0-3

1963-4
Round 1   Coventry City (a) 6-4
Round 2   Aston Villa (a) 0-2

1964-5
Round 1   Northampton Town (h) 7-1
Round 2   Birmingham City (h) 4-4
Replay   Birmingham City (a) 3-2
Round 3   Wolverhampton Wanderers (h) 1-1
Replay   Wolverhampton Wanderers (a) 0-2

1965-6
Round 2   Nottingham Forest (h) 0-0
Replay   Nottingham Forest (a) 1-2

1966-7
Round 1   Walsall (a) 4-4
Replay   Walsall (h) 1-1
2nd Replay   Walsall (h) 1-0
Round 2   Birmingham City (a) 0-2

1967-8
Round 1   Aston Villa (a) 2-1
Round 2   Nottingham Forest (a) 2-1
Round 3   Stoke City (a) 1-4

1968-9
Round 2   Aston Villa (a) 4-0
Round 3   Stoke City (h) 2-0
Round 4   Coventry City (a) 3-0
Round 5   Chelsea (a) 2-1
Semi-final   Manchester United (h) 3-2
Semi-final   Manchester United (a) 2-1
Final   Sunderland (h) 3-0
Final   Sunderland (a) 0-6

1969-70
Round 2   Derby County (h) 3-0
Round 3   Nottingham Forest (a) 0-1

1970-71
Round 2   Stoke City (h) 3-0
Round 3   Birmingham City (h) 2-2
Replay   Birmingham City (a) 1-1
2nd Replay   Birmingham City (a) 0-3

1971-2
Round 2   Mansfield Town (h) 2-0
Round 3   Aston Villa (a) 2-3

1972-3
Round 2   Derby County (a) 1-2

1973-4
Round 2   Aston Villa (h) 1-0
Round 3   Queen's Park Rangers (a) 2-0
Round 4   Stoke City (h) 5-0
Round 5   Sheffield United (h) 1-0
Semi-final   Huddersfield Town (h) 0-1
Semi-final   Huddersfield Town (a) 1-1

1974-5
Round 2   Leicester City (a) 1-0
Round 3   Kettering Town (h) 3-1
Round 4   Arsenal (a) 1-3

1975-6
Round 2   Coventry City (h) 3-0
Round 3   Charlton Athletic (h) 3-1
Round 4   Ipswich Town (h) 1-1
Replay   Ipswich Town (a) 2-1
Round 5   Manchester United (h) 2-2
Replay   Manchester United (a) 4-1
Semi-final   Crystal Palace (h) 3-2
Semi-final   Crystal Palace (a) 2-0
Final   Wolverhampton Wanderers (a) 2-0
Final   Wolverhampton Wanderers (h) 3-0

1976-7
Round 2   Aston Villa (h) 1-1
Replay   Aston Villa (a) 3-1
Round 3   Swindon Town (a) 4-0
Round 4   Wolverhampton Wanderers (h) 4-0
Round 5   Crystal Palace (a) 0-3

1977-8
Round 2   Derby County (a) 1-1
Replay   Derby County (h) 1-0
Round 3   Arsenal (h) 2-0
Round 4   Oldham Athletic (h) 2-1
Round 5   Peterborough United (a) 0-0
Replay   Peterborough United (h) 2-0
Semi-final   Crystal Palace (a) 1-1
Semi-final Crystal Palace (h) 0-0
Replay   Crystal Palace (h) 2-2
2nd Replay   Crystal Palace (a) 0-3

1978-9
Round 2   Aston Villa (h) 1-1
Replay   Aston Villa (a) 0-1

1979-80
Round 2   Nuneaton Borough (a) 1-0
Round 3   Peterborough United (a) 2-0
Round 4   Luton Town (h) 3-1
Round 5   Aston Villa (h) 1-1
Replay   Aston Villa (a) 2-3

1980-81
Round 2   Wrexham (h) 0-0
Replay   Wrexham (a) 0-0
2nd Replay   Wrexham (h) 0-2

1981-2
Round 2   Sheffield Wednesday (a) 3-4

1982-3
Round 1   Shrewsbury Town (a) 3-2
Round 2   Manchester United (h) 0-1

1983-4
Round 1   Nottingham Forest (a) 1-0
Round 2   Aston Villa (h) 0-3

1984-5
Round 1   Hednesford Town (a) 0-0
Replay   Hednesford Town (h) 1-2

1985-6
Round 1   Grimsby Town (h) 2-0
Round 2   Leicester City (h) 3-6

1986-7
Round 1   Derby County (h) 1-0
Round 2   Coventry City (h) 0-0
Replay   Coventry City (a) 0-3

Albert McPherson (far left), trainer and Fred Horne, assistant secretary for the club in 1959.

Mike McCartney, Scottish Youth International, 1973.

228

A disconsolate Albion team are comforted by trainer Jimmy Dunn after losing 6-0 to Sunderland in the 1969 FA Youth Cup Final 2nd leg.

Stewart Woolgar scored two goals in the 1st leg of the 1969 FA Youth Cup Final at The Hawthorns.

Derek Monaghan, on the score-sheet in the 2nd leg of the 1976 FA Youth Cup Final.

FA Youth Cup Finals

1954-5
First leg
April 27 v Man United (a) 1-4
McGuinness (og)
Cashmore; Whale, Rogers, Drury, Hughes, Cooke, Maynes, Setters, McCartney, Jackson, G.Williams.
Att: 16,696
Second leg
April 30 v Man United (h) 0-3 (agg 1-7)
Cashmore; Whale, Rogers, Setters, Hughes, Cooke, Maynes, Harris, McCartney, Jackson, G.Williams.
Att: 8,335

1968-9
First leg
April 28 v Sunderland (h) 3-0
MacLean, Woolgar 2
Nisbet; Minton, Bell, Hughes, Holton, Robertson, Woolgar, Hartford, Morton, Cantello, MacLean. Sub: Butler.
Att: 15,613
Second leg
May 3 v Sunderland (a) 0-6 (agg 3-6)
Nisbet; Minton, Bell, Hughes, Holton, Robertson, Woolgar, Hartford, Morton, Cantello, MacLean. Sub: Butler.
Att: 8,040

1975-6
First leg
April 27 v Wolves (a) 2-0
Summerfield, Trenter
Grew; Cooper, Statham, Loveridge, Clarke, Davies, Lynex (Hood), Gregson, Trenter, Hughes, Summerfield.
Att: 11,875
Second leg
May 3 v Wolves (h) 3-0 (agg 5-0)
Berry (og), Loveridge, Monaghan
Grew; Cooper, Statham, Loveridge, Clarke, Davies, Monaghan (Hood), Gregson, Trenter, Hughes, Summerfield.
Att: 15,558

Programme Parade

THE first edition of the *Albion News* — the official programme of West Bromwich Albion Football Club — was issued on Saturday, 2 September 1905, for Albion's home Second Division match against Burnley.

The programme consisted of eight pages and was priced at one old penny. About 2,000 copies were printed.

By 1907-08 the *Albion News* enjoyed a circulation of some 5,000, with readers as far afield as Canada, Singapore and West Africa.

Before 1905, Albion issued a team-sheet which was handed out to spectators. In the earliest days the club posted notices outside the ground, listing the players' names. Sometimes the teams were also chalked up on a blackboard which was carried around the pitch before kick-off.

The editor of the *Albion News* for many years was Mr Harry Keys who, even though a director of the club, would sit in the Press box rather than in the more comfortable director's box. Between 1915 and 1919, the *Albion News* was not published and from 1940 until 1945 it was produced on a restricted scale because of the wartime paper shortage.

There have been over 25 changes to the front cover design of the Albion programme through the years with a multi-coloured front page appearing for the first time in season 1974-5.

During the 1960-1 campaign, reserve match programmes, which had previously been identical to first-team programmes, were altered to a two-page edition costing two 'old' pence.

Peerless Press Limited took over the printing of the *Albion News* in 1961 and in 1965 the cost of the programme was increased from 4d to 6d (2p) with the inclusion of the popular *Soccer Review* (later called the *Football League Review*).

At the start of the 1969-70 season, a match-day magazine was introduced to replace the traditional programme. Under the editorship of commercial manager Les Thorley, who succeeded secretary Alan Everiss, it was voted top football programme of the season by the magazine *Soccer Star*. In 1979 the *Albion News* was selected top Football League programme by the Birmingham *Evening Mail*.

In 1979-80 the Albion club programme cost 30p. The price rose steadily and in seasons 1985-6 and 1986-7 it was 60p.

Over the past five seasons the contents have been of an exceptionally high standard. Indeed, the *Albion News* has always claimed a high placing in the annual programme awards up and down the country.

In 1985-6 it consisted of 32 pages, but following relegation to Division Two, Peerless Press, who have had the franchise on the programme since 1980 reduced this to 24.

Albion's Grounds

The Hawthorns

During the summer of 1898 the Albion board set in motion the activities which were to eventually lead to the transfer of the club to The Hawthorns two years later.

The directors found a number of pitfalls in front of them before a piece of land was finally located at the corner of Halford's Lane and the adjoining Birmingham Road. Local tradesmen got wind of the news via two Albion directors, Tom Brennand and Harry Powell, who were themselves traders. Representations were made to Albion because shopkeepers feared that they would lose business on match days. Meanwhile, the Board secured an option on a piece of ground on the Birmingham Road but this option was later withdrawn.

In May, 1899 a meeting of shareholders was convened to consider the club's position, and a syndicate offered to put up enough money to improve the existing facilities at Stoney Lane. Nothing came of this scheme and the Albion board, under the wise leadership of Harry Keys, pressed on with their plans.

The lease on Stoney Lane expired in 1899 and by that year it was one of the worst grounds in the First Division. And because it was rented, the directors were unwilling to spend much money on it. Nevertheless, the lease was renewed for a further year while the ground committee searched around for a suitable site, and on 14 May 1900, the club's seal was affixed to a 14-year lease on the field that was to become known as The Hawthorns.

Why was the new ground called The Hawthorns? It was the suggestion of the then club secretary, Frank Heaven, who noted that the area was shown on the surveyor's map as The Hawthorns Estate. As a hawthorn copse had apparently flourished there at one time, it seemed an obvious choice of name.

The field had a marshy appearance because of the presence of a brook which formed the boundary between Smethwick, Handsworth and West Bromwich, but this did not deter the Albion management who forged ahead. It was a tremendous gamble but the alternative was stagnation and probable extinction at Stoney Lane.

A number of ground improvements have been made to The Hawthorns down the years. Successive Albion boards have not been slow to improve facilities at the ground but even more could have been achieved but for the crippling entertainments tax which was introduced during World War One and which was not abolished until 1959; in ten years after World War Two, Albion had to pay out £134,038 in this iniquitous tax, £17,600 in season 1954-5 alone.

Aerial view of The Hawthorns in 1977-8.

Calendar 1900-1987

1900 Opening match played at The Hawthorns between Albion and Derby County (1-1). Steve Bloomer scored the first goal recorded at The Hawthorns.

1904 The old Stoney Lane stand, the 'Noah's Ark', was burnt down on Guy Fawkes' Night.

1906 A new stand was constructed at the Smethwick end.

1911 Main stand overhauled. Banking increased on Handsworth side.

1913 Freehold purchased for £5,350.

1914 Halford's Lane stand extended.

1920 Concrete terracing constructed. A concrete wall replaced wooden fencing around the playing area.

1922 A half-time scoreboard was erected.

1923 Handsworth embankment extended further back and stand heightened.

1931 Terracing finally completed. Tip-up seats installed in wing stands. The Hawthorns Halt station on the Great Western Railway was opened on Christmas Day.

1934 A new stand was completed at the Smethwick corner in Halford's Lane (750 extra seats).

1935 New oak panelled tea-room constructed.

1939 The wooden roof of the Halford's Lane stand was dismantled and replaced by asbestos sheets resting on five steel stanchions. The roof was also extended to the front of the terraces.

1939-45 Only the bare necessities were done to the ground because building licenses could not be obtained. Even directly after the war, repairs were difficult to put into effect because of the shortage of building materials.

1947 A new block of turnstiles erected on the Handsworth side behind the Woodman Inn.

1949 The wooden terraces in front of the Main Stand were replaced with the extension of the front of the stand, providing 750 extra seats. First electronic turnstile aggregator to be installed on any British sports ground was housed at The Hawthorns.

1950 New directors' box was provided and offices and dressing-rooms were remodelled.

1951 Eight new turnstiles introduced at the Smethwick end.

1957 Installation of floodlights at a cost of £18,000.

1958 A wing was added to the Main Stand at the West Bromwich end of the ground.

1961 A new car park, for 600 cars, was opened in Middlemore Road. By September 1964 there were four car parks within 800 yards of the ground.

1964 Rainbow Stand erected on the Handsworth side, containing over 4,000 tip-up seats, paid for with funds from the Development Association. The Handsworth Stand was re-erected on the previously uncovered bank at the Birmingham Road End.

1965 First Throstle Club opened at The Hawthorns.

1967 Buffet bars renovated at a cost of £20,000.

1968 The Hawthorns Halt used for the last time in April.

1969 First 'open' day for supporters.

1970 Renovation of floodlights — illumination increased four-fold for colour TV transmissions.

1976 Fourteen executive boxes erected on Handsworth side. 750 extra paddock seats also constructed.

1977 Executive box complex completed. Terracing reconstructed at Smethwick and Birmingham Road ends of ground. New crush barriers erected.

1979 Commencement of new £2 million stand on the Halfords Lane side of ground (built in two phases, 1979-82).

1983 Closure of The Hawthorns Throstle Club, situated next to The Woodman public house on the Handsworth side of the ground. Electronic scoreboard erected at Smethwick End (removed 1985).

1985 Smethwick End stand re-roofed. New safety measures installed at ground.

1986 Crowd control video cameras installed.

Cooper's Hill

West Bromwich Strollers (later Albion) contested their earliest kick-abouts on open land at Cooper's Hill between Walsall Street and Beeches Road, now occupied by St Philip's Church. Coats and hats were originally used as goalposts and then a crude form of woodwork was erected with a piece of string tied to the top serving as a crossbar.

A local cricket club also played here so, to save wear and tear on the ground, the Strollers also used a pitch in Dartmouth Park. When the players went there they carried their goalposts with them, erecting them as best as they could, with the aid of bricks. Sometimes the pitch they intended to use was already occupied on arrival so the posts had to be taken back to Beeches Road.

Albion's first recorded match at Cooper's Hill was on 20 December 1879 when Bullock's Club were overcome 4-0 by this team: S.Biddlestone; H.Bell, R.Roberts, H.Twist, E.Turner, E.T.Smith, W.Bisseker, H.Evans, J.Stanton, H.Aston, J.Round, J.Armstrong. Billy Bisseker was captain.

Dartmouth Park

Albion played at Dartmouth Park on a regular basis in 1880-81 under skipper Jimmy Stanton. Their regular pitch was on a square near to the main entrance to the park, although occasionally a pitch was utilised at the Herbert Street end of Dartmouth Park. The teams changed at the Glebe Inn in Reform Street.

Even after Albion had transferred to Bunn's Field and The Four Acres, the occasional pre-season friendly was played in Dartmouth Park, usually against Wednesbury Old Athletic to celebrate the opening of the West Bromwich Flower Show.

Bunn's Field

Albion's first enclosed ground was at Bunn's Field in Walsall Street (now Alfred Street), West Bromwich. The move here was made in August 1881 when a nine-month lease was taken out, and the Albion players equipped the field themselves, levelling and rolling it and then erecting goal posts which were linked by a nailed tape which served as a crossbar. The entrance to the field was opposite Christ Church School where so many of the earliest Albion players were educated. The field was so muddy at times that supporters used to bring their own planks to stand on in wet weather. There was no covered accommodation of any sort; indeed, one of the original Albion pioneers, Jimmy Stanton, once told the founder of the Football League, William McGregor, that the only thing resembling a grandstand was a manure heap.

The new headquarters of Albion was known as The Birches, and it was here that the club was able to charge admission to their matches for the first time. Not everyone paid to witness those early contests, however, as one of Albion's first season ticket holders, Joe Stringer, recalled many years later:

"As a youth in those days I did not have many coppers to spend in paying for admission to football matches. But I was one of the privileged few who had the pleasure of going into the yard of Mr W.Ward's candle factory.....fronting New Street, and by standing on a wagon was able to overlook the ground and see the match for nothing."

The players dressed at the White Hart public house which stood at the junction of Herbert Street, Bull Street and Walsall Street, and for some obscure reason the changing rooms were known as 'Charlie Lamper's'. Once they were togged out, the players went through a back-yard of the pub, over a wall and on to the pitch. More suitable dressing-rooms were subsequently found at the Roebuck Inn, at the corner of New Street and Walsall Street.

Albion's first match at The Birches is believed to be the 5-1 victory over Oldbury on 10 September 1881. Although a full fixture list for the only season at Bunn's Field is not available, it appears that Albion were a difficult side to beat on their own patch. Among the results at The Birches were a 12-0 defeat of Milton on 8 October, a 9-1 destruction of Nechells on 3 December, a 6-1 defeat of West Bromwich Rovers on 4 February, a 5-0 win over Fallings Heath Rovers on 25 February, and a 10-0 victory against St Luke's on 4 March.

Albion's colours in the only season at The Birches were yellow and white quartered jerseys with the Staffordshire knot embroidered on the front, and also chocolate and blue halves. By the end of a successful first season, in which Albion reached the semi-final of the Birmingham Cup, it was found that the Dartmouth Cricket Club were willing to share their much more comfortable accommodation with the Albion and so Bunn's Field faded into the history books as Albion transferred to the Four Acres.

The Four Acres

In September 1882, Albion moved from their primitive ground at Walsall Street to more comfortable accommodation at The Four Acres, the home of West Bromwich Dartmouth Cricket Club who played there for over 80 years after their formation in 1834.

The Four Acres was a well-known local centre where athletics races were held at festivals and on public holidays; it was originally dedicated by William, fourth Earl of Dartmouth, for the recreation of local inhabitants.

One of the conditions Albion had imposed upon them by the Dartmouth club was that football matches could be played there on two days of the week only — Saturdays and Mondays. Season tickets at 2s 6d (12p) were issued at the start of the first season at The Four Acres. The opening fixture played there by Albion was a friendly against Stourbridge Standard on 7 October 1882, and the Throstles celebrated in style, winning 10-0 with goals from Billy Bisseker (6), John Stokes and Harry Aston (3). The Albion team was: Roberts; H.Bell, Stanton, Horton, Bunn, While, Whitehouse, Aston, Bisseker, Stokes, G.Bell.

Some improvements were made to The Four Acres in the summer of 1883 when the playing pitch was enclosing by a form of tubing instead of by ropes, and wooden racks were laid around the reserve portion of the ground so that spectators could stand on them. At the Albion AGM in July 1883 it was disclosed that the Dartmouth club had agreed to let The Four Acres for a further two years at a rental of £15 per annum, and to pay a third of the cost of a new ticket office and pavilion.

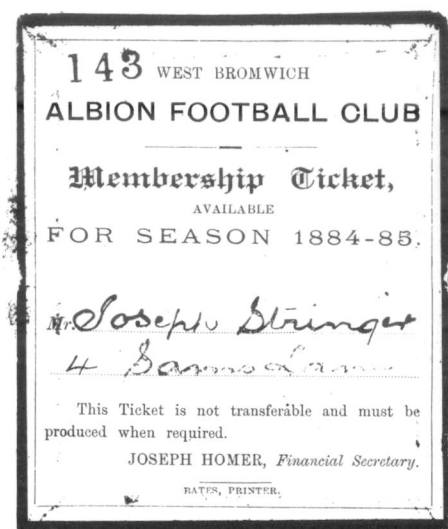

Season ticket for 1884-5, priced £3, when The Four Acres was Albion's home ground.

Albion's biggest match at The Four Acres was a sixth round FA Cup tie against Blackburn Rovers on 21 February 1885 when a crowd of 16,393 saw a thrilling confrontation. According to *The Athlete*, the spectators were 'thickly packed round the field of play, in stands temporary and stands permanent, on the walls and house-tops, everywhere, in fact, where a footing could be obtained...'

The optimistic Albion supporters wore in their hats a funeral card with a black border inscribed thus: 'In memorium. Blackburn Rovers defeated in the English Cup competition, West Bromwich, February 21, 1885'. Rovers had other ideas, however, and took the lead just before half-time, whereupon (according to the Birmingham *Daily Gazette*) 'the supporters of the West Bromwich team immediately upon this ascended a small balloon, bearing the inscription 'Play up Albion'. This aeriel injunction passed slowly over the field and was observed by the home players, who, as if in answer to its bidding, played up strenuously...'

At the interval, pigeons were despatched to various Black Country locations to announce the news that Albion were trailing to the FA Cup holders. Rovers were 2-0 winners at the conclusion of the game which prompted *Saturday Night* to surround their report of the match with black lines — as if a royal personage had passed away.

Even as this Cup tie was being played, the Albion committee were on the look-out for new premises as The Four Acres (now part of Park Crescent in Seager Street) was already too small for the club's requirements. The last senior match Albion contested at The Four Acres before the move to Stoney Lane in the summer of 1885 was against Wednesbury Old Athletic on 6 April 1885, when this team wore the cardinal and blue halves: Roberts; H.Bell, Green, Horton, Bunn, Bradbury, Woodhall, Aston, Smith, Loach, G.Bell. Albion were 3-2 winners.

The Four Acres Facts and Figures

Record Victory 26-0 v Coseley, Birmingham Cup 1st round, 11 Nov 1882.

Record defeat 5-1 v Stoke, Friendly, 20 Oct 1882.

Most goals by one player Six, by W.Bisseker (v Stourbridge Standard, 1882) and by H.Aston (v Birmingham Junior Association, 1883).

Complete playing record:

P	W	D	L	F	A
61	48	6	7	268	56

In three seasons Albion played 22 Cup ties at the ground, in the FA Cup, Staffordshire, Birmingham and Wednesbury Charity Cups. Albion were defeated only twice.

Stoney Lane

In the playing sense Stoney Lane was the headquarters of the Albion club from 1885 to 1900, but the Throstles' administration was dealt with at the nearby Plough and Harrow public house and afterwards at offices in High Street, West Bromwich.

The move from The Four Acres to Stoney Lane came about in 1885 because the Albion committee wanted more spacious accommodation in keeping with the growing reputation of the club. A ground committee was established and a number of sites were inspected before it was decided to lease a field at the back of the Sandwell Brewery in Stoney Lane.

It was not far from the Four Acres and close to the club's headquarters at the Plough and Harrow. On 27 February 1885 the committee were authorised to secure the tenancy of the field which belonged to the local undertaker, Mr Webb. The lease was for a seven-year term at an annual rent of £28, and work was begun almost immediately to convert the field into a suitable home for Albion.

The field was returfed and levelled and ashes were laid around the ground which was 120 yards long by 82 yards wide, the playing area being 110 yards by 78. A wooden grandstand was erected with planking serving as seats and it became affectionately known as the 'Noah's Ark'. It was on the Sandwell Road side of the ground (the brewery side) and the centre, which was covered, allowed for 600 people. The uncovered portions at each end accommodated a further 1,500 spectators. The opposite side of the ground was covered in ash and it was gradually raised towards the back so that everyone had a good view although it had no covered accommodation of any sort. Fencing and a boundary wall were also put in place and two simply furnished brick 'dressing tents', sporting corrugated iron roofs, were also constructed. Three refreshment stalls were added. Wagonettes and other vehicles were permitted to drive into the ground and were stationed behind the bank at the Stoney Lane entrance.

The pitch had a pronounced slope towards the Stoney Lane end of the ground and the sight of Albion's attack in full cry down the gradient gave many a goalkeeper the jitters. At first there were five pay boxes situated in Stoney Lane but these were found to be inefficient, so admission was gained by purchasing tickets through openings in the walls. On the opposite side of the road from the ground, tickets could also be purchased at the Plough and Harrow and, on important match-days, neighbouring houses were utilised to sell tickets. The cost of equipping the ground was £370 and to help pay for the cost, Albion arranged a series of home friendlies in September 1885.

In future years the standards slumped at Stoney Lane because the directors were reluctant to spend much money on a ground which was only rented, and in time it became the poorest Division One ground for amenities.

The first season-tickets at Stoney Lane cost five shillings (25p), and Albion's total gate receipts in their opening campaign there amounted to £1,190. The first groundsman was a Mr Russell who was paid the princely sum of 5 shillings a week. The usual admission charge to matches at Stoney Lane was sixpence (2p).

The opening fixture at Stoney Lane was a friendly against Third Lanark Rifle Volunteers of Glasgow on 5 September 1885, and the Albion selection was: Roberts; H.Bell, H.Green, Horton, Bunn, Timmins, Woodhall, Bayliss, T.Green, Lavender, G.Bell. Albion were 4-1 winners with goals from T.Green (3) and Woodhall. Tom Green was the scorer of the first goal on the ground after five minutes play.

The first team to win at Stoney Lane was Burnley (3-0) on 23 November 1885, and the same club took part in the first Football League fixture there, on 29 September 1888. Albion said goodbye to Stoney Lane on 16 April 1900, defeating Nottingham Forest 8-0 in a Division One game. Preston North End were the most successful visitors to the ground in League matches, winning six times. Aston Villa and Sunderland were also rather successful with five wins apiece.

Albion played over 350 games at Stoney Lane, winning 223 of them and losing only 70. They scored almost 900 goals and were undefeated in 14 consecutive FA Cup-ties between 1885 and 1893.

Attendances at The Hawthorns

These are the 'top ten' crowds at The Hawthorns:

1. 64,815	v Arsenal	FAC	6 Mar 1937
2. 64,612	v Aston Villa	FAC	21 Feb 1925
3. 61,088	v Newcastle United	FAC	20 Feb 1954
4. 60,945	v Wolves	Div One	4 Mar 1950
5. 59,674	v Aston Villa	Div One	14 Nov 1931
6. 59,448	v Portsmouth	FAC	28 Jan 1956
7. 58,163	v Nottingham Forest	FAC	25 Jan 1958
8. 57,843	v Chelsea	FAC	12 Feb 1949
9. 57,574	v Manchester United	FAC	1 Mar 1958
10. 57,503	v Sheffield United	FAC	19 Feb 1958

And the ten lowest 'gates' at The Hawthorns:

1. 1,050	v Sheffield United	Div One	30 Apr 1901
2. 1,206	v Burton United	Div Two	5 Apr 1902
3. 1,495	v Nottingham Forest	Div Two	19 Mar 1930
4. 2,072	v Gainsborough T	Div Two	28 Jan 1905
5. 2,366	v Bradford City	Div Two	25 Mar 1905
6. 2,533	v Leeds City	Div Two	6 Jan 1906
7. 2,675	v Barnsley	Div Two	17 Dec 1904
8. 3,103	v Blackpool	Div Two	16 Apr 1910
9. 3,104	v Leicester Fosse	Div Two	8 Apr 1905
10. 3,109	v Norwich City	Div Two	29 Apr 1939

This table shows how The Hawthorns crowd record has been broken down the years.

20,104	Albion v Derby County	3 Sep 1900	Div One.
35,417	Albion v Aston Villa	8 Sep 1900	Div One.
35,529	Albion v Derby County	23 Feb 1907	FAC Rd 3.
36,727	Albion v Birmingham	11 Jan 1908	FAC Rd 1.
38,049	Albion v Birmingham	26 Dec 1908	Div Two.
45,203	Albion v Aston Villa	30 Sep 1911	Div One.
48,057	Albion v Aston Villa	4 Oct 1913	Div One.
49,488	Albion v Birmingham	26 Dec 1921	Div One.
56,474	Albion v Sunderland	3 Feb 1923	FAC Rd 2.
64,612	Albion v Aston Villa	21 Feb 1925	FAC Rd 3.
64,815	Albion v Arsenal	6 Mar 1937	FAC Rd 6.

Crowd Facts & Figures

The lowest FA Cup crowd for an Albion home tie is one of 5,230, v Leicester Fosse on 14 January 1905 (Intermediate Round).

In the League Cup, before the competition was sponsored, the smallest turnout is the 8,294 v Millwall on 10 September 1974.

A total of 6,288 fans witnessed Albion's Milk Cup clash with Port Vale at The Hawthorns on 24 September 1985.

And only 6,765 spectators were present at the Albion-Derby County Littlewoods Challenge Cup match on 7 October 1986.

The lowest 'European' gate to assemble at The Hawthorns — 16,745 — did so on 30 September 1981 when Albion played hosts to Grasshoppers (Zurich) in the UEFA Cup.

Albion's best 'wartime' home crowd was 38,077, against Wolverhampton Wanderers, Football League South on 23 April 1946 although, of course, the war had ended some months before but League football proper had not resumed.

In non-competitive football, Albion's top home gate is 55,497 against an Invitation XI for Norman Heath's benefit match on 25 April 1956.

In the Central League, Albion Reserves boast a record home crowd of 22,372, versus Aston Villa on 3 March 1934.

The attendance of 15,613 for the Albion versus Sunderland 1969 FA Youth Cup Final (first leg) is the highest below reserve team level at The Hawthorns.

The attendance figure was broken at the following grounds when Albion played there. The list is given in chronological order.

The Oval. FAC Final, 1885-6, v Blackburn Rovers	15,156
Derby (County Ground). FAC Final Replay, 1885-6, v Blackburn Rovers	16,144
Trent Bridge. FAC Semi-final, 1886-7, v Preston NE	16,068
The Oval. FAC Final, 1886-7, v Aston Villa	15,534
Cape Hill, Smethwick. FAC Rd 2, 1887-8, v Mitchell's St George	7,805
The Oval. FAC Final, 1887-8, v Preston North End	18,904
Bramall Lane, Sheffield. FAC Semi-final, 1888-9, v Preston North End	22,688
The Links, Chatham. FAC Rd 3, 1888-9, v Chatham	17,092
Victoria Ground, Stoke. FAC Semi-final, 1890-1, v Blackburn Rovers	21,774
Edgbaston. Birmingham Cup, 1890-1, v Aston Villa	12,000
Molineux Grounds. FAC Semi-final, 1891-2, v Nottingham Forest	21,076
The Oval. FAC Final, 1891-2, v Aston Villa	32,710
Goodison Park. FAC Rd 1, 1892-3, v Everton	23,867
The Crystal Palace. FAC Final, 1894-5, v Aston Villa	42,652
Derby (County Ground). FAC Semi-final, 1894-5, v Sheffield Wednesday	25,013
Blundell Park. FAC Rd 2, 1895-6, v Grimsby Town	7,108
Dallow Lane, Luton. FAC Rd 1, 1896-7, v Luton Town	6,898
Home Park, Plymouth. Friendly, 1897-8, v Devon County	4,000
Baseball Ground. Div One, 1902-3, v Derby County	21,909
Elland Road. Div Two, 1905-6, v Leeds City	6,802
Stamford Bridge. Div Two, 1905-6, v Chelsea	10,123
The Dell. FAC Rd 2, 1907-8, v Southampton	18,728
Elland Road. FAC Rd 2, 1911-12, v Leeds City	21,320
Roker Park. FAC Rd 3, 1911-12, v Sunderland	43,383
Villa Park. Div One, 1912-3, v Aston Villa	55,064
Elland Road. FAC Rd 2, 1913-4, v Leeds City	29,733
Villa Park. Div One, 1919-20, v Aston Villa	58,273
Villa Park. Div One, 1920-21, v Aston Villa	66,094
Goodison Park. Div One, 1920-21, v Everton	59,964
Meadow Lane. FAC Rd 1, 1920-21, v Notts County	32,995
Stalybridge. FAC Rd 1, 1922-3, v Stalybridge Celtic	9,753
The Den. FAC Rd 1, 1923-4, v Millwall	30,922
Bramall Lane. FAC Rd 4, 1924-5, v Sheffield United	57,197
Racecourse Ground, Wrexham. FAC Rd 3 1929-30, v Wrexham	16,570
Old Trafford. FAC Semi-final, 1930-31, v Everton	69,241
St Andrew's. Div One, 1931-2, v Birmingham	57,806
Edgeley Park. FAC Rd 5, 1934-5, v Stockport County	24,684
Victoria Ground, Stoke. FAC Semi-final, 1934-5, v Bolton Wanderers	49,110
Highfield Road. FAC Rd 5, 1936-7, v Coventry City	44,492
Bootham Crescent. FAC Rd 4, 1937-8, v York City	18,795
Sincil Bank. FAC Rd 3, 1948-9, v Lincoln City	19,602
Redheugh Park. FAC Rd 4, 1948-9, v Gateshead	16,855
The Dell. Div Two, 1948-9, v Southampton	30,856
Kings Lynn. Benefit Match, 1952-3, v Kings Lynn	9,200
Dean Court. FAC Rd 3, 1954-5, v Bournemouth	19,498
City Ground. Div One, 1957-8, v Nottingham Forest	41,675
City Ground. FAC Rd 4, 1957-8, v Nottingham Forest	46,455
Tiflis, Russia. Friendly, 1957, v Dynamo Tblisi	35,000
National Stadium, Peking. Friendly, 1977-8, v China	89,400
St Martin's Ground, Guernsey. Friendly, 1978-9, v Birmingham City	4,400
Marriott's Close Stadium, Witney. Benefit Match, 1978-9, v Nottingham Forest	3,558

Albion best average home League attendance for a single season is 38,819 — set in 1949-50. The aggregate total of fans who saw the 21 home First Division matches was 815,217.

On 26 December 1933, Albion's 'A' team played a home game at The Hawthorns against Cheltenham in a Birmingham Combination fixture — and a record crowd of 3,340 turned up to see it.

In their 1957-8 FA Cup run, Albion were watched by a total of 227,263 spectators in four home ties — which gave an average of 56,816 per game.

Albion played four away games against Tottenham Hotspur between January 1947 and January 1949 — three in the League and one in the FA Cup. The four-match crowd total was a staggering 226,459, and at the time both teams were in the Second Division.

The best attendance figure for an-opening-of-season match at The Hawthorns is 49,596 (receipts. £5,133) for Albion's First Division 'return' match against Charlton Athletic on 20 August 1949.

The lowest 'opening day' crowd is 4,123 — Albion v Grimsby, Div Two, 10 September 1904.

The lowest attendance figure for any Albion home League game (September 1888 to date) is a mere 405 — for the visit of Derby County to Stoney Lane in a First Division match on 29 November, 1890.

Albion's average home Football League attendance (September 1888-May 1987) is 19,673 — aggregate (1,726 matches) 33,956,484. The average League attendance at The Hawthorns (September 1900-May 1987) is 21,209 — aggregate (1,556 matches) 33,001,999.

In the FA Cup, Albion's average home gate (1883-1987) is 28,064 — aggregate (150 matches) 4,209,651.

And in the Football League Cup (including Milk Cup and Littlewoods Cup) the average crowd for an Albion home game at The Hawthorns is 19,543 — aggregate 859,915 (44 matches).

When the policeman watched the match, not the spectators. Crowd scene from The Hawthorns in soccer's so-called Golden Age which spanned the late 1940s and early 50s.

The last time a 50,000-plus gate assembled at The Hawthorns was for ▶ the FA Cup tie — Albion v Spurs in February 1962.

Here is a detailed account of Albion's home League attendances 1888 to 1987 inclusive:

Season	Played	Average	Aggregate	Largest	Smallest	Season	Played	Average	Aggregate	Largest	Smallest
1888-9	11	4,582	50,409	8,515	2,079	1936-7	21	21,707	455,855	33,962	7,022
1889-90	11	5,241	57,650	10,122	1,550	1937-8	21	23,246	488,183	55,444	8,028
1890-1	11	4,418	48,605	8,537	405	1938-9	21	18,467	387,828	30,943	3,109
1891-2	13	7,162	93,114	14,185	1,109	1946-7	21	24,642	517,498	42,031	10,506
1892-3	15	4,620	69,301	11,239	607	1947-8	21	30,856	647,985	51,945	13,349
1893-4	15	5,123	76,852	13,997	2,024	1948-9	21	33,379	700,961	47,028	13,009
1894-5	15	6,921	103,818	19,720	2,535	1949-50	21	38,819	815,217	60,945	16,780
1895-6	15	5,711	85,671	17,510	560	1950-1	21	31,082	652,741	44,543	17,912
1896-7	15	5,857	87,855	10,291	1,105	1951-2	21	29,712	623,962	47,782	18,903
1897-8	15	7,006	105,102	12,244	3,455	1952-3	21	31,527	662,063	54,480	16,250
1898-9	17	4,879	82,955	15,896	1,571	1953-4	21	38,279	803,852	53,210	20,306
1899-1900	17	5,491	93,353	14,905	1,717	1954-5	21	31,247	656,201	51,833	7,764
1900-01	17	11,938	202,950	35,417	1,050	1955-6	21	26,922	565,361	45,306	16,141
1901-02	17	7,822	132,974	23,697	1,206	1956-7	21	23,343	490,217	37,255	6,397
1902-03	17	15,657	266,176	28,536	4,148	1957-8	21	32,558	683,717	56,904	16,518
1903-04	17	12,651	215,057	31,418	4,467	1958-9	21	31,547	662,495	48,898	17,071
1904-05	17	4,884	83,032	10,105	2,072	1959-60	21	27,504	577,595	40,739	12,204
1905-06	19	8,637	164,093	23,021	2,533	1960-1	21	24,707	518,840	41,903	15,099
1906-07	19	12,126	230,397	25,562	5,034	1961-2	21	20,998	440,953	39,071	13,894
1907-08	19	11,100	210,902	30,026	4,140	1962-3	21	18,637	391,381	32,450	10,759
1908-09	19	17,845	339,061	38,049	4,982	1963-4	21	20,552	431,601	37,189	10,715
1909-10	19	11,705	222,398	30,104	3,103	1964-5	21	19,405	407,508	28,504	10,511
1910-11	19	15,601	296,427	30,135	3,577	1965-6	21	19,781	415,414	29,669	13,079
1911-12	19	18,042	342,803	46,203	3,122	1966-7	21	23,352	490,393	37,969	16,832
1912-13	19	17,047	323,908	40,589	6,565	1967-8	21	25,837	542,580	45,992	15,490
1913-14	19	20,629	391,948	48,057	12,057	1968-9	21	25,091	526,924	38,299	16,483
1914-15	19	10,823	205,657	19,492	4,410	1969-70	21	27,871	585,309	45,120	18,512
1919-20	21	30,532	641,187	43,579	19,058	1970-1	21	25,691	539,526	41,134	12,684
1920-1	21	27,802	583,835	44,023	17,242	1971-2	21	25,784	541,471	46,992	16,702
1921-2	21	21,691	455,514	49,488	11,026	1972-3	21	21,438	450,207	39,209	12,215
1922-3	21	18,817	395,152	39,576	5,520	1973-4	21	16,001	336,023	43,119	11,456
1923-4	21	17,381	365,010	42,096	8,003	1974-5	21	12,679	266,260	29,614	7,812
1924-5	21	20,596	432,522	41,990	9,892	1975-6	21	17,233	361,900	26,640	10,496
1925-6	21	18,595	390,507	52,322	8,287	1976-7	21	24,523	514,995	41,867	16,434
1926-7	21	21,710	455,919	50,392	10,043	1977-8	21	24,133	506,798	36,067	17,053
1927-8	21	19,596	411,517	37,342	8,116	1978-9	21	26,702	560,745	35,166	17,499
1928-9	21	13,220	277,263	24,902	6,994	1979-80	21	22,735	477,442	35,093	11,735
1929-30	21	14,023	294,501	25,221	1,495	1980-1	21	20,382	428,038	34,195	14,833
1930-1	21	21,722	456,179	52,415	11,037	1981-2	21	16,851	353,874	23,378	11,733
1931-2	21	24,251	509,284	59,674	7,796	1982-3	21	15,260	320,460	25,331	9,221
1932-3	21	22,799	478,781	45,038	8,933	1983-4	21	14,620	307,037	27,954	10,313
1933-4	21	20,078	421,647	32,660	10,493	1984-5	21	13,958	293,132	26,401	7,423
1934-5	21	22,350	469,342	44,503	10,420	1985-6	21	12,194	256,076	25,068	6,021
1935-6	21	23,064	484,345	42,402	7,893	1986-7	21	9,280	194,893	15,329	6,198

FIGURES given in this section have been taken from the official records of the club and may differ from those published in certain newspapers. Today, for safety reasons, the official capacity of The Hawthorns is a shade over 39,000. Yet before World War Two it was said that 70,000 fans could have been packed into the ground.

However, obvious and necessary ground improvements, including the insertion of extra seats — there are now 12,159 — have cut the official capacity quite dramatically, especially over the last 20 years.

The biggest attendance for a soccer match at The Hawthorns was on Saturday, 6 March 1937, when Albion beat Arsenal 3-1 in a sixth round FA Cup tie. That day 64,815 spectators paid £3,914 in receipts to see the action. The top League 'gate' at The Hawthorns — 60,945 — gathered on Saturday 4 March 1950, for the Albion-Wolves First Division game. And the best Second Division audience was the 52,415 for the Albion-Charlton Athletic match on 2 May 1931 — the day Albion clinched that wonderful Cup and promotion double. In the Football League Cup, Walsall were Albion's visitors for a second round tie on 22 September 1965, when a record 41,188 supporters flocked to The Hawthorns to see Albion win 3-1 under floodlights.

Fashions had changed dramatically by the time this photograph was taken of The Hawthorns in the 1970s.

England at The Hawthorns

England have played two full international matches at The Hawthorns — in 1922 and 1924 — and one Victory international in 1945.

Here are details of those three internationals on Albion soil, with team line-ups, results, scorers and attendances.

England 2 Ireland 0 – 21 October 1922

Attendance: 20,173   *Scorer: Chambers 2*

ENGLAND: Taylor (Huddersfield Town); Smith (West Bromwich Albion), Harrow (Chelsea), Moss (Aston Villa), Wilson (Sheffield Wednesday), Grimsdell (Tottenham Hotspur), Mercer (Sheffield United), Seed (Tottenham Hotspur), Osborne (Fulham), Chambers (Liverpool), Williams (Clapton Orient).
IRELAND: Harland (Linfield); Rollo (Blackburn Rovers), Curran (Pontypridd), Emerson (Burnley), Smith (Cardiff City), Morgan (Linfield), Lyner (Manchester United), Irvine (Everton), Nellis (Nottingham Forest), Gillespie (Sheffield United), Burns (Glenavon).

Both goals came in the second-half after an even first 45 minutes. The deadlock was broken in the 66th minute when Harry Chambers, who later played for Albion, forced home Mercer's right-wing corner. Six minutes from time the same player, put through by Williams, netted past Harland's right hand with a sweetly struck shot from 15 yards.

England 4 Belgium 0 – 8 December 1924

Attendance: 15,405   *Scorers: Bradford 2, Walker 2*

ENGLAND: Hardy (Stockport County); Ashurst (Notts County), Bower (Corinthians), Magee (West Bromwich Albion), Butler (Arsenal), Ewer (The Casuals), Osborne (Tottenham Hotspur), Roberts (Manchester City), Bradford (Birmingham), Walker (Aston Villa), Dorrell (Aston Villa).
BELGIUM: Debie (R.Racing C.B.); Swartenbroeks (Daring C.B.), Baes (C.S. Brugge), Cnudde (Union St.Gilliose), Augustus (Antwerp), Braine (Beerschot), Dries (Berchen), Gillis (Stannard), Adams (Anderlecht), Grimonprez (R.C.Gand), Bastin (Antwerp).

Although the scoreline suggests that this was an easy victory for England, the Belgians put up a tremendous fight and deserved better reward for their efforts. But England took their chances well, despite a missed penalty by Villa's Billy Walker.
It was Walker, in fact, who set up England's first goal in the 17th minute, his pass finding Joe Bradford who netted from fully 25 yards. On the hour Bradford set up Walker for goal number two and immediately afterwards Bradford ran on to Ewer's through ball to make it 3-0. Ten minutes from time Osborne and Roberts linked well down the right and Walker finished off in style.

England 0 Wales 1 – 20 October 1945

Attendance: 54,611   *Scorer: Powell*

ENGLAND: Williams (Wolves); Scott (Arsenal), Kinsell (West Bromwich Albion), Soo (Leicester City), Franklin (Stoke City), Mercer (Everton), Matthews (Stoke City), Fenton (Middlesbrough), Stubbins (Newcastle United), Barrass (Bolton Wanderers), Watson (Huddersfield Town).
WALES: Sidlow (Wolves); Winter (Bolton Wanderers), Hughes (Birmingham), Dearson (Birmingham), Davies (Nottingham Forest), Burgess (Tottenham Hotspur), Powell (Leeds United), Astbury (Chester), Lowrie (Coventry City), Lucas (Swindon Town), Edwards (Birmingham).
This was a tough international and two players, Harry Kinsell of the Albion, performing in front of his own fans, and Coventry's George Lowrie were sent-off for fighting. The winning goal was scored by the

Spectators perch on top of the stand at The Hawthorns for the England-Wales wartime international.

Leeds United outside-right, Powell, in the first-half following some good work on the left by George Edwards.

The gate receipts of £8,573 created a new record for The Hawthorns.

238

International and Representative Matches at The Hawthorns

7 Oct 1914	Football League 2 Irish League 1	(9,250)
9 Feb 1920	England 2 The South 1	(14,427)
21 Oct 1922	England 2 Ireland 0	(20,173)
8 Dec 1924	England 4 Belgium 0	(15,405)
23 Jan 1928	England 5 The Rest 1	(9,345)
27 Feb 1935	England 2 The Rest 2	(12,845)
20 Oct 1945	England 0 Wales 1	(54,611)

Other Representative Matches at The Hawthorns

4 Apr 1908	England Juniors 4 Scotland Juniors 0	
18 Apr 1925	England Juniors 4 Scotland Juniors 1	
13 Apr 1935	England Juniors 3 Scotland Junors 1	
15 Mar 1972	England Schools 1 Northern Ireland Schools 1	
9 Jan 1974	England Youth 1 Wales Youth 0	
13 Feb 1974	England Youth 1 Holland Youth 1	
9 Mar 1977	England Youth 1 Wales Youth 0	
1 May 1978	England Schools 6 Wales Schools 0	
13 May 1983	Scotland Youth 3 USSR Youth 0	
21 Mar 1986	England Schools 4 Scotland Schools 2	
10 Nov 1986	England Youth (U-17) 3 Sweden Youth 3	

Cup Semi-Finals at The Hawthorns

15 Mar 1902	Derby County 1 Sheffield United 1, FA Cup	(33,603)
26 Mar 1960	Wolverhampton Wanderers 1 Aston Villa 1, FA Cup	(55,596)
5 Apr 1967	Hendon Town 1 Skelmersdale United 3, FA Amateur Cup	(5,225)
18 Dec 1968	Swindon Town 3 Burnley 2, FL Cup replay	(20,155)
3 Apr 1971	Telford United 3 Yeovil Town 1, FA Trophy	(9,058)

FA Trophy Final Replay

12 May 1987 Burton Albion 1 Kidderminster Harriers 2 (15,865)

The main stand, Halfords Lane at The Hawthorns, 1904-05.

Half-time scoreboard at The Hawthorns, surmounted by the throstle erected in 1979.

The Hawthorns Facts and Figures

First Match Albion 1 Derby County 1 (Football League, Div One) 3 September 1900. Albion team: J.Reader; A.Adams, W.Williams, A.Dunn, A.Jones, H.Hadley, J.Chadburn, T.Pickering, C.Simmons, F.Wheldon, R.Roberts.

First Albion goalscorer 'Chippy' Simmons, against Derby County, 3 September 1900.

First Albion League win 3-2 v Manchester City, 6 October 1900.

Record League victory 9-2 v Manchester City, 21 September 1957.

Record League defeat 1-6 v Nottingham Forest, 20 October 1900, and v Sunderland, 23 October 1937.

Highest attendance 64,815 v Arsenal (FA Cup 6th round), 6 March 1937.

Highest League attendance 60,945 v Wolverhampton Wanderers, 4 March 1950.

Lowest attendance 1,050 v Sheffield United, 30 April 1901.

Record receipts £79,494.76 v Tottenham Hotspur, FL Cup Semi-final (1st leg), 3 February 1982.

Record League game receipts £69,835.80 v Manchester United, Div One, 21 September 1985.

Point of Interest

It is believed that The Hawthorns is the highest Football League ground, lying about 550 feet above sea-level. The next highest appear to be those of Port Vale (just two or three feet lower than Albion's) and Oldham Athletic (500 feet).

In the 1919-20 season Wolverhampton Wanderers were permitted to play two Second Division matches at The Hawthorns after Molineux had been closed because of crowd disturbances. On 6 December 1919 Wolves drew 2-2 with Stockport County and on 29 November 1919 they lost 4-2 to Barnsley.

The Hawthorns staged the Telford United-Leeds United FA Cup third-round tie on 11 January 1987. A crowd of 6,460 saw Leeds win 2-1.

On 11 May 1931, HRH The Prince of Wales (later King Edward VIII and then Duke of Windsor) called in at The Hawthorns while on a visit to the Midlands. He offered his congratulations on the unique double achievement and to pose for a photograph with the FA Cup winning team.

On 7 August 1944, American and Canadian army teams staged a baseball match at The Hawthorns before a crowd of over 5,000 spectators.

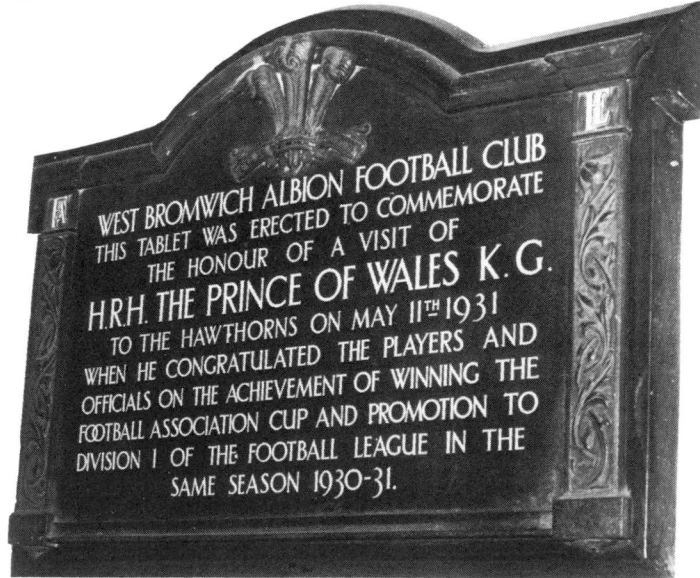

The tablet erected inside The Hawthorns to commemorate the visit of HRH The Prince of Wales in May 1931.

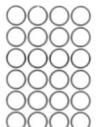
Floodlights were installed at The Hawthorns in 1957, and the first game played by Albion under their new lights was a League Division One match against Chelsea on Wednesday, 18 September 1957. The result was a 1-1 draw and the attendance was 36,835. Allen scored Albion's goal from the penalty spot.

Six weeks later, on 29 October — the CDSA side (the Centralniy Dom Krasnoy Armiy — Central Home of the Red Army), one of Russia's leading club sides, opposed Albion in an international friendly to 'officially' inaugurate The Hawthorns' floodlighting system. The game, played in torrential rain, was covered live by BBC television; it ended in a 6-5 win for Albion in front of 52,805 spectators.

BEAMS OF LIGHT

On Monday, 24 September 1888, Albion played out a 2-2 away draw with Walsall Town Swifts in a friendly under 'electric lights'. A 7,000 crowd saw the game which was restricted to half-an-hour each way.

A local sportspaper — 'Saturday Night' — carried this quote: 'The heavy mist enveloping the ground considerably dimmed the brilliancy of the artificial luminant provided, and it was a temptation to mirth at times to see the surprise evinced by one and another of the players, as when under the impression that the sphere was in safe custody in a remote part of the field, it suddenly dropped at their feet.'

This game against Walsall Town Swifts was not an entirely successful experiment and Saturday Night went on '...taken altogether, football by electric light in a Scotch Mist cannot be pronounced a qualified success.'

On 20 March 1896, Albion beat Thames Ironworks (now West Ham United) 4-2 in a friendly in London. The game was played under lights and the turnout was 1,500.

Albion first senior post-World War Two game under floodlights was a friendly against Wolverhampton Wanderers at Hednesford on 24 March — a match which officially opened the Hednesford club's newly installed floodlighting system. The result was a 4-2 win for Wolves and the crowd was recorded as 3,500.

Five months earlier, on 29 October 1952, Albion reserve side had played Kidderminster Harriers, away, in a floodlit Staffordshire Cup tie.

The 1954 FA Charity Shield game between Albion and Wolverhampton Wanderers at Molinuex on 29 September was played partly under floodlights. The result was a 4-4 draw.

Under the floodlights of the Heysel Stadium, Brussels, on 6 October 1954, Albion lost 5-3 to the crack Hungarian side, Honved, in a tournament game before a full-house crowd of 55,000. This was the first time an Albion side had played abroad under any form of lighting.

And on Wednesday, 24 September 1958, Albion played Port Vale in a match arranged to officially open Vale Park's new floodlights. Albion were beaten 5-3.

Albion's floodlighting system was renovated in the close-season of 1970, to bring it up to the standard required for colour television transmission.

Tuesday, October 29th, 1957

KICK-OFF 7.15 p.m.

Nº 1190

WEST BROMWICH ALBION v. CENTRAL SOVIET ARMY
(C. D. S. A.)

at The Hawthorns, West Bromwich

ADMISSION TERRACE

2/6

Entrance Turnstile
Smethwick Corner **L**

E. Smith
Secretary,
W.B. Albion F.C. Ltd.

Spectators are advised in their own interests to attend early.
This portion to be retained

This portion to be given up at turnstile

CONGESTED FIXTURE LIST

At the end of the 1911-12 season, Albion had to play seven games in ten days owing to the postponement of so many early-season matches coupled with a long Cup run.

This was their programme for April, 1912:
Sat 20 April — Barnsley (FA Cup Final, away) 0-0
Mon 22 April — Everton (away, League) 0-3
Wed 24 April — Barnsley (FA Cup Final replay)0-1
Thu 25 April — Blackburn (away, League) 1-4

Fri 26 April — Bradford City (home, League) 0-0
Sat 27 April — Sheffield Wednesday (home, League) 1-5
Mon 29 April — Oldham Athletic (home, League) 0-0
(Albion's score given first in each case)

For the game against Everton on 22 April Albion put out their reserve side, and although all but two of the eleven players had previously appeared in the League team, they were fined £150 by the Football League for the 'offence', of fielding a weakened side.

CLUB COLOURS

In more than a century of football activity Albion have experienced quite a number of colour variations and changes as the following table indicates:

1880-1 Cardinal red and blue quarters, also maroon jerseys
1881-2 Yellow and white quarters, also chocolate and blue halves
1882-3 Chocolate and blue halves, also red and white hoops
1883-4 Chocolate and white jerseys
1884-5 Cardinal red and blue halves
1885-9 Blue and white stripes
1889 Scarlet and blue broad stripes
1889-1941 Navy blue and white stripes
1941-7 Navy blue jerseys
1947-61 Navy blue and white stripes
1961-72 Navy blue and white stripes with white sleeves
1972-9 Navy blue and white broad stripes
1979-87 Traditional Navy blue and white vertical stripes

It was not until 15 September 1885 that it was decided at a committee meeting to adopt the blue and white stripes which have since become famous the world over. A number of the committee favoured the blue and white quarters of Blackburn Rovers, but a majority preferred stripes and these colours were worn in the club's first FA Cup Final appearance at The Oval in 1886. Prior to 1885 the Albion players wore whatever colours were available for purchase locally; thus it was that when Albion won the Staffordshire Cup for the first time in 1883, red and white hoops were sported but later that year, when Wednesbury Town were entertained in the FA Cup at the Four Acres, Albion turned out in chocolate and white.

At another committee meeting in August, 1889, it was resolved to alter the colours from blue and white stripes and white knickers to a much more exotic design. The new attire was a scarlet and blue broad striped jersey with red collar and cuffs and black knickers — they could hardly be described as shorts in those days — with scarlet stripes on each side. Hardly surprising, the Albion players soon attracted wolf whistles and

became known as the 'nigger minstrels'. Fortunately, sanity prevailed and within a month or two, the blue and white stripes (which had been donated to the second team) were hastily re-introduced.

During World War Two, striped jerseys could not be manufactured and so for some six years navy blue shirts were adopted. Albion first wore striped jerseys after the war for a home FA Cup tie against Leeds United on 11 January 1947. Even then, however, it was difficult to obtain supplies of playing kit because of the shortage of clothing coupons and for a time appeals were made through the *Albion News* for supporters to donate coupons.

Since 1885, Albion's players have sported white shorts, but a recent innovation has been the use of navy blue shorts which were permanently adopted at the start of the 1986-7 season. In 1969 red numbers were added to the sides of players' shorts for the first time. Albion's traditional navy blue stockings with white hoops have been abandoned in latter years; in the 1960s a white stocking with navy blue hoops was introduced but since then the design has varied between all-white and all-navy blue.

Change Colours

The change colours of the Albion were white jerseys with black shorts as long ago as the 1890s, but for the 1935 FA Cup Final against Sheffield Wednesday, when both sides' colours clashed, the Baggies adopted navy blue jerseys. Towards the end of the 1950s, an all-red design (jerseys and shorts) was preffered but after the disastrous Football League Cup Final of 1967 it was discarded for an all-white strip which was favoured during the 1968 Cup run.

All-red was again preferred as the 1970s approached and then Albion used yellow jerseys with green trimmings and blue shorts with a white stripe, and yellow stockings topped by a green band. These change colours were in use from 1971 until the 1974-5 season when the green and yellow striped jerseys with green shorts were brought into use.

Yellow shirts with blue shorts followed next and in 1986 the all-red change strip was re-introduced with yellow and blue 'in reserve'.

Substitutes · 12 Substitutes 12

SUBSTITUTES were introduced into the Football League in 1965-6, initially for injured players only, although this was later changed to allow for tactical replacements. In that first season, 746 substitutions were made in League matches and Albion's contribution was eight.

Two substitutes were permitted in European competitions from 1968-9 (from five named), and two subs were also allowed in Full Members' Cup ties and Littlewoods Challenge Cup matches in the mid-1980s. The FA Cup competition saw two substitutes on the bench in 1986-7.

Firsts

Denis Clarke has the distinction of being the first substitute to be called off the bench to play in an FA Cup Final — for Albion against Everton at Wembley, 1968.

Albion's first League substitute used was Graham Lovett (for Ken Foggo) at Northampton Town in a Division One match on 10 September 1965. Lovett was also Albion's first FA Cup sub, replacing Dick Krzywicki at Colchester on 27 January 1968.

Krzywicki had the honour of being Albion's first sub in a League Cup tie, going on in place of Doug Fraser against Manchester City at The Hawthorns 5 October 1966 — and he scored. Lovett subsequently completed a 'hat-trick' when he took over from Jeff Astle in the away leg of Albion's European Cup-winners' Cup tie against FC Bruges on 18 September 1968 to become the club's first sub in a European competition.

Several players made their Albion debuts as substitute, including Len Cantello (1968), David Shaw (1973), David Mills (1979), Gary Robson (1983), Carlton Palmer (1985) and Colin Anderson (1985).

'Super-Sub' Nicky Cross was named substitute by Albion in almost 70 competitive matches between 1980 and 1985, and in season 1981-2, he was on the bench no fewer than 18 times — a club record.

Albion reached the Final of every cup competition they entered in season 1887-8; the FA Cup, the Staffordshire Senior Cup, the Birmingham Cup, the West Bromwich Charity Cup and the Walsall Cup. Indeed, Albion's record in cup matches this term was quite magnificent — P23 W19 D2 L2 (losing in the Staffordshire and Birmingham Cup Finals). Their goal-record was 78 for and 19 against.

The hottest weather in which Albion have played a Football League game was that on the opening Saturday of the 1906-07 season (11 September) when the temperature was recorded at 90°F in the shade at Burnley's Turf Moor ground. When Albion toured East Africa in 1968, a temperature of 102°F was registered at their game with the Kenya National XI on 1 June.

BRIBERY!

In November 1913, prior to an Albion-Everton League game at The Hawthorns, Jesse Pennington was offered £55 by a man who wanted him to 'fix' the result of the match so that Everton would not lose.

Pennington immediately informed Albion officials who in turn notified the local police. A trap was set, and on the day of the match — 29 November 1913 — Pascoe Bioletti, alias Samuel Johnson, alias Frederick Pater, was arrested near The Hawthorns. He was later sentenced to five months imprisonment by Lord Justice Lush at Stafford Assize Court.

n.b. The match ended in a 1-1 draw, the £55 being equally divided between two West Bromwich charities.

On 20 September 1964, the *Sunday People* newspaper alleged that certain Everton players had collected a sum of money on their Hawthorns-bound coach for the purpose of bribing Albion players to lose the vital League game on 7 May 1963, the winning of which would ensure the League Championship for the Merseyside club. The *People* stated: "We have no evidence that the bribe was accepted by any of the West Brom players, but the fact is that Everton won the match by the wide margin of 4-0." During the game Albion lost left-half Ron Bradley with a broken arm, Graham Williams put through his own goal and Everton were awarded a penalty. Separate enquiries by both clubs failed to establish any truth in the article.

Jesse Pennington, the West Bromwich captain, and one of the best known men in the football world, telling how he laid a trap for the man who is alleged to have approached him. An amazing story of an alleged attempt to bribe a famous footballer, so that he might arrange that his team, West Bromwich, might not win their match with Everton on Saturday, was told at Smethwick Police Court yesterday when a man giving the name of Pater was remanded on a charge under the Corrupt Practices Act.

Above: A unique newspaper cutting showing Pennington giving evidence.

Albion have had four English Test cricketers on their books down the years — Warwickshire's Tom Dollery, Cyril Washbrook of Lancashire and the Worcestershire duo of Don Kenyon and Jack Flavell.

On 2 April 1926, Albion travelled south to play Tottenham Hotspur in a League match at White Hart Lane (a 256-miles round trip). Twenty-four hours later they switched due north and visited Burnley at Turf Moor in another First Division match (a-248 miles round trip). That meant 504 miles covered in two days.

On 24 April 1912, Albion played Barnsley, at Sheffield, in the replay of the FA Cup Final. They returned home that same night. The next morning the team travelled north to play Blackburn Rovers in a League match — returning to West Bromwich afterwards. On 26 April they entertained Bradford City, played hosts to Sheffield Wednesday the next day, and ended the season — and this hectic period — with another home game, against Oldham Athletic on 29 April.

On 20 April 1912, Albion fielded this team in the FA Cup Final goalless draw with Barnsley: Pearson; Cook, Pennington, Baddeley, Buck, McNeal, Jephcott, Wright, Pailor, Bowser, Shearman.
Two days later, against Everton in a League match, they made 11 changes. The side read: Moorwood; Smith, Wood, Hibbert, Waterhouse, Manners, Wollaston, Gregory, Deacey, Morris, Lloyd.
Albion were fined £150 by the Football League for fielding a weak side.

Albion's fourth Round FA Cup tie against Chelsea in 1953 lasted for 427 minutes, covering four matches. Chelsea finally won 4-0 in the third replay at Highbury after previous draws at Stamford Bridge, The Hawthorns and Villa Park, the last two after extra-time.

Albion's captains in the 1912, 1954 and 1968 FA Cup Finals, were all left-backs: Pennington, Millard and Williams respectively.

Tony Millington, a Welsh international goalkeeper, made his Albion debut in 1961-2, and his first five League outings all ended in draws — a unique record. In three of these matches his colleague, centre-half Stan Jones, conceded three own-goals.

Millington made two visits to Molineux in 1962-3 as Albion's 'keeper. On 16 March he was on the receiving end of a 7-0 Wolves onslaught in a First Division match, and on 1 May, as Albion's Central League custodian, he let in eight more as Wolves reserves hammered the Baggies' second string 8-3.

Willie McCullum was an Albion full-back for four and a half months in 1891, and winger Edward Burton had a shade under four months at The Hawthorns in 1905.

Twenty-three players made their League debuts for Albion in 1946-7, the first season after the war; 20 were introduced into League competition in 1888-9, and 19 in 1904-5.

Strikes and Rebellions

Players' Strike 1886

In January 1886, a letter was sent from the Albion committee to the club's reserve players, which read:

The committee have reluctantly been compelled, owing to the state of the funds, to discontinue paying the second team, but if the balance at the end of the season will permit, a bonus will be given to the second-team players according to the number of matches played. Of course, travelling expenses and refreshments, with payment for necessary loss of time, will be paid by the club.

The players were so displeased that they refused to play against Small Heath Alliance second eleven and the match had to be cancelled. After the first month of the season, Albion's reserve players had already been on half-pay and this latest action by the committee was the last straw. After a number of the malcontents had been briefly suspended, they were reinstated to the team but a number of them left at the season's end to join Crosswell's Brewery FC (later Oldbury Town).

In fact, when the Crosswell's team came to play Albion at Stoney Lane on 16 October 1886, in a Walsall Cup tie, seven of the team were ex-Albion players: Matthews, Bradbury, Stanton, F.Bunn, W.Bunn, Neale and Bradbury.

Transfer Rebellion 1963

On Monday 9 December 1963, ten Albion players — Don Howe, Graham Williams, Ray Potter, Doug Fraser, Terry Simpson, Stan Jones, Clive Clark, Bobby Hope, John Kaye and Ronnie Fenton — asked for transfers because 'we can't get on with manager Jimmy Hagan.'

Alec Jackson was already on the transfer list and he, too, joined in the rebellion. Howe, Albion's captain and spokesman, said "No-one is getting any satisfaction out of his football, and we feel the main reason for this is the failure to get on with the manager. Training is too stereotyped, Mr Hagan shows a lack of understanding and imposes too many restrictions."

The upheaval went on for four days, and after having their transfer requests turned down by the Albion board on 11 December, the ten rebels finally agreed to return to normal duties as West Bromwich Albion footballers, agreeing jointly that a way was open for happy relations in the future between players and the managerial staff at The Hawthorns.

Mr J W Gaunt, the Albion chairman, said at a press conference on 13 December 1963:

"This kind of situation is always arising in industry and politics, and can only be settled by give and take on both sides.

"No side has given way. It has been mutually agreed that no information other the statement which Mr Everiss, the club secretary will pass on to you, shall be released."

The statement read out by Mr Everiss, went as follows:

"The players are satisfied with the interview this morning with the chairman and manager. The various points have been fully discussed and we now feel the way is open for happy relations in the future.

"We are confident that the machinery exists to iron out any troubles that may arise. The requests for transfer have been withdrawn."

Track-Suit Saga 1963

On Thursday, 19 December 1963, further trouble flared at The Hawthorns when nine other 'rebels' (plus Jackson) joined the ten who had asked for a transfer ten days before, and refused to train in shorts in the cold weather. After being refused permission to wear track suits, the 20 players, again led by Howe, walked out of their Spring Road training ground at Smethwick, and went off for a special meeting.

Howe had been training with the England party at Birmingham University, on Tuesday and Wednesday, and when he walked into the training ground on the Thursday morning he was met by a number of disgruntled Albion players, who told him that earlier in the week (Tuesday), they had been refused permission to wear track suits on a bitterly cold morning. They asked Howe what had gone on during the England practice sessions regarding the wearing of track suits. Howe replied; "They let us use our own discretion, and treated us like adults. We could wear trouser bottoms if we wished."

At the time when the Albion players staged their walk-out, the temperature in West Bromwich and surrounding area was 27.7° F — four degrees below freezing.

The dispute, involving manager Hagan, trainer Wilf Dixon, and the 20 players, went on for five days, and at one stage the players threatened to go out into a local park to do their training — without their boss. Poison pen-letters were sent to the players, and Howe even received some offensive telephone calls. Four players — Howe, Clark, Williams and Jones — were each fined £5 by Hagan for refusing to train.

At last, on 23 December 1963, Albion chairman, JW Gaunt announced a settlement in the 'track suit saga' and the following day the Albion players began their afternoon training stint by lapping their practice pitch in sweaters and shorts. It is understood that this was their own decision.

Manager Hagan made no comment on the settlement, but a brief statement issued by the club contained these facts: 'The players and manager have come to a mutual agreement. All is settled now.'

The additional 'rebels' who joined the ten transfer-seekers, were: Tony Millington, Bobby Cram, Ray Fairfax, Ron Bradley, Bill Williams, 'Chuck' Drury, Geoff Carter and Brian Macready. First-teamer Bobby Hope, who was under treatment at the time, also pledged his support.

Three days after the decision to 'return to normal duties' was made, Albion played out a tremendous 4-4 home draw with Tottenham Hotspur in a League game, and followed this up by winning the return 2-0 in London two days later. The track suit rebellion was forgotten in a relatively short time.

Manager Hagan remained at The Hawthorns until April 1967, and under his guidance Albion won the League Cup (1966) and lost in the Final of the same competition eight weeks before his departure.

In season 1892-3, Albion met neighbours Aston Villa no fewer than eight times at first-team level: two League games, one Birmingham Cup tie and five friendlies.

Former Albion players, Joe Wilson, Ezra Horton, Jem Bayliss and Alf Green were all elected to the list of Football League referees on 14 May 1895.

The two longest footballing campaigns Albion have played in are those of seasons 1886-7, when their season ran from 19 July to 20 June, and 1965-6 when games were played from 7 July to 5 June.

One of Albion's 13 goals at Swansea in a friendly game on 20 April 1899, was credited to referee T.Kinney who diverted a shot from Billy Bassett into the net.

Goals and Goalscorers

Top 20 League Goalscorers for Albion (1888-1987)

1. Tony Brown 218
2. Ronnie Allen 208
3. 'W.G.'Richardson 202
4. Derek Kevan 157
5. Joe Carter 145
6. Jeff Astle 137
7. Tommy Glidden 135
8. Freddie Morris 112
9. Jimmy Cookson 103
10. Dave Walsh 94
11. Freddie Buck 90
12. Cyrille Regis 82
13. Clive Clark 80
14. Stan Davies 77
15. 'Chippy' Simmons 75
16. Ally Brown 72
17. Tom Pearson 72
18. Teddy Sandford 72
19. Sid Bowser 64
20. Billy Bassett 61

Top 20 Goalscorers (all competitions)

1. 'W.G.'Richardson 328
2. Tony Brown 279
3. Ronnie Allen 234
4. Jeff Astle 174
5. Derek Kevan 173
6. Billy Elliott 156
7. Joe Carter 155
8. Tommy Glidden 140
9. Freddie Morris 118
10. Cyrille Regis 112
11. Jimmy Cookson 110
12. Harry Jones 104
13. Dave Walsh 100
14. 'Ike' Clarke 99
15. Clive Clark 98
16. Freddie Buck 94
17. Tom Pearson 88
18. Ally Brown 85
19. Stan Davies 83
20. 'Chippy' Simmons 81

Leading League Cup scorers for Albion (including Milk Cup and Littlewoods Challenge Cup)

1. Jeff Astle 19
2. Tony Brown 17
3. Cyrille Regis 16
4. Clive Clark 10
5. Bobby Hope 7

European competition marksmen (leading group)

1. Tony Brown 8
2. Laurie Cunningham 4
3. Asa Hartford 3
4. Cyrille Regis 3
5. Bryan Robson 2

Top FA Cup marksmen for Albion

1. Tony Brown 27
2. 'W.G.'Richardson 26
3. 'Jem' Bayliss 24
4. Ronnie Allen 23
5. Derek Kevan 16
6. Jeff Astle 14
7. Tom Pearson 12
8. Joe Wilson 12
9. Billy Bassett 11
10. Joe Carter 10
11. Cyrille Regis 10
12. George Woodhall 10

Top Ten Wartime scorers for Albion (1939-46) (Not including 1939-40 League and 1945-6 FA Cup)

1. Billy Elliott 117
2. 'W.G.'Richardson 100
3. 'Ike' Clarke 55
4. Harry Jones 47
5. Sammy Heaselgrave 41
6. Charlie Evans 31
7. Robbie Newsome 28
8. Joe Johnson 25
9. Frank Hodgetts 23
10. Jack Sankey 22

Albion centre-forward, Dave Walsh, scoring against Fulham at The Hawthorns in December 1949. Albion won the game 4-1.

'W.G.' Richardson scored 202 League goals for Albion.

Goal Talk

Ronnie Allen scored all his 208 League goals in the First Division — a club record. Jimmy Cookson (103) has scored most Division Two goals for Albion.

Albion had five goals disallowed in their home match against Bristol City on 2 October 1906. They had four goals ruled out against Burslem Port Vale (away) on 23 December 1905.

Jimmy Cookson, against Blackpool (home) Division Two, 17 September 1927; and 'W.G.' Richardson, against Luton Town (home), League South, 22 November 1941, are the only two players to have scored six goals in a senior competitive match for Albion.
 George Bell (1882), William Bisseker (1882), Harry Aston (1883), 'Jem' Bayliss (1884), Billy Bassett (1890), Billy Garraty (1909), 'W.G.'Richardson (1941) and Bobby Robson (1959) are the other Albion players who have netted six goals in a game.

Freddie Morris (against Notts County, October 1919) and Derek Kevan (against Everton, March 1960) are the only players to score five goals in a League game for Albion.

During a six-month period (May-Oct 1921) Albion played six home League matches and failed to score a goal in any of them.

In 16 away games during 1923-4 season Albion failed to find the net — a club record. And from 1 September to 25 December 1923, Albion did not register a single goal in ten successive away League matches.

Albion's defence did not concede a goal in any of their last six League games of season 1949-50.

Albion failed to gain promotion in season 1908-09 by just 1/56th of a goal, Tottenham Hotspur pipping them at the post with a goal tally of 67-32 to Albion's 56-27.

During the Albion-Lincoln Division Two game at The Hawthorns on 21 December 1907, five goals were scored in 11 minutes inside the last quarter of an hour and in that time Albion missed a penalty.

Albion scored five goals in 13 minutes of their home First Division match against Arsenal on 14 October 1922. And five goals came in 12 minutes of the Albion-Huddersfield League game on 6 October 1923, four of which were credited to the visitors.

In nine tour games in Canada and the USA in May-June 1959, Albion netted 59 goals, an average of 6.55 per game.

Albion scored in every recorded home game they played during the first four seasons of their history, 1879-1883 inclusive.

In seven successive home League matches in 1925-6, Albion ran up a total of 32 goals. In 12 consecutive games in this same season they managed 44 goals, including three five-goal romps and one seven-goal burst against West Ham United.

In their 21 home League games in 1929-30 Albion scored 73 goals — a club record.

Albion's top first-team victory is 26-0 against Coseley (home) Birmingham Cup, 11 November 1882. In an away friendly against Studley and District in September 1888, Albion ran out 23-2 winners; and against Burton Wanderers (home) in a Staffordshire Cup in February 1890, Albion won 23-0.

Albion's heaviest defeat (any competition) is 10-3 at Stoke (Division One) February 1937. They lost 10-5 at Hereford United (testimonial) in November 1954.

The highest score by an Albion team is 36-0 — against Bearwood Juniors in a Handsworth Junior League match on 8 September 1951. An amateur, Keith Knight, scored 15 of the goals.

Johnny Nicholls scores for Albion in the 4-2 defeat of Newcastle United at The Hawthorns on 1 September 1954.

A goal by Alec Jackson in Albion's 3-0 win over Everton at The Hawthorns on 25 March 1961.

Ronnie Allen scores Albion's first goal in the 1954 FA Cup Final against Preston North End.

One of the great FA Cup Final pictures — Ronnie Allen's penalty equaliser for Albion against Preston North End at Wembley in the 1954 Final. Albion's goalkeeper, Jimmy Sanders, hugs a post and prays for success.

Billy Williams scored a goal from fully 60 yards against Nottingham Forest (FA Cup) in February 1898; Bill Ashurst's goal against Blackburn at The Hawthorns (Division Two) in 1927 came from 55 yards; and Len Millard found the net from 50 yards against Cardiff City (home) in 1954-5.

During World War Two, Harry Jones was a scorer in 11 successive Midland Regional League games (Oct-Dec 1939); Billy Elliott was on target in nine consecutive League South matches between September and December 1941.

'W.G.'Richardson scored in each of seven consecutive League games in 1935-6; Fred Morris scored in ten successive League matches in 1919-20; and Dave Walsh netted in each of his first six League matches at the start of the 1946-7 season.

Ronnie Allen scored in nine consecutive Division One matches in 1954-5 and in ten games altogether (including the FA Charity Shield).

246

Albion have scored a century of League goals in a season on two occasions — 104 in 1919-20 and 105 in 1929-30. In the 1945-6 transitional season, Albion scored 104 League South goals.

Albion's best scoring season in modern times came in 1958-9 when they netted 160 goals — 88 in the League, five in the FA Cup, and 66 in friendlies, plus one in an abandoned match.

The fastest recorded League goal by an Albion player came from George James against Nottingham Forest (home) Division One, 13 December 1924 — timed at five seconds after the kick-off. Ronnie Allen netted after 12 seconds against Manchester United (away) on 15 December 1951, and Ally Brown in 22 seconds against Ipswich Town at The Hawthorns on 19 August 1978. Brown's goal was the first by any player in the League that season. He had also hit the League's first goal in 1971-2, when with Leicester City.

Freddie Morris scored two goals for Albion in the first 58 seconds of a League game against Manchester City on 13 December 1919.

'W.G.'Richardson hit four goals in five minutes for Albion at West Ham (Division One) on 7 November 1931, his strikes coming in the fifth, seventh, eighth and ninth minutes.

Cyrille Regis created a unique record during the years 1977 and 1978 when he scored on his debut for Albion in five different competitions. He netted twice in the League Cup against Rotherham 31 August 1977; scored once against Middlesbrough (Division One) 3 September 1977; notched a goal in a home FA Cup-tie against Blackpool on 7 January 1978; registered one goal against Southampton at Ibrox Park in a Tennent-Caledonian Cup game on 5 August 1978; and scored once against Sheffield Wednesday Reserves (home) on 27 August 1977 (Central League).

Alf Bentley made a great start to his career with Albion when he scored all four goals in his debut game against Burnley (home) on 6 September 1913 (Division One).

Two other players who registered hat-tricks on their Albion debuts were Willie Jordan (against Gainsborough Trinity, Division Two, 16 February 1907) and Albert Lewis (against Burnley, Division Two, 3 September 1904).

Several players celebrated their Albion debuts with two goals, including Derek Kevan (1955), Colin Suggett (1969) and Cyrille Regis (1977).

A goal for Ronnie Allen against Doncaster Rovers in an FA Cup replay in 1957.

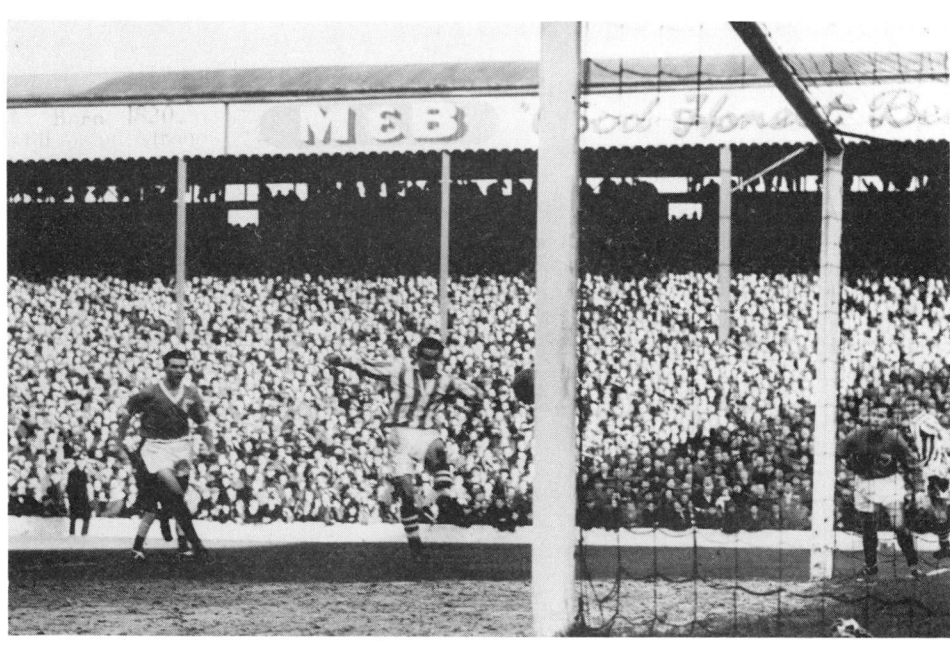

Ronnie Allen scoring against Blackpool at The Hawthorns in a fifth round FA Cup replay in February 1957. Albion won 2-1.

Ray Treacy scored on his two debuts for Albion: against Sunderland (away) on 8 October 1966 and then against Derby County (away) on 25 September 1976 after re-signing for the Throstles after a break of eight years.

The most own-goals received by Albion in a complete season is four, in 1965-6 (Division One), two coming from Leicester's John Sjoberg.

Albion centre-half Stan Jones scored three own-goals past Tony Millington during 1961-2 season (September-October), a club record.

Jesse Pennington conceded three own-goals in 1906-07 and another full-back, George Shaw, did likewise in 1931-2.

Alf McMichael (Newcastle United) scored an own-goal for Albion 12 seconds after the start of a Division One game at The Hawthorns on 5 September 1951 — the fastest on record in any game involving Albion.

Ten different players figured on the scoresheet when Albion beat Coseley 26-0 in 1882.

Centre-half Bill Richardson and outside-right Jimmy Prew were Albion's marksmen in the 2-1 win over Wolverhampton Wanderers on 17 October 1936 — they were the only goals these two players scored for Albion's senior XI; Richardson played over 350 times for the club.

'W.G.' Richardson scored in 24 of his 41 League games for Albion in 1935-6 — a club record.

Albion scored a total of 18 goals in three away League games against Birmingham City in successive seasons; won 5-3 in 1957-8; won 6-0 in 1958-9; won 7-1 in 1959-60.

Ronnie Allen is the only player to have scored in League games in every season from 1946-7 to 1964-5 inclusive, doing so for Port Vale (1946-50), Albion (1950-61) and Crystal Palace (1961-5). Allen also scored for Vale in season 1945-6, giving him the unique record of a goal in each of the first 20 post-war seasons.

Tony Brown shares the League record for most goals scored by a half-back in a season — 15 in 1968-9. This equalled the record set in 1951-2 by former Albion player Jack Lewis who netted 15 for Reading.

The following Albion players topped the First Division scoring charts in the seasons stated: Freddie Morris 1919-20 (37 goals), Ronnie Allen 1954-5 (27) Derek Kevan 1961-2 (33*), Jeff Astle 1969-70 (25), Tony Brown 1970-1 (28).
*Shared with Ray Crawford (Ipswich).

Jimmy Cookson (38 goals) was Division Two's top scorer in season 1927-8.

▲
Jeff Astle's 100th League goal for Albion, scored against Sheffield Wednesday at The Hawthorns on 22 November 1969. Albion won 3-0.

Asa Hartford scoring Albion's equaliser against 'double winners' Arsenal in the 2-2 draw at The Hawthorns in April 1971.
▼

Hat-Tricks
Hat-Tricks
Hat-Tricks

From December 1879 to May 1987, over 250 hat-tricks have been scored for Albion in first-team matches, with around half of them coming in the Football League.

Here is a breakdown of these competitive trebles:

Football League (Divisions One & Two)	124
FA Cup	15
League Cup (Milk Cup, Littlewoods Cup	4
European Competitions	1
FA Charity Shield	1
Wartime Matches (WWI & WWII)	47
Other games (Friendlies etc)	60
Total	**252**

W.G.Richardson hit 12 League hat-tricks for Albion (1929-39), three more than fellow striker Jimmy Cookson. Derek Kevan notched eight, Ronnie Allen seven and Jeff Astle six. Tony Brown, Fred Shinton and Tom Pearson claimed five apiece.

In the FA Cup, 'Jem' Bayliss registered three hat-tricks and W.G. Richardson two.

Astle netted two trebles in the League Cup, whilst Allen recorded Albion's only hat-trick in the Charity Shield (1954).

To date Tony Brown is Albion's lone 'European' hat-trick star with three goals against DOS Utrecht (home), Fairs Cup, 1966.

TONY BROWN

In wartime competition W.G.Richardson again topped the list with 12 hat-tricks, ten of which came in competitive matches; 'Ike' Clarke scored ten and Harry Jones and Billy Elliott eight each.
Tom Pearson scored Albion's first League hat-trick, at home to Bolton Wanderers on 4 November 1889.

'Jem' Bayliss notched the first Albion hat-trick in the FA Cup, against Old Westminsters (home) on 13 February 1886.

Jeff Astle (v Coventry City, home, 10 November 1965) netted Albion's initial League Cup hat-trick.

Two defenders have scored hat-tricks for Albion — Sid Bowser (v Bradford City, Division One, home, 27 September 1919) and Bobby Cram (v Stoke City, home, Division One, 12 September 1964).

W.G.Richardson hit a hat-trick in three minutes for Albion at West Ham on 7 November 1931 — and added a fourth in this same game to capture the unique record of four goals in five minutes. Two years later, against Derby County in September 1933, 'W.G.' netted three goals in nine minutes as Albion won 5-1.

Bobby Blood slammed home a hat-trick in five minutes for Albion v Nottingham Forest (away) on 3 March 1923, and Charlie 'Tug' Wilson's treble (v West Ham, home, on 15 November 1924) came in 11 minutes.

Jimmy Cookson scored three of his six goals against Blackpool (home, September 1927) in eight minutes, early in the second half. His last four goals came in 13 minutes from the 57th minute.

Six hat-tricks were scored in the Staffordshire Cup tie between Albion and Burton Wanderers on 1 February 1890. Billy Bassett grabbed six goals. Albion won 23-0.

Albert Lewis (v Burnley, 1904), Wille Jordan (v Gainsborough Trinity, 1907) and Alf Bentley (v Burnley, 1913) scored hat-tricks on their League debuts for Albion. Bentley netted a four-timer.

W.G.Richardson (1935-6), Jimmy Cookson (1927-8) and Fred Shinton (1906-7) each scored four hat-tricks in a season for Albion. Shinton's tally included three four-goals romps.

Jeff Astle heads Albion's first goal against Sheffield Wednesday on 4 September 1965 from Ken Foggo's corner kick. This goal put Astle on the way to his first hat-trick for the club.

Penalties

The penalty-kick was introduced by the Irish FA during season 1890-1. The English FA accepted it in September 1891 and it was immediately brought into operation in League matches.

The first penalty awarded to Albion was against Aston Villa (home) in a friendly match on 11 January 1892. Tom Pearson missed the kick, firing the ball over the bar.

Albion's first League penalty came in their home Division One game against Nottingham Forest on 3 April 1892. This time John Reynolds scored from the spot to earn Albion a 2-2 draw.

The first spot-kick conceded by Albion was at Wolverhampton Wanderers in a League game on 19 September 1891. Jack Horton was the culprit but luckily for him, Wolves' Harry Allen missed the kick, ballooning the ball over the bar.

The first penalty scored against Albion was by J.Campbell (Sunderland) in an away League game on 24 October 1891.

In 1958-9, Albion had 14 penalties awarded to them (all games). Ronnie Allen scored nine of them. Allen beat Sid Bowser's record of eight penalty conversions (set in 1919-20) and in 1977-8 Tony Brown stepped up to create a new penalty record for Albion by scoring from the spot on ten occasions.

Goalkeeper Hubert Pearson scored two penalty goals for Albion in 1911-12.

Goalkeeper Jim Sanders saved 28 penalties in his career (1940-59), and 20 of them were for Albion, including nine saves in League matches in 1948-9 when Albion won promotion from Division Two.

Full-back Cecil Shaw had a 100-per-cent scoring record from penalty-kicks while with Wolves, but after leaving Molineux for The Hawthorns in 1936 he missed his first spot-kick for Albion, at Coventry City in an FA Cup match in February 1937.

Ronnie Allen is one of only a handful of players to have scored a penalty goal in an FA Cup Final at Wembley, doing so for Albion against Preston North End in 1954.

Roddy McLeod was the first player to miss a penalty for Albion in a competitive match, against Blackburn Rovers in an FA Cup match on 27 February 1894. Albion lost the match 3-2.

Freddie Buck's penalty-goal winner against Huddersfield Town at The Hawthorns on 29 April 1911 gave Albion the two points which clinched promotion from Division Two.

Tony Brown has been Albion's most successful penalty-taker, netting a total of 53 in all competitions including friendlies. Ronnie Allen had almost 40 successes from the spot.

Tony Brown sends the Coventry City 'keeper the wrong way to score in 1979.

AMOS ADAMS

Born: West Bromwich, June 1880. Died: January 1941.

Career: West Bromwich Baptist and Bratt Street Schools, Geo. Salter Works, Springfields FC, Albion (June 1897-April 1910). Retired to become sportsmaster at a local school (West Bromwich) and later coached the Amiens Club (France), becoming manager in 1926-7.

Amos Adams was an intelligent, versatile and stylish full-back, accurate in kicking, strong in the tackle, and an excellent clubman. He spent 13 seasons with Albion and during that time appeared in well over 200 senior games. He won a Second Division Championship medal in 1902 and if Albion had been a more fashionable club, in the First Division, then Adams would have surely won international honours in the early 1900s. He arrived at the club in 1897 and after a year or so in the reserves, made his first-team debut at centre-forward. But it was at full-back where he made good, and after Billy Williams had been forced to quit football in 1901, Adams made the No.3 slot his own until Jesse Pennington came along, when he switched to the right-hand side.

Albion debut v Notts County (away) Division One, 9 March 1899.

JIMMY ADAMS

Born: Norton Canes, Cannock, January 1908. Died: Birmingham, 1983.

Career: Cannock Schools, Cannock Chase Colliery, Cannock Town, Albion (July 1929 -May 1945) Retired.

'Doc' Adams was a fine, competent goalkeeper, hefty but extremely mobile, whose career at Albion coincided with those of Harold Pearson,

George Ashmore and Billy Light. He was one of the club's heaviest players, tipping the scales at 14st 10lb during World War Two when he played most of his 221 matches for the Throstles. Albion debut v Notts County (home) Division Two, 23 November 1929.

RONNIE ALLEN

Born: Fenton, Stoke-on-Trent, January 1929.

Career: Hanley High School, Bucknall Boys Brigade, Wellington Scouts, Northwood Mission, Port Vale (1944), RAF, WBA (March 1950-May 1961), Crystal Palace (£4,500), Wolves (coach, later manager), Athletic Bilbao (manager), Sporting Lisbon (manager), Walsall (manager), Albion (January 1977 as scouting advisor, then manager June 1977-December 1977), Panathinaikos, (Greece), Albion (manager, July 1981-May 1982, then general manager until 1983).

The 'complete footballer' and the kingpin of Albion's wonderful attack of the 1950s, Ronnie filled every forward position for the club, with centre-forward undoubtedly his favourite. He possessed a powerful shot in both feet, was a superb volleyer of the ball and an ace penalty taker. Winner of five England caps (1952-54) he

also represented the Football League, the England 'B' team, the FA XI and the RAF. Allen won an FA Cup winners' medal in 1954 when his two goals helped Albion beat Preston North End 3-2 at Wembley, and in 1967 he led Wolves back into the First Division. Two years later he was with Bilbao when they won the Spanish Cup. For Albion alone Allen appeared in 415 League games (all in Division One, 306 at centre-forward) and scored 208 goals — a club record until passed by Tony Brown in 1978. He also played in 42 FA Cup-ties (23 goals) and hit a hat-trick for Albion in the 1954 Charity Shield match v Wolves. In his magnificent career Allen amassed a grand total of 637 League appearances (276 goals) and in all matches he played over 800 times, and scored 354 goals. Allen holds the honour of being the only player to have scored in each of the first 20 post-war seasons (1945-6-1964-5 inclusive). He was the First Division's leading marksman in 1954-5 with 27 goals.

Albion debut v Wolves (home) Division One, 4 March 1950.

GEORGE ASHMORE

Born: Plymouth, May 1898. Died: Birmingham, May 1973.

Career: South Devon & District Schools, Nineveh Wesley, Albion (November 1919-October 1931), Chesterfield. Retired 1935.

An agile, daring goalkeeper, George Ashmore was in the shadows of Hubert Pearson for a number of seasons at The Hawthorns. 'Cap', as

he was known, played once for England (1926) and appeared in 268 senior games for the Throstles. A loyal club-man, he worked for the MEB for several years after announcing his retirement at the age of 37.
Albion debut v Blackburn Rovers (away) Division One, 9 October 1920, lost 1-5.

JEFF ASTLE
Born: Eastwood, Nottinghamshire, May 1942.
Career: Devonshire Drive and Walker Street Schools, Holy Trinity YC, West Notts Boys, John Player FC (Nottingham), Notts County, Albion (September 1964-July 1974), Hellenic (South Africa), Dunstable Town, Weymouth, Atherstone Town, Hillingdon Borough, WBA All Stars. Retired 1977.
Jeff Astle was a real bargain-buy for Albion, manager Jimmy Hagan paying £25,000 for this superb striker in 1964. Nicknamed the 'King', Astle was indeed a brilliant centre-forward, brilliant in the air and not bad on the ground either. He won five England caps (1969-70); had outings for the Football League and England 'B' teams, and collected an FA Cup winners' medal in 1968 when his extra-time special beat Everton at Wembley. Two years earlier he gained a League Cup winners' tankard and was in Albion's side in both the 1967 and 1970 League Cup Finals, scoring in the latter (against Manchester City) which gave him the record of becoming the first player to find the net in both the FA and League Cup Final at Wembley. In 1968 he was voted Midland Footballer of the Year.

Altogether, in a really wonderful career, Astle accumulated more than 450 appearances in senior football — 361 of them with Albion. He scored 168 League goals with 25 coming in 1969-70 when he topped the First Division charts. His tally for Albion in the League was 137 which included six hat-tricks, two in a week in September 1965 and two in 72 hours at the end of the 1967-8 campaign. In August 1986 Astle returned to Albion in the capacity of President of the club's newly-formed Challenge Club.

HAROLD BACHE
Born: Churchill, Nr Kidderminster, August 1889. Died: France (killed in action) February 1916.
Career: King Edwards's Grammar School (Birmingham), Cambridge University, The Corinthians, West Bromwich Springfield, Staffordshire Youths, Eastbourne, Albion (February 1914-February 1916).
Harold Bache was a quite brilliant amateur international centre-forward, destined for all the major soccer honours until tragedy struck when serving with the Lancashire Fusiliers in France, in 1916, when he was only 26 years of age. Standing at 5ft 8in tall and weighing barely 10st, Bache was so skilful and positive in everything he did that his height and build were insignificant. He sadly played in only 14 games for Albion (four goals scored) but had been a regular performer for the England AFA international side long before he moved to The Hawthorns in 1914. In all he collected seven caps (1910-13) and in one game, against France at Ipswich in 1910, he scored no fewer than seven of England's goals in their 20-0 victory. Bache also played for the Football League XI (1914) and besides being a superb soccer player he excelled on the Rugby Union field, on the cricket square (with Worcestershire), on the tennis court and around the athletics track. He was a grand sportsman in every sense of the word — and a man who was liked and respected throughout the sporting world.
Albion debut v Aston Villa (away) FAC, 21 February 1914.

GEORGE BADDELEY
Born: Fegg Hayes, Staffs, May 1874. Died: West Bromwich, July 1952.
Career: Pitshill FC, Biddulph FC, Stoke City, Albion (June 1908-May 1914). Retired 1914 cs.
George Baddeley was strong in all aspects of half-back play — being safe, difficult to pass

and above all a fine feeder of the attack. He was captain of Stoke for several years before moving to The Hawthorns. As an Albion man he made in excess of 150 first-team appearances and he won a Second Division Championship medal in 1911 and an FA Cup runners-up medal a year later. After his retirement he became a publican in West Bromwich.
Albion debut: v Grimsby Town (away) Division Two, 5 September 1908.

RAY BARLOW
Born: Swindon, August 1926.
Career: Sandford Street School Swindon, Swindon Town(trial), Garrards FC, Albion (June 1944 - June 1960), Birmingham City, Stourbridge. Retired 1962. Guested for Swindon Town in World War Two and played for WBA All Stars(1969-81).

A tall, rangy player, who was poised, elegant, skilful, fast over 20 yards, wholehearted with heaps of energy, Ray Barlow was converted successfully by Albion from an inside-forward into a classy, international left-half where he developed a singularly sound tackle. He strutted across the field majestically, sending passes straight to his man from distances of up to 40 yards His powerful runs into the opposing penalty-areas caused all sorts of trouble and it was his forward dash into the 'box' in the 1954 FA Cup Final that resulted in a penalty being awarded to Albion as they strove to beat Preston. Barlow also turned out from time to time in the centre-half and centre-forward positions but it was in the No.6 shirt that he is best remembered. He was extremely unlucky not to win more than one cap for England (gained against Northern Ireland in 1954), but he did play for the 'B' team, the Football League XI and the FA representative side on many occasions, as well as being a regular England reserve. He skippered Albion during the late 1950s and during his professional career, with Albion and Birmingham City, amassed a total of 490 competitive matches, in 17 years. He toured South America with the FA in 1953. On terminating his playing career, Barlow went into the newsagents' and tobacconists' trade in West Bromwich, and later at Stourbridge. Albion debut v Walsall (home) Wartime League Cup, 3 February 1945. League debut v Newport County (away) Division Two, 28 September 1946, and he scored in a 7-2 Albion win.

PETER BARNES
Born: Manchester, June 1957.
Career: Chorlton Park Juniors, Chorlton High Grammar School, Whitehall, Gatley Rangers, Manchester & District Boys, Manchester City (1972, professional 1974), Albion (July 1979 -July 1981), Leeds United, Real Betis (Spain), Leeds United, West Ham United, Coventry City, Manchester United, Manchester City.
Highly skilled outside-left, winner of 22 full England caps, one at 'B' level, nine at Under-21, and a former Schoolboy and Youth International, 'Barnsey' cost Albion a club record £748,000 when they signed him from Manchester City in the summer of 1979. And when he left The Hawthorns, for Elland Road, Leeds, in 1981, Albion collected £930,000, a record incoming fee. A player who flitted in and out of the game, Barnes had speed, a fine body swerve and powerful shot. He scored a splendid goal for Manchester City in the 1976 League Cup Final against Newcastle United — and it helped City lift that coveted silver trophy for the second time. Barnes had a wonderful first season with Albion (1979-80) when he scored 15 goals, including a hat-trick against Bolton at The

Hawthorns in March. After leaving Albion he never really settled down again and although he had a good spell in Spain, his career slowly wound down until in 1986-7 he was basically a reserve at Old Trafford. Albion debut v Derby County (home) Division One, 18 August 1979.

BILLY BASSETT
Born: West Bromwich, January 1869. Died: West Bromwich, April 1937.
Career: Christ Church School, Oak Villa, West Bromwich Strollers (not Albion), Old Church Club, Albion (August 1886-April 1899), Retired. Became Club Director (September 1900), and elected Chairman in 1908, serving in that capacity until his untimely death in 1937 hours before Albion met Preston North End in the FA Cup semi-final at Highbury. League Management Committee (1930-7) and a member of the England International Selection Committee (1936-7). He was also a JP (appointed in 1935).
One of the great names in Albion's history, Billy (William Isaiah) Bassett was a brilliant footballer. Fast and clever, determined and dedicated, he played mostly as an outside-right, hugging the touch-line and putting in many darting runs. His centres were immaculate and

his shooting red-hot. He was a wonderful club-man who gained 16 England caps(eight against Scotland) as well as performing regularly, and consistently, for the Football League representative side, and the FA XI. He played in three FA Cup Finals — 1888, 1892 and 1895 — picking up winners medals in the first two. He was associated with the Albion club for 51 years.
Albion debut v Wednesbury Old Athletic (home) FAC, 15 October 1887.
League debut v Stoke (away) 8 September 1888.

BRENDON BATSON
Born: St George's, Grenada, West Indies, February 1953.
Career: St Mary's Junior School (Tilbury), McEntee Technical College, Walthamstow, Waltham Forest Boys, Arsenal, Cambridge United, Albion (February 1978-May 1984). Retired. Assisted WBA All Stars 1984-87.
Brendon Batson was a highly efficient right-back who began his playing career with Arsenal as either a midfielder or central-defender. Steady, easy-going and sincere, Batson was Ron Atkinson's first signing for Albion — and he turned out to be one of his best — a £30,000 bargain. With Arsenal he won an FA Youth Cup-winners' medal (1971) and later, as Cambridge United's captain, he helped his team win the Fourth Division Championship (1977). Gained England 'B' recognition (three caps) in 1980 — his only representative honours. Sadly in 1984 he was forced to retire from competitive football through injury and Albion granted him a testimonial to say 'thank you' for his magnificent service to the club. Batson, an intelligent, articulate man, became assistant secretary of the PFA in 1984-5 and also assists a local radio station, covering football matches.
Albion debut v Birmingham City (away) Division One, 28 February 1978.

'JEM' BAYLISS
Born: Tipton, August 1863. Died: West Bromwich, August 1933.
Career: Great Bridge and Horseley Heath Schools, Great Bridge Unity, Tipton Providence, Wednesbury Old Athletic, Albion (August 1884, professional August 1885-March 1892), guested for Walsall Town. Retired, became Club Director — a post he initially held whilst an active player with the club (1891-1905).

'Jem' Bayliss — a nickname taken from three of his Christian names (Edward James Matthias) — was a grand all-round footballer, always full of running, always willing to work and always likely to score a spectacular goal. He played at wing-half, inside-right and centre-forward for Albion and gained one England cap in 1891. He was Albion's 'leader' in the 1886, 1887 and 1888 FA Cup Finals, scoring the first goal in the latter tie against Preston North End. He made his Albion debut at the start of the 1884-5 season against Aston Villa (away), scoring 20 goals in his first year with the club. In 1885-6 he notched another 20 or so, including a hat-trick in the FA Cup-tie v Old Westminsters; his 1886-7 haul was around the 40 mark and in 1887-8 he topped the charts wth 50. Bayliss was a real 'gem' when it came to finding a way past the 'keeper — and for Albion his goal total was in excess of 150 (all competitions and friendlies). He virtually retired in 1891 but was 'recalled' for an FA Cup semi-final replay against Nottingham Forest, his last appearance for Albion. A real gentleman in more ways than one, Bayliss actually read his own 'obituary' notice in the local newspaper in 1897. He had gone on holiday to Gibralter and while he was away from his Great Bridge home, rumours gained currency that he had died. He returned and proved he was alive and kicking and quickly had the 'notice' framed for posterity. He lived for another 36 years.
Albion FA Cup debut v Derby Junction Street School (away), 25 October 1884 (scoring twice in a 7-1 win).
League debut v Stoke (away) Division One, 8 September 1888.

MARTYN BENNETT
Born: Birmingham, August 1961.
Career: Pheasey Junior School, Birmingham, Aldridge Comprehensive School, Aston Schools, Aldridge and Brownhills Schools, Walsall Schools, West Midlands County Schools, Streetly FC. Albion (August 1977, professional August 1978-
A talented defender, tall, dominant and quick, Martyn Bennett won nine Schoolboy caps for England. He understudied John Wile and Ally Robertson for a number of years before establishing himself in Albion's first team during the 1980-81 season. Injuries have troubled him

from time to time and have twice prevented him from representing his country. When Bennett was called up by England in 1982-3, he was described by Jimmy Greaves as 'the fastest covering defender I've ever seen.' Bennett was named Albion club captain at the start of 1986-87.
Debut for Albion v Everton (home) Division One, 7 April 1979, in the right-back position.

ALF BENTLEY
Born: Alfreton, Derbyshire, September 1887. Died: April 1940.
Career: Church of England School (Alfreton), Derby County, Bolton Wanderers, Albion (June 1913-May 1922), Burton Albion, Alfreton Town. Retired 1926, aged 38.
Alf Bentley was an 'eager-beaver' type of centre-forward who cost Albion £650 when he signed from Bolton shortly before World War One. 'Nobby' or 'Snobby' as he was called by colleagues and supporters, made an immediate impact when he scored four goals on his Albion debut, against Burnley at The Hawthorns in

September 1913. He was dangerous around the penalty area, always ready to take a shot at goal, and his League striking record was good — over 160 goals in 265 appearances. For Derby alone he scored 99 goals in 151 League games, twice breaking the Rams' individual scoring record for a season. Derby needed his goals, too, for they had parted company with the great Steve Bloomer. Bentley won a League Championship medal with Albion in 1919-20 when his 15 goals were bettered only by the prolific Freddie Morris with whom he had drawn up a fine understanding.
Albion debut v Burnley (home) Division One, 6 September 1913, scoring four goals.

BOBBY BLOOD
Born: Harpur Hill, near Buxton, March 1894
Career: Harpur Hill School, Buxton, Buxton Lime Firms, Leek Alexandra, Port Vale, Albion (February 1921-December 1924), Stockport County, Winsford United, Mossley, Ashton National. Retired 1931, aged 37.
Bobby Blood was a dynamic centre-forward, renowned for his cannonball shooting. He stood only 5ft 7in tall but was a brave player. A real terrier around goal, he scored well over 70 goals in less than 150 League matches during his career. In all types of football, after leaving school until his retirement in 1931, Blood claimed somewhere in the region of 400 goals, including 100 in two seasons immediately prior to joining Port Vale. For Vale, he hit 44 goals in only 53 League games, including 24 in his first season, 1919-20. In 1986-7 he was still alive, living in a Salvation Army hostel in Buxton, and still enjoying five and six mile walks in his 92nd year.
Albion debut v Tottenham Hotspur (home) Division One, 19 February 1921, when he scored a penalty in Albion's 3-1 win.

SID BOWSER
Born: Handsworth, Birmingham, January 1892. Died: Birmingham, February 1961.
Career: Wattville Road School, Astbury

Richmond, Willenhall, Birmingham (trial), Albion (July 1908-April 1913), Belfast Distillery, Albion (February 1914-August 1924), Walsall. Retired 1927. Guested for Southport Vulcan and Notts County during World War One.

A tenacious, resilient and hard-working player, Sid Bowser divided his immense talents between two widely differing roles, those of inside-forward and centre-half. A big, strong fellow, Bowser had two spells with Albion and in each of them he achieved personal success. In 1910-11 he helped Albion win the Second Division Championship and a year later played for them in the FA Cup Final. On his return he was a key member of the League Championship winning side of 1919-20, helping himself to eight penalties and a hat-trick from centre-half against Bradford City. A sterling performer, Bowser won an England cap, against Ireland in 1919, and represented the Irish League whilst a Distillery player. He was a publican (in Dudley) for 25 years following his retirement in 1927.

Albion debut v Grimsby Town (home) Division Two, 2 January 1909, scoring twice in Albion's 7-2 win.

WALLY BOYES

Born: Killamarsh, Sheffield, January 1913.
Died: September 1960.
Career: Netherthorpe Council School, Sheffield Boys, Woodhouse Mills United, Albion (February 1931-February 1938), Everton, Notts County (player-coach), Scunthorpe United (player-trainer), Retford Town (manager), Hyde United (manager), Swansea Town (trainer 1959). Retired (ill-health) 1960. Guested for Aldershot, Brentford, Clapton Orient, Leeds United, Manchester United, Middlesbrough, Millwall, Newcastle United, PNE and Sunderland during World War Two.

A spirited little footballer who was perhaps best known as an orthodox left-winger, Wally Boyes also competed ably at left-half and inside-left. He was a purposeful player with an accurate shot which he allied to quickness off the mark.

A schoolboy prodigy in Sheffield — where he once scored 17 goals in one game — Boyes took over from Stan Wood in the Albion team and scored in the 1935 FA Cup Final against Sheffield Wednesday at Wembley. After leaving The Hawthorns he gained a League Championship medal with Everton in 1938-9, netting four goals in 36 appearances for the Merseysiders. He won four full international caps (two with Albion, two with Everton) and at 5ft 4in tall was one of the smallest wingers ever to represent England. Boyes' career was even more remarkable when one remembers that he had one leg shorter than the other.

Albion debut v Aston Villa (home) Division One, 14 November 1931, in front of a near-60,000 attendance.

ALLY BROWN

Born: Musselburgh, Scotland, April 1951.
Career: Musselburgh and Edinburgh District Schools, Leicester City, Albion (March 1972-March 1983), Crystal Palace, Walsall, Port Vale. Retired 1986, aged 35. Played for Portland Timbers (NASL) May-August 1981.

Ally Brown cost Albion the unusual fee of £61,111 when he signed from Leicester City on the 1972 transfer deadline. He scored on each of his first two outings in Albion's senior side and went on to prove a good professional for the

rest of his 11-year career with the Throstles, finishing leading marksman in 1975-6 and 1978-9. He had a couple of lean seasons (1973-4 and 1974-5) when Don Howe was manager but overall he served the club consistently in all competitions. When he retired in the summer of 1986, Brown became a publican in West Bromwich. He scored a total of 157 League and Cup goals for his five English clubs and was Leicester's leading scorer when they won the Second Division title in 1970-71.

Albion debut v Crystal Palace (home) Division One, 11 March 1972.

TONY BROWN

Born: Oldham, Lancashire, October 1945.
Career: Columba RC School (Manchester), St Peter's (Wythenshawe) and St Clare's (Blakely) Schools, Manchester and District Boys, Lancashire Boys, Albion (April 1961, professional October 1963-October 1981), Torquay United, Stafford Rangers. Played for New England Teamen and Jacksonville Teamen (NASL, 1980-1981). WBA All Stars. Returned to The Hawthorns as coach (1984-6).

Albion's record League appearance maker, Tony 'The Bomber' Brown enjoyed 20 wonderful years with the Throstles, during which time he gave many sparkling displays in many different positions. A wholehearted player, Brown packed a deadly shot in his right foot, and was no slouch with his left. He converted over 50 penalties for Albion and created many club records. When he netted at Leeds on 14 October 1978, he overtook Ronnie Allen's record of 208 League goals, ending his Albion career with 218 goals in a record 574 League games; and in all first-team games (including friendlies) he made 819 appearances and scored 312 goals. His 459 First Division appearances is also an Albion record, as is his 146 senior Cup appearances. Brown won a League Cup winners' tankard (1966) and an FA Cup winners' medal (1968) as well as playing in the 1967 and 1970 League Cup Finals at Wembley. He played for the England Youth team and gained one full cap, against Wales in 1971. Brown also represented

the Football League, was Midlands Footballer of the Year in 1969, 1971 and 1979, and topped the First Division goalscoring list with 28 goals in 1970-71. He returned to The Hawthorns in 1984, as coach under Johnny Giles' managership, but lost the job when Ron Saunders was appointed. He still plays regularly for the WBA All Stars charity team looking as fit as he did 20 years ago,
Albion debut v Ipswich Town (away) Division One, 28 September 1963, scoring in a 2-1 win.

FRED BUCK
Born: Newcastle-under-Lyme, Staffs, July 1880. Died: June 1952.
Career: Newcastle-under-Lyme District Schools, Stafford Wesleyans, Stafford Rangers, Albion (November 1900-May 1903), Liverpool, Plymouth Argyle, Albion (April 1906-May 1914), Swansea Town. Retired 1917.
One of the great little players Albion have had on their books, Fred Buck, of slight physique, was fast and dangerous, possessed wonderful judgement and was ever-dangerous in front of goal. He began his career as an inside-forward and spent his first three years with Albion in the forward line. During his second spell with the club he was converted into a safe, solid centre-half and despite his size — he stood only 5ft 4in, but weighed 11st — he was regarded as one of the finest in the country. Buck represented the Football League in 1911, won a Second Division Championship medal the same year, and was Albion's centre-half in the 1912 FA Cup Final against Barnsley. Buck was a brilliant footballer who made well over 500 appearances during his lengthy career with four different clubs.
Albion debut v Bolton Wanderers (home) Division One, 8 December 1900, and he scored once in Albion's 7-2 win.

DAVY BURNSIDE
Born: Bristol, December 1939.
Career: Kingswood School, Bristol & District Boys, Bristol City (amateur), Albion (December 1955, professional February 1957-September 1962), Southampton (£17,000), Crystal Palace, Wolves, Plymouth Argyle, Bristol City, Colchester United, Bath City (manager), Walsall (assistant-manager), Cadbury Heath, Bridgwater Town, (player-manager), Taunton Town. Retired May 1980, later FA coach; appointed England youth team manager 1983.

Davy Burnside was a talented inside-forward with exceptional ball skills which he displayed to capture the acclaim of the paying customers. Unfortunately Burnside's play was spasmodic. In 1957 — during the half-time interval of the Albion v CDSA (Russia) friendly — he showed off his individual artistry 'live' on TV and afterwards was offered a lucrative contract to appear regularly on shows all over the world. He turned the offer down to concentrate on football. In 1960 Burnside entered the *'Sunday Despatch'* 'Get-a-Header' contest, which was organised to find out whether Britain possessed a footballer capable of capturing the world's heading record which at the time was held by the Austrian George Kaul, aged 19. Burnside managed 495 clean headers without a break; Kaul's record was 3,025. In 135 games for Albion, he scored 42 goals. He represented England Youth, and the Under-23s (two caps) as well as serving with the FA XI. He was in Wolves' 1966-7 promotion-winning side.
Albion debut v Leeds United (away) Division One, 19 October 1957.

JACK BYERS

JACK BYERS
Born: Selby, Yorkshire, January 1897. Died: November 1931.
Career: Selby Schools, Knaresborough (Harrogate), Huddersfield Town, Blackburn Rovers, Albion (January 1924-July 1928), Worcester City, Torquay United, Kidderminster Harriers, Retired close season 1931.
An outstandingly quick and dangerous outside-left, who had loads of skill and a powerful shot, Jack Byers joined Albion as cover for Howard Gregory (looking to retire) and Arthur Fitton. Byers, in fact, went immediately into Albion's League side, but injuries cropped up now and again, and during the second half of the 1923-4 season he was in and out of the side. In the following campaign he was a consistent performer but then began to lose his form, and flair, and subsequently found himself 'recovering' in the reserves. During his League career — with Huddersfield, Blackburn and Albion — he accumulated a total of 143 appearances.
Albion debut v Burnley (away) Division One, 26 January 1924.

LEN CANTELLO
Born: Newton Heath, Manchester, September 1951.
Career: Albert Memorial School, Manchester & Lancashire Boys, Newton Heath Schools, Albion (July 1967, professional October 1968-May 1979), Bolton Wanderers, Burnley (trial), Altrincham, Eastern FC (Hong Kong), Hereford United (N/C), Bury (N/C), SC Cambuur (Holland; player-coach), Peterborough United (trial), Northwich Victoria (1986-7). Assisted Dallas Tornados (NASL, May-August 1978).
Len Cantello carried out many duties for Albion during his professional career at The Hawthorns, donning ten different numbered shirts in the first team and performing with style and artistry, mainly as a midfielder. He certainly had flair, and he drew up an excellent understanding, first with Asa Hartford and afterwards with Johnny Giles and Bryan Robson. As a defender, lining up at left-back, Cantello

tackled hard and was always eager to attack down the flank. He gained international honours for England at Schoolboy (six caps), Youth (four caps) and Under-23 (eight caps). He played in well over 360 games for Albion including an appearance in the 1970 League Cup Final, at the age of 18. He left Albion for Bolton immediately after his testimonial in 1979.
Albion debut v Ipswich Town (away) Division One, 7 December 1968 (as substitute).

JOE CARTER
Born: Aston, Birmingham, April 1901. Died: Handsworth, Birmingham, January 1977.
Career: Farm Street & Hockley Hill Schools (Birmingham), Westbourne Celtic, Albion (April 1921-May 1936), Sheffield Wednesday (for six days), Tranmere Rovers, Walsall, Vono Sports FC (player-manager). Retired 1940 aged 39.
Joe Carter gave Albion 15 years loyal service from the inside-right position. He was upright, had a grand dribbling technique, a magnificent body-swerve, expert positional sense and a pretty useful goalscoring record. He formed a wonderful partnership with outside-right Tommy Glidden and together the 'twins', as they were called by The Hawthorns' faithful, performed together on Albion's right flank in well over 350 senior matches. Carter himself made over 450 appearances for Albion (155 goals). He won three England caps (1926-29), and represented the Football League. He was a key figure in Albion's 'double-winning' team of 1930-31, and played in both of Albion's FA Cup Finals in the 1930s, collecting a winners' medal in 1931. He left Albion for Sheffield Wednesday in 1936 but was rejected by the Hillsborough club on medical grounds owing to complications with his right leg which resulted in him having a cartilage operation prior to switching his allegiance to Tranmere. Carter had a particularly sad death, of dehydration at his Handsworth home in 1977, aged 75.
Albion debut v Bolton Wanderers (away) Division One, 9 December 1922.

WILF CARTER
Born: Wednesbury, Staffs. October 1933.
Career: Wednesbury High School, SE Staffs Boys, Birmingham & District Schools, Birmingham County Youths, Albion (April 1949 Professional January 1951-May 1957), Plymouth Argyle, Exeter City, Bath City. Retired 1970.
Wilf Carter was initially an inside-forward at The Hawthorns, and therefore had to battle it out for a first-team place with some pretty useful players — Allen, Nicholls, Kevan and Robson among them. All told he made only 61 senior appearances for the club, 11 of them in the left-back position during 1956-7 when he replaced the injured Len Millard. After leaving Albion in 1957, Carter went on to perform majestically for Plymouth and in 252 League games for the Devon club he scored 133 goals. He was Argyle's leading marksman for five successive seasons (1957-62) and helped his club win the Third Division (S) title in 1959. In 1957 Carter was selected for the Third Division (S) representative side but had to miss the game through injury.
Albion debut v Fulham (away) Division One, 22 September 1951.

HARRY CHAMBERS
Born: Willington Quay, Nr Newcastle-upon-Tyne, February 1896. Died: June 1949.
Career: Percy Main School (Tynemouth), Willington United Methodists, North Shields Athletic, Liverpool, Distillery and Glentoran (wartime guest), Liverpool, Albion (March 1928-July 1929), Oakengates Town (player-manager). Retired June 1948 after playing his last game at the age of 52.
'Smiler' Chambers was a player of ice-cool temperament who had a brilliant football brain. Bow-legged, he could 'bend' a ball at will and occasionally surprised opponents with a fierce left-foot shot. He played inside-left for most of his career but during his spell at Albion reverted

to centre-half with good effect. He moved to Anfield just before World War One and during the war guested for Irish League clubs, Distillery and Glentoran, playing in the latter club's losing 1919 Irish Cup Final team. He returned to Liverpool and became an immediate success with the fans. When the Merseysiders won the League Championship in successive seasons (1921-2 and 1922-3) Chambers scored 41 goals in 72 League matches. In all he netted 151 goals for the Reds (338 appearances) for an average of a goal almost every two games. He topped Liverpool's scoring charts in each of the first five post-war seasons. Chambers won eight England caps (four goals scored) and played five times for the Football League XI.
Albion debut v Fulham (home) Division Two, 10 March 1928, scoring in a 4-0 win.

CLIVE CLARK
Born: Leeds, December 1940.
Career: Harehills and Leeds City Schools,

Ashley Road Methodists Club, Huddersfield Town (trial), Leeds United, QPR, Albion (January 1961-June 1969), QPR, Preston North End, Southport, Telford United, Washington Diplomats, Dallas Tornados, Philadelphia Fury, Skegness Town. Retired 1976-7.

'Chippy' Clark was an accomplished left-winger, fast, direct and courageous — and a great goalscorer. He cost Albion £17,000 in 1961, the year he won an England Under-23 cap, and repaid the Throstles with 98 goals in over 350 games, a figure which made him Albion's greatest goalscoring winger after Tommy Glidden. He took over the No.11 shirt from Derek Hogg and was a virtual ever-present until injury sidelined him in 1968, soon after he had helped Albion win the FA Cup. A year earlier, in March 1967, he scored two goals in the first-half of the League Cup Final against his old club, QPR, but after the break Rangers fought back to take the trophy in the first Final of that competition to be staged at Wembley. In 1966, Clark was in Albion's League Cup winning side against West Ham. In the 1966-7 competition he became the first player to score in every game up to and including the Final. He helped Preston win the Third Division title in 1970-71 and his entire League career spanned 447 matches and 98 goals. Today he lives in Filey, North Yorkshire.

Albion debut v Preston North End (home) Division One, 14 January 1961.

IKE CLARKE
Born: Tipton, January 1915.
Career: Prince's End Baptists, Coseley Juniors, Toll End Wesley, Albion (January 1937-November 1947), Portsmouth (£5,000), Sittingbourne (manager), Yeovil Town (manager), Canterbury City (manager), Ashford Town (manager). Retired from football 1973, aged 58. Guested for Walsall and Nottingham Forest during World War Two.
Ike Clarke was a fearless competitor with a strong kick, boundless energy and a solid frame able to take the fiercest of challenges. A former England Junior international (1937), he played inside or centre-forward for Albion for ten

years, either side of World War Two, participating in 213 games and scoring almost 100 goals. A true Black Country man, born and bred in the industrial area near West Bromwich and Dudley, Clarke was a great favourite of The Hawthorns fans and they were in uproar when Albion sold him to Pompey in 1947. He prospered at Fratton Park, and helped Portsmouth win the First Division Championship in successive seasons, 1949 and 1950, scoring 49 goals in 116 League matches. In 1951, at the tail-end of his playing career, he toured Australia with the FA XI and appeared in five 'internationals' against the Aussies.

Albion debut v Charlton Athletic (away) Division One, 11 September 1937.

IAN COLLARD
Born: South Hetton, Co. Durham, August 1947.
Career: South Hetton Primary and Senior Schools, Durham Boys, Albion (June 1962, professional November 1964-May 1969), Ipswich Town, Portsmouth (on loan, 1975). Retired 1976. Coach to the Kuwait Sporting Club 1978-9.
Ian Collard was a player who always put maximum effort into his performances. He started off as a talented inside-forward but later did splendid work as a left-half and left-back. He joined Ipswich in a player-exchange deal, plus £55,000, involving Danny Hegan. Collard played in the 1967 League Cup Final and in the 1968 FA Cup Final for Albion, gaining a winners' medal in the latter when he lined up in midfield with Bobby Hope and Tony Brown. Brother of Bruce Collard, the former Scunthorpe United defender, he made over 90 appearances for Albion, almost 100 for Ipswich and just one for Pompey.

Albion debut v Burnley (home) Division One, 26 September 1964.

JIMMY COOKSON
Born: Manchester, December 1904. Died: December 1970.
Career: Johnston Street School, Manchester, South Salford Lads' Club, Clayton FC, Manchester North End, Manchester City, Southport (trial), Chesterfield, Albion (June

1927-August 1933), Plymouth Argyle, Swindon Town. Retired 1938. Became a publican, but still played local football in Swindon up to 1952.
A powerful and most prolific goalscoring inside or centre-forward, Jimmy Cookson notched 92 goals in only 103 League appearances for Albion in just three full seasons (1927-30), including a club record six-goal haul in a Second Division match versus Blackpool at The Hawthorns in September 1927. In his 15 years' career in top-class football, 'Cooky' scored 255 League goals — 85 for Chesterfield, 103 for Albion, 37 for Argyle and 30 for Swindon — and he appeared in only 290 matches — a magnificent record for a truly remarkable striker. He was leading scorer in Division Three (N) in 1925-6 and in Division Two in 1927-8. The 100th League goal of his career came in only his 89th match — playing for Albion v South Shields in December 1927 — which is the quickest individual century of goals in League history from the start of a player's League career. He also scored more Second Division goals than anyone else in Albion's history. Cookson eventually lost his place in Albion's front line to another great marksman, W.G. Richardson.

Albion debut v Oldham Athletic (away) Division Two, 27 August 1927, and he scored in a 3-1 Albion defeat.

BOBBY CRAM
Born: Hetton-le-Hole, Co. Durham, November 1939.
Career: Hetton-le-Hole Schools, Durham & District Boys, Albion (September 1955, professional January 1957-August 1967), Bromsgrove Rovers, Vancouver Royals, Vancouver All Stars, Paul Taylors's (coach), Colchester United, Royal Canada FC, Bath City, Canada (coach). Retired 1974.
Bobby Cram was a determined and versatile footballer who played at right-back, wing-half and inside or centre-forward during his 12 years with Albion. He wore the No.2 shirt in the 1967 League Cup Final at Wembley — his last game for Albion — and all told appeared in 163 senior games for the club, scoring 26 goals, a third of which came from penalty-kicks. Cram is one of only two players to have scored hat-tricks in League football from a full-back position — his treble coming against Stoke City in Albion's home Division One match on 12

September 1964. He is the uncle of athlete Steve Cram.
Albion debut v Bolton Wanderers (away) Division One, 17 October 1959.

JACK CRISP
Born: Hamstead, Birmingham, November 1896. Died: February 1939.
Career: Hamstead School, Leicester Fosse, Ordnance FC, Albion (May 1914-May 1923), Blackburn Rovers, Coventry City, Birmingham,

Cheltenham Town. Retired 1935.
Jack Crisp played on both wings for Albion and gained a League Division One Championship medal in 1920, when he missed only four matches. He preferred the right-wing and this was where most of his better displays came from. He had rapid acceleration and a useful shot, but was inconsistent. He represented the Football League in 1919-20 and during his career, with Albion, Blackburn, Coventry and Blues, he made well over 250 senior appearances, and scored 40 goals.
Albion debut v Everton (away) Division One, 5 December 1914, scoring his side's goal in a 2-1 defeat.

JIM CUMBES
Born: East Didsbury, Manchester, May 1944
Career: Didsbury Grammer School, Didsbury & Manchester Boys, Whalley Range FC, Runcorn, Tranmere Rovers, Albion (August 1969-November 1971), Aston Villa (£36,000), Portland Timbers (NASL), Coventry City, Runcorn, Southport, Worcester City, WBA All Stars, Kidderminster Harriers. Retired 1984. Played county cricket for Lancashire, Surrey, Worcestershire, and Warwickshire, and is currently Commercial Manager of Warwickshire CCC at Edgbaston.
Jim Cumbes was a tall goalkeeper, acrobatic, with a safe pair of hands but who sometimes lacked total concentration. He cost Albion £33,350 when signed from Tranmere in 1969. Later he won a League Cup tankard with Aston Villa in 1975 (v Norwich City). A friend of ex-Albion 'keeper John Osborne, he went into business with Osborne in the sports outfitters trade in 1978. Cumbes made well over 400 League and Cup appearances during a splendid career.
Albion debut v Arsenal (home) Division One, 16 August 1969.

LAURIE CUNNINGHAM
Born: Archway, London, March 1956.
Career: Stroud Green School, Highgate Wood Boys, Haringey Schools, SE Counties Schools, Orient, Albion (March 1977-June 1979), Real Madrid, Olympique Marseilles, Manchester

United, Sporting Gijon, Leicester City.
Laurie Cunningham, who joined the Throstles for £110,000, was called the 'second Pele' when he starred for Albion in the late 1970s. Nicknamed the 'Black Pearl' and 'Black Beauty' by the Baggies' supporters who idolised him, Cunningham had pace, intricate footwork, fine finishing

technique, power, expert reflexes, determination and wonderful balance. He became the first coloured footballer to wear an England international jersey in a major representative match when he lined up against Scotland in an Under-21 match in 1977. Later he added a further five Under-21 caps, a 'B' cap, and six full caps to his collection. He left Albion, for the Spanish giants Real Madrid for an Albion club record fee of £995,000, and at once assumed the nickname 'El Negrito'. He appeared in the 1981 European Cup Final with Real, and was in their team which won the Spanish League and Cup double in 1979-80. Cunningham attempted a comeback in English League Football with Manchester United and Leicester in the mid 1980s after a series of niggling leg injuries, but sadly failed to re-establish himself.
Albion debut v Tottenham Hotspur (away) Division One, 12 March 1977.

STAN DAVIES
Born: Chirk, March 1898. Died: January 1972.
Career: Chirk Schools, Rochdale, Preston North End, Everton, Albion (November 1921-November 1927), Birmingham, Cardiff City, Barnsley, Manchester Central, Dudley Town, Chelmsford City (trainer). Retired 1936. Became a publican in West Bromwich 1937-46.
Stan Davies was a Welsh international who skippered his country twice, and who won a total of 19 caps in six different positions — an indication of his wonderful versatility. Big and strong, Davies, who cost Albion £3,300, possessed a good shot, he could head a ball hard and true, and he had lots of stamina. He joined Albion in 1921, when the centre-forward position was becoming something of a problem at The Hawthorns, and stayed with the Baggies for six years during which time he became a big hit with the fans, scoring 83 goals in 159 League and Cup games. Two years after leaving Albion, Davies went on tour to Canada with the Welsh

FA. During his career he scored 110 goals in almost 250 senior appearances for seven League clubs (1919-31). In World War One he distinguished himself with the Welsh Fusiliers and was awarded the Military Medal and the Croix de Guerre.
Albion debut v Manchester City (home) Division One, 26 November 1921.

GEORGE DORSETT
Born: Brownhills, August 1881: Died: April 1943.
Career: Brownhills & District Shools, Shireoaks Athletic, Small Heath (trial), Brownhills Albion, Albion (November 1901-December 1904), Manchester City, Retired 1912, through injury.
George Dorsett was an excellent ball-playing outside-left. He had splendid control and an unflurried demeanour which certainly graced his game. He was clever and altogether a cultured performer who, when sold to Manchester City in 1904, cost £400, then a record transfer

fee for a wing-forward. Dorsett played in exactly 100 senior games for Albion (22 goals). He won a Second Division Championship medal in 1902 when he was part of an excellent front line which also included McLean, Simmons, Smith, Worton and Lee. This season Dorsett netted seven important goals in 32 outings and his assistance went a long way in helping Albion regain their First Division status after only one season in the lower division. Nicknamed 'Sos' and brother of Joe, also an Albion player, he was converted into a classy left-half by City and in 1910 helped himself to another Second Division Championship prize. In 1905-6 he represented the Football League, his only international honour. A penalty expert, he replaced Ben Garfield as Albion's regular outside-left.
Albion debut v Preston North End (away) Division Two, 4 January 1902.

CHARLES 'CHUCK' DRURY
Born: Darlaston, July 1937.
Career: Darlaston & Wednesbury Schools, SE Staffs Boys, FH Lloyds FC, Albion (September 1954, professional February 1955-June 1964), Bristol City (£7,500), Bradford (Park Avenue), Tamworth, Warley, Bromsgrove Rovers. Retired 1974.
An England Youth international (1955), 'Chuck' Drury was a hard-working, dour, solidly-built half-back and a hard tackler. He was a regular in the Albion side for four seasons (1959-63), linking up with such players as Bobby Robson and Stan Jones in the middle line. After leaving The Hawthorns, he helped Bristol City win promotion to the Second Division in 1964-5, and when he retired from competitive football in 1969, he had amassed in excess of 250 League and Cup appearances, including 160 for Albion.
Albion debut v Bolton Wanderers (away) Division One, 22 February 1958.

JIMMY DUDLEY
Born: Gartcosh, Glasgow, August 1928.
Career: Hill Top Schools (West Bromwich), Walsall Conduits FC, Albright YC, Albion (August 1944, professional 1945-December 1959), Walsall (£4,000), Stourbridge, Guest Motors FC. Retired 1966.
Originally an inside-forward, Scotsman Jimmy Dudley became a competent footballer in all aspects of half-back play, performing diligently and without fuss or bother in Albion's No.4 shirt for a number of years, and chalking up 166 consecutive League appearances for the club (1952-56), a record beaten later by Ally Robertson, another Scot. In 1954, Dudley won an FA Cup winners' medal with Albion (after scoring a vital goal in the semi-final against Port Vale), as well as a Scottish 'B' cap — his only representative honour. He made a total of 320 senior appearances for Albion and later, with Walsall, added another 175 to his collection, helping the Saddlers win the Division Four title in 1960, and promotion to Division Two in 1961. While at The Hawthorns, Dudley was part of a wonderful half-back line which included Joe Kennedy or Jimmy Dugdale and big Ray Barlow. Brother George was with Albion from 1937 to 1946, and Jim himself is the cousin of the late Jimmy 'Iron' Edwards, a left-half with Albion before World War Two. Jim Dudley still works for Guest Motors in West Bromwich.
Albion debut v Manchester City (away) Division One, 10 December 1949.

JIMMY DUGDALE
Born: Liverpool, January, 1932.
Career: Liverpool Collegiate FC, Harrowby FC, Albion (January 1950-February 1956), Aston Villa, QPR. Retired 1963.
Jimmy Dugdale was an outstanding centre-half who could control the heart of the defence with efficiency and authority. Unfortunately he had Joe Kennedy as a rival pivot at Albion, and eventually he opted for a transfer and moved to neighbours Aston Villa for a fee of £25,000 in 1956 — this after helping Albion win the FA Cup in 1954. In 1957 he went to Wembley again — with Villa — and collected another winners' medal as Manchester United, with goalkeeper Ray Wood injured, were pipped 2-1 by a Peter

McParland-inspired Villa side. In 1960, a Second Division Championship medal came Dugdale's way and a year later he added a League Cup winners' tankard to his silverware. He also won three England 'B' caps and represented the Football League side. He is the uncle of former Coventry City, Charlton and Barnsley defender, Alan Dugdale. After retiring he became a publican, first in Aston, then in Moseley and today he is pulling pints in Halesowen.
Albion debut v Bolton Wanderers (home) Division One, 13 December 1952.

CLIFF EDWARDS
Born: Chase Terrace, Nr Cannock, March 1921.
Career: Rawnsley School, Chase Terrace United, Cannock Town, Albion (October 1938, professional May 1939-June 1948), Bristol City, Gravesend & Northfleet. Albion director 1971, retired 1986). Guested for Bath City, Blackpool and Carlisle United during World War Two.
A short, thick-set half-back of natural ability, quick in the tackle and eminently solid in defence, where he usually occupied the centre-half berth, Cliff Edwards was a reliable performer, who always gave a good account of himself despite being only 5ft 7in tall. His career was obviously disrupted by the war and when Albion recruited the services of Irish international Jack Vernon in 1947, Edwards' days were sadly

numbered at The Hawthorns. He left the club in a player-exchange deal with Cyril Williams from Bristol City in the summer of 1948. He made 33 League appearances for the Bristol club before dropping to non-League to join Gravesend and Northfleet in 1950. He returned to The Hawthorns in 1971 when he was elected to the Board of Directors, staying in office until his retirement in 1986 at the age of 65.
Albion debut v Blackburn Rovers (away) Wartime League Cup, 25 May 1940.
League debut v Birmingham City (away) Division Two, 25 September 1946.

JIMMY EDWARDS
Born: Tipton, December 1905. Died: April 1982.
Career: Horseley Bridge and Tipton Schools, Tipton Park, Newport Foundry FC, Stourbridge, Great Bridge Celtic, Stourbridge, Albion (May 1926-May 1937), Norwich City, Bilston, Kingswinford, Dudley Town. Retired 1944.
Jimmy Edwards — nicknamed 'Iron' — was converted by Albion from an aggressive inside-forward into an indefatigable, solid and highly efficient left-half. He had legs like tree-trunks and possessed a formidable tackle. A grand clubman, Edwards appeared in over 200 first-team games for Albion in his 11 years at The Hawthorns. He was a member of Albion's 1931 and 1935 FA Cup Final teams, collecting a winners' medal in the former. Also in 1931 he represented the Football League. When he played alongside his centre-half partner, Bill Richardson, the pair were often referred to as 'Iron' and 'Steel.'
Albion debut v Hull City (away) Division Two, 31 March 1928.

BILLY ELLIOTT
Born: Harrington, Cumberland, August 1919. Died: November 1966, holidaying in the Canary Islands.
Career: Carlisle Grammar School, Carlisle United, Wolverhampton Wanderers, Bournemouth, Albion (December 1938-July 1951), Bilston United (player-manager) Retired 1954.
A brilliant outside-right, fast with incredible close ball-control and a powerful shot in his right foot, Billy Elliott might have had a good international career had he not played at the

same time as Stanley Matthews. Both Elliott's England appearances came in wartime soccer. He had one particularly smart trick — that of checking when running at top speed, by drawing his foot quickly over the top of the ball. An Achilles tendon injury finished his career with Albion when he was only 32 and still an active member of the First Division side. After a brief association with Bilston, he became a publican in Handsworth, Birmingham and was still a licensee when he died on holiday in 1966. For Albion he played in 330 senior matches and scored 157 goals, most of his strikes coming during the wartime period. He was a qualified FA coach and a member of the Players' Union committee. In season 1941-2, Elliott scored in 11 successive games for Albion and thus equalled Harry Jones' club record.
Albion debut v Luton Town (away) Division Two, 24 December 1938.

RAY FAIRFAX
Born: Smethwick, November 1941.
Career: Corbett Street Junior and James Watt Technical Schools Smethwick, Smethwick & Birmingham Boys, Staffs County FA & Boys, Albion (May 1959, professional August 1959-June 1968), Northampton Town, Wellingborough, Olney Town, WBA All Stars. Retired 1979. Albion commercial assistant May 1974, assistant secretary 1976. To Port Vale as club secretary 1985.
Stern tackling distinguished Ray Fairfax's displays at full-back, his kicking being strong and safe. He had some good defenders with him at The Hawthorns and consequently had his work cut out to establish himself in the senior side. He battled through, however, and managed almost 100 outings for the first team in his nine professional seasons with the club. Later he played 116 League games for Northampton. He won a League Cup winners' tankard with Albion in 1966, and scored just one goal — a

blockbuster against Bologna (Italy) in a Fairs Cup-tie at The Hawthorns in 1967.
Albion debut v Liverpool (away) Division One, 20 March 1963.

RONNIE FENTON
Born: South Shields, September 1940.
Career: South Shields Schools, Durham Boys, Albion (trial 1955), South Shields, Burnley, Albion (November 1962-January 1965), Birmingham City (£7,500), Brentford, Notts County. Later coach at Meadow Lane, then manager (1975-77), assistant manager-coach Nottingham Forest (October 1977-).

An inside-forward, Ronnie Fenton cost Albion £15,000 when secured from Burnley in 1962. His performances for Albion were assertive, yet occasionally he struggled to make an impression. He scored 18 goals in 66 outings for the Throstles; and after leaving The Hawthorns he netted 26 goals in League football for Birmingham and Brentford. During his League career, Fenton made a total of 195 appearances and scored 43 goals. He is now in his tenth season as Brian Clough's assistant at Forest.

Albion debut v West Ham United (away) Division One, 1 December 1962.

BOB FINCH
Born: Hednesford, Staffs. August 1908.
Career: Hill Top and West Hill School Hednesford, Hednesford Prims, Hednesford Town, Albion (April 1925, professional September 1925-May 1939), Swansea Town, Hednesford Town, Tamworth. Retired 1947. Joined police force in 1942, serving as a constable until 1956.
Bob Finch was a redoubtable full-back, dour, zealous and quick to spot danger. He gave Albion 14 years splendid service, playing in 234 League and Cup matches, without ever scoring a goal. He had to contest the full-back positions with some useful players including internationals Bill Ashurst and George Shaw, Bert Trentham and Hughie Foulkes (Wales) and later Cecil Shaw, among others. He was a first-team regular for three seasons (1927-30) missing only 10 out of 126 League games. During the 1930s he won three Central League Championship medals with Albion, skippering the reserves on many occasions. Earlier, in 1927-8, he had played in two international trials for England.
Albion debut v Leicester City (home) Division One, 27 February 1926.

ARTHUR FITTON
Born: Melton Mowbray, May 1902. Died: Kinver, September 1984.
Career: Edgecliff School (Kinver), Kinver Swifts, Cookley St Peter's, Kidderminster Harriers, Albion (October 1922-March 1932), Manchester United, Preston North End, Coventry City, Kidderminster Harriers. Retired June 1939, aged 37. Albion assistant trainer-coach (October 1948-July 1950); first-team trainer (August 1951-June 1956). Became game warden at Kinver National Trust Park.
'Mother' Fitton was a penetrative left-winger who gave Albion eminent service both on and off the field, for the reserves and first team alike. A very popular character indeed, he had 99 first-team outings and 261 for the Central League side (56 goals) — an existing club record. He won three Central League Championship medals with Albion (1923, 1924 and 1927), and in September 1954 was trainer to the Football League side which met the League of Ireland in Dublin. Four months earlier he had

seen Albion win the FA Cup at Wembley. At Preston he helped the Deepdale club win promotion from Division Two in 1934 and assisted Coventry City to the Third Division (S) title in 1936. Outside soccer Fitton was a fine cricketer, playing behind the stumps for Stourbridge CC, West Bromwich Dartmouth and the Staffordshire Minor Counties team. During World War One he worked in a factory which produced hand-grenades.
Albion debut v Manchester City (away) Division One, 11 November 1922.

KEN FOGGO
Born: Perth, Scotland, November 1943.
Career: Peebles High School, Peebleshire & Scotland Schools, Peebles YMCA, St Johnstone (trial), Albion (August, 1959, professional November 1960-October 1967), Norwich City

(£15,000), Portsmouth, Brentford (loan), Southend United, Chelmsford City, Brereton Social. Retired 1982.

Diminutive outside-right often roughly treated by the bigger defenders, Ken Foggo was a clever footballer whose accurate crosses on the run were a feature of his play. He came down from Scotland to The Hawthorns with fellow schoolboys Bobby Hope, Campbell Crawford and Bobby Murray, following their performances for Scotland Boys against England Boys in 1959. He had earlier represented Scotland Boys on the Rugby field. Foggo took over from Alec Jackson on Albion's right-wing in 1963 and went on to make in excess of 130 senior appearances for the club (29 goals scored). After leaving Albion he had 187 League outings for Norwich (54 goals), 60 for Portsmouth (3 goals) and 30 for Southend (6 goals) which gave him a career record of 406 League appearances and 92 goals. He went to work in London after retiring from soccer.

Albion debut v Fulham (home) 8 September 1962, assisting in three goals in Albion's 6-1 victory.

DOUG FRASER

Born: Busby, Lanarkshire, December 1941.

Career: Busby Junior and Senior Schools, Rolls Royce FC, Eaglesham Amateurs, Blantyre Celtic, Aberdeen, Albion (September 1963-January 1971), Nottingham Forest (£35,000), Walsall. Manager at Fellows Park, 1975). Retired from football 1977 to become a prison warder at Nottingham.

A fine, compact wing-half, who cost Albion £23,000, Doug Fraser was uncommonly fast in gathering the ball and passing it in almost one smooth movement. He had a fine tackle and was an overall stylish player. He did good work in the right-back position in later years. He played for Albion in the 1966, 1967 and 1970 League Cup Finals, skippering the team in the latter. And in 1968 he was in Albion's FA Cup-winning team against Everton. After appearing

in 325 games for Albion, he added a further 120 to his tally with Forest and Walsall. He had 70 outings for Aberdeen (1960-63). A Scottish international, he won two caps, in the mid-1960s against Holland and Cyprus.

Albion debut v Birmingham City (home) Division One, 18 September 1963.

ARTHUR GALE

Born: Salford, November 1904. Died: May 1976.

Career: Salford & District Schools, South Salford Lads' Club, Sedgley Park (Salford), Bury, Chester, Albion (June 1931-December 1936), Chester, Macclesfield, Altrincham (coach 1939), Northern Nomads (manager 1967-7).

A fast, direct and forceful outside-right or centre-forward, Arthur Gale was an 'unlucky' stand-in for Tommy Glidden during Albion's 1935 FA Cup run. Gale, a schoolteacher by profession, had played in every round of that season's competition, including the semi-final, and had scored in four ties, one goal being a brilliant diving header in the sixth round against Preston at The Hawthorns. Glidden, however, was brought back for the Wembley meeting with Sheffield Wednesday, only to break down injured as Gale sat on the bench and cried. Albion lost the Final 4-2 to the Owls. He managed a mere 29 first-team appearances for Albion (12 goals), yet won three Central League Championship medals in the 1930s and for the reserves his record was quite remarkable — 136 matches and 146 goals, 41 coming in season 1934-5 when Albion's second string netted 121 goals in winning the title for the third season running. It was unfortunate for Gale that he understudied such fine players as Glidden and W.G. Richardson during his five and a half years at The Hawthorns.

Albion debut v Newcastle United (home) Division One, 2 April 1932.

ALF 'JASPER' GEDDES

Born: West Bromwich, April 1871. Died: October 1927.

Career: Christ Church and Bratt Street Schools (West Bromwich), Causeway Green Villa, Albion (May 1891-March 1894), Clapham Rovers, Millwall Athletic, Albion (April-May 1895), Millwall Athletic, Bedminster, Bristol City. Retired 1908, aged 37.

A mercurial outside-left, fast, enthusiastic and able to centre in splendid style, Jasper Geddes was also a temperamental player. A little greedy at times, he nevertheless had some outstanding games for Albion. He served them in two separate spells, the second at a crucial stage in the season whereby Albion had to win their remaining two matches to stay in Division One. Albion won those two fixtures, and Geddes scored in both of them. He then returned to Millwall. Only 5ft 4in tall and barely 10st in weight, he won an FA Cup winners' medal with Albion (1892) and was reputedly Millwall's first professional footballer, skippering the Lions in their two Southern League Championship winning seasons of 1894-5 and 1895-6. He played over 100 times for Albion, including friendlies.

Albion debut (first spell v Everton (away) Division One, 7 November 1891.

JOHNNY GILES

Born: Cabra, Dublin, November 1940.

Career: Brunswick Street School (Dublin), St Colombus FC, Dublin Schools, Dublin City FC (later Munster Victoria), The Leprechauns, Stella Maris, Home Farm, Manchester United, Leeds United, Albion (as player-manager June 1975-May 1977), Shamrock Rovers (player-manager), Philadelphia Fury, Vancouver Whitecaps (coach), Albion (manager February 1984-September 1985). Player-manager of Republic of Ireland national team (1973-80). WBA All Stars.

Arguably one of the most brilliant midfield players Albion have ever had, Johnny Giles combined his magnificent ball skills with vision and thought. He possessed a useful shot and was a great asset to Albion when he arrived at the club in 1975, in a £48,000 deal from Leeds. In his first season at The Hawthorns he saw Albion win promotion from the Second Division and then set them firmly back among the big boys before leaving to return home to his native Ireland. He came back to Albion as manager in

1984 but this time things went wrong and he left as the team were heading back into Division Two. With Leeds, Giles won First and Second Division Championship medals, FA Cup, Football League Cup and Fairs Cup winners' prizes, and appeared in several other Finals including the 1975 European Cup, which was to be his last game for Leeds. Earlier, with Manchester United, he had gained an FA Cup winners' medal in 1963. In all, he played in 11 FA Cup semi-finals (including replays) and shares the record for most FA Cup Final appearances (five). In fact, he played in six, counting the 1970 replay. As a lad he played for the Republic of Ireland Schools against England

and then proceeded to become the first Eire player to win 50 full caps for his country; his final tally was 60. He was played in 'The Three' v 'The Six' game at Wembley in 1973, for the Irish XI v Brazil in the same year, and for an Eire XI v Manchester United in 1974. Giles won an FAI Cup winners' medal with Shamrock Rovers in 1978. In a truly wonderful playing career, Johnny Giles amassed 554 League games and scored 99 goals (1959-77). In all competitions (League, Cup and representative matches) his playing record was 863 appearances and 125 goals. For Albion he netted five times in 88 games.
Albion debut v Chelsea (home) Division Two, 20 August 1975.

TOMMY GLIDDEN
Born: Coxlodge, Newcastle-upon-Tyne, July 1902. Died: West Bromwich, July 1974.
Career: Castletown School, Sunderland Schools, Durham Boys, Sunderland (amateur), Bristol City (trial), Colliery Old Boys, Bolden Villa,

Sunderland West End, Albion (April 1922-May 1936). Retired summer 1936. Became coach at The Hawthorns (1936-9); Director (1951 until his death).
An outside or inside-right and one of Albion's celebrities during the 1930s, Tommy Glidden was an extremely nimble player, a fine ball-artist who was always on hand to cash in on a half-chance. He had the knack of scoring direct from corner-kicks. Glidden skippered Albion in both the 1931 and 1935 FA Cup Finals, collecting the trophy in 1931 after Albion had pipped arch-rivals Birmingham 2-1 at Wembley. During his long and loyal association with Albion, he appeared in 479 competitive matches, scoring 140 goals. He got into the senior side in 1922, at the expense of Jack Crisp, and, but for a few games, was Albion's first-choice outside-right for 14 years. He represented England Schoolboys in 1914 and figured in an international trial in 1925-6. He received a special award in April 1972 when celebrating 50 years' association with Albion. He died after a heart attack.
Albion debut v Everton (away) Division One, 25 November 1922.

TONY GODDEN
Born: Gillingham, August 1955.
Career: Napier Secondary Modern School,

Gillingham, Leonard Star FC, Eastcourt United. Gillingham & District Schools, Gillingham (amateur), Ashford Town, Wolverhampton Wanderers (trial), Albion (August 1975-May 1986), Chelsea. Also on loan to Preston North End, Luton Town, Walsall and Chelsea.
In October 1981, goalkeeper Tony Godden set an Albion record which will take some beating — he appeared in his 228th consecutive first-team game. He then lost his place in the side to Mark Grew. Four and a half years earlier Godden had made his Albion debut against Tottenham and immediately was said to have a bright future ahead of him. He went from strength to strength and when he had his testimonial match at The Hawthorns in May 1986 he had 360 senior games to his name, 329 of them for Albion. A safe 'keeper with fine reflexes, Godden appeared in the 1978 FA Cup semi-final. Eventually he became disillusioned with life at The Hawthorns and towards the end of 1985-6, his loan period to Chelsea ended with a permanent transfer to Stamford Bridge.
Albion debut v Tottenham Hotspur (away) Division One, 12 March 1977.

HOWARD GREGORY
Born: Aston Manor, Birmingham, May 1894, Died: August 1954.
Career: Gower Street and Aston Schools, Aston Manor FC, Birchfield Trinity, Albion (May 1911-May 1926). Retired through injury. Licensee of the Woodman Inn, (Handsworth) 1927-32, and remained in trade until 1953.
Howard Gregory was a quick-witted outside-left, fast and plucky, who was always likely to produce something out of the ordinary. He formed a tremendous left-wing partnership with that fine goal-grabber, Freddie Morris,

and in Albion's Championship-winning season of 1919-20 they scored between them a total of 49 First Division goals. Nicknamed the 'Express Man', Gregory once struck a soaking-wet ball so hard, playing against Wolves at Molineux, that en-route to goal, the casing split, the bladder going into the net and the casing itself over the bar. He took some time to get into Albion's first team but when he did, he performed consistently well, making a total of 181 senior appearances and scoring 45 goals before announcing his retirement, through injury, in 1926.
Albion debut v Everton (away) Division One, 22 April 1912.

FRANK GRIFFIN
Born: Pendlebury, Manchester, March 1928.
Career: Pendlebury Central School, St Augustine's Youth Club, Newton Heath, Hull City (trial), Bolton Wanderers (amateur 1944-48), Eccles Town, Shrewsbury Town, Albion (April 1951-June 1959), Northampton Town, Wellington Town, Sankey's FC, Worthen United (manager) Retired 1966.
Frank Griffin was the toast of West Bromwich back in 1954 when he scored the winning goal for Albion against Preston in the FA Cup Final. A right-winger, he was worth every penny of the £9,500 transfer fee Albion paid Shrewsbury Town in 1951. Albion signed Griffin to replace Billy Elliott and he was an instant success in the No.7 shirt. Fast and clever, and always eager to try a shot at goal, he appeared in 275 senior games for Albion (52 goals) in his eight years with the club. He was showing international form in 1958 when he broke his right leg in a collision with Sheffield United's Joe Shaw in an FA Cup tie at The Hawthorns. He failed to regain his form and wound down his career slowly with Northampton (18 appearances) and then with a handful of non-League teams.
Albion debut v Sunderland (away) Division One, 28 April 1951.

BILLY GRIPTON
Born: Princes End, Tipton, July 1920. Died: July 1981.
Career: Prince's End and Tipton Schools, Dartmouth Vics, Bush Rangers Brownhills Albion, Albion (June 1935, professional November 1937-June 1948), Luton Town (£3,000), Bournemouth, Worcester City. Retired 1956 to become local works' groundsman in Tipton.
Billy Gripton was a hard but fair centre-half who was a dominant force at the heart of Albion's defence for a number of years. A great tactician, he managed to total more than 200 first-team appearances despite the fact that his career was interrupted by war. In 1945 he was replaced in the Albion side by George Tranter who, in turn, lost his place to Jack Vernon.
Albion debut v Millwall (home) Division Two, 8 April 1939.

WILLIE GROVES
Born: Leith, Scotland, November 1869. Died: February, 1908.
Career: Thistle Club (Edinburgh), Hibernian, Everton, Celtic, Albion (October 1890-September 1893), Aston Villa, Hibernian, Rushden FC. Retired 1902.
An exciting footballer who, although having no claims to greatness in heading and goalscoring, was second to none in foraging and distribution skills. A play-anywhere performer, Groves had immense enthusiasm and dedication for the game. In a splendid career, which saw him converted by Albion from a centre-forward to a wing-half, he won three Scottish caps, in 1888, 1889 and 1890, scoring a hat-trick against Ireland in his second game. He also represented the Football League (1891-2) and played for Edinburgh in an inter-city match. In his first

spell with Hibernian he won a Scottish Cup winners' medal in 1887, and a runners-up medal in the same competition in 1896. With Celtic he gained a Cup runners-up medal in 1889 and for Albion he made two of the three goals in the 1892 FA Cup Final when Aston Villa were beaten 3-0 at the Crystal Palace. Later, as a

Villa player, Groves gained a First Division Championship medal (1894). He scored 10 goals in 67 League and Cup games for Albion. In his career (with Hibs, Albion and Villa) he scored over 30 goals in almost 200 matches. He did not appear in Everton's first team.
Albion debut v Wolverhampton Wanderers (home) Division One, 13 December 1890.

HARRY HADLEY
Born: Barrow-in-Furness, April 1878. Died: circa 1950.
Career: Cradley Heath & District Schools, Colley Gate United, Halesowen, Albion (February 1897-February 1905), Aston Villa, Nottingham Forest, Southampton, Croydon Common, Halesowen, Merthyr T. (manager on four separate occasions commencing May 1919 and ending September 1931), Chesterfield (manager),

Aberdare Athletic (manager), Gillingham (manager), Bangor City (manager). Retired 1936.

Harry Hadley was a good player, cool, calculated, energetic and a half-back who was keen in the tackle, forceful in attack and determined to win. Capped by England once (in 1903) he gained a Second Division Championship medal with Albion in 1902, and in his eight years with the club appeared in some 181 games. Normally he filled in at left-half, and at the turn of the century figured in a useful middle-line comprising himself, right-half Dan Nurse and centre-half Jim Stevenson. Brother of Ben Hadley, another Albion player, Harry became a successful manager after retiring as a player, and was sought by many leading clubs. He preferred to remain in the lower divisions and did exceptionally well, particularly with Merthyr Town.
Albion debut v Notts County (away) Division One, 19 March 1898.

from the City Ground to Goodison Park in that same year before Manchester City paid £350,000 to Everton to recall him to Maine Road in 1981. A Scottish international at Youth, Under-21, Under 23 and full levels, Hartford won a total of 50 senior caps for his country. He played for Albion in the 1970 League Cup Final, won a League Cup winners' medal with Manchester City in 1976, and a Milk Cup medal with Norwich City in 1985, when his deflected shot beat Sunderland. Hartford has now amassed well over 800 appearances (all competitions, including his spell in the NASL and on the international front). He was named Asa by his parents after the celebrated American singer Al (Asa) Jolson.
Albion debut v Sheffield United (away) Division One, 10 February 1968, aged 17.

NORMAN HEATH
Born: Wolverhampton, January 1924. Died: Great Barr, Birmingham, November 1983.
Career: Bushbury Hill School, Wolverhampton Boys, Henry Meadows FC, Albion (May 1942, professional October 1943-June 1955). Forced to retire following serious spinal injury suffered in League match at Sunderland in March 1954. Manager of junior side Great Barr Gunners (1971-73).
In his time Norman Heath was a fine, courageous goalkeeper whose agility and brilliant reflexes were key features of his splendid displays between the posts in 169 senior matches for Albion. He came to The Hawthorns during the war and understudied Jimmy Sanders for a number of years before that tragic injury in 1954 — and it was Sanders who stepped into goal for that year's FA Cup Final against Preston.
Albion League debut v Sheffield Wednesday (away) Division Two, 13 December 1947.

ASA HARTFORD
Born: Clydebank, Scotland, October 1950.
Career: Faifley Primary School, Clydebank High School, Dunbartonshire Boys, Drumchapel Amateurs, Albion (April 1966, professional October 1967-November 1971), Leeds United (for 24 hours), Albion (November 1971-August 1974), Manchester City (for £225,000; a club record sale at the time), Nottingham Forest, Everton, Manchester City, Fort Lauderdale Sun, Norwich City, Bolton Wanderers.
Richard Asa Hartford was a midfield dynamo, a player who darted and danced all over the park each and every time he donned a football jersey. Full of energy, always buzzing around in search of an opening, he was the player who, on medical advice, was rejected by Leeds in 1971 because of a 'hole in the heart' condition. At the time Albion and Leeds had agreed on a £170,000 fee. Three years later Hartford moved from The Hawthorns to Maine Road for £225,000. His transfer from City to Forest in 1979 cost £450,000; it was a £400,000 deal which took him

SAMMY HEASELGRAVE
Born: Smethwick, October 1916. Died: Birmingham, April 1975.
Career: Smethwick & District Schools, Bearwood Swifts, Warley Lions, Smethwick Highfield, Brierley Hill Alliance, Albion (October 1934-October 1945), Northampton Town. Retired 1947-8. Guested for Walsall in 1945-6. All-England Bowls Champion in 1963.
Sammy Heaselgrave was a hard-working, seemingly tireless, utility forward, constantly on target with his powerful shooting. A Junior international in 1936, he broke into Albion's first team in March 1937 and from then until his departure, to Northampton in 1945, he appeared in well over 160 senior games, scoring 57 goals — an extremely creditable record. Initially he had to bide his time before establishing himself in the League side but, once in, he stayed put and did a splendid job, especially during the wartime period when he played alongside such great players as Len Duns, Jack Acquaroff, W.G. Richardson, Ike Clarke and Billy Elliott, to name but a few. Indeed, Heaselgrave was one of only four Albion players to represent the club in each of the seven wartime seasons (1939-46 inclusive). After his playing days were over he became a solicitor in Bearwood, a business which is still in the family today.
Albion debut v Brentford (home) Division One, 27 March 1937.

FRANK HODGETTS

FRANK HODGETTS

Born: Oakham, Dudley, September 1924.
Career: Rowley Regis School, St Mary's Sunday School FC, Accles & Pollock Works FC, Albion (September 1939, professional October 1942-May 1949), Millwall (£6,000), Worcester City. Retired through injury. Returned to Albion as coach (1958-62). Currently Chairman of the Herefordshire and Worcestershire County Tennis Association and Chief Organiser of Coaching.
Winger Frank Hodgetts was just 16 years, 26 days old when he made his first appearance for Albion's senior team against Notts County in a wartime game at The Hawthorns in October 1940. That made him the youngest-ever player to don Albion's first-team jersey - a record that still holds good today. Nominally an outside-left, Hodgetts was likely to bob up anywhere in the attack — sometimes to the annoyance of his colleagues. A cheerful character with a fierce shot, he played well over 200 competitive matches during his career (Albion and Millwall, 1940-53), and scored 44 goals. Most of his outings for Albion were during World War Two. Today he lives in retirement at Hagley near Kidderminster.
Albion League debut v Swansea Town (away) Division Two, 31 August 1946, and he scored in his side's 3-2 win.

DEREK HOGG

Born: Stockton-on-Tees, November 1930.
Career: Middleforth C of E School, Preston North End (trial), Lostock Hall FC, Chorley, Leicester City, Albion (£20,000 April 1958-October 1960), Cardiff City (£12,500), Kettering Town, Retired 1965.
An ingenious and fleet-footed outside-left who responded best to a ball-playing inside partner, Derek Hogg had the marked tendency to over-elaborate with his footwork. He arrived at The Hawthorns to replace George Lee and was then himself dislodged by both Geoff Carter and Andy Aitken before leaving Albion for Cardiff City. Hogg, who had occasional game on the right flank, received Football League recognition in 1955-6 and the following season helped Leicester City win the Second Division title. During his League career he appeared in 283

matches (44 goals); his Albion record was 81 outings and 11 goals.
Albion debut v Luton Town (away) Division One, 23 August 1958.

BOBBY HOPE

Born: Bridge of Allan, Stirlingshire, September 1943.
Career: Clydebank High and Dunbartonshire West Schools, Drumchapel Amateurs, Scotland Boys, Sunderland (trial, 2 weeks), Albion (August 1959, professional September 1960-May 1972), Birmingham City (£66,666), Philadelphia Atoms, Dallas Tornados, Sheffield Wednesday, Bromsgrove Rovers (player-coach, appointed manager 1983). WBA All Stars 1979-87.
Bobby Hope was a player who displayed a masterly generalship in midfield. His superb ball skills and telling passes were highlights of a wonderful association with Albion for whom he won a League Cup winners' tankard in 1966 and an FA Cup winners' medal in 1968, as well as runners-up prizes in the League Cup in 1967 and 1970. Capped by Scotland at Schoolboy, Under-23 and full levels, he appeared in over 400 senior games for Albion scoring 42 goals, one of which was Albion's first in Europe — against DOS Utrecht (Holland) in 1966-7. For Albion, Blues and Wednesday, Hope's League record was 407 matches and 45 goals. Today, besides looking after non-Leaguers Bromsgrove Rovers, Hope runs a Post Office in Handsworth Wood, Birmingham, as well as turning out in various charity matches for WBA All Stars.
Albion debut v Arsenal (home) Division One, 30 April 1960, aged 16.

EZRA HORTON

Born: West Bromwich, August 1861. Died: West Bromwich, July 1939
Career: Christ Chruch and Beeches Road Schools, George Salter Works FC, West Bromwich FC, Albion (August 1882, professional August 1885-June 1891). Retired. Became a referee in 1895. Guested for Aston Villa in 1884-5 season. In later years he turned out for the West

Bromwich hockey team as a centre-half and became only the second Midlander to play for England at this sport.
As a footballer, Ezra Horton — nicknamed 'Ironsides' — was a very sporting player and a largely defensive right-half who was good at heading, strong at kicking and fearsome in the tackle — hence his nickname. He played in three successive FA Cup Finals for Albion (1886-7-8), being a winner at the third attempt. He skippered Albion in 1884-5 and had the distinction of playing in each of Albion's first 36 FA Cup-ties. He played in around 300 matches for the Baggies (all competitions including friendlies) during his nine years with the club. Brother of John Horton, Ezra was a member of the first League side fielded by Albion (at Stoke) in September 1888.
Albion debut v St George's (away), 1882.
FA Cup debut v Wednesday Town (home), 10 November 1883.

JOHN HORTON

Born: West Bromwich, February 1866. Died: January 1947.
Career: Dartmouth School, Oak Villa, Burslem Port Vale, Wednesday Old Athletic, Albion (October 1882, professional September 1885-May 1899). Retired summer 1899, aged 33.
A schoolteacher by profession, 'Jack' Horton was a grand full-back who could never be faulted when it came to resolute tackling and clearing his lines, which he did in fine style. A

magnificent clubman — 17 seasons with Albion — he clocked up over 250 games for the Throstles (all competitions, including friendlies). He was right-back in Albion's first-ever League match, against Stoke in 1888, and during his association with the club he was never critical of the way it was run. He came back in 1895 to play in the FA Cup Final against Aston Villa after missing all the previous rounds. 'Jack' also put in appearances as a half-back and as a centre-forward, but it was in the full-back position where he excelled best of all. Brother of Ezra Horton, who played in the same team for a number of seasons up to 1891.
Albion debut v Wednesbury Old Athletic (home) FAC, 6 December 1884.
League debut v Stoke (away), 8 September 1888.

DON HOWE
Born: Wolverhampton, October 1935.
Career: St Peter's School (Wolverhampton), Wolverhampton Boys, Wolves (trial), Albion (December 1950, professional November 1952-April 1964), Arsenal (£40,000). Retired 1967, to become coach at Highbury, then assistant-manager 1969. Albion manager (July 1971-April 1975), Galatasary (coach), Leeds United (coach), Arsenal (coach, then manager), England 'B' team coach, then chief coach. Saudi Arabia (coach 1986-7), Bristol Rovers (coach 1987).
Deft positioning and reliability were the hallmarks of Don Howe's play at right-back for Albion and England. Although in later years he did play at right-half and inside-right, the No.2 shirt was always his favourite — and best. He took over at Albion from Stuart Williams after making his debut early in the 1955-6 season.

Howe held his place and went on to make over 375 appearances for Albion besides winning 23 consecutive caps for England. He also collected six Under-23 caps, played for England 'B', represented the Football League and turned out for the FA XI in 1956 and 1962. He was club captain at Albion for a number of years. With Arsenal he fractured his leg in March 1966 and the injury ended his playing career. He coached the Gunners when they lifted the 'double' in 1970-1. Howe came back to Albion as manager in the summer of 1971 but disaster struck in 1973 and the Throstles were relegated. Perhaps Howe's best day as Albion boss was when he signed Willie Johnston from Rangers. When he returned to Highbury, Howe coached Arsenal to three successive FA Cup Finals (1978-9-80).
Albion debut v Everton (home) Division One, 24 August 1955.

ALEC JACKSON
Born: Tipton, May 1937.
Career: Park Lane Secondary Modern School, Tipton St John's FC, W.G. Allen's FC, Albion (May 1954, professional September 1954-June 1964), Birmingham City (£12,500), Walsall, Nuneaton Borough, Kidderminster Harriers, Warley, Oldbury Town, Warley Borough, Darlaston, Blakenhall, Gornal, Rushall Olympic, Bush Rangers, WBA All Stars. Retired 1985. Coach to Coseley Rovers Youth Club 1980-82.
Alec Jackson was a pluckily little utility forward, fleet of foot and able to perform in any position with a great deal of success. A brilliant dribbler at times, 'Jacko' chose the right-wing berth as his best and represented the Football League against the Scottish League in 1962, wearing the No.7 shirt. He made his Albion debut as a 17-year-old and was still playing charity football for the WBA All Stars in 1985, at the age of 48. He scored a goal on average every four games for Albion — and during his League career with Albion, Birmingham City and Walsall, he amassed 307 appearances and hit 67 goals. Jackson broke his leg playing against Spurs at White Hart Lane in 1958.
Albion debut v Charlton Athletic (away), Division One, 6 November 1954, scoring in a 3-1 victory.

GEORGE JAMES
Born: Oldbury, February 1899. Died: December 1976.
Career: Oldbury & District Schools, Bilston United, Albion (January 1920-May 1929), Reading, Watford, Retired 1933 to become a West Bromwich licensee.
A shortish, heavily-built inside or centre-forward of the bustling type, George James was a player who was fearless, with a telling shot and big heart. He was a chatterbox both on and off the field, but he certainly gave Albion good service during his stay at The Hawthorns. He scored 57 goals in 116 matches for Albion, including a quick-fire effort against Nottingham Forest in December 1924 which was reputedly timed at five seconds from the kick-off. James scored four of Albion's five goals that afternoon —and he finished the season with 30 under his belt for a personal record. He linked up wonderfully well with Joe Carter, 'Tug' Wilson and Stan Davies, and was forever searching for an opening. He played in an England trial in 1925.
Albion debut v Bolton Wanderers (away) Division One, 12 November 1921.

CLAUDE JEPHCOTT
Born: Smethwick, October 1891. Died: October

1950.
Career: West Smethwick School, Olive Mount FC, Brierley Hill Alliance, Stourbridge, Brierley Hill Alliance, Albion (April 1911-May 1923). Retired. Albion Director (January 1934 until his death).

A brilliant outside-right who made full use of his tremendous pace, Claude Jephcott was wonderfully consistent and always rose to the big occasion. A Junior international in 1911, he suffered a fractured leg in 1922, against Aston Villa, which ended his career a shade prematurely — this after he had played in almost 200 first team-matches for the Throstles (16 goals). He appeared in the 1912 FA Cup Final against Barnsley, and in 1919-20 won a First Division Championship medal with Albion, his form on the right wing during this campaign being quite superb. He represented the Football League and an England XI between 1913 and 1919.
Albion debut v Sunderland (away) Division One, 9 December 1911.

JOE JOHNSON
Born: Grimsby, April 1911. Died: West Bromwich, August 1983.
Career: Grimsby junior football, Scunthorpe United, Bristol City, Stoke City, Albion (November 1937-May 1946), Northwich Victoria, Hereford United, Retired 1949-50. Guested for Notts. County, Leicester City and Crewe Alexandra during the war.
An excellent little player who achieved a useful record as a goal-scoring left-winger, most of Joe Johnson's good work was done with Stoke when he had Stan Matthews on the opposite flank. He gave Albion splendid service, too, before and during the war, appearing in 145 senior games and scoring 47 goals. Capped by England on five occasions (1936-7), he won a Second Division Championship medal with Stoke in 1933. He ran the Dartmouth Park cafe-restaurant in West Bromwich for a number of years after retiring.
Albion debut v Huddersfield Town (away) Division One, 11 December 1937.

WILLIE JOHNSTON
Born: Glasgow, December 1946.
Career: Lochore Welfare, Rangers, Albion (£138,000, December 1972-March 1979), Vancouver Whitecaps (£100,000), Birmingham City (loan) Vancouver Whitecaps, Rangers, Vancouver Whitecaps, Hearts (player, then player-coach), East Fife (coach). Retired 1985 to become a publican in Glasgow.
With his ability to beat a defence with either footwork or speed, and to cap a move with a fierce shot, Willie Johnston was a welcome acquisition to Albion in a defence-orientated game. On the debit side, Johnston's tendency to hold the ball a shade too long, and a short, fiery temper that had him in trouble on several occasions (he was sent-off 15 times during his career), often went against him. Nevertheless, he was a fine winger. For Rangers (two spells) he played in over 400 games (160-plus goals) and collected medals galore in League, Cup, League Cup and European competitions. In 1971 he scored a hat-trick of penalties for Rangers against St Johnstone after coming on as substitute, and a year later hit two goals against Moscow Dynamo in the European Cup-winners' Cup Final. For Albion his appearance tally topped 250 and he added further games with Blues, Hearts and East Fife, ending with almost 700 appearances at club level. As a Scottish international, Johnston won 22 full caps — 13 with Albion, nine with Rangers. He made two appearances for the Scottish League side. and two at Under-23 level, as well as winning Youth recognition. At his best, nobody was faster than Willie Johnston

over 30 to 40 yards.
Albion debut v Liverpool (home) Division One, 9 December 1972.

HARRY JONES
Born: Haydock, October 1911. Died: February 1957.
Career: Haydock Schools, Haydock & District Junior Leagues, Preston North End, Albion (May 1933-August 1943). Retired through injury and illness. Albion scout (1946-7).
Harry 'Popeye' Jones was a jovial character, able to play equally well in any forward role although he particularly enjoyed the centre-forward spot. He had an aggressive style and would often bundle the ball and goalkeeper over the line as he tore in from deep positions. A big favourite with The Hawthorns crowd, he had an appetite for goals and during his career with Albion he netted no fewer than 104 in only 169 senior outings. In 1939-40 he rattled home 50 goals in only 40 matches (League, Cup and friendlies) including six hat-tricks and a goal in each of 11 consecutive matches — a club record equalled later by winger Billy Elliott. During the war Jones guested for Everton (in goal) and for Blackburn Rovers. In earlier years he was awarded a Royal Humane Society medal after he had dived into a canal to save a child from drowning.
Albion debut v Sheffield Wednesday (away) Division One, 1 January 1935.

IVOR JONES
Born: Merthyr, Wales, July 1899. Died: 1974.
Career: Merthyr Schools, Merthyr Town, Caerphilly, Swansea Town, Albion (April 1922-May 1926), Swansea Town, Aldershot, Thames FC, Aberystwyth (coach). Retired 1935.
A grand little inside-forward with good control, Ivor Jones was difficult to dispossess, yet was erratic at times with his shooting. A Welsh international (ten caps won between 1920 and 1926), he also played for the Welsh League against the Southern League at Aberdare in 1921. Jones played 67 times for Albion. He got into the first team immediately and spread his games out evenly in the No.8 and No.10 berths, forming a fine link with wingers Howard Gregory, Jack Byers and Tommy Glidden. His son, Cliff Jones, is the former Tottenham Hotspur and Wales winger of the 1960s.

Albion debut v Newcastle United (away) Division One, 15 April 1922.

STAN JONES

Born: Highley, Shropshire, November 1938.
Career: Highley Council and Bridgnorth Grammar Schools, Staffordshire Youths, Kidderminster Harriers, Wolves (amateur), Walsall, Albion (£7,000, May 1960-March 1968), Walsall, Burton Albion, Kidderminster Harriers, Hednesford Town, Coleshill Town (coach), Walsall (trainer), WBA All Stars (1979-87).
An inspiring defender, big and strong, who rarely put a foot wrong, Stan Jones was a cool player, extremely useful in the air. He played 267 games for Albion's senior team and over 250 for Walsall. However, in one five-match spell in the mid-1960s he had the dubious record of scoring three own-goals. Bought by Albion to replace Joe Kennedy, he largely held on to the No.5 shirt up to 1967 when Eddie Colquhoun and John Talbut arrived at The Hawthorns. He missed the 1966 League Cup

Final through injury and was dropped for the 1967 Final, playing in only one more first-team game after that.
Albion debut v Birmingham City (away) Division One, 31 August 1960.

JOHN KAYE

Born: Goole, March 1940.
Career: Goole & District Schools, Goole Boys, Goole United, Goole Dockers FC, Hull City (amateur), Goole Town, Scunthorpe United, Albion (£44,750, May 1963-November 1971), Hull City (£28,000, player, thereafter coach and manager), Scunthorpe United (assistant manager). Retired to go into hotel business.
John Kaye, known as 'Yorky', was a goalscoring inside-right when he was signed by Albion manager Jimmy Hagan in 1963 for a club record fee. He was converted into a defensive half-back during Albion's successful season of 1967-8 and in the No.6 shirt, he performed with steadiness, dedication and wholehearted endeavour, committing himself 100 per-cent to the game. He gained a League Cup winners' tankard in 1966, a runners-up prize in the same competition a year later, and added an FA Cup winners' medal in 1968, following that with another League Cup runners-up award in 1970. Kaye represented the Football League twice, in 1965-6, and was voted Midland Footballer of the Year in 1966 and 1970. He played in more than 360 games for Albion and during his League career he made 433 appearances and scored 79 goals — 25 for Scunthorpe, 45 for Albion and nine for Hull.
Albion debut v Leicester City (home) Division One, 24 August 1963.

JOE KENNEDY

Born: Cleator Moor, Nr Whitehaven, November 1925. Died: West Bromwich, September 1986.
Career: St Patrick's School (Whitehaven), Whitehaven & District Boys, Cleator Moor Celtic, Brentford (trial), Millwall (trial), Gravesend League football with Freelands FC, Altrincham, Albion (December 1948-June 1961), Chester, Stourbridge (1962), Brockhouse Works FC. Retired 1966.
Joe Kennedy began his career as an inside-right, developed into a steady, reliable right-half and ended up as a solid centre-half, tremendous in the air, so sound and sure on the ground. Raven-haired Kennedy seemed destined for full international honours with England after being a permanent reserve during the early 1950s, but injury forced him out of action at crucial times in his career and the only representative calls he received were to skipper England 'B' on three occasions, and play for the

FA XI. He played at right-back in Albion's Cup-winning side of 1954 after being out of the team with leg trouble since January. Jack Vernon was in control of the No.5 shirt when Kennedy first arrived at Albion; then Jimmy Dugdale came along and Kennedy was the regular from 1955 to 1960, with the odd exception when Ray Barlow filled the berth. He appeared in a total of 397 senior games for Albion in his twelve and a half years stay at the club, playing in a wonderful middle line with Dudley and Barlow. He collapsed and died at his workplace (Brockhouse Ltd) aged only 60.
Albion debut v Luton Town (away) Division Two, 9 April 1949.

DEREK KEVAN

Born: Ripon, March 1935.
Career: Ripon Secondary Modern School, Harrogate & District Schools, Ripon City, Ripon YMCA Sheffield United (trial), Bradford (Park Avenue), Albion (£3,000, July 1953-

March 1963), Chelsea (£50,000), Manchester City, Crystal Palace, Peterborough United, Luton Town, Stockport County, Macclesfield Town, Boston United, Stourbridge, Ansells FC, WBA All Stars (1972-85). Now manager of the All Stars XI. Was with Albion's Lottery Department in the early 1980s.

Big Derek Kevan was an Albion 'great'. Standing 6ft tall and weighing 13st, he had power in every department; a big heart, stamina and a lust for goals. He could head a ball as hard as some players could kick one, and he possessed a fierce shot in his right foot, as well as a fair one in his left. A marvellous competitor in every sense of the word, Kevan won 14 full caps for England (eight goals scored), played four times for the Under-23s and had an outing with the Football League XI. In ten years at The Hawthorns he hit 173 goals in 291 League and Cup appearances, including one 'five' against Everton (home) in 1960. After leaving Albion amid some controversy, he won a Fourth Division Championship medal with Stockport in 1967, and created a new post-war scoring record for Manchester City in 1963-4 with 30 League goals. In his League career Kevan scored 235 goals in 440 games, and he topped the First Division scoring charts in 1961-2 with 33. A little clumsy when he first set out with Albion, Kevan developed into one of the greatest strikers the club has ever seen.

Albion debut v Everton (home) Division One, 24 August 1955, scoring both goals in a 2-0 win.

HARRY KINSELL
Born: Cannock, May 1921.
Career: Cannock Central & Cannock Senior Schools, Albion (May 1935, professional June 1938-June 1949), Bolton Wanderers (£12,000), Reading, West Ham United, Bedford Town. Retired 1957, aged 36. Guested for Blackpool, Mansfield, Middlesbrough, and Southport during World War Two, playing left-back in the 1944 League War Cup Final for Blackpool v Aston Villa.

In his day Harry Kinsell was a wonderful left-back, fast, intelligent, a good footballer who loved to overlap. He partnered Idris Bassett, Cecil Shaw and Jim Pemberton during his stay at The Hawthorns and with all three he performed admirably, winning for himself international recognition in 1945, when he played for England in two Victory games and for the FA XI. In 1939, he had gained a Junior cap for his country. A key member of Albion's promotion team of 1948-9 — a season when he lined up once in the outside-left berth — Kinsell played in 158 senior matches for the Throstles and his transfer to Bolton in 1949 realised a record fee for the Lancashire club.

Albion debut v Walsall (home) Wartime game, 14 May 1940.
FA Cup debut v Cardiff City (away), 5 January 1946.
League debut v Swansea Town (away) Division Two, 31 August 1946.

PETER LATCHFORD
Born: King's Heath, Birmingham, September 1952.
Career: Broadmeadow Juniors and Brandwood Secondary Modern School, South Birmingham Boys, Monyhull Hospital FC, Redditch Town, Sutton Coldfield Town, Albion (May 1969, professional October 1969-February 1975), Celtic (initially on loan, February 1975, signing full-time July 1975 for £35,000).

A goalkeeper of exceptional agility for a big man, Peter Latchford became rather inconsistent during the latter part of his stay with Albion. He comes from a footballing family with brothers Dave and Bob perhaps better known nationally. Peter Latchford was at The Hawthorns at a time when the club had some good 'keepers on their books and therefore his stay was short-lived. He went to Celtic, did very well at first, but then dropped into the reserves, and by the time he had a testimonial in 1985 he was a permanent fixture in Celtic's second team. He won two England Under-23 caps in 1973-4 and appeared in 104 senior games for Albion. With Celtic he has gained considerable European experience as well as winning medals in League and Cup competitions. He was voted Celtic's

'Player of the Year' in 1977-8 and as a lad represented England at basketball.
Albion debut v Sheffield United (home) Division One, 26 August 1972.

GEORGE LEE
Born: York, June 1920.
Career: York City Schools, Yorkshire County Boys, Acomb FC, Scarborough, York City, Nottingham Forest, Albion (July 1949-June 1958), Lockheed Leamington, Vauxhall Motors FC, Albion (trainer-coach 1959-63), Norwich City (trainer-coach 1963-87).

'Ada' Lee was a wholehearted outside-left who varied his game, and style, judiciously. Strongly built, he had powerful legs, a useful turn of speed and a good left-foot shot. He came to Albion when their outside-left position was causing some concern and got into the side immediately to hold on to the No.11 shirt well into the late 1950s, apart from an occasional lapse of form. Lee helped Albion win the FA Cup in 1954, laying on the first goal. He scored 65 goals for the Throstles in close on 300 outings. After leaving The Hawthorns for a second time, Lee was trainer to Norwich when they lifted the Second Division crown in 1971-2.
Albion debut v Charlton Athletic (home) Division One, 20 August 1949.

BILLY LEE
Born: West Bromwich, August 1878. Died: November 1934.
Career: West Bromwich Baptist, West Bromwich Standard, Bournville Athletic, Albion (September 1901-September 1904), Bournemouth Wanderers, (loan), Portsmouth, Chesterfield Town, New Brompton, Darlaston. Retired 1911-12.

Billy Lee's unerring marksmanship made him a consistent scorer from the centre-forward position. He arrived at Albion soon after the club had dropped into the Second Division for the first time, but his presence in the side, plus his goalscoring expoits, soon had the fans cheering - and promotion was gained immediately. He played in three Junior internationals for

England (1899-1900) and scored 25 goals in 76 games for Albion.
Albion debut v Chesterfield (away) Division Two, 28 September 1901

GRAHAM LOVETT
Born: Sheldon, Birmingham, August 1947.
Career: Cockshutt Hill, Sheldon Heath and Camp Lane Schools Birmingham, Birmingham & County Schoolboys, Albion (February 1964, professional November 1964-June 1972), Southampton (loan), Worcester City, Solihull Borough, Greaves FC, WBA All Stars (1979-85). Retired 1986.
In the mid-1960s Graham Lovett — nicknamed 'Shuv' — was being talked of as the 'new Duncan Edwards' of Midlands' soccer. A skilful inside-forward or wing-half, he plied his fellow forwards with scoring chances, displaying clever, close ball control in the process. He was solidly built, strong in the tackle and had stamina to match. Lovett won an FA Cup winners' medal with Albion in 1968, after he had survived two horrific car crashes. Sadly, the injuries he received in those collisions eventually forced him to give up League soccer at the early age of 26, although he did play some football until 1986. He made 156 appearances for Albion

and was showing international form when tragedy struck. In 1973, at Birmingham Crown Court, Lovatt was awarded £14,000 damages against the West Midlands Passenger Transport Executive, after one of the accidents, in Quinton, Birmingham.
Albion debut v Chelsea (home) Division One, 5 December 1964.

STEVE MACKENZIE
Born: Romford, Essex, November 1961.
Career: Byron Red Star (Romford), Havering and Essex Schools, Crystal Palace, Manchester City, Albion (£650,000, July 1981).
Steve Mackenzie joined Albion almost immediately after scoring one of the most spectacular goals seen in a Wembley FA Cup Final — for Manchester City against Spurs. Yet his first move in professional football — from Palace to Maine Road — caused something of a stir, because the £250,000 splashed out by Malcolm Allison was for a player who had not featured in a senior League or Cup game. He had been a key figure in Palace's youth team of 1977 and 1978 but was a novice as far as playing in the big time was concerned. However, Mackenzie pulled through. He made over 75 appearances for City and then carried on the good work with Albion, although he missed virtually all of the 1982-3 season because of a serious pelvic injury. A midfielder, powerful and with good skills, he prefers a central role, which enables him to come forward and unleash one of his thunderbolt shots. On the international front he has won caps for England at Youth, (15), Under-23 (three) and 'B'(one) team levels. He collected an FA Youth Cup winners' medal in 1978.
Albion debut v Manchester City (away) Division One, 29 August 1981.

RODDY McLEOD
Born: Kilsyth, Stirlingshire, February 1872. Died: December 1931.
Career: Kilsyth School, Partick Thistle, Albion (January 1891-April 1897), Leicester Fosse, Brighton United, Southampton, Brentford. Retired 1905-6.
Roddy McLeod was a grand little player, occupying the inside-right position most of the time. He had intricate footwork and his passing

and shooting ability were outstanding. He was the perfect foil to Billy Bassett with whom he performed, so wonderfully well in many games for Albion during the 1890s. McLeod's own record for Albion was a useful one — 65 goals in over 180 major appearances. He played in the 1892 and 1895 FA Cup Finals and helped Brentford win the Southern League Division Two title in 1901.
Albion debut v Sheffield Wednesday (away) FAC, 14 February 1891
League debut v Accrington(home) Division One, 7 March 1891.

'SANDY' McNAB
Born: Glasgow, December 1911. Died: September 1962.
Career: Glasgow Schools, Tuesday Waverley,

Pollock FC (Glasgow), Sunderland, Albion (March 1938-April 1946), Newport County (£1,000), Dudley Town, Northwich Victoria. Retired 1952 to take a pub in West Bromwich. Guested for Newport County, Nottingham Forest, Northampton Town and Walsall during World War Two.

A marvellous 'pint-sized' left-half whose tackling was done judiciously without him losing his poise, Sandy McNab was the brave and seemingly tireless redhead who rallied Sunderland to victory in the 1937 FA Cup Final, a year after he had helped the Wearsiders win the First Division Championship. McNab gained two caps for Scotland (1937 and 1939), represented the Football League, toured Canada and USA with the Scottish FA party in 1939, and all-told amassed almost 190 first-team appearances for Albion, the majority of which came during wartime when he skippered the club for a short while.

Albion debut v Derby County (home) Division One, 12 March 1938.

TOMMY MAGEE

Born: Widnes, May 1899. Died: May 1974.

Career: St Mary's School Widnes, Appleton Hornets (Rugby League), St Helen's Recs (Rugby League), Widnes Athletic (amateur), Albion (January 1919-May 1934), Crystal Palace (player-coach), Runcorn (player-manager, later coach). Retired 1947.

Tommy Magee was a 'midget' right-half who was formerly an outside-right or inside-right. He played with evident enjoyment, tenacity, wonderful consistency and constructiveness. Nicknamed 'Pocket Hercules' and the 'Mighty Atom' by players and supporters alike — for he stood only 5ft 2ins tall and weighed 10 stone — he was a great favourite at The Hawthorns, and for Albion 'wee Tummy' played in over 400 senior games in 15 splendid years. He was initially signed-up whilst serving in the trenches in France during World War One, sending the appropriate papers back to Albion by air. He won five England caps (as a wing-half), toured Canada with the FA party in 1926 and again in 1931, and is the only Albion player to have won a First Division Championship medal (1920) and an FA Cup winners' medal (1931). Magee is reputedly the smallest player ever to wear an England shirt — and he was certainly the smallest first-team player Albion have ever had.

Albion debut v. Derby County (h) MVL, 5 April 1919

League debut v. Oldham Athletic (h) Division One, 30 August 1919.

JACK MAHON

Born: Gillingham, December 1911.

Career: Doncaster Grammar School, New Brompton Excelsior, Doncaster Rovers, Leeds United, Albion (September 1935-September 1938), Huddersfield Town, York City, Leeds United (coach). After the war he coached in Denmark, and during the hostilities guested for

Aldershot, Bradford City, Chelsea, Halifax Town, Leeds United, Millwall, QPR, Reading, Torquay United and West Ham. Coach to Hull City 1953-4.

A resourceful and swift outside-right with a good shot, Jack Mahon never used robust tactics. He came to Albion as a replacement for Tommy Glidden and appeared in well over 120 games (44 goals scored) before switching to Huddersfield. He made a sad start with his new club, however, breaking his right leg in his debut game. Mahon bounced back, though, and toured South Africa with the FA party in 1939, playing in one Test Match. He amassed around 250 senior appearances during his playing career.

Albion debut v Liverpool (away) Division One, 28 September 1935.

JACK MANNERS

Born: Morpeth, March 1878. Died: May 1946.

Career: Morpeth YMCA, Morpeth Harriers, Albion (May 1904-June 1913), Hartlepools United, (player, then manager).

Jack Manners was a useful half-back, usually found on the left-hand side. He had a biting tackle, good powers of distribution and maintained a consistent level of performance

BOBBY McNEAL

Born: Hobson Village, Co Durham, January 1891. Died: May 1956.

Career: Hobson Wanderers, Albion (June 1910-May 1925). Retired through injury. Albion coach. Guested for Port Vale, Fulham, Notts County and Middlesbrough during World War One. Later became a publican in West Bromwich.

Bobby McNeal was a stylish left-half with a footballing brain. He distributed the ball accurately and defended with commendable steadiness. He came to Albion as a 19-year-old and made his debut in the inside-left position, but was switched to wing-half almost immediately and remained in that position until injuries began to plague him in 1924-5. An English international (two caps) Bobby McNeal also represented the Football League five times (1912-14) and won three medals with Albion — League Championship 1919-20, Division Two Championship 1910-11, and FA Cup runners-up in 1911-12. He was a penalty-expert, stood only 5ft 6in tall and appeared in more than 400 games for Albion — a magnificent clubman who went into the licensed trade after retiring.

Albion debut v Leeds City (home) Division Two, 8 October 1910.

during his nine years at The Hawthorns. He played in a total of 209 League and Cup games for Albion (7 goals scored) and was a mainstay of the side for five seasons (1905-10) forming a solid middle line with first 'Cock' Pheasant and Arthur Randle, and then with George Baddeley and Sammy Timmins. Manners also appeared in the outside-left and centre-half berths for Albion but it was as a left-half that he became a formidable performer, winning a Second Division Championship medal in season 1910-11.
Albion debut v Burnley (away) Division Two, 3 September 1904.

MICK MARTIN
Born: Dublin, July, 1951.
Career: Whitehall School, St Vincent's CBS (Football & Hurling Club), Reds United, Home Farm, Greenfields-in-Santry FC, Home Farm, Bohemians, Manchester United, Albion (loan October 1975; signed for £30,000 December 1975-December 1978), Newcastle United (£100,000), Vancouver Whitecaps, Wolverhampton Wanderers, Cardiff City, Peterborough United, Rotherham United, Preston North End.
Son of Con Martin, the former Aston Villa and Republic of Ireland player, Mick Martin was a versatile performer, who preferred a midfield role. He spent almost five years at Old Trafford without really establishing himself in the United first team. Then Johnny Giles brought him to The Hawthorns, and he developed into a classy player, helping Albion win promotion to the First Division (1976). In later years he did wonderfully well at Newcastle (over 160 apps), and then dropped down into the lower divisions before retiring after well over 500 games as a professional footballer. He made 52 appearances for the Republic of Ireland (1971-83), collected one cap at Under-23 level and also received one as an amateur while a Bohemian player. He also represented the League of Ireland. Martin had a testimonial match at Dalymount Park, in August 1983.
Albion debut v Oldham Athletic (home) Division Two, 4 October 1975.

LEN MILLARD
Born: Coseley, Nr Wolverhampton, March 1919.
Career: Christ Church School, Coseley FC, Wallbrook FC, Coseley Town, Bilston Town, Sunbeam FC, Albion (May 1937, professional September 1942-June 1958), Stafford Rangers (manager). Retired 1961. Guested for Bilston Borough in 1938.
'Len the Dependable' was Albion's left-back for a number of years, skippering the side to success in the 1954 FA Cup Final. A defender who stuck to his task, he gave fine service to several wing-halves and left-wingers he played behind, always being fair in the challenge, strong with his kicks and honest in his approach to the game. Millard began as a centre-forward, scoring two hat-tricks; he then had a spell as a wing-half before finally settling down in the No.3 berth in 1949, following the departure of Harry Kinsell. Nicknamed the 'Agitator', he appeared in 645 first team games for Albion, including friendlies, with 436 coming in the League alone. Without doubt he was a truly great servant to West Bromwich Albion for 21 years, and missed only 13 games in the first ten post-war League seasons.
Albion debut v Northampton Town (away) League (South), 29 August 1942.
League debut v Swansea Town (away) Division Two, 31 August 1946.

DAVID MILLS
Born: Robin Hood's Bay, Nr Whitby, North Yorkshire, December 1951.
Career: Whitby Schools, North Yorks Boys, Scarborough & District Youths, Middlesbrough, Albion (£516,000, January 1979-January 1983), Newcastle United (loan), Sheffield Wednesday, Newcastle United, Middlesbrough, Darlington (n/c 1986-7).
David Mills was Britain's costliest footballer when he joined Ron Atkinson at West Bromwich in 1979, but he never lived up to the big price-tag which Albion had placed on his head. An inside-forward, hard-working with a distinctive goalscoring flair, Mills had netted 76 goals in 295 League games for 'Boro before switching to the West Midlands. After some four years and 76 matches for Albion he moved to Sheffield

Wednesday, then to Newcastle with whom he had served on loan a year earlier. When he retired, through a series of niggling injuries, Mills had assembled a useful set of statistics — 126 goals in 515 competitive matches for his four major clubs. He gained eight England Under-23 caps whilst with 'Boro, and also collected a Second Division Championship medal in 1974.
Albion debut v Liverpool (away) Division One, 3 February 1979, coming on as substitute.

FRED MORRIS
Born: Tipton, August 1893. Died: Great Bridge, July 1962.
Career: Great Bridge Primary School, Ball Street Primitives, Tipton Victoria, Redditch, Albion (May 1911-August 1924), Coventry City, Oakengates Town (1925), Retired 1930. Guested for Fulham, Watford and Tipton Excelsior during World War One.
Fred Morris was a strongly built, courageous centre or inside-forward who displayed glorious talents, neat control, rapid acceleration, dynamic shooting powers and intelligent off-the-ball running. He formed a tremendous left-wing duo with Howard Gregory just after World War One. A Junior international (1911) and winner of two England caps in 1920, as well as receiving Football League and FA recognition, Morris scored a then record 37 League goals when Albion won the First Division Championship in 1919-20, and in 287 appearances for The Baggies he notched 118 goals. In 1922 he became the first player to reach 100 League goals for Albion — and he is one of only three men to have scored five goals in a League match for the club, doing so against Notts County in October 1919.
Albion debut v Sunderland (home) Division One, 30 April 1912, scoring in a 1-0 win.

PADDY MULLIGAN

Born: Dublin, March 1945.
Career: Dublin Schools, Stella Maris, Home Farm, Bohemians, Shamrock Rovers, Boston Beacons (NASL), Shamrock Rovers, Chelsea, Crystal Palace, Albion (September 1975-August 1979), Shamrock Rovers, Panathinaikos, (assistant-manager), Galway Rovers (manager 1981). Retired 1982 to become an insurance agent in Leighton Buzzard.

An attacking right-back, an expert at overlapping, steady and thoughtful, and a player with ability who was never completely dominated by a winger, Paddy Mulligan was a wonderful capture by Albion player-manager Johnny Giles and his presence in the defence went a long way

in helping the side gain promotion in 1976. A Republic of Ireland Schoolboy international (1960-1), Mulligan went on to gain a total of 51 full caps for his country (1969-80) and he also served the League of Ireland (1965-69). He collected four FAI Cup winners' medals (1965, 66, 67 & 69); and was a member of Chelsea's League Cup Final team which lost to Stoke in 1972. He appeared as substitute for the Londoners in the European Cup-winners' Cup Final of 1971, against Real Madrid in Athens. For Albion, Mulligan made 132 senior appearances and during his professional career in England amassed in excess of 250 League and Cup games for his three clubs.
Albion debut v Fulham (home) FLC, 9 September 1975.
League debut v Blackburn Rovers (away) Division Two, 11 October 1975.

JIMMY MURPHY

Born: Ton Pentre, South Wales, August 1908.
Career: Ton Pentre Village School, Ton Pentre Boys, Treorchy Thursday FC, Treorchy Juniors, Mid-Rhondda Boys, Albion (February 1928-March 1939), Swindon Town, Morris Commercial FC, Manchester United (Coach and later assistant-manager. Caretaker manager 1958. Scout and Adviser at Old Trafford, to 1982). Welsh international team manager October 1956 to June 1963, taking Wales to the 1958 World Cup Finals in Sweden.
'Spud' or 'Twinkletoes' Murphy, as he was so aptly called around The Hawthorns, was a

vigorous attacking wing-half, skilled in tackling and a glutton for hard work. He had already gained Welsh schoolboy honours (1924 against England at Cardiff) when he joined Albion and he went on to total 15 full internationals for his country as well as playing in 223 games for Albion, including the 1935 FA Cup Final. He replaced the 'Mighty Midget' Tommy Magee in Albion's middle-line — and did a splendid job. Murphy served overseas during World War Two, with the Eighth Army, and here he met Matt Busby, in Bari, Italy, in 1945 when he was asked to join United as Busby's assistant in rebuilding the club. United won the League title three times, finished runners-up on four occasions, carried off the FA Cup, and twice won the Charity Shield — all inside ten seasons before the Munich air disaster destroyed the team. Murphy took over from Busby and when the boss returned, together they reach further heights — more Championships, further Cup success, all culminating in that great triumph in 1968 when the European Cup came to Old Trafford. Murphy resigned in 1971 but has remained loyal to the club ever since.
Albion debut v Blackpool (away) Division Two, 5 March 1930.

JOHNNY NICHOLLS

Born: Wolverhampton, April 1931.
Career: Prestwood Road, Holy Trinity and Springfield Road Schools (Wolverhampton), Heath Town FC, Albion (trial, 1946-7), Heath Town Wesley, Heath Town United, Wolverhampton Wanderers (trial 1949), Albion (August 1950, professional August 1951-May 1957), Cardiff City, Exeter City, Worcester City, Wellington Twon, Oswestry Town, Sankeys Works FC, H. Meadows FC (technical advisor), Red Dragon FC (West Bromwich League), WBA All Stars (1969-73). Retired June 1973.
One of the greatest goal 'poachers' of his day, Johnny Nicholls was a player who could run into the right spot instinctively, unleash a cracking shot or delicately place the ball into the net with either foot or with his head.

Nicholls formed a magnificent scoring partnership with his Albion 'twin' Ronnie Allen in the mid-1950s and in two successive seasons (1953-55) they scored 105 goals between them in League and Cup. He gained two England caps (with Allen) in 1954, collected a 'B' cap and one at Under-23 level (against Italy). He was a key performer in Albion's wonderful 1953-4 season when they came so close to achieving the double, collecting for himself an FA Cup winners' medal against Preston. His record for Albion was 64 goals in 145 League and Cup appearances. For Albion's reserves he netted 46 goals, notched another 50 for the intermediates and 40 for the juniors. In his entire career — with Albion, Cardiff and Exeter — Nicholls secured a total of 95 goals in 225 outings.
Albion debut v Blackburn Rovers (away) FAC, 23 February 1952.
League debut v Chelsea (home) Division One, 1 March 1952.

SAMMY NICHOLLS
Born: West Bromwich, January 1870. Died: October 1912.

Career: Spon Lane School (West Bromwich), Kidderminster Olympic, West Bromwich Victoria, Albion (February 1890-June 1892), London CBC, Albion (July 1893-July 1894). Retired through injury.

Any lack of ball finesse was more than atoned for by Sammy Nicholls' dashing, fearless displays in and around the opponents' penalty-area. He had two spells with Albion, and during his first helped the team win the 1892 FA Cup Final, scoring once in the 3-0 win over Villa. Perhaps he found it hard to settle into the team early on, but once he had made the breakthrough, he was an eager player, always wanting to be in the thick of the action. He lined up in all three central forward positions for Albion, but seemed to prefer to be leader of the attack. He left football for a year (1892-3) to work for the London County Borough Council, and a serious knee injury terminated his career at the early age of 24.

Albion debut v Everton (away) Division One, 8 March 1890.

MARK NICHOLSON
Born: Oakengates, Shropshire, June 1871. Died: circa 1943.
Career: Oakengates Fellowship School, Oswestry Town, Albion (May 1891-May 1894), Luton Town, Cairo, Vienna (when he became associated with the Austrian FA, coaching their national team in 1899-1900). Was the first President of the Austrian Football Union, and had a team named after him (Nicholson FC) in 1900. Was one of the pioneers of Austrian football, playing for Cricket FC and Vienna FC.

Mark Nicholson was a fine full-back, whose footwork and speed in recovery were outstanding features of his consistent play. His three seasons with Albion coincided with those of Tom McCulloch, Seth Powell, Jack Horton and Bob Crone, and he had to be in tip-top form to hold on to his senior position. He won an FA Cup winners' medal in 1892, against Aston Villa.

Albion debut v Everton (home) Division One, 5 September 1891.

GORDON NISBET
Born: Wallsend, September 1951.
Career: Wallsend Grammar School, Wallsend & Northumberland Boys, Willington Boys' Club, Albion (August 1968, professional September 1968-September 1976), Hull City, Plymouth Argyle. Had trials with Blackpool, Leicester City, Preston North End and Sunderland before signing for Albion.

An always thoughtful and composed right-back, Gordon Nisbet actually started his League career as a First Division goalkeeper. He played reserve-team football with Albion in a number of positions, including right-half and centre-forward, but then under Don Howe's management he was converted into a full-back. He gained one England Under-23 cap in 1972 and when he left The Hawthorns in 1976, following the arrival of Paddy Mulligan, he had accumulated in excess of 160 senior appearances. Nisbett was a member of Plymouth's FA Cup semi-final team in 1984 and he led the Pilgrims to promotion from Division Three in 1985-6.

Albion debut v Coventry City (away) Division One, 12 August 1969.

DAN NURSE
Born: Princes End, Tipton, June 1873. Died: West Bromwich, April 1959.

Career: Prince's End School, Princes's End FC (Sunday), Coseley FC, Wolverhampton Wanderers, Albion (May 1901-April 1905). Retired through injury. Became an Albion director (August 1910), staying in office until May 1927). Elected a Life Member of the club in 1920 in recognition of his sterling efforts to help keep Albion in existence during the summer of 1910.

A powerful right-half who was instrumental in helping Albion win promotion, at the first attempt in 1901-02, Dan Nurse was not always at ease when faced with intricate dribblers, but he was mighty efficient in going forward and breaking up attacks aimed down the right-hand side of the defence. He skippered Albion for three years after having made over 40 appearances for Wolves in eight years. Nurse made 88 senior appearances for Albion (four goals) and in 1902-3 represented the Football League. He was a player who led by example.

Albion debut v Glossop (home) Division Two, 2 September 1901.

JOHN OSBORNE
Born: Barlborough, Derbyshire, December 1940.
Career: Staveley Netherthorpe Grammar School, Chesterfield Boys, Derbyshire & District Schools, Barlborough Colliery Miners' Welfare, North-East Derbyshire Boys, Netherthorpe FC, Chesterfield & District Youths, Bolton Wanderers (amateur), Chesterfield, Albion (£10,000 January 1967-June 1972). Retired. Rejoined Albion (January 1973-July 1978), Walsall (loan), Shamrock Rovers, Preston North End (N/C), Telford United (N/C), Coventry City (N/C), BPM Rangers, Walsall (amateur), Corinthians FC (manager), WBA All Stars (1982-7). Currently commmercial manager of Worcestershire CCC.

John Osborne was nicknamed the 'bionic goalkeeper' after having a plastic joint inserted into his finger. He served Albion magnificently over a period of some ten years, divided into two spells. A product of Chesterfield's famous goalkeeping 'academy' Osborne occasionally performed miracles between the posts for Albion and was undoubtedly one of the club's finest post-war 'keepers. Standing 6ft 2in tall, he had a safe pair of hands, was alert in positioning, and a courageous and dedicated clubman. Initially an outfield player, he won England Schoolboy honours and appeared in the FA Cup Final of 1968 and the 1970 League Cup for

Albion, as well as helping the team win promotion in 1976. He replaced Ray Potter and Dick Sheppard at Albion, and but for a brief spell in the 1970s when Peter Latchford and Jim Cumbes took over in goal, he was Albion's first-choice 'keeper in 312 competitive matches. He made over 420 appearances during his career. He loves ornothology, sports quizzes and cricket, and once ran a sports oufitters' business with his fellow 'keeper Jim Cumbes. In later years he worked in the promotions department of the *Birmingham & Sandwell Evening Mail*. His testimonial in 1978, realised £32,000, a record for a Midlands player.
Albion debut v Nottingham Forest (home) Division One, 7 January 1967.

GARY OWEN
Born St Helens, Lancashire, July 1958.
Career: Warrington & District Schools, Manchester City, Albion (£465,000, May 1979-July 1986). Panionios of Greece, on a two-year contract.
Skilful midfielder Gary Owen's career with Albion was ruined by a series of injuries, including a fractured shin and a gashed calf which required a skin graft. There was no doubting Owen's ability. He was a fine ball-player, with vision and craft, but his days at Albion were numbered when Ron Saunders took over as manager in 1986, after Owen had been a permanent fixture in the side for five years (1979-84). Earlier, with Manchester City, he won England recognition at Youth, 'B', and Under-21 levels, and holds the record for most England Under-21 caps (22). He also played for the Football League. Owen appeared in 123 games for City (23 goals) and in 229 for Albion (26 goals). He opted for a move to Greece when released by Albion at the end of the 1985-6 season.

Albion debut v Derby County (home) Division One, 18 August 1979.

BOB PAILOR
Born: Stockton-on-Tees, July 1887. Died: Hartlepool, January 1976.
Career: Galley's Field School, St Oswald's FC, West Hartlepool, Albion (October 1908-July 1914), Newcastle United. Retired 1915 because of a kidney complaint.
Bob Pailor was a player made for scoring goals. His hefty weight, allied with pace and agility, made him such an effective centre-forward. He averaged a goal every two games for Albion, and helped his side reach the 1912 FA Cup Final with an extra-time winner in the semi-final against Blackburn Rovers. He topped Albion's scoring charts in 1911-12 and 1912-13, and during his six year stay at The Hawthorns, won many friends. He made his Newcastle debut against Albion in September 1914. After his footballing days were over he became a successful bookmaker in Hartlepool, later having to hand over his license when he became blind.
Albion debut v Bradford (Park Avenue) (away) Division Two, 30 January 1909.

HAROLD PEARSON
Born: Tamworth, May 1908.
Career: Tamworth & Amington Schools, Glascote United, Glascote Methodists, Belgrave YMCA,

Belgrave United, Two Gates FC, Nuneaton Borough, Tamworth Castle, Albion (April 1925, professional May 1927-August 1937), Millwall. Retired 1940 after guesting for West Ham.. Returned to Albion as coach (1948-52).
For a man who stood 6ft 2in tall and weighed 13st 12lb, Harold Pearson made goalkeeping look so simple. Equally adept with high or low crosses, he had a tremendous reach and kicked vast distances out of his hands; and he could throw the ball a fair way, too. 'Algy', as he was known, was on Albion's books along with his father, Hubert, (1925) and went on to make a grand total of 303 senior appearances for the Throstles, winning an FA Cup winners' medal in 1931 and a runners-up prize in 1935, and later collecting a Third Division (S) Championship medal with Millwall (1938). Earlier in his career he gained a Junior international cap (1927) and added a full cap in 1932, playing against Scotland. Pearson replaced George Ashmore in Albion's first team and was himself dislodged by Billy Light (briefly) and then Jimmy Adams in 1937.
Albion debut v South Shields (home) Division Two, 17 December 1927.

HUBERT PEARSON
Born: Kettlebrook, Tamworth, May 1886. Died: Tamworth, October 1955.
Career: Kettlebrook Oakfield, Tamworth Castle, Tamworth Athletic, Albion (February 1906-May 1926). Retired 1926. Guested for Oldbury Town 1915-16.
A board-shouldered goalkeeper, Hubert Pearson was efficient, sound and dependable, a player whose usefulness was not confined to his goal-line. He would advance some distance to avert danger, fly-kicking to safety if need be, although he was never reckless. A Junior international for England in 1907, Pearson was selected to play for the full England side against France in 1923 but was forced to withdraw through injury. He never got another chance. Nicknamed 'Joe', he won a Second Division Championship medal in 1911, added a First Division winners' medal to his collection in 1920 and in between played for Albion in the 1912 FA Cup Final against Barnsley. He represented the Football League in 1914 and 1922, and played in more League games than any other Albion 'keeper. In all Pearson made 377 appearances for the Throstles, and took over the goalkeeper's jersey in 1909-10 from big Joe Stringer. His son, Harold Pearson, was another fine Albion custodian. Scored two penalties for Albion in 1911-12.

Albion debut v Birmingham City (away) FAC, 15 January 1908.
League debut v Clapton Orient (away) Division One, 18 January 1908.

TOM PEARSON
Born: West Bromwich, 1866. Died: West Bromwich, July 1918.
Career: Christ Church School, Oak Villa, West Bromwich Sandwell, Albion (April 1886-May 1894). Retired through injury.
Albion's first really great marksman, Tom Pearson, was leading scorer in each of the first five Football League seasons, 1888-1893. He was a wonderful inside-left, with endurance, resolution, shooting power — in both feet — and a distinctive short gait. He was certainly a natural goal-getter, whose alertness and presence of mind brought him well over 100 goals during his Albion career. He played in the 1887, 1888 and 1892 FA Cup Finals, picking up winners' medals in the last two. It was a sad day when he was forced to quit the game, through injury, in 1894 at the relatively young age of 28. He was a cripple by the age of 30.
Albion debut v Halliwell (away) April 1886.
Senior debut v Notts County (away) FAC, 19 February 1887.
League debut v Stoke City (away) Division One, 8 September 1888.

JIM PEMBERTON
Born: Wolverhampton, April 1916.
Career: Willenhall Road School, Wolverhampton Boys, Ward Street Clinic FC, Round Oak FC, Brownhills Albion, Birmingham (amateur), Albion (September 1937, professional August 1938-March 1951). Retired through injury and ill-health.
Jim Pemberton was a strong, confident right-back, hard and wiry, who had a fine physique, solid kick and good positional sense. A member of Albion's 1948-9 promotion side, he was virtually an ever-present in the team for the first four post-war seasons and was then injured playing against Aston Villa on the opening day

of the 1950-1 campaign. Sadly, he never played again. He chalked up 172 League and Cup appearances for the Throstles, all in the No.2 shirt.
Albion debut v Swansea Town (away) Division Two, 31 August 1946.

JESSE PENNINGTON
Born: West Bromwich, August 1883. Died: Kidderminster, September 1970.
Career: Smethwick Schools, Summit Star, Smethwick Centaur, Langley Villa, Langley St Michael's, Dudley Town, Aston Villa (amateur), Dudley Town, Albion (March 1903-May 1922), Oldbury Town (guest 1915-16). Retired to become Albion coach until August 1923; Kidderminster Harriers (coach), Malvern College (coach), Wolves (scout), Albion (scout 1950-60).
One of the greatest names in the annals of West Bromwich Albion Football Club, Jesse 'Peerless' Pennington was a superbly equipped left-back, and scrupulously fair. Notably quick in recovery

and a player with beautiful balance, a keen eye and lovely kick out of defence, he was a magnificent captain, wonderful sportsman and a grand clubman who played in 455 League games for Albion (plus 39 FA Cup-ties and one Charity Shield match). He held the club appearance record for 44 years before losing it to Tony Brown in 1976. Pennington won 25 England caps (1907-20), represented the Football League XI on nine occasions, played for an England XI five times and also appeared in five international trials (1910-12). He skippered England twice and the League XI once, all in 1920 when aged 36. He guided Albion to the Second Division title in 1911, led them in the FA Cup Final a year later and in 1920 captained the team that won the First Division Championship for the only time to date. In his entire footballing career, Pennington never scored a goal; he was dropped from Albion's team only once and he was universally regarded as the nonpareil of Albion and England left-backs. He formed a superb duo in international circles with Blackburn's Bob Crompton, lining up as Crompton's partner in 23 of his 25 matches for his country. Pennington had the experience of playing his first and last League game for Albion against the same team — Liverpool. In 1910 he had a minor dispute with Albion regarding pay and signed for Kidderminster Harriers. That dispute, was soon sorted out and the forms cancelled when he returned to The Hawthorns. In 1913 he was the subject of a bribe scandal when he was approached with cash to 'fix' a League game between Albion and Everton. Pennington informed the police, the culprit was apprehended and later got six months' imprisonment. In November 1969, Pennington was made a Life Member of West Bromwich Albion at the age of 86, a fitting tribute to a most wonderful footballer, one of Albion's greatest.
Albion League debut v Liverpool (away) Division One, 26 September 1903.

CHARLIE PERRY
Born: West Bromwich, January 1866. Died: West Bromwich, July 1927.

Career: *Christ Church School (West Bromwich), West Bromwich Strollers (not Albion), Albion (March 1884, professional August 1885-May 1896). Retired. Albion director (1896-1902).*

Charlie Perry was a superb player and a great captain. He had a polished style, was determined in everything he did, cool under pressure, and a man who marshalled his defence magnificently from the centre-half position, which was undoubtedly his best. Brother of Tom and Walter, he won three England caps (1890-3), had two outings for the Football League XI and appeared in four international trials (1889-91). He was Albion's pivot in the 1886, 1887, 1888 and 1892 FA Cup Finals, collecting winners' medals in the last two. He missed the 1895 Final through injury, which eventually forced him to retire from top-class football. Tall and strong, Perry was Albion's first 'great' centre-half and served the club in more than 200 senior games.

Albion debut v Blackburn Rovers (The Oval) FAC Final, 3 April 1886.

League debut v Stoke (away), 8 September 1888.

TOM PERRY

Born: West Bromwich, August 1871. Died: West Bromwich, July 1927.

Career: *Christ Church School, Christ Church FC, West Bromwich Baptist FC, Stourbridge, Albion (July 1890-October 1901), Aston Villa (for four months). Retired 1902-03.*

A stalwart right-half for Albion during the ten years leading up to the club's move to The Hawthorns, Tom Perry was a capable, efficient and enthusiastic performer, wholehearted in every way, whose hard-working approach to the game made him such a key figure in the 1890s. He made his Albion bow in the outside-left position but soon became noted for his displays in the middle-line where he served alongside his elder brother, Charlie. Tom won one England cap (1898); he played three games for the Football League (1894-98); and turned out for the League XI against Aston Villa in 1894. He was Albion's right-half in the 1895 FA Cup Final and appeared in 277 League and Cup matches for the Throstles, lining up at full-back, and inside-forward as well as his 'best' role. He died two weeks after brother Charlie, and his older brother Walter (also an Albion player) passed on a year later, in 1928.

Albion debut v Preston North End (away) Division One, 13 September 1890.

TED PHEASANT

Born: Darlaston, February 1877. Died: Leicester, July 1910.

Career: *Joseph Edward Cox School (Wednesbury), Wednesbury Excelsior,*

Wednesbury Old Athletic, Wolverhampton Wanderers, Albion (November 1904-July 1910), Leicester Fosse. Died of peritonitis two weeks after leaving The Hawthorns.

'Cock' Pheasant was 6ft 2in tall and weighed almost 15st. He could play centre-half or centre-forward. As hard as nails, 'Cock' made over 150 senior appearances for Albion (22 goals) and when taking penalties, his powerhouse shooting was done almost without a run at the ball. A fearless player, he skippered Albion (1906-08) after moving to The Hawthorns from nearby Molineux. For Wolves he appeared in well over 150 League and Cup matches (17 goals) between 1896 and 1904, and missed only one League game in three seasons (1899-1902 inclusive). He was once selected to play for the Football League but refused the honour because he wanted to play for Wolves the same day. He died in a Leicester hospital soon after leaving Albion, at the age of 33.

Albion debut v Manchester United (home) Division Two, 5 November 1904.

RAY POTTER

Born: Beckenham, May 1936.

Career: *Beckenham & District Schools, Beckenham Boys, Kent Schools XI, Millwall*

(amateur), Beckenham FC, Crystal Palace, Albion (June 1958-May 1967), Portsmouth, Colchester United (assistant commercial manager), Bournemouth (assistant commercial manager and secretary), Portsmouth (administration).

Goalkeeper Ray Potter gave Albion excellent service between the posts for a number of years. Never flashy, he did his job professionally and well. He arrived at The Hawthorns at a time when there was a goalkeeping problem, with Jackman having been injured. Yet Potter, plunged in at the deep end, made the No.1 position his own from his first game and he went on to appear in over 230 senior games for the Throstles, including the 1966 League Cup Final against West Ham. When he retired at the end of the 1969-70 season, he had amassed a tally of 264 League appearances — 217 with Albion.

Albion debut v West Ham United (home) Division One, 18 October 1958.

ARTHUR RANDLE

Born: West Bromwich, December 1880. Died: West Bromwich, September 1913.

Career: *Springfield School (West Bromwich), Lyng Rovers, Oldbury Town, Darlaston, Albion (April 1901-May 1908), Leicester Fosse. Retired May 1912, aged 32 (ill-health).*

The perfect right-half, always foraging and possessing superb close control, excellent passing ability and an accurate shot, Arthur Randle's forte was probably his tactical genius. A Junior international in 1901, he joined Albion just as the team were relegated for the first time in the club's history. He spent practically two seasons in the reserves but in 1903-04 began to force himself forward, making 17 League appearances. He finally settled into the senior side in 1904-05 and held his place for three complete terms before handing over his jersey to Sammy Timmins at the start of the 1907-08 season. He had 143 first-team outings for Albion.

Albion debut v Newton Heath (away) Division Two, 9 November 1901.

JOE READER

Born: West Bromwich, February 1866. Died: West Bromwich, March 1954.

Career: *Beeches Road and St Phillip's School (West Bromwich), Albion (January 1885, professional August 1885-April 1901). Retired*

to become trainer-coach at The Hawthorns, later steward until 1950. His association with Albion spanned 65 years.

Joe Reader was a goalkeeper to rank with the finest the game has produced. Superb in handling and with marvellous reflexes, Reader used his feet as much as anything else to divert goalbound shots or headers. He appeared in over 350 games for Albion, his only club. He played in the 1892 and 1895 FA Cup Finals, won one England cap (against Ireland in 1894), represented the Football League three times and played for a League XI once. A dedicated clubman, he turned out in one match with his arm in a sling. Nicknamed 'Kicker', he is the only player to have served Albion on three different home grounds — The Four Acres, Stoney Lane and The Hawthorns. He was Albion's goalkeeper for 16 years and he was forced to give up the game through illness rather than injury, yet he was still a keen and active member of the club during his spell as coach till shortly before World War One. It is believed that Reader was the last of the 'keepers to discard the customary long white trousers, doing so in the mid-1890s. He took over between the posts from the great Bob Roberts, and was himself replaced by Ike Webb in 1901.
Albion debut v Aston Villa (away) Division One, 26 October 1889.

FRED REED
Born: Scotswood-on-Tyne, March 1894. Died:

West Bromwich, December 1967.
Career: Scotswood School, Newburn FC, Wesley Hall, Benwell FC, Lintz Institute, Albion (February 1913-July 1927), Newcastle United (guest 1919). Retired to become trainer at The Hawthorns until 1950.
Fred Reed's performances at centre-half for Albion were typical of a rugged North-Easterner, especially in the tackle where he was solid, determined and so efficient. When he arrived at Albion he understudied Frank Waterhouse and Sid Bowser and had to wait almost ten years before claiming a regular first-team place. Indeed, Reed amassed well over 150 reserve appearances before establishing himself in the senior side as captain. He stayed in the League side for three and a half seasons, during which time he made 138 League appearances before giving way to a younger man in 1927. As Albion's trainer he saw them win the FA Cup in 1931, lose to Sheffield Wednesday in the 1935 Final and win promotion from Division Two in 1948-9. He was 'sponge-man' to the Football League in 1934-5 and trainer in the England v the Rest trial matches in 1927-8 and 1934-5. During the mid-1930s he was Masseur to Warwickshire CCC. He was succeeded by Arthur 'Mother' Fitton as Albion's trainer.
Albion debut v Tottenham Hotspur (home) Division One, 6 April 1915.

CYRILLE REGIS
Born: Maripiasoula, French Guyana, February 1958.
Career: Cardinal Hinsley School (Harlesden), Harlesden Borough Boys, Brent Valley, Mosley FC, Chelsea (trial), Hayes, Albion (May 1977-October 1984), Coventry City (£300,000).
Big Cyrille Regis had seven good years at The Hawthorns, scoring 140 goals in 370 matches (including friendlies). A big favourite with the fans, he scored twice on his debut in 1977 and netted some quite spectacular goals in League and Cup football. Indeed, he created a record

by scoring on his debuts for Albion in each of five different competitions. Strong, muscular and aggressive, 'Smokin Joe' had terrific pace, a powerful shot and superb heading ability. He would often collect a ball 40 yards from goal and head towards his target with devastating pace and mobility before unleashing a fierce shot. He was certainly a bargain buy at £5,000 when Albion snapped him up after he had scored 40 goals in two seasons of non-League football. Capped by England at full, 'B' and Under-21 levels, Regis was voted PFA Young Footballer of the Year in 1979 and was runner-up to Footballer of the Year Steve Perryman (Spurs) in 1982. His transfer to Coventry was a shock to all Albion fans and Regis himself found it a big wrench to leave The Hawthorns. He scored five for Coventry against Chester in a Milk Cup game in October 1985 and was their top-scorer in 1986-7, helping the Sky Blues to Wembley glory. Regis was the Midland Sports-writers' Player of the Year in 1987.
Albion debut v Rotherham United (home) FLC, 31 August 1977.
League debut v Middlesbrough (home) Division One, 3 September 1977.

JOHN REYNOLDS
Born: Blackburn, February 1869. Died: 1917.
Career: Park Road FC (Blackburn), Witton FC, Blackburn Rovers, Park Road FC, East Lancashire Regiment, Distillery, Ulster, Albion (March 1891-April 1893), Aston Villa, Celtic, Southampton, Bristol St George, New Zealand (as coach), Stockport County, Willesden Town. Retired close season 1905. Guested for Droitwich Town (1891-2).
'Baldy' Reynolds was a marvellous wing-half who sometimes bewildered his team-mates as well as the opposition. He mastered every trick in the book and aided by some quite remarkable ball skills, his footwork was at times exceptionally brilliant. Reynolds played international football for both Ireland and England, winning a total of 13 full caps — five for Ireland. He also played for the Football League on four occasions, for the Professionals XI three times and appeared in one England trial in 1894. As Albion's right-half he gained an FA Cup winners' medal in 1892, scoring a fine goal in the 3-0 defeat of Aston Villa, and in 1895 he helped Villa beat Albion 1-0 in the Final. The following year he won a First Division Championship medal and in 1897 was a member of Villa's League and Cup double-winning team. He helped Celtic win the Scottish First Division Championship in 1898, and won an Irish Cup winners' medal, in 1891. Reynolds had the pleasure of scoring Albion's first penalty-kick, against Nottingham Forest in April 1893. He left Albion after falling

out with the committee. His League debut for Villa was against Albion on 2 September 1893. Albion debut v Blackburn Rovers (home) Division One, 3 October 1891.

SAMMY RICHARDSON

Born: West Bromwich, February 1892. Died: September 1959.

Career: Whitehall Road School, Greets Green Prims, Great Bridge Juniors, Great Bridge Celtic, Albion (February 1913-August 1927), Newport County, Aldershot. Retired 1931. Guested for Oldbury Town and Coventry City during World War One.

A wing-half mainly noted for his workmanlike displays as a defensive rather than an attacking player, Sammy Richardson was a physically strong and dominant player in the air, and an accurate passer of the ball and biting in the tackle. He was a key member of Albion's League Championship-winning team in 1919-20, and was virtually a permanent fixture in the side during the first three campaigns after World War One. He lost his place to Tommy Magee in 1923 but returned as a left-half in seasons 1924-5 and 1925-6. Brother of Bill Richardson, Albion's centre-half, Sammy played in well over 200 games for Albion and he represented the Football League and the FA in 1921.

Albion debut v Sheffield United (away) Division One, 16 January 1915.

BILLY 'G' RICHARDSON

Born: Framwellgate Moor, Co Durham, May 1909. Died: Birmingham, March 1959.

Career: Framwellgate Moor and Easington Colliery Schools, Durham Schools, Horden Wednesday FC, United Bus Company (Hartlepool), Hartlepools United, Albion (June 1929-November 1945), Shrewsbury Town, Albion (assistant trainer-coach, June 1946. Was still on Albion's training staff when he collapsed and died playing in a charity match). Guested for Derby County and Walsall during World War Two.

On his day 'W.G.' Richardson had few equals and no superiors at snapping up the half-chance, especially those which flew hard and low across the face of the goal from either wing. A truly dynamic centre-forward who depended largely on his alertness rather than his weight, he was quick, assertive and so sharp inside the 'box'. During the 1930s, 'W.G.' was seemingly always hitting the headlines — and the net. He scored both goals in the 1931 FA Cup Final; secured the match-winning goal against Charlton at The Hawthorns in 1931 which clinched Albion's Cup and promotion double; he grabbed four goals in five minutes against West Ham at Upton Park in November 1931; hit three in six minutes past Derby County in 1933; set an Albion record (which still stands) with 40 League and Cup goals in season 1935-6; and claimed a total of 14 League and Cup hat-tricks, including four 'fours' (1933-5). During World War Two he continued to crack in the goals and twice he netted six times in a match — against Luton Town and the RAF (1941-2) — and he notched up five against Swansea in 1941 and five versus Aston Villa in 1943. His wartime goalscoring exploits were exceptional — 123 in 106 games, including friendlies. For Shrewsbury in 1945-6 he netted 55 goals in only 40 outings before returning to The Hawthorns as a trainer-coach. In his brilliant scoring career, 'W.G.' surprisingly won only one England cap, against Holland in 1935. He weighed in with 202 League goals for Albion, a further 26 in the FA Cup, plus those he netted during the war. His career total was around 450 (all matches) and his appearance record was not far short of 500 games. He scored 50 Central League goals in his first season in Albion's reserves, including eight hat-tricks. The 'G' was for 'Ginger', added to help distinguish him from the other

W.Richardson who was on Albion's books at the same time.

Albion debut v Millwall (home) Division Two, 26 December 1929, scoring in a 6-1 victory for his team.

BILL RICHARDSON

Born: Great Bridge, Tipton, February 1908. Died: West Bromwich, June 1985.

Career: Whitehall Road Schools, Greets Green Boys, Greets Green Prims, Great Bridge Celtic, Albion (November 1926-May 1937), Swindon Town, Dudley Town, Vono Sports. Retired June 1941.

Bill Richardson, no relation to 'W.G' but brother to Sammy, although a shade casual at times, was a splendid pivot, unflagging and especially good in the air. He gave Albion grand service for almost 11 years, making over 350 appearances. He first set foot inside The Hawthorns when the centre-half and wing-half positions were causing some concern, and settled down in the middle line halfway through the 1928-9 campaign, with little Tommy Magee on one side and Len Darnell on the other. From then on Richardson played steadily and was always a popular and reliable servant in the Albion ranks. From December 1928 (his debut) to February 1937, Albion played a total of 347 League matches and Richardson appeared in 319 of them — testament to his tremendous dedication and consistency.

Albion debut v Middlesbrough (away) Division Two, 1 December 1928.

STAN RICKABY

Born: Stockton-on-Tees, March 1924.

Career: Stockton & District Schools, South Bank FC, Middlesbrough, Albion (£7,500, February 1950-June 1955), Poole Town (player-manager), Weymouth, Newton Abbot Spurs. Retired July 1964. Went into accountancy, emigrating to Australia in 1969.

Rickaby was a strong, accomplished right-back, good in the tackle, a player who was never flustered. He arrived at The Hawthorns as cover for Jim Pemberton but inside six months he had replaced him when injury forced the full-back to quit the game. Rickaby himself

Walter Robbins was a competent outside-left with 'tree-trunk' legs which enabled him to release a thunderbolt shot. He once hit five goals from the left-wing for Cardiff City against Thames at Ninian Park on 6 February 1932 — a League record. An ex-motor engineer and brewery lorry driver, he came to Albion as deputy to Stan Wood but had to contest the left-wing berth with Wally Boyes as well. Robbins had a few outings at inside forward before finally settling for a more controlled role in centre-field. He even played at centre-half twice in 1938. He made over 90 appearances for Albion and gained 11 caps for Wales (1930-35). In 1929 he toured Canada with the Welsh FA and collected three Central League Championship medals with Albion in successive seasons (1932-35). As Swansea's trainer he sat on the bench in the 1964 FA Cup semi-final against Preston North End and also won honours when doing the same job at Cardiff, with whom he won a Welsh Cup-winners' medal in 1929-30. He also played in three Divisions of the League with the Welsh club. Robbins had a testimonial match against Albion in May 1971 after spending ten years at The Vetch Field.
Albion debut v Chelsea (away) Division One, 23 April 1932.

posts. He won three England caps, his first against Scotland in 1886-7, and also played for the Football Alliance and in three international trials. Roberts was Albion's 'custodian' in the 1886, 1887 and 1888 FA Cup Finals, collecting a winners' medal in the latter against Preston North End when he played superbly. He had two spells with Albion — the second being for only a season — and during his 12 years' association with the club he amassed around 400 appearances including 84 in League and Cup action.
Albion debut v Wednesbury Town (home) FAC, 10 November 1883.
League debut v Stoke (away), 8 September 1888.

ALLY ROBERTSON
Born: Philpstoun, Lothian, Scotland, September 1952.
Career: Bridgend Junior and East Lothian Schools, Linlithgow Academy, Uphall Saints, Albion (July 1968, professional September 1969-September 1986), Wolverhampton Wanderers.
After 18 years and more than 700 first-team games, Ally Robertson said farewell to West Bromwich Albion at the beginning of the 1986-7 season, following the arrival at The Hawthorns of manager Ron Saunders who said that there was no room for the likeable Scot in his long-term plans for the club. It was a sad occasion for Robertson who had made his debut as a 17-year-old in 1969 against high-flying Manchester United before a 45,000 crowd in the First Division. Since that initial outing, Robertson had served in Albion's defence as a steady, centre-back, solidly built with powerful shoulders, a crunching trackle and dogged determination. A real 'tough-nut', he drew up a splendid understanding with co-defender, John Wile, and together they appeared in 573 games, helping Albion win promotion in 1975-6, reach three Cup semi-finals, as well as containing some exciting European forwards during Albion's exploits in the UEFA Cup. In 1979, Robertson passed Jimmy Dudley's record of 166 consecutive League appearances for Albion, and when he left the club he was one of only three players to have made over 500 League appearances for Albion (the other being Wile and Tony Brown). In fact, Ally Robertson's grand total of 718 plus 11 as a substitute for Albion (all matches, including

WALTER ROBBINS
Born: Cardiff, November 1910. Died: Swansea, February 1979.
Career: Cardiff Boys, Ely Brewery FC, Ely United, Cardiff City, Albion (April 1932-May 1939), Newport County, Cardiff City (trainer), Swansea (trainer, then assistant-manager until 1971, then chief scout). During the 1950s was trainer to the Welsh national team.

BOB ROBERTS
Born: West Bromwich, April 1859. Died: October 1929.
Career: Christ Church School, Salters Works, Albion (Strollers 1879) (professional August 1885-May 1890), Sunderland Albion, Albion (May 1891-May 1892), Aston Villa. Retired June 1893.
Albion's first international, goalkeeper Bob Roberts was a giant of a man, measuring 6ft 4in in height and weighing 13st. He was so well built that he could deal comfortably with any player who dared brush with him. He had a tremendous reach, a safe pair of hands, wore size-13 boots (which helped him kick enormous distances), and above all had a wonderful temperament. He started his footballing career as an outfield player, occupying many different positions, before settling down between the

was lucky with injuries during his stay at Albion — that is until the FA Cup semi-final against Port Vale in 1954. He was hurt in that tie and had to miss the Cup Final against Preston. Capped once by England, against Northern Ireland in 1953, he appeared in 205 senior games for Albion, all of them in the No.2 shirt. He left the club in 1955 after a disagreement.
Albion debut v Manchester City (home) Division One, 29 April 1950.

friendlies) makes him the second-highest appearance maker in the club's history behind Tony Brown. When only 18, Robertson had the misfortune to break a leg playing against Charlton in a League Cup-tie, but he bounced back to become one of Albion's finest defenders. As a lad he won four Scottish Schoolboy international caps, and added six Youth caps between 1968 and 1970. One disappointment was that he never made an impression on the full Scottish team selectors. In five seasons (1975-80) he missed only seven League games out of 210 as Albion returned to the First Division and established themselves as one of the country's top sides. In 1986-7, Robertson helped Wolves to the Division Four promotion play-offs.

Albion debut v Manchester United (home) Division One, 25 October 1969.

BRYAN ROBSON
Born: Witton Gilbert, Co Durham, January 1957.
Career: Chester-le-Street Junior and Birtley Comprehensive Schools, Chester-le-Street Cubs, Washington Schoolboys, Chester-le-Street Boys, Albion (September 1972, professional August 1974-October 1981), Manchester United (£1.5 million). Had trials with Burnley, Coventry City, and Newcastle United before joining Albion.
Bryan Robson became Britain's costliest footballer when he left The Hawthorns for Manchester United soon after the start of the 1981-2 season. The deal, worth around £2 million included Remi Moses, rated at the time in the £500,000 class. Regarded by many as the best midfielder since the war, Robson has been plagued by injury over the past three years and after starting England's World Cup challenge in Mexico in 1986 he had to sit out the rest of the tournament with a damaged shoulder. 'Pop' as he is known by players and fans alike, has great stamina, aggression and an abundant supply of soccer's most precious commodity —skill. He suffered three broken legs in 1976-7 when trying to establish himself in Albion's first team. He recovered full fitness and helped the

Throstles into the UEFA Cup. Robson won Youth honours for England and added Under-21, 'B' and full caps to his collection as he became one of the most gifted players in European football during the 1980s. He skippered United to FA Cup glory in 1983 and 1985 and has captained his country on many occasions. He was *Sports Argus-Sportsco* Footballer of the Year 1979; Midland Footballer of the year and Midland Sportswriters' Player of the Year 1980. He scored the fastest-ever goal in the World Cup Finals — for England against France — 27 seconds after kick-off on 16 June 1982. Brother of Gary Robson who joined Albion in 1981.
Albion debut v York City (away) Division Two, 12 April 1975.

BOBBY ROBSON
Born: Sacriston, Co Durham, February 1933.
Career: Waterhouses Secondary Modern School, Langley Park Juniors, Chester-le-Street, Middlesbrough, Southampton (trial), Fulham, Albion (£25,000 March 1956-August 1962), Fulham (£20,000), Oxford University (trainer-coach), Vancouver Royals (player-manager), Fulham (manager), Chelsea (scout), Ipswich Town (manager). Appointed England manager in July 1982. Was England 'B' team manager, January 1978-July 1982).
During his Fulham days, Bobby Robson was part of a useful inside trio which included Bedford Jezzard and Johnny Haynes. After leaving Craven Cottage for The Hawthorns in 1956 he was converted from a goalscoring inside-right into an international right-half by manager Vic Buckingham, going on to win 20 full caps (1957-62) before returning to Fulham where he ended his League career in 1967 after 585 appearances. A model competitor whose play oozed confidence, Robson's temperament was a shining example to his colleagues. A hard-worker, always full of fight, he inspired his fellow team-mates and proved a tireless wing-half and inside-forward. Besides his score of full caps, Robson played five times for the League XI, once for the Under-23s, once for the 'B' team, and represented the FA XI on tour to South Africa in 1956. He was in the 1958 and 1962 World Cup Finals squads and netted twice on his England debut, against France at Wembley in 1957. He played for the FA XI against

Tottenham in the 1962 Charity Shield game and as manager of Ipswich saw the Portman Road club celebrate success in the FA Cup (1978) and UEFA Cup (1981), as well as winning the Texaco Cup in 1973. He was also Town manager when they were pipped for the League title by Aston Villa in 1981. During his playing career (for Fulham, Albion and England at all levels) Robson made 673 senior appearances and scored 151 goals. For Albion his record was 257 games and 61 goals. He was a good cricketer too, playing for Sacriston, Worcester Park (London), and for West Bromwich Dartmouth. As England team manager Robson was in charge during the 1986 World Cup Finals in Mexico and celebrated his 50th international as manager when England played Sweden in Stockholm in September 1986.
Albion debut v Manchester City (home) Division One, 10 March 1956.

REG RYAN
Born: Dublin, October 1925.
Career: Merino School (Gaelic Football), Claremont School (Blackpool), Blackpool Boys, S.S. Cars FC, Sheffield United (trial), Jaguar Cars FC, Nuneaton Borough, Nottingham Forest (trial), Coventry City, Albion (April 1945-June 1955), Derby County (£3,000), Coventry City. Retired November 1960. Coventry City FC Pools Organiser. Joined Albion. December 1961, on similar basis. Became club's chief scout September 1962-October 1976. Later acted as scout for Hereford United and Leeds United.
A stocky, mobile player who gave many impressive displays from both wing-half positions and as an inside-forward for clubs and country, 'Paddy' Ryan took time to stake a claim in Albion's senior side, but once in he was a consistent

performer, helping them win promotion from Division Two in 1949 and gaining an FA Cup winners' medal in 1954, when he linked up tremendously well in centre-field with Jimmy Dudley and Ray Barlow. After leaving Albion he inspired Derby County to the Third Division (N) Championship in 1956-7 when he skippered the Rams. On the international front, Ryan won 17 caps, sixteen for the Republic of Ireland and one for Northern Ireland. He amassed 432 League appearances (234 for Albion) and netted a combined figure of 70 goals in the competition. In 1955, he played left-half for the Third Division (N) team against the Third Division (S) side and scored a penalty. He still follows football today and is always eager to attend re-unions of old players at The Hawthorns.
Albion debut v Millwall (away) Football League South, 10 November 1945.
Albion League debut v Chesterfield (away) Division Two, 4 September 1947.

JIM SANDERS
Born: Hackney, London, July 1920.
Career: Hackney Grammar and North London Schools, Longlands FC, Liverpool (trial), Charlton Athletic, Albion (£2,250, November 1945-June 1958), Coventry City, Hinckley Athletic. Retired 1960. Guested for Albion, Southampton, Chelsea, West Ham, Fulham and Liverpool during World War Two.
Jim Sanders was a very consistent goalkeeper, never acrobatic but always steady and capable. He was something of an expert at stopping penalties — preventing some 25 from entering the net in his 19-year career. He was invalided out of the RAF during the war after many operational flights as an air-gunner, but recovered full fitness and acted as Albion's last line of defence in 391 games, including the 1954 FA Cup Final when he came into the team as a late replacement for the injured Norman Heath. He was a key member of Albion's 1948-9 promotion-winning side, and at The Valley was understudy to the great Sam Bartram. Sanders was Albion's first choice 'keeper for the period 1948-51 and again from 1954 to 1958 when he handed over the duties to Clive Jackman, before moving to nearby Coventry. After his footballing days were over, Sanders became a

publican, first in Derby, then in Birmingham. Today he lives in Tamworth and can still be seen sporting his bow-tie and FA Cup-winners' medal, which hangs proudly on a chain around his neck.
Albion debut in November 1945.
FA Cup debut v Cardiff City (away), 5 January 1946.
League debut v Swansea Town (away) Division Two, 31 August 1946.

TEDDY SANDFORD
Born: Handsworth, Birmingham, October 1910.
Career: Wattville Road School, Tantany Athletic, Overend Wesley, Birmingham Carriage Works FC, Smethwick Highfield, Albion (October 1929-March 1939), Sheffield United, Morris Commercial FC, Retired 1943. Albion coach during 1950s, scout 1961-67.
Teddy Sandford had ten fine years at The Hawthorns. He arrived at the club when Albion were reasonably well-off for inside-forwards, and spent a season in the reserves before making his first-team debut in 1930-31, the season which ended in triumph with that Cup and promotion double. Sandford was a quiet type of player, never flashy, but nevertheless an excellent goalscoring inside-left who was exceedingly quick to pounce and dispossess an opponent who in turn found it hard to dispossess him. He had an enviable physique which held him in good stead later in his career when he lined up to good effect at centre-half. He won an FA Cup winners' medal with Albion in 1931 and collected a loser's prize in 1935 after scoring a goal in his side's 4-2 defeat by Sheffield Wednesday. He won one England cap, against Wales in 1932, and appeared in 317 games for Albion, scoring 75 goals. He is one of the youngest players ever to win an FA Cup medal with Albion, being just 20 years, six months when The Throstles took the trophy in 1931.
Albion debut v Preston North End (away) Division Two, 15 November 1931, scoring in a 3-2 Albion victory.

JACK SANKEY
Born: Moulton, March 1912. Died: Handsworth, Birmingham, January 1985.
Career: Moulton C of E School, Moulton Wanderers, Winsford United, Albion (November

1930-October 1945), Northampton Town, Walsall (guest 1945-46), Hereford United (player, then assistant-trainer). Albion (coach 1955-64, then scout 1965-6).
Jack Sankey was an industrious and highly efficient wing-half or inside-forward whose overall play was characterised by some powerful long-range shooting. He spent three and a half seasons playing for Albion's reserve team before making the major breakthrough into the first eleven in 1933-4, taking over from Jimmy Edwards. From then until the outbreak of World War Two, Sankey's senior outings were frequent and by 1939 his Albion appearances had reached the 150 mark. During the hostilities he added over 120 more competitive matches to his tally and ended his career at The Hawthorns in 1945 with a record of 290 first-team games and 27 goals. He had a testimonial match (Hereford versus Albion) in 1954 when 4,500 fans saw Hereford win 10-5.
Albion debut v Chelsea (away) FAC, 13 January 1934.
League debut v Blackburn Rovers (home), Division One, 20 January 1934.

MAURICE SETTERS
Born: Honiton, Devon, December 1936.
Career: Honiton & Cullompton Schools, Exeter City, Albion (£3,000, January 1955-January 1960), Manchester United (£30,000), Stoke City, Coventry City, Charlton Athletic, Doncaster Rovers (manager), Sheffield Wednesday (coach), Rotherham United (assistant-manager), Newcastle United (chief scout). Assistant-manager of Republic of Ireland national team (1986-7).
With his bandy-legs and crew-cut hair, Maurice Setters looked what he was on the field of play — a real terrier, as hard as nails, determined and fearless despite standing only 5ft 6in tall. After winning Schoolboy recognition, he went on to gain one Youth cap and 16 at Under-23 level for England. He also played twice for the FA XI and represented Young England in 1958. He appeared in 132 League and Cup games for Albion and 186 for United. For Exeter, Stoke, Coventry and Charlton, his senior outings totalled 170 — and he finished his League career with 434 games to his name. Setters won an FA Cup winners' medal with United in 1963. A tremendous competitor in every sense of the word, Setters tasted major

football in seven different outfield positions but was at his best in midfield.
Albion debut v Huddersfield Town (away) Division One, 26 November 1955.

CECIL SHAW
Born: Mansfield, June 1911. Died: Handsworth, Birmingham, January 1977.
Career: Mansfield Schools, Mansfield Invicta, Blidworth Juniors, Rainworth Church FC, Rufford Colliery FC, Wolverhampton Wanderers

(1930), Albion (£7,500, December 1936-June 1947), Hereford United. Retired 1949 Guested for Nottingham Forest and Blackpool during World War Two. Refereed in Oldbury & District Leagues 1950-60. Albion scout 1961-64.
Cecil Shaw was a tough full-back, a resolute and robust tackler who played some 200 games for Wolves (176 in the League) before transferring to Albion in 1936 for a record fee of £7,500, paid in two instalments. He gained a first-team place with Wolves late in 1932 and played with such consistency and reliability that up to the middle of September 1936 he had missed only one match in the senior side, making 126 consecutive appearances. He was Wolves' skipper and their penalty expert. Alas, Shaw missed the first spot-kick he took for Albion, in an FA Cup-tie at Coventry in February 1937. Standing 5ft 9ins tall and weighing 12st 7lb, he went straight into Albion's League team, holding his place at left-back until the war and partly through it. He is one of only a handful of players who served Albion before, during and after World War Two. Towards the end of 1936-7 and at the start of 1937-8, he lined up alongside his namesake, George, in the full-back position in 15 League matches for Albion. Shaw made 251 appearances for Albion (League, Cup and wartime competitions) and he scored 14 goals. He represented the Football League in 1935 when a Wolves player.
Albion debut v Liverpool (away) Division One, 28 December 1936.

GEORGE SHAW
Born: Swinton, October 1899. Died: March 1973.
Career: Swinton Schools, Bolton-on-Deane FC, Rossington Main Colliery, Doncaster Rovers, Gillingham, Doncaster Rovers, Huddersfield Town, Albion (November 1926-May 1938), Stalybridge Celtic, Worcester City (player-manager), FC Floriana, Malta (player-manager-coach 1948-51). Retired cs 1951, returning to Hamworth Colliery, Doncaster.
Like several of his contemporaries, George 'Cocky' Shaw — nicknamed 'Teapot' — gave long and loyal service to Albion. Admirably built for a full-back, he was dominant in the air, strong on the ground and decidedly safe with his kicking. He was a grand volleyer of the ball and a useful penalty-taker. Shaw was an occasional member of Huddersfield's League Championship winning teams of 1923-4, 1924-5

and 1925-6, making 24 appearances in three seasons. With Albion he won an FA Cup winners' medal in 1931, a runners-up award at Wembly in 1935, one England cap, against Scotland in 1932, and had an outing with the Football League XI. He went on two FA Tours, to Belgium, France and Spain in 1929, and to Canada in 1931. After making his Albion debut he missed only five of the next 300 League games to January 1934, and when he left The Hawthorns, shortly after the end of the 1937-8 campaign, he had amassed 425 senior appearances for the Baggies. Shaw cost Albion £4,100 when signed from Huddersfield — a club record at the time. An ex-naval man, he was a useful singer and his hobby was mat-making.
Albion debut v Sheffield United (away), 4 December 1926.

BEN SHEARMAN
Born: Lincoln, June 1884. Died: October 1958.
Career: Attercliffe, High Hazels (Sheffield Amateur League), Worksop, Rotherham Town, Bristol City, Albion (June 1911-August 1919) Nottingham Forest, Gainsborough Trinity, Norton Woodseats. Retired 1938.
Ben Shearman was an elusive outside-left, quick off the mark and strikingly accurate with his crosses, whether hit high or low. He replaced Amos Lloyd on Albion's left-wing and was a consistent performer in that position until Howard Gregory and Jack Crisp came along immediately after World War One to contest the No.11 spot, Shearman rejoined Nottingham Forest. He appeared in 143 games for Albion, and was in their 1912 FA Cup Final side against Barnsley. He played for the Football League XI on two occasions in 1911, and during his career in League football amassed more than 180 appearances.
Albion debut v Notts County (home) Division One, 2 September 1911, scoring in a 2-1 Albion victory.

FRED SHINTON
Born: Wednesbury, March 1883. Died: Leicester, April 1923.
Career: St James' School (Wednesbury),

Hawthorn Villa, Moxley White Star, Wednesbury Old Athletic, Hednesford Town, Albion (April 1905-December 1907), Leicester Fosse, Bolton Wanderers, Leicester Fosse. Retired (ill-health) 1912.

Fred Shinton was a deadly marksman who scored 46 goals in only 64 League games for Albion in two and a half years with the club. A very sporting character, he played with dash and tenacity; he had a never-say-die attitude and thoroughly enjoyed scoring goals. Nicknamed 'Appleyard' and 'Tickler' by his colleagues, he had perhaps one of the best overall scoring records in terms of goals-per-matches, than any other player. In the first half of the 1906-7 campaign he scored 26 goals in 21 matches, including three 'fours'. He had a remarkable knack of finding the net. He was recruited by Albion following the problem of filling the centre-forward spot in 1904-5 when no fewer than six different players were tried. Shinton stepped in and made such an impact that when he left, upset fans caused a rumpus at the ground. His place as leader of the attack was taken by a number of players — yet again — until finally Bob Pailor arrived to fit the bill in 1908.
Albion debut v Bolton Wanderers (home) Division Two, 22 April 1905.

'CHIPPY' SIMMONS
Born: West Bromwich, September 1878. Died: Wednesbury, December 1937.
Career: Beeches Road School, Trinity Victoria, Oldbury Town, Worcester Rovers, Albion (April 1898-July 1904), West Ham United, Albion (May 1905-March 1907), Chesterfield Town, Wellington Town, Royal Rovers (Canada). Retired 1922, returning to West Bromwich where he became a publican, having learnt the trade in 1909.
Charlie Simmons, always known as 'Chippy', was a regular scorer from the inside-right or centre-forward positions. He teamed up well with first Billy Bassett, and then Jimmy McLean and Fred Buck, and later with Fred Shinton after he had returned to West Bromwich following a brief association with West Ham. A player with a cracking shot, Simmons had plenty of pace and craft. He was a big favourite with the fans, especially the ladies, and scored 81 goals in 193 first-team games for the Throstles. He gained a Second Division Championship medal

in 1902 when he top-scored with 23 League goals, and it was in this same year that he figured in an England international trial, later representing the Professionals of the South v The Amateurs of the South in 1905. He was an England reserve on three occasions during the 1901-2 season.
Albion debut v. Burnley (away) Division One, 19 November 1898.

JOE SMITH
Born: Darby End, Nr Dudley, April 1890. Died: June 1956.
Career: Halesowen Road Council School, Netherton St Andrew's, Darby End Victoria, Cradley Heath St Luke's, Albion (May 1910-May 1926), Birmingham, Worcester City (player-manager). Retired 1933. Guested for Everton and Notts County in World War One.
Joe Smith was a right-back strategist who more than balanced any deficiency in speed by good positional sense. He often cleared his lines with long, telling kicks and was sound in the tackle

for a relatively small man. His remarkably high level of performance over a long period is illustrated by the number of League appearances

he made from 1919-20 to 1924-25 inclusive: 247 out of a possible 252, and all in the First Division. Joe Smith formed fine partnerships at full-back with Jesse Pennington and later with Billy Adams and Arthur Perry. A Junior international in 1909, Smith obtained two full England caps, in 1919-20 and 1922-3, and gained a Second Division Championship medal in 1911 and a First Division winners' medal in 1920. He also played for England in a 1919 Victory international. A wonderful clubman, a studious performer, Joe Smith made more than 470 senior appearances for Albion — 434 in the League alone.
Albion debut v Bolton Wanderers (away) Division Two, 5 September 1910.

DEREK STATHAM
Born: Whitmore Reams, Wolverhampton, March 1959.
Career: St Mary's Primary and St Edmund's Junior Schools (Wolverhampton), Albion (July 1975, professional April 1976-).
Derek Statham was one of the finest left-backs in England in the early 1980s, but he had Arsenal's Kenny Sansom to contest the No.3 shirt with on the international front and won only three full caps, in 1982-3 against Wales and Australia (2). A cheerful, buoyant character who tackles tigerishly and loves to go forward, Derek Statham scored against one of the finest 'keepers in the country when making his Albion debut in 1976 — that man being Peter Shilton, then with Stoke. Earlier, Statham had gained an FA Youth Cup winners' medal with Albion and went on to win seven Youth caps for his country, following up with more at Under-21 and 'B' team levels before breaking into the senior side in 1983 after ex-Albion man, Bobby Robson, had taken over as team-manager. Statham has had injury problems but when fit he has tremendous talent. His weaving, darting runs from deep in his own half directly into the opposing penalty area have highlighted his displays. In 1986-7 a proposed £250,000 transfer to Liverpool fell through on medical grounds.
Albion debut v Stoke City (away) Division One, 18 December 1976, scoring once, in a 2-0 win.

JIM STEVENSON
Born: Bonhill, Dumbarton, August 1875. Died: Dumbarton, March 1925.
Career: Bonhill St Augustine's School, Dumbarton

Fereday, Dumbarton, Preston North End, Bristol St George, Preston North End, Albion (October 1900-June 1904), Dumbarton. Retired cs 1910. Albion (trainer 1914-16). Died following an accident at Leven Shipyard.

Jim Stevenson was a resilient, strong-tackling centre-half who also played and performed admirably at centre-forward. He was aided by his height (6ft 2in) and qualities of coolness and precise judgment. Signed by Albion at a time when the team was at a low ebb, he failed to save them from relegation but was instrumental in helping them regain their First Division status the following season, when he appeared in all 34 League matches, lining up in the middle of wing-halves Dan Nurse and Harry Hadley. Stevenson commanded the defence and had a wonderful spell at The Hawthorns, making 129 League and Cup appearances and winning a Second Division Championship medal in 1902. He gained one minor representative honour — a game for the Anglo-Scots v Scotland in 1902-3.

Albion debut v Stoke (home) Division One, 3 November 1900.

JIM STRINGER
Born: Netherton, May 1878. Died: Dudley, December 1933.
Career: Netherton & District Schools, Netherton

Rovers, Wolverhampton Wanderers, Albion (April 1905-October 1910), Dudley Town, Port Talbot (trainer). Retired.

Jim Stringer was a sound, vigilant goalkeeper, whose height and weight enabled him to dominate when high crosses looped over, or there was a tight situation near his goal. Albion secured him from neighbouring Wolves to take over between the posts from Ike Webb. Stringer did well, holding his place in the side for four and a half seasons before handing over to Hubert Pearson halfway through the 1909-10 campaign.

Albion debut v Leicester Fosse (home) Division Two, 8 April 1905.

COLIN SUGGETT
Born: Washington, Co Durham, December, 1948.
Career: Washington Grammar School, Chester-le-Street and Co Durham Schools, Sunderland, Albion (£100,000, July 1969-February 1973), Norwich City, Newcastle United (August 1978). Retired 1979 to become coach at St James' Park.

Colin Suggett was Albion's first £100,000 signing, in 1969, and he got off to a flying start, scoring twice on his debut against Southampton at The Dell at the start of the 1969-70 season. He arrived at The Hawthorns with a big reputation as a goal-getter and left as a highly efficient midfielder who cost Norwich £70,000. He made his League debut for Sunderland in March 1967 as an 18-year-old, and whilst at Roker Park played in the 1966 and 1967 FA Youth Cup Finals. He won England Schoolboy and Youth honours (1963-4 and 1966-7 respectively) and was in Albion's 1970 League Cup Final team at Wembley. He played for Norwich in the 1975 League Cup Final against Aston Villa, and during his career amassed a grand total of 440 League games, scoring 65 goals. For Norwich he netted 21 times in 203 League matches; and for Sunderland his record was 24 goals in 86 League games. He was a keen pigeon fancier and also enjoyed a wager on the horses and

dogs, owning a greyhound while an Albion player.

Albion debut v Southampton (away) Division One, 9 August 1969 (scoring two goals).

JOHN TALBUT
Born: Headington, Oxford, October 1940.
Career: South Shields Grammar School, South Shields Schools, Durham Boys, Burnley, Albion (December 1966-May 1971), KV Mechelen (Belgium, player-manager). Retired 1974 to become a licensee in Belgium, taking the 'Kup Winna' bar in Mechelen.

John Talbut was already an experienced centre-half when he came to Albion halfway through the 1966-7 season, having played in 138 League games for Burnley, besides gaining England caps at Schoolboy (1955) and Under-23 levels (seven appearances). He was recruited to Albion by manager Jimmy Hagan as a replacement for Stan Jones and repaid every penny of the £30,000 fee placed on his head, by appearing in well over 190 senior games for Albion, including the 1968 FA Cup and 1970 League Cup Finals. He broke into League football with Burnley in December 1958, against Leicester, and during the first four months of his Albion career had to sit and watch the team battle through to Wembley in the League Cup, having already played for Burnley in that season's competition. Twelve months later, however, he gained a winners' medal as Albion beat Everton 1-0 in extra-time to take the FA Cup.

Albion debut v Tottenham Hotspur (home) Division One, 26 December 1966.

BERT TRENTHAM
Born: Chirbury, Salop, April 1908. Died: Birmingham, June, 1979.
Career: Chirbury St John's School, Knighton Town, Knighton Victoria, Knighton United, Hereford United, Aston Villa (trial), Albion (April 1929-May 1937), Hereford United, Darlaston. Retired 1942. Went into ironmongers business in Ward End, Birmingham.

'Corker' Trentham was a useful full-back, able and willing to play in either the right or left hand

berth. A model of consistency, he was sound rather than brilliant and always carried a handkerchief in his withered right hand. He drew up a fine relationship on the field with his co-partner, George Shaw, and together they played in over 230 games for Albion during the 1930s, including appearances in both the 1931 and 1935 FA Cup Finals. Trentham was a member of Albion's 'double' team of 1930-1, and during his splendid career he won a Junior international cap (1929) and represented the Football League in 1933. He never scored a goal in more than 270 senior appearances for Albion.

Albion debut v Blackpool (away) Division Two, 5 March 1930.

JACK VERNON
Born: Belfast, September 1919. Died: Belfast, August 1981.
Career: St Paul's School (Belfast), Springfield Road Juniors, Dundela Juniors, Liverpool (trial, 1937), Belfast Celtic, Albion (February 1947-July 1952), Crusaders, Retired June 1954, to continue his father's butchers business in Belfast, a job he did until his untimely death.

Jack Vernon was unquestionably among the greatest of West Bromwich Albion centre-halves, supreme in the air and masterful on the ground —a true sportsman of the highest calibre. Albion signed Vernon on a five-year agreement in 1947, handing over a then club record fee of £9,500 to Belfast Celtic. He had to wait five weeks for his Albion debut due to the atrocious weather which gripped England that winter — and when he did finally step out for his Albion baptism, at Upton Park, he was on the receiving end of a hat-trick from the home striker Neary as the Hammers won 3-2. But Vernon soon settled into the routine of commanding the back division — a job he did so successfully, not only for Albion but for Northern Ireland as well. He collected 22 full caps (two with the Republic) and skippered Northern Ireland on 17 occasions. He also captained the United Kingdom side against Wales in 1951 and was at centre-half for the Great Britain XI v the Rest of the World at Hampden Park in 1947, an honour which confirmed him as the game's top pivot at that time. Before he arrived at The Hawthorns, Vernon — nicknamed 'Twinkletoes' because of his small size-5 feet — won Irish Cup winners' medals in 1941, 1943 and 1944, and Irish League Championship medals in 1939 and 1940, as well as playing for the Irish Select XI on three occasions and the Irish League 12 times between 1941 and 1946. He led Albion to promotion in 1948-9 and played in exactly 200 League and Cup matches for the Baggies, scoring just one goal —against Sheffield Wednesday on Christmas morning 1948.

Albion debut v West Ham United (away) Division Two, 15 March 1947.

DAVE WALSH
Born: Waterford, April 1924.
Career: St Joseph's (Waterford), The Corinthians, Shelbourne of Waterford, Glen Rovers, Limerick, Shelbourne of Dublin (on loan), Linfield, Albion (£3,500, May 1946-December 1950), Aston Villa (£25,000), Walsall, Worcester City. Retired June 1957. Ran successful sports outfitters in Droitwich before retiring to Torquay in 1984.

Dave Walsh had an ideal build for a centre-forward, a job he did so well with speed and thrust. He was a consistent scorer throughout his career which saw him win 11 caps for Northern Ireland and 20 for the Republic. He also represented the Irish League twice in 1946, and helped Albion win promotion in 1949, when he scored 23 goals. As keen as mustard in and around the 'box', he had netted over 60 goals for Linfield in 1945-6 when they won the Irish League Championship. He also scored two in the Irish Cup Final against Distillery — and this record promoted Albion boss Fred Everiss to travel to Ireland and secure Walsh's services. Walsh had scored well over 120 goals in Irish football, winning other Cup medals in 1944 (runners-up) and 1945 (winners), and in each of his first six League matches in England he scored at least once to create an Albion record. He notched exactly 100 goals in 174 games for Albion and his record with Villa and Walsall sent his statistics in League football up to 137 goals in 293 outings before he drifted into non-League soccer with Worcester in 1956.

Albion debut v Swansea Town (away) Division Two, 31 August 1946, when he scored twice in a 3-2 Albion win.

IKE WEBB
Born: Worcester, October 1874. Died: March 1950.
Career: Worcester Park School, St Clement's Rangers, Berwick Rangers (Worcester League), Evesham Town, Mansfield Town, Lincoln City, Small Heath, Albion (May 1901-December 1904), Sunderland, QPR. Retired 1910. Made a 'comeback' for Albion's first team in August 1918 at the age of 43.

Ike Webb was a goalkeeper of outstanding reflexes and quickness off his line. Spectacularly agile at times, his actions were usually so perfectly timed, although occasionally he tended to be rather casual. He is believed to have played with a fractured skull during an interesting career which took him to all parts of the country. He was secured by Albion to replace the retiring Joe Reader and he did a wonderful job between the posts for three and a half seasons, making 101 senior appearances. He gained a Second Division Championship medal in 1902 and was in terrific form during that campaign, his first with Albion.

Albion debut v Glossop (home) Division Two, 2 September 1901.

CLIVE WHITEHEAD
Born: Northfield, Birmingham, November 1955.
Career: Alston Junior school, Waverley Grammar School, Bordesley Green, Northfield Juniors, Wolves (trial) Bristol City, Albion (£100,000, November 1981-87). On loan to Wolverhampton Wanderers, January 1986.

Former England Youth international Clive Whitehead is a good professional, gritty, unselfish and a player who will do a worthwhile job in any position. Whitehead's Albion career was revitalised following the appointment of manager Ron Saunders in February 1986. He had been on loan to Wolves but had a new lease of life when told by the boss that he was Albion's best right-back and the position was his if he put his mind to it. He played 256 games for Bristol City prior to joining Albion and whilst at Ashton Gate had a long spell on the left-wing and another one in the left-back berth. He helped City win promotion to Division One in 1975-6 by scoring the all-important winning promotion goal against Portsmouth. In season 1982-3 he was used in six different positions by Albion, but always preferred a full-back role. In May 1987, Whitehead's career at The Hawthorns seemed finally over when he was given a free-transfer.

Albion debut v Tottenham Hotspur (away) Division One, 7 November 1981.

JOHN WILE

Born: Sherburn, Co Durham, March 1947.
Career: Sherburn Secondary Modern School, Eppleton Juniors (Hetton), Durham City, Peterborough United (trial), Sunderland, Peterborough United, Albion (£32,000, December 1970-June 1983), Peterborough United (player-manager, retiring as a player in 1986 and as manager later that year). Played in the NASL with Vancouver Whitecaps 1982.

John Wile's last game for Albion, against his former club, Sunderland, at Roker Park on 14 May 1983, was his 500th in League competition for the Baggies. It crowned a magnificent 13 years with The Throstles, during which time he made many friends, both inside and outside football; he was a fine 'ambassador' in China in 1978. He was an astute, reliable, commanding and powerful centre-half. Indeed, he was acknowledged by the fans as being one of Albion's finest-ever pivots. He had the will to win and certainly gave Albion everything each time he pulled on the club jersey. Fans still

recall his tremendous display in the 1978 FA Cup semi-final against Ipswich Town at Highbury when he played on with his head swathed in blood-stained bandages, albeit to no avail as Albion lost 3-1. But that was the essence of John Wile. He was a born fighter, a true battler and a great sportsman. He retired from first-class football at the end of the 1985-6 season. He took over the No.5 shirt at Albion from John Talbut and was succeeded by Ken McNaught in 1983. During his reign at The Hawthorns, Albion fulfilled 525 League fixtures, and 'Wiley' played in 500 of them. He missed only one Cup-tie, and in 1978-9, Albion played a total of 76 first team matches, and Wile turned out in 75 of them — the most games played by an Albion footballer in a single season. He played more matches at centre-half than any other Albion player — 616 plus one as substitute (just two at left-half). And in the League alone he played in the No.5 position on 497 occasions, plus once as a substitute. He is the third-highest appearance maker for Albion with 714 (plus one) games. Sadly he never won a major honour, despite playing in three major Cup semi-finals with Albion, reaching the quarter-finals of the UEFA Cup in 1979 and being a dominant figure in Albion's promotion-winning side in 1975-6. He was an ever-present for Albion in seven seasons — a club record. Former manager Johnny Giles once said of John Wile: "If he could play football from nine in the morning till nine at night, seven days a week, 52 weeks a year, he still wouldn't be satisfied."

Albion debut v Blackpool (home) Division One, 19 December 1970.

BILLY WILLIAMS

Born: West Smethwick, June 1875. Died: West Bromwich, January 1929.
Career: Oldbury Road School (Smethwick), West Smethwick FC, Old Hill Wanderers, Albion (May 1894-June 1901). Forced to quit the game after a cartilage injury. Became Albion trainer for a while, later acting as coach at The Hawthorns (1910), before taking over a

pub in West Bromwich.
Billy Williams was a brilliant full-back, stylish, dedicated and above all safe and sure under pressure. He possessed a long, raking kick and scored a few goals from far distances including one from fully 60 yards against Nottingham Forest (FAC) in February 1898. He was also an expert with penalty-kicks. He gained six England caps and played for the Football League and the Professionals in representative matches. He collected a runners-up medal with Albion in the 1895 FA Cup Final and made 208 senior appearances for the Baggies. Williams' enforced retirement was a bitter blow to Albion who suffered relegation for the first time at the end of his farewell season.

Albion debut v Sheffield United (away) Division One, 1 September 1894.

CYRIL WILLIAMS

Born: Bristol, November 1921. Died: Bristol, January 1980.
Career: Luckwell Road School (Bristol), Bristol Boys, Bristol City Albion (June 1948-August

1951), Bristol City (£4,500), Chippenham Town (manager), Gloucester City (manager). Guested for Reading and Tottenham Hotspur during World War Two.

Cyril Williams was a capable and efficient inside-forward who had enthusiasm as well as skill. A goalscorer who found the net 20 times in 77 League and Cup games for Albion, he was a key figure in the 1948-9 promotion team and later shone at left-half for Bristol City, for whom he played in nearly 300 League matches (68 goals), winning a Third Division (S) Championship medal in 1954-5. He came to The Hawthorns in a player-exchange deal involving Cliff Edwards plus £500. Cyril Williams was killed in a car crash on 21 January 1980.
Albion debut v Chesterfield (away) Division Two, 4 September 1948.

GRAHAM WILLIAMS
Born: Hellan, North Wales, April 1938.
Career: Emmanuel Secondary Modern School, Flintshire Boys, Burnley (trial 1953), Rhyl Athletic, Albion (September 1954, professional April 1955-April 1972), Weymouth (player-manager), Sports Klub Kuwait, OFI (Greece, coach)), Poole Town (manager), Cardiff City (coach, then manager), Newport County (scout).
Graham Williams had 18 years' association with Albion, first as an outside-left and later as a powerful left-back. He also put in a few enterprising displays at left-half but it was in the No.3 shirt where he blossomed, skippering Albion to FA Cup Final success in 1968, after having led his team to a League Cup triumph two years earlier. He also played in the 1967 and 1970 League Cup Fnals, collecting a runners-up prize each time. He was capped 26 times by Wales and had two outings for the Under-23s. For Albion, his only League club as a player, he appeared in well over 350 competitive matches, including 314 in the First Division. It was not until 1962-3 that he became a firm fixture in Albion's senior eleven — this after his

namesake, Stuart, had left for Southampton. It is interesting to note that Graham and Stuart Williams played together as full-backs for both Albion and Wales. In 1981, Graham Williams took Poole Town to the Final of the Anglo-Italian Tournament. Today he lives in Weymouth with his wife and family.
Albion debut v Blackpool (home) Division One, 19 November 1955.

STUART WILLIAMS
Born: Wrexham, July 1930.
Career: Aston Park and Grove Park Grammar Schools (Wrexham), Victoria Youth Club, Wrexham, Albion (November 1950-September 1962), Southampton (£15,000), Albion (trainer 1967-69), Aston Villa (trainer) Payhaan (manager), Morton (trainer-coach), Southampton (coach and assistant-manager), Carlisle United (scout), Stavanger (Norway, manager).
One-time inside-right Stuart Williams was converted by Albion into a grand full-back who gave the Baggies 12 years' yeoman service. He had a sure kick, splendid positional sense and a first-rate temperament. Whilst at The Hawthorns he gained 33 Welsh caps (an Albion record for most-capped player) and after leaving for The Dell, he added another ten to his total. He had 246 senior outings for Albion (nine goals scored) and for the Saints, whom he helped win promotion to the First Division in 1966, his appearance tally topped the 175 mark, 147 coming in the League. He looked likely to replace Stan Rickaby in Albion's 1954 FA Cup Final side but was left out in favour of the more experienced Joe Kennedy.
Albion debut v Huddersfield Town (away) Division One, 16 February 1952.

CHARLIE WILSON
Born: Heeley, Sheffield, July 1905. Died: Kidderminster, 1985.
Career: Netherthorpe School, Stonehouse FC, Chesterfield (trial), Sheffield United (trial), Hallam FC, Albion (December 1920, professional November 1922-February 1928), Sheffield Wednesday, Grimsby Town, Aston Villa, Coventry City, Kidderminster Harriers, Worcester City, Kidderminster Harriers. Guested for Charlton Athletic and Aldershot during World

War Two and played for Kidderminster Police in 1946. Became a publican in 1947, retiring in 1971.
Charlie Wilson was an opportunist inside or centre-forward, who had an unquenchable thirst for goals — he hit 45 in 133 games for Albion. 'Tug', with his film-star looks, was a constant threat to opposing defenders; he could shoot from any angle and from seemingly any distance with either foot — and he usually hit the target. He had the reputation of keeping himself clean on the muddiest of pitches, yet he was still a 'grafter' who moved to left-half late in his career. He has the distinction of being the youngest player ever to appear in a League game for Albion — his debut coming at Oldham in October 1921 when he was 16 years 63 days old. In the 1920s he gained three Central League Championship medals with Albion and assisted Sheffield Wednesday during their First Division title-winning seasons of 1928-9 and 1929-30. He linked superbly up front for Albion with Stan Davies, George James, Joe Carter, and both Arthur Fitton and Jack Byers, his left-wingers.
Albion debut v Oldham Athletic (away) Division One, 1 October 1921.

JOE WILSON
Born: Handsworth, Birmingham, January 1861. Died: Acocks Green, Birmingham, October 1952.

Career: Hamstead Swifts, Aston Unity, Stoke, Walsall Town, Aston Villa, Walsall Town, Albion (September 1887-May 1890), Kidderminster Harriers, Birmingham St George's. Retired. Became Football League referee (1894-1910). Was a goldsmith by trade.

Joe Wilson had the distinction of scoring Albion's first-ever League goal — at Stoke on 8 September 1888. Six months earlier he had helped Albion win the FA Cup at The Oval after scoring half-a-dozen goals in the earlier rounds. An aggressive outside-left of dashing style, he kept defences alert with his wing play. He formed a fine partnership with Tom Pearson and was virtually an ever-present in Albion's first two League campaigns. After playing the game he took up refereeing, and did a fine job for 16 seasons, officiating in most divisions, in the FA Cup and at non-League level. He played 53 League and Cup matches for Albion and scored 20 goals.

Albion debut in September 1887.

FA Cup debut v Wednesbury Old Athletic (home), 15 October 1887, scoring twice in a 7-1 victory.

League debut v Stoke (away), 8 September 1888.

RAY WILSON

Born: Grangemouth, Stirlingshire, April 1947.
Career: Dundas Primary and Grangemouth High Schools, Stirlingshire Boys, Woodburn Athletic, Albion (July 1963, professional May 1964-March 1977). Forced to retire through serious knee injury.

Ray Wilson began with Albion as an outside-left but made a big name for himself as a steady left-back, who gained Scottish Under-23 recognition in 1970. A good covering player, who tackled hard, he had exceptional speed which enabled him to recover quickly. He loved to overlap and was a fine 'chipper' of the ball, left-footed down the touchline. He appeared in the 1970 League Cup Final for Albion — one of

284 senior games for the club. He established himself in the first team (at left-back) in the late 1960s, taking over initially from Graham Williams. His last game in Albion's colours was at Luton during the promotion season of 1975-6. He had a testimonial at The Hawthorns in May 1975 when Albion met Villa.

Albion debut v Chelsea (home) Division One, 2 October 1965.

DOUG WITCOMB

Born: Cwm, Nr Ebbw Vale, Gwent, April 1918.
Career: Ebbw Vale Schools, Cwm Villa, Tottenham Hotspur (amateur), Northfleet FC, Enfield, Albion (October 1937-February 1947), Sheffield Wednesday (£6,500), Newport County, Llandudno. Retired June 1965, later played works football with H.D. Alloys and Alkamatic in South Wales. Guested for Grimsby, Leicester, Swansea, Lovells Athletic and Newport during World War Two.

Doug Witcomb was a wing-half or inside-forward of enormous talent; a quick and cunning distributor of timely passes, and a player with a powerful shot in his right foot. He had almost ten years at The Hawthorns, during which time he appeared in a total of 122 games (55 in the League). He won ten Welsh caps, including wartime internationals, and in 1939 represented the All-British XI v The Football League at Wolverhampton. His career in League football earned him a total of 303 matches, 223 for Wednesday whom he assisted to promotion from Division Two in 1950 and again in 1952.

Albion debut v Burnley (away) Division Two, 17 September 1938.

STAN WOOD

Born: Winsford, July 1905. Died: Halifax, February 1967.
Career: Meadow Bank School (Winsford), Whitegate Victoria, Winsford United, Albion (April 1928-May 1938), Halifax Town (player, then trainer). Retired 1949. Guested for Huddersfield Town during World War Two.

Stan Wood nicknamed 'Splinter' and the 'Singing Winger', was a wiry, slippery outside-left whose cleverness stood him in good stead for ten fine seasons with Albion. He made 280 League and Cup appearances for Albion, scoring 66 goals. He starred in the 1931 FA Cup Final and a year later represented the Football League. Wood staked a claim in the Albion side in 1928 and eventually took over the mantle from Arthur Fitton, holding the position on the left-wing until Wally Boyes came along in 1934. He was in and out of the side during the latter part of the 1930s, but always gave 100 per-cent effort when he did play. A fine footballer.

Albion debut v Notts County (home) Division Two, 3 September 1928.

GEORGE WOODHALL

Born: West Bromwich, September 1863. Died: West Bromwich, September 1924.
Career: Hateley Heath School, West Bromwich All Saints, Churchfield Foresters, Albion (May 1883, professional August 1885-July 1892), Wolves, Berwick Rangers (Birmingham League), Oldbury Town. Retired 1898.

'Spry' Woodhall was singularly well-nicknamed, for he was indeed a sprightly outside or inside-right, centering with great accuracy and combining especially well with Billy Bassett. A regular member of Albion's front line for nine seasons, he won two England caps in 1888, the same year he gained an FA Cup winners' medal after scoring the clinching goal against Preston in the Final. He also played in the 1886 and 1887 Finals and scored 20 goals in 74 senior games for Albion. With his delightful personality,

Woodhall was one of the most popular players of 'the old brigade', being remembered as a generous and wholehearted sportsman by the older generation who lived to tell the tales of his fine play on Albion's right flank.

Albion debut v Blackburn Rovers (away), November 1883.

FA Cup debut v Junction St School (Derby), (away), 25 October 1884.

League debut v Stoke (away), 8 September 1888.

AGE

There have been instances where footballers have been known to have played the top-class game at the ages of 14 and 52. Albion have had no one who has fallen into these categories but they have had several players down the years who have been both relatively young and quite old when they turned out for the club at first-team level.

Oldest Players

The oldest player ever to appear for Albion in a Football League game is Jesse Pennington, who, at the age of 38 years, 256 days, lined up against Liverpool at The Hawthorns in a First Division match on 6 May 1922. It was his last game for the club.

Pennington also holds the club record of being the oldest player to appear in an FA Cup-tie — doing so on 22 February 1922 against Notts County (a) when 38 years, 183 days old.

The oldest player to wear Albion's colours in any sort of first-team game, other than in practice matches and benefit games, is Ike Webb, who was 43 years, 222 days old when he played in goal against Wolverhampton Wanderers on 10 August 1918, in a wartime friendly.

Albion's oldest League debutant is Johnny Giles, the diminutive midfield general from Dublin, who, at the age of 34 years, 287 days, played at inside-left versus Chelsea in a Second Division game at The Hawthorns on 20 August 1975.

Scot Jimmy Millar (born 2 March 1870), was 34 years, 220 days old when he played centre-forward for Albion against Burton United (h) in a Second Division game on 8 October 1904. It was Millar's only outing for the club, and he captained the team to a 4-0 win.

JIMMY MILLAR

The honour of being Albion's oldest debutant in the FA Cup competition also goes to Giles, who was 35 years, 58 days old when he skippered Albion in their home third round against Carlisle United on 3 January 1976. And Giles also holds the tag of being the oldest player to play for Albion in a League Cup tie — against Brighton (h) 22 September 1976, aged 35 years, 320 days.

Youngest Players

The youngest player ever to appear in Albion's League side is Charlie 'Tug' Wilson (born 20 July 1905), who was 16 years, 73 days old when he lined up at inside-left in the game at Oldham on 1 October 1921.

The youngest Albion player to appear in the FA Cup is Sid Bowser, who at the age of 16 years, 359 days, performed against Bolton Wanderers (h) in a first round tie on 16 January 1909 — a fortnight after his League baptism against Grimsby.

Bobby Hope (born September 28 1943), was 16 years, 215 days old when he played his first game in Albion's League side, against Arsenal (h) 30 April 1960. He was, of course, still an amateur at the time — the apprentice-professional scheme had not been introduced.

BOBBY HOPE

FRANK HODGETTS

Frank Hodgetts was 16 years 26 days when he played his first game for Albion — against Notts County (h) F. League South 26 October 1940; Albion's youngest first team player in any competitive match.

SNIPPETS:

The oldest player ever to appear against Albion in the League is Billy Meredith, who at the age of 48 years, 72 days played outside-right for Manchester City in a First Division game at The Hawthorns on 4 November 1922.

Stanley Matthews (born 1 February 1915), was 45 years, 10 months old, when he wore the number 7 shirt for Blackpool in a Division One game against Albion at The Hawthorns in December, 1960.

The youngest footballer ever to oppose Albion at senior level was Cameron Buchanan of Wolverhampton Wanderers, who was a shade over 14 years of age when he played in a regional wartime fixture at Molineux on 26 September 1942.

Albion's League team against Chesterfield (h) on September 9 1901 had an average age of 24, with all eleven players in their 20s. The team was: Taylor; Kifford, Adams, Nurse, Stevenson, Hadley, McLean, Simmons, Smith, Worton, Garfield.

Going to the other extreme, Albion's team which played Everton (h) in the League on November 1976 had an average age of 29. It read: Osborne (35); Mulligan (31), Cantello (25), T.Brown (31), Wile (29), Robertson (24), Martin (25), Treacy (30), Cross (25), Giles (36), Johnston (29). Sub: A.Brown (25). This is one of the oldest teams ever fielded by Albion and another 'aged one' is the 1935 FA Cup Final side whose average age was 28 years, six months.

Len Millard was 38 years, 226 days, when he played his last League game for Albion, against Leeds United, away, on 19 October, 1957.

Millard is also the oldest Albion player to win an FA Cup winners' medal — he was 35 years of age when Preston were beaten in the 1954 Final. Billy Bassett is the youngest Albion man to win a Cup medal — being 19 years, two months, when Preston were defeated 2-1 in the 1888 Final.

Tommy Magee is the youngest player ever to win a League Championship medal with Albion. He was just 21 when he received his medal in 1920.

Graham Lovett (born 5 August 1947) is Albion's youngest recepient of a League Cup winners' tankard being 18 and a half years of age when Albion played West Ham (a) in the first leg of the 1966 Final.

Bassett (aged 19) is Albion's youngest ever international at senior level, playing for England against Ireland in 1888.

Mickey Lewis was only 16 years, 303 days old when he made his debut for Albion in the League Cup-tie at Crystal Palace in December 1981.

Players: most and least, used in season

The fewest players utilised by Albion in a complete 42-match League season is 17 — in 1977-8 and 1978-9. Before then the lowest was 18 —in 1919-20.

The most players Albion have called upon in a League season is 33 — in 1904-5 and in season 1985-6 when a total of 34 players were used — 33 in the First Division plus goalkeeper David Powell in the Full Members Cup game against Crystal Palace.

In 1942-3 Albion, playing in the Football League South, had to utilise 43 players during the course of the campaign. In all games (including friendlies and cup-ties) they called up 54 — a club record.

HEIGHT AND WEIGHT

Tallest — the tallest player to appear in League matches for Albion is goalkeeper Bob Roberts. He was a member of the club's first eleven during the late 1800s and stood 6ft 4in tall. In 1986-7 Albion had Stewart Evans (6ft 3in), George Reilly (6ft 3in), Carlton Palmer (6ft 2in), Stuart Naylor (6ft 2in) and Paul Dyson (6ft 2in) on their books. Albert Iremonger, goalkeeper of Notts County and Lincoln City (1904-27), and Stuart Taylor, centre-half of Bristol Rovers (1970-9), are the tallest players to have opposed Albion in League combat, both measuring 6ft 5in. Micky Droy of Chelsea was 6ft 4¾in tall when he defended against Albion in 1976-7.

Shortest — the shortest player to appear in Football League matches for Albion is 'Wee' Tommy Magee. He was 5ft 2½in high when he first joined the club in 1919. Syd Tufnell of Blackpool is the shortest man to have opposed Albion in the League, being a mere 5ft 2¾in tall when he played left-half in a First Division match on 5 September 1931.

Other small Albion League players include: Hughie Reed, Jimmy Prew, Jimmy McLean and Jimmy Spencer — all outside-rights — Alf Geddes, and the 1986-7 duo of Wayne Dobbins and Andy Thompson.

The Middlesbrough forward line which played against Albion in a First Division game at Ayresome Park on 1 September 1934, was collectively the smallest and probably the lightest ever to have taken part in a first-class soccer match. Yorston, the centre-forward, was only 5ft 4¾in tall, and inside-right Bruce was just a quarter-of-an-inch taller. Outside-right Chadwick and his left-wing partner, Warren, each stood at 5ft 6in, and the 'giant' of them all, inside-left Baxter, was a mere 5ft 9in. The combined weight of those five footballers was recorded as 56st 4lb.

Albion's forward line against Ipswich Town (a) on 28 September 1963, was Ken Foggo, Tony Brown, Ron Fenton, Alec Jackson and Clive Clark. Each player stood under 5ft 9in tall and therefore this is probably one of the shortest front lines Albion have fielded.

Hughie Reed, midget right-winger.

Heaviest — William 'Fatty' Foulke is the heaviest player to appear in a League game against Albion —doing so for Bradford City in a Second Division match at The Hawthorns on 17 November 1906, when he weighed around 22st.

The heaviest player to turn out for Albion's first team is probably goalkeeper Jimmy Adams, who tipped the scales at 14st 10lb when he appeared during World War Two. Ted Pheasant (1904-10) weighed 14st 9lb, Fred Shinton (1905-07) was 14st 7lb and Idris 'Killer' Bassett (1936-43) weighed in at 14st 2lb.

Lightest — among the lightest players to have donned Albion colours are: Hughie MacLean (1967-74) 9st, Mike Lee (1956-8) 8st 10lb, and outside-right Harry Parkes (1906-08 and 1914-19) 9st 2lb.

Hugh MacLean, light-weight ▶ outside-left.

◀ Albion's 'tiny' forward line in September 1963. Left to right: Ken Foggo, Tony Brown, Ron Fenton, Alec Jackson and Clive Clark.

293

Albion in the Transfer Market

The highest fee paid by Albion is the £748,000 which brought Peter Barnes from Manchester City in July 1979.

Albion's previous record fee was for David Mills who cost £516,000 from Middlesbrough six months before Barnes' arrival.

The biggest fee received by Albion is the £1.5 million which Manchester United paid for Bryan Robson in October 1981. The 'package' was actually worth £2 million because it included Remi Moses who was valued at £500,000.

DAVID MILLS

BRYAN ROBSON

Albion's record outgoing transfer fee has progressed as follows:

£4,000 for Bobby Blood (Port Vale), February 1921.
£4,100 for George Shaw (Huddersfield T), December 1926.
£7,500 for Cecil Shaw (Wolves), December 1936.
£9,500 for Jack Vernon (Belfast Celtic), February 1947.
£20,000 for Ronnie Allen (Port Vale), March 1950.
£25,000 for Bobby Robson (Fulham), March 1956.
£44,750 for John Kaye (Scunthorpe U), May 1963.
£100,000 for Colin Suggett (Sunderland), June 1969.
£138,000 for Willie Johnston (Rangers), December 1972.
£516,000 for David Mills (Middlesbrough), January 1979.
£748,000 for Peter Barnes (Manchester C), July 1979.

The second-highest incoming fee is the £995,000, paid by Spanish giants, Real Madrid, for Laurie Cunningham in June 1979.

LAURIE CUNNINGHAM

BOBBY ROBSON

SENDINGS OFF ▶ ▶ ▶ ▶

The first player to be sent off whilst representing West Bromwich Albion was also one of the club's all-time greats, William Isaiah Bassett. He was dismissed for using 'unparliamentary language' in a friendly game against Millwall (away) on 28 April 1894.

FOOTBALL LEAGUE

Joe READER	v Bolton Wanderers	(a) 13 Apr 1895
Abraham JONES	v Stoke	(a) 21 Oct 1899
Jackie KIFFORD	v Aston Villa	(a) 12 Sep 1903
Stan DAVIES	v Sheffield United	(a) 4 Dec 1926
Joe CARTER	v Blackburn Rovers	(h) 19 Sep 1931
Teddy SANDFORD	v Blackburn Rovers	(a) 30 Jan 1932
Teddy SANDFORD	v Tottenham Hotspur	(a) 17 Mar 1934
Wally BOYES	v Middlesbrough	(a) 1 Jan 1937
Derek HOGG	v Leeds United	(a) 27 Dec 1958
Maurice SETTERS	v Sheffield Wednesday	(a) 31 Oct 1959
Clive CLARK	v Aston Villa	(a) 6 Oct 1962
Graham WILLIAMS	v Aston Villa	(a) 17 Oct 1964
Dick KRZYWICKI	v Manchester City	(a) 4 Oct 1969
Len CANTELLO	v Sheffield Wednesday	(a) 10 Mar 1970
Willie JOHNSTON	v Swindon Town	(a) 8 Sep 1973
David SHAW	v Portsmouth	(a) 3 Feb 1974
Willie JOHNSTON	v Bristol City	(h) 16 Nov 1974
Ray WILSON	v Oxford United	(a) 15 Mar 1975
Len CANTELLO	v Chelsea	(h) 20 Aug 1975
John GILES	v Luton Town	(a) 13 Dec 1975
John WILE	v Hull City	(a) 21 Feb 1976
Paddy MULLIGAN	v Stoke City	(a) 18 Dec 1976
Ally ROBERTSON	v Coventry City	(a) 13 Dec 1980
Steve MACKENZIE	v Middlesbrough	(a) 9 Mar 1982
Cyrille REGIS	v Aston Villa	(h) 8 May 1982
Gary OWEN	v Notts County	(a) 15 May 1982
Garry THOMPSON	v Wolverhampton W	(a) 28 Apr 1984
Cyrille REGIS	v Sunderland	(a) 8 Sep 1984
Ally ROBERTSON	v Watford	(h) 8 Dec 1984
Martyn BENNETT	v Stoke City	(a) 12 Mar 1985
Jimmy NICHOLL	v Stoke City	(a) 12 Mar 1985
Steve HUNT	v Coventry City	(a) 28 Sep 1985
Jimmy NICHOLL	v Queen's Park Rangers	(h) 9 Nov 1985
Martin DICKINSON	v Southampton	(h) 29 Mar 1986
Carlton PALMER	v Leeds United	(h) 6 Dec 1986
Garth CROOKS	v Ipswich Town	(a) 3 Mar 1987

FA CUP

Willie JOHNSTON	v Everton	(h) 30 Jan 1974
Mick MARTIN	v Ipswich Town (Highbury)	8 Apr 1978

LEAGUE CUP (including MILK CUP and LITTLEWOODS CHALLENGE CUP)

Willie JOHNSTON	v Brighton & Hove Albion	(h) 22 Sep 1976
Len CANTELLO	v Leeds United (Maine Road)	2 Oct 1978
Ally BROWN	v West Ham United	(a) 1 Dec 1981
Maarten JOL	v Tottenham Hotspur	(h) 3 Feb 1982
Gary OWEN	v Aston Villa	(h) 30 Nov 1984
Martin DICKINSON	v Derby County	(a) 23 Sep 1986

EUROPEAN CUP-WINNERS' CUP

Ronnie REES	v Dinamo Bucharest	(a) 13 Nov 1968

UEFA CUP

Ally BROWN	v Carl Zeiss Jena	(h) 3 Oct 1979

WARTIME FOOTBALL

Eddie CONNELLY	v Coventry City	(h) 23 Mar 1940
Eddie CONNELLY	v Coventry City	(h) 9 Nov 1940

Four players — Harry Kinsell and Maurice Setters (England), Mick Martin (Republic of Ireland) and Willie Johnston (Scotland) — were all sent off representing their country.

Two Bradford City players — Leigh Palin and David Evans — were sent-off in the Second Division match at The Hawthorns on 9 May 1987, bringing the total number of sendings-off on the ground (senior level — 1900-87) to 40, six in season 1986-7.

Tom Hutchinson, playing against Small Heath in a Birmingham Cup semi-final at Wolverhampton in March 1895, was sent off in extra-time, this after he had scored the winning goal.

Asa Hartford and Jim Holton were both ordered off in the second leg of the 1969 FA Youth Cup Final at Sunderland. Albion won the first leg 3-0, but crashed to a 6-0 defeat at Roker Park.

Skipper John Wile, Mick Martin and manager Ronnie Allen, were all banished to the dressing room during Albion's Trofeo Costa Blanca game against FC Hercules in Spain in August 1977 — Allen was ordered from the touchline dug-out.

And in Seville, in August 1981, Derek Statham was dismissed for dissent.

Mick Martin's dismissal in the 1978 FA Cup semi-final (v Ipswich) at Highbury, was the first sending-off in a semi-final for more than 40 years.

Graham Williams and Asa Hartford were sent off during Albion's tour of East Africa in 1968, and Graham Lovett was dismissed in two games when Albion played in South America in 1966.

Besides having the unenviable record of having been dismissed more times than any other Albion player, Willie Johnston has been sent off on 15 occasions in his career: seven times with Glasgow Rangers, four with Albion, twice with Heart of Midlothian, once with Vancouver Whitecaps and once for Scotland. This could well be an all-time record.

In Central League football, both Ernest Pattison and Jimmy Poxton of Albion were ordered off during the away game at Sheffield Wednesday in October 1927. And goalkeeper, Fred Brown, received his marching orders when Albion reserves opposed Wolves at Molineux in February 1956.

In the Albion v Sunderland First Division game on 6 April 1935, 'Patsy' Gallacher was sent off for ungentlemanly conduct — it was not until 37 years later that another visiting player was ordered off in a League game at The Hawthorns, and the culprit then was Peter Cormack of Liverpool, 9 December 1972.

More have followed since, including Terry Gibson (Coventry — now Manchester United) and Tony Galvin (Spurs).
In the Stoke City v Albion League match on 12 March 1985, three players were dismissed: Keith Bertschin (Stoke) and Martyn Bennett and Jimmy Nicholl (Albion). This was the first time that two Albion players had been sent off in the same League match and the first time there had been three dismissals in any sort of first eleven game involving Albion.
Albion's Carlton Palmer, with John Stiles and Ian Snodin (now Everton) of Leeds, were sent off in the space of two minutes either side of half-time at The Hawthorns on 6 December 1986.

On 10 November 1973, Kenny Stephens (Bristol Rovers) and Duggie Fraser (Walsall), who were both in Albion's 1968 FA Cup semi-final side v Birmingham City, were sent off for fighting each other in a Third Division match at Walsall.

Four players — Harry Kinsell and Maurice Setters (England), Mick Martin (Republic of Ireland) and Willie Johnston (Scotland) — were all sent off representing their country.

SUSPENSION:
The first Albion player to be suspended by the Football League for misconduct was centre-forward, Willie Hendry, who was reported to the League for fighting with a Bolton Wanderers defender on 5 November 1888. Both players were suspended for a month in December of that year. Willie Johnston joined Albion in December 1972 after having just served a record 67 days suspension imposed by the Scottish FA.

Albion Players' Career Records

The following is a list of all Albion players who have appeared in first-class matches for the club. Club joined from and transferred to are also shown. The League appearances and goals total includes the three games of the abandoned 1939-40 season. The 'others' total includes wartime matches, Full Members' Cup, Anglo-Scottish Cup, Anglo-Italian Tournament, Watney Cup, Texaco Cup, FA Charity Shield and all other first-team competitive games not included in the preceding totals.

PLAYER	BIRTHPLACE & YEAR	POSN	FROM (year) — TO (year)	League App	Gls	FA Cup App	Gls	Lge Cup App	Gls	Euro App	Gls	Others App	Gls	TOTALS App	Gls
ADAMS A	West Bromwich 1880	FB	Springfields 1897 — Retired 1910	209	3	15								214	3
ADAMS J	Norton Canes 1908	G	Cannock T 1929 — Retired 1945	103		10						108		221	
ADAMS W	Blackheath 1892	FB	Rowley V 1919 — Barrow 1928	92		6								98	
ADDERLEY JB	Birmingham 1922	FB	Bournville Youths 1941 — Released 1946									1		1	
AITKEN AFS	Craigmillar, Edinburgh 1934	W	Hibernian 1959 — Falkirk 1961	22	2									22	2
ALDERWICK J	Birmingham 1921	G	New Oscot FC 1940 — Released 1946									1		1	
ALDRIDGE AJ	Walsall 1864	FB	Walsall Swifts 1886 — Walsall TS 1888			15								15	
ALDRIDGE N	Coventry 1921	FB	Foxford 1945 — Northampton T 1948	1										1	
ALLAN SJ	Wallsend-on-Tyne 1884	CF	Newcastle U 1911 — Nottingham F 1912	19	4	1								20	4
ALLEN R	Fenton, Stoke 1929	CF	Port Vale 1950 — Crystal P 1961	415	208	42	23					1	3	458	234
ALSOP G	Frampton Cotterill, Bristol 1908	CF	Walsall 1935 — Ipswich T 1937	1										1	
ANDERSON CR	Newcastle 1962	FB-M	Torquay U 1985 —	34(5)	1	1	1	2(1)				0(1)		37(7)	2
APPLEBY B	Burton-on-Trent 1878	CF	Burton U 1901 — Bristol R 1903	1										1	
ARMSTRONG GJ	Belfast 1954	F	Real Mallorca 1985 — Brighton & HA 1986	7(1)				2	1			1		10(1)	1
ARTHUR DR	Bushbury, Wolverhampton 1960	FB	School 1976 — Walsall 1982	2(1)				3						5(1)	
ASHLEY H	Smethwick 1913	F	Smethwick Highfield 1934 — Derby C 1937									13	6	13	6
ASHMORE GS	Plymouth 1898	G	Nineveh Wesley 1919 — Chesterfield 1931	246		22								268	
ASHURST W	Willington, Co Durham 1894	FB	Notts C 1926 — Newark T 1928	22	1	1								23	1
ASKIN GW	West Bromwich 1861	IF	Elwells 1882 — Hednesford 1889			1								1	
ASTLE J	Eastwood, Notts 1942	CF	Notts C 1964 — Hellenic (South Africa) 1974	290(2)	137	23	14	28	19	10	1	8	3	359(2)	174
ASTON JH	Redditch 1881	CF	Durham Light Infantry 1904 — Willenhall Swifts 1905	25	9	1	1							26	10
ASTON H	Bloxwich 1855	IF	George Salter Works 1879 — Wolves 1885			7	3							7	3
BACHE HG	Churchhill, Worcs 1889	CF	Eastbourne 1914 — Killed 1916	12	4	2								14	4
BADDELEY G	Fegg Hayes, Staffs 1874	HB	Stoke 1908 — Retired 1914cs	145	1	12								157	1
BALDWIN HJA	Birmingham 1920	G	Sutton T 1937 — Brighton & HA 1939	5										5	
BALL HG	West Bromwich 1921	CF	Golds Green Meths 1939 — Darlaston 1946									16	9	16	9
BAMFORD AE	Weedon, Northants 1880	OL	Wellingborough T 1905 — Wellingborough T 1906	3										3	
BANKS GE	Wednesbury 1919	CF	Brownhills A 1933 — Mansfield T 1947	4	3							13	7	17	10
BANKS J	West Bromwich 1871	LH	Oldbury Broadwell 1894 — Newton Heath 1901	119	5	12	1					3		134	6
BANNISTER J	Chesterfield 1942	HB	School 1958 — Scunthorpe U 1964	9										9	
BARKER RC	Kinglassie, Glenrothes 1927	OL	Kelty Rangers 1945 — Shrewsbury T 1950	14	2									14	2
BARLOW RJ	Swindon 1926	LH	Garrards 1944 — Birmingham C 1960	403	31	46	5					33	12	482	48
BARNES PS	Manchester 1957	OL	Manchester C 1979 — Leeds U 1981	76(1)	23	4	1	9(1)	1	1				90(2)	25
BARNSLEY GR	Bilston 1935	G	Erdington A 1951 — Plymouth A 1957	1										1	
BARRON PG	London 1953	G	Crystal P 1982 — Queen's Park R 1985	63		6		4						73	
BASSETT ICH	Brithdir 1915	FB	Sutton T 1936 — Retired 1943	8								92		100	
BASSETT WI	West Bromwich 1869	OR	Old Church Club 1886 — Retired 1899	261	61	40	11					10	5	311	77
BATSON BM	Grenada, West Indies 1953	FB	Cambridge U 1978 — Retired 1984	172	1	13	1	21		12		2		220	2
BAUGH R	Wolverhampton 1898	FB	Cardiff C 1924 — Exeter C 1928	61		4								65	
BAYLISS AEJM	Tipton 1863	WH/CF	Wednesbury Old Athletic 1884 — Retired 1892	56	12	39	24							95	36
BEDFORD L	Birmingham 1904	W	School 1920 — Walsall 1922	3										3	
BELL G	West Bromwich 1861	OL	George Salter Works 1879 — Kidderminster H 1888			16	7							16	7
BELL H	West Bromwich 1862	FB	George Salter Works 1879 — Retired 1888			15								15	
BELL SLT	Langbank, Strathclyde 1875	F	Brentford 1904 — Hibernian 1905	16	6	1								17	6
BELL T	Airth, Falkirk 1917	IF	Cambuslang Rangers 1939 — Retired 1946									15	5	15	5
BENJAMIN IT	Nottingham 1961	M	Sheffield U 1979 — Peterborough U 1982	1(1)										1(1)	
BENNETT M	Birmingham 1961	D	Streetly 1977 —	174(1)	8	13		18	1			3		208(1)	9
BENTLEY A	Alfreton 1887	CF	Bolton W 1913 — Burton Albion 1922	97	46	5	1					3(1)		105(1)	47
BETTELEY RH	Bradley, Bilston 1880	FB	Wolves 1906 — Bilston U 1912	85		4								89	
BETTERIDGE RM	Redditch 1924	W	Warslow Celtic 1948 — Swindon T 1951	5										5	
BILLINGHAM PA	Pensnett, Nr Dudley 1938	WH	Walsall 1960 — Worcester C 1962	7										7	
BISSEKER W	West Bromwich 1863	CF	George Salter Works 1879 — Retired 1884			1								1	
BLAGDEN J	Sheffield 1893	IF	Cresswell Colliery 1921 — Worksop T 1923	16	2	4	2							20	4
BLOOD R	Harpur Hill, Nr Buxton 1894	CF	Port Vale 1921 — Stockport C 1924	53	26									53	26
BOOKMAN LJ	Dolphin Bar 1890	OL	Bradford C 1914 — Luton 1919	16	1							2		18	1
BOSTOCK AMW	Brecon, mid Wales 1869	CF	Shrewsbury T 1892 — Burton Swifts 1894	26	11							8	2	34	13
BOSTON HJ	Nantwich 1899	OR	Bolton W 1929 — Swansea T 1931	27	6									27	6
BOURNE RA	Roundle 1881	OL	Clapton O 1907 — Walsall 1908	9	1									9	1
BOWDEN J	Manchester 1882	HB	Handsworth R 1904 — Southampton 1906	8										8	
BOWEN TH	West Bromwich 1924	F	West Bromwich Ath 1941 — Newport C 1946									6	2	6	2
BOWEN WE	Hednesford 1891	CH	Nuneaton T 1914 — Hednesford T 1915	1										1	
BOWSER S	Handsworth 1892	CH/IF	Willenhall 1908 — Belfast Distillery 1913 / Belfast Distillery 1914 — Walsall 1924	341	64	28	8					2		371	72
BOWSER W	Handsworth 1886	F	Dudley T 1907 — Walsall 1909	1										1	
BOYD H	Lanchester 1866	IF	Burnley 1892 — April 1893	7	1	1						2	1	10	2
BOYD J	Consett 1925	RB	Sunderland 1948 — Consett T 1949	1										1	
BOYES WE	Killamarsh, Nr Sheffield 1913	WH/OL	Woodhouse Mills U 1931 — Everton 1938	151	35	14	3							165	38
BRADLEY CH	Smethwick 1882	OR	Invention Street Boys 1905 — Dudley T 1905	3										3	
BRADLEY DM	Birmingham 1965	M	Aston Villa 1986 —	24	1									24	1
BRADLEY DJ	Annerley, Notts 1924	FB	Clipstone Colliery 1942 — Mansfield T 1949									2		2	
BRADLEY EJ	Dudley 1882	WH/IF	Dudley T 1905 — Luton T 1908	25	6	2								27	6
BRADLEY RJ	Ellingshall, Wolverhampton 1939	FB	SE Staffordshire Boys 1954 — Norwich C 1964	13										13	
BRADSHAW PW	Altrincham 1956	G	Vancouver Whitecaps 1985 — Bristol Rovers 1987	8				5				1		14	
BRETT R	Chester 1878	F	Army Medical Corps 1898 — Wellingborough T 1899	12	3									12	3
BRETT SS	St Asaph, North Wales 1879	F	Southport Central 1898 — Wellingborough T 1902	8	2	2	1							10	3
BRITTAIN JW	Wednesbury 1880	FB	Wednesbury OA 1902 — Willenhall Swifts 1906	9		1								10	
BROAD T	Stalybridge 1887	OR	Openshaw LC 1905 — Chesterfield 1908	11		4	1							15	1
BROCKHURST WJ	Brownhills 1913	CH	Cannock CC 1935 — Hednesford T 1938	5										5	
BROMAGE E	Mickleover, Derby 1898	OL	Gillingham 1928 — Nottingham F 1929	10	2									10	2
BROOKES WA	Dudley 1931	WH	Churchfields 1947 — Allen's Cross 1958	19								1		20	
BROOKS J	Stairfool, Yorks 1886	OL	Barnsley 1907 — Barnsley 1908	21	1	1								22	1
BROWN A	Musselburgh, Lothian 1951	F	Leicester C 1972 — Crystal P 1983	254(25)	72	26(2)	6	27	2	10	1	14(1)	4	331(28)	85
BROWN A	Oldham 1945	WH/F	Manchester Schools 1961 — Torquay U 1981	561(13)	218	53(1)	27	46(1)	17	16(1)	8	28	9	704(16)	279
BROWN F	Leyton 1931	G	Aldershot 1955 — Portsmouth 1958	11										11	
BROWN H	Northampton 1883	IF	Northampton T 1903 — Southampton 1905	35	5	1								36	5

PLAYER	BIRTHPLACE & YEAR	POSN	FROM (year) — TO (year)	League App	League Gls	FA Cup App	FA Cup Gls	Lge Cup App	Lge Cup Gls	Euro App	Euro Gls	Others App	Others Gls	TOTALS App	TOTALS Gls
BROWN JF	Brierley Hill 1886	IF	Stoke 1908 — Kidderminster H 1910	8										8	
BUCK F	Newcastle-Under-Lyme 1880	CH/IF	Stafford R 1900 — Liverpool 1903 / Plymouth A 1906 — Swansea T 1914	287	90	32	4							319	94
BULL S	Tipton 1965	CF	Tipton Town 1984 — Wolverhampton W 1986	2(2)	2			2	1			1(2)		5(4)	3
BUNN AF	West Bromwich 1861	CH	George Salter Works 1879 — Crosswell's B 1886			12	1							12	1
BURGIN M	Sheffield 1911	IF	Nottingham F 1938 — Retired 1942	14	9							2		16	9
BURNS JA	Liverpool 1865	OL	London Cals 1889 — Notts C 1892	15	5	2								17	5
BURNS J	Walsall 1871	IF	Fairfield Villa 1893 — Stafford R 1894	1										1	
BURNSIDE DG	Bristol 1939	IF	Bristol C 1955 — Southampton 1962	127	39	8	3							135	42
BURROWS D	West Bromwich 1968	FB	School 1985 —	13(3)	1	1		0(1)						14(4)	1
BURTON EC	Birmingham 1881	OR	Walsall 1905 — Walsall 1905	1										1	
BURTON HA	West Bromwich 1872	FB	Sheffield W 1909 — Scunthorpe U 1911	32		4								36	
BUSHELL G	Wednesbury 1864	F	West Bromwich FC 1883 — Wednesbury Old Ath 1889			1								1	
BUTLER S	Stellington 1919	OL	Scunthorpe U 1938 — Southport 1947	4		2						30	8	36	8
BYERS JE	Selby, Yorks 1897	OL	Blackburn R 1924 — Worcester C 1928	104	11	7	1							111	12
BYTHEWAY G	Shuttlewood, Derbyshire 1908	W	Staveley T 1927 — Coventry C 1933	16	2									16	2
CAMERON JR	Currie, Nr Edinburgh 1875	CF	Everton 1896 — Blackburn R 1897	13	2	2								15	2
CAMPBELL D	Manchester 1944	CH	Droylsden 1961 — Los Angeles W 1968	8				3						11	
CAMPBELL JC	St Pancras, London 1937	OR	Maidenhead 1954 — Portsmouth 1959	31	9									31	9
CANTELLO L	Newton Heath, Manchester 1951	M	School 1967 — Bolton W 1979	297(4)	13	22	3	21	3	7		18	2	365(4)	21
CARTER G	Moulton, Cheshire 1943	OL	Moulton FC 1959 — Bury 1966	25	3									25	3
CARTER JH	Aston 1901	IR	Westbourne C 1921 — Tranmere R 1936	414	145	37	10							451	155
CARTER W	Wednesbury 1933	F	SE Staffordshire Boys 1949 — Plymouth A 1957	57	12	3						1		61	12
CASTLE J	Birmingham 1871	WH	Birmingham St George 1891 — Brierley Hill 1892	4										4	
CAVE GH	Great Bridge 1874	FB	Great Bridge U 1896 — Retired 1901	77		6								83	
CHADBURN J	Mansfield 1873	RB/OR	Wolves 1900 — Liverpool 1903	43	3	5	1							48	4
CHAMBERLAIN HG	Langley, West Midlands 1901	FB	Cradley Heath 1922 — Brighton & HA 1926	4										4	
CHAMBERS H	Willington Quay, Co Durham 1896	IF	Liverpool 1928 — Oakengates T 1929	40	4	6	1							46	5
CHAPMAN G	Burton-on-Trent 1920	F	Donisthorpe FC 1938 — Brighton & HA 1946									14	2	14	2
CHARSLEY CC	Leicester 1864	G	Small Heath A 1891 — Small Heath A 1891	1										1	
CHILDS GPC	Birmingham 1964	M	School 1980 — Walsall 1983	2(1)										2(1)	
CLARK B	Wednesbury 1900	OL	Seaforth Highlanders 1919 — Blakenhall 1920	1										1	
CLARK C	Leeds 1940	OL	Queen's Park R 1961 — Queen's Park R 1969	300(1)	80	25(1)	7	19	10	7	1			351(2)	98
CLARKE D	Stockton-on-Tees 1948	FB	School 1963 — Huddersfield T 1969	19		4(1)		1		1				25(1)	
CLARKE I	Tipton 1915	IF	Toll End Wesley 1937 — Portsmouth 1947	108	39	9	4					96	55	213	98
CLEMENTS HW	Worcester 1884	OR	Worcester C 1903 — Worcester C 1904	10										10	
COEN RWL	Lowestoft 1914	OL	Milford Haven 1932 — Coventry C 1938	7	4	2								9	4
COLE HJ	Hill Top, West Bromwich 1885	IR	Bloxwich St 1901 — Wellingborough T 1904	9	3									9	3
COLLARD I	South Hetton, Co Durham 1947	M	School 1962 — Ipswich T 1969	63(6)	7	12		7	1	7(1)		1		90(7)	8
COLQUHOUN EP	Prestonpans, Edinburgh 1945	D	Bury 1967 — Sheffield U 1968	46	1	5		2						54	1
CONNELLY E	Dumbarton 1916	IF	Luton T 1939 — Luton T 1946	3	1	4	1					54	13	61	15
CONNOR JJM	Lochee, Dundee 1880	OR	Gordon Highlanders 1898 — Walsall 1899	10										10	
COOK AF	Stafford 1890	FB	Wrexham 1911 — Swansea T 1922	38		12						5		55	
COOK F	Rugby 1880	G	Northampton T 1902 — Portsmouth 1905	28		1								29	
COOKSON J	Manchester 1904	CF	Chesterfield 1927 — Plymouth A 1933	122	103	9	7							131	110
CORBETT FJ	Willenhall 1903	FB	Hednesford T 1926 — Coventry C 1931	12										12	
CORBETT G	North Warbottle, Co Durham 1925	FB	Spennymoor 1951 — Workington 1953	1										1	
CORBETT R	Wolverhampton 1887	FB	Willenhall SW 1909 — Walsall 1911	3										3	
CORFIELD S	Tipton 1883	CH	Toll End W 1902 — Retired 1904	8										8	
COWDRILL BL	Birmingham 1957	D	Sutton Town 1979 —	95(4)		5	1	9(1)				1		110(5)	1
COX FJA	Reading 1920	W	Arsenal 1953 — Bournemouth 1956	4										4	
COX S	Mexborough 1920	FB	Denaby U 1948 — Accrington S 1951	2										2	
CRABTREE FW	West Bromwich 1865	W	Christ Church 1887 — Old Stephen's 1889	1	1									1	1
CRAM R	Hetton-le-Hole, Co Durham 1939	FB/WH	Durham Boys 1955 — Bromsgrove R 1967	141	25	8	1	13		1				163	26
CRAWFORD CHR	Alexandria, Dumbarton 1943	FB	Scotland Boys 1959 — Exeter C 1967	10				2		2				14	
CRAWFORD R	Portsmouth 1936	CF	Wolves 1965 — Ipswich T 1966	14	6	1		2	1					17	7
CRESSWELL F	South Shields 1908	IF	Sunderland 1929 — Chester 1930	30	6	1								31	6
CRISP J	Hamstead, Birmingham 1896	W	Ordnance FC 1914 — Blackburn R 1923	115	22	7	1					2		124	23
CRONE R	Belfast 1870	FB	Middlesbrough 1893 — Burton Swifts 1895	40		1						10		51	
CROOKS GA	Stoke-on-Trent 1958	F	Tottenham H 1985 — Charlton A 1987	39	16	1		6	2			4	3	50	21
CROSS D	Heywood, Lancashire 1950	CF	Coventry C 1976 — West Ham U 1977 / Vancouver Whitecaps 1984 — Bolton W 1985	54	20	2		5	2			0(1)	1	61(1)	23
CROSS NJR	Birmingham 1961	F	School 1977 — Walsall 1985	68(37)	15	5	1	6(2)	3	0(1)				79(40)	19
CROWE E	Stourport, Worcs 1910	G	Stourport Swifts 1930 — Swansea T 1936	15		1								16	
CROWSHAW AA	Willenhall 1932	W	Bloxwich W 1946 — Derby C 1956	11	2									11	2
CRUMP A	Smethwick 1886	D	Reading 1908 — Dudley T 1910	1										1	
CUMBES J	East Didsbury, Manchester 1944	G	Tranmere R 1969 — Aston Villa 1971	64		4		4				7		79	
CUNNINGHAM LP	Archway, London 1956	F	Orient 1977 — Real Madrid 1979	81(5)	21	7(3)	3	6		8	4	4	2	106(8)	30
CUTLER RV	Blackheath 1935	OL	Schools 1950 — Bournemouth 1956	5										5	
DALE RA	Willington, Co Durham 1903	HB	Birmingham 1922 — Tranmere R 1931	19		2								21	
DARNELL L	Irchester, Northants 1905	HB	Rushden 1924 — Reading 1930	57		5								62	
DAVENPORT A	Springfield, Wolverhampton 1924	D	Springfield 1942 — Released 1946									1		1	
DAVIES A	Bodhovel 1880	OR	Druids 1904 — Middlesbrough 1904	12	1									12	1
DAVIES C	West Bromwich 1917	CH	Kidderminster H 1935 — Stourbridge 1947	7								8		15	
DAVIES LC	Bodhovel 1883	D	Wrexham 1904 — Wrexham 1905	3										3	
DAVIES RW	Tipton 1933	G	Palethorpes 1949 — Walsall 1955	4										4	
DAVIES SC	Chirk 1898	F	Everton 1921 — Birmingham 1927	147	77	12	6							159	83
DAVIES WC	Rhayadar 1884	OL	Crystal P 1906 — Crystal P 1910	52	4	3								55	4
DAWES J	Smethwick 1881	OL	Smethwick C 1903 — Smethwick C 1905	2										2	
DEACEY C	Wednesbury 1888	CH/CF	Wednesbury Old Athletic 1910 — Hull C 1914	18		1	1							19	1
DEAN A	West Bromwich 1878	OR	Walsall 1896 — Walsall 1898	7	3	1								8	3
DEEHAN JM	Solihull 1957	F	Aston Villa 1979 — Norwich C 1981	44(3)	5	2				1				47(3)	5
DENNISON R	Banbridge, Northern Ireland 1963	F	Glenavon 1985 — Wolves 1987	9(7)	1	2		1				1		13(7)	1
DICKEN HJ	Wednesbury 1890	HB	Bilston 1909 — Bilston U 1910	1										1	
DICKINSON MJ	Leeds 1963	M	Leeds U 1986 —	33(1)	1			2						35(1)	1
DILLY T	Arbroath 1882	OL	Everton 1906 — Derby C 1907	30	9	7	1							37	10
DIXON R	Felling-on-Tyne 1936	OL	Workington 1959 — Hereford U 1960	7	1									7	1
DOBBINS W	Bromsgrove 1968	M	Burlish Olympic 1984 —	3(3)				1						4(3)	
DONAGHY B	Consett 1956	OR	School 1971 — Workington 1975	4(2)										4(2)	
DONNACHIE C	Invergowrie, Strathmore 1869	HB	Dundee 1880 — Cambuslang R 1890	2										2	
DORSETT G	Brownhills 1881	OL	Brownhills A 1901 — Manchester C 1904	95	22	5								100	22
DORSETT JA	Brownhills 1888	OL	Brownhills A 1907 — Manchester C 1910	18	3									18	3
DRURY CE	Darlaston 1917	WH	FH Lloyds 1954 — Bristol C 1964	146	1	14								160	1
DRURY GB	Hucknall, Notts 1914	IF	Arsenal 1946 — Watford 1948	29	8	2	1							31	9
DUDLEY G	Gartcosh, Glasgow 1916	F	Vono Sports 1937 — Banbury Sp 1946	6	2							19	3	25	5
DUDLEY JG	Gartcosh, Glasgow 1928	WH	Albright YC 1944 — Walsall 1959	285	9	34	2					1		320	11

PLAYER	BIRTHPLACE & YEAR	POSN	FROM (year) — TO (year)	League App	League Gls	FA Cup App	FA Cup Gls	Lge Cup App	Lge Cup Gls	Euro App	Euro Gls	Others App	Others Gls	TOTALS App	TOTALS Gls
DUGDALE JR	Liverpool 1932	CH	Harrowby 1950 — Aston Villa 1956	63		11						0(1)		74(1)	
DUGGAN J	Droitwich, Worcs 1920	IF	Droitwich OB 1935 — Hereford U 1947	25	8	2								27	8
DUNN A	Bridgton, Glasgow 1878	FB	Gordon Highlanders 1898 — Bristol R 1901	71	2	10	1							81	3
DUTTON HR	Edmonton, London 1900	LH	Schools 1921 — Bury 1927	57	2	3								60	2
DYER F	Bishopbriggs, Strathclyde 1870	HB	Warwick Co 1890 — Woolwich A 1892	41	2	5	1							46	3
DYSON PI	Birmingham 1959	CH	Stoke C 1986 —	53	2	1		2				1		57	2
EASTOE P	Dorden, Tamworth 1953	F	Everton 1982 — Sporting Farense 1985	30(1)	8	2	1	1						33(1)	9
EBANKS MWR	Birmingham 1964	D	School 1981 — Port Vale 1984	6(1)										6(1)	
EDWARDS CI	Chase Terrace, Cannock 1921	HB	Cannock T 1938 — Bristol C 1948	40	1	2						60	2	102	3
EDWARDS EJ	Dudley Port, Tipton 1893	CF	Old Hill U 1913 — Walsall 1920	7	3	1	1					2	2	10	6
EDWARDS IR	Wrexham 1955	CF	Rhyl A 1973 — Chester 1976	15(3)	3			2				2		19(3)	3
EDWARDS J	Tipton 1905	IL/LH	Stourbridge 1926 — Norwich C 1937	182	9	19						1		202	9
EDWARDS S	Wolverhampton 1885	CH	Brades Park 1904 — Stafford R 1905	1										1	
ELLIOTT WB	Harrington, Cumbria 1919	OR	Bournemouth & BA 1938 — Bilston U 1951	170	39	12	1					148	117	330	157
ELMORE GV	Wednesbury 1884	IR	Broadheath FC 1902 — Bristol R 1903	3	1	1								4	1
EVANS AJ	Barnard Castle, North Yorks 1874	FB	Aston Villa 1907 — Retired 1909	37		3								40	
EVANS AJ	Penrhycadery, South Wales 1922	IF	Wilden FC 1943 — Retired 1948	18		1						10	2	29	2
EVANS CJ	West Bromwich 1923	IF	Cordley Vics 1937 — Stafford R 1950	1								129	31	130	31
EVANS EE	Ferndale, Glamorgan 1926	IF	Cardiff C 1952 — Wrexham 1955	17	3									17	3
EVANS G	Sutton-in-Ashfield 1865	IF	Derby C 1889 — Brierley Hill A 1890	14	8	2								16	8
EVANS JT	Darlaston 1906	CH	Darlaston 1922 — Retired 1931	88	8	2								90	8
EVANS S	Maltby, Yorks 1960	F	Wimbledon 1986 — Plymouth A 1987	13(1)	1			2				1		16(1)	1
EVANS TT	Wolverhampton 1872	FB	Fairfield FC 1896 — Tottenham H 1897	21		1								22	
EVENSON I	Manchester 1882	WH	Clapton Orient 1907 — Plymouth A 1908	8	1									8	1
FAIRFAX RJ	Smethwick 1941	FB	School 1959 — Northampton T 1968	79(2)		1		9		1	1			90(2)	1
FARRINGTON SG	Burslem, Stoke-on-Trent 1884	CF	Hanley Swifts 1902 — Bristol C 1903	1	1									1	1
FELLOWS E	West Bromwich 1870	F	Cooper's Hill Meths 1892 — Kings Heath 1897 Kings Heath 1899 — Studley Rovers 1899	12								2		14	
FENTON F	Gainsborough 1878	W	Preston NE 1903 — Bristol C 1904	6	1									6	1
FENTON R	South Shields 1940	IF	Burnley 1962 — Birmingham C 1965	59	16	7	2							66	18
FIELDING RA	Stoke 1884	OR	Stoke 1908 — Stoke 1909	10	1									10	1
FINCH EAR	Hednesford 1908	FB	Hednesford T 1925 — Swansea T 1939	216		18								234	
FINCH R	Barry Island 1922	OL	Swansea T 1944 — Lincoln C 1949	15	1	1	1					6		22	2
FITTON GA	Melton Mowbray 1902	OL	Kidderminster Harriers 1922 — Manchester U 1932	96	11	3								99	11
FLAVELL AE	West Bromwich 1875	G	West Bromwich Baptists 1896 — Bournbrook 1898	2										2	
FLETCHER F	Caversham, Berkshire 1874	IR	Reading 1892 — Grimsby T 1895	2										2	
FLEWITT AW	Beeston, Notts 1872	IF	Everton 1896 — Bedminster 1899	65	18	7	3					4	2	80	23
FOGGO KT	Perth, Scotland 1943	OR	Peebles YMCA 1959 — Norwich C 1967	128(1)	29	5		2						135(1)	29
FOLKS WT	Tottenham, London 1886	OR	Clapton FC 1904 — Clapton FC 1904	1										1	
FORD EF	Chingford, Essex 1897	OL	Ilford FC 1922 — Retired 1923	1										1	
FORD WG	Dundee 1872	IF/WH	Dundee 1896 — Hereford T 1896	12	1									12	1
FORRESTER AC	Parkstone, Bournemouth 1940	OR	Dorset Boys 1955 — Southend U 1959	6	3									6	3
FORSYTH ME	Liverpool 1966	D	Earlswood Juniors 1982 — Derby C 1986	28(1)		2		1	1					31(1)	1
FOSTER J	Darlaston 1879	OR	Berwick R 1898 — Blackpool 1899	1										1	
FOULKES HE	Llandudno 1908	FB	Llandudno T 1930 — Guildford 1937	15										15	
FRASER DM	Busby, Scotland 1941	FB/WH	Aberdeen 1963 — Nottingham F 1971	255(2)	8	24		29	4	10		5		323(2)	12
FREEMAN RP	Newark 1945	CF	Stourbridge 1968 — Lincoln C 1970	2										2	
FRYER ER	South Yardley 1904	WH	Harborne L 1923 — Shrewsbury T 1930	21										21	
FUDGE MH	Bristol 1945	IF	Bristol Boys 1961 — Exeter C 1967	13	5	3								16	5
GALE AR	Salford 1904	OR/CF	Chester 1931 — Chester 1936	23	8	6	4							29	12
GALLAGHER M	Cambuslang, Nr Glasgow 1932	OL	Bolton W 1952 — Selkirk 1953	1										1	
GARFIELD BW	Burton-on-Trent 1872	OL	Burton W 1896 — Brighton & HA 1902	109	34	8	4							117	38
GARRATT GT	Byker, Newcastle upon Tyne 1884	OR	Plymouth A 1907 — Crystal P 1908	29	3	1								30	3
GARRATY W	Saltley, Birmingham 1878	F	Leicester Fosse 1908 — Lincoln C 1910	53	20	6	2							59	22
GEDDES AJ	West Bromwich 1871	OL	Causeway GV 1891 — Clapham 1894 Millwall 1895 — Millwall 1895	73	25	9	6					11	7	93	38
GILES JM	Cabra, Dublin 1940	M	Leeds U 1975 — Shamrock R 1977	74(1)	3	4		4	1			5	1	87(1)	5
GLIDDEN TW	Coxlodge 1902	OR	Sunderland WE 1922 — Retired 1936	445	135	33	5					1		479	140
GLOVER AR	Staines, Middlesex 1950	M	Queen's Park R 1969 — Orient 1977	84(8)	9	4		4(2)				0(3)	1	92(13)	10
GODDEN AL	Gillingham 1955	G	Ashford T 1975 — Chelsea 1986	267		19		27		12		4		329	
GOLLINGS P	Winson Green, Birmingham 1878	HB	Hereford Th 1899 — Brierley Hill A 1904	5										5	
GOMM BA	Castle Cary, Somerset 1918	CF	Dudley TC 1935 — Released 1946									4	1	4	1
GOODMAN D	Leeds, May 1966	F	Bradford C 1987 —	10	2									10	2
GORDON DW	Wolverhampton 1924	W	Oxford City 1947 — Brighton & HA 1952	27	10	3								30	10
GOULD RA	Coventry 1946	CF	Wolves 1971 — Bristol C 1972	52	18	1		4				3	1	60	19
GREALISH AP	Paddington, London 1956	M	Brighton & HA 1984 — Manchester C 1986	55(10)	5	1		7(1)						63(11)	5
GREEN H	West Bromwich 1860	FB	George Salter Works 1881 — Old Hill W 1891	33		32								65	
GREEN T	Worcester 1863	IF	Mitchell St George — 1885 — Aston Villa 1887			16	8							16	8
GREEN T	Droitwich 1913	IF	Droitwich Com 1931 — West Ham U 1936	13	3							3	2	16	5
GREEN T	Kings Heath, Birmingham 1873	IF	Coles Farm U 1894 — Small Heath 1895	8	2									8	2
GREGORY H	Aston Manor, Birmingham 1894	OL	Birchfield T 1911 — Retired 1926	162	39	13	3					6	3	181	45
GREW MS	Bilston 1958	G	School 1975 — Leicester C 1983	34		5		8		0(1)				47(1)	
GRIFFIN FA	Pendlebury 1928	OR	Shrewsbury T 1951 — Northampton T 1959	240	47	34	5					1		275	52
GRIMLEY TW	Dinnington 1920	G	Swallownest 1939 — New Brighton 1948	30										30	
GRIPTON WE	Princes End, Tipton 1920	CH	Brownhills A 1935 — Luton T 1948	16								192	3	208	3
GROVES W	Leith 1869	WH/CF	Glasgow Celtic 1890 — Aston Villa 1893	58	7	9	3					2		69	10
GUY H	Wolverhampton 1932	CH	Springfield OB 1948 — Peterborough U 1956	1										1	
HADLEY B	West Bromwich 1871	WH	Hereford Th 1892 — Hereford T 1896	7	1							1		8	1
HADLEY H	Barrow-in-Furness 1878	HB	Halesowen 1897 — Aston Villa 1905	167	2	14								181	2
HAINES JTW	Wickhamford 1920	IF	Leicester C 1948 — Bradford 1949	59	23	3								62	23
HANCOCK H	Levenshulme, Manchester 1878	IF	Manchester C 1909 — Brierley Hill A 1910	2										2	
HARPER WE	Nechells, Birmingham 1876	OL	Smethwick WR 1899 — Leicester Fosse 1903	8	1									8	1
HARRIS GA	Halesowen 1878	LH	Aston Villa 1909 — Coventry C 1910	18		2	1							20	1
HARRIS W	Oakham, Dudley 1918	G	Whiteheath 1936 — Oldham A 1946	2								15		17	
HARTFORD RA	Clydebank 1950	IF	Drumchapel A 1966 — Manchester C 1974	206(9)	18	19	2	15	2	6	3	20	1	266(9)	26
HATTON S	West Bromwich 1892	U	West Bromwich Baptists 1912 — Shrewsbury T 1922	6										6	
HAYCOCK FJ	Smethwick 1886	IF	Coombs Wood 1904 — Crewe A 1907	15	8									15	8
HAYNES GA	West Bromwich 1865	IF	WB Sandwell 1887 — Coles Farm U 1892	10	1									10	1
HAYWARD A	Oldham 1886	OL	Blackburn R 1896 — Chorley 1897	3										3	
HAYWARD AB	Horninglow, Burton-on-Trent 1875	IF	Wolves 1905 — Blackpool 1907	62	25	5	2							67	27
HAYWARD S	Bloxwich 1968	D	School 1985 — Released, May 1987									1		1	
HAYWOOD T	Walsall 1880	HB	Aston Villa 1905 — Crewe A 1908	15										15	
HEASELGRAVE SE	Smethwick 1916	IF	Brierley Hill A 1934 — Northampton T 1945	49	16	3						111	41	163	57
HEATH NH	Wolverhampton 1924	G	H Meadows FC 1942 — Retired 1955	121		13						35		169	
HEGAN D	Coatbridge 1943	IF	Ipswich T 1969 — Wolves 1970	13	2			4						17	2
HENDRY WH	Dundee 1864	CF	Dundee W 1888 — Stoke 1889	18	4									18	4

PLAYER	BIRTHPLACE & YEAR	POSN	FROM (year) TO (year)	League App	League Gls	FA Cup App	FA Cup Gls	Lge Cup App	Lge Cup Gls	Euro App	Euro Gls	Others App	Others Gls	TOTALS App	TOTALS Gls
HEWITT C	Greatham, Cleveland 1884	IF	Llverpool 1908 — Spennymoor U 1910	60	26	4	2							64	28
HIBBERT JW	Hebburn-on-Tyne 1890	IF/WH	Pelaw 1910 — Hartlepool U 1912	3										3	
HIGGINS T	Halesowen 1874	HB	Stourbridge 1894 — Retired 1898	78	4	12						4	1	94	5
HOBSON AF	Tipton 1878	U	Wednesbury T 1899 — Brentford 1904	13	4	2								15	4
HODGETTS F	Oakham, Dudley 1924	W	Accles & Pollock 1939 — Millwall 1949	67	11	3						108	23	178	34
HODKISSON WK	West Bromwich 1933	IF	Greets Green P 1949 — Walsall 1955	21	4									21	4
HOGG D	Stockton-on-Tees 1930	OL	Leicester C 1958 — Cardiff C 1960	81	11	6	1							87	12
HOLDEN GH	West Bromwich 1858	OR	Wednesbury Old Athletic 1886 — Wednesbury Old Ath 1887			4	1							4	1
HOOD GO	Pen-twyn, Monmouth 1925	WH	Nuffield FC 1943 — Retired 1951	69		4						1		74	
HOPE R	Bridge of Allan, Perthshire 1943	IF	Drumchapel A 1959 — Birmingham C 1972	331(5)	33	19		29	7	9	1	10	1	398(5)	42
HOPKINS R	Hall Green, Birmingham 1961	F	Manchester C 1986 —	25	4	1								26	4
HORNE LH	Netherton, Dudley 1925	CH	Netherton W 1944 — Plymouth A 1952	13		3								16	
HOROBIN R	Brownhills 1935	OL	Walsall Wood 1950 — Notts C 1958	54	6	13	2							67	8
HORTON E	West Bromwich 1861	RH	West Bromwich FC 1882 — Retired 1891	47		36	1							83	1
HORTON JH	West Bromwich 1866	FB	Wednesbury Old Athletic 1882 — Retired 1899	129		13						10		152	
HOWARTH N	I' o' the Heights, Shropshire 1905	WH	Bolton W 1926 — Retired 1929	61	1	2	1							63	2
HOWE D	Wolverhampton 1935	RB	Wolverhampton Boys 1950 — Arsenal 1964	342	17	37	2							379	19
HOWSHALL GT	Stoke-on-Trent 1944	WH	Plymouth A 1960 — Norwich C 1967	43	3									43	3
HOYLAND E	Thurnscoe, South Yorkshire 1914	OR	Blackpool 1938 — Lincoln C 1939	1										1	
HUGHES BW	Port Talbot 1958	M	Brinton Ferry FC 1974 — Cardiff C 1979	3(3)	2	0(1)						0(1)		3(5)	2
HUGHES LJ	Smethwick 1950	WH	Smethwick Boys 1964 — Peterborough U 1975	91(9)	3	5		7				15	1	118(9)	4
HUMPAGE WLF	Birmingham 1870	G	Wednesbury Old Athletic 1893 — Hereford T 1896	4										4	
HUNT S	Witton, Birmingham 1956	M	Coventry C 1984 — Aston Villa 1986	68	15	2	1	11	3			3	1	84	20
HURST GC	Ashton-under-Lyne 1941	IF	Stoke C 1975 — Seattle Sounders 1976	10	2			2						12	2
HUTCHINSON T	Glasgow 1872	CF	Nelson 1894 — Stockport C 1897	45	19	10	2					3		58	21
INWOOD GF	Kislingbury, Northants 1928	OL	Rushden T 1946 — Hull C 1950	10		2	1							12	1
JACK WR	Grangemouth 1875	CF	Bristol R — Clyde 1905	25	13	1								26	13
JACKMAN CEJ	Aldershot 1936	G	Aldershot 1957 — Retired 1960	21										21	
JACKSON A	Tipton 1937	UF	WG Allen's FC 1954 — Birmingham C 1964	192	50	16	2							208	52
JACKSON WH	Oldbury 1894	CF	Langley SM 1912 — 1917 Killed during World War One	3										3	
JAMES GC	Oldbury 1899	CF	Bilston U 1920 — Reading 1929	106	52	10	5							116	57
JAMES RW	Smethwick 1897	LH	Smethwick H 1919 — Brentford 1922	9	4									9	4
JEPHCOTT AC	Smethwick 1891	OR	Brierley Hill A 1911 — Retired 1923	174	15	15	1					1		190	16
JOHNSON G	West Bromwich 1871	UF	Wrockwardine W 1895 — Walsall 1896	1		1						1		3	1
JOHNSON JA	Grimsby 1911	OL	Stoke C 1937 — Norwich Victoria 1946	55	22	5						85	25	145	47
JOHNSON LG	Vancouver, Canada 1951	CF	Vancouver Sp 1969 — Vancouver R 1972	2										2	
JOHNSTON WM	Glasgow 1946	OL	Glasgow Rangers 1972 — Vancouver Whitecaps 1979	203(4)	18	24(2)	6	15	2			12(1)	2	254(7)	28
JOHNSTONE WR	Kirriemuir, Angus 1877	CF	Dundee Harp 1889 — Alloa 1890	3										3	
JOL MC	The Hague, Holland 1956	M	FC Twente Enschede 1981 — Coventry C 1983	53(1)	4	5		10						68(1)	4
JONES A	Tipton 1875	CH	Cameron Highlanders 1896 — Middlesbrough 1901	104	6	13	4							117	10
JONES CL	Penn, Wolverhampton 1925	IF	Penn FC 1941 — Released 1947									1		1	
JONES EN	Stirchley, Birmingham 1915	OR	Portsmouth 1939 — Brentford 1945	3	4							19	3	22	7
JONES GA	Nuneaton 1932	OR	Erdington A 1947 — Wrexham 1955	2		1								3	
JONES H	West Bromwich 1881	G	Brierley Hill A 1902 — Brierley Hill A 1904 Brierley Hill A 1905 — Shrewsbury T 1907	2										2	
JONES HJ	Haydock 1911	UF	Preston North End 1933 — Retired 1943	120	54	9	3					40	47	169	104
JONES I	Merthyr 1899	IF	Swansea T 1922 — Swansea T 1926	63	9	4	1							67	10
JONES SG	Highley, Shropshire 1938	CH	Walsall 1960 — Walsall 1968	239	2	14	1	12	2					267	3
JORDAN WC	Langley, West Midlands 1885	CF	Langley SM 1904 — Everton 1909	31	14	4	4							35	18
KAYE J	Goole 1940	LH/IF	Scunthorpe U 1963 — Hull C 1971	281(3)	45	25	2	31	6	10	1	11		358(3)	54
KELSEY AG	Wallingford, Berkshire 1871	LH/IF	Worcs Regt Aldershot 1895 — Brierley Hill A 1896	11										11	
KENNEDY JP	Cleator Moor, Cumberland 1925	CH	Altrincham 1948 — Chester 1961	364	3	32	1					1		397	4
KENT K	Stoke-on-Trent 1965	F	School 1981 — Newport C 1984	1(1)										1(1)	
KEVAN DT	Ripon 1935	F	Bradford 1953 — Chelsea 1963	262	157	29	16							291	173
KIFFORD J	Paisley, Nr Glasgow 1878	FB	Portsmouth 1901 — Millwall 1905	96	8	3								99	8
KING AE	Luton 1956	M/IF	Queen's Park R 1981 — Everton 1982	21(4)	4	4	1	8(1)	1					33(5)	6
KINSELL TH	Cannock 1921	FB	School 1935 — Bolton W 1949	83		8						67		158	
KNOWLES JW	Wednesbury 1879	IF	School 1897 — Dudley T 1898 Dudley T 1900 — Dudley T 1901	3										3	
KRZYWICKI RL	Penley, Flint 1947	OR	Leek YC 1962 — Huddersfield T 1970	51	9	4(1)		4(3)	2			1	1	60(4)	12
LATCHFORD PW	Sheldon, Birmingham 1952	G	Sutton T 1969 — Glasgow Celtic 1975	81		9		8				6		104	
LAW A	Wealdstone 1874	G	Millwall A 1896 — Stafford R 1897	1										1	
LAW WD	Pleck, Walsall 1882	OL	Doncaster R 1905 — Watford 1906	10		1								11	
LEE GT	York 1920	OL	Nottingham F 1949 — Lockheed Leamington 1958	271	59	23	6					1		295	65
LEE JM	Mold, Flint 1938	OL	Saltney Juniors 1956 — Crewe A 1958	1										1	
LEE W	West Bromwich 1878	CF	Bournville A 1901 — Portsmouth 1904	71	25	5								76	25
LEEDHAM F	Lye 1909	OR	Kidderminster H 1926 — Kidderminster H 1929	4										4	
LEGGE SG	Willenhall 1881	OL	Willenhall SW 1906 — Worcester C 1907 Worcester C 1908 — Coventry C 1910	9	3									9	3
LEWIS AE	Wolverhampton 1884	IL	Stafford R 1904 — Northampton T 1906 Northampton T 1913 — South Shields 1914	47	9	1								48	9
LEWIS M	Birmingham 1965	M	School 1981 — Derby C 1984	22(2)		4		4(1)						30(3)	
LIGHT WH	Woolston, Hampshire 1913	G	Southampton 1936 — Colchester U 1938	28		2								30	
LLOYD JA	Pelsall 1889	OL	Hednesford T 1910 — Swansea T 1914	45	8	1	1							46	9
LOACH AA	West Bromwich 1863	IF	George Salter Works 1882 — Aston Villa 1888			14	9							14	9
LONG WR	Tividale, West Midlands 1899	OL	Hednesford T 1919 — Hednesford T 1920	2										2	
LOVATT J	Burton-on-Trent 1941	CF	Erdington A 1956 — Nuneaton B 1963	18	5									18	5
LOVETT GJ	Sheldon, Birmingham 1947	M	Sheldon Schools 1964 — Worcester C 1972	106(8)	8	12(2)		13(1)		4(2)	1	6(3)		141(15)	9
LOWE JA	West Bromwich 1876	G	Coombs Wood 1899 — Willenhall P 1903	4										4	
LOWERY A	Wallsend-on-Tyne 1961	M	Ashington 1981 — Mansfield T 1983	1										1	
LOWERY H	Moor Row, Cumberland 1918	WH	Moor Celtic 1934 — Northampton T 1945	17								27		44	
LUKE NE	Birmingham 1964	M	School 1980 — Mansfield T 1984	8(1)	1	2(2)		1						11(3)	1
LUNN WJ	Lurgan, Northern Ireland 1923	IF	Glenavon 1946 — Bournemouth & BA 1948	10	5									10	5
LYNEX SC	West Bromwich 1958	W	Sandwell R 1974 — Shamrock R 1977 Leicester C 1987 —	10	1									10	1
McCALL A	Hamilton 1925	IF	Blackpool 1951 — Leeds U 1952	31	3	1								32	3
McCULLOCH T	Strathblane, Stirlingshire 1868	FB	Glasgow U 1891 — Stirling 1893	46		9						2		57	
McCULLUM WD	Paisley 1870	FB	Glasgow Celtic 1891 — Dumbarton 1891	3										3	
McKENNAN PS	Airdrie 1918	IF	Partick T 1947 — Leicester C 1948	11	4	1						15	13	27	17
McKENZIE AD	Greenock 1875	IF	Millwall A 1897 — Dumbarton 1899	51	9	4								55	9
MACKENZIE S	Romford 1961	M	Manchester C 1981 —	153(3)	23	8	1	16(2)	1	2				179(5)	25
MacLEAN H	Stornoway 1952	OL	School 1967 — Swindon T 1974	4				1				1(2)		6(2)	
McLEAN J	Stoke-on-Trent 1877	OR	Walsall 1901 — Preston North End 1903	57	10	3								60	10
McLEOD R	Kilsyth, Dumbarton 1872	IF	Partick T 1891 — Leicester Fosse 1897	149	50	20	7					16	8	185	65
McMANUS P	Winchburgh, West Lothian 1873	WH	Hibernian 1896 — Warmley 1898	28	1									28	1
McNAB A	Glasgow 1911	WH	Sunderland 1938 — Newport C 1946	52	2	3						131	2	186	4
McNAUGHT K	Kirkcaldy, Fife 1955	CH	Aston Villa 1983 — Sheffield U 1985	42	1	4		4						50	1

PLAYER	BIRTHPLACE & YEAR	POSN	FROM (year)　　　TO (year)	League App	Gls	FA Cup App	Gls	Lge Cup App	Gls	Euro App	Gls	Others App	Gls	TOTALS App	Gls
McNEAL R	Hobson, Co Durham 1891	LH	Hobson W 1910 — Retired 1925	370	9	30						3	1	403	10
MACREADY BL	Leicester 1942	OR	Hull C 1959 — Mansfield T 1964	14	1	1								15	1
McVITIE GJ	Carlisle 1948	OR	Carlisle U 1970 — Oldham A 1972	42	5	5		2				3		52	5
MADDEN C	Manchester 1958	CF/IF	Bury 1986 — Blackpool 1987	10(2)	3									10(2)	3
MAGEE TP	Widnes 1899	IR/RH	Widnes A 1919 — Crystal P 1934	394	15	34						6	3	434	18
MAHON J	Gillingham 1911	OR	Leeds U 1935 — Huddersfield T 1938	113	39	10	5							123	44
MALE NA	West Bromwich 1917	FB	Bush R 1933 — Walsall 1938	3	1							1		4	1
MANN JF	West Bromwich 1891	CF	Great Bridge Juniors 1912 — Newport C 1918	2										2	
MANNERS JA	Morpeth 1878	WH	Morpeth H 1904 — Hartlepools U 1913	193	7	16								209	7
MARTIN DW	Edinburgh 1947	W	Kettering T 1967 — Carlisle U 1970	14	1	4		0(1)	1	1		1(2)		20(3)	2
MARTIN MP	Dublin 1951	M	Manchester U 1975 — Newcastle U 1978	85(4)	11	12	2	5(1)	2	0(1)		6(1)		108(7)	15
MATTHEWS J	West Bromwich 1860	G	Aston Unity 1883 — Crosswell's B 1885			1								1	
MAYO J	Tipton 1951	CF	Walsall 1973 — Orient 1977	67(5)	16	7	1	5				5(1)	3	84(6)	20
MERRICK AR	Selly Oak, Birmingham 1950	D	School 1966 — Kiddermisnter H 1976	131(8)	5	6(2)	9					10(3)		156(13)	5
MILLAR J	Annbank, Ayrshire 1870	CF	Sunderland 1904 — Chelsea 1905	1										1	
MILLARD A	West Bromwich 1868	D	West Bromwich Victoria 1888 — Halesowen 1892	5										5	
MILLARD L	Coseley, West Midlands 1919	FB	Sunbeam FC 1937 — Stafford R 1958	436	7	40						149	11	625	18
MILLINGTON AH	Hawarden, Nr Chester 1943	G	Sutton T 1959 — Crystal P 1964	40										40	
MILLS DJ	Robin Hood's Bay 1951	F	Middlesbrough 1979 — Sheffield W 1983	44(15)	6	2(3)		6(2)		3(1)				55(21)	6
MINTON RC	Moseley, Birmingham 1951	FB	Schools 1966 — Dunstable T 1975	24(2)	1			2				1		27(2)	1
MONAGHAN DJ	Bromsgrove 1959	F	Astwood Bank 1976 — Port Vale 1984	14(5)	2	1		2(1)	1	0(1)				17(7)	3
MOORWOOD L	Wednesbury 1888	G	Bilston U 1909 — Burnley 1920	30		3								33	
MORLEY AW	Ormskirk 1954	W	Aston Villa 1983 — Den Haag 1986	26	4	4	2	1						31	6
MORRIS F	Tipton 1893	IL	Redditch 1911 — Coventry C 1924	263	112	20	4					4	2	287	118
MORROW JHE	Larne, Northern Ireland 1930	OR	Nuneaton B 1945 — Nuneaton B 1950	5	2									5	2
MOSES RM	Manchester 1960	M	Corpus Christi Boys Club 1977 — Manchester U 1981	63	5	2		7	1	1				73	6
MOUNTFORD D	Hanley 1931	UF	Crewe A 1951 — Crewe A 1953	4	1									5	1
MULLIGAN PM	Dublin 1945	FB	Crystal P 1975 — Shamrock R 1979	109	1	11		7				5	1	132	2
MURPHY JP	Ton Pentre 1908	WH	Mid Rhondda Boys 1928 — Swindon T 1939	204		19								223	
MURRAY M	Falkirk 1935	CF	Glasgow Rangers 1962 — Third Lanark 1963	3										3	
NAYLOR SW	Leeds 1962	G	Lincoln C 1986 —	54		1		2				1		58	
NEALE W	West Bromwich 1872	CF	Grove Hall Sts 1893 — Brierley Hill A 1894	6	3	1								7	3
NEVIN JW	Gosforth, Tyne and Wear 1887	WH	Hobson W 1910 — Bristol R 1912	2										2	
NEWALL JT	West Bromwich 1894	IF	Great Bridge Celtic 1912 — Retired 1922	21	3							1		22	3
NEWALL WT	Lye 1869	OL	Stourbridge 1894 — Worcester R 1895	14	2							1		15	2
NEWSOME R	Hebden Bridge, Yorks 1919	OR/CF	Congleton 1939 — Coventry C 1947			4	2					55	28	59	30
NICHOLL J	Hamilton, Canada 1956	RB	Toronto Blizzard 1984 — Rangers 1986	56		3		6				2	1	67	1
NICHOLLS F	Handsworth 1884	OR	Handsworth R 1904 — Goldenhill W 1906	7										7	
NICHOLLS HJ	Walsall 1891	OL	Hednesford T 1913 — Cannock T 1914	4										4	
NICHOLLS J	West Bromwich 1867	U	St John's U 1889 — Kidderminster O 1890	4		2								6	
NICHOLLS J	Wolverhampton 1931	IF	Heath TU 1950 — Cardiff C 1957	131	58	14	6							145	64
NICHOLLS S	West Bromwich 1870	CF	West Brom Victoria 1890 — London CBC 1892 London CBC 1893 — Retired 1894	41	14	9	3							50	17
NICHOLSON MD	Oakengates 1871	FB	Oswestry T 1891 — Luton 1894	56		8						4		68	
NISBET GJM	Wallsend-on-Tyne 1951	FB/G	Willington Boys Club 1968 — Hull C 1976	136		13	1	8				10		167	1
NOCK JF	West Bromwich 1875	OL	Halesowen T 1897 — Langley R 1899	15	6									15	6
NORMAN O	West Bromwich 1866	UF	Wednesbury Old Athletic 1893 — Hereford T 1896	18	4							2		20	4
NURSE DG	Princes End, Tipton 1873	RH	Wolves 1901 — Retired 1905	85	4	3								88	4
OLIVER HSM	Birmingham 1863	LB	Small Heath 1888 — Small Heath 1889	1										1	
OSBORNE J	Barlborough, Derbyshire 1940	G	Chesterfield 1967 — Shamrock R 1978	250		24		16		8		14		312	
OWEN AG	Coalbrookdale, Shropshire 1880	Ol	Ironbridge 1903 — Walsall 1905	7	1									7	1
OWEN GA	St Helens 1958	M	Manchester C 1979 — Panionios (Greece) 1986	185(2)	21	12(2)	3	24	2	4				225(4)	26
OWERS EH	Bromley 1889	CF	Blackpool 1907 — Chesterfield 1909	4										4	
PADDOCK JW	West Bromwich 1877	W	School 1894 — Walsall T 1896 Brierley Hill 1899 — Halesowen 1900	20	5									20	5
PADDOCK W	West Bromwich 1862	OL	West Bromwich U 1886 — Retired 1888			8	3							8	3
PAILOR R	Stockton-on-Tees 1887	CF	West Hartlepool 1908 — Newcastle U 1914	79	40	13	7							92	47
PALMER CL	Rowley Regis, West Midlands 1965	D	Youth Training Scheme 1983 —	52(5)	1	1		3(1)				3		59(5)	1
PARKER AE	Tipton 1925	FB	School 1942 — Hereford U 1946									5	1	5	1
PARKES HA	Gorsty Hill, Halesowen 1888	OR	Halesowen 1906 — Coventry C 1908 Coventry C 1914 — Newport C 1919	27	4	4								31	4
PARRY J	Glan Mule, Montgomeryshire 1871	OL	Newtown 1895 — Aberystwyth 1895	1										1	
PEARS WG	Aston, Birmingham 1922	CF	Wolseley FC 1943 — Kidderminster H 1947									4	2	4	2
PEARSON HF	Tamworth 1908	G	Tamworth Castle 1925 — Millwall 1937	281		21						1		303	
PEARSON H	Kettlebrook, Tamworth 1886	G	Tamworth Ath 1906 — Retired 1926	341	2	29						7		377	2
PEARSON T	West Bromwich 1866	IF	WB Sandwell 1886 — Retired 1894	138	72	26	12					7	4	171	88
PEMBERTON JHA	Wolverhampton 1916	RB	Birmingham 1937 — Retired 1951	162		10								172	
PEMBERTON JT	Brierley Hill 1925	LB	Round Oak FC 1943 — Round Oak FC 1944									1		1	
PENDREY GJS	Lozells Birmingham 1949	D	Birmingham C 1979 — Torquay U 1981	18										18	
PENNINGTON J	West Bromwich 1883	FB	Dudley T 1903 — Retired 1922	455		39						2		496	
PERKINS EE	Astwood Bank, Worcs 1874	OL	Worcester C 1904 — Worcester C 1907	33	1	1								34	1
PERKINS E	West Bromwich 1924	FB	Hill Top F 1952 — Walsall 1956	2										2	
PERRY AA	West Bromwich 1897	FB	West Brom Baptists 1921 — Wellington 1927	74		7								81	
PERRY C	West Bromwich 1866	HB	West Brom Strollers 1884 — Retired 1896	171	12	39	3					9	1	219	16
PERRY M	Wimbledon 1964	F	School 1980 — Torquay U 1984	14(6)	5	1		2						17(6)	5
PERRY T	West Bromwich 1871	HB	Stourbridge 1890 — Aston Villa 1901	248	14	29						14	1	291	15
PERRY W	West Bromwich 1868	IF	West Brom Excelsior 1886 — Wolves 1889 Warwick C 1894 — Burton S 1895	11	4	4	3							15	7
PETERS S	West Bromwich 1886	WH	Churchfields 1904 — Crewe A 1907	6	1									6	1
PHEASANT E	Darlaston 1877	CH/CF	Wolves 1904 — Leicester Fosse 1910	140	20	12	2							152	22
PICKEN T	Hednesford 1883	G	Shrewsbury 1905 — Rood End 1910	2										2	
PICKERING TG	Wednesbury 1879	IF	Brierley Hill A 1900 — Kettering T 1901	10	2									10	2
PIKE RSGA	Finchley 1917	CF	Banbury Sp 1937 — Banbury Sp 1946	1										1	
PITTAWAY J	West Bromwich 1867	UF	West Brom Wednesday 1889 — Stourbridge 1890	2	1									2	1
POTTER RC	Wolverhampton 1948	CH	School 1964 — Swindon T 1970	8										8	
POTTER RJ	Beckenham, Kent 1936	G	Crystal P 1958 — Portsmouth 1967	217		13		6		2				238	
POULTON A	Wolverhampton 1896	CF	Priestfield FC 1913 — Merthyr T 1919	9	1									9	1
POWELL D	Hednesford 1967	G	Cherry Valley FC 1984 —									1		1	
POWELL S	Pulford, Clwyd 1865	FB	Oswestry 1890 — Burton S 1892	30		5								35	
POYNTON W	Hill Top, West Bromwich 1883	OR	Brittania Vics 1902 — Retired 1903	2	2									2	2
POXTON JH	Staveley 1904	Ol	Staveley T 1924 — Gillingham 1928	9	1									9	1
PREW JH	Coventry 1914	OR	Hinckley U 1936 — Walsall 1938	7	1									7	1
PRICE GW	Wolverhampton 1888	CF	Chillington R 1910 — Cradley SL 1911	1										1	
RAMSEY AR	Collington, Hereford 1867	RB	Kidderminster H 1888 — Kidderminster H 1900	1										1	
RANDLE A	West Bromwich 1880	RH	Darlaston 1901 — Leicester Fosse 1908	132	1	11	1							143	2
RANKIN B	Liverpool 1880	W	Everton 1906 — Manchester C 1907	29	5	2	1							31	6

PLAYER	BIRTHPLACE & YEAR	POSN	FROM (year) TO (year)	League App	League Gls	FA Cup App	FA Cup Gls	Lge Cup App	Lge Cup Gls	Euro App	Euro Gls	Others App	Others Gls	TOTALS App	TOTALS Gls
RAW H	Tow Law, Co Durham 1903	WH/IF	Huddersfield T 1931 — Lincoln C 1936	25	7	1						1		27	7
RAWLINGS JDS	Wombwell, Yorks 1913	OR	Huddersfield T 1935 — Northampton T 1936	10	1									10	1
REA JC	Lledrod, Cardigan 1870	OL	Aberystwyth 1894 — Aberystwyth 1895	1										1	
READER J	West Bromwich 1866	G	School 1885 — Retired 1901	315		39						16		370	
READFERN TE	Crook, Co Durham 1944	CF	Langley Park Juniors 1960 — Kidderminster H 1964	4		1								5	
REED FWM	Scotswood-on-Tyne 1894	CH	Lintz Inst 1913 — Retired 1927	138	4	16	1					3		157	5
REED HD	Alexandria, Dumbarton 1950	OR	Drumchapel A 1966 — Plymouth A 1971	5(3)	2							0(1)		5(4)	2
REES RR	Ystradgynlais, Brecknock 1944	OR/OL	Coventry C 1968 — Nottingham F 1969	34	9	1(1)	2	2	1	3				40(1)	12
REGIS C	Maripiasoula (French Guyana) 1958	S	Hayes 1977 — Coventry C 1984	233(4)	82	25	10	27(1)	16	10	3	2	1	297(5)	112
REID GA	Handsworth, Sheffield 1872	CF	Sheffield W 1897 — Walmley 1898	11	3	2								13	3
REILLY GG	Bellshill, Lanarkshire 1957	CF	Newcastle U 1985 —	29	9	2	1							31	10
REYNOLDS J	Blackburn 1869	WH	Ulster 1891 — Aston Villa 1893	37	3	7	2					2	1	46	6
RICHARDS AJ	Knighton 1888	RB	New Invention 1910 — Kilnhurst 1911	1										1	
RICHARDS GM	Bilston 1929	OR	Albion Works 1943 — Stafford R 1952	3	1									3	1
RICHARDS J	Martley, Worcester 1873	OR	City Ramblers (London) 1895 — Loughborough T 1896	14		2	1					4	1	20	2
RICHARDS W	West Bromwich 1874	CF	West Brom Standard 1894 — Newton Heath 1901	123	35	21	6					4	1	148	42
RICHARDSON F	Middlestone Moor, Durham 1925	CF	Barnsley 1950 — Chester 1952	29	8	2								31	8
RICHARDSON S	West Bromwich 1892	WH	Great Bridge Celtic 1913 — Newport C 1927	191	1	15						6		212	1
RICHARDSON W'G'	Framwellgate Moor, Durham 1909	CF	Hartlepool U 1929 — Shrewsbury T 1945	320	202	34	26					90	100	444	328
RICHARDSON W	Great Bridge 1908	CH	G Bridge Celtic 1926 — Swindon T 1937	319	1	32						1		352	1
RICKABY S	Stockton-on-Tees 1924	RB	Middlesbrough 1950 — Poole T 1955	189	2	15						1		205	2
RIDYARD A	Shafton, South Yorkshire 1908	CH	Barnsley 1932 — Queen's Park R 1938	31		3								34	
RILEY JH	West Bromwich 1869	UF	Wednesbury Old Athletic 1889 — Walsall TS 1891	3	1									3	1
RIX J	Lintz, Bursopfield 1908	WH	Lintz Colliery 1927 — Lincoln C 1939	64		4								68	
ROBBINS WW	Cardiff 1910	OL	Cardiff C 1932 — Newport C 1939	84	28	7	3							91	31
ROBERTS F	West Bromwich 1874	D	West Brom Standard 1893 — Smethwick C 1895	2										2	
ROBERTS RHC	Marchweil, Wrexham 1870	OL	Wrexham 1890 — Corwen 1891	1										1	
ROBERTS RJ	Redditch 1878	W	West Brom Excelsior 1899 — Newcastle U 1901	43	8	9	2							52	10
ROBERTS RJ	West Bromwich 1859	G	George Salter Works 1879 — Sunderland Albion 1890 Sunderland Albion 1891 — Aston Villa 1892	49		35								84	
ROBERTS TF	Smethwick 1868	FB	School 1890 — Birmingham St George 1891 Birmingham St George 1893 — Retired 1895	2										2	
ROBERTSON AP	Philpstoun, West Lothian 1952	D	Uphall Saints 1968 — Wolverhampton W 1986	504(2)	8	34(2)		53	3	12	1	19		622(4)	12
ROBINSON B	Wheelton, Lancashire 1865	FB	Bolton W 1889 — Bolton W 1890 Bolton W 1891 — Hyde U 1891			4								4	
ROBINSON EV	Walsall 1922	FB	Hilary Street Old Boys 1938 — Shrewsbury T 1948									1		1	
ROBINSON EM	Manchester 1935	IF	Altrincham 1957 — Rotherham U 1959	1										1	
ROBINSON MJ	Rochdale 1968	W	School 1985 — Released, May 1987	2				0(1)						2(1)	
ROBSON B	Witton Gilbert, Co Durham 1957	M	Schools 1972 — Manchester U 1981	194(4)	39	10(2)	2	17(1)	2	12	2	9	1	242(7)	46
ROBSON G	Chester-le-Street 1965	M	Whitehill 1981 —	27(12)		0(1)		4(1)				1(1)		32(15)	1
ROBSON RW	Sacriston, Co Durham 1933	IF/WH	Fulham 1956 — Fulham 1962	239	56	18	5							257	61
ROOKE E	Hockley 1899	CH	Brierley Hill A 1921 — Nuneaton T 1929	41	1	1								42	1
ROUSE FW	Bracknell, Berkshire 1885	CF	Chelsea 1909 — Croydon Common 1910	5	2									5	2
ROWLEY GA	Wolverhampton 1926	IF	Blakenhall SL 1944 — Fulham 1948	24	4	1	1					16	10	41	15
RUSHBURY DG	Wolverhampton 1956	D	St Chad's College 1972 — Sheffield W 1977	28		3								31	
RUSSELL TJ	Walsall 1924	F	Brockhouses FC 1943 — Kidderminster H 1948									4	1	4	1
RYAN RA	Dublin 1925	WH/IF	Coventry C 1945 — Derby C 1955	234	28	20	2					18	1	272	31
SAMBROOK C	Smethwick 1896	F	Coventry C 1915 — Retired 1920									2	1	2	1
SANDERS JA	Hackney, London 1920	G	Charlton A 1945 — Coventry C 1958	327		36						28		391	
SANDFORD EA	Handsworth 1910	IF	Smethwick Highfield 1929 — Sheffield U 1939	286	67	30	8					1		317	75
SANKEY J	Moulton, Cheshire 1912	WH	Winsford U 1930 — Northampton T 1945	147	5	13						130	22	290	27
SAUNDERS DG	Birmingham 1927	OL	W.B.Hawthorne 1942 — Banbury Sp 1948			1						5	3	6	3
SAUNDERS S	West Bromwich 1872	OL	Unity Gas 1895 — Birmingham Centinels 1896	2										2	
SAUNDERS W	Banbury 1916	G	Banbury Spencer 1938 — Banbury Spencer 1946	2								32		34	
SAVAGE G	Birmingham 1903	F	Willenhall 1921 — Wrexham 1922	2										2	
SCREEN J	Oldbury 1915	FB	Smethwick Highfield 1933 — Wrexham 1939	1										1	
SETTERS ME	Honiton, Devon 1936	U	Exeter C 1955 — Manchester U 1960	120	10	12								132	10
SHAW CE	Mansfield 1911	FB	Wolves 1936 — Hereford U 1947	113	10	14						124	4	251	14
SHAW CR	Willenhall 1862	OL	Walsall TS 1888 — Walsall TS 1888	1	1									1	1
SHAW GD	Huddersfield 1948	IF	Oldham Ath 1969 — Oldham A 1975	65(17)	17	7	1	4	1			2(1)	1	78(18)	20
SHAW GE	Swinton 1899	FB	Huddersfield T 1926 — Stalybridge C 1938	393	11	31						1		425	11
SHEARMAN BW	Lincoln 1884	OL	Bristol C 1911 — Nottingham F 1919	126	18	15						2		143	18
SHELDON A	West Bromwich 1871	FB	Smethwick Carriage Wks 1892 — Worcester R 1893									1		1	
SHEPHERD E	Wombwell, Yorks 1919	OL	Fulham 1948 — Hull C 1949	4										4	
SHEPPARD RJ	Bristol 1945	G	Gloucester Schools 1960 — Bristol R 1969	39		4		11						54	
SHINTON F	Wednesbury 1883	CF	Hednesford T 1905 — Leicester Fosse 1907	64	46	4								68	46
SHORE EW	Kings Hill, Wednesbury 1891	FB	Willenhall Swifts 1913 — Stourbridge 1919	5										5	
SHORT JS	Norbrigg, Chesterfield 1903	IF	Seamore FC 1923 — Retired 1930	39	17	2								41	17
SIMMONS C	West Bromwich 1878	CF	Worcester Rov 1898 — West Ham U 1904 West Ham U 1905 — Chesterfield T 1907	178	75	15	6							193	81
SIMPSON G	Sheffield 1883	OL	Sheffield W 1909 — North Shields 1910	19	5	5	1							24	6
SIMPSON TJN	Southampton 1938	WH	Peterborough U 1963 — Walsall 1967	71	3	5		1	1					77	4
SINGLETON MD	Banbury, Oxon 1963	M	Bradford C 1986 —	5(2)		0(1)								5(3)	
SMITH AW	Camberwell 1896	IF/CH	Birmingham 1919 — Stoke 1923	79	20	1						1	2	81	22
SMITH AW	Slamannan, Stirling 1879	F	Newton Heath 1900 — Bristol R 1903	23	8	2								25	8
SMITH A	West Bromwich 1880	OR	Worcester C 1903 — Brierley Hill A 1904	8	1	2	1							10	2
SMITH A	West Bromwich 1878	IF	West Brom Baptists 1898 — Retired 1900	6	1									6	1
SMITH AE	Whetstone, Leicester 1921	OL	Leicester C 1948 — Plymouth A 1952	49	12	3	1							52	13
SMITH D	Armadale, Leicester 1921	OL	Coltness U 1939 — Chesterfield 1948	7	1									7	1
SMITH E	Old Hill 1880	IF	Old Hill W 1899 — Brierley Hill A 1900 Brierley Hill A 1901 — Brierley Hill A 1904	10	4									10	4
SMITH GWC	Liverpool 1947	G	Colchester U 1971 — Cambridge U 1973	10										10	
SMITH H	Netherton, Dudley 1903	W	Hingley's FC 1922 — Blackpool 1927	2										2	
SMITH J	Northfield, Birmingham 1964	D	School 1980 — Telford U 1984					1						1	
SMITH J	Darby End, Cradley 1890	RB	Cradley Heath St Luke's 1910 — Birmingham 1926	434		30						7		471	
SMITH KW	Woodville, Leics 1940	IF	Coalville Boys 1957 — Peterborough U 1963	63	30	7	4							70	34
SMITH WA	Old Hill 1882	IF	Worcester C 1902 — Brierley Hill A 1905	21	3	1								22	3
SOUTHAM JH	Willenhall 1920	FB	Shornhill Rec FC 1939 — Newport Co 1946									34		34	
SPENCER G	Shavington, Staffs 1913	OR	Nantwich Vic 1933 — Brighton & HA 1939	13	2									13	2
SPENCER JL	Masborough 1900	OR	Beighton YC 1922 — Aston Villa 1927	59	3	7								66	3
SPOONER J	West Bromwich 1871	CF	Hednesford T 1895 — Retired 1896	2										2	
SPROSON T	Stoke-on-Trent 1903	G	Audley FC 1922 — Port Vale 1928	9										9	
STANTON J	West Bromwich 1862	FB/WH	George Salter Works 1879 — Newton Heath 1885			6								6	
STATHAM DJ	Whitmore Reams 1959	LB	School 1975 —	297(1)	8	28	1	34	1	12		6		377(1)	10
STEELE SF	Fenton, Stoke-on-Trent 1937	IF	Port Vale 1961 — Port Vale 1961	1										1	
STEGGLES KP	Ditchingham, Norfolk 1961	D	Ipswich T 1987 —	10										10	
STEPHENS KJ	Bristol 1946	OR	Phildown R 1962 — Walsall 1968	21(1)	2	1(2)		1	1			1		24(3)	3

PLAYER	BIRTHPLACE & YEAR	POSN	FROM (year) — TO (year)	League App	Gls	FA Cup App	Gls	Lge Cup App	Gls	Euro App	Gls	Others App	Gls	TOTALS App	Gls
STEVENSON J	Bonhill, Dumbarton 1875	HB/CF	Preston North End 1900 — Dumbarton 1904	120	9	9								129	9
STRINGER J	Netherton, Dudley 1878	G	Wolves 1905 — Dudley T 1910	160		12								172	
STYLES AJ	Smethwick 1939	WH	School 1956 — Wrexham 1960	1										1	
SUGGETT C	Washington, Co Durham 1948	IF	Sunderland 1969 — Norwich C 1973	123(5)	20	10	2	15	4			17	4	165(5)	30
SUMMERFIELD K	Walsall 1959	F	School 1975 — Birmingham C 1982	5(4)	4			2						7(4)	4
SUMMERS GT	Small Heath 1933	WH	Erdington Albion 1950 — Sheffield U 1957	22		3								25	
SWALLOW J	Sheffield 1860	WH	Oldbury 1883 — Wednesbury T 1884			1								1	
SWIFT A	West Hartlepool 1892	CF	Hartlepool Expansion 1913 — Crystal P 1920	28	11									28	11
SWINDEN SA	Smethwick 1913	FB	Smethwick Highfield 1931 — Swindon T 1937	4										4	
TAGGART J	Belfast 1872	HB	Middlesbrough 1893 — Walsall 1896	68	4	11						14		93	5
TALBUT J	Headington, Oxford 1940	CH	Burnley 1966 — KV Mechelen 1971	143(1)		21		15	7			6	1	192(1)	1
TAYLOR AS	Lozells, Birmingham 1925	CF	Handsworth Wood 1941 — Retired 1951	4	5									4	5
TAYLOR GA	Trehaford 1905	OR	Trehaford 1927 — Leamington T 1929			1								1	
TAYLOR H	Dudley 1893	CF	Dudley Bean 1920 — Barrow 1922	9	2									9	2
TAYLOR O	Wednesfield 1880	G	Bilston 1901 — Coventry C 1903	5										5	
THOMAS MR	Mochdre, Montgomeryshire 1954	M	Chelsea 1985 — Witchita Wings 1986	20		2	1	5				1		28	1
THOMPSON AR	Wolverhampton 1967	M	Featherstone FC 1984 — Wolves 1986	18(5)	1	2		0(1)				1(1)		21(7)	1
THOMPSON GL	Birmingham 1959	CF	Coventry C 1983 — Sheffield W 1985	91	39	5	1	9	5					105	45
THOMPSON JT	North Shields 1955	FB	Northumberland Boys 1970 — Newport C 1978	20				2						22	
THOMPSON W	Morpeth, Northumberland 1886	OR	Morpeth H 1908 — Sunderland 1911	54	6	3								57	6
TIGHE J	Aghamore, Northern Ireland 1923	G	Larkhall Th 1945 — Hednesford T 1948	1										1	
TIMMINS G	West Bromwich 1858	WH/IF	George Salter Works 1879 — Old Hill W 1891	33		28	1							61	1
TIMMINS S	West Bromwich 1879	WH	Nottingham F 1906 — Retired 1911	111	3	5								116	3
TRANTER GH	Yardley, Birmingham 1915	CH	Rover Works 1934 — Hereford U 1947	16		4						50		70	
TREACY RCP	Dublin 1946	CF	Home Farm 1961 — Charlton A 1968 / Preston North End 1976 — Shamrock R 1977	22(4)	7	2								24(4)	7
TRENTHAM HF	Chirbury, Shropshire 1908	FB	Hereford U 1929 — Hereford U 1937	246		25						1		272	
TREWICK J	Bedlington, Northumberland 1957	M/FB	Schools 1972 — Newcastle U 1980	83(13)	11	12		10(2)		6(2)	1	5(1)		116(18)	12
TREVIS ASSRTBG	Blackheath 1910	CH	Leamington T 1929 — Chester 1936	1										1	
TUDOR WH	Shotton, Chester 1918	CH	Lavender FC 1934 — Wrexham 1946	31		3								34	
TURNER I	Netherton, Dudley 1876	G	Dudley St James 1898 — Stourbridge 1899	1										1	
TURNER SI	Langley, West Midlands 1882	IL	Darlaston 1904 — Coventry 1905	1										1	
TWIGG L	Buxton, Derbyshire 1921	G	Buxton FC 1945 — Retired 1947			1						1		2	
VALENTINE CH	Manchester 1958	W	Vancouver Whitecaps 1984 — Wichita Wings 1986	44	6			6				3	1	53	7
VARADI I	Paddington, London 1959	CF	Sheffield W 1985 — Manchester C 1986	30(2)	9	2		5	4			2		39(2)	13
VARNEY H	Belper, Derbyshire 1885	OR	Belper T 1905 — Belper T 1907	5										5	
VARTY JW	Scotswood-on-Tyne 1890	WH	Scotswood R 1911 — Hartlepools U 1913	3										3	
VERNON J	Belfast 1919	CH	Belfast Celtic 1947 — Crusaders 1952	190	1	10								200	1
VIGROW S	Muirhead, Angus 1878	IL	Dundee 1896 — Airdrie 1897	1										1	
VINCENT EA	Dudley Wood 1922	WH	Toll End Wesley 1939 — Worcester C 1946									1		1	
WALKER D	Oakdene, Walsall 1884	IL	Bristol R 1907 — Leicester Fosse 1908	36	15	3								39	15
WALKER L	West Bromwich 1860	FB	West Brom Royal 1883 — West Brom Standard 1891	18		1								19	
WALKER WW	Horseley Heath, Tipton 1879	IF	Toll End Wesley 1898 — Brierley Hill 1903	32	5	2								34	5
WALKER W	Walsall 1888	CF	Halesowen 1910 — Willenhall Swifts 1911	1	1									1	1
WALLACE JMB	Wallyford, Edinburgh 1935	G	Airdrie 1959 — Bedford T 1962	69		7								76	
WALSH DJ	Waterford 1924	CF	Linfield 1946 — Aston Villa 1950	165	94	9	6							174	100
WARD RA	West Bromwich 1953	G	Imperial Star 1972 — Blackpool 1977	9								1		10	
WATERHOUSE F	Langley Green, West Midlands 1889	HB	Wednesbury Old Athletic 1908 — Derby C 1920	172	6	12						4		188	6
WATSON A	Sheffield 1868	W	Mansfield T 1896 — Lincoln C 1899	28	2	2	1							30	3
WATSON E	West Bromwich 1901	RH	Tanfield FC 1922 — Hereford U 1923	1										1	
WEBB AR	Wrockwardine Wood, Salop 1963	D	School 1979 — Port Vale 1984	23(1)				0(1)						23(2)	
WEBB I	Worcester 1874	G	Small Heath 1901 — Sunderland 1904	96		5								101	
WEBSTER H	Walsall 1909	G	Burtonwood Villa 1928 — Swindon T 1929	1										1	
WHELDON GF	Langley Green, West Midlands 1869	IF	Aston Villa 1900 — Queen's Park R 1901	26	3	3								29	3
WHELDON S	Smethwick 1865	WH	Langley Green Vics 1891 — Walsall 1892	1										1	
WHITE H	Wednesbury 1916	RB	Darlaston 1937 — Worcester C 1946	39		3						36	1	78	1
WHITEHEAD CR	Northfield, Birmingham 1955	U	Bristol C 1981 — Free-transfer, May 1987	157(11)	6	10	2	14(2)	1			2		183(13)	9
WHITEHEAD NJ	Tamworth 1914	OR	Birmingham University 1932 — Birmingham 1935	1										1	
WHITEHOUSE B	West Bromwich 1935	IF	Vono Sports 1950 — Norwich C 1960	37	13	9	4							46	17
WHITEHOUSE JW	West Bromwich 1861	OR	West Brom Rovers 1880 — Retired 1884			1								1	
WILCOX EE	Blaengarw, Glamorgan 1927	CF	Oxford C 1947 — Worcester C 1951	12	3									12	3
WILCOX HM	Hockley, Birmingham 1881	IF	Leicester Fosse 1907 — Plymouth A 1908	17	5	3	2							20	7
WILCOXSON GH	Heanor, Derbyshire 1925	IF	Heanor Town 1943 — Heanor Town 1946									1		1	
WILE JD	Sherburn, Co Durham 1947	CH	Peterborough U 1970 — Peterborough U 1983	499(1)	24	42	2	42	2	12	1	23		618(1)	29
WILKES AG	Hagley, Worcs 1918	CF	Kidderminster H 1938 — Blackheath 1946			1						4	5	5	5
WILLETTS G	West Bromwich 1920	G	Clanborough FC 1941 — Retired 1946									1		1	
WILLIAMS CE	Bristol 1921	IF	Bristol C 1948 — Bristol C 1951	71	19	6	1							77	20
WILLIAMS G	West Bromwich 1925	WH	Harvills Hawthorn FC 1943 — Banbury Sp 1949	7		2						28		37	
WILLIAMS GE	Hellan, Rhyl 1938	FB	Rhyl A 1954 — Weymouth 1972	308(6)	10	25		15	1	5		1		354(6)	11
WILLIAMS GO	Wednesbury 1879	HB	Wednesbury Old Athletic 1899 — Brierley Hill 1902	16		2								18	
WILLIAMS J	Brownhills 1882	OR	Aston Villa 1905 — Brownhills A 1909	31	1	4								35	1
WILLIAMS NE	Wolverhampton 1924	FB	Featherstone FC 1944 — Released 1946									1		1	
WILLIAMS O	Smethwick 1874	IF	Oldbury T 1893 — Oldbury T 1895	14	7	1						4	2	19	9
WILLIAMS SG	Wrexham 1930	FB	Wrexham 1950 — Southampton 1962	226	6	20	3							246	9
WILLIAMS W	West Smethwick 1875	FB	Old Hill Wanderers 1894 — Retired 1901	180	8	23	2					5	2	208	12
WILLIAMS WT	Esher, Surrey 1942	CH	Queen's Park R 1963 — Mansfield T 1966	1										1	
WILLIAMSON R	Glasgow 1961	CF	Glasgow Rangers 1986 —	30(1)	8	1		2				1		34(1)	8
WILSON C	Heeley, Sheffield 1905	IF	Hallam FC 1920 — Sheffield W 1928	125	41	8	4							133	45
WILSON JJ	Handsworth, Birmingham 1861	OL	Walsall T 1887 — Kidderminster H 1890	40	8	13	12							53	20
WILSON RT	Grangemouth, Stirling 1947	OL/FB	Woodburn A 1963 — Retired 1977	230(2)	3	21		11		4		16		282(2)	3
WITCOMB D	Cwm, Gwent 1918	WH	Enfield 1937 — Sheffield W 1947	55	3	9	1					58	6	122	10
WOLLASTON W	Willenhall 1886	OR	Willenhall Pickwick 1910 — Darlaston 1913	25	2	1	1							26	3
WOOD HF	West Bromwich 1870	IF	Oldbury T 1891 — Walsall 1893	1	1									1	1
WOOD MC	Hobson, Co Durham 1890	FB/CH	Hobson W 1911 — Kidderminster H 1922	17										17	
WOOD S	Winsford, Cheshire 1905	OL	Winsford U 1928 — Halifax T 1938	256	58	24	8					1		281	66
WOODHALL G	West Bromwich 1863	OR/IR	Churchfield For 1883 — Wolves 1892	44	10	30	10							74	20
WOOLGAR S	Chesterfield 1952	M	School 1968 — Doncaster R 1974	2(2)				0(1)				1		3(3)	
WORTON T	Wolverhampton 1878	IF	Wolves 1901 — Retired 1905	72	23	3								75	23
WRIGHT F	Wednesbury 1872	D	Wednesbury Old Athletic 1895 — Rowley RS 1896	2										2	
WRIGHT HF	West Bromwich 1890	IF	West Brom Wednesbury A 1906 — Stourbridge 1909 / Stourbridge 1910 — Wolves 1919	89	17	10	3					6		105	20
YOUNG G	Kirkintilloch, Dumbarton 1880	FB	Portsmouth 1905 — West Brom Strollers 1906	16										16	
YOUNG WC	Chadsmoor, Staffs 1884	RH	Hednesford T 1907 — Hednesford T 1910	19	2	3								22	2
ZONDERVAN R	Surinam (Dutch Guinea) 1959	M	FC Twente Enschede 1982 — Ipswich T 1984	82(2)	5	5		6						93(2)	5

Top League Appearances for Albion

Substitute appearances in brackets.

1.	Tony Brown	561(13)
2.	Ally Robertson	504(2)
3.	John Wile	499(1)
4.	Jesse Pennington	455
5.	Tommy Glidden	445
6.	Len Millard	436
7.	Joe Smith	434
8.	Ronnie Allen	415
9.	Joe Carter	414
10.	Ray Barlow	403
11.	Tommy Magee	394
12.	George Shaw	393
13.	Bobby McNeal	370
14.	Joe Kennedy	364
15.	Don Howe	342
16.	Sid Bowser	341
17.	Hubert Pearson	341
18.	Bobby Hope	331(5)
19.	Jim Sanders	327
20.	'W.G' Richardson	320
21.	Bill Richardson	319
22.	Joe Reader	315
23.	Graham Williams	308(6)
24.	Clive Clark	300(1)
25	Len Cantello	297(4)
26.	Derek Statham	297(1)
27.	Jeff Astle	290(2)
28.	Freddie Buck	287
29.	Teddy Sandford	286
30.	Jimmy Dudley	285
31.	John Kaye	281(3)
32.	Harold Pearson	281
33.	Ally Brown	254(25)
34.	George Lee	271
35.	Tony Godden	267
36.	Freddie Morris	263
37.	Derek Kevan	262
38.	Billy Bassett	261
39.	Doug Fraser	255(2)
40.	Stan Wood	256
41.	John Osborne	250

Tony 'Bomber' Brown scores from the penalty spot midway through the second half of the game against Leeds United on 22 January 1977. This was Albion's only goal in their 2-1 defeat at The Hawthorns, both Leeds' goals coming in the first half.

Tony Brown in action as a stand-in for goalkeeper John Osborne in the 3-1 defeat by Blackpool at Bloomfield Road in 1970.

Top Appearances (all competitions)

1.	Tony Brown	704(16)
2.	Len Millard	627
3.	Ally Robertson	622(4)
4.	John Wile	618(1)
5.	Jesse Pennington	496
6.	Ray Barlow	482
7.	Tommy Glidden	479
8.	Joe Smith	471
9.	Ronnie Allen	458
10.	Joe Carter	451
11.	'W.G.' Richardson	444
12.	Tommy Magee	434
13.	George Shaw	425
14.	Bobby McNeal	403
15.	Bobby Hope	398(5)
16.	Joe Kennedy	397
17.	Jim Sanders	391
18.	Don Howe	379
19.	Derek Statham	377(1)
20.	Hubert Pearson	377
21.	Sid Bowser	371
22.	Joe Reader	370
23.	Len Cantello	365(4)
24.	Jeff Astle	359(2)
25.	John Kaye	358(3)
26.	Graham Williams	354(6)
27.	Ally Brown	331(28)
28.	Clive Clark	351(2)
29.	Bill Richardson	352
30.	Billy Elliott	330
31.	Tony Godden	329
32.	Doug Fraser	323(2)
33.	Jim Dudley	320
34.	Freddie Buck	319
35.	Teddy Sandford	317
36.	John Osborne	312
37.	Billy Bassett	311
38.	Harold Pearson	303
39.	Cyrille Regis	297(5)

Tony Brown netting the only goal of the game from the penalty-spot against Leeds United at The Hawthorns on 31 December 1977.

MANAGERS

The post of Albion team manager was first created in the 1948 close season when Fred Everiss retired as Secretary-manager after 46 years unstinting service to the club. It was considered that the post was too demanding for one man and so the position of team manager was advertised.

Jack Smith
1948-1952

Career: Albion trialist at 16. Wolverhampton Wanderers, Swindon Town, Chelsea, Wolverhampton Wanderers (coach), Albion (manager 1948-52), Reading (manager 1952-4). Albion wartime guest.
Died, 1975, aged 63.

Jesse Carver
1952

Career: England Schoolboy international. Blackburn Rovers, Newcastle United, Bury, Huddersfield Town (assistant trainer), Dutch FA (coach), Marzotto (coach), Lazio (coach), Juventus (coach), Valdagno (coach), Albion (manager 1952), Torino (coach), AC Roma (manager), Coventry City (joint manager), Lazio (coach), Tottenham Hotspur (trainer-coach), Portugal (coach).

Vic Buckingham
1953-1959

Career: Tottenham Hotspur, Middlesex County (FA coach), Oxford University (coach), Pegasus (coach), Bradford (manager), Albion (manager 1953-9).
After leaving Albion for personal reasons in 1959, Vic Buckingham held managerial appointments with the following clubs: Ajax Amsterdam, Plymouth Argyle, Sheffield Wednesday, Ajax, Fulham, Ethnikos, Barcelona, Sevilla.
England wartime international.

Gordon Clark
1959-1961

Career: Goldthorpe United, Southend United, Manchester City, Waterford, Hyde United (player-manager), Distillery (manager), Aldershot (manager), Albion (chief scout 1955, then assistant-manager and manager until 1961), Sheffield Wednesday (assistant manager), Peterborough United (manager), Arsenal (chief scout), Fulham (assistant manager), Philadelphia Fury (coach).

Archie Macaulay
1961-1963

Career: Camelon Juniors, Glasgow Rangers, West Ham United, Brentford, Arsenal, Fulham, Guildford City (manager), Dundee (coach), Norwich City (manager), Albion (manager 1961-3), Brighton and Hove Albion (manager).
Winner of 13 Scotland caps.

Jimmy Hagan
1963-1967

Career: England Schoolboy international. Trial for Albion as youngster. Washington Colliery, Liverpool, Derby County, Sheffield United, Peterborough United (manager), Albion (manager 1963-7), Manchester City (scout), Benfica (manager), Kuwait (coach), Sporting Lisbon (manager).
One England cap, plus 16 in wartime.

Alan Ashman
1967-1971

Career: Sheffield United, Nottingham Forest, Carlisle United, Penrith (coach), Carlisle United (manager), Albion (manager 1967-71), Olympiakos (manager), Carlisle United (manager), Workington (manager), Manchester United (scout), Walsall (manager), Derby County (chief scout, then assistant manager), Hereford United (assistant manager).

Don Howe
1971-1975

Career: St Peter's School, Wolverhampton Wanderers, Albion (player 1950-64), Arsenal (player, coach and assistant manager), Albion (manager 1971-5), Galatasary (coach), Leeds United (coach), Arsenal (chief coach, then manager), England 'B' (coach), England (chief coach), Saudi Arabia (coach 1986-7).
Twenty-three England caps.

Johnny Giles
1975-1977 and 1983-1985

Career: Republic of Ireland Schoolboy international. St Columbus, Dublin City, Munster Victoria, The Leprechauns, Stella Maris, Home Farm, Manchester United, Leeds United, Albion (player manager 1975-7), Shamrock Rovers (player manager), Philadelphia Fury, Vancouver Whitecaps (coach), Republic of Ireland (manager), Albion (manager 1983-5). Capped 60 times by the Republic of Ireland.

Ronnie Allen
1977 and 1981-1982

Career: Bucknall Boys Brigade, Wellington SC, Northwood Mission, Port Vale, Albion (player), Crystal Palace (player and coach), Wolverhampton Wanderers (coach and manager), Atletico Bilbao (coach), Sporting Lisbon (manager), Walsall (manager), Albion (scout then manager 1977), Saudi Arabia national team (manager), Panathinaikos (manager), Albion (scout then manager 1981-2).
Five England caps.

Ron Atkinson
1978-1981

Career: Lea Village School, BSA Tools, Wolverhampton Wanderers, Aston Villa, Headington United, Oxford United, Kettering Town (player-manager), Cambridge United (manager), Albion (manager 1978-81), Manchester United (manager 1981-6).

Ron Wylie
1982-1983

Career: Clydesdale Juniors, Scotland Schoolboys, Notts County, Aston Villa, Birmingham City, Aston Villa (coach), Coventry City (coach then assistant manager), Cyprus (coach), Bulova Hong Kong (manager), Albion (manager 1982-3), Aston Villa (coach).

Nobby Stiles
1985-1986

Career: St Patrick's School, Lancashire Schools, England Schoolboys, Manchester United, Middlesbrough, Preston North End (player then manager), Vancouver Whitecaps (coach), Albion (coach-assistant manager 1983, then manager 1985-6, coach 1986-7). Capped 28 times by England.

Ron Saunders
1986-

Career: Birkenhead and Liverpool District Schools, Everton, Tonbridge, Gillingham, Portsmouth, Watford, Charlton Athletic, Yeovil Town (manager), Oxford United (manager), Norwich City (manager), Manchester City (manager), Aston Villa (manager), Birmingham City (manager), Albion (manager 1986-).

Coaches

Albion's first officially appointed coach was the former Aston Villa defender Albert Evans, whose career was terminated by a broken leg. He was at The Hawthorns as coach in 1910-11. A number of other ex-players have since held coaching positions at Albion, among them Jesse Pennington, (1922-3), Tommy Glidden (1936-8), 'W.G.'Richardson (assistant-trainer-coach, 1946-59) George Lee (trainer-coach, 1959-63), Graham Williams (1970-72), Brian Whitehouse (1971-81), Tony Brown (1985-6).

Other coaches employed by Albion in recent times have included Albert McPherson (trainer-coach 1964-84), Geoff Hudson (1970-72), Bill Asprey (1972-4), Jimmy Dunn (also trainer, 1965-71), Colin Addison (1979), Mick Brown (1980), and since then Mike Kelly, Norman Hunter, Nobby Stiles and Keith Leonard.

Former player and coach Brian Whitehouse

Trainers

Albion appointed their first trainer in March 1883. He was Dick Oxenbould of Birchfield Harriers Athletic Club. Later that year, another Harrier, Joey Law, an old George Salter's employee, was engaged as a permanent trainer at the fee of 2s 6d (12p) per week, which was later increased to five shillings (25p) and then 7s 6d (37p). For a time Law was assisted by Billy Nicholls but in August 1886 he was joined by Jack Paddock who was subsequently confirmed as sole trainer of Albion in 1888 when Law joined Burnley for a brief spell.

Trainer Fred Reed (extreme left) with the players at the start of the 1935-6 season.

Albion's first-team trainers 1883-1987

Joe Law (1883-8), Jack Paddock (1888-1901), Bill Brierley (1901-04), Tom Dempster (1904), Jimmy Millar (1904-05), Bill Barber (1905-22), T.H. 'Bill' Gopsill (1922-7), Fred Reed (1927-50), Arthur Fitton (1950-56), 'Dick' Graham (1956-60), George Lee (1960-61), Wilf Dixon (1961-4), John Jarman (1964-5), Albert McPherson (1965-7), Stuart Williams (1967-9), Jimmy Dunn (1969-71), George Wright (1971-9), Richard Roberts (1979-83), Colin Saunders (1983-4), George Wright (1984-6), Graham Doig (1986-7).

Assistant-trainers have included:-

Bill Nicholls, Jimmy Fainter (from 1888), Bill Barber (1900-5), Harry Bell (1906-07), Eddie Jones (1907-08), Bob Crone (1908-09), Ted Paddock (1909-10), Jim Stevenson (1914-15), Sam Guest (1919-39), Sammy Short (1930-46), 'W.G.'Richardson (1946-8), Arthur Fitton (1948-50), Fred Pedley (1950), Wilf Dixon (1959-60) and John Jarman (1961-4).

Albion have not officially appointed an assistant-trainer since 1964-5. Several people have, however, done the job on a temporary basis.

Masseurs & Physiotherapists

Albion's first masseur was T.H.'Bill' Gopsill, when the First Division Championship was won in 1919-20. He died, prematurely, in 1927.

Since the last war, Fred Pedley (from 1950 to 1965), Tom Jones (1966-71), George Wright (1971-9 and 1984-6), Richard Roberts

Physiotherapist George Wright in a pensive mood.

(1971-2 and 1979-83), Colin Saunders (1983-4) and Colin Doig (1986-7) have been physiotherapists at Albion.

Training 'Honours'

J.Paddock, Football League v Irish League, 1896-7.
W.Barber, Football League v Scottish League, 1908-09.
W.Barber, Football League v Irish League, 1914-15.
T.H.Gopsill, FA XI v Oxford University, 1922-3.
T.H.Gopsill, England v Belgium, 1924-5.
S.Guest, Belgium v England, 1924-5.
S.Guest, FA XI v Staffordshire, 1926-7.
S.Guest, The Rest v England, 1927-8, 1934-5.
F.Reed, England v The Rest, 1927-8, 1934-5.
F.Reed, Football League v Irish League, 1934-5.
F.Reed, England v Wales, 1945-6.

Albion Directors

THE FOOTBALL club director is responsible for the club's financial matters and the overall direction of its administration, and it is fair to say that the majority of directors concerned with West Bromwich Albion have been men who have put their money and minds forward to work for the good of the game.

Until 1891, Albion's fortunes were guided by a committee which, in 1882, consisted of six players (Fred Bunn, George Bell, Harry Bell, James Stanton, William Bisseker and John Stokes) and five non-playing members of the club. Meetings were held at the club's headquarters, the Plough and Harrow, where the committee selected the team in these days. A number of other players who also served on the committee during the 1880s included Ezra Horton, Bob Roberts, 'Jem' Bayliss and George Timmins, while the leading lights on the non-playing side were such local worthies as Dr Herbert Manley, Thomas Cotterili, J.J.Raybould, John Bowen, Dr Robert Rees, James Couse, William Mould, Dr Isaac Pitt, John Homer and Dr W.Lawson.

Two gentlemen not named above are worthy of particular mention, these being Mr Henry S.Jackson and Edward W.W.Heelis. The former was the chairman of the Albion committee when the momentous move to Stoney Lane was made in 1885. He was the clerk to the local magistrates at the time, and was rewarded for all the hard work he put in when Albion won the FA Cup for the first time in 1888. Mr Heelis joined the committee in 1887 when he was Mayor of West Bromwich, and he was elected club chairman in 1888 in succession to Mr Jackson. He resigned in December, 1890 and left the committee in April 1891 but joined the club's board of directors some months later.

Albion's first board of directors was elected at the Plough and Harrow on 1 September 1891, at a shareholders' meeting. It consisted of George Salter, Edward Heelis, James Couse, Henry Jackson, John Phillips, Dr Robert Rees, William Bache, James Lavender and 'Jem' Bayliss, who was then still a playing member of the club.

Albion Directors (1891-1918)
George Salter (1891-5), Edward W.W.Heelis (1891-5), James Couse (1891-2; 1895-6), Henry Jackson (1891-3), John Phillips (1891-3), Dr Robert Rees (1891-5), William Bache (1891-2), James Lavender (1891-2), 'Jem' Bayliss (1891-1905), Louis Ford (1892-6), Harry Roberts (1892-7), Enoch Wood (1892-5), Dr Isaac Pitt (1893-1904), T.Harris Spencer (1896-1902; 1905-07), W.Hall Keys (1896-7), Harry Powell (1896-1904), J.A.Fellows (1896-9), Harry Keys (1896-1903; 1905-08; 1919-29), Charles Perry (1896-1902), Thomas Brennand (1897-1900), Joseph Lones (1900), George W.East (1901-05), George Mason (1902-05), Joseph S.Round (1903-05; 1927-40), Richard Mason (1904-05), J.W.B.Stephens (1904-05), Thomas Hedges (1904-05), W.I. 'Billy' Bassett (1905-37), Charles Couse (1905-10), J.V.Webster (1907-8), R.Fellows (1908-9), Major (Lt Col) Harold Ely (1909-27), Dan Nurse (1910-27), Albert Seymour (1910-22).

All these gentlemen faced a common problem: Albion's chronic lack of funds. Things became so bad in March 1905 that the entire board — under pressure from the bank and the club's many creditors —resigned and only the intervention of Harry Keys, W.I.Bassett, T.Harris Spencer and Charles Couse, who offered to stand in their places, saved the day. Several of the directors listed above deserve particular mention:

Harry Keys

He was the outstanding personality on the Albion board for many years and even when he was not a director he kept in close touch with the club's affairs. He was first elected chairman of Albion in 1899 but resigned after a disagreement with his fellow board members in 1903. He was a blunt, outspoken man who was once described by Fred Everiss as a man 'who called a spade a spade and, sometimes, a sanguinary shovel'. Despite this approach he was a warm and friendly character who was a great favourite with legions of Albion players who nicknamed him 'John Bull'. In 1905 he was elected to the Football League management committee and five years later he became vice-president of the League, a position he was to hold until his death in 1929. He was also an FA councillor and a member of the international selection committee. Two of his brothers were closely connected with the Albion club, one as a director, the other as secretary and auditor, and his son, Major H.Wilson Keys, also joined the Albion board, shortly after his father's death.

'Jem' Bayliss

Albion's first Cup Final captain was a dominant character both on and off the field. He was so proud of his Staffordshire county cap that he wore it in every match in which he participated, either as a fearless bustling centre-forward of the old school or, in the twilight of his playing career, as a crafty wing-half. He won a solitary England cap in 1891, against Ireland. He was first elected to the Albion committee in 1886 and was a director of the club in 1891 while still a player. He became chairman of Albion in September 1903, when financial troubles were coming to a head, and he resigned a few months later along with the entire board.

George Salter

A former goalkeeper for West Bromwich FC, in 1881-2, George Salter retired from playing through injury and turned his attentions to the non-playing side of the game, first as a supporter and then as a director of the Albion club. Educated at Malvern College and a keen West Bromwich Dartmouth cricketer, he was, like many Albion directors over the years, a prominent Freemason. Mr Salter was Mayor of West Bromwich in 1891-2 and 1895-6. He was Albion's first president, in August 1882 and he became chairman of the Albion board in 1891.

Joe Round

A local publican who gave Albion unstinting service as a director in two separate spells, he was passionately interested in local junior football, helping to found the Birmingham and District League and being associated with it for over 50 years. He served as chairman and president and was also a member of the Birmingham County FA council for a similar length of time. Mr Round became an FA councillor in 1929 and was elected vice-chairman of Albion in 1937.

Dan Nurse

A former Wolverhampton Wanderers right-half who was signed for a meagre amount in 1901, Dan Nurse captained West Brom when they won the Second Division Championship in 1901-02, but was forced to retire in 1904 because of injury. After part-guaranteeing the players' summer wages in 1910, when another financial crisis loomed, he was elected to the board, remaining there until he resigned in 1927.

W.I.Bassett

When he died in April 1937, the *Albion News* described him as 'guide, philosopher and friend' to the Albion club, and Football League secretary, Fred Howarth, declared him to be 'the most popular man in the game'. Billy Bassett was one of the greatest footballers of the Victorian era with 16 international caps earned between 1888 and 1896, and after he retired from the playing side in 1899, he went into the licensed trade and later had interests in the cinema business. He became a director in March 1905 and was elected chairman in September 1908, rarely missing a board meeting between 1905 and 1932. His influence at the Albion was incalculable and it was recognised at the club's AGM in August 1936 when he was presented with a silver casket and an illuminated scroll on the occasion of his reaching 50 years with Albion. From 1930 to 1937 he was a member of the Football League management committee.

Albion Directors (1918-1987, excluding those already mentioned)
Louis J.Nurse (1922-48), Walter W.Hackett (1927-37), Major H.Wilson Keys (1930-65), James Everiss (1930-2), A.Claude Jephcott (1934-50), W.Horace Thursfield (1937-64), Norman W.Bassett (1937-52), W.Ellery Jephcott (1941-53), Fred Everiss (1948-51), Tommy W. Glidden (1951-74), Jim W.Gaunt (1951-76), Sam R.Shepherd (1952-63), Len Prichards (1953-71), Clive H.James (1963-70), F.A. 'Bert' Millichip (1964-84), Tom H.Silk (1965-80), John Gordon (1970-84), Cliff Edwards (1971-86), J.Sid Lucas (1975-87), D.Brian Boundy (1976-87). Alan E.Everiss (1981-86) Trevor J.Summers (1984-7), John G.Silk (1984-7), Mick McGinnity (1986-7), Joe Brandrick (1986-7).

Since 1918 the club's finances have been more stable than in the earlier days, and the Albion directors have rarely had to face the financial pressures which almost brought about the end of the club on two separate occasions, in 1905 and 1910. But the present board had to face up to a worrying period during the 1970s when Albion were in the Second Division. In the season in which Albion were relegated, a record loss of £104,000 was announced, followed by two further seasons in which losses of £126,000 and £139,000 were incurred. Despite those figures the board remained resolute and the reward for maintaining a First Division set-up at The Hawthorns came at the conclusion of the 1975-6 season when Albion climbed back into Division One.

A number of the directors listed above gave the club particularly outstanding service:

Louis Nurse

Brother of Dan, 'Lou' Nurse was an Albion scout for a number of years before his election to the board. He had a particular interest in the reserve team and during a 15-year period missed only two Central League games. He was elected Albion chairman in the summer of 1937, in succession to Mr W.I.Bassett and he became an FA councillor in 1941.

W.Horace Thursfield

Although vice-chairman of Albion from 1950 until 1962, Horace Thursfield was nevertheless keenly fond of local junior football and was chairman and later president of the Staffordshire FA. His sporting interests also extended to the cricket field (as did Mr Gaunt's) and he was chairman and president of West Bromwich Dartmouth CC. Mr Thursfield was an FA councillor from 1957 to 1964.

Jim Gaunt

As Albion chairman from 1 April 1963 to September 1974, Mr Gaunt guided Albion through some of their most significant post-war seasons. A year before he retired from the board he was elected president of the club, a position he held until August 1984 when he handed over the role to Bert Millichip.

Tommy Glidden

A former schoolboy international of 1914 who was most unlucky not to win a full England cap, Tommy Glidden was part of Albion for 53 years (1922-74) as a player, coach, shareholder and director He was a goalscoring outside-right who could also play at inside-forward and such was his stature at The Hawthorns that he became captain of the unique double winning side of 1931. He held the position of vice-chairman from 1963 until 1969.

H.Wilson Keys

Elected Albion chairman in 1947 after 10 years as vice-chairman, he was an influential figure at The Hawthorns, like his father before him, and also in the wider spheres of football. Whereas Harry Keys was an important Football League official, his son became a leading light in FA circles, eventually being elected FA vice-president in December 1969. A more complete portrait of his career in football appears in the *Albion Centenary Brochure*. Up to the present time no director has served longer than the 'Major's' 35 years on the Albion board.

A.Claude Jephcott

Associated with Albion for nearly 40 years as a player, shareholder and director, Claude Jephcott hailed from an 'Albion family'. His father was a journalist who covered Albion home and away for many years and had his own seat at The Hawthorns, while his brother, Ellery, spent over 50 years in journalism and edited the *Albion News* for a number of years before World War Two. He was also the club's first historian and joined Claude on the Albion board for 10 years. Claude was a dashing right-winger in his playing days, with a terrific turn of pace, and he was on the verge of full international recognition when a broken leg ended his career in 1922.

Presidents

The position of Albion president is an honorary one and does not confer a seat on the board, although Mr Jim Gaunt had a dual role as a director and club president for a year in 1964-5. Club presidents have been as follows:

George Salter (elected 1882)
Sir Ernest J.Spencer (September 1904-July 1937)
The Earl of Dartmouth (August 1937-February 1958)
Walter W.Hackett (September 1958-April 1964)
Major H.Wilson Keys (August 1964-September 1974)
Jim W.Gaunt (September 1974-August 1984)
F.A.'Bert' Millichip (August 1984-1987)

▲ Bert Millichip, President of West Bromwich Albion in 1987.

It is not always appreciated by supporters that the director is an unpaid official of the club and that the only remuneration he can receive from the football club is the end-of-year dividend on the shares he holds, and the payment of expenses incurred on club business. The club does not always pay a dividend on shares held; indeed, it was not until 1911 that Albion were able to announce a five-per-cent tax-free dividend for the first time ever. The members of the Albion board are normally elected by the club's shareholders at the AGM which is usually held in August or September, and each year two directors offer themselves for re-election at this meeting, when they can be challenged by other candidates, although this is a very rare occurrence indeed.

Cliff Edwards, the last in a long line of former players to join Albion's board before retiring in 1986. ▼

Albion have had at least one former player on the board or committee of the club almost since its inception in 1879, right up until the summer of 1986 — a record unique in football. Seven former professionals have become directors of the Albion club — 'Jem' Bayliss, Charlie Perry, Billy Bassett, Dan Nurse, Claude Jephcott, Tommy Glidden and Cliff Edwards, who broke the long line when he left in 1986.

Albion Chairmen:-

1885-8	Henry Jackson	1905-08	Harry Keys
1888-90	Edward W.Heelis	1908-37	William S.Bassett
1891	Henry Jackson	1937-47	L.J.'Lou' Nurse
1891-5	George Salter	1947-63	Major H.Wilson Keys
1895-9	T.Harris Spencer	1963-74	'Jim' W.Gaunt
1899-1903	Harry Keys	1974-83	F.A.'Bert' Millichip
1903-05	A.J.'Jem' Bayliss	1983-	J.'Sid' Lucas

Albion Chairman Sid Lucas

Sid Lucas was elected to the Albion board at the club's annual meeting in September 1975, moving into the vacancy caused by the untimely death of Mr Tommy Glidden. A local businessman, Sid has followed the fortunes of Albion since he was a lad and was a regular terrace supporter for many years, standing behind the Birmingham Road goal. He was appointed chairman of the club in August 1984, taking over from 'Bert' Millichip.

F.A. 'Bert' Millichip

A partner in Sharp and Millichip (solicitors) of High Street, West Bromwich, for many years solicitors to the Albion club. Became an Albion director in August 1964, in place of the late W.H.Thursfield, and ten years later, on 2 September 1974, was elected chairman as replacement for the retiring chairman J.W.Gaunt. He had become Albion vice-chairman in 1970.

In December 1969, Mr Millichip was elected to the FA Council as a replacement for Major H.W.Keys. On 27 June 1981 he was elected chairman of the FA Council. Subsequently he has also become a vice-president of the Football Association (1984 to present). On 26 August 1983 he resigned as Albion chairman because of the pressure of his FA commitments and he left the Albion board in August 1984, at which time he was elected president of Albion, succeeding J.W.Gaunt. He has been chairman of the FA Council during a most difficult period and has had to deal with unprecedented problems relating to hooliganism and the control of crowds.

Albion Secretaries

The Everiss Era

FROM 1902 to 1980 the position of Albion secretary was held by three members of the same family over a period of 78 years — a truly remarkable record of service to the Albion club. Fred Everiss held the post for 46 years and was followed by his brother-in-law, 'Eph' Smith, for 12 years before Fred's son, Alan, took over.

Fred Everiss JP was born at Spon Lane in May 1882. He was secretary of Albion for 46 years during which time his devotion to the club cannot be measured. He joined Albion as an office boy in September 1896 and was put in charge of programmes and given general clerical duties. He acquitted himself so well that the directors had no hesitation in appointing him secretary at the age of 20 in 1902, a tremendous responsibility for one so young.

He became a much-loved figure in the game and with the assistance of Billy Bassett and Harry Keys in particular, he earned great respect for the Albion club. In 1926 an unusual tribute was paid to him by past and present Albion players who presented him with an illuminated address as a tangible token of the high regard in which he was held.

From 1927 he was secretary of the Football League Secretaries and Managers Association and later he became its chairman. During World War Two he had to combine the jobs of secretary-manager, typist, telephonist, office-boy, part-time groundsman and ARP night-watchman. In October 1946 he was presented with a silver casket and an illuminated address on the occasion of his 50 years' service with Albion.

FRED EVERISS

'EPH' SMITH

For the last three years of his life, Fred Everiss was a director of Albion, and when he died in 1951 he had served the club for over 54 years. He is undoubtedly one of the greatest names in the history of the club.

'Eph' Smith started his Albion career in September 1906 as an office boy and became Fred Everiss' assistant in 1911. He gave Albion loyal and devoted service until he retired in May 1960, after 12 years as successor to Everiss and over 53 years at The Hawthorns. In August 1956 he was made a Life Member of the club on the occasion of his reaching 50 years with Albion.

Alan Everiss JP, as secretary and later director, accompanied the club all over the world and is probably the most travelled Albion employee of all time. He initially came Albion in August 1933, as a £1-a-week office junior, and carried on the family tradition of long service magnificently. Like his father before him, he became a Justice of the Peace, in 1968. He was chairman of the Football League Secretaries, Managers and Coaches Association, and he would readily endorse the remark once made in the *Albion News* that a First Division secretary needs to have a knowledge of every occupation 'from estate agent to travel agent.'

On stepping down from his secretarial duties in 1980 he moved into directorship (February 1981), a position he held until retiring in the summer of 1986 — thus severing the Albion-Everiss association which had been maintained since 1896, a total of 91 years. Alan Everiss himself had been with Albion for 53 years. He was voted a Life Member of the club on 11 August 1980, and three years later he was elected to the Football League Management Committee.

ALAN EVERISS

GORDON DIMBLEBY

WBA Club Secretaries

1880-1 John Bisseker
1881-2 John While
1882 Arthur E.Eld and F.Seymour (joint secretaries)
1883-4 Arthur E.Eld (honorary secretary) and Joseph Hughes (honorary financial secretary)
1884-9 Tom Smith (honorary general secretary)
1884 John Homer (honorary financial secretary)
1884-7 Thomas Foster (honorary financial secretary)
1887-9 Louis Ford (honorary financial secretary)
1890-2 Louis Ford (general secretary) and W.Pierce Dix (honorary financial secretary)
1892-4 Henry 'Swin' Jackson (general secretary)
1892-5 Clement Keys (financial secretary)
1894-5 E. Stephenson (general secretary)
1895-6 Clement Keys
1896-1902 W.Frank Heaven
1902-48 Fred Everiss JP
1948-60 Ephriam 'Eph' Smith
1960-80 Alan Everiss JP
1980-4 Tony Rance
1984-5 Gordon Dimbleby
1985-6 John Westmancoat
1986- Gordon Bennett

International and Representative Honours

Note: Before 1924 there was only one 'Ireland' team. Then the Republic of Ireland began separate international matches. In this section, 'Ireland' refers to the all-Ireland team of pre-1924 and to the Northern Ireland team thereafter. England Under-23 ceased to play international matches in 1976-7 when England Under-21 took over.

Full, Wartime and Victory internationals

England

A.Aldridge (1) 1887-8 Ireland
R.Allen (5) 1951-2 Switzerland; 1953-4 Scotland (1 goal), Yugoslavia; 1954-5 Wales, West Germany (1 goal)
G.S.Ashmore (1) 1925-6 Belgium
J.Astle (5) 1968-9 Wales; 1969-70 Portugal, Scotland, Brazil, Czechoslovakia
R.J.Barlow (1) 1954-5 Ireland
P.S.Barnes (6) 1979-80 Denmark, Wales; 1980-81 Spain (sub), Brazil, Wales, Switzerland (sub)
W.I.Bassett (16) 1887-8 Ireland; 1888-9 Wales (1 goal), Scotland (1 goal); 1889-90 Wales, Scotland; 1890-91 Ireland (1 goal), Scotland; 1891-2 Scotland; 1892-3 Wales (1 goal), Scotland; 1893-4 Scotland; 1894-5 Ireland (1 goal), Scotland; 1895-6 Ireland, Wales (1 goal), Scotland (1 goal)

BILLY BASSETT

A.J.Bayliss (1) 1890-91 Ireland
S.Bowser (1) 1919-20 Ireland
W.E.Boyes (2) 1934-5 Holland; 1935-6 Scotland (Jubilee)
A.Brown (1) 1970-71 Wales
J.H.Carter (3) 1925-6 Belgium (1 goal); 1928-9 Belgium (1 goal), Spain (2 goals)
L.P.Cunningham (3) 1978-9 Wales, Sweden, Austria

W.B.Elliott (2) 1943-4 Wales (Wartime); 1945-6 Scotland (Victory)
B.Garfield (1) 1897-8 Ireland
H.Hadley (1) 1902-03 Ireland
J.T.W.Haines (1) 1948-9 Switzerland (2 goals)
D.Howe (23) 1957-8 Wales, Ireland, France, Scotland, Portugal, Yugoslavia, USSR (3 times), Brazil, Austria; 1958-9 Ireland, USSR, Wales, Scotland, Italy, Brazil, Peru, Mexico, USA; 1959-60 Wales, Sweden, Ireland
S.Hunt (2) 1983-4 Scotland (sub), USSR (sub)
D.T.Kevan (14) 1956-7 Scotland (1 goal); 1957-8 Wales, Ireland, Scotland (2 goals), Portugal, Yugoslavia, USSR (3 times — 2 goals), Brazil, Austria (1 goal); 1958-9 Mexico (1 goal), USA (1 goal); 1960-61 Mexico

***DEREK KEVAN** (grounded) scoring on his England debut v Scotland at Wembley in 1957.*

T.H.Kinsell (2) 1945-6 Ireland, Wales (both Victory)
R.McNeal (2) 1913-14 Wales, Scotland
T.P.Magee (5) 1922-3 Wales, Sweden; 1924-5 Belgium, Scotland, France
F.Morris (2) 1919-20 Scotland (1 goal), 1920-21 Ireland
J.Nicholls (2) 1953-4 Scotland (1 goal), Yugoslavia

***JOHNNY NICHOLLS** heads England's second goal in his first international v Scotland at Hampden Park in April 1954.*

H.F.Pearson (1) 1931-2 Scotland
J.Pennington (25) 1906-07 Wales, Scotland; 1907-08 Ireland, Wales, Scotland, Austria; 1908-09 Wales, Scotland, Hungary (twice), Austria; 1909-10 Wales, Scotland; 1910-11 Ireland, Wales, Scotland; 1911-12 Ireland, Wales, Scotland; 1912-13 Wales, Scotland; 1913-14 Ireland, Scotland; 1919-20 Wales, Scotland
C.Perry (3) 1889-90 Ireland; 1890-91 Ireland; 1892-3 Wales
T.Perry (1) 1897-8 Wales
J.Reader (1) 1893-4 Ireland
C.Regis (4) 1981-2 Ireland, Wales, Iceland; 1982-3 West Germany
J.Reynolds (3) 1891-2 Scotland; 1892-3 Wales (1 goal), Scotland (1 goal)
W.G.Richardson (1) 1934-5 Holland
S.Rickaby (1) 1953-4 Ireland

BOBBY ROBSON (extreme right) scores England's second goal in the 4-0 defeat of France at Wembley in November 1957. Robson scored two goals in this his international debut.

R.Roberts (3) 1886-7 Scotland; 1887-8 Ireland; 1889-90 Ireland
B.Robson (13) 1979-80 Republic of Ireland, Australia; 1980-81 Norway, Rumania (twice), Switzerland (twice), Spain, Brazil, Wales, Scotland, Hungary; 1981-2 Norway
R.W.Robson (20) 1957-8 France (2 goals), USSR (twice), Brazil, Austria; 1959-60 Spain, Hungary; 1960-61 Ireland, Luxembourg, Spain, Wales, Scotland (1 goal), Mexico (1 goal), Portugal, Italy; 1961-2 Luxembourg, Wales, Portugal, Ireland, Switzerland
E.A.Sandford (1) 1932-3 Wales
G.E.Shaw (1) 1931-2 Scotland
J.Smith (3) 1919-20 Wales (Victory), Ireland; 1922-3 Ireland
D.Statham (3) 1982-3 Wales, Australia (twice)
W.Williams (6) 1896-7 Ireland; 1897-8 Ireland, Wales, Scotland; 1898-9 Ireland, Wales
G.Woodhall (2) 1887-8 Wales (1 goal), Scotland

Scotland

D.M.Fraser (2) 1967-8 Holland; 1968-9 Cyprus
R.A.Hartford (6) 1971-2 Peru, Wales, England, Yugoslavia, Czechoslovakia, Brazil

ASA HARTFORD

R.Hope (2) 1967-8 Holland; 1968-9 Denmark
W.M.Johnston (13) 1976-7 Sweden, Wales, Ireland, England, Chile, Argentina, Brazil; 1977-8 East Germany, Czechoslovakia, Wales (twice), England, Peru
A.McNab (1) 1938-9 England

Wales

S.Davies (11) 1921-2 Scotland (1 goal), England, Ireland; 1922-3 Scotland; 1924-5 Scotland, Ireland; 1925-6 Scotland, Ireland, England; 1926-7 Scotland; 1927-8 Scotland
W.C.Davies (2) 1908-09 England; 1909-10 Scotland
H.E.Foulkes (1) 1931-2 Ireland

Three of Albion's Welsh internationals from the 1930s — Walter Robbins, Hugh Foulkes and Jimmy Murphy.

I.Jones (4) 1922-3 England, Ireland; 1923-4 Scotland; 1925-6 Ireland
R.L.Krzywicki (2) 1969-70 East Germany, Italy
A.H.Millington (3) 1962-3 Scotland, Hungary, England
J.P.Murphy (15) 1932-3 England, Ireland, France; 1933-4 Scotland, England; 1934-5 England, Scotland, Ireland; 1935-6 Scotland, England, Ireland; 1936-7 Scotland, Ireland; 1937-8 Scotland, England
S.Powell (4) 1890-91 England, Scotland; 1891-2 England, Scotland
R.R.Rees (2) 1967-8 West Germany; 1968-9 Italy
W.W.Robbins (6) 1932-3 Scotland, England, Ireland (2 goals), France; 1933-4 Scotland (1 goal); 1935-6 Scotland
M.R.Thomas (2) 1985-6 Hungary, Saudi Arabia (sub)
G.E.Williams (26) 1959-60 Ireland; 1960-61 Republic of Ireland, Scotland, England; 1962-3 Hungary, Ireland; 1963-4 England, Scotland, Ireland; 1964-5 Scotland, Denmark, England, Greece (twice), Ireland (1 goal), Italy, USSR; 1965-6 Ireland, Brazil (twice), Chile; 1966-7 Scotland, England, Ireland; 1967-8 Ireland; 1968-9 Italy

JIMMY MURPHY (striped shirt) is congratulated on winning his first Welsh cap by (left to right) Wally Boyes, Teddy Sandford and Joe Carter.

S.G.Williams (33) 1953-4 Austria; 1954-5 England, Ireland; 1955-6 England, Scotland, Austria; 1957-8 England, Scotland, Israel (twice), Ireland, Hungary (twice), Mexico, Sweden, Brazil; 1958-9 Scotland, England, Ireland; 1959-60 England, Scotland, Ireland; 1960-61 Republic of Ireland, Ireland, Spain (twice), Hungary; 1961-2 England, Scotland, Ireland, Brazil (twice), Mexico

The Williams's — Stuart and Graham — Albion's Welsh international full-backs.

D.F.Witcomb (9) 1939-40 England (twice); 1940-41 England (twice — 1 goal); 1941-2 England (twice) (all Wartime); 1945-6 Scotland (Victory); 1946-7 Scotland, England

Ireland (Northern Ireland)

G.J.Armstrong (4) 1985-6 Turkey, Rumania (sub), England (sub), France (sub)
D.Hegan (1) 1969-70 USSR

J.M.Nicholl (11) 1984-5 Finland, England, Spain, Turkey; 1985-6 Turkey, Rumania, England, France, Algeria, Spain, Brazil
R.A.Ryan (1) 1949-50 Wales
J.Vernon (15) 1946-7 Wales; 1947-8 Scotland, England, Wales; 1948-9 England, Scotland, Wales; 1949-50 Scotland, England; 1950-51 England, Scotland, Wales, France; 1951-2 Scotland, England
D.J.Walsh (9) 1946-7 Scotland, Wales; 1947-8 Scotland, England (1 goal), Wales; 1948-9 England (2 goals), Scotland (2 goals), Wales; 1949-50 Wales

DAVE WALSH – JACK VERNON – REG RYAN
Three Irish internationals in 1949.

Republic of Ireland

M.J.Giles (7) 1975-6 Turkey; 1976-7 England, Turkey, France (twice), Poland, Bulgaria
A.Grealish (10) 1983-4 Poland, China; 1984-5 Mexico, USSR, Norway, Denmark, Spain (sub), Switzerland; 1985-6 USSR, Denmark
M.P.Martin (10) 1975-6 Turkey, Norway, Poland; 1976-7 England, Turkey, France (twice), Spain, Poland, Bulgaria
P.M.Mulligan (16) 1975-6 Turkey, Poland; 1976-7 England, Turkey, France (twice), Poland, Bulgaria; 1977-8 Bulgaria, Norway, Denmark; 1978-9 England, Denmark, Bulgaria, West Germany, Argentina
R.A.Ryan (15) 1949-50 Sweden, Belgium; 1950-51 Norway (twice), Argentina; 1951-2 West Germany (twice), Austria, Spain; 1952-3 France, Austria; 1953-4 France (twice — 1 goal), Luxembourg (1 goal); 1954-5 Norway (1 goal)
R.C.Treacy (6) 1965-6 West Germany; 1966-7 Spain, Czechoslovakia; 1967-8 Czechoslovakia (1 goal); 1976-7 France, Poland
D.J.Walsh (14) 1945-6 Portugal, Spain; 1946-7 Spain (2 goals), Portugal; 1947-8 Portugal, Spain (1 goal); 1948-9 Switzerland, Portugal, Sweden (1 goal), Spain; 1949-50 England, Finland, Sweden; 1950-51 Norway (1 goal)

Canada

C.Valentine (1) 1985-6 Honduras

R.Allen (2) 1953-4 Scotland, Switzerland

RONNIE ALLEN also holder of five full England caps, from 1952-54.

J.Astle (2) 1969-70 Columbia (1 goal), Ecuador XI (3 goals)
R.J.Barlow (2) 1951-2 France; 1952-3 Scotland
P.S.Barnes (1) 1980-81 USA
B.M.Batson (3) 1980-81 USA, Australia, Spain
L.P.Cunningham (1) 1978-9 Czechoslovakia
J.R.Dugdale (3) 1953-4 Scotland, Yugoslavia, Switzerland
D.Howe (1) 1956-7 Scotland
J.P.Kennedy (3) 1951-2 France; 1955-6 Yugoslavia, Scotland
J.Nicholls (1) 1953-4 Switzerland (sub)
C.Regis (3) 1978-9 Czechoslovakia (sub); 1980-81 USA, Australia
B.Robson (2) 1978-9 Austria; 1979-80 Spain
D.J.Statham (2) 1980-81 USA (1 goal), Spain (1 goal)

Scotland

J.G.Dudley (1) 1953-4 England

Under-23 and Under-21 representative honours

England

D.G.Burnside (2) 1960-61 Danish XI; 1961-2 Turkey

L.Cantello (8) 1971-2 East Germany; 1972-3 Wales, Holland (twice), Denmark, Czechoslovakia; 1973-4 Poland, Denmark
C.Clark (1) 1960-61 Wales
L.P.Cunningham (6) 1976-7 Scotland (1 goal), Finland, Norway (sub); 1977-8 Norway, Finland (1 goal), Italy

LAURIE CUNNINGHAM the first coloured player to wear the white shirt of England in a major international.

D.Howe (6) 1955-6 Scotland; 1956-7 France, Scotland; 1957-8 Bulgaria, Scotland, Wales
D.T.Kevan (4) 1956-7 Bulgaria, Rumania, Czechoslovakia; 1957-8 Bulgaria

DEREK KEVAN made 14 full international appearances for England, scoring eight goals.

314

P.W.Latchford (2) 1973-4 Poland, Wales
S.Mackenzie (3) 1981-2 Norway, Scotland (twice)
R.Moses (7) 1980-81 Norway (sub), Switzerland (twice), Republic of Ireland, Rumania, Hungary; 1981-2 Norway (sub)
J.Nicholls (1) 1953-4 Italy
G.J.M.Nisbet (1) 1971-2 East Germany
G.A.Owen (12) 1978-9 Bulgaria, Sweden (sub); 1979-80 Denmark, Scotland (twice — 1 goal), East Germany; 1980-81 Switzerland (1 goal), Rumania; 1981-2 Norway (sub), Hungary; 1982-3 West Germany (twice — 2 goals)
C.Regis (6) 1978-9 Denmark, Bulgaria (1 goal), Sweden (1 goal); 1979-80 Scotland, East Germany; 1982-3 Denmark (1 goal)
B.Robson (7) 1978-9 Wales, Bulgaria (sub), Sweden (1 goal); 1979-80 Denmark, Bulgaria, Scotland (twice — 1 goal)
M.E.Setters (11) 1957-8 Bulgaria, Rumania, Scotland, Wales; 1958-9 Poland, Czechoslovakia, France, Italy, West Germany; 1959-60 Hungary, France
D.J.Statham (6) 1977-8 Finland; 1978-9 Wales, Bulgaria, Sweden; 1979-80 Denmark; 1982-3 Greece

DEREK STATHAM played three times for the England senior side at full-back.

Scotland

E.P.Colquhoun (1) 1967-8 England
R.A.Hartford (5) 1969-70 Wales; 1970-71 Wales; 1971-2 England; 1972-3 England, Wales
R.Hope (1) 1966-7 Wales
R.T.Wilson (1) 1969-70 Wales

Wales

B.W.Hughes (3) 1976-7 England, Scotland; 1977-8 Scotland
R.L.Krzywicki (3) 1966-7 Scotland, England; 1969-70 Scotland

A.H.Millington (4) 1961-2 Scotland, Ireland; 1962-3 Scotland, Ireland
G.E.Williams (2) 1959-60 Scotland; 1960-61 Wales

Republic of Ireland

J.Anderson (5) 1977-8 Ireland; 1978-9 USSR, Argentina, Hungary, Yugoslavia.
R.C.P.Treacy (1) 1965-6 France

Amateur Internationals

England

R.Banks (1) 1933-4 Wales
L.F.Cooling (1) 1924-5 Wales
W.C.Jordan (2) 1907-08 France (6 goals); 1909-10 Ireland (2 goals)

Football League Honours

R.Allen (1) 1957-8 Scottish League (1 goal)
J.Astle (2) 1969-70 Scottish League (2 goals); 1970-71 Irish League (2 goals)
H.G.Bache (1) 1914-5 Irish League
R.J.Barlow (5) 1952-3 League of Ireland, Danish Combination; 1953-4 League of Ireland; 1954-5 League of Ireland; 1957-8 League of Ireland
W.I.Bassett (3) 1891-2 Scottish League (1 goal); 1892-3 Scottish League (1 goal); 1896-7 Irish League
W.E.Boyes (1) 1935-6 Irish League (1 goal)
A.Brown (2) 1970-71 Irish League (sub) (1 goal), Scottish League
F.Buck (2) 1911-2 Southern League, Irish League
J.H.Carter (1) 1930-31 Scottish League
J.Crisp (1) 1919-20 Irish League
J.R.Dugdale (1) 1953-4 League of Ireland
J.Edwards (1) 1931-2 Scottish League
W.Groves (1) 1891-2 Scottish League
T.Higgins (2) 1895-6 Scottish League; 1896-7 Irish League
D.Howe (6) 1956-7 Scottish League; 1957-8 Scottish League; 1958-9 League of Ireland; 1959-60 Irish League; 1960-61 Scottish League; 1961-2 Irish League
A.Jackson (1) 1961-2 Scottish League
A.C.Jephcott (2) 1913-4 Scottish League; 1919-20 Irish League
J.Kaye (2) 1965-6 League of Ireland (2 goals), Scottish League
D.T.Kevan (1) 1957-8 Scottish League (3 goals)
R.McNeal (5) 1912-3 Southern League, Irish League; 1913-4 Southern League, Scottish League; 1914-5 Scottish League
F.Morris (1) 1919-20 Scottish League (2 goals)
D.G.Nurse (1) 1902-03 Irish League
H.Pearson (2) 1914-15 Irish League; 1922-3 Irish League
J.Pennington (9) 1906-07 Scottish League; 1910-11 Scottish League; 1911-2 Southern League, Irish League, Scottish League; 1912-3 Irish League; 1913-4 Irish League, Southern League; 1919-20 Scottish League
C.Perry (1) 1892-3 Scottish League
T.Perry (3) 1893-4 Irish League; 1895-6 Scottish League; 1896-7 Irish League
J.Reader (3) 1891-2 Scottish League; 1893-4 Irish League; 1896-7 Irish League
J.Reynolds (2) 1891-2 Scottish League; 1892-3 Scottish League
S.Richardson (1) 1921-2 Irish League
S.Rickaby (1) 1953-4 League of Ireland
R.W.Robson (5) 1957-8 Scottish League; 1959-60 Scottish League; 1960-61 Italian League, Scottish League; 1961-2 League of Ireland
G.E.Shaw (1) 1933-4 Scottish League
B.W.Shearman (2) 1911-2 Southern League, Irish League
J.L.Spencer (1) 1924-5 Irish League
H.F.Trentham (1) 1933-4 Irish League
W.Williams (5) 1895-6 Scottish League; 1896-7 Irish League, Scottish League; 1898-9 Irish League; 1899-1900 Irish League
S.Wood (1) 1932-3 Irish League (1 goal)

Miscellaneous Representative Honours

England XI: J.Astle, W.I.Bassett, D.Howe, D.T.Kevan, C.Perry, C.Regis, R.W.Robson

Scotland XI: E.P.Colquhoun, J.G.Dudley, D.M.Fraser, R.Hope

Wales XI: A.Evans

Republic of Ireland: A.Grealish, M.P.Martin, P.M.Mulligan

Great Britain XI: J.Vernon

Rest of United Kingdom: J.Vernon

All British XI: D.F.Witcomb

Football League XI: W.I.Bassett, A.McNab, R.McNeal, H.Pearson, J.Pennington, T.Perry, J.Reader

Young England XI: A.Brown, M.E.Setters

FA XI: W.Adams, R.Allen, G.S.Ashmore, R.J.Barlow, W.I.Bassett, D.G.Burnside, J.H.Carter, J.Cookson, J.R.Dugdale, W.B.Elliott, D.Howe, C.E.Jackman, J.P.Kennedy, D.T.Kevan, T.H.Kinsell, T.P.Magee, G.J.McVitie, F.Morris, H.Pearson, S.Richardson, S.Rickaby, R.W.Robson, M.E.Setters, G.E.Shaw

Scottish FA XI: A.McNab

FA Amateur XI: N.J.Whitehead

'**PADDY RYAN**' (dark shirt), who played for both Irish countries during the 1950s, seen here in action for the Republic v Austria at Dalymount Park, Dublin in March 1953.

International Trials:

Note: The term 'International Trial' used here includes fixtures such as Professionals against Amateurs, Possibles against Probables, North against South, England against The Rest, Whites against Stripes, Whites against Blues, Players against Gentlemen, England against South, England against North.

England: W.I.Bassett, A.J.Bayliss, J.H.Carter, J.Crisp, A..Finch, T.W.Glidden, T.Green, G.C.James, A.C.Jephcott, T.P.Magee, F.Morris, H.F.Pearson, J.Pennington, C.Perry, J.Reynolds, S.Richardson, W.Richardson, R.Roberts, E.A.Sandford, G.E.Shaw, J.Simmons, J.Smith, J.L.Spencer, W.Williams

Scotland: J.Stevenson

Miscellaneous Representative Honours with other clubs

England: A.Aldridge, W.Ashurst, P.S.Barnes, W.E.Boyes, H.Chambers, C.C.Charsley, R.Crawford, W.Garraty, G.H.Holden, G.C.Hurst, J.A.Johnston, A.W.Morley, W.W.Morris, J.Reynolds, G.F.Wheldon.

Scotland: E.P.Colquhoun, A.Goram, W.Groves, A.Hannah, R.A.Hartford, J.Holton, W.M.Johnston, A.McNab, J.Miller, D.Stewart.

Wales: A.M.Bostock, A.Davies, L.C.Davies, S.Davies, W.C.Davies, I.R.Edwards, P.A.Griffiths, A.Hughes, I.Jones, R.L.Krzywicki, T.Martin, A.H.Millington, D.Nardiello, S.Powell, R.R.Rees, W.W.Robbins, M.R.Thomas, G.O.Williams, S.G.Williams, D.F.Witcomb.

Ireland: G.J.Armstrong, L.O.Bookman, J.Connor, R.Crone, A.Elleman, D.Hegan, W.McCabe, J.M.Nicholl, J.Reynolds, J.Taggart, J.Vernon, D.J.Walsh.

Republic of Ireland: M.J.Giles, A.Grealish, M.P.Martin, P.M.Mulligan, R.A.Ryan, R.C.P.Treacy, J.Vernon, D.J.Walsh

Canada: L.G.Johnson, C.Valentine

USA: K.Crow

Holland: M.C.Jol, R.Zondervan

Rhodesia: B.Grobbelaar

Zimbabwe: B.Grobbelaar

Yugoslavia: I.Katalinic, D.Muzinic

England 'B': S.Mackenzie, A.W.Morley, G.A.Owen, G.A.Rowley

England XI: P.S.Barnes, I.Clarke, G.C.Hurst, J.Mahon, A.W.Morley, B.Robson

England Under-23: G.C.Hurst, D.J.Mills, A.W.Morley, R.W.Robson, M.E.Setters, J.Talbut.

England Under-21: P.S.Barnes, P.Bradshaw, G.A.Crooks, J.M.Deeham, P.Dyson, A.E.King, R.Moses, G.A.Owen, G.Thompson

England (amateur): H.G.Bache, J.G.Shield

Football League: W.Ashurst, W.E.Boyes, T.Broad, H.Chambers, R.Crawford, G.Dorsett, A.Evans, D.Hogg, G.C.Hurst, J.Reynolds, F.W.Rouse, G.A.Rowley, C.E.Shaw, G.F.Wheldon

Football League XI: P.S.Barnes, G.C.Hurst, G.A.Owen

Football Alliance: R.Roberts

Third Division (South): S.F.Steele

Third Division (North): R.V.Cutler, R.A.Ryan

Southern League: E.Bradley, A.Lewis, W.Thompson, H.M.Wilcox

Southern League XI: A.Geddes, A.McKenzie

FA XI: W.Ashurst, N.W.Bassett, I.Clarke, R.Crawford, D.Howe, J.Mahon, M.E.Setters, G.T.Summers

FA International Trials: W.Ashurst, H.Chambers, W.Garraty, J.A.Johnson, B.Rankin, J.Reynolds, B.Robinson

Scotland Under-23: J.Holton, W.M.Johnston, M.Murray, D.Stewart

Scotland Under-21: A.Goram, R.A.Hartford

Scotland (amateur): M.Murray

Scottish League: L.Bell, W.M.Johnston, P.S.McKennon, J.Millar

Scottish League XI: J.M.B.Wallace

Scottish International Trials: W.Groves, J.Millar

Wales Under-23: R.R.Rees, M.R.Thomas

Wales Under-21: I.R.Edwards, D.Nardiello, M.R.Thomas

Wales (amateur): A.Hughes

Welsh League: I.Jones, W.Taylor

Welsh International Trials: A.Davies, L.C.Davies

UK-Ireland-Denmark XI: M.J.Giles

Ireland-Northern Ireland XI: G.J.Armstrong, J.M.Nicholl, J.Vernon

Northern Ireland Under 21: J.M.Nicholl

Irish League: S.Bowser, G.B.Drury, P.S.McKennan, J.Vernon, D.J.Walsh

All Ireland XI: M.J.Giles, M.P.Martin, P.M.Mulligan

Republic of Ireland XI: M.J.Giles, A.Grealish, M.P.Martin, P.M.Mulligan, R.C.P.Treacy

Republic of Ireland Under 23: M.P.Martin, P.M.Mulligan

Republic of Ireland (amateur): M.P.Martin

League of Ireland: J.Dainty, M.P.Martin, P.M.Mulligan, R.C.P.Treacy

Holland 'B': M.C.Jol, R.Zonderan

Holland Under-23: M.C.Jol

Holand Under-21: M.C.Jol, R.Zonderan

Malaysian FA XI: R.Crawford

International and Representative Records

First International Cap: Goalkeeper Bob Roberts, England against Scotland at Blackburn, 29 March 1887

First Major Representative Honour: Goalkeeper Bob Roberts, North against South, in London, 26 January 1884.

Youngest International: Billy Bassett (19 years 2 months) against Ireland, 7 April 1888.

Most Capped Albion Player: Full-Back Stuart Williams with 33 Welsh appearances between 1954 and 1962. After leaving Albion for Southampton he gained a further ten Welsh caps between 1962 and 1965. He captained Wales on 14 occasions.

Most Capped Player to Represent Albion: Right-back Jimmy Nicholl made 73 appearances for Northern Ireland between 1976 and 1986 while serving Manchester United, Toronto Blizzard, Sunderland, Rangers and Albion.

Three great post-war internationals. Left to right: Billy Wright (Wolves & England) and the Albion duo of Dave Walsh and Jack Vernon (Ireland).

Most Internationals on Albion's Books: Nine, in 1933-4 (Sandford, Pearson, Shaw, Carter and Magee of England and Robbins, Foulkes, Griffiths and Murphy of Wales) and in 1935-6 (Sandford, Pearson, Shaw, Carter, Boyes and Richardson of England and Robbins, Foulkes and Murphy of Wales).

Most Players in an International Team: Four, in 1976-7 (Giles, Martin, Mulligan and Treacy for the Republic of Ireland against France at Dublin and against Poland, also at Dublin).

International Captains: Jesse Pennington (England), Stan Davies, Jimmy Murphy, Graham Williams and Stuart Williams (Wales), Jack Vernon (Northern Ireland) and John Giles, Mick Martin, Paddy Mulligan and Tony Grealish (Republic of Ireland) have each captained their respective countries while on Albion's books. Vernon also skippered the United Kingdom XI.
Jesse Pennington, Billy Williams, Ray Barlow, Don Howe and Bobby Robson have captained the Football League representative side while Gary Owen and Cyrille Regis have led out the England Under-21 team.
Doug Fraser was skipper of the Scotland XI which toured Israel, Hong Kong, Australia, New Zealand and Canada in 1967.
Asa Hartford captained the Scotland Under-23 team whilst with Albion, and Don Howe and Maurice Setters captained England Under-23.
Joe Kennedy was skipper of England 'B' during the 1950s.

Debut Goals: Seven Albion forwards have scored on their first international appearance — all for England: George Woodhall (1888), Fred Morris (1920), Joe Carter (1926), Jack Haines (1948), Johnny Nicholls (1954), Derek Kevan (1957) and Bobby Robson (1957). Haines and Robson both scored twice, Haines against Switzerland in 1948 and Robson against France in 1957. In an amateur international in 1908, centre-forward Billy Jordan scored six goals against France on his debut.
In his first full appearance for Wales, against Malta in season 1978-9, former Albion centre-forward Ian Edwards of Chester scored four goals.

Most Goals In Representative Football: Jimmy Cookson scored 24 times in 11 matches on the FA tour of Canada in 1931.

Consecutive Appearances: Between 1907 and 1920 Jesse Pennington made nine consecutive appearances against Scotland and between 1889 and 1896, Billy Bassett played for England against Scotland on eight consecutive occasions. When England defeated Scotland for the third successive year in 1893, Bassett was one of four England players who were each awarded a special international cap.
Between October 1957 and November 1959 Don Howe's 23 England appearances were consecutive.

Successful Partnerships: Between March 1907 and April 1914 Sam Hardy (Aston Villa), Bob Crompton (Blackburn Rovers) and Jesse Pennington formed a resolute last line of defence for England in 14 internationals. Crompton and Pennington played at full-back together in 23 England internationals.

Dual Internationals: Albion's right-half of the early 1890s, John 'Baldy' Reynolds, was capped by both Ireland and England. Before he signed for Albion he had appeared five times in the Irish national side while with the Distillery and Ulster clubs but on arriving at Stoney Lane it was discovered that he was born at Blackburn and thus eligible to play for England. He was subsequently chosen eight times for England while with Albion and Aston Villa. Other Albion 'dual' international players were Dave Walsh, Reg Ryan and Jack Vernon, all whom played for both Northern Ireland and the Republic of Ireland.

International Miscellanea

In 19 international appearances for Wales, with Preston North End, Everton, Albion and Rotherham United, Stan Davies filled six different positions — right-half, left-half, inside-right, centre-forward, inside-left and outside-right. He also served in one match as a goalkeeper when the regular Welsh 'keeper retired injured.

Albion's Reg Ryan filled five different positions for the Republic of Ireland — right-half, left-half, and the three inside-forward positions.

The first Albion player to take part in a World Cup match was centre-forward David Walsh for the Republic of Ireland against Sweden at Stockholm on 2 June 1949.

One of the unluckiest players of all was goalkeeper Bert Pearson who was selected to play for England against Wales in 1923 after 16 years as an Albion professional. He had to forego the honour because of injury and never again had the opportunity to win full international honours.

The only Albion player to win an international cap, a League Championship medal and an FA Cup winners' medal was pint-sized Tommy Magee who, at 5ft 2½ins, was one of the smallest half-backs to play for England.

Four Albion players have been sent off whilst representing their country. The first to go was Harry Kinsell who was dismissed along with Lowrie of Wales in the England-Wales Victory international match at The Hawthorns on 20 October 1945. Willie Johnston was sent off whilst playing for Scotland against Argentina at Buenos Aires on 18 June 1977, and Mick Martin was twice dismissed in Republic of Ireland colours, against Turkey at Dublin on 29 October 1975 and against Bulgaria at Sofia on 1 June 1977. Maurice Setters received his marching orders playing for England Under-23 against West Germany at Bochum on 10 May 1959.

In his first 36 appearances for the Republic of Ireland, Mick Martin of Bohemians, Manchester United, Albion and Newcastle United received only one international cap. Apparently the FA of Ireland could not afford a cap for every match.

The first international player to sign for Albion was the Wednesbury Old Athletic captain George Holden, who played four times on England's right-wing between 1881 and 1884. He joined Albion in time for the 1886-7 season but was not a great success as observed by the journal *Saturday Night* which reported that 'his great fault is that he attempts to dribble the ball alone, while the rest of the team play the short passing game.'

When George Woodhall was honoured by selection for the England-Scotland match in Glasgow in March 1888, it was by no means certain that he would be allowed to play. Some members of the Albion committee wanted him to play in the Staffordshire Cup semi-final but it was narrowly agreed — by eight votes to five — to release him to play for his country.

Albion's Steve Hunt was the last substitute to be used in the Home International Championship when he made his England debut against Scotland at Wembley on 26 May 1984. The competition was terminated at the end of the 1983-4 season.

By playing against Rumania Under-21 on 28 April 1981, Albion's Gary Owen created a record of 18 England Under-21 appearances. He completed a record 22 appearances for England Under-21 in October 1982 of which ten were as captain. In those 22 games England were defeated only twice.

Billy Williams was chosen for Football League honours against the Irish League in November 1897 but he declined to play, preferring to help Albion out in a League match against Everton. For his loyalty to the club a special medal was struck and was duly presented to him.

Unluckiest Albion international debutant was Bobby Hope whose first appearance for Scotland against Holland on 30 May 1968 lasted only 15 minutes. He was then carried off injured and he took no further part in the game.

During the 1980s several former Albion personalities were simultaneously connected with the full England international team: F.A. 'Bert' Millichip was the chairman of the FA Council, Bobby Robson was the England team manager, with Bryan Robson as his captain and Don Howe and Mike Kelly were England coaches. In addition, David Burnside was manager of the England Youth XI.

Several Albion players have made 50 or more full international appearances during their complete careers, among them Bryan Robson (England), Asa Hartford (Scotland), Mickey Thomas (Wales), Jimmy Nicholl and Gerry Armstrong (Ireland) and John Giles, Paddy Mulligan and Mick Martin (Republic of Ireland). Geoff Hurst made 49 appearances for England and remains the only player ever to score three goals in a World Cup Final.

Subscribers

4 Tony Matthews	80 Hans Peters	156 Bruce Wilson	232 Anthony B Hopkins
5 Colin Mackenzie	81 Gordon Small	157 Stephen John Rose	233 Brian Tabner
6 Moira & Frederick Furness	82 Jack Mills	158 Frank Andrews	234 Mike Purkiss
7 Graham Belt	83 Roger Hudson	159 Frank Grande	235 P Baxendale
8 Christopher Prinn	84 F J Lee	160 Mark Cleminson	236 D P Baxendale
9 Michael Cornell	85 Malcolm Hartley	161 Kenneth L Proud	237 G K Hughes
10 Graham Smyth	86 Brian H Hobbs	162 John Barry Hickling	238 Matthew Christian Jones
11 Keith Mullarkey	87 Antonio Accili	163 A J Washington	239 Ian Griffiths.
12 Andrew Mackie	88 D R Seaby	164 R F Woodhouse	240 G Protheroe
13 A R Johnson	89 John A Harris	165 Neil & Janette Williams	241 Melvin Scott
14 Ian Musikant	90 A & J A Waterman	166 Norman Green	242 D Fryer
15 Chris Scrine	91 Dave Hillam	167 Andrew Patrick	243 Philip Wain
16 Warren S Dosanjh	92 Glyn D Round	168 Graham H Silk	244 John Billingsley
17 John Murchington	93 Torvid Høiland	169 Philip J H Silk	245 H R Noon
18 Kevan Hobbis	94 James Menzies	170 G & PJ Hampson-Silk	246 S W Noon
19 Jim Saul	95 Robert Whitelaw Mills	171 D Wheatley	247 J W Gaunt
20 K D Dodd	96 Michael Barnett	172 H F Mitchell	248 Paul Manell
21 Richard Wilmot	97 Peter Baxter	173 Ron Humphreys	249 Alfred A Clark
22 Ivor J Hodgetts	98 Jim Wattam	174 P D Barker	250 Oliver Edward Hayes
23 John Homer	99 A A Dunmore	175 Roger F Buckley	251 W G J & M E Walton
24 A J Timmins	100 Carsten Grønning	176 D F Fitzgerald	252 Alan L Buttress
25 Thomas Paul Cooke	101 Søren Skafte Jensen	177 W J Narbett	253 Martin Chatwin
26 Miss P S Bates	102 R D King	178 S W Clayton	254 Alfred L Harper
27 Joe Waters	103 Keith Coburn	179 R D Narbett	255 Roger Buckingham
28 John Motson	104 Peter John Wild	180 J V Narbett	256 Thomas Perrins
29 Richard Szreter	105 Graham Wood	181 L Bone	257 Roger T Collett
30 Raymond Parkes	106 Richard Pierce	182 William Needs	258 Martin C Collett
31 Derek Hyde	107 B M Cowley	183 R H White	259 Maurice Yarwood Sayce
32 Stephen Laski	108 John R Nicholls	184 Christopher Smith	260 Peter Stevens
33 A J Saunders	109 Paul Foster	185 Mark William Raybould	261 David Edwin Dew
34 John Rowlinson	110 Angus W Rodger	186 S G Moore	262 Neil Morris
35 Gordon Fowkes	111 M Swart	187 C W Denning	263 R C Pullin JP
36 Dr Philip Bickley	112 Domenico Polimeno	188 John V Tuzzio	264 Alan John Clements
37 Graham W Doughty	113 K M Torgrimsen	189 N C A Downes	265 Arthur Edward Unwin
38 Brian Sawyer	114 Tim Baseley	190 Simon Paul Cherry	266 J Wilcox
39 Stephen Woodfield	115 Stephen Carr	191 Christopher Pearce MSc	267 P R Davies
40 R A Aiken	116 M J Rollason	192 A Unwin	268 T A Oliver
41 Steven Mann	117 J D Ensor	193 Garry R Breakwell	269 Vernon Plover
42 David Downs	118 Robin Woolman	194 John M Davis	270 J P Langley
43 David Keats	119 Neil Piggott	195 J F Hudson	271 Mervyn Golden
44 Rob Turbitt	120 Colin Cameron	196 David John Watkin	272 William John Moore
45 George Ernest Wiles	121 David Sullivan	197 M J O'Connor	273 D A Andrews
46 B H Standish	122 Geir Juva	198 K P Wood	274 Kevin T Mills
47 Stephen Hughes	123 Richard Sanders	199 Robert Lilliman	275 Robert L Mills
48 Peter Hall	124 Christian Wilkes	200 Keith Farley	276 John R Harman
49 Peter Westwood	125 J W Morgan	201 Carl Mosch	277 I L Powleson
50 Martin Banner	126 Robert S Bradley	202 D J Harrison	278 Mark Peckham
51 P S J Robottom	127 Warren James Poole	203 Ian Oakton	279 Michael W Stanley
52 Kenneth Anthony Salt	128 Douglas Lamming	204 A D Bodley	280 Roger M Stanley
53 Jeffrey Perry	129 Robin H Harman	205 Philip James Whitehouse	281 P Harris
54 Terry Frost LCIOB	130 Neil Reynolds	206 B Hourston	282 B Knight
55 Ralph Mortimer	131 Nathan Reynolds	207 Roderick J Dean	283 David J Prust
56 John Byrne	132 Charles Reynolds	208 Keith Lowe	284 A E Harvey
57 Robert Jex	133 C R Evans	209 Neil P Roche	285 T A Pegler
58 Reg Marbleboot	134 Philip Smith	210 John Hicklin	286 Keith Wheeler
59 J Ringrose	135 M H Clapham	211 Michael A Carden	287 Arthur Westwood
60 Duncan Watt	136 Jarl Midtun	212 R W D Hampton	288 Harold Francis Thomson
61 Derek T Bryant	137 Christer Svensson	213 Stephen Deeley	289 William Blunt
62 Davis G Parnaby	138 T J Beech	214 Martin Reynolds	290 Simon David Allsopp
63 Jon Robinson	139 Gilbert Thomas Cox	215 Carl Dellicott	291 R P Mills
64 Michael Phipps	140 Sheila V Berryman	216 John Reeves	292 Brian Turner
65 Mr & Mrs J Mees	141 Colin G H Moore	217 Peter T Walker	293 Lee Francis
66 M R Jones	142 Lars-Olof Wendler	218 J Gardiner	294 Robert James Hawkins
67 John G Brown	143 Philip John Cartwright	219 Cyril George	295 Douglas Hughes
68 Harry Thompson	144 Neil Congrave	220 L A Zammit	296 T J H Price
69 P L M Lunn	145 Colin E Jones	221 M W D Perks	297 Trevor John Yates
70 Richard Wells	146 Mike Vass	222 David Michael Woods	298 Alan Ison
71 A P Wheatley	147 T K Guy F.C.A.	223 Harald Lohr	299 David Cattell
72 Philip Soar	148 Robert Briggs	224 John Qvarnberg	300 Alan Powell
73 Roy Frank Edward Parsons	149 David Grant	225 Richard Stocken	301 David Craige
74 Anthony P J F Hayward	150 Eric Joseph	226 Mark Southwell	302 Derek J Mycock
75 T K Tromans	151 W W Hooper	227 Peter Pickup	303 R W Godfrey-White
76 Alan Topping	152 D Ingram	228 Simon John Handy	304 Frederick John Grigg
77 W G Morgan	153 Frank Pizzey	229 Anthony Dalton	305 Elsa Alajuuma
78 J W D Wilkes	154 Maurice Golesworthy	230 Stewart Fell	306 Jack Carley
79 Earl Cliff	155 Geoffrey Wright	231 Ian Harraden	307 Ferd Ramsell

308 Len Grindrod	393 N L Round	478 Stephen Boddy	563 Stanley Edwards
309 Stephen J Matthews	394 Carl Price	479 Kenneth Hughes	564 Robert Cox
310 Roger Bullock	395 Anthony Price	480 Brian Forsbrook	565 Robert H Thomas
311 R F Batchelor	396 Duncan Howell	481 John Lee Caudle	566 Andrew Jones
312 J K Aston	397 Paul Dunn	482 Colin Sevier	567 P Farmer
313 Anthony Michael Eric Stanger	398 Gary Millard	483 Peter Lamburn	568 John Fox
314 Lewis Clews	399 Jonathan Walton	484 John Goodwin	569 Carol Round
315 Mr & Mrs R A Webb	400 John Alfred Clarke	485 F K Lowe	570 Alistair James Hickinbottom
316 Michael J Nicklin	401 Melvyn John Farr	486 Dean Russell Easthope	571 Alfred Griffin
317 Graham Hill	402 S Robson	487 David & Roger Homer	572 Jeff Merchant
318 Neil Biddlestone	403 M Kain	488 David J Holloway	573 Paul Glover
319 Giles Bates	404 Raymond T Rawlins	489 Michael Thomas	574 Jacqueline Anne Walker
320 R Grice	405 Mrs J M Carter	490 Peter Alan Beddard	575 Mrs J A Kite-Lightfoot
321 G K Ashman	406 Alan Davies	491 Donald Alan Beddard	576 Brian Kite
322 Jack Cooper	407 M Howes	492 Neil Rose	577 Ian Atkins
323 Richard Truscott	408 Mr & Mrs K Daubney	493 Dale Walker	578 Keith G Lewis
324 Barry Marsh	409 Nigel Andrew Cox	494 Ray Lawley	579 Ina Summers
325 Michael Murphy	410 W Mansell	495 E S Woodhall	580 Brian Ward
326 Andrew Lowe	411 R Gainham	496 Nicholas B E Wharton	581 Stuart Cooper
327 Kenneth Bernard Connor	412 W E Care	497 M V Dutton	582 Asa Hickman
328 Anthony James Scott-Wise	413 W A Care	498 Roger A Fallon	583 Mr A H & Mrs M Heath
329 Nigel John Bellmore	414 Anthony Purchase	499 Brian Thompson	584 Gunnar Kjeilen
330 David Turton	415 Alan Bunch	500 Stanley F Gould	585 Bjørn Langerud
331 Mrs Wendy Young	416 A W Pitt	501 Alison Grimley	586 Bjørn Granskogen
332 A W Hadley	417 John Baggott	502 E F Simpson	587 Arve Stubberud
333 Robert Alexander George MacVie	418 Robert John Bytheway	503 Andrew Trumper	588 Jack Denis Wood
334 J G Murphy	419 D Ruby	504 Arthur Raymond Worley	589 Martyn Graham Rigby
335 Ian Riddell	420 M S Joyce	505 Andrew John Withers	590 Paul Darren Rigby
336 Dennis F Dauncey	421 P Wilkes	506 Graham Cole	591 G J S Bassett
337 Steven Turner	422 J J Wakelam	507 R J Hart	592 David Taylor
338 Martyn K Witts	423 V T Harvey	508 David Shaw	593 John Gerrard Baldwin
339 Reginald Walter Collett	424 D Salter	509 James Roger Jukes	594 D R Hughes
340 John Stanley	425 Chas F Groves	510 John Steele	595 Martin C Adams
341 M A Waring	426 D L Smith	511 R Eagle	596 Neil Wilkinson
342 John Treleven	427 David Richard Jones	512 H R Dursley	597 Trevor A Griffiths
343 Leonard Denigan	428 Graham Hill	513 J Hodgkiss	598 Brian Butler
344 Gordon Davies	429 Graham Peter Harpin	514 W J Matthews	599 Neil Hinkinson
345 Sammy Salt	430 Michael David Green	515 Ronald David Wilcox	600 Jonathan C Eden
346 Richard Barton	431 Derek Michelman	516 Mike Tregidgo	601 Scott Wills
347 Roy Barton	432 K S Lovekin	517 David J A Butler	602 E Williams
348 R J Allen	433 Tony Duncan	518 David McCabe	603 Peter Reeves
349 Pter M Owen	434 D R Morley	519 A Springthorpe	604 Paul A Williams
350 Miss N Letzer	435 Peter W Woodward	520 Alan Branfield	605 John Priest
351 Peter Alan Jones	436 David Rogers	521 Kevin Griffiths	606 Terence Neil Wall
352 Michael Henry Bagnall	437 Steven Stokes	522 B McKay	607 Melvyn Turner
353 David Drew	438 Stanley Stokes	523 J Deakin	608 Paul Reynolds
354 Henry William Thomas Morgan	439 N G Walker	524 Stuart Hudson	609 Dave Knott
355 Ian Hoult	440 Michael Allen	525 A W Swann	610 Andrew Ward
356 D Bailey	441 E K Lloyd	526 Simon Evans	611 Trevor E Davies
357 Mark John Davis	442 T W Bowdler	527 Philip Ainsbury	612 Martin Simons
358 John Northcutt	443 P Poxton	528 B Wright	613 Andrew Charles Payne
359 Olly Ridge	444 M J P McKiernan	529 Paul Tromans	614 Neil G Parkes
360 J R Bissell	445 A E Beetlestone	530 Arthur Leslie Weston	615 G Roberts
361 Neville David Powell	446 Robert Lockett	531 Philip Rogers	616 Mark Whitehouse
362 K W Taylor	447 A Heywood	532 Dax Morris	617 Andrew John Detheridge
363 Richard Waplington	448 Reginald E Stephens	533 Annette Williams	618 Richard C Haynes
364 Paul Eades	449 Phillip A Walters	534 Steven Davies	619 Alastair R Preece
365 Wesley Ball	450 John Shingleton	535 Albert Thomas Shotton	620 Christopher R Watts
366 Michael Bishop	451 Andrew Norton	536 D N Elcock	621 Peter Geobey
367 G T Allman	452 John Beech	537 Dennis Corbett	622 Ian Mills
368 J Musgrove	453 Kenneth Skelding	538 Ashley Jonathon Kemshall	623 Barry Brisland
369 Donald Noble	454 Clive Noble	539 Adam Robert Franklin	624 Alan Davies
370 Juri Pawlovich Lukosiak	455 H J Martin	540 A P Hughes	625 Peter J Driver
371 Colin Jose	456 Allister J Collings	541 Paul Clayton	626 Alan Hingley
372 A Evans	457 D J Amos	542 Robert Lloyd	627 Tony Purchase
373 Jean Hoult	458 Robert Charles Lucas	543 Stuart Glover	628 David & Noreen Bearcroft
374 Andrew Whitehouse	459 Judy Simcox	544 Gary Reynolds	629 WBA Supporters Club (Malta)
375 Adam C Lees	460 A A Hewett	545 L W Price	630 Mark Crockett
376 D A Westwood	461 Jack Parkes	546 Giles Grant	631 Jean, Gordon & Martin Wilkes
377 Leslie A Loach	462 Paul N Startin	547 Michael Heeley	632 Stuart Anderson
378 Maxwell Davies	463 Derek Raymond Dunn	548 J V Handley	633 Philip Watkin
379 John Michael Paddock	464 Norman A Adams	549 G Brownhill	634 E R T Burn
380 Roger Sellars	465 J Tromans	550 Paul Douglas Henderson	635 Stuart M Hackett
381 Norman B Neal	466 Barry Hilton	551 Frank Benson	636 Wayne Rushton
382 Robert D Mullard	467 Ken S Meredith	552 Philip Charles Matthews	637 Derek Jones
383 Peter Marks	468 Keith Lawley	553 Timothy G Nock	638 Paul A Jones
384 S Ridgway	469 Ronald Fisher	554 Robert Clive Priest	639 M A T Smith
385 E D Freeth	470 Neil A Steventon	555 A J MacKenzie	640 Andrew Christopher Cull
386 Michael Tipple	471 Arthur George Hughes	556 Anthony William Bishop	641 W T Wood
387 Mrs Gillian Barker	472 Norman Lamb	557 Antony J Osborne	642 Raymond Faulkner 648 Geoff Ward
388 S L Lucas	473 S N Cox	558 N A C Adams	643 Michael Kerry 649 Lee Jones
389 T E Robbins	474 Stephen J Davis	559 Duncan Chadwick	644 J B Whitton 650 Richard B T F Da᷿
390 Ken Goodwin	475 Darren John Perry	560 Edward A Billington	645 Stephen McLaughlin 651 Alan J Lowe
391 J R Mills	476 Barry Swash	561 W A Bragg	646 David Instone 652 Peter J Colley
392 P J Mills	477 Michael Dennis Stevens	562 K Cox	647 Simon Bensley 653 Ivan Williams